*Hierarchy, Commerce, and Fraud
in Bourbon Spanish America*

Hierarchy, Commerce, and Fraud in Bourbon Spanish America

A POSTAL INSPECTOR'S EXPOSÉ

Ruth Hill

Vanderbilt University Press

Nashville

Publication of this book has been supported by a generous subsidy
from the Program for Cultural Cooperation between Spain's Ministry of
Culture and United States Universities.

Library of Congress Cataloging-in-Publication Data

Hill, Ruth, 1966–
Hierarchy, commerce, and fraud in Bourbon Spanish America :
    a postal inspector's expose / Ruth Hill.
p. cm.
Includes bibliographical references.
ISBN 0-8265-1492-8 (cloth)
    1. Concolorcorvo, b. ca. 1706. Lazarillo de ciegos caminantes.
        2. Latin America—History—To 1830.
        3. Spain—Colonies—America—Commerce.
        4. Oligarchy—Latin America—History—18th century.
        5. Social classes—Latin America—History—18th century.
        6. Corruption—Latin America—History—18th century.
        7. Fraud—Latin America—History—18th century.   I. Title.
F2221.H55 2005
946'.054—dc22

                                                    2005005459

For my parents

Contents

Illustrations

Acknowledgments

I would not have written this book were it not for kind words spoken by the late eighteenth-century specialist Antony Higgins at the Carolina Conference at Chapel Hill in the spring of 2001. Although I hardly knew Tony, I greatly admired his work. I regret very much that we did not talk more about this project then and that now we never will.

A mere chapter of my two-volume dissertation (1994) was devoted to Alonso Carrió's exposé, but the imprint of my graduate studies and of my dissertation committee on this study is clearly visible: Cedomil Goic and Charles Fraker will readily recognize this influence. My general thinking about the eighteenth century has changed since that time, thanks to not only my colleagues in the American Society for Eighteenth Century Studies (ASECS) who teach and research the viceregal period but also to a number of graduate students at the University of Virginia, the University of Rhode Island, and the University of Massachusetts who have taken my courses in Charlottesville and Salamanca. I owe a great deal to members of the Iberoamerican Society, an ASECS affiliate, and to Karen Stolley, Pedro Lasarte, Rolena Adorno, Raquel Chang-Rodríguez, Margaret Ewalt, L. Elena Delgado, Raúl Marrero-Fente, Maureen Ahern, Ralph Bauer, and Mariselle Meléndez.

A large chunk of this study was inspired by my conversations at the John Carter Brown Library with James Muldoon, whose generosity of intellect and spirit I can never repay. Other colleagues in history (Joan Bristol, Karen Racine, Lance Grahn) aided me in ways that they have probably forgotten. Colleagues at the University of Virginia, such as Richard Handler, Alison Weber, David Gies, David Haberly and Michael Gerli, each contributed to this book in different ways.

I am grateful to friends and loved ones who kept me going with their love, music, color, and company: Letizia Modena, Teresa Sanhueza, María Carrión, Regina Rush, Adina Galan and Donald Breen, Elizabeth Giráldez, Diane Mulroney and Brad Ellis, and Raina O'Neal.

Generous financial and logistical support for this study was provided by the National Endowment for the Humanities; the John Carter Brown Library and the John Hay Library at Brown University; the Interlibrary Loan Office, the dean of the College of Arts and Sciences, the vice president for Research and Graduate Studies, and Special Collections at the University of Virginia; and Special Collections at the Johns Hopkins University Milton S. Eisenhower Library. I am especially grateful to the directors, curators, librarians, and support staff at the

Milton S. Eisenhower Library and at the John Carter Brown Library for their professionalism and kindness. Both of these institutions also gave their kind permission when I asked to include in this study reproductions of maps and illustrations from their holdings.

I am indebted to Joan Vidal for her fine copyediting, and to Andix Indexing Associates for producing the index. Finally, I thank everyone at Vanderbilt University Press who has had a hand in this project. I am eternally grateful to my superb editor, Betsy Phillips, who had confidence in this book when my own teetered. Sue Havlish and Dariel Mayer were helpful beyond belief. Anonymous readers generously offered a wealth of feedback that has made this a better book. All opinions herein and any errors that remain are my own. Translations, too, are mine unless otherwise indicated.

Introduction

Overview

E*l lazarillo de ciegos caminantes* (*Guide for Blind Rovers* or *Guide for Blind Traders*) (1775), published under pseudonym, is the best-known work of the Spanish American eighteenth century. Its author, Alonso Carrió de Lavandera (1715–1783), was a Spaniard who spent nearly fifty years in the viceroyalties of New Spain and Peru, trading, serving the Crown in a variety of capacities, and building a family and lifelong friendships.[1] In 1767 the Crown commissioned Carrió de Lavandera to escort the exiled Jesuits out of Peru. A few years later, between 1771 and 1773, he was commissioned to conduct a review and personal inspection of the postal system in the Viceroyalty of Peru. This was the motivation for *El lazarillo de ciegos caminantes*.

The relationship between Concolorcorvo (the alleged Inca scribe to whom Carrió attributed his exposé) and Calixto Bustamante (the man who accompanied Carrió on part of his inspection) and the historical relationship between Bustamante and Carrió are issues that I explore later. Here I wish to point out that Carrió, like the inspector of the posts with whom Concolorcorvo dialogues in the account, possessed more than a passing interest in law and economics, and his writings and experiences confirm that he was versed in not only imaginative literature but also philosophy, geography, and history. His experience with a variety of peoples and places compels us to remember that he was directing much of the information in his account to business travelers and that he was speaking to them in a manner designed to make their load seem lighter and their trip shorter. The image of Carrió as bluff and hearty inspector of the posts is largely one of his own account's making, but much of what the Spaniard wrote in jest about Bourbon Spanish America was no laughing matter.

In the jocose anecdote that closes *El lazarillo de ciegos caminantes*, the riddle of the 4Ps from Lima (which appears over and over in Carrió's narration) is posed to Spanish residents of Lima by a Spanish resident of Guatemala and then solved in two different ways at the archbishop of Guatemala's palace in 1746. It was around 1990 that I began to ask myself, "Why Santiago de Guatemala? It was not even part of Carrió's inspection route. And why 1746, nearly twenty-five years *before* his inspection of the posts?" Little attention had been paid to the setting of this mock trial, or to its participants, but I became convinced that asking some obvious questions would answer many mysteries about Carrió that remained even after the publication of so many critical studies. I did not realize then that answering my own questions would take more than a decade or that the answers would also speak to key issues in the fields of Hispanic, colonial, and imperial studies.

The riddle and its solutions together undercut current theoretical notions about colonial identity in general, but there is far more to it than that. My research into the riddle and its solutions prompted me to confront a *discursive* reality particular to viceregal Spanish America that is not supported by *history*, or what I loosely call here *material* reality: the rivalry between *criollos* (Spaniards born in the New World) and peninsulars (Spaniards born in the Old World).[2] The riddle of the 4Ps from Lima laughingly conveys the existence of reform-resistant, mixed (i.e., *criollo* and peninsular) oligarchical clans (or *roscas*) who understood hierarchy, commerce, and fraud only too well. This fact in turn holds important implications for Latin Americanists who employ the *middle period* model. The *middle period* is a category devised some two decades ago to replace the *colonial, late colonial,* and *independence* periods by setting the second half of the eighteenth century against the first.[3] It assumes that Bourbon reforms in the second half of the eighteenth century set Spanish America on a course that it would traverse during the nineteenth century. Carrió's witty anecdote suggests otherwise. It further suggests that scholars have sold Carrió and his century short by approaching *El lazarillo de ciegos caminantes* as a baroque echo that was deaf to the material reality and discursive options of eighteenth-century Spanish America, which were no less contradictory and polyphonic than those of seventeenth-century Spanish America and were probably more cosmopolitan than those of eighteenth-century France or England.

In sum, the mock trial that supposedly took place in Santiago de Guatemala in 1746 was Carrió's way of putting the cultural practices of his century, and several of his contemporaries from Mexico City to Lima, on trial. To productively engage with Carrió, who has entertained and confounded readers for centuries, we must get on our feet and get our bearings, not in discourse theory but in history.

This book is divided into three parts. Part I comprises Chapters 1 and 2. Chapter 1 examines the four areas represented by the first solution to the riddle of the 4Ps from Lima: *Pila, Puente, Pan,* and *Peines*—literally, "Fountain," "Bridge," "Bread," and "Los Peines." Carrió reduced the economic and cultural rivalry between Lima and Mexico City to absurdity—to the four elements mentioned— after it served him, ideologically (as a pretext) and rhetorically (as a proemium), for the Guatemalan tale. My reading of the first solution to the riddle of the 4Ps from Lima makes it clear that *Pila, Puente, Pan,* and *Peines* were contemporary phenomena for Carrió in 1775. It does so by examining the ostensibly enlightened regime of Viceroy Manuel de Amat y Junient of Peru—a quintessential Bourbon technocrat if there ever was one—and the inspector's portrait of it throughout *El lazarillo de ciegos caminantes.* Lima's claim to fame, I argue, would truly have been a claim to shame had the majority of its elites possessed any. Instead, they manifested an impeccable duplicity, presenting to the Crown in Madrid an image of propriety and sobriety—of Bourbon modernity—while engaging in behaviors that had traditionally been associated with deviants, miscreants, and paupers.

Chapter 2 explains the importance of the Pardo de Figueroa clan to eighteenth-century Spain and Spanish America by examining *Pedro, Pardo, Paulino,* and *Perulero,* the second solution to the riddle of the 4Ps from Lima. Archbishop Pedro Pardo de Figueroa's sexual and financial profile provides us with the crucial link between this second solution and the first. My close reading of the mock trial that solves the riddle of the 4Ps from Lima reveals that shame (*infamia*) was still formidable in Carrió's times, and it made even a dead archbishop fair game. I do not provide a systematic account of the two types of shame (*infamia iuris* and *infamia facti*) then operative in the Spanish world. Instead, I show (1) how the solution *Pedro, Pardo, Paulino,* and *Perulero* is tied to both types and (2) the links between the codification of *infamia,* which began in the twelfth century, and the codification of purity (*limpieza*) in the Hispanic world, which began in the fifteenth.

In closing, Chapter 2 demonstrates that the archbishop's brother, José Pardo de Figueroa, was a prolific author of riddles and a provincial governor (*corregidor*) in Carrió's aquaintance. Moreover, among Europeans (thanks largely to the French), he was the best-known Spanish American of the first half of the eighteenth century, and his reputation as a Bourbon encyclopedia of the arts and sciences would continue into the second half of the century. Carrió's roughing up of both Pardo de Figueroa brothers in *El lazarillo de ciegos caminantes* is an ignored aspect of the inspection report that goes to the very heart of discussions about Bourbon reform and Carrió's views on Enlightenment culture.

Part II addresses the most significant of the economic and political continuities that *El lazarillo de ciegos caminantes* brings to the fore. Chapter 3 shows (1) that, during the first half of the eighteenth century, illegal trade and the diversion of gold, silver, and mercury were interrelated practices of commerce in the viceroyalties of New Spain, New Granada, and Peru and (2) how they relied on the posts, which were already the target of Bourbon reformers. This culture of creative accounting, winks and nods, and outright fraud contributed to the formation of elites in Lima, Santiago de Guatemala, Mexico City, and Buenos Aires. Rather than attempt to point out all of the economic and social inflections of commerce and fraud, I detail where and why Carrió's exposé repeatedly returns to this problem, both directly and indirectly, as I bring various critical voices and approaches into a dialogue on the issues.

Chapter 4 examines the trade in illegal goods and the diversion of precious metals in the second half of the eighteenth century, when Carrió became directly involved in the rolling reforms of the post. I contend that, to a large degree (and one largely unmeasured by scholars), *El lazarillo de ciegos caminantes* pivots around the economic and social pretensions of Buenos Aires and Lima, the former on the rise and the latter in decline. Carrió's exposé is, among other things, a tale of how Buenos Aires eclipsed Lima by using the same illegal means that merchants in Lima had used centuries earlier to defeat merchants in Seville. An examination of significant continuities between the first and second halves of the eighteenth century provides an alternative to the *middle period* model. Also examined is the fact that, just as blindness was a moral and intellectual trope in the iconological and literary explorations of Ignorance and Error in France, Italy, England, and Spain, blindness in Carrió's *Guide for Blind Rovers* (or *Guide for Blind Traders*) impinges on different types of travelers—merchants, muleteers, readers of exotic travelogues (armchair travelers), government officials—and what they were packing, so to speak.

Chapters 5, 6, and 7 constitute Part III. Chapter 5 argues that the prevailing scholarly approaches to hierarchy in viceregal Spanish America must reverse course: we cannot continue to use modern and postmodern categories and models of hierarchy to analyze viceregal society. Carrió's cultural geography was not a postmodern one. This means that any examination of *texts* (in the postmodern sense) that were used to *legitimate* a social hierarchy—treatises on the circulation of blood, on faculty psychology, paintings of *castas,* the literature of heraldry, genealogical paintings and histories, poems and dramas about various *castas* and *estados*—cannot be analyzed without attending to *the principles of that hierarchy* and how they were negotiated in particular, or local, situations by the Crown, church, and individuals who lived that hierarchy as a material reality. Local hierarchies in the parts of viceregal Spanish America under examination were constituted from the intersecting principles of *casta, estado,* and *limpieza (de sangre* and *de oficio).* Although all of these hierarchical principles had their own discursive realities, none was materially biological or genetic; none was what would become known in the nineteenth century as *race.* Because genealogy could legally be (and often was) a discursive reality at odds with material reality, extralegal climbing within the social hierarchy—what the inspector in *El lazarillo de ciegos caminantes* terms *passing*—was commonplace.

Chapter 6 explores how social privileges, responsibilities, and taxonomies are figured in Concolorcorvo's transformations. It also presents some fictional and historical inspirations for Carrió's invention of Concolorcorvo, including *Don Quijote de la Mancha* (Cervantes 1983), which Carrió appropriated in order to give his opinion about several hot-button issues: the origins of the Indians, Crown and church policies of integration and assimilation that developed from the Reconquest period into the late eighteenth century, culture versus biology. Recalling the partly Indian man who accompanied Carrió on part of his inspection tour, Calixto Bustamante, this chapter suggests that his legal troubles and shame (*infamia*) shaped Carrió's invention of Concolorcorvo as an impostor and a blowhard. That *infamia* was caused partially by his various manifestations of *hybridity*.[4] Finally, the chapter looks at how the debates about the rights and responsibilities of provincial governors are figured in *El lazarillo de ciegos caminantes*. Carrió's opinions in these controversies placed him squarely in the camp opposed to Bourbon technocrats in Peru, which explains not only the inspector's cantankerousness but also the legal problems that dogged Carrió after the clandestine publication of his exposé.

Chapter 7 analyzes Carrió's sense of humor and conceptualization of wit. It also explains how the Guatemalan tale functions rhetorically, as a unit within the broader unit that is *El lazarillo de ciegos caminantes*, and how closely Carrió followed rhetorical authorities (classical and modern) in his construction of the tale and the 4Ps from Lima riddle embedded in it. It suggests links between the Guatemalan tale, medieval tournaments, and mock trials in eighteenth-century Peru and France and then deliberates on the weighty legal and literary question "Is Carrió's joke merely a friendly insult, or is it instead a piece of defamation?" Finally, the case is made again that Carrió's exposé is not as baroque as literary historians believe it to be: the Guatemalan anecdote in which the riddle and its solutions are embedded could have been written in Cicero's times or in Montesquieu's. Its very presence reminds us that the baroque borrowed as much from antiquity as it bequeathed to the Enlightenment.[5]

Because most postmodern theorists believe that they are in some form or fashion reacting against the Enlightenment—against the eighteenth-century business of perfectability, against the costs of doing that business borne by cultures and institutions that were not valued within Enlightenment models—it is surprising that Carrió has not been claimed by colonial and postcolonial critique as an aged poster child for Enlightenment dissonance or difference à la Montesquieu. However, most of the criticism of Carrió's account has de-emphasized the material conditions in which he lived and worked and wrote, choosing to focus instead on *race, class,* and other postcolonial approximations using structuralist, poststructuralist, and other largely ahistorical tools.

To avoid the *postcolonial trap,* I do not approach Carrió's report as fictional discourse or historiography in general as invented narrative; my objections to this approach have been aired on other occasions. I also call attention here to the fact that I have elected to speak of *viceregal,* rather than *colonial,* Spanish America for the same reason that Anglo-Americanists speak of *colonial,* rather than *viceregal,* New England: where a concept or category did not exist, it is not helpful to Anglo- or Ibero-Americanists to pretend that it did. The primary goal of this book is to uncover the messages that Carrió's inspection report conveys about hierarchy, commerce, and fraud in eighteenth-century Spanish America within the geographical limits established earlier. Consequently, beyond the discussion of genre and audience in this Introduction, only Chapters 6 and 7 directly engage with *El lazarillo de ciegos caminantes* qua literary discourse.

Carrió, Double Consciousness, and the Criollo/Peninsular Rivalry

The 1768 trial (*probatio*) that resulted in Carrió's recognition as an untitled nobleman (*hidalgo*) yielded the bulk of the information that we have about his immediate family. His father, Justo de Carrió y Lavandera, an *hidalgo* and permanent alderman in Gijón, Galicia, married Teresa Carreño Argüelles in 1705. They had several children: Fernando, a Benedictine monk; second-born Antonio, a Carmelite monk in New Spain; first-born Cosme, a priest; Justo; José; and Alonso, the fifth child, who was born on July 3, 1715 (Gómez-Tabanera 1984, 230–34). The inspector in *El lazarillo de ciegos caminantes,* Carrió's textual secret sharer, reveals that the young Spanish merchant left Gijón for New Spain in 1735. At the age of thirty, after spending four or five years trading in New Biscayne, he moved to Mexico City (see Figure 1), where he lived for more than five years (Carrió 1973, 459).[6] In an unpublished *Manifiesto* written in 1777, Carrió stated that he had covered New Spain from Vera Cruz to Chiguagua as a merchant and from Mexico City to Guatemala (then part of New Spain) (see Figure 2) as a traveler (Real Díaz 1956, 4). Attempts to reform the bureaucracy in Mexico were especially intense in the 1740s and 1750s (Arnold 1991, *passim*); as a merchant and as a traveler, Carrió could not have ignored this fact.

The Spanish Crown's attempts at bureaucratic reform, which aimed to bolster its authority, are in fact a constant of Spanish history, according to Bertrand (1999b). A continuity stretches from the reforms instituted by Ferdinand and Isabella to those enacted by the Bourbon monarchs in the second half of the eighteenth century. The latter witnessed a deepening, or evolution, of the reform measures from the early eighteenth century rather than an overhaul of the administrative apparatus.[7] Recognizing this continuity spurs us "to relocate the Bourbon reforms of the second half of the eighteenth century, traditionally baptized as enlightened, within a long-term historical perspective" (Bertrand 1999b, 325).

This study approaches the Crown's efforts at reform as inseparable from the processes of identity formation among Spanish residents in the viceroyalties of New Spain, Peru, and later New Granada and the Riverplate. *El lazarillo de ciegos caminantes* confirms that identity formation was very different from the narrative of it that elite *criollos* began to write at the end of the eighteenth century, when their monopoly of the high courts and of the production and distribution of goods and services—a monopoly made possible by the alliance of elite *criollos* with elite and aspiring-to-be-elite peninsulars—was challenged by the Crown. (Their story, which has been masterfully recorded by David Brading [1991] and Anthony Pagden [1992], is not the tale I wish to tell here.) The discourse of disenfranchisement that began at that point, unlike the earlier rebuttals of European attacks on *criollos,* was the father of the *Spanish American Middle Ages* narrative that served as a cornerstone of nation building for nineteenth-century Spanish American intellectuals and politicians. This refashioning of viceregal history, aided by the refashioning of Spanish history undertaken by their European contemporaries, portrayed viceregal Spanish America as a feudal comedy of errors in which *criollos* were victimized by European Spaniards.[8] That so many Spanish American politicians and magnates were descendants of elite *criollos* who had pillaged their own lands in tandem with European Spaniards (who were often their wives, husbands, sons-in-law or daughters-in-law) is history. It is often ignored by the *Sturm und Drang* school of Spanish American identity that I have just sketched. My critique of current scholarly discussions of colonial subjectivity and discourse is therefore linked to my particular understanding of the *criollo*-peninsular rivalry, which privileges the long-term, microhistorical dimensions of social relationships in eighteenth-century Spanish America.[9]

Even in the eighteenth century, the viceroyalties of Peru and New Spain were commonly called empires (*Imperio Peruano, Imperio Mexicano*), not *colonies* in the Anglo or French sense, and what Anglo and French scholars call the Spanish Empire was the *Monarquía* for the individuals who lived within it.[10] I do not dispute in this study that attempts were made to turn the Empires of Peru and Mexico into colonies during the late eighteenth century.[11] (Indeed, in 1774 the term *colony* [*colonia*] was used in the Anglo sense by Pedro Rodríguez Campomanes, Charles III's minister and a keen student of Adam Smith.) What I question is the unqualified success of those attempts at administrative and economic reform, and I give evidence that those attempts did not significantly alter local and regional structures of power. Again I emphasize that questions of identity in the large chunk of Bourbon Spanish America that is the subject of this study—their practices of inclusion and exclusion and our interpretations of those practices in the postcolonial period—cannot be isolated from economic and bureaucratic matters in the *Monarquía*.

The 1746 trial of wits in Santiago de Guatemala, at which the riddle of the 4Ps from Lima is posed and solved in two different ways, has several identity markers, as well as oblique references to what or who was in need of reform. Before the Spaniard from Guatemala poses the riddle, the inspector sets up the story:

> Para que Vm. dé fin, señor inca, a un viaje tan pesado, le concluirá Vm. con una burla chistosa que hizo un guatemalteco gachupín, a ciertos chapetones limeños. Para evitar toda equivocación y sentido siniestro, es preciso advertir que fuera de Lima se dicen limeños a todos aquellos que tuvieron alguna residencia en esta capital, ya sean criollos o europeos. En la Nueva España los llaman peruleros, y en la península mantienen este nombre hasta en sus patrias, y así en Madrid, a mi cuñado y a mí y a los demás criollos nos reputaban igualmente por peruleros o limeños. Se hallaban seis u ocho de éstos en Gua-

temala a tiempo que gobernaban aquel reino los ilustrísimos señores Araujo y Pardo, peruleros, a quienes hacían la corte los chapetones o gachupines, como dicen allende y aquende el mar. (Carrió 467–68)

[In order to bring such a tiresome journey to a close, Mr. Inca, you shall conclude it with a practical joke that a Guatemalan *gachupín* played on some Liman *chapetones*. To avoid any ambiguity or sinister interpretations, it is necessary to note that, outside of Lima, all of those who resided for a time in this capital, whether they are *criollos* or Europeans, are called *Limans*. In New Spain they call them *peruleros,* and in the Peninsula they keep this name even in their homelands, and so in Madrid they treated my brother-in-law and me and the other *criollos* alike as *peruleros* or *Limans*. Six or eight of the latter found themselves in Guatemala at a time when the most illustrious lords, Araujo and Pardo, *peruleros,* were governing that kingdom, to whom the *gachupines* or the *chapetones*—as they say on this and that side of the Ocean, respectively—were paying court.]

What is jarring about this passage is the fact that in the inspector's declaration Carrió, who left Spain for New Spain when he was a grown man and then moved to Peru when he was about forty, refers to himself as an American Spaniard: "so in Madrid, they treated my brother-in-law and me and the other *criollos* alike as *peruleros* or Limans." As if this "me and the other *criollos*" were not perplexing enough, given what we know about Carrió and what the inspector tells us in the Spaniard's exposé, the inspector soon designates the archbishop and the governor of Guatemala, who were born and raised in Lima, as *peruleros,* a designation that was not restricted to American Spaniards: European-born Spaniards who took up residence in Lima were also called *peruleros*. None of this, I am convinced, was mere rhetorical slippage on the part of the Spanish author of *El lazarillo de ciegos caminantes*. The inspector's multiple sites of enunciation, in fact, represent a multilayered subjectivity. They bring to the surface a positional hybridity, or double consciousness, that is closer to what theorists of colonial situations have assigned to the colonized indigenous person or African or to the colonizing/colonized creole or *criollo*.[12]

What I have said of Carrió can be said equally of the Spaniard from Guatemala and of the Spaniards from Peru. Carrió's Guatemalan tale refers to the former and the latter in language used to deride Spaniards who were not born in America: "El Gachupín Guatemalteco reparó en los muchos elogios que hacian de Lima los Chapetones." ("The Guatemalan *gachupín* noted the many praises that the *chapetones* sang of Lima.") (Carrió 1775, n.p.). After the Spaniard from Guatemala officially challenges the Peruvian delegation to solve the riddle of the 4Ps from Lima, the spokesman for the delegation replies in part:

Señores, el Enigma que propuso nuestro Paysano el Gachupín, y el Desafío que hizo, prueban el poco conocimiento que tiene de las cosas que pasan allende el Mar, y que reputa a los Chapetones por unos Hombres que solo pensamos en nuestros particulares Intereses, sin atender a las particularidades del Pays. De todo estamos muy bien impuestos aunque Forasteros. (Carrió 1775, n.p.)

[Sires, the Riddle that the *Gachupín,* our Countryman, posed, and the Challenge that he issued, confirm the little knowledge that he has about things that happen yonder the Sea and that he assumes us *Chapetones* are a bunch of Men who only look out for our particular Interests, without thinking about the particulars of the Country. Though Outsiders, we are on top of everything.]

Here the spokesman for the Peruvian delegation refers to the Spaniard from Guatemala as a *gachupín,* the term that Spaniards born and raised in the Viceroyalty of New Spain used to designate Spaniards born in Spain. The same man refers to himself and the other members of the Peruvian delegation as *chapetones,* the term that Spaniards born and raised in the Viceroyalty of Peru applied to Spaniards born in Spain. He addresses the Spaniard from Guatemala as one of his countrymen *and* as a *gachupín,* which suggests two different ideas: (1) the Spaniard from Peru and the Spaniard from Guatemala are members of the same community and (2) the person speaking is a *criollo,* precisely a Spaniard born and raised in the Viceroyalty of New Spain (where the term *gachupín* was used), whereas the person to whom he is speaking is a Spaniard born and raised in Spain. To further complicate matters, the Spaniard from Peru identifies the Peruvian delegation as *chapetones,* which again suggests two different ideas: (1) he and the men whom he represents are European Spaniards and (2) the person speaking is a *criollo,* specifically a Spaniard born and raised in the Viceroyalty of Peru (where the term *chapetón* was used).

Why does Carrió speak, by turns, as a European Spaniard, as an American Spaniard (*criollo* or *español americano*), and as a *perulero* (a Spaniard, European or American, who resides or once resided in Peru)? Why does the spokesman for the *peruleros* identify himself and his opponent from Guatemala as European Spaniards by employing the slang of first a *criollo* from New Spain and then a *criollo* from Peru? The answers to these questions, which have not been posed in the more than 225 years that have passed since the clandestine publication of Carrió's exposé, are only hinted at in the autobiographical revelations and the inspector's Guatemalan tale that have led me to pose the questions. We must look past Carrió's discourse, and beyond the fetishization of the *criollo,* at the material reality of eighteenth-century Spanish America to find satisfactory answers.

For those of us who are interested in issues of identity, Carrió's *perulero* concept throws a spanner in our works: it disrupts the prevailing scholarly distinction between European and American Spaniard, positing an experiential identification (residence in Peru) rather than a geographical and pseudobiological one (birth in Spain or Spanish America). This is no simple matter: a Spaniard from Europe, Carrió nonetheless appears to be the colonized subject, or perhaps the colonizer/colonized subject, of postmodern cultural studies. However, my point herein is not to postulate a middle category between *criollo* and peninsular: indeed, I could very easily coerce Bhabha's concept of hybridity into playing that role, and there would be no need for me to carry the issue forward. Instead, I argue that a peninsular like Carrió, as well as any *criollo,* could have a double consciousness and that the elite *criollos* and peninsulars of the Guatemalan tale *viewed themselves and functioned, historically* and in spite of the double consciousness and ribbing, *as one group.*

I believe this is what both the historical record and Carrió's exposé tell us. It is also what several Latin American scholars have been telling us for decades. *Perulero* (or *criollo,* for that matter) is a discursive reality that can be fully grasped only by examining the material conditions—the historical relationships—in which it arose, conditions obfuscated by the discourse of elite *criollos* in the late viceregal period and Spanish American politicians in the nineteenth century and beyond.

The elite tale of identity in late viceregal Spanish America assumes that *criollo* (American Spaniard) or *europeo* (European), like the modern concept of *race,* was an immanent category. According to this tale, birth in a particular place (i.e., place of origin) determined one's identity, or framed what colonial and imperial studies scholars commonly call the *colonial subject.* Critical discussions about *colonial subjectivity,* including the *criollo*-peninsular rivalry, need to be reinscribed in material reality, I am persuaded, and this can be expedited by focusing on the microhistorical dimensions of social relationships, especially economic relationships. Microhistorical approaches to such relationships analyze social networks—organized relations between family, friends, and colleagues. They take us beyond the shared interests of professional groups (e.g., archbishops, judges, merchants, governors), geographic groupings (e.g., Europeans, Mexicans, Limans, Spaniards), and affective and ostensibly antagonistic communities (*peninsulares* and *criollos*), and they help us to understand the failure of Bourbon reforms in general and the ideological impetus of *El lazarillo de ciegos caminantes* in particular. As Bertrand explains in his study of the social networks of royal treasury officials in eighteenth-century New Spain:

> This framing in terms of social networks can therefore contribute to a re-framing of the issue of the Bourbon reforms, the transformation of the colonial state and its impact on the affirmation of protonational aspirations among the *criollo* elite. One can surmise that the reforms did not mean a whole lot as long as the values of the actors charged with applying them persisted without

radically changing. From this point of view, the passage from the Old Regime to modernity must be analyzed more from the point of social practice than from the norm imposed from above. (1999a, 49–50)[13]

Since the sixteenth century, elite *criollos* and *peninsulares* organized themselves through patterns of marriage and inheritance in order to defend their family and economic interests. Rejecting the notion that *criollo*-peninsular relations in eighteenth-century New Spain were antagonistic, Gloria Artís has reconstructed the genealogy of Mexico City's elite families to understand how the old *criollo* aristocracy retained its economic and political dominance. It did so, in part, by incorporating peninsular merchants who had accumulated fortunes in New Spain. Thus, a dozen or so families enjoyed an increasing concentration of power and wealth.[14] "In view of that, the vision of the oligarchy as a single group eliminates the distinction between *criollos* and peninsulars. Both formed part of the oligarchy and they were integrated into a single social organization sharing economic and family interests" (1994, 21).

Bertrand makes a similar case against the "elitist and *criollista*" marriage model identified in previous studies of *criollo* elites: "Strong geographical endogamy, translated for the Spanish-American elite in terms of the *criollo*-peninsular dichotomy, cannot be verified for these [royal treasury] officials: 75% of the marriages reconstructed for a group of some three-hundred individuals do not obey this rule as they take place between a peninsular—the royal official—and a *criollo* woman." When subjected to a rigorous examination by historians and anthropologists who do not ignore the microhistorical dimension of identity in viceregal Spanish America, the vaunted *criollo*-peninsular rivalry breaks down on both sides. When Bertrand tells us that 75% of the officials from Spain married women born in Spanish America, he also tells us that *criollo* elites were ready, willing, and able to marry their daughters to treasury officials who were from Spain. What is even more striking is that, according to Bertrand's research, *criollo* elites were even willing to "marry down" their daughters to peninsulars: "The same thing occurs with social homogamy, or the tendency to fall back on one's own social group, which translates into a difficulty with integrating newcomers in view of defending 'honour' and 'blood.' This behavior, frequently ascribed to the colonial elite, cannot be totally confirmed in the case of royal officials' marriages, since 30%, or a very strong minority, of their marriages are forged with [*criollo*] families of much greater social prestige than their own" (1999a, 47). Bertrand's research is replete with examples of marriage choices that link *criollo* elites in Mexico with elites in Madrid, Lima, and so forth. Social homogamy and geographic endogamy, he argues, yielded to familial endogamy (1999b, 224). The selling of offices and of licenses to marry a woman native to one's jurisdiction was Crown policy, and it enabled social networks to form and sustain themselves.

In the face of overwhelming evidence presented by scholars of social networks in New Spain, it is high time that we discard the "elitist and *criollista*" marriage model, as well as the Romantic tales of *criollo* and peninsular hatreds. Yet to fully grasp that Carrió's exposé is a tale of such networks throughout Spanish America, it is necessary to establish that elites in Peru, notwithstanding the economic and literary rivalries between Lima and Mexico City, were not unlike those in New Spain. This spadework has, in fact, already been done: Artís's and Bertrand's findings for New Spain are matched by Guillermo Lohmann Villena's findings for Peru. According to his research, a handful of families dominated the religious and political posts of the Viceroyalty of Peru until the last quarter of the eighteenth century.[15] Between the years 1700 and 1775, *criollos* were not underrepresented at the high court in Lima. In numerical terms, they held 46 percent of the posts. Natives of Lima alone occupied 33 percent of the judgeships; natives of Chile, 7.5 percent; and natives of New Granada, 2.5 percent. No less significant are his marriage statistics, which imply that elite marriage patterns in Peru were similar to those in eighteenth-century New Spain. A full 48 percent of the Lima-born judges married women from Lima, as did 4 percent of the judges from other parts of the Viceroyalty of Peru. Only half of the traditional model for elite *criollo* marriage (elite *criollos* marry their equals) can be confirmed here (*criollos* marry *criollas*), because Lohmann Villena did not specify the ancestry or wealth of the *criollas,* or *criollo* wives. Yet his analysis of the marriage choices made by peninsular judges on the high court in Lima calls into question even that half, because only 21 percent of them married women from Spain. A hefty 79 percent percent of them married *criollas*: 10 percent married *criollas* from outside Peru, 39 percent married women from Lima, and the remaining 30% found wives in Peruvian cities other than Lima.[16]

As Socolow has observed:

> To govern America the Spanish Crown had always strived, in theory if not in practice, to create a disinterested bureaucracy, a corps of civil servants unencumbered by personal and familial ties to local groups. . . . One of the ways envisaged . . . was to prohibit marriage with local women. As a result, Hapsburg legislation decreed that no Audiencia oidor, nor any of his children, could marry a native of the same Audiencia district. Indeed, a magistrate could only marry a criolla from another area after special royal permission had been secured. Regardless of legislation, in the Audiencias of Mexico, Lima, Santiago de Chile, and Santa Fe de Bogotá, criollos and Spaniards married to local women came to dominate the halls of justice and the fiscal administration of the colony. (1987, 193)

Perhaps no one captured the concept of marriage as a mechanism of the *criollo*-peninsular oligarchy in eighteenth-century Lima better than Antonio de Ulloa and Jorge Juan, who stated that their observations about elite *criollo*-peninsular marriages in Lima were generally true for all of Spanish America:

> Among distinguished families, in particular, the same thing occurs in Lima as in Quito, and it is a general rule in all of the Indies that some families have been established there for years and others have settled there recently. Because Lima is the seat of all the commerce in Peru, many more Europeans flock there than to any other city, be it for this reason or because of the government and magistrate posts to which they are appointed when in Spain. For both types the most noble individuals are chosen, and although many return to their hometowns after they have completed their appointments, normally most of them stay on, and charmed by the abundance and the good climate, get married to ladies of nobility who, beyond their dowry of material assets, tend to have one of natural assets, and so this is how new families are continually established. (1748, 3:70)

It was not supposed to be this way, of course. Lawyers for the Spanish Crown had been aware of potential problems, but royal dispensations (often purchased along with posts in Spain) thwarted the rationale of the laws that walled off the halls of justice and the vaults of the royal treasury from the loyalties of family.

In the Viceroyalty of New Granada, too, European Spaniards paired off with elite *criollas*. As Ulloa and Juan reported, the former were merchants and the latter were offspring of the landed gentry, whose ancestors had come to Cartagena from Spain as government officials:

> The white homeowners that live in Cartagena can be divided into two types: the Europeans and the *criollos,* or natives of the country. The former, whom they call *chapetones,* are not many in number because they either return to Spain after they have made a respectable fortune or move to the interior provinces to better their fortune. . . . The families of *criollos* are the ones who own the land and farms, and among these are some of great nobility because their ancestors [in Spain] moved to those places with government appointments and their families, settled down there, and [the descendants] have tried to maintain the lustre of their ancestors by marrying either their *criollo* equals or Europeans who arrive in the *armadas.* (1748, 1: 40)

A native of Madrid, Dionisio de Alcedo y Herrera (1690–1777) was appointed provincial governor of Canta, Peru, in 1721 and was designated governor and president of the high court in Quito in 1728 (González Palencia in Alcedo y Herrera 1915, v–xi.). In his *Plano geográfico e hidrográfico del Distrito de la Real Audiencia de Quito* (*Geographic and Hydrographic Map of the District of the High Court in Quito*), originally published in 1766, he wrote about "European Spaniards who leave these kingdoms [of Spain], appointed to positions, and the accompanying entourage that serve them, and [that in the Kingdom of Quito] they call both of these groups *chapetones*" (60). He went on to describe the situation of the two groups of peninsulars after their arrival in the kingdom:

> And upon arriving there, it is hard to find a man who continues in service because the latter is generally reserved for black, mulatto and *sambo* slaves, and others commonly devote themselves to trade, in which many tend to make a fortune, and the noble ones with families or without them marry into the families of the other patrician Spaniards who are called *criollos,* descendants of the conquerors and holders of *encomiendas,* and of others who have gone there with the same charge. . . . Thus the successions grow, the treasures, lands and farms increase and are distributed and shared, and their owners confine themselves to the comfort and utility of their commodities to maintain their houses and families with abundance, regalement and the utmost propriety, leading restful and quiet lives. (60–61)

The Habsburgs had fought and lost the battle against the formation of *criollo*-peninsular oligarchies in Spanish America. The Bourbons, for their part, were hamstrung by financial pressures and political goals during the first half of the eighteenth century and could scarcely fight the battle. During the heyday of sales, Spaniards purchased their judgeship and marriage dispensation together before they left for the New World.[17] (This was also true of *criollos,* as we shall see.) Socolow has correctly signaled the purpose of some of the vaunted reforms attempted by the Spanish Bourbons. "The Bourbon reforms," she writes, "especially the policies of the third Bourbon king, Charles III, signaled a reaction against this growth of local influence; one of the cardinal objectives of Charles's program was to reconquer America from the hands of the creoles" (1987, 193). But despite the royal order of 1779 that reinforced the marriage prohibitions and added royal finance officials to the list, social practice undermined the stated intent of that and subsequent legislation. "The Spanish crown," Socolow notes, "showed itself only two [*sic*] willing to disregard its own policies, granting permission to all those who petitioned the crown" (194). As an engineer from Spain who resided in Paraguay in the 1780s bragged, "The *chapetones* are practically owners of the daughters, farms and wills of the *criollos* upon becoming their relatives" (qtd. in Rípodas Ardanaz, 1977, 36). From New Spain to Peru, historical evidence does not support prevailing approaches to identity and subjectivity in viceregal Spanish America, which merely extend the Manichean identity tale spun by *criollo* elites in the late eighteenth century and by their successors in the independence period.

The uneven, oscillating subjectivity of Carrió and the spokesperson for the Peruvian delegation refracts material reality; it is illuminated by, and it obliquely confirms, the historical evidence concerning elite marriages, inheritance patterns, and the levels of *criollo* and peninsular participation in the high court, royal treasury, and other hubs of viceregal power. A historical, or material, analysis of both yields a conclusion that escapes theories of colonial and postcolonial discourses as they are presently constituted: the object within one hierarchy is, simultaneously, the subject within another, and so it mattered little if Spaniards in Spain devalued a *criollo* in Mexico City who controlled, say, wheat production. Within the hierarchy of Spain and its dominions (i.e., the *Monarquía*) that was constructed by residents of Castile, the *criollo* and "criollized" elites in Peru—the cream of the *perulero* crop—could be envied or rewarded, disparaged or admired as fellow members of the *Nación*. At the very same time, the local cultures of viceregal Spanish America had their own hierarchies articulated and coiffed by the very same *criollo*-peninsular *roscas*, simultaneously articulator and articulated, subjects and objects of hierarchy.

Unlike revolutionary Spanish America, viceregal Spanish America is a tale of local resentments and struggles that were not waged primarily against a Crown that the lower orders did not know: they were waged against its representatives who, more often than not, were either locals or European Spaniards who were tied to locals by blood, marriage, or occupation. Local resentments are irreducible to the vertical concerns of local elites, for the resentments of plebeians are unassimilable to those concerns. Thus, the alleged *criollo*-peninsular rivalry had nothing at all material to do with indigenous rebellions, plebeian food riots, and the like, although *discursively* the *criollo*-peninsular opposition could be deployed in hopes of deflecting the lower order's resistance to the oligarchical practices of the local elites.[18] The inspector's Guatemalan tale is an *exemplum*, a type of allegory by which Carrió captured social networks that were thwarting reform in Bourbon Spanish America.

Multiple Audiences, Multiple Genres

As José J. Real Díaz points out, Carrió sent a number of technical reports, itineraries, postal guides, updates, and summaries of his reforms to the viceroy of Peru and to postal administrators in Madrid between 1771 and 1774. Unlike his prior writings, *El lazarillo de ciegos caminantes* provides information of a nontechnical nature (1956, 20). His varied aims corresponded to different segments of his readership. On one hand, Carrió's account is directed to material *caminantes:* persons who traveled throughout Peru for professional reasons—to sell mules, to trade goods, to get to their Crown or church posts, and so on. The very term *caminante* implied both travel and trade,[19] and business travelers, no matter what their profession, needed to know about the posts and postal routes and about the different locales and their inhabitants. On the other hand, it is directed to armchair travelers, especially the supposedly enlightened literati and ministers in Europe who had never been to the New World.[20] The majority of the first group in Carrió's times valued experience; the majority of the second valued theory. The first group he often worked with; the second group he often worked for.

Just as Carrió's eighteenth-century readership was a motley assortment of potential interlocutors, so his discourse is a mixture of the popular and the highbrow.[21] Yet it would be a mistake to associate the popular with the first audience, the highbrow with the second. The wit—insinuation, caricature, jest, riddle, tale—that is meant to entertain the material *caminantes* often operates at the expense of the second audience, because influential authors and officials during the first century of Spanish Bourbon rule in the main disparaged the culture (including humor) of previous generations of Spanish courtiers and tastemakers. Like the Benedictine Benito Jerónimo Feijoo y Montenegro, the internationally renowned cultural critic of the Spanish Enlightenment, many of these armchair travelers belonged to the mob (*el vulgo*) for Carrió, in spite of their education, personal libraries, and positions of influence.

It was Baltasar de Gracián, not Feijoo y Montenegro, whom Carrió trusted; it is the *theatrum mundi* of *El criticón* (*The Faultfinder*), not the rationalist theater of *Teatro crítico* (*Critical Theater*), through which the inspector and Concolorcorvo move. In the second part of Gracián's *El criticón,* Critilo and his naïve disciple Andrenio enter the "Plebs' Square and Mob's Theater." The mob from various countries are huddled together, "speaking, but not reasoning" about politics, religion, and reform. Among the "shuffled fools," Andrenio is astonished to see so many noblemen:

> "I never thought I would see," pondered Andrenio, "so many wise fools in one place, and yet here I see them of every estate and type, even lay-brothers." "Why, of course," the wise man said, "for the mob can be found everywhere, and no matter how distinguished a community is, there are ignoramuses in it who have something to say about everything and take it upon themselves to pass judgment on things, without a bit of sense. . . . Do you think that a man is wise just because he is carried on a litter, or that he is well informed because he is well dressed? There are some who are just as base [*vulgares*] and ignorant as their footmen. And note that even if he is a prince, when he does not know certain things, but decides to take it upon himself to talk about them—to give his opinion about things he does not know or understand—right then and there he declares himself a base and plebeian man [*un hombre vulgar y plebeyo*]; because the mob is nothing more than a synagogue of presumptuous ignoramuses, and the less they understand things, the more they talk about them." (1967, 730–31)

Critical issues of genre and audience are inseparable from the instability of signifiers in *El lazarillo de ciegos caminantes.* There is a high dose of what I call *semantic variegation* in Carrió's exposé: his use of words such as *bisoño* ("rookie" or "naïf"), *caminante* ("journeyman," "traveler," or "trader"), *vulgo* ("the mob," "commoners," or "ignorant people"), and *ciego* ("blindman," "naïf," or "scamp") make translation into English a slippery art. Therefore, this study provides an English translation and the Spanish original when Carrió's exposé is quoted. It is even more important to note that this semantic variegation allowed Carrió to speak to different audiences at the same time, delivering a different message to each, which was absolutely essential to his negotiation of the Bourbon cultural paradigm imposed by the men who hired him.

A clear example of semantic variegation is *sátira* (*satire*). When Carrió caught wind of claims by some Limans that parts of *El lazarillo de ciegos caminantes* were libelous or defamatory (one of the meanings of *sátira*), he wrote to the head of the post in Madrid in defense of his work: "Yo estoy cierto de la ingenuidad, claridad y veracidad con que la escribí, hasta ocultar el nombre de los sujetos que agraviaron a las Rentas de Correos, por lo que suplico a V. V. S. S. que si fuera cierta esta noticia mande se señalen los puntos que contienen sátira para satisfacer puntualmente" (qtd. in Carilla 1976, 35–36) ("I am certain of the ingenuousness, clarity and veracity with which I wrote it, even shielding the names of the individuals who assaulted the Revenues of the Postal Service; I thereby beg Your Lords to order, were this information correct, that the points that contain libel be identified so I can give an exact response"). It is clear that Carrió distinguished between libelous satire, which some officials had accused him of having written, and a narration that folded in jocose bits (*jocosidades,* as he called them) in the spirit of Menippean satire. A great many people still enjoyed these jests in Carrió's times, but the literati and ministers who supported the Crown's attempts to remake Spain, and whom the Bourbon monarchs protected for this purpose, did not share Carrió's sense of humor. What he viewed as urbane witticisms, or friendly insults rooted in truth and exchanged among respectable people, they viewed as sins and insults that rose to the level of *sátira* in the legal sense—defamation.

Numerous critical attempts to categorize Carrió's narration have been made.[22] Many scholars have viewed *El lazarillo de ciegos caminantes* as a picaresque novel (Gómez-Tabanera 1984, 228). It is often inscribed within the carnivalesque, but the halfhearted deployment of this analytical concept has, paradoxically, underweighted the subversive freight of Carrió's exposé. A privileging of form over content has unwittingly defused the text's explosive charge: the material reality that prompted Carrió's mockery has been displaced by what could properly be called a "descent into discourse."[23] Several scholars specifically site *El lazarillo de ciegos caminantes* within the Menippean tradition,[24] and the deformations of material reality and the parody of various genres in Carrió's work support this critical approach.[25] The inspector's secretary, Don Calixto Bustamante Carlos Inca, also known as Concolorcorvo, represents a significant transformation of material reality.[26] In actuality, Calixto Bustamante was Carrió's assistant for ten months, but he did not accompany Carrió beyond Potosí and he did not write the inspector's report as the title page claims (Carilla 1976, 63–66). Furthermore, Carrió's parody of several genres leaves no doubt that his exposé continues the carnivalesque and often corrosive Menippean tradition. The latter was full of the witticisms that Spaniards had practiced for centuries, and the most famous work of Spanish literature glorified the Menippean tradition and weighed heavily on Carrió.

Although the collation of *Don Quijote de la Mancha* and *El lazarillo de ciegos caminantes* has often yielded parallels stripped of their ideological dimensions, the similarities between these works reveal a good deal about Carrió's aims. From my point of view, a truly significant sharing is to be found in Carrió's ideological motivations for writing and clandestinely publishing his account. After Don Quijote dies, the alleged author Cide Hamete Benengeli hangs up his quill (*pluma*). The last words of the novel are ones that he speaks to his quill: "for my desire has been none other than to make men hate the fake and nonsensical tales in the books of chivalry, which because of the tales of my true Don Quijote are now merely stumbling along, and will soon collapse altogether, without a doubt. *Vale*" (1983, 2:609). The alleged author of *El lazarillo de ciegos caminantes,* Concolorcorvo, ends his prologue after a *sententia* from Tacitus, saying, "con la que doy fin, poniendo el dedo en la boca, la pluma en el tintero y el tintero en un rincón de mi cuarto, hasta que se ofrezca otro viaje, si antes no doy a mis lectores el último. *Vale*" (121) ("with which I come to an end, putting my finger on my mouth, the featherpen in the inkwell, and the inkwell in a corner of my room, until another journey presents itself, if I do not rather give my readers their last one. *Vale*"). Both alleged authors express the desire of the actual authors of the narrations to extinguish certain genres of literature: Cide Hamete intends to debunk chivalric romances; Concolorcorvo intends to debunk geographical and historiographical romances.[27]

Scholars have been quick to classify Carrió's account as a travelogue (*libro de viajes*)[28] or to view facts in Carrió's exposé as mere digressions (Pupo-Walker 1982). These critical positions both stem from a lack of clarity about the responsibilities of the inspector of the posts and his options. True, both *Don Quijote* and *El lazarillo de ciegos caminantes* involve travel and travelers—just as *The Odyssey, The Adventures of Spiderman, Invisible Cities,* and countless other works of literature have. Yet the veiled explosive charge of Carrió's exposé, as I unveil it in subsequent chapters of this study, provides us with a more likely motive for his parody of travelogues and *Don Quijote de la Mancha.* It is undeniable that Menippean satire, in which travel motivates the narration and provides the protagonists with their privileged, most often otherworldy, access to the objects of the narration's disdain and ridicule had a purchase on Carrió.[29] At the very same time, we should not forget that travel was a *material* motive for Carrió: he had been commissioned to inspect and reform the posts and to write up a report. Many of his supposed digressions, I assert, were motivated by the different segments of his readership.

Note the generous title that he gave to his narration: *EL LAZARILLO DE*

CIEGOS CAMINANTES desde Buenos-Ayres hasta Lima con sus Itinerarios segun la mas puntual observacion, con algunas noticias utiles a los Nuevos Comerciantes que tratan en Mulas; y otras Historicas. SACADO DE LAS MEMORIAS QUE hizo Don Alonso Carrió de la Vandera en este dilatado Viage y Comision que tubo por la Corte para el arreglo de Correos y Estafetas, Situacion y ajuste de Postas, desde Montevideo (*Guide for Blind Travelers/Traders from Buenos Aires to Lima [Complete] with Itineraries/Routes Based on the Most Precise Observation and Some Useful Information for New Merchants Dealing in Mules and Other Historiographic Information. Excerpted from the Memoirs Prepared by Don Alonso Carrió de Lavandera during the Lengthy Journey and Commission That He Had Been Given by the Court [in Lima] for the Improvement of Delivery of Letters and Parcels, Location and Relocation of the Posts from Montevideo [to Lima]*). A title such as this compels us to distinguish between rhetorical, or literary, features of Carrió's account and the subject matter of his account, which was practical and historiographical/geographical (geography belonged to historiography in Carrió's times), in part.[30] He does, indeed, include plenty of material that today appears dry, but to the contemporary traveler, trader, or minister in the New World, that very same material was timely and practical. A brief look at two eighteenth-century works, one in manuscript and the other published, will bear this out.

The manuscript by an unknown writer bears the following desert-like title: *Itineraries and Courses in the Provinces of [the Viceroyalty of] Peru Declaring the Leagues and Stopovers Commonly Taken from Buenos Aires to Lima, from Lima to Potosí, to Potosí from Paita, from La Plata to the Cities in [the Kingdoms of] Buenos Aires and Chile, from Lima to Arequipa, and the Route That Mules Follow from Tucumán to the Inspection and Auction Houses in [the Kingdom of] Peru, and in Which the Distances from One Principal City or Village to Another Are Also Noted, Along with Some Useful Advisories for Those Who Might Have to Travel through Said Provinces.*[31] This work is basically a skin-and-bones sketch of what we today call Spanish-speaking South America, in which the author aims to help future travelers to the Viceroyalty of Peru prepare for their trip. Like Carrió's account, it includes basic information about distances between towns and stopovers or post offices (*mansiones*) from Buenos Aires to Lima, the routes taken by mule traders from Tucumán to the auction sites in the Kingdom of Peru, and so forth. Carrió's own "itinerario histórico" ("historiographical/geographical itinerary"), with his "advertencias" ("advisories") designed to ensure that mail was properly sent and delivered (433), could have adopted the same format.

Alcedo y Herrera's *Plano geográfico e hidrográfico* was a comprehensive geographical report accompanied by a *Demostración*, or detailed map. The arrangement of his report corresponded to the routes (*carreras*) or roads (*caminos*) that led to San Francisco de Quito as shown in the *Demostración:* "For the communication, trade and commercial correspondences of such a vast and stretching province with the others in South America, and even with Middle America by the

South Sea and ports that they commonly call *on the other coast* [*de la otra costa*], there are three routes or roads that lead to the capital city" (1915, 8). The first road led from Cartagena de Indias, under the jursidiction of the high court in the New Kingdom of Granada, to Quito. The second stretched from Piura, in the jurisdiction of the high court in Lima, to Quito. The third and final road connected Guayaquil, in the province of Quito, to the capital city, San Francisco de Quito (4). Two (Cartagena-Quito and Quito-Piura) of these three highways (*carreras*) were postal routes (*los Correos*) that linked the two high courts and viceroyalties of New Granada and Peru (8–11). A fourth highway was the third postal road that linked Lima, in the Viceroyalty of Peru, to Santiago in Chile, and Buenos Aires and Montevideo in the Riverplate ("carrera del tercer Correo del gobierno de aquel virreinato que llaman *de la costa*") (59). Like many geographical reports written in this period, Alcedo y Herrera's reads more like an encyclopedia volume today: from mines to rivers, customs duties, volcanoes, distances, exports and governors, it covers all the bases (Hill 1996a). Yet Alcedo y Herrera elected to guide his readers through the area described by referring to postal routes and postal carriers, because the post was so very central to communications and commerce in viceregal Spanish America.

Like the two aforementioned works, Carrió's exposé involves travel, but not exploration or exotic travel. Certain historical distinctions among types of travel and travelers should be recalled here. In eighteenth-century Peru, business travel was the bulk of travel (again, *caminantes* meant *traders,* not just *rovers*); leisure travel basically consisted of trips to the country, or promenades.[32] Adventure trips to Peru were popular among Europeans who could afford them, and such adventure travel produced a substantial number of travelogues from which I quote throughout this book. Just as many drivers today use rest areas to refuel and get a bite to eat, business travelers in eighteenth-century Spanish America visited the offices of the post in sparsely populated areas to exchange mules or horses and to purchase supplies for the rest of their trip, and they often followed the postmen's routes. In the main, *El lazarillo de ciegos caminantes* is historiographical (which included the geographical), and the manner in which Carrió presents his materials should not mislead us.

Works that belonged to the catchall genre of the almanac and contained astronomical explanations, geographical descriptions, predictions about weather, harvests and political events, riddles, and even jokes left a deep imprint on his exposé. As left field as these works appear today, they bear on the title of Carrió's exposé and on his shuffling of genres, registers, and audiences in it. Cosme Bueno, a Spanish resident of Lima whom Carrió admired, published his almanacs with the title *Lazarillo de los ciegos* (*Blindmen's Guide*) (Stolley 1994, 249). Yet he did not invent this classification. Numerous almanacs published in Spain bear this or a similar title. Many were authored by the Spanish moralist, satirist, and college professor Diego de Torres Villarroel, including *Los ciegos de Madrid. Almanak, pronóstico y diario de quartos de luna para el año bisiesto de 1732. Juizio de los sucessos elementares y políticos de la Europa* (*The Blindmen of Madrid. Almanac, Forecast and Diary of Moon Quarters for the Leap Year of 1732. Judgment of the Elemental and Political Events in Europe*) (Aguilar Piñal 1978, 61). Some almanacs promised to be guides to naïve, or "blind," mortals in Madrid, as in the following title: *Gran Piscator nuevo. Pronóstico para 1735. El lazarillo de los ciegos de esta Corte* (*The New Great* Piscator. *Forecast for 1735. Guide for Blindmen in This Court*) (64). Another, titled *El segundo Lazarillo y Piscator de aventura en una escuela de niños. Pronóstico para 1737* (*The Second Guide and* Piscator *of Adventure at a Children's School. Forecast for 1737*), played off the same suggestion (67). Like the seers of old, many astrologers of the eighteenth century were blindmen (or they represented themselves as blindmen), and many blindmen represented themselves as astrologers. Hence the title of one almanac directed at residents of Burgos: *El ciego astrólogo. Nuevo Piscator burgense para 1751* (*The Blind Astrologer. New* Piscator *from Burgos for 1751*) (88). Still another almanac, published in Madrid in 1759, suggested that a council of blind seers had issued predictions about the weather, courts, and political events in Europe: *Los ciegos. Pronóstico diario de quartos de luna, con los sucessos elementales, áulicos y políticos de la Europa para el año de 1760* (*The Blindmen. Forecast Diary of Moon Quarters, with the Elemental, Royal and Political Events in Europe for the Year 1760*) (104).

Moreover, almanacs were not an exclusively Spanish affliction. There was a plethora of English guides, or "almanacs-plus," published in Carrió's lifetime— many of which included information that we find in *El lazarillo de ciegos caminantes*—including *The English Chapman's and Traveller's Almanack for the Year of Christ, 1711, Wherein All the Post-Roads, . . . the Marts, Fairs and Markets in England and Wales Are Alphabetically Disposed in Every Month* (1711). Other examples are the twenty-first (1766) and twenty-second (1772) editions of *Vade mecum, or The Necessary Pocket Companion,* which contained Samuel Moreland's *Perpetual Almanack,* as well as tables explaining how to cast Portuguese gold; the postal rates for letters; the story of the penny post; the principal roads in England; the rates charged by coachmen, carmen (men who loaded and unloaded goods for sale), and watermen; and so forth. The tenth edition (1765) of *A Complete Guide to All Persons Who Have Any Trade or Concern with the City of London and Parts Adjacent . . . Designed for the Use of Persons of All Degrees, as Well Natives as Foreigners* provided the names of streets, squares, churches, meetinghouses, companies, merchants, and trading houses. It also surveyed the rates and schedules of coaches; the rates of carmen, watermen, porters, and coachmen; and the rates, schedules, locations, and destinations of the general post and the penny post. It even provided charts to determine interest payments and the value of commodities, as well as maps of the Royal Exchange and the city of London. In my view, Carrió was very much a man of his times, and his exposé straddles different genres and registers with the same ease that authors of almanacs straddled them.

Two works attributed to Daniel Defoe deserve separate mention here, both because they were very popular and because they bear striking resemblances to *El lazarillo de ciegos caminantes.* The first is called *The Compleat Tradesman, or The Exact Dealers Daily Companion. Instructing Him Thoroughly in all things absolutely Necessary to be known by all those who would thrive in the World; and in the whole ART and MYSTERY of TRADE and TRAFFIC; and will be of constant use for all MERCHANTS, WHOLE-SALE-MEN, SHOP-KEEPERS, RETAILERS, YOUNG TRADESMEN, COUNTREY-CHAPMEN, INDUSTRIOUS YEOMEN, TRADERS in Petty Villages, and all FARMERS, AND Others that go to Countrey FAIRS and MARKETS; and for all Men whatsoever, that be of any TRADE, or have any considerable Dealings in the WORLD.* Chapter 35 gives the principal cities and towns in England and Wales and their distances from one another. Chapter 46 is called "Of the Post-Office" (Merchant 1684a, 161–62), and it discusses how letters are sent by post and on which days and to where, how men can go on horseback using post horses, and even how men and women "of better rank" can travel from London to nearby villages by stagecoaches called Flying Coaches for a small fee and how they can travel very quickly with the post (162). Chapter 47 is titled "The several rates that now are, and have been taken for the Carriage of Letters, Pacquets and Parcels, to or from any of His Majesties Dominions, to or from any other Parts or Places beyond the Seas . . ." (163–66). Chapter 48 is titled "The Rates and Orders of Coach-men" (166–68), and Chapter 49, "The Rates for Car-men" (168–71). Chapter 50, titled "Orders for Car-Men" (171–72), deals with the men who pack and unpack merchant carts. Chapter 52 is "A Table of Kings" (175), and Chapter 53 is titled "The Fairs in England" (176–80). The author provided a great deal of practical information of the same sort that is found in *El lazarillo de ciegos caminantes,* but he also incorporated proverbs, poetry, and quotes in Latin borrowed from "the Satyrist" in *The Compleat Tradesman.* A work such as this held undeniable appeal for a seasoned merchant and traveler like Carrió, and if a popular foreign guide for traders mixed the mundane and the moronic, why could he not do the same in an account whose target audience included "tradesmen"? Remember, *caminantes* did not mean only "rovers"; the semantic field of this word also included traders, journeymen, and others involved in commerce. Moreover, the edition of *The Compleat Tradesman* that I consulted was published at The Black Raven, and Carrió's exposé attributes authorship to Secretary Concolorcorvo ("Crow-with-Color").

The sequel to this guide is *The Pleasant Art of Money-Catching, Newly and Fully Discovered.* The last (and unnumbered) chapter is "A full account of the Penny-Post" (Merchant 1684b, 139–42), but several of the unnumbered chapters that precede it are cautionary tales, anecdotes, and satirical rebukes of con artists, adventurers, and bums. One is titled "How to Travail all England over Without a Farthing of Money, with an Account of those that have tried the Experiment" (71–75). In this chapter the author discusses a shyster called the False-galloper, who tells rich farmers that he has been robbed and needs to borrow money to continue his travels. This impostor can travel throughout England on someone else's dime: "And thus with the Feathers of other Birds is this Monster stuck, making wings of sundry fashions, with which he thus basely flies over a whole Kingdom" (73). Another sort of impostor scams innkeepers: "There is a Twin-brother to this False-galloper, and he cheats Inn-keepers only, or their Tapsters, by . . . bringing counterfeit Letters of commendations" (73).

Almanacs and guides for foreign tourists and business travelers can be seen as literature on travel, but they are not the same as travelogues, or *libros de viaje:* they advise for future travel (leisure or business) rather than narrate an explorer's past travels. *El lazarillo de ciegos caminantes* was closer in purpose to those pocketbook almanacs, travel guides, and trade guides, although its witticisms most often target historical persons and events rather than social types or prototypes like Defoe's False-galloper. In sum, a significant influence on Carrió was exercised by works that today are found in a bookstore's travel section. Still, I contend that Carrió did not intend to write a travelogue: this was only one of many literary genres parodied by Carrió; to read his exposé as a travelogue would be like reading *Don Quijote de la Mancha* as a straight-up chivalric romance.

Wit was upheld by the courtiers of the late medieval, renaissance, and baroque periods, but it was also appreciated well into the eighteenth century by anyone who could read. Getting the jokes in *El lazarillo de ciegos caminantes* requires a certain diachronic flexibility in addition to a synchronic analysis of the material conditions in which Carrió lived, worked, and wrote. Central to Carrió's report on the posts is the scathing riddle of the 4Ps from Lima, and it is difficult to ignore the influence of collections of jokes, scams, riddles, and laconics on Carrió's exposé.

Many *jest books,* which one Hispanist has qualified as the least critically defined subgenre of European *fool's literature,* date from the sixteenth century (Márquez Villanueva 1979, 234–35). During the Spanish renaissance, several jest books, or collections of wit, brought together riddles, tales (*casos*), witty sayings, and retorts. Numerous editions of *Floresta española* (*Spanish Anthology*) by Melchor de Santa Cruz (originally published in 1574) were published well into the eighteenth century (1702, 1728, 1751, 1769, 1777, 1787, 1790) (Santa Cruz 1997, lvii–lviii). I refer several times in this book to *Miscelánea o varia historia (Miscellaneous or Various Tales)* (written in 1589) by Luis Zapata de Chaves (1999) and *Las seiscientas apotegmas y otras obras en verso (Six-Hundred Apothegms and Other Works in Verse)* (written in 1596) by Juan Rufo (1972). Unflattering tales of postmen were included in these collections.[33] Rufo's apothegms appeared in a 1718 Portuguese collection by Pedro José Supico de Moraes and more than fifty times in the 1730 *Segunda parte de la Floresta española (Spanish Anthology Part Two)* by Francisco Asensio (Rufo 1972, xxv–xlv). In the eighteenth century, original compilations other than Asensio's *Floresta española* continued the jest book tradition.

Bernardino Fernández de Velasco y Pimentel's *Deleite de la discreción y fácil escuela de la agudeza* (*The Delight of Wit and Easy School of Acuity*) was published several times (1743, 1749, 1764, 1770). *Tertulia de la aldea* (*Village Chat*), a periodical collection of short stories, was published between 1775 and 1777 (and perhaps as early as 1768). Both of these texts contained riddles built from glyphs or initials (Fernández Insuela 1990, 850–53).

The title of Carrió's exposé and his claim of offering travelers a bit of relief and advice together recall in spirit two collections of wit by Joan Timoneda: *Buen aviso y Portacuentos* (*Fair Warning and Story Carrier*) (1564) and *El Sobremesa y alivio de caminantes* (*Afterdinner Book and Travelers'/Traders' Relief*) (1563). His short stories are classified as either *cuentos* or *dichos*, following Juan de Boscán's terminology in the Spanish version of Baldassare Castiglione's masterpiece, *Los cuatro libros de El cortesano* (*The Courier*) (1994; originally published in 1534). Some had erudite sources: apothegms derived from Erasmus, and witty tales taken from Italian collections, whereas others were traditional, or rooted in lore. The majority of Timoneda's stories are jocose, although some sententious tales appear as well (Timoneda 1990, 8–19). Timoneda's *El sobremesa y alivio de caminantes,* read by many, echoed in Quevedo's poetry and in a later (1728) edition of Santa Cruz's *Floresta española* (21–24). He was not, however, the only author of a jest book to cross over, so to speak, from a seriocomic genre to a decidedly serious one. In Gracián's *Arte de ingenio, Tratado de la agudeza* (*Art of Wit, Treatise on Acuity*), for example, he referred to Rufo more than thirty times, and in *El criticón* he again borrowed from Rufo's collection (Rufo 1972, xxv–xlv).

Carrió's exhibition of wit in *El lazarillo de ciegos caminantes* should not be interpreted as a concession to journeymen or muleteers. Fool's literature was not a phenomenon of Spanish popular culture: the masses in Spain did not read, and many men of Carrió's standing and temperament devoured such books of wit. In Britain too, moreover, the long eighteenth century was the age of wit. In Richard Head's *Nugae venales, or Complaisant Companion, Being New Jests, Domestick and Foreign, Bulls, Rhodomontados, Pleasant Novels and Miscellanies,* his "Epistle to the Reader" equated ignorance and blindness: "You ignorant brisk Fops, who being internally blind, can discern no farther than you can see, whose gaping mouthes dam'd up with silent Non-sense speaks loudly that ye are full of emptiness" (1675, n.p.). His first section, titled "Domestick Jests, Witty Reparties, &c.," consists of witty short tales (1–132). The second section is "Foreign Jests: Witty Reparties, &c." (133–98), and the third is "Witty Sayings of a French Jester" (199–205); clearly, a jestbook was a cross-cultural enterprise. "A Bull Prologue" (206), "A Bull Letter" (207), and "Bulls" (208–43) follow. A section titled "Pleasant Stories" (244–75) precedes "A Cluster of Choice Novels" (276–311), which Head laughably claimed to have gotten from a gentleman who was standing in front of a pasquinade tacked to White Chapel Church, adding that they "may be more properly called Jests than Stories" (276–77). Another section is titled "Lyes and Improbabilities" (312–14), which is followed by "Miscellanies" (315–23). In his last section, "A Preachment on Malt," Head elected to provide serious and jocose interpretations of the riddle M.A.L.T. (324–27). Nathaniel Crouch's *Winter-Evening Entertainments* (the seventh edition dates from 1737) contained tales and riddles with their solutions. There were also *Jack Smart's Merry Jester, or, The Wit's Compleat Treasury* (1750s), *The Polite Companion, or Wit a-la-mode, Adapted to the Recreation of All Ranks and Degrees, from the Prince to the Peasant* (1760), and the seventh edition of *Ben Johnson's Jests, or, The Wit's Pocket Companion* (1760?), all of which contained many of the same types of literature that we find in Santa Cruz and sprinkled throughout Carrió's exposé: epigrams, inscriptions in jest and in earnest, tall tales, maxims, puns, moral tales, bulls and sundry jokes, retorts, and riddles.

Comic theater's contributions to *El lazarillo de ciegos caminantes* have not gone unnoticed. Several critics have studied the relationship of Concolorcorvo to the fool (*bobo*) of Spanish comedy, the closing epitaph's relationship to eighteenth-century Peruvian opera, and the similarities between Carrió's targets of censure and those found in a satirical dialogue written in Lima during the same period.[34] Carrió borrowed a great deal from drama, as did the blindmen who sold theatrical broadsides (*pliegos teatrales*), or recited them from memory.[35] Rustics and their mules were often portrayed in baroque theater, and they are ever present in Carrió's exposé. In one *entremés* (skit), a singing mule "turned monkey" laughed at and urinated on the play's *bobo* (Ávila 1911, 205). Secretary Concolorcorvo is a *serrano*—a native of the Peruvian highlands—and often speaks like one, whereas one of his female counterparts (*serrana*) in a Spanish skit spoke of her *Seor* (instead of *Señor*) and had to choose between a wagoneer with his mule and a nobleman (Mendoza 1911, 332–35). Under "Author's Obligations," in the 1777 *Reglamento para los teatros de Madrid* (*Ordinances for the Playhouses in Madrid*) (Cotarelo y Mori 1904, 666–71), the list of "props and sundry items that [owners] must provide for their plays" included these: "Cardboard mules," "Hempen Cloth Mule's tail," "Mule Harnesses and Saddles," "Geese, bunkers and a bag-of-bones donkey," and "Journal and Perfume Bottle" (668–70).[36] Mules were still a part of everyday life in the Spanish world, even in capital cities, and comic theater during the Enlightenment still reflected their role in travel, trade, and communications.

Indian painters and sculptors are "comic actors" ("*comediantes*"), the inspector observes (387), by which he meant that they were nobody's fools. When Secretary Concolorcorvo asks for more time to describe the magnificence of his native Cuzco, the inspector responds with stage instructions, and the Secretary begins to mimic as a comic actor:

> *Pasito*, como digo yo; *aparte*, como dicen los cómicos españoles, y *tout bas*, como se explican los franceses, porque si lo oyen las mulatas de Lima le han de poner en el arpa, que es lo mismo que un trato de cuerda, con que ellas castigan a lo político. *Molatas* y *molas*, todo es uno, porque se fingen *mansas* por dar una *patada a so satisfacción*. Muy bien imita Vm [Concolorcorvo] a sus paisanos, porque no le cuesta trabajo. (395)

[*Keep it down,* as I say; *aside,* like the Spanish writers of comedies say, and *tout bas,* as the French express themselves, because if the mulattas in Lima hear you, they will string you like a harp, which is the same thing as getting the cords treatment, with which they punish diplomatically. *Mowlattas* and *mowles,* they are one and the same, because they pretend to be *tame* just to *kick yow harder.* You imitate your countrymen quite well, [Mr. Concolorcorvo,] because it does not cost you any effort.]

In *Il Cannocchiale Aristotelico* (*The Aristotelian Telescope*), published in the mid-seventeenth century, Emanuele Tesauro discussed symbols of wit that worked through words or content, noting that mimic performances were "animated hypotyposis." They were metaphors built from hypotyposis in content, or things: "all this that represents some Action with a lifelike quality and energy and movement" (1968, 616). Like the fool of fool's literature, Concolorcorvo often mimics others, and this adds a theatrical quality to *El lazarillo de ciegos caminates.* Yet make no mistake: Concolorcorvo is no fool; he just *acts* like one. As Don Quijote tells the *bachiller* Sansón Carrasco: "To tell witticisms and to write jokes is proper to great wits: the most astute figure in a drama is that of the fool (*bobo*), because he who wishes to let on that he is naïve, must not be" (2:53). In *El lazarillo de ciegos caminantes,* Carrió employs Concolorcorvo as a *bobo* to air his own wit, or *discreción,* on numerous occasions.

Journalism and the Culture Wars: Carrió's Indictment

Significant links between newspapers and Carrió's exposé have been conspicuously absent in discussions around the genre and audience of his narration. Newspapers and almanacs alike contained historical, geographical, and political news, as well as riddles. The practice of paying blindmen, who were often appropriated in the titles of almanacs, to sell newspapers was so pervasive that it had already yielded a popular adage to refer to a person who was going blind: "Está ya para vender gazetas" ("He's already fit to sell newspapers").[37] Newspapers and journalists were the objects of contempt for many in Spain and Spanish America who decried their flattery, omissions, and plagiarism.[38] Carrió himself was a critical reader of foreign news. In Montevideo, for example, Carrió's alter ego, the inspector, laughs at an unidentified newspaper reporter from London who reported on a state dinner: "Venga ahora a espantarnos el gacetero de Londres con los trozos de vacas que se ponen en aquella capital en las mesas de estado. Si allí el mayor es de a 200 libras, de que comen doscientos milords, aquí se pone de a 500 sólo para siete u ocho gauderios" (136) ("Now let the gazetteer from London shock us with the pieces of beef that are served on state tables in that capital. If the biggest there weighs 200 pounds, which feeds 200 *milords,* here a piece weighing 500 pounds is served to just 7 or 8 *gauchos*").

Because Benedict Anderson (1983) has assigned to newspapers a significant role in the birth of nationalism, Latin Americanists by and large focus on Spanish-language newspapers published in the last third of the eighteenth century.[39] Yet Spanish American newspapers published earlier help us to understand Carrió's skepticism and his inclusion of an *enigma* (or riddle) in his exposé. Before addressing the specifics, it is important to have a general sense of what constituted journalism under the Spanish Bourbons and how the circulation of Spanish-language newspapers relied directly on the mail ferries and roads of the Spanish postal service.

Like all literate residents in Spanish America, Carrió was familiar with Spanish newspapers such as *Gaceta de Madrid* (*Madrid Gazette*) and *Mercurio histórico y político* (*Historiographical and Political Mercury*). These, like letters and packages and commercial goods, traveled the postal routes of Spanish America. Even before they arrived in Spanish America, newspapers were dependent on the postal system in Spain. As Luis Miguel Enciso Recio has explained, "The shipments were done through La Coruña using the packetboats of the Postal Service. The routes were two: by way of Havana, from which they were distributed to New Spain, Cartagena and the Islands of Barlovento; and by way of Buenos Aires, which delivered to Peru, Chile and other points" (1957, 83). As a traveling merchant and later as postal inspector, Carrió was familiar with ports, postal routes, and mail ferries that traveled between Spanish America and La Coruña in his native Galicia. He had to have been familiar with the *Gaceta de Madrid* and the *Mercurio histórico y político,* which were sent to Spanish America by mail ferry in the years leading up to *El lazarillo de ciegos caminantes* and were distributed by the postal service. [40]

The *Gaceta de Madrid* dates from the seventeenth century. The eighteenth-century version was modeled after the French *Gazette.* In a royal decree that confirmed the publisher's privileges in 1707, Philip V noted that he subscribed to and read issues of the *Gaceta* every week. In February 1761, publishing rights were incorporated by the Crown, and the publisher was compensated with monies taken from the postal service. By 1762, the *Gaceta de Madrid* was being managed by the secretary of state and his staff (Enciso Recio 1957, 25–32). *Mercurio histórico y político* had a more checkered past. *Mercure historique et politique* was published in Paris during the eighteenth century, and another *Mercure historique et politique,* which opposed the political flattery of the Parisian version, was published in Parma. Still another version was published at The Hague. According to one scholar of this last version, "Spain received extensive treatment and general condemnation in the *Mercure historique et politique* during the ascendancy of the Queen Elizabeth Farnese during the period 1714–1746. . . . In the 1750's editorial fear of Spain as a force disruptive to the peace of Europe declined and editorial interest in Spain diminished from then on. For example, the enlightened despotism of King Charles III (1759–1788) went unpraised in stark contrast to the hero worship offered to Frederick the Great and Catherine the Great" (Crawford 1969, 181–83). The Spanish *Mercurio histórico y político,* which began publishing in 1738, translated news not only from the *Mercure* published in Parma but also from "different *Diarios, Mercurios, Gacetas* from all countries" (qtd. in Enciso Recio 1957, 44) for its reports. The editor also included geographical descriptions of Europe, stories, and recent developments in the arts and sciences. Since 1739, it was required that both the *Gaceta de Madrid* and *Mercurio histórico y político* be approved by one of the king's ministers before going to press (Enciso Recio 1957, 26–44).[41]

Politics, rationalism, and economic desires underpinned the optimism of publishers and editors in eighteenth-century New Spain. The first newspaper to be published in Mexico City, *Gaceta de México y noticias de Nueva España* (*Mexico City Gazette and News from New Spain*) (1722) and the second, *Gaceta de México* (*Mexico City Gazette*) (1728–1739) were monthly publications. The editor of the first noted that, during the tenure of the marquis de Castell-dos-Rius, the first Bourbon viceroy of Peru, sheets of news had been printed in Lima and that a gazette was not without "utility," since it was "a most faithful account of what occurs in these far-flung regions." Journalists also could please those in Europe who "ask[ed] for news of America in order to enrich their histories with novelty" (qtd. in Agüeros de la Portilla 1911, 400). Europeans relied on newspaper accounts "to enrich . . . their histories," a reliance shared by many of their Spanish American counterparts, and journalism played a significant role in the construction of learned versions of Spanish American events. As we shall see, that reliance could irritate participants in the same events whose memories of them differed from those "most faithful account[s]."[42] The last issue of *Gaceta de México y Noticias de Nueva España* was published in June 1722.

Roughly six years later, on January 1, 1728, the Holy Office's publisher, Joseph Bernardo de Hogal, launched Mexico City's second regularly published newspaper, *Gaceta de México* (*Mexico City Gazette*) (1728–1739). The publisher's comments in the first issue confirm that the distinction between journalists and historians was becoming fuzzy and that rationalism was bolstering confidence in the work product of both sets of intellectuals:

It has not been precisely determined when *Gazettes* came into fashion, but one can safely assume that it was over two centuries ago, for the great Historian, Father Famián de Estrada, put together the eloquent History of the Wars in Flanders for the most part from the *Gazettes* that he had read, and though knowledge of when they began in Spain has retreated from inquiry, their utility to Chronicles is public knowledge, and more so to the most recent ones, for the *Gazettes* of Madrid since 1700, which was [the year of] the precious death of the pious Lord Don Charles II, contain the Reign of our August Philip, and with their news the discreet Historian, Dr. Don Juan de la

Cruz, published four books, very pleasant though small. (qtd. in Agüeros de la Portilla 1911, 405–6)

The editor of *Gaceta de México* noted that a viceroy of Peru had relied heavily on newspapers (including those published sporadically in Lima since the turn of the eighteenth century) to inform his mandates. (Guatemala, too, imitated Lima's example: *Gaceta de Guatemala* [*Guatemala Gazette*] first rolled off Sebastián de Arévalo's press in 1729 [Vela 1960, 1:160; Agüeros de la Portilla 1911, 400–407].) He then added, "In many courts in Europe, Gazettes roll off the press every week, and every month, like in Paris and Parma, . . . with the title of *Mercurio Histórico y Político,* which contains the actual state of Europe and what is happening in its Courts, the affairs of its Princes and their intentions" (qtd. in Agüeros de la Portilla 1911, 406).

As the messenger to the gods and as the god of eloquence, commerce, theft, and travel, Mercury (*Mercurio*) was adopted as the name of many newspapers. Mercury made his appearance in Mexico City, in *Mercurio de México* (*Mexico City Mercury*), first published in 1742. Political and religious officials who worked outside of the Capital served as regional correspondents of the *Mercurio de México* by mailing their news to the editor (Agüeros de la Portilla 1911, 399–410). The first issue of *Gaceta de Lima* (*Lima Gazette*) was published in 1744, and in the early years of the *Gaceta,* Mercury appeared at the top of the front page (Figure 3). While Carrió was inspecting the posts from Lima to Buenos Aires/Montevideo, a vehicle of Enlightenment science, *Mercurio Volante con noticias importantes y curiosas sobre varios asuntos de Física y Medicina* (*Flying Mercury with Important and Curious News about Various Matters of Physics and Medicine*) was published in Mexico City. True to its name, *Mercurio Volante* had a fleeting existence: it began circulation in November 1772 and ceased in February 1773 (413–16).

In the late sixteenth century, historians had tried to guide travelers in their journeys; in the eighteenth century, travelers (including newspaper correspondents) were guiding historians. Spanish American newspapers allowed and even encouraged the learned—intellectuals and Crown officials alike—to become armchair travelers, while newspaper editors in the capitals relied on correspondents whose reports from the provinces reached the editors by post. But because travelers and armchair travelers alike required rest, newspapers in Europe and Spanish America frequently offered their readers a bit of intellectual entertainment in the form of a riddle (*enigma*). Sebastián de Covarrubias Orozco's definition from 1611 confirmed that the learned of the renaissance knew of riddles: "ENIGMA. Is a Greek name . . . ; [it] is an obscure allegory, or a deceptive and intricate matter or question invented at the pleasure of the person who presents it" (1943, 520). Collections of riddles were very popular in Spain, and not only among renaissance humanists: Cristóbal Pérez de Herrera's collection (1733, 1943), first published in 1608, was republished numerous times well into the eighteenth century.

Emanuele Tesauro treated the marvelous (*il mirabile*), of which the last species was "the RIDDLE, which our Author [Aristotle] calls, *A witty oration composed of the most disparate terms*" (1968, 459). One sort of riddle that was published in collections and newspapers was aptly described by Tesauro in his treatment of ambiguity, or equivocation: "Likewise many Riddles are born from this, like when you call a Rainbow *A bow without a string and without arrows.* And the crane for lifting heavy objects, *I am a Crane, but I do not fly.* And threatening [someone] with the apple [*pomo;* i.e., handle] of a sword, *I will make you eat an apple that will break your teeth*" (389). These examples are of the sort of riddle often written in verse and called *adivinanza* ("guess") in Spanish because it requires readers to guess (*adivinar*) the thing, person, or action to which the riddle alludes.[43] In *Arte de ingenio*, Gracián discussed another type of riddle that was included in newspapers. In "On the Conceits of Questions" ("De los Conceptos por Qüestión"), Gracián wrote, "Every Question demands thought and is pleasant food for wit: through difficulty it gives pause and through the witty solution it pleases. The artfulness and wit of this principal form of sharpness consists, then, of a queer, hidden and moral question, in the extravagant solution to which the intellect finds enjoyment" (1998, 19). He added, "When there are variety and competitiveness in the answers, facing off against each other, they make the question more pleasant" (320). This last claim makes Carrió's closing with a trial of wits understandable from a literary vantage.

Yet we should recognize that Carrió's decision to use a riddle to hold together the account of his inspection of the posts was not especially Spanish or especially baroque. The Spanish penchant for riddles came out of renaissance humanism, continued into the seventeenth and eighteenth centuries, and was a cultural constant even outside the Hispanic world. In Great Britain, for example, collections of riddles such as *Thesaurus aenigmaticus, or, A Collection of CXL of the Most Ingenious and Diverting Aenigmas or Riddles With Their Explanations, Being Designed for Universal Entertainment and for the Exercise of the Fancies of the Curious* (1731), and *The Book of Knowledge, or, The Trial of Wit Containing Above An Hundred Riddles for the Benefit of All That Desire to Try Their Wits* (1766) invited readers to test their wits. A French periodical also incorporated a variety of riddles. *Mercure de France,* later called *Mercure galant,* began in 1678 as a monthly composed of three hundred to four hundred pages. Its editor from 1710 to 1714 was Charles Riviere Dufresny. Under the title of *Amusements,* which formed the second part of *Mercure galant,* Dufresny included rhymes, riddles (*énigmes*), songs, and *questions galantes.* These riddles were widely read;[44] in addition, a best-selling collection of riddles was published in Paris in 1717 (Moureau 1982, 126 n. 7).

The first Spanish American newspaper to incorporate riddles was *Mercurio de*

México. Cognizant of the European precedent, the editor explained that he was including

> for the greater satisfaction of studiousness and the exercise of wits, a RID-
> DLE, summarized in the brevity of a *décima* [ten-line stanza], that will be un-
> raveled in a few words the following month along with the name of whoever
> solves it, and exquisite Talents, in whom this Court abounds, will be able to
> summarize whatever RIDDLES they like in the same meter, and by contact-
> ing the Author [the Editor] they will earn the reward of having the riddles
> with their names shared with the public in succeeding months. (*Gaceta de
> México* 1986, 3:216)

The first issue of the *Mercurio de México* that ends with a riddle was dated January 1742 (*Gaceta de México* 1986, 3:222), some four years before the merchant Carrió left the Viceroyalty of New Spain. Moreover, throughout the 1740s and 1750s, a riddle was published at the end of the *Gaceta de Lima* (Figures 4, 5, and 6), and the correct solution to each riddle was mailed to the editor by a reader and published in the subsequent issue.[45] I am convinced that Carrió's invention of an *enigma* parodied a staple of the newspapers that he and other residents were reading in New Spain and Peru.

Given the increasingly rationalist claims of their founders, Spanish American newspapers were not as practical or as useful as Carrió would have liked. In the early issues of the *Gaceta de Lima,* the section of Spanish American news (from Lima, the Viceroyalty of Peru, the Viceroyalty of New Spain) came first, and the European section—whenever reports arrived to the editor by post—followed. Often, however, the order was reversed. In the February 8–March 28, 1745, issue, under the headline "CONTINUACION DE NOTICIAS DE EUROPA" ("NEWS FROM EUROPE CONTINUED"), the following editorial note appeared:

> In the preceding issue of the *Gaceta,* that which was judged most signifi-
> cant from the news of Europe, and which the small space of this periodical
> permitted, was included. In the current issue the summary of other news
> [from Europe] will be shared, with the hope of satisfying the curious [*curiosos*]
> who live in areas distant from this Court and who do not have the facility or
> the occasion to read *Mercurios* and other papers [*papeletas*] that come from
> Europe. (n.p.)

This reversal signaled, in my estimation, a more general shift in Spanish America's learned and popular cultures: one that valued the foreign or faraway more highly than the autochthonous and local, the theoretical or universal more highly than the practical and particular. The passage just quoted also conveys how newspapers in capitals such as Lima shaped the opinions of faraway events for "curious" people who did not live in large cities. In *El lazarillo de ciegos caminantes,* Carrió has Concolorcorvo feign enthusiasm for the contemporary paradigm of highbrow culture—intellectual curiosity—at the same time that he undercuts it by mentioning the riddle of the 4Ps from Lima:

> En este dilatado reino no hay, verdaderamente, hombres curiosos, porque jamás hemos visto que un cuzqueño tome postas para pasar a Lima con sólo el fin de ver las cuatro prodigiosas PPPP, ni a comunicar ni oír las gracias del insigne Juan de la Cova, como asimismo ningún limeño pasar al Cuzco sólo por ver el Rodadero y fortaleza del Inca, y comunicar al Cojo Nava, hombre en la realidad raro, porque, según mis paisanos, mantiene una mula con una aceituna. (104)

> [In this extensive kingdom there truly are no curious men, because we have never seen a Cuzcan ride the post to get to Lima with the express purpose of seeing the 4 prodigious Ps or to contact or listen to the witty tales of the remarkable Juan de la Cova, just as we have not seen any Liman go to Cuzco just to see the Inca's rounded boulders and fortress and to contact Nava the Cripple, a man truly unusual because, according to my countrymen, he maintains a she-ass with an olive.]

In Carrió's exposé, the eloquence, travels, thievery, and commerce of Mercury's beneficiaries are spoofed, and the literature that is parodied includes newspapers and other periodicals named after the god.

Special Deliveries: The Cultures of Theft in Bourbon Spanish America

Like journalists and like blindmen, postmen did not enjoy a solid reputation in Madrid, New Spain, or Peru; they were the butt of jokes. In *Teatro universal de todas ciencias y artes* (*Universal Theater of All Arts and Sciences*), a bestseller published in 1615 and republished, after many revisions, as late as 1733, the Spaniard Cristóbal Suárez de Figueroa defined the mission and nature of postal carriers:

> The profession of these men is to walk on foot or run the posts on horseback, carrying personal letters, tenders, documents, monies and such things, serving Princes, lords, gentlemen, merchants and whoever sends them. . . . Nor are the mister postmen devoid of vices and faults, for, without mentioning the betrayal, that reigns in many, of opening someone else's letters, of exposing their seals and of revealing their secrets, they are also the inventors of a thousand frauds, breaking into the bags and pretending to have been robbed

on dangerous routes. . . . In everything else, almost all the people in this profession are most vile, blasphemous, and they constantly tie themselves to the bottle, not a single one ever reaching old age, all of them dying, worn out, in the prime of their lives (1615, Discourse 40, 150).[46]

An unflattering portrait of postmen appears in Spanish America too. In 1749 the Council of the Indies noted that the post offices and horses used by the postal carriers in Santiago de Guatemala were located in Indian villages. Although the carriers themselves were low on the social pecking order in Bourbon Spanish America, this did not discourage them from looking down on the Indians: "The mulatto postmen being of a depraved and lowly estate [*depravada vil condición*], and astute, they dominate and treat Indians with disdain" (Bose 1939, 268–69).

By appropriating the post and postmen in satire, usually *political* satire, European literature from the seventeenth and eighteenth centuries reflected the contempt in which they were held. In Italian we have Ferrante Pallavicino's *Il corriero svaligiato* (*The Postman Stripped of His Mailbags*) (1660b)[47] and *Continuazione del Corriero svaligiato* (*The Postman Stripped of His Mailbags Continued*) (1660a).[48] The pretext of the letter reading and commentary is that a Milanese postman had his mail robbed by order of an Italian prince who wanted to find out what the Spanish were plotting. No money or packages were taken, only letters, which suggests that, although the theft was blamed on bandits, a powerful person ordered the mailman's route to be interrupted. At least one of Pallavicino's works was known in Peru in the eighteenth century, for the famed *criollo* savant Peralta Barnuevo mentioned Pallavicino's work as *Correo desvalijado* in his satirical defense of a viceroy of Peru, *El templo de la Fama vindicado* (*The Temple of Fame Vindicated*) (1996b). Also significant is Traiano Boccalini's *Ragguagli di Parnaso e Pietra del paragone politico* (*Reports from Parnassus and Political Paragon's Stone*) (1910–1948), in which numerous letters travel to Parnassus by post, where they are read by Apollo.

In English we have Charles Gildon's *The Post-Man Robb'd of his Mail. Or, the Packet broke open*, in which he refers to a successful previous effort from the second half of the seventeenth century that he had given a similar title (1717, pref., xiv). We have Edmund Curll's biting parodies of Alexander Pope and other famed authors, *Post-office Intelligence, or, Universal Gallantry, Being a Collection of Love-Letters* (1736), which he attributed to several persons, claiming that these letters were returned to a London post office because their recipients had died or moved away. If the post and postal workers were pilloried, the post was also a common literary device used to pillory; it was a pillorying post in the truest sense of the phrase.

In Spanish there is Diego de Torres Villarroel's *Correo del otro mundo* (*Mail from the Other World*), perhaps inspired by Pallavicino. In one of the letters written by the dead, an Italian astrologer makes fun of Torres Villarroel's "theatrical metaphor"—his jocose appropriation of theatre and music—in the almanac for 1724 titled *Melodrama astrológica* (*Astrological Melodramma*) (2000, 120 and n. 83). In his reply to the letter written by a dead mystic, the narrator-protagonist of *Correo del otro mundo* states, "From the very start my life took the wrong course in its directions, and I was so unfortunate that, though guided by many signs, I would lose heart on the roads. And, walking astray, night would come upon me on the slopes of fate, my blindness [*ceguedad*] never finding a traveler [*caminante*] to put me on the path of life" (187). Blindness is figured epistemologically and morally here, just as it is in Carrió's exposé. Similarly, at the end of *Correo del otro mundo*, Torres writes, "If [this work] does not please you, reader, take a number [*paciencia*]. I shall not force you to buy it, but at least the newspapers and the blindmen [*ciegos*] are going to stick you with it, whether you want it or not" (191–92).

Carrió's blind contemporary in Lima, Friar Francisco del Castillo Andraca y Tamayo, wrote a mock *quaestione,* or debate, on lying in Lima that reveals how central the Peruvian post was to everyday life in Carrió's times and how it was manipulated by various groups and interests: "Coloquio y Disputa en que se indaga el dónde, el cuándo y el pretexto con que se miente más en Lima" ("Coloquium and Debate That Ascertains Where, When and under Cover of What One Lies the Most in Lima") (Castillo 1948, 88–96) is argued by two idle residents of Lima. One of these jousters points out the various "guilds" of liars, "for example, muleteers/who, when they go herding/carry more lies than/supplies in their saddlebags" ("verbigracia, borriqueros/que cuando van arreando/más que materiales, llevan/mentiras en los capachos") (90), which suggests to me that the oblique and obvious references to smuggling in *El lazarillo de ciegos caminantes* are not satirical fiction. Further, most of the verses in this *Coloquio y Disputa* concern "the volcano . . . of Lima's talking-shop" (91): "Este es el Correo, el cual/está siempre destinado/a seguir en tres veredas/correspondencias y estado/pero en estos nuestros tiempos/tenemos bien observado/que es el del Cuzco y de Valle/ocasión de mentir largo" (92) ("This is the Post, which/is always designated/to track, along three routes,/private corrrespondence and state,/but in these times of ours,/we have clearly noticed/that the post from Cuzco and from the Valley/is an occasion for telling long lies").

In 1747 Domingo de Basavilbaso—who would later endear himself to Carrió as the postmaster general of the maritime post (1767) and postmaster general of the maritime and ground post (1769)—offered the viceroy of Peru a proposal to extend the royal posts into the Riverplate region. Basavilbaso, future postmaster of Buenos Aires, modeled his proposal on the delivery schedule that was operating in the rest of the Viceroyalty of Peru, and is revealed in Castillo's verses: "Observadles que lo fuerte/del mentir va principiando,/ocho días antes de esto/y después dura otros tantos" (1948, 94–95) ("Note that the bulk/of the lying gets started/eight days before this/and lasts for about the same"). One of the proposal's stipulations reads in part "that every eight days a *chasqui* must be sent out with every type of letter and papers (*cartas y pliegos*), but without any goods (*sin especie ninguna*) in his charge" (Bose 1934, 341). Near the close of Castillo's poem, the resolution of this debate boils down to two possibilities: "porque o esta es la mentira/ que especie nos está enviando/*simpliciter* infinita/que así hay quien llama al peca-do/o es la criatura *omnium/mentirissima,* notando/que en ella la iniquidad/dejó su ser agotado" (1948, 95–96). The gist of these lines is that either lying is sending out countless goods as letters ("simpliciter" plays off *simple* or *sencilla*—roughly, letter rate) or the post is the most mendacious creature of all. Friar Castillo was insinuating that postal carriers (*chasquis*) who were not supposed to be delivering goods or packages (*fardos* or *especies*), because they pertained to a separate branch and tariff structure of the postal service in Peru, were doing so under the cover of letters and papers.

In the closing verses of the blind Friar Castillo's "Coloquio y Disputa" about lying in Lima, the poetic self has the last word on the postal system, using allusion (*significatio*) to remind us of the relations between communications and trade: "y por la regla que hoy se usa,/de irlo todo calculando,/digo que si por cada onza/ de una de éstas, poco hablo,/por cada libra o arroba,/fueran un cuartillo dando/ de real, doce millones/de pesos dieran cada año./Así lo sentimos todos,/el etcétera está en salvo,/porque en todo lo demás/se entiende lo que callamos" (1948, 96) ("and by the standard used today/to go adding it all up/I say that, if for every ounce/of one of these—but I undershoot—/if for every pound or *arroba,/* they were to start giving a mere quarter/of a *real,* twelve million/ *pesos* they would con-tribute per year./That is what we all believe,/the *etcetera* can be spared,/because in all the rest,/everyone knows what we are keeping quiet"). Here "ounce" ("onza") can be read literally as a reference to lies (*mentiras*) or to a class of mail that was heavier than the *carta sencilla* or *simple,* or the *pliego sencillo:* it was a package or parcel. Literally, then, this litigant's "these" (*estas*) can be understood in reference to either correspondence or lies contained in correspondence. However, I am per-suaded that Castillo's verses are deliberately ambiguous: "these" simultaneously refers to ounces, pounds, and large quantities (*arroba* is a measurement equal to 11.5 kilograms) of *pastas metálicas,* or diverted silver and gold ore. Like contraband goods and like the bars of gold and silver that had been taxed and stamped by the mint in Lima (*barras quintadas y selladas*), diverted silver and gold got to ports, and into foreign hands, by traveling the posts.

Castillo's contestant suggests something hidden yet notorious, something related to the post and merchandise: "Así lo sentimos todos,/el etcétera está en salvo,/porque en todo lo demás/se entiende lo que callamos." What these men keep secret or quiet is understood, according to the last verse, but for twenty-first-century readers to understand it we must somehow get at the main threads of the culture of Castillo, Carrió, and others in the eighteenth century and their pliable registers of discourse. I wish to comment again on *semantic variegation,* a tech-nique that compels us to study the textual clues contained in Castillo's verses and Carrió's prose.

Semantic variegation does not result merely from rhetorical imperatives such as variety or prolepsis, and it does not simply telegraph Carrió's penchant for the "instabilities" and "protean possibilities" of baroque "discursivity," to use the critical clichés. I view eighteenth-century Spanish American culture as a kaleidoscope: changes in the size, shape, and location of the bits of material reality were reflected in an endless variety of cultural patterns that are visible in patterns of discourse, or texts, written in that period. For example, it is clear today what *correo* means, and, according to the first dictionary ever published by the Spanish Royal Academy of Language, *Diccionario de la lengua castellana* (1726–1739), it meant the same thing in the eighteenth century: the mail or the postman who delivered it (Real Academia Española 1979, 1:611). However, *correo* had several other meanings that Castillo and Carrió took for granted. In the criminal courts, *correo* meant the co-conspirator or accomplice in a crime (*con* + *reo*) (1:611). In the vernacular of the underworld, *correo* meant the lookout: the thief who stood guard while others stole (1:611). Given that the postal profession was legally and socially dishonorable—a "dirty job," or *vil oficio*—it is not surprising that *correo* found its way into the argot of criminals. The verb *correr* in that same context was "a popular expression" that meant to mug someone or to knock off or rob something (1:612).

Carrió was well traveled, and he had a wealth of experience with burglars, con artists, and gangs of bandits who belonged to the lower orders: "Todos tienen a los gitanos por sutilísimos ladrones, pero estoy cierto que si se aparecieran en El Cuzco y Huamanga tuvieran mucho que aprender, y mucho más en Quito y México, que son las dos mayores universidades que fundó *Caco*" (387) ("Everyone takes the gypsies for the most clever of thieves, but I am certain that if they showed up in Cuzco or Huamanga, they would have a lot to learn, and even more so in Quito and Mexico City, which are the two greatest universities founded by Cacus"). Cacus was the mythical bandit who inhabited Mt. Aventino, one of the seven peaks of ancient Rome. In the prologue to *Don Quijote de la Mancha,* the implicit author's friend offers him a series of well-treaded allusions and stories to fill out his work. "If you deal with thieves," he assures, "I will tell you the story of Cacus, since I know it by heart" (Cervantes 1983, 1:60). Even Feijoo y Montenegro mentioned him in print, noting that Virgil had called Cacus's cave—a den of thieves—a "royal palace" (1773–1774, 7:190). In Carrió's times, educated people knew that the Spanish adjective *ciego* ("blind") was derived from the Latin *caecus,* just as *Caco* was. (Hto San Joseph Giral del Pino recorded, "CIEGO, adj. blind. Latin *caecus*" [1763, n.p.].) Carrió's characterization of Mexico City and Quito as great places for students of Cacus to get an education was not far off the mark.

Theft cast a long shadow on the cultural landscape in New Spain well after Carrió left for Peru. In the official account of his viceregal administration (1746–1754) that Francisco de Güemes y Horcasitas left his successor, he stated that Mexico City, other cities in New Spain, and the roads linking them had been infested by roving thieves. The capital itself had been a den of thieves and drunks until he corrected this social problem:

From the idleness that I have mentioned already, or due to the malignant propensity of the plebs—which is a most copious and unbudging number of low, uncivil persons who are for the most part of bad inclinations, because this capital is the cave, woods or refuge for every depraved tramp there is in the Kingdom, and they come to this one from others—the vices that necessarily become predominant are theft and drunkenness; and although in the past the former ran roughshod over the entire Kingdom, with such impudence that squadrons of bandits were infesting the roads with robberies and murders, and in the city not even the light of day could prevent robberies nor were the sacred temples exempt from sacrileges, this disorder was corrected. (1867, 8)

Such problems were long-standing. Some four decades before Carrió arrived there, an interim viceroy of New Spain, Juan de Ortega Montañés (February 27–December 1696), had taken effective measures to remove panhandlers and unlicensed food sellers from the main squares of Mexico City (see Figure 1, nos. 3, 6, and 9), and had also taken, by his own admission, unsuccessful measures to crack down on robbery and assaults in the streets and other public places (Ortega Montañés 1965, 60–63, 168–70, 172–74). It appears that in the booths and stalls set up in the public plazas, thieves hid from police, and people engaged in sexual acts (173), problems also endemic to the main plaza in Lima during Carrió's residence there.

According to the Jesuit priest Mario Cicala, who had lived in the Kingdom of Quito in the 1740s, the principal vice of residents there was theft. Break-ins at churches and commercial establishments were rampant. Thieves would literally steal the hat off a person's head (1994, 216). In home invasions, burglars used potions made from crushed human bones that caused temporary blindness and amnesia (216–17). "Indians are greatly inclined to theft, but usually they steal silly things, food items, never daring to commit serious robberies" (215). "But among the *mestizos* and others," he wrote in 1771, "I did indeed meet countless [thieves], and some of them [were] major" (216).

When Carrió was conducting his inspection of the posts, thieves and armed bandits were legion in the Viceroyalty of Peru. According to the *Memoria de gobierno (Administration Memoir)* that Manuel de Amat y Junient, the most renowned viceroy (1761–1776) of the Bourbon period, left his successor, a ring of burglars was terrorizing Lima's residents by night. He claimed that he had caught them and executed them in 1772. The highways too were infested with thieves: three leagues from Lima, in the hills of Carabeillo Valley, groups of black men were going out to the streets, raping, robbing, and committing other violent crimes. Viceroy Amat ordered the governor of Port Callao to surround the hills and arrest the men. Four men were sentenced to death, and four others were sentenced to forced labor at Port Callao (1947, 165–66). For Carrió to compare the cultures of theft in cities in the Viceroyalty of Peru, the Viceroyalty of New Granada, and the Viceroyalty of New Spain was not flattering to any viceroyalty, but it was not a comparison that could imperil Carrió. As we shall see, although theft by members of the lower orders is explicitly addressed in his exposé, theft committed by members of the higher orders, including Crown and church officials, is conveyed by indirect means that rely on semantic variegation or some other rhetorical device.

It is significant that Carrió alternates *riddle* (*enigma*) and *mystery* (*misterio*) in his exposé. Recall the definitions of *enigma* with which every eighteenth-century reader in the Hispanic world was familiar. As for *misterio*, Covarrubias explained, "that is how we call anything that is enclosed beneath a veil, a deed, or words or other signs" (1943, 807). According to the *Diccionario de la lengua castellana*, *misterios* in the plural meant "state secrets": "by extension, the secrets of princes and the dealings of great consequence and importance, which for whatever reason are kept hidden, are called [*mysteries*]. In Latin, *Mysterium*" (Real Academia Española 1979, 2:639). *Mystery* was also part of "to speak in riddles" (literally, "to speak mysteriously"), a phrase that meant to speak cryptically, implying that one knew more than one could say and creating intrigue: "*to speak in riddles* [*hablar de misterio*]. Phrase that means to speak cunningly and reservedly [*cautelosa y reservadamente*], or to affect obscurity in what one says in order to make those who are listening infer and figure out something" (2:639). Castillo, in his versified trial of wits, and Carrió, in his inspection report, speak in riddles. What is more, because Carrió chooses to structure his exposé with the riddle of the 4Ps from Lima, we readers are constantly aware that the inspector knows much more than he is saying (or than Secretary Concolorcorvo is extracting). As we shall see, simple mail fraud or the con games of travel guides and journeymen were not Carrió's (or Castillo's) target: theft was being engineered by merchants and by entrepeneurial officials on a grand scale in Spanish America.[49]

PART I

CHAPTER I

Mexico City versus Lima: Pila, Puente, Pan, and Peines

In the mock trial that closes Alonso Carrió de Lavandera's exposé, a Spanish resident of Guatemala poses the riddle of the 4Ps that surfaces repeatedly along the itinerary to Spanish residents of Lima in 1746, the very same year in which Carrió left Mexico City for Lima. The litigants are participating in a trial of wits at the archbishop of Guatemala's palace in Santiago, the capital of the Kingdom of Guatemala, which belonged at that time to the Viceroyalty of New Spain (see Figure 2).

> El Gachupin Guatemalteco reparó en los muchos elogios que hacian de Lima los Chapetones, pero al mismo tiempo advirtió que no habian hecho mencion de las quatro principales P.P.P.P. y una Noche las mandó poner con Almagre en la Puerta principal del Señor Arzobispo, con un Cartel de Desafio a los Chapetones, para que descifrasen su significacion. (1775, n.p.)

> [The Guatemalan *Gachupín* noted the many praises that the *Chapetones* sang of Lima, but at the same time he noticed that they had not made mention of the four illustrious Ps, and one Night he had them painted in Red Lead on the Distinguished Archbishop's front Door along with a Letter of Public Challenge to the *Chapetones* to decipher their meaning.]

The 4Ps riddle is thereafter given two disparate solutions. The senior member of the Peruvian delegation—Carrió describes him as *decano,* a term that indicated seniority in a Crown post—rises and presents the first interpretation, according to which Lima outdoes Mexico City in four areas:

> El Decano de los Peruleros era un Hombre serio y de pocas palabras. Luego que hicieron señal los dos Señores Governadores, Jueces y Presidentes de la Asamblea, se puso en pie, y tocando con la mano derecha su Gorra, arrengó en el modo siguiente. Señores, el Enigma que propuso nuestro Paysano el Gachupín, y el Desafio que hizo, prueban el poco conocimiento que tiene de

las cosas que pasan allende el Mar, y que reputa a los Chapetones por unos Hombres que solo pensamos en nuestros particulares Intereses, sin atender a las particularidades del Pays. De todo estamos muy bien impuestos aunque Forasteros. Vastante pudor me cuesta descifrar un enigma tan publico que hasta los Muchachos de Lima lo saben. Finalmente las quatro P.P.P.P. que fixó el Gachupín a la Puerta de este Palacio Arzobispal no significan otra cosa, como a V.S. Illustrissimas les consta, que Pila, Puente, Pan y Peynes, en que excede Lima a la ponderada Ciudad de Mexico. (1775, n.p.)

[The Senior Member of the Peruleros was a grave Man of few words. After the two Honourable Governors, Judges and Presidents of the Assembly gave the signal, he stood up and, after touching his Cap with his right hand, began to harangue as follows: Sires, the Riddle that the *Gachupín,* our Countryman, posed, and the Challenge that he issued, confirm the little knowledge that he has about things that happen yonder the Sea and that he assumes us *Chapetones* to be a bunch of Men who only look after our particular Interests, without thinking about the particulars of the Country. Though Outsiders, we are on top of everything. It causes me no small embarrassment to solve a riddle so obvious that even the Kids in Lima know it. In short, the four Ps that the *Gachupín* tacked to the Door of this Archbishop's Palace mean nothing more, as your most illustrious sires know full well, than *Pila, Puente, Pan* and *Peines,* in which Lima outdoes the fabled City of Mexico.]

Although the inspector tells his secretary that the Guatemalan tale was a practical joke played on some distinguished gentlemen from Lima in 1746, the 4Ps were also contemporary phenomena for Carrió, and the inspector refers to them on several occasions. Residents of Cuzco did not rush to Lima to see them, according to Carrió's report (104), and the inspector tells Concolorcorvo to praise them when they are traveling through Potosí (280). *Pila, Puente, Pan,* and *Peines* encodes Carrió's opinion of his society in the 1770s and transforms a postal inspector's report into social history and cultural critique.

Scholars have assumed that *Pila, Puente, Pan,* and *Peines* are self-explanatory terms, but the senior Peruvian's interpretation, which establishes Lima's superiority to Mexico City, actually represents Carrió's rebuke of high society, whose excesses were fomented (when not spearheaded) by its Bourbon rulers. Principal among these was Viceroy Amat, who was also Carrió's boss. Because of his successes as a soldier and general, Manuel de Amat y Junient, a member of the Order of Santiago, was assigned to govern the Kingdom of Chile (1754–1761) and later the Viceroyalty of Peru (1761–1776). The Spanish postal inspector's contempt for the viceroy is expressed in equations of negative superiority throughout *El lazarillo de ciegos caminantes.* Nevertheless, Carrió's attitude toward Amat and other members of his regime has gone largely unexamined, in part because of the false publication date of his exposé.

Carrió's cryptic allusions to Amat and his operatic mistress, Micaela Bastidos (also known as "La Perricholi"), along with the key dates of their affair, prove that his exposé was not published in 1773. In light of the fact that Carrió did not finish his inspection of the posts until late that year and in April 1776 wrote to postal administrators in Madrid that he had been too busy in 1774 to think about publishing his account (Real Díaz 1956, 409–11), the exposé could not have been published before 1775. Documents from the same period show that in August or September 1773, before a live audience, La Perricholi slapped the Italian actor and producer who dominated the playhouse in Lima. She was banned from the theater, and Amat broke off their relationship. However, in mid-September 1775, Amat took up with Micaela again, and in early November 1775 she was back on stage (Sánchez 1971, 101–2, 110, 113–14). As we shall see, Amat and Bastidos were still together while Carrió was writing his exposé, which means that it was finished either before their notorious breakup in late 1773 or after their very public reconciliation in late 1775. According to Carrió's own statements in April 1776, the first option is untenable; therefore, *El lazarillo de ciegos caminantes* could not have been published until late 1775, giving Carrió plenty of time to witness the continuing saga of Bourbon reform and renewal in Amat's viceroyalty.

It is always necessary to read between the lines in *El lazarillo de ciegos caminantes,* even when the inspector's topic is good taste and public order in Lima: "El actual virrey, excelentísimo señor don Manuel de Amat y Junient, decoró mucho esta ciudad en paseos públicos y otras muchas obras convenientes al estado. No puedo referirlas todas porque sería preciso escribir un gran volumen de a folio, y otra pluma, pero nadie puede negar que su genio e ingenio es y ha sido superior a todos los virreyes en materia de civilización y buen gusto" ("The current viceroy, the Most Excellent Lord, Don Manuel de Amat y Junient, greatly adorned this city with public promenades and many other works befitting the State. I cannot report on them all because that would require a great volume of folios, and another feather pen, but no one can deny that his nature and cleverness are and have been superior to those of all viceroys in the area of polity and good taste") (445–46). This ironic praise—the invisible winks and nods between the lines—can be detected through the material analysis of *Pila, Puente, Pan,* and *Peines* presented in the following pages.

Peines

Although at first blush the first solution to the riddle promises to involve combs (*peines*), the reference to Peines is actually topographical. In Carrió's times, Los Peines formed part of Lima's fabled promenade, La Alameda (see Figures 7, 8 and 9). The inclusion of Los Peines in the first solution to the riddle of Lima's 4Ps ridicules the excesses of Lima's elite—in particular, those of General Amat and his cronies—and, when properly interpreted, it reveals the true nature of several seemingly innocuous and unrelated passages in Carrió's exposé.

Persons in Lima who had to go downtown on a daily basis confronted an unwinning combination of coaches, excrement, and people. According to the Spanish traveling scientists Antonio de Ulloa and Jorge Juan, it was necessary to travel by coach or wagon in the city proper because of the constant flow of mule trains, which "has the streets continuously covered with dung, and when this is dried by the sun and the wind, it turns into a dust so annoying that it is unbearable to walk on, as well as nasty to breathe" (1748, 3:68). The French tourist Courte de la Blanchardiere noted the mixture of dung, insects, coaches, mule trains, and plebeians that crowded the city's streets: "The majority of individuals travel on horseback or by coach, there are but blacks, mulattoes and Indians who go on foot. . . . One is annoyed by the dust that rules the length of the streets and roadways. . . . What is worse is that this powder produces a prodigious quantity of two kinds of very pesky insects" (1751, 121–22). On the way out of the city, crossing the River Rimac, those same persons could enter a different world: one with a leisurely rhythm, lush greenery, wide streets, fresh air, and fountains. Durret's *Voyage de Marseille a Lima* praised the River Rimac and La Alameda, highlighting the variety of people who frequented the promenade and their motives for doing so:

> The locale of the promenade is charming; it is a beautiful pathway, very long and with a wide-open view, with four rows of the most beautiful trees, all of them orange and citrus; two streams of clean water running on either side, and at the far end one sees in the distance the front of one of the best built convents, which forms a perspective that gives great pleasure to foreigners. The coaches and wagons promenade by the hundreds in the afternoon, and it is the gathering place for all the persons of distinction in the city, curious people and foreigners. Lovers talk up their mistresses, and they honor them by following them on foot, leaning on the door of their coach; it is there that they proffer their tender thoughts and they regale them with all sorts of sweets, fruits and refreshing liqueurs. This place is full of slaves who sell all these sorts of things, and they take nothing there but their best and most beautiful; they thus make the transiting lovers pay on that basis, who spare nothing to shine on the promenade and to get in the good graces of their mistresses. These sorts of slaves do whatever they want, they feed and entertain themselves on their own, by means of a certain sum that they pay their masters; there are some of them who are quite industrious and who have plenty of means to procure their liberty with the profits that they make. It is a pleasure for the masters to give it to them because of the emulation that it inspires in the others, for whom parallel examples serve as an incentive to get themselves up from the slavery they are in, and in which the majority find themselves

even before they have the use of reason. . . . There are slaves who are paid to wet down the pathways of the promenade and spread a lot of water every day, so that the dust does not inconvenience those who promenade there. (1720, 255–56)[1]

A social institution rooted in the Enlightenment ethos, Lima's promenade progressed as the century did, becoming the site of various social functions and dysfunctions.

The annual Royal Battle Standard Parade (Paseo del Real Estandarte), which took place in early January, commemorated the Spanish conquest of Lima, the City of Kings (La Ciudad de los Reyes). The viceroy of Peru and accompaniment (judges, members of the merchants' guild, and others) rode with the royal battle standard to the cathedral to attend vespers on January 5. Later he and the dignitaries rode with the battle standard through the main streets of Lima and the promenade. On the morning of January 6, Day of the Kings in the Spanish world, they carried the standard to a *misa de gracias* to celebrate the birth of Christ and the conquest of Lima. Accounts of this parade are found in the *Gaceta de Lima* from early 1758, when Viceroy José Antonio Manso de Velasco, count de Superunda, led the parade:

On the afternoon of this day, the 6th, the customary public parade down Alameda and Peines was held, which was honored by His Excellency in his open carriage drawn by six horses, carrying in the opposite seat two lords of the high court, and on either side of the vehicle rode the new mayors-ordinary on two handsome beasts splendidly decked out, who were followed by a great many retainers in excellent uniforms. This pomp was preceded by 100 soldiers on horseback, His Excellency's [palace] guard . . . , and by the archers who marched directly nearby, protecting the carriage of the Lord Viceroy. (*Gaceta de Lima* 1982–1983, 2:116)

From this newspaper report and other sources that I have examined, it is clear that Los Peines and one other street were in fact joined to La Alameda to form Lima's promenade.[2] This configuration, which was already famous in Europe and America, was described by Cosme Bueno in 1764 as "a beautiful promenade, sumptuously renovated by the Most Excellent Lord Don Manuel Amat in 1762, at the same time that a Coliseum was established for cockfights" (1951, 19). Several poems by Friar Francisco del Castillo Andraca y Tamayo confirm that La Alameda consisted of "three lovely streets" lined with trees, flowers, springs, bells, "crystalline *Peines*," and "gorgeous canopies" made of precious stones.[3] One avenue of La Alameda was the Paseo de los Descalzos, another was the Paseo de Aguas (then called also La Navona), and the third was the Paseo Militar (Los Peines or Plazuela de San Cristóbal) (see Figure 8, nos. 65 and 66, and Figure 9, nos. 66, 67, and 69).[4] Under Viceroy Amat, however, even a military exercise at Los Peines could become a sexual exercise, for the two types were inextricably linked within Amat and his administration.

The robust Viceroy Amat dedicated a section of *Memoria de gobierno* to the public works undertaken during his reign (1947, 167–72), confirming that his attention to Lima's promenade was not paid on a whim. The following passage tells us that La Alameda was of paramount importance not only to Lima's image as a modern urban center but also to his own image:

> Shortly into my reign I inspected the public promenade, La Alameda, whose fountains were out of order, and the trees without that lush green that offers diversion and pleasantness. In all well-ordered cities these sites are maintained for the unwinding of the soul in those moments that are given over to rest, and, therefore, right away I sought to remedy the disorder that was noticeable by getting its fountains operational, replanting trees and creating seating and streets for the common folk so that they would not get in the way of the many coaches and wagons that assemble on the holidays, especially on the first days of the year when the Viceroy and the mayors-ordinary pass by, according to tradition. (169–70)

In truth, Amat did far more than dress up La Alameda for special occasions: he extended it by adding the ornate waterworks that gave La Navona its other name, Paseo de Aguas: "I thought that the promenade should extend further, so waterworks have been set up whose apparatus, modeled after that which is in Rome, upon completion will be one of the most beautiful recreations that any city could have, and I must let Your Excellency know that my wishes have been to adorn this republic by every possible means, giving it that splendor that it deserves" (1947, 170).

In 1768 a permanent bullfighting ring was opened in Lurigancho Valley, within view of the country estate owned by Viceroy Amat (and occupied by his mistress), on the corner of a cul-de-sac of El Prado (see Figure 8 and Figure 9, no. 52). The ring was built to accommodate ten thousand people. Instead of a circular wall around the sand, to which the bullfighter could run for cover, barriers were built so that people who had rented private rooms around the ring, beneath the stands, could see (Sánchez 1971, 80–81). The ring was built after the viceroy had renovated Piedra Lisa, the road that led out of the city to Lurigancho Valley. This was one of Viceroy Amat's proudest public works: "The road that they call Piedra Lisa, which leads to the amenable Lurigancho Valley, also was impassable, and what was then a roughshodden crag that one could hardly set foot on is today so level and paved that it is one of the leisurely rides in coach that residents have, with a roomy and lush walkway that I have built and improved at my own expense" (1947, 167–68). No viceroy of Peru was more personally and professionally invested in Lima's public recreation venues than General Amat.

The Alameda lost some if its charm (and Viceroy Amat's presence) after the paving of Piedra Lisa and the building of the bullfighting ring in Lurigancho Valley. According to the season, Viceroy Amat frequented either the streets of La Alameda or Piedra Lisa and the Valley, and the people followed his lead.[5] Although Los Peines and La Alameda may have been fertile ground for what Amat in his *Memoria* called "the unwinding of the soul," men and women did not go there to experience the pleasures of the contemplative life. According to Friar Castillo, "undercover bulls" ("toros encubiertos")—young studs in coaches—bolted down La Alameda, ostensibly for fresh air but truly in search of firewood for their burning passions.[6] It stands to reason that what even a blind friar knew, Carrió could not have ignored. However, there is another dimension to Peines that ties the inspector directly to the place.

Carrió was not only an experienced merchant; he was a veteran soldier. In 1762 and 1763, during the war with England, he belonged to Lima's regiment of noble cavalrymen. Doubtless he participated in the military exercises that Viceroy Amat and his subordinates designed for public consumption. In an issue dated December 3, 1762, the *Gaceta de Lima* lauded General Amat's military flair. On November 8, Amat had met with members of his War Council:

> In this meeting the general inspection of the troops was ordered, which His Excellency began that very afternoon and continued for a period of fifteen afternoons with only a day's break; and to conduct it he had his tent set up at the site called Los Peines, where it meets La Alameda, so that these two large terrains could accommodate the multitude of coaches and plebeians that gathered to see the troops, who per his orders were presenting themselves for inspection; only a few odd companies did not report because they had asked His Excellency to wait a few days so that they could appear in the uniforms that were being finished for them, which was granted them, and we are all eagerly awaiting the day when they will present themselves because we know how splendidly they will shine and that they are already trained in the Prussian exercise. (*Gaceta de Lima* 1982–1983, 3:14–15)

In Carrió's exposé, a decidedly unflattering assessment of the military exercises at La Alameda and Los Peines is buried in ironic praise for gazettes and for the post's role in providing journalists with information about the courts in Europe (102–4). A mock heroic spirit is injected into the inspection report on numerous occasions. One apparently innocuous passage, in which a French Jesuit's satire of the Age of Reason is introduced without attribution, in fact transmits a breakdown in military discipline and an underlying *cultural* breakdown in the Viceroyalty of Peru:

> Los que tienen espíritu marcial apetecen, con razón, ver y reconocer dos grandes ejércitos opuestos en campaña, principalmente si los mandan testas coronadas o príncipes de la sangre. El autor de la inoculación del buen juicio dice: que llegó a tal extremo en este siglo el fausto de los franceses, que sólo faltó entapizar las trincheras y sahumar la pólvora, y tomar cuarteles en verano, para refrescarse con las limonadas. No se puede dudar que estos ejércitos en campaña causarán una notable alegría. La corte estará allí más patente. Las tiendas de campaña del rey, príncipes y grandes señores, se compararán a los grandes palacios. Servirá de mucho gusto oír y ver las diferentes maneras que tienen de insinuarse tan distintas naciones de que se compone un gran ejército, como asimismo los concurrentes. Solamente reparo la falta que habrá del bello sexo de distinguidas, que apenas tocará a cada gran señor u oficial general una expresión de abanico. Los demás oficiales, que son los Adonis de este siglo, se verán precisados a hacer la corte a las vivanderas. (103–4).

[Those with military spirit rightly relish seeing and inspecting two great opposing armies on the field, especially if crowned heads or royal princes are leading them. The author of *L'inoculation du Bon Sens* says that the pomp of the French reached such an extreme in this century that the only thing they did not do was carpet the trenches and perfume the gunpowder, and report for duty in the summer so they could freshen up with lemonades. No one can deny that these field exercises will cause great joy. The court will be more present there. The tents of the king, princes and great lords will be compared to great palaces. It will be a great pleasure to hear and see the different ways in which the so very different peoples who make up a great army, as well as the gathering crowds, get along. I only point out that there will be a lack of the fair sex of distinguished ladies, for there will scarcely be a fan's signal for every great lord or general officer. The other officers, who are the Adonises of this century, will be forced to pay court to the female sutlers.]

Here Carrió slyly turns Father Nicholas Josef Selis's *Inoculation du Bon Sens*[7] against General Amat and lower-ranking military officials who made military exercises and parades at Los Peines and La Alameda into *fêtes galantes,* with the enthusiastic participation of Lima's residents, rich and poor. Selis had contrasted gunpowder and talcum powder: Prussian soldiers who loved to fight and French soldiers who loved to chase girls (1761, 12). He had claimed that his countrymen preferred the novelesque and impious to true history, actors and actresses to honest men and women, and theater to the great events in Europe (23, 29). Roughly fifteen years after Selis, and some three years after Selis's satire made its way into a Spanish satire of high culture, Carrió availed himself of the Frenchman's polemic to belittle the cultural paradigm set down by Bourbon elites in Lima.[8]

Lima, not Paris, had armies composed of soldiers of different cultural groups (*naciones* or *castas*) and different estates or orders (*estados* or *condiciones*): there were battalions of Spaniards made up of, for example, noblemen or plebeians, *mestizos,* or unenslaved blacks known as *grays* (*pardos*).[9] Lima, not Paris, had a population composed of different *castas* and *estados:* the fact that the original Alameda and General Amat's brainchild, Los Peines, formed a melting pot was lost on neither travelers to Lima nor longtime residents of Peru like Carrió. Moreover, one specific phrase in the previously cited passage, "Solamente reparo la falta que habrá del bello sexo de distinguidas, que apenas tocará a cada gran señor u oficial general una expresión de abanico," is nothing if not a scantily clad allusion to Viceroy Amat and his off-duty activities. Several pieces of historical evidence support this reading.

First, General Amat is identified throughout *El lazarillo de ciegos caminantes* as "Gran Señor," and he and other military men attracted prostitutes and actresses with "fan" in hand rather than "distinguished ladies." The passage in question tells us that officers other than generals were reduced to courting female sutlers, the women who trailed armies and sold them provisions. Still, this passage most likely refers not to dashing military men such as Amat's own nephew, who was the middleman in many of his uncle's sexual transactions, but to the general and viceroy himself. After Amat left office, the daughter of a *mestiza* and a grocer (*pulpero*) sued him. It was public knowledge in Lima that she had sexually serviced the viceroy at his country estate, *Rincón del Prado,* and even at the viceregal palace, where Amat's black slave Francisco would let her in the private entrance off the Square of the Church of the Desamparados (Lohmann Villena 1976, 199 and n. 161) (Figure 7; Figure 8, no. 4; and Figure 9, no. 4).

Second, numerous passages in *El lazarillo de ciegos caminantes* confirm what twentieth-century historians have independently proven: Amat was a seventy-year-old at his sexual peak, truly the Gran Señor of Lima. Although early on the inspector divides journeymen (*caminantes*) into "rookies" ("bisoños") and veterans ("veteranos"), this opposition is later transferred from human to beast as we read that a provincial governor (*corregidor*) must mix his fresh horses ("ganado bisoño") with his seasoned ones ("mulas veteranas") (231). Burros constitute a hierarchical republic, and the inspector draws a comparison between rules of engagement in a pack of mules and rules of engagement in the harems of the Gran Señor, General Amat: "Los burros, que llaman hechores, son tan celosos que defienden su manada y no permiten, pena de la vida, introducirse en ella caballo alguno capaz de engendrar, y sólo dan cuartel a los eunucos, como lo ejecuta el Gran Señor, y otros, en sus serallos" (225) ("The burros that they call studs are so jealous that they defend their pack and do not allow any horse capable of breeding to come near it, on penalty of death, and they give quarter only to eunuchs, just as the *Gran Señor* and others execute in their harems").[10] The historical record tells us that this was precisely the viceroy's sexual *modus operandi:* he imprisoned, exiled, or killed rivals for the affection of "La Perricholi," the derogatory moniker assigned to the opera singer and actress Micaela Bastidos, who bore him at least one child.[11] Again, Carrió's exposé accurately reflects the historical record: only "eunuchs"—the *castrati* of the opera house in Lima—were permitted to interact with the Gran Señor's "harem."[12]

If Los Peines was one measure of Lima's superiority to Mexico City, it was certainly not something that respectable people should have been proud of: it was a negative, or false, superiority. Yet sexual indiscretions are sprinkled throughout *El lazarillo de ciegos caminantes,* in the form of banter that is socially harmless because the participants are supposedly plebeians or through veiled allusions that appear to be bouts of praise for Lima's elites. An especially revealing example of the latter is the inspector's mention of two characteristics particular to Lima: "La primera es la grandeza de las camas nupciales y la segunda, [la grandeza] de las cunas y ajuares de los recién nacidos en casa opulentas. Las primeras casi son *ad pompam,* y las segundas, *ad usum*" (462) ("The first thing is the grandeur of the matrimonial beds, and the second, [that] of the cradles and swaddling clothes of the newborns in luxurious houses. The first are almost *ad pompam,* and the second, *ad usum*"). The matrimonial beds are almost for show ("*ad pompam*"), which is to suggest that most of Lima's elite married couples do not have much use for them. The cradles and baby outfits of newborns in opulent houses are, on the other hand, customary ("*ad usum*"), or for actual use. Now, if elite married couples are hardly making use of their matrimonial beds and yet they have well-appointed cradles and baby clothes in their homes, Carrió's implication is that the children are not products of these marriages but of adulterous sexual unions. From several poems by the Peruvian friar Castillo, and from recent studies in history and anthropology (Mannarelli 1999; Twinam 1999), I suspect that this implication might very well have embarrassed some of Carrió's readers in Lima, but it could not have surprised them.

Furthermore, when the inspector ridicules the lavish bedrooms and nurseries of Lima's *criollo* elite, he is also taking a stab at Viceroy Amat and his traveling "harem," for the very notion of Lima's two "particularities" in fact springs from the same fount of ironic praise as the first solution to the riddle of Lima's 4Ps. After a detailed description of beds, cradles, and baby clothes, the inspector concludes that American-born Spaniards (*criollos*) of modest fortune can brag that they were reared in finer diapers than all the rulers of Europe, even if the Gran Señor comes in with all of his harem: "Los criollos de casas de mediana opulencia pueden jactarse de que se criaron en mejores pañales que todos los príncipes de la Europa, aunque entre el Gran Señor con todo su serrallo" (462).[13] Here again it is the historical record that can help us make sense of this veiled allusion to Viceroy Amat, for it is well documented that Amat received prostitutes procured by his nephew Juan or by a young confidant from Mallorca named Jaime Palmer, who owned the Rincón del Prado estate located behind the religious quarters of El Prado (see Figure 7, A; Figure 8; and Figure 9, no. 52) and near Amat's own estate (Eguiguren 1945, 37; Sánchez 1971, 126–27). The lavish rooms and gardens of Jaime's estate, to which he or Juan used to transport "the Goddesses" for the viceroy's trysts, was jocosely known as "The Great Room" ("Gran Cámara") or, more to the point, "The Little Room of Whoring" ("Cuartito de Putaísmo") (Eguiguren 1945, 218). It was public knowledge in Carrió's Lima that the money the Gran Señor earned from the illegal sale of *corregidor* posts he then spent in his "Gran Cámara" (Lohmann Villena 1976, 205).

The inspector tells Concolorcorvo that black female slaves (*negras*) do not make and unmake the beds that he has just described: "Estas las hacen y deshacen señoritas que se mantienen de néctar y ambrosía" (463) ("Young ladies who live off nectar and ambrosia make and unmake these"). Taken metaphorically, these "young ladies" are not unlike the "distinguished ladies" whom we saw earlier in the spoof of military exercises at Los Peines. Still, Concolorcorvo takes literally the inspector's characterization of the women who make and unmake the matrimonial beds in Lima's wealthy houses: he objects that, to the contrary, he has seen many women in Lima eat the same cracklings, tripe, and cheese stew as his female kin in the mountains (463). This deployment of Concolorcorvo as a naïf sets up the inspector's correction, which clarifies Carrió's intent:

> Esas, señor inca, son damas de la Arcadia, que se acomodan al alimento pastoril y bailan al son de los alboques del semicapro dios; pero éstas de que yo hablo son ninfas del Parnaso, presididas del sacro Apolo, que sólo se mantienen, como llevo dicho, de néctar y ambrosía, como los dioses. Sus entretenimientos son elevadas composiciones en prosa y verso, y cuando alguna quiere pasear todo el orbe en una hora, monta en el Pegaso, que siempre está pronto y paciendo alrededor del sacro coro. (463–64)

> [Those, Mr. Inca, are dames from Arcadia who adapt to rustic fare and dance to the sound of the half-goat god's flute, but these women that I am talking about are nymphs from Parnassus—presided over by the sacred Apollo—who, as I have said, eat only nectar and ambrosia like the gods. Their amusements are elevated compositions in prose and verse, and when one of them wishes to parade about the entire world in an hour, she mounts Pegassus, who is always ready and grazing about the sacred chorus.]

The first are the ostensibly respectable women of Lima whose crude alimentary and sexual habits Carrió engages facetiously, defining these women who make and unmake the matrimonial beds of Lima's elites as residents of Arcadia with its happiness and innocence. This confronts the image of Lima as a *locus amoenus,* an image forged in Europe by the overwhelming success of Jacques Vanière's *Praedium rusticum* (1750), first published in 1706.[14] Carrió's true opinion of such women in fact confirms those offered by several French travelers, despite his tendency to dismiss French works on Spanish America as mere *brochures.* Le Gentil, for example, had asserted that the fair sex in Lima was proud of their wantonness, or "libertinage," and that the only topic of conversation among the city's residents would make even the most libertine blush (1728, 1:101). The clergy, not the climate, was to blame, and his travelogue included tales of religious dignitaries and relatives of the viceroy who consorted publicly with women, had several children with them, and engaged in violent confrontations with male rivals (1:102–3). Unfortunately, the clergy preached what they practiced, teaching respectable women a morality of convenience—"une morale fort pratique" (1:102).

That the second group of women named by the inspector—those who eat like the gods—are Amat's mistresses can be inferred from the fact that *Goddesses* (*las Diosas*) was the term used by one of Amat's two procurers of prostitutes to describe the numerous women who had sex with the viceroy at his Rincón del Prado estate (Lohmann Villena 1976, 205; Eguiguren 1945, 218). The "elevated compositions in prose and verse" is a reference to either Lima's playhouse or the private theater and sexual shenanigans at Amat's country estate as described by historians. "Pegassus" is a bit of circumlocution for Amat's coach or horse, which was always ready outside of his country home (or Jaime Palmer's), next to the convent of El Prado, to ferry women and Amat between El Prado and the viceroy's palace, across from the cathedral in the Plaza Mayor. In 1778 the mayor of Lima declared under oath that the diva Micaela followed Amat's coach to his house in Miraflores, on horseback or in coach, disguised as a man (Lohmann Villena 1976, 197–99 and n. 158).

The illicit sexual behavior of Viceroy Amat and other elites in Lima becomes entangled textually with the favorite leisure activity of rural plebeians, who had no good name to lose and therefore could not be expected to behave like proper gentlemen and ladies. A clear example of this can be found in Carrió's description of a country feast in Tucumán (247–52)—one of the most memorable in all of *El lazarillo de ciegos caminantes,* for it would appear to foreshadow the nineteenth-century's fascination with gauchos and local color. And yet the rustic revelry, including a folk ballad with an obscene fourth stanza that was allegedly invented by a friar, is better understood as an element of Carrió's overall strategy to excoriate the moral failings of Lima's elites. The ballad is about a country courtier who competes for the affections of a woman, and its fourth stanza is uttered by the gallant: "Salga a plaza esa tropilla,/salga también ese bravo,/y salgan los que quisieren/para que me limpie el r——" (251), which is, very roughly translated,

"Bring on the troops,/bring on that brave bull too,/and bring on whoever else dares/so that I can clean my t[ail]." The missing word here is "rabo," which conjures a bull's tail as much as the front or back "tail" of a man. If the challenger's desire to meet his rivals so that he can "clean his tail" suggests their kissing his ass or his entering theirs, it clearly has a meaning that goes beyond simply defeating the "troop" of "young bulls" who are competing for his damsel's affections.

As Concolorcorvo states later, the inspector censored these verses: "Me hizo sustituir la cuarta copla, por contener sentido doble, que se podía aplicar a determinados sujetos muy distantes de los gauderios" (275–76) ("He made me replace the fourth *copla* because it had a double-meaning that could be applied to certain individuals far-removed from the gauchos"). That a friar would invent such a ballad is consonant with Le Gentil's characterization of the clergy in Lima, not Tucumán. Furthermore, the risqué and slippery nature of the friar's verses, which are placed in the mouth of macho rustics, fits that French traveler's characterization of the register used by courtiers in Lima: "A young man does not give off good airs unless all of his words are, I would not say equivocal, but *parlantes*. A cheap and uncouth love there passes for a beautiful passion, and debauchery and self-interest are the gods that women there adore" (1728, 1:101). Concolorcorvo's explanation of the inspector's fear—that the verse could be applied to individuals far-removed from the cowpokes in Tucumán—suggests that the entire stanza mocks Viceroy Amat, who frequented the bullfighting ring in Lurigancho and was famous for destroying his much younger rivals (bullfighters among them) for La Perricholi (Eguiguren 1945, 216–17; Sánchez 1971). This interpretation is supported by another fact: the racy verses allegedly penned by an unnamed friar in Tucumán are on a par with many written by Carrió's famed contemporary Friar Castillo, in Lima.

Another example of transporting the sexual sins of Lima's elites to rustic plebeians occurs when the inspector and his secretary visit Potosí. The inspector facetiously reports that men there are constant only in their love for true coquettes. A true coquette can compel her last suitor to marry her or to find her a hard-headed husband or one who will not hold a woman's past against her:

Sólo son constantes en las pasiones amorosas, por lo que se experimenta que las verdaderas coquetas hacen progresos favorables, y se han visto más de cuatro de pocos años a esta parte retirarse del comercio ilícito con competente subsistencia, ya obligando a su último galán a casarse con ellas o a buscar marido de aquellos que se acomodan a todo y tienen una fuerte testa, o al que lleva la opinión de que lo que fue en su año, no es en su daño. (295–96)

[They are constant only in their amorous passions, which is why experience shows that the true coquettes make favorable advances, and in the past few years more than four have retired from the illicit trade with a decent living, either by forcing their last gallant to marry them or to find them one of those husbands who put up with anything and have a hard head, or one who holds the opinion that what she was in her day is no skin off his chin.]

The truth is, their heads must be strong enough to sustain the cuckoldry that their wives—former prostitutes—cause them. In other words, they must be able to accept that their wives once consorted, and perhaps still consort, with "young bulls" of the sort mentioned by the friar-poet Castillo in Lima and by the inspector's friar-poet in Tucumán. Like the men in Potosí the inspector describes in this passage, men in Lima who chase after prostitutes whom they support, according to another saucy poem by Castillo, must have a strong head ("fuerte testa"): "Lo mismo es tocar a toros/que tocar a cornería,/y cada uno de éstos piensa/sacar la cabeza limpia" ("Touching bulls is the same/as touching horniness,/and every one of these men plans/to come out of it with his head unscathed").[15]

Given the international fame of La Alameda and its streets, the boasts of the Peruvian delegation in Carrió's mock trial were not outlandish: proud residents of Lima most likely bragged that one street of their promenade, Los Peines, "outdid"—was grander than—Mexico City's. However, Carrió's exposé as a whole compels us to interpret this superiority in a different light. What was truly happening at Los Peines—and nearly everywhere else where Amat pitched his tent—was not a display of battle readiness as the *Gaceta de Lima* reported; it was a battle of the sexes that created stress points in the social fabric insofar as members of different *castas* and *estados* interacted in ways that the social hierarchy condemned. A brief look at what was happening in Mexico City confirms my interpretation of Los Peines in the 1746 Guatemalan tale as an element of Lima's negative superiority vis-à-vis Mexico City.

The capital of New Spain could be justifiably proud of its elegant promenades in the eighteenth century, thanks to Juan Vázquez de Acuña y Bejarano (1658–1734), marquis de Casa Fuerte. The marquis was named viceroy on April 22, 1722, and he began his tenure on October 15 of that year (Rubio Mañé 1955, 167–68). Detractors labeled him *Gran Dux* for his Francophile ways and imperial airs. He always wore the wig and fine clothes of a military officer favored by Philip V, and he made sure that his viceregal court of New Spain echoed the protocols and tastes of the court in Paris.[16] He expended his personal energies and the royal treasury's resources to beautify Mexico City, paying special attention to the oldest promenade, La Alameda, established in 1572. In 1727 the viceroy was appointed mayor of La Alameda, a post coveted by Mexico City's elite. Dissatisfied with the pace of the work being carried out by his subordinates, he handpicked the next mayor of La Alameda in 1730, and soon after over one thousand trees were planted and the canals were cleaned up (Núñez y Domínguez 1927, 225–26). In 1771, Viceroy C.

Francisco de Croix (1766–1771), perhaps following the lead of General Amat in Lima, extended La Alameda. Not to be outdone by his predecessor, Viceroy Antonio María de Bucarelli (1771–1779) built two more avenues that crossed the original La Alameda and installed several fountains (Viqueira 1999, 171).

Having already established the prurient side of Los Peines and the other streets of Lima's promenade, it is not difficult to recognize that Lima's true competition among Mexico City's promenades was not La Alameda, but El Paseo de Jamaica, or the "Jamaican Stroll." This was a promenade along the royal canals of Mexico City that led from a neighborhood called Jamaica to that of Ixtacalco and from there to La Viga (Viqueira 1999, 112). Viceroys in the eighteenth century issued a series of reform measures to contain the debauchery associated with the Paseo de Jamaica. In 1733, a year before his death, the marquis de Casa Fuerte decided to clamp down on the revelry, as the April issue of the *Gaceta de México* confirms: "On the 13th an edict was made public by order of His Excellency in which (wishing to avoid offenses against God that arise from going to El Paseo de Jamaica at night) he orders and demands that no one dare to embark after the ringing of the bells, and that the guards not permit any watercraft whatsoever, under severe penalties that will be executed unsparingly, according to his order" (Nuñez y Domínguez 1927, 248).

That viceregal decree appears to have done little to dampen nocturnal spirits along the royal canals. When Carrió left New Spain in 1746, the Paseo de Jamaica was crowded with food sellers, musicians, and sellers of spirits. It was an immensely popular pastime that encouraged sexual romps and drunken melees among members of various *estados* and *castas*. According to Francisco de Güemes y Horcasitas, viceroy of New Spain (1746–1754), he acted to put a stop to these activities by rounding up or banishing prostitutes and setting a curfew for promenaders:

> Hidden sexual incontinence, here and everywhere else, becomes completely untreatable, while prudent rulers are content to avoid its public manifestations, as I have done during my tenure, by exiling and confining women who are free-wheeling, rambunctious and the object of public scandal. And because on this point the Paseo de Jamaica or Ixtacalco, with the selling of wines and other foodstuffs during the nocturnal gatherings, and the musical attractions, tended to lead to dissolution, fights and disturbances, I gladly took the measure of issuing an annual decree so that at exactly nine o'clock at night there would no longer be a foodstand operating and the promenade would shut down, ordering guards at La Viga not to open it after that time or permit any canoes to cross, assigning there a horseback patrol led by an officer from the cavalry company of this royal palace. (1867, 10)

In Carrió's opinion, the immoral activities that were taking place along Lima's

Paseo Militar, or Los Peines, surpassed even those that were taking place along Mexico City's Alameda and Paseo de Jamaica.

Pan

Given the scholarly disinterest in interrogating *Pila, Puente, Pan* and *Peines,* it is worth asking if a literal interpretation of *Pan* (or "bread") makes any sense. Does the first solution to the riddle of Lima's 4Ps suggest that there was more bread—that there were more bakeries and local grocers stocked with bread—in Lima than in Mexico City?

In 1697, Viceroy Juan de Ortega Montañés lamented the shortages of wheat, corn, and meat that had plagued New Spain for five years. He warned his successor that the mob blamed their rulers for such shortages: "The careless plebs blame those of us who govern as if it were within our power to bring into existence grains and corns and an abundance of livestock" (74). In the eighteenth century, wealthy residents of New Spain consumed *pan especial,* or "special bread" (also sold as *pan español* or *pan francés*), and, more frequently, *pan floreado.* Other residents consumed either "common bread" (*pan común*) or "cheap bread" (*pambazo* or *pan bajo*) or, the cheapest of all, *semita* (*acemita*), which was often sold as *pan bajo* (García Acosta 1989, 158–59). The poor, including many Indians, *mestizos,* and *mulatos,* bought *pan común* at their local grocer (*pulpería*). The wealthy, including many European and American Spaniards, bought *pan floreado* at bakeries, which also produced *pan común* and distributed it to the local grocers (García Acosta 1989, 29). The adulteration of bread was common. Bakers mixed flours of different qualities and then sold *pan común* as *pan floreado* or *pambazo* as *pan común.* They added extra water and leavening to the dough so that the baked bread weighed more, or they processed inferior types of wheat (*trigo mojado, trigo picado*) in ways that yielded more flour (García Acosta 1989, 160–64; Ortega Montañés 1965, 57, 75, 171). Viceroy Ortega Montañés had recommended stringent regulation of wheat, flour, and bread to confront the manipulation of scales and prices, which he considered detrimental to "the rational government of any republic" (1965, 77).

The production and consumption of bread in Peru was not an entirely different matter. In the late seventeenth century, the wheat supply in Lima was shaped by a poorly organized irrigation system, crop losses, an expansion of the rural population and its demand for bread, crop diversification, hoarding, and earthquakes. An organized reaction to these conditions was hampered by the lack of steady incentive for wheat farmers in the valleys of Lima: wheat was imported through Port Callao from the valleys of northern Chile (Ramos Pérez 1967, 26–34). During the War of the Spanish Succession (1700–1713), the suspension of the Portobelo trade fair, coupled with the illegal and legal trade of the French who crossed the Atlantic Ocean to the Pacific through Cape Horn, caused Valparaíso and Concepción to become key suppliers of wheat to cities in the Kingdom of Peru. However, weather and the Araucanian resistance depressed harvest levels in central and northern Chile, producing scarcity and rising costs in Lima between 1723 and 1727. The weak supply and strong demand encouraged farmers in Lima's valleys to return to planting wheat in 1727. This proved helpful when a major earthquake in Chile wiped out numerous estate farms and mills in 1730 (Ramos Pérez 1967, 55–57, 62–64, 67).

In an epic poem titled *Lima fundada o Conquista del Perú* (*Lima Founded, or The Conquest of Peru*), Peralta Barnuevo set down in verse Chile's contributions to Lima's bread industry. He explained in a footnote that the sterility of wheat fields in Lima and the coastal areas had lasted for forty years. During that period, the fertile valleys of Chile, especially Valparaíso, had supplied his native city with copious amounts of wheat (1732, can. 8, st. 53, n.). The production of wheat in the Kingdom of Peru and the importation of wheat from Chile were still pressing matters in 1736 when Peralta Barnuevo penned the outgoing Viceroy Armendáriz's *Relación del Gobierno* (*Administration Account*) (2000, 351–618):

> As to the city's provisions, its main one consisting in the wheat that it feeds on, and its granary having been the Kingdom of Chile, since the beginning of the sterility of its fields, Lima has never been without wheat; and only rarely have I had to take action, at the request of the farm owners [*hacendados*] of the Valley and with the support of the royal council, to obligate bakers to buy grains [from the Valley] at the same price that Chilean grains had, once the amount of grains that were held in the granaries and the amount of bread that is consumed were determined, based on the evidence that the *hacendados* presented of the damage that they incurred from the disparity [in prices], of the disincentive that would exist for the cultivation of their farms, and, consequently, the prolongation of the financial ruin that they were experiencing.
>
> Although even after these measures, neither the abundance nor the quality of the wheat has proven to be sufficient, independently of Chilean wheat, without which these wheat fields still do not enjoy the fortune of fertility that would supply Lima's demand, it has not been left at the whim of those who bring it from that Kingdom or those who store it in Port Callao to raise the price, I having set a price that seemed fair. (2000, 543–44)

That very same year Peralta Barnuevo inveighed against Chile's control of the wheat market in Lima and lauded the new viceroy of Peru (1736–1745), Mendoza Sotomayor y Camaño, marquis de Villagarcía, for having stabilized bread supplies and prices in Seville. Desiring that the same be achieved in Lima, Peralta Barnuevo called on the poets of Lima to compose a jocose poem on this topic (1736, f. 213).

History tells us that Lima's problems with bread were known outside of Peru, even in the period in which the mock trial allegedly took place in Santiago de Guatemala. The Spanish scientists Antonio de Ulloa and Jorge Juan offered a detailed commentary on wheat shortages in Lima (1748, 3:122–23), while another viceroy of Peru (1745–1761), Manso de Velasco, count de Superunda, took several measures to make the Kingdom of Peru independent of the Kingdom of Chile, where he had served as governor (1983, 271–74). His protectionism angered not only the shipping magnates in Lima who were profiting from the importation of Chilean wheat through Port Callao but also Amat y Junient, then governor of Chile.[17] Manso de Velasco commissioned the legal opinion of a judge on the high court, Pedro José Bravo de Lagunas y Castilla, which was published under the rubric of *Voto consultivo*. This opinion gives us a hard fact of interest in our comparison of the bread industry in Mexico City and Lima: as of May 1754, when this jurist delivered his opinion, there were forty-three bakeries open or preparing to open in Lima (1755, 152).

There appears to be no material evidence, however, to support the possibility that Lima had a higher consumption or supply or quality of bread than Mexico City. In the eighteenth century, the consumption of bread was higher in Mexico City (the most populous city in Spanish America) than in European cities with larger populations (García Acosta 1989, 27–29). And although it is true that residents of Peru need not have had a material basis in order to make such a claim, it seems much more likely that Carrió intended the term *Pan* to be taken figuratively rather than literally. The *Pan* in *Pila, Puente, Pan,* and *Peines* is ripe with sexual and occupational connotations that have not been explored by scholars.

In numerous texts from the viceregal period, the lexicon of the bakery functions figuratively. In Friar Castillo's mock debate on lying that we saw earlier, bakers in Lima were twitted for manipulating grades of wheat and prices of bread: "Los panaderos no se hable/pues con su trigo picado,/cuando empiezan a mentir/ echan pan al mismo diablo" (1948, 90) ("Do not even talk to me about bakers/ since, with their half-meal,/when they start lying/their bread feeds the devil"). Here "pan" forms part of a figurative expression (*echar pan al diablo*) that communicates how the bakers' fraud serves the devil's cause. Customers in Lima, like their counterparts in Mexico City, encountered fraud of the sort targeted in Castillo's verses. One of the "stretching" measures taken by bakers in Lima was the adulteration of bread dough, which often was achieved by mixing in generous amounts of barley flour (Ramos Pérez 1967, 71).

The reputation of bakers was further sullied by their association with the criminal world. Since the late seventeenth century and well into the nineteenth century, bakeries in Peru were staffed by plebeians ranging from Indians and Spaniards to *pardos* and freed *mulatos* and by petty criminals and slaves who were commonly sentenced by the high court in Lima to labor at bakeries for their wrongdoings. Bakers had to feed, clothe, and pay a nominal sum to their laboring convicts. At times the prisoners lived under house arrest at a bakery along with the baker and his family, which led in some cases to sexual relationships between the male convicts and members of the baker's family (Arrelucea 1996, *passim*). Not only *Peines,* then, but *Pan* too had a wealth of seedy connotations that a respectable Peruvian would not praise in earnest.

What has been lost on Carrió's modern and postmodern readers is that *pan* and *trigo* were common circumlocutions around prostitution, adulterous affairs with non-Spanish women, and illegitimate children. In the Peruvian satirist Juan del Valle y Caviedes's "A un personaje que era amigo de negras, vistiéndose de negro" ("To a Character Who Was a Friend of Black Girls by Wearing Black"), he used an economic irregularity (i.e., the scarcity of bread after the earthquakes of 1687) to make a point about moral irregularities. Of the male character's philandering with black women, the poet jokes, "Aunque ahora juzgo que no/le valdrán un pan por ciento,/porque éste es año de hambre/y anda caro lo trigueño" (1984, 149–50, vv. 29–32). In other words, his consorting with one hundred freed black lassies (*pardillas*) will not be worth a thing—they will not yield him a loaf of bread (or fetus in the womb)—because this is a famine year and all things wheat are expensive. According to the *Diccionario de la lengua castellana,* bread made of different grains (*panis mixtus*) was called *mixtura.*[18] In Peru, however, *mixtura* (or *mistura*) also served the function that scholars of the viceregal period commonly assign to *casta:* it designated exclusively a person of mixed ancestry or mixed faith.[19] In several of Friar Castillo's poems, too, we read of sex-for-gifts arrangements between Spanish men and non-Spanish women, sexual diseases, unplanned pregnancies, and abortions in the deadend streets created by the protective wall around the city of Lima (see Figures 7, 8, and 9). One deadend street is entered by men and women who represent numerous lowly professions, and Friar Castillo does not spare the baker: "También entra el panadero/por esta vereda misma/y deja la levadura/fermento de masa inicua" (1948, 42), which roughly translates as "The baker too gets there/by the very same path/and leaves behind his yeast,/leavening for iniquitous dough."

In Carrió's treatment of a religious festival in Cuzco, the reader encounters the mock-heroic spirit that permeates all things, places, and persons military in *El lazarillo de ciegos caminantes* as baked goods, bulls, and ladies of the night converge:

> Estos caballeros forman sus cuadrillas acompañando al corregidor y alcaldes, que se apostan en las bocas de las calles para ver las corridas de toros y correr a una y otra parte para defenderse de sus acometidas y ver sus suertes, como asimismo para saludar a las damas y recoger sus favores en grajeas y aguas olorosas, que arrojan desde los balcones, a que corresponden según la pulidez de cada uno, pero lo regular es cargarse de unos grandes *cartuchos de confite grueso* para arrojar a la gente del *bronce,* que corresponde con igual *munición* o *metralla,* que recoge del suelo la gente plebeya y vuelve a vender a la caballería. (412)

> [These knights form their squads accompanying the provincial governor and mayors, who station themselves at intersections to watch the running of the bulls and run this way and that to escape their charges and see their outcomes, as well as to greet the dames and collect their favors in sugarplums and co-

lognes that they throw from the balconies, to which (the knights) respond, each according to his polish, but it is typical for them to load up on certain large cornets filled with confetti to toss to the folk from the *bronce,* who answer with a similar munition or shrapnel that the plebeian folk pick up from the ground and resell to the cavalry.]

Here the inspector describes one-half of the gifts-for-sex equation as if it were a military engagement. The "cartuchos de confite grueso" are paper or cloth cornets filled with assorted candies, or what Italians call *confetti.* Yet the eighteenth-century definition of *cartucho* was rather different, as Carrió knew from personal experience: "Artillery term. A small cloth or paper pouch in which the powder for each blast is put, and many times they are filled with bits of bullets and broken nails in order to use them instead of bullets in order to do more damage. Little cartridges are also made whereby soldiers have every round of their rifle ready in order to load it more easily" (Real Academia Española 1979, 1:205). Here we have two meanings of *cartucho:* (1) the sort of materials that today could be used in a pipe bomb or included in explosives worn by suicide bombers to wreak more havoc and (2) a gun cartridge. The *Diccionario de la lengua castellana* explains that *munición* has two meanings: "The equipment and supplies necessary to maintain an army, Square, etc. They can be divided into mouth munitions and war munitions [*municiones de boca y municiones de guerra*]. Those of the mouth are the supplies and provisions for eating, and those of war consist of all kinds of offensive and defensive arms, uniforms and other supplies" (2:631). In the passage from Carrió's report, *munición* belongs to the category of "mouth munitions," and yet the instrument for delivering the candy is a *munición* that belongs to the category of "war munitions." Elsewhere in *El lazarillo de ciegos caminantes,* Carrió refers explicitly to *pan de munición*—"soldier's bread," or "bullet bread"—that was made from unsifted flour (which made it hard as a rock) and was fed to troops.[20] Finally, the eighteenth-century usage of *metralla* made it a synonym of *cartucho* in the first sense of the latter, according to the same *Diccionario* (2:561). Thus, for Carrió's eighteenth-century readers, the connotations of *Pan* and *Peines* overlapped in military as well as sexual terms.

The gifts-for-sex equation is suggested by the inspector as he describes the women who regale the nobility and the persons regaled by the nobility and the gifts themselves. The inspector refers to the women on the balcony as "dames" and to the recipients of the candies as "gente del bronce." It has already been established how Carrió jocosely employed the first term; the second term is no less rich in suggestion. The phrase "gente del bronce" appears in a poem on Lima's bullfighting ring by Friar Castillo. The midget don Domingo, veteran wagoneer (*carretonero*), describes the nocturnal promenades of disorderly persons who travel in glorified carts (*carretones*), rather than coaches or wagons (*coches* or *calesas*). The blind friar's verses reveal that there were whorehouses in the Plaza Mayor of Lima:

prostitutes asked *carretoneros* to take them to the plaza when they were in trouble. The nocturnal aspect and the fact that these persons do not travel in coaches indicate that the persons involved are plebs. Don Domingo expresses his exasperation: "Cuántas gentes del bronce,/—cholas, mulatas y chinas—/se embarcan con algazara/con sus amigos y amigas" (n.d., Fondo Varios, vol. 805, vv. 137–40) ("So many folks from the bronce—*cholo,* mulatto and *chino* girls—set off with their male and female friends amid shouts").[21] All of these suggest a lack of social respectability: the variety of mixed *castas* present; the shouting or whooping, which is described with a term belonging to the Moors ("algazara"); the mingling of the sexes, who are described as female friends and male friends of the "gente del bronce." Who were these people so described, and how did they wind up in Carrió's exposé?

The term *bronce* is a figurative one for "artillery," and it is possible that the "gente del bronce" in Cuzco were folks associated with the military as soldiers, prostitutes, cooks, and the like. From this perspective, *bronce* in Carrió's description of the religious festival in Cuzco can be seen as a mock-epic element. However, it seems more likely that these persons were described as "gente del bronce" because they frequented the bronze fountain in Lima's main square, washing clothes, fetching water, working as food sellers, flower sellers, prostitutes, messengers, and so on. These persons also tended to have bronze-colored skin because of their ancestry or because they worked outdoors. By antonomasia, then, similar types in Cuzco became *gente del bronce,* a term that captured a lower order of Spanish-American society in the eighteenth century. Of course, soldiers were quite often members of the lower orders, or "cannon fodder," so the two interpretations of *gente del bronce* are not mutually exclusive.

Now we turn to the gifts themselves: Carrió tells us that the noblemen on horseback collect sugarplums and cologne from the "dames" on the balconies— that is, prostitutes or mistresses—and respond to them as their polish permits. Typically, the knights arm themselves with packages of bulk sweets that they toss to the "gente del bronce," who respond in kind. According to Castillo's poem about the midget Don Domingo, men in Lima visited prostitutes night and day. They supported these women by lending them money or by giving them money outright to buy flowers and a variety of baked goods, including bread from the fish market: "¿Qué les dieron para flores,/para chischás o manillas,/para bizcochos, rosquetes,/pan de la pescadería,/para pasteles y sango/y las demás porquerías?/Que estas tarascas tragonas/embuten de noche y día" (n.d., Fondo Varios, vol. 805, vv. 225–32) ("How much did they give them for flowers,/for jangles or bracelets/for cookies, cakes,/bread from the fish market,/for pastries and porridge/and the other garbage?/'Cause these dragon ladies/stuff themselves day and night"). Castillo's enumeration of bakery items (*bizcochos, rosquetes, pan*) is joined to "de la pescadería" (from the fish market), which can be shown to further spin out the sexual connotations of *pan* in Carrió's times.

In another poem by Castillo (1996, 905–12), a guide (*lazarillo*) takes the blind friar through the Plaza Mayor to the corner of the Calle de los Mercaderes, one of the four sides of the plaza (see Figures 7, 8, and 9) and a main thoroughfare crowded with stagecoaches, packhorses, mule trains, commercial agents and officials, laborers, and slaves. There the poet is dumbfounded by shouts and a sudden halt in the flow of traffic. After the two men get out of the crowd, the guide laughs and explains that two black coachmen had stopped in the intersection, holding up more than sixty stagecoaches (910). The two black coachmen were arguing about who had the fastest mule. After some heated discussion, one offered the other a cigarette, and then, the poem tells us, a firestorm was ignited by a black female slave "who let one of them know with her piggish ways that she could fry some fish" ("a uno de ellos una negra/que a entender daba en lo puerco,/ser ella chicharronera" [910]).[22] Her shtick is fried fish for a *real,* but the black man has more gills, or guts, than a fish that does not let go of the bait ("pero él tiene más agallas/que el pescado que no suelta" [911]). A dispute ensues, and the poet observes equivocally that "some damned pieces of merchandise" (i.e., female slaves like this one) have enslaved commerce: "que está el comercio hecho esclavo/de unas tan malditas piezas" (911). By joining *pan* and *pescadería,* Friar Castillo was poking fun of a reality well-known to his eighteenth-century readers: there were black women among the women "visited" by monied men in Lima—a fact acknowledged earlier and in similar language by Valle y Caviedes. Moreover, Castillo's verses implied a relationship between the *gente del bronce* and prostitution in downtown Lima that is not unlike the gifts-for-sex equation in Carrió's description of the religious celebrations in Cuzco.

Pan can be understood in still another figurative sense. Pan was the Greek god and shepherd who was half-man and half-goat. As we have seen, several veiled references to Amat in *El lazarillo de ciegos caminantes* characterize him as the great lord of the mules, and the god Pan, like a mule, was a hybrid. Before the Spaniard from Guatemala challenges the Spaniards from Peru to solve the riddle, the inspector jocosely explains to his Inca secretary that the women in Lima who eat food similar to the secretary's are the dames of Arcadia: "Esas Señor Inca son Damas de la Arcadia, que se acomodan al alimento Pastoril y baylan al son de los Alvogues del Semi-Capro Dios" (1775, n.p.) In the bucolic portrait of Peru that was fashioned by foreigners and residents alike, there was no theft, no prostitution, no philandering viceroy, and no women of mixed and plebeian ancestry who bore him children out of wedlock. Surreptitiously, Carrió parodies that bucolic discourse: General and Viceroy Amat is transformed into "the half-goat god," Pan, god of the shepherds in Arcadia; Micaela is transformed into one of the "damsels of Arcadia" who eat country food and dance to the sound of his rustic flutes. One of the Inca secretary's epigraphs is taken from Ovid's *Metamorphoses,* in which a nymph is transformed into empty reeds, leaving Pan more in love with her than with fluted reeds (Cagiga y Rada 1739, n.p.). If the actress Micaela had transformed herself into the viceroy's mistress, making Amat love what he should not, the deadend streets or alleyways where the working poor—especially the non-Spanish working poor—lived were characterized as "flutes" by the friar-poet Castillo in a poetic conceit that turned on the usage of "flutes" as an imprecation, a sort of mild curse word. The alleys are the flutes, or escape valves, in houses of every estate, through which bad air comes in. They are the cause of fluted—that is, pregnant—women and illegitimate children.[23]

In *Pila, Puente, Pan, y Peines,* the term *Pan* alludes to an occupational and sexual economy. The literal interpretation of *Pan* does not pass muster: there is no evidence to support the claim that Lima had a more plentiful supply of bread or bakeries than Mexico City had. The sexually illicit, often criminal, activities associated figuratively with *Pan* during the long eighteenth century involved Amat and *criollo* elites as much as plebeians. On this score, Lima defeated Mexico City in Carrió's opinion, and he obviously believed that customs were better corrected through ironic praise than through sermons—especially when members of the clergy were themselves engaged in immoral behavior.

Having deciphered *Peines* and *Pan,* we now turn to another of the four terms in the Peruvian delegation's solution to the riddle of the 4Ps: *Puente,* or *Bridge.*

Puente

In his *Nouveau Voyage au tour du monde,* Le Gentil singled out the bridge through which one entered Lima proper from the other side of the River Rimac:

> Upon entering the city from the side of the promenade, one encounters a large neighborhood in which the houses are very well built, and one crosses the River on a bridge made of stones. The view is most beautiful. From that vantage point, one sees, on one side, the winding sea get lost in the distance, and, on the other side, the celebrated Valley of Lima, of which the poets of this city have sung enough, and which in effect deserves a portion of the praises that they have given it. The gate to the city, which is joined to this bridge, has a certain look of grandeur, and it is the only bit of architecture that is even slightly uniform. (1728, 1:96)

In *Lima fundada o Conquista del Perú,* Peralta Barnuevo praised Juan del Corral, the architect who designed "the grand Bridge of Lima" through which one entered the city (1732, can. 5, st. 75, n. 73; can. 7, st. 268, n. 246). Ulloa and Juan remembered how Lima looked in 1740: "It has a stone bridge very handsome and wide, and at the far end of it an arch that matches the rest of the work in the majesty of its architecture. This bridge serves as the entrance to the city and leads to the main Plaza nearby, which is square, very expansive and well decorated with magnificent structures" (1748, 3:39). After the earthquake of 1746, Viceroy

Manso de Velasco ordered "that a new arch be constructed at the entrance to the bridge because the old one had been completely destroyed, the lack of which was a notable eyesore." He described the bridge in detail: "The bridge that joins the most distinguished population to the residents of San Lázaro parish, which extends to the other side of the River, is an outstanding structure and is clearly visible, and as the constant flow of waters, because of the fury with which the waters come down from the mountains in the summer, takes its toll, it requires inspection and even repairs every year, and the pillars on which its arches and vault rest, with all the stone that the waters wash away, are damaged at the foundation." Manso de Velasco ordered repairs, and he put Judge Pedro José Bravo de Lagunas y Castilla, author of *Voto consultivo,* in charge of seeing that they were done (1983, 258–59).

In *Nouveau voyage fait au Pérou,* Courte de la Blanchardiere praised the bridge, which he saw as he passed through Lima in 1747: "The River over which there is a stone bridge adorned with a parapet that all together makes for a most handsome structure and has for the most part escaped the overall destruction enters Lima from the neighboring mountains that are called the *Cordilleras*" (1751, 119). Italian readers, too, became familiar with Lima's most famous bridge, through Jesuit Giandomenico Coleti's entry on Lima in his *Dizionario storico-geografico dell'America Meridionale* (*Historico-Geographical Dictionary of South America*): "It is situated on a spacious plain called the *Valley of Rimac,* which was later called, corruptedly, *Lima.* . . . Its walls are bathed by the River Rimac, over which there is a beautiful stone bridge with five arches that Viceroy Marquis de Montesclaros had built" (1771, 1:186).

Further alterations and improvements to the famed *Puente* were done under the supervision of Viceroy Amat, according to his *Memoria de gobierno,* because the owners of estates, as well as merchants engaged in a very active trade with the lowlands and the highlands, had to cross it regularly (1947, 169). During Amat's tenure, the "disguised bulls" who frequented La Alameda were only too familiar with the city's *Puente* because it connected La Alameda to the city proper. On the way back from their promenade, they used to race to the bridge, where, according to Friar Castillo, they stopped to engage in malicious gossip, flirting, and speculation about who was riding with whom and in whose coach. Even though La Alameda might offer them the recreations of the Elysian Fields, he wrote in one poem, Hell was on the bridge on their way back.[24] Viceroy Amat was no stranger to such activities, as we have already seen, and he took a curious measure that served his own interests: he had the lattices on balconies (from the Plaza Mayor to the bridge) destroyed so that he could monitor the comings and goings of his subjects (Lohmann Villena 1976, 115, 171). When monks passed that way, for instance, he reported them to their prelates and accused them of violating their monastic vows (Eguiguren 1945, 216). Certainly, there was no shortage of opportunities for monks to violate their vows on the *Puente*—or just beyond it, at Los Peines—as the Gran Señor knew from personal experience. What was good for the goose, it appears that he decided, was not good for the gander.

In Carrió's times, *puente* had other sexual, and even financial, overtones. A *puente* was a short-term loan to tide someone over until he or she could pay the debt. It also meant the bridge on a musical instrument—that is, what keeps the strings elevated. Cords, or strings, was a slippery concept in Spanish. In a poem by Castillo, a white-faced she-mule overhears a prostitute of mixed ancestry complain "del que la tiene enfermiza/o dos incordios le ha puesto,/porque la que ha sido yegua/tenga los potros por premio" (1996, 917). A fair rendering of these verses is "about the one who has gotten her sickly, or strung her like a guitar, so the woman who has played a mare will have colts as a reward." The sexual servant's condition was buboes: the initial stage of syphilis is marked by "strings," or *incordios* (also *encordios*).[25] In *El lazarillo de ciegos caminantes,* the inspector and Concolorcorvo discuss *mulatas* and their torture treatment, "the harp," in a passage quoted for a different purpose in the Introduction herein: "*Pasito,* como digo yo; *aparte,* como dicen los cómicos españoles, y *tout bas,* como se explican los franceses, porque si lo oyen las mulatas de Lima le han de poner en el arpa, que es lo mismo que un trato de cuerda, con que ellas castigan a lo político" (395) ("*Keep it down,* as I say; *aside,* like the Spanish writers of comedies say, and *tout bas,* as the French express themselves, because if the mulattas in Lima hear you they will string you like a harp, which is the same thing as getting the cords treatment, with which they punish diplomatically"). Scholars have overlooked the significance of this passage, and yet it employs a salty expression that was well known in eighteenth-century Lima: Peralta Barnuevo put it in the mouth of a character in his Menippean satire, *Diálogo de los muertos: La causa académica* (*Dialogue of the Dead: An Academic Trial*).[26] The inspector's warning about *mulatas* and their "harp" or "cords treatment" insinuates equivocally the illicit sexual activities fostered by Lima's famous bridge, a musical bridge and the "cords" suggestive of syphilis, which was widespread in Lima.

In 1746, the year in which Carrió arrived there, the *Gaceta de Lima* advertised a cure for syphilis (*específico antigálico*) developed by Dr. Pablo Petit, which could be sent to the afflicted by regular post.[27] The Parisian physician lamented in his *Breve tratado de la enfermedad venerea* (*Brief Treatise on Venereal Disease*) that so many in Lima still believed that sex with a healthy female would heal an infected man (1730, 29–32). Dr. Petit went on to identify some striking connectives between demographic realities and urban legends in Lima:

> Since I have been in this land, I have seen countless persons of distinction and others [of the lower estates] who are taken by this error, who have assured me that this could occur, and that to be absolutely sure, it is best to choose among two healthy women, one white and the other black, and this could very well be one of the main reasons why there are so many and so different

kinds of peoples, and what further supports my opinion is that I have seen more than ten little black girls, from age 8 to age 10 or 11, who had ulcers and purging, and four of them had this poison in the opening or lips of the vulva, [and] through the many questions that I asked these poor creatures, I came to realize that men had attempted coitus with them. (32)

When one thinks of a bridge, one thinks of water, and in Castillo's poem, the white-faced she-mule relates to her black-faced colleague another story she over-heard: "o del que le hizo a patadas/sudar todo aquel refresco/de aquellos recién venidos/que con ansioso deseo/le feriaron ricas aguas,/por ver si les daba puerto" (1996, 917). A simple translation of these verses in English is "or of the one who by kicks made her sweat all that refreshment from the recent arrivals, who with *clamoring* desire had regaled her with precious waters just to see if she would offer them port." The bordello is the site of illicit, or impure, trade (*comercio ilícito* or *impuro*) between women and men. It is also a market (*feria*) to which new arrivals come just as merchants visited Lima when they went to the trade fair in Portobelo. The phrase "ricas aguas" alludes to the men's exchange of cologne (*agua de colonia*) or liquor for sex ("to be given port"), which is precisely the equation I discerned in Carrió's description of the religious festival in Cuzco. Of course, the phrase "precious waters" can also be understood as a metaphor for sperm and "port" as the matrix of the prostitute. Neither should we forget that *bread* and *fish* alike had sexual connotations not at all unlike those of *water* and *bridge.* Thus, *Puente* does not signify simply a physical structure that was internationally renowned; it alludes to financial and sexual transactions that were facilitated by the bridge that connected *Peines* and the rest of the promenade to Lima proper.

Mexico City was not famous for its bridges; rather, as we saw earlier, its canals played an important role in the social activities of residents, rich and poor. Its vacation hideaways, or *Casas de Recreación,* were reached by navigating the canals (see Figure 1, no. 15), and we already know the broad outlines of "recreation" in New Spain and Peru.

It remains to be seen what a historical interpretation of the first element in *Pila, Puente, Pan,* and *Peines* has to tell us about Bourbon Spanish America.

Pila

Carrió noted that the principal houses in La Plata had "una fuente o pila" ("a fountain or *pila*") on the patio (292), but he was no fan of urban fountains in general: "Las fuentes de las ciudades grandes, además de las impurezas que traen de su origen, pasan por unos conductos muy sospechosos, y en partes muy asquero-sas" (293) ("The fountains in big cities, besides the impurities that they carry from their source, pass through some very suspect canals and very disgusting areas").

These ubiquitous fountains in the cities of the Viceroyalty of Peru were not as internationally known as the *Pila* in Lima mentioned in the discussion of *Pan*.

Le Gentil described the Plaza Mayor in Lima, showcasing the *Pila* that distinguished it from other public squares: "The great Plaza of Lima is a uniform square. The Cathedral and the Archbishop's palace form one of its sides; the Viceroy's palace forms another. The other two sides are made up of several uniform houses that are not beautiful simply because the others are not. In the center of this Plaza there is a great jet of water decorated with bronze figures that direct the water into a large and spacious basin that serves as a public fountain" (1728, 1:97–98). Durret also remarked on the Plaza Mayor, and he mentioned both the *Pila* and the multitude of black slaves and Indians who sold foodstuffs there:

> The Cathedral is dedicated to St. John the Evangelist; it is very beautiful and makes up one side of the Plaza Mayor; the Viceroy's palace, another; the third side is packed with the shops of merchants, and the fourth is a great building supported by several pillars, that holds the ministers of justice; it is what is called the *Palais* in France. This entire Plaza Mayor is filled with the booths of black slaves and Indian girls who for the most part supply food, raw and cooked . . . ; all sorts of grains, herbs, strawberries, eggs, milk, butter, chickens . . . in short, everything that one could desire according to the season. In the middle of this Plaza there is a great basin, but without a jet of water, it is plated in bronze, with certain vases of flowers spread out in relief; in the middle rises a beautiful pyramid composed of three basins, one on top of the other. . . . At all four corners there are small basins that would be well-suited for fetching water there, but there is none, because that would hurt a great number of slaves who have no means to earn a living other than the water that they [take from the *Pila* and] supply to individual homeowners; they place it in small barrels onto asses that carry three barrels at a time. (1720, 253–54)

Peralta Barnuevo singled out the architect Francisco Noguera, who had designed the fountain in the main square ("la pila de la Plaza") (*Lima fundada*, can. 7, st. 268, n. 246). He again glorified the *Pila* as it looked during the celebrations of Viceroy Mendoza's entrance in Lima: "It was decorated with singular beauty, the admirable fountain that occupies the center of that ample Forum and surpasses all of those that were flowing marvels in Antiquity and all of those today that are splendors in the greatest capitals, like the crystal soul of an Emporium so rich; it appears that it inherited from the Miracle at Rhodes all of its bronze, and all of its lines from that one there in Olympus" (1736, ff. 74–75).

Ulloa and Juan, too, fondly remembered the fountain they had seen so many times in 1740, when they visited Lima: "In its center or middle point it has a magnificent fountain, no less distinguishable for its beauty than for a statue of Fame that crowns it; and all of it, along with four other small basins that surround it in circles, is made of bronze; it sends out water in abundance from the principal figure and from those of eight lions, made of the same material, which beautify with their crystalline spouts at the same time that they adorn the work with polish" (1748, 3:39–40). After the devastating earthquake of 1746, La Blanchardiere recalled the remnants of the fountain in his *Nouveau voyage fait au Pérou:* "In the middle there was a fountain with three jets of water that come from a pyramid surrounded by a *renommée*. The whole thing is made of bronze, just like the basin; this fountain is completely demolished" (1751, 118–19).

Viceroy Manso de Velasco oversaw the rebuilding of the Cathedral and numerous other structures in Lima after they were damaged or destroyed by the earthquake. With respect to waterworks, he ordered

> that the water well, at its origins, be repaired and a new, fairly extensive pipeline be built to carry the water that the city's fountains provide, which was being greatly wasted because the old pipeline [was] almost destroyed, its loss being felt in detriment to the common good; that the main *Pila* in the Plaza [Mayor] not only be made operational, but that it be restored to its original beauty, and that the pipes that cross the streets be repaired, among other minor projects. (1983, 258)

The fame of Lima's *Pila* stretched into the second half of the eighteenth century. Alcedo y Herrera mentioned the Kingdom of Quito's wholesale outlets in Lima "that they call the *Clothiers of Quito,* one at the city water well, on Archbishop's Street" (1766, 29). Bueno wrote of the fountain for which Lima was famous in one of the descriptions included in his 1764 almanac: "A fountain made of bronze is praised, a handsome and splendid structure that the Count de Salvatierra ordered cast and placed in the middle of her spacious Plaza" (1951, 19). Even the Jesuit Coleti singled out the *Pila* in his entry on Lima: "The Plaza Mayor is square and large. . . . The buildings that flank it are majestic, and in the middle there is a beautiful fountain made of bronze that the Count de Salvatierra had erected" (1771, 1:186). This *Pila* was one of many for which Lima was famous: its water system was perhaps the most sophisticated in Spanish America.

At the same time, the culture (I hesitate to use the term *subculture* because members of all estates engaged in these activities) of the square in which Lima's most famous *Pila* was located was foremost in Carrió's mind when he included *Pila* in the first solution to the riddle of the 4Ps from Lima. As my interpretation of *Pan* suggests, the Plaza Mayor was a hub of the sex trade in Lima that brought together members of different *castas* and *estados*. Immediately after the earthquake, the Plaza Mayor became a de facto refugee camp for survivors. Viceroy Manso de Velasco himself lived there for three months, and in 1747 he finally had to order all of the shacks, lean-tos, and tents dismantled and the homeless removed (Ramón

2002, 269). The bronze *Pila* was the Plaza Mayor's official main attraction, as Manso de Velasco and later Amat knew very well. Members of the lower orders in Lima could be seen at the *Pila* working as messengers, hawking their sexual attributes, getting water, selling goods, and so on.

Of course, residents of New Spain considered their own water system to be the more sophisticated of the two. During the Marquis de Casa Fuerte's administration, a fountain was constructed on Mexico City's La Alameda, and the underground water pipes and faucets along *La Alameda* and the drainage ditches were cleared (Núñez y Domínguez 1927, 225–26). Its advances and the engineers who achieved them were detailed in the *Gaceta de México* (1986, 3:87–88). Mexico City also had Los Baños, or Baths (see Figure 1, no. 1), and we need not tax our imagination about those.

In the late eighteenth century, compilers and encyclopedists in Europe had described Mexico City and Lima in terms that highlighted their opulence. Coleti painted Lima in glowing terms: "Its trade is the greatest and the richest in all of South America. . . . Lima is the emporium of that New World: large, densely populated, wealthy, beautiful and the queen of all the cities in South America" (1771, 1:187–88). This was the economic image of Lima in Europe during Carrió's inspection of the posts. It was an image forged largely from Ulloa and Juan's *Relación histórica,* which had been penned by the first of these traveling scientists. Coleti merely reiterated the Spanish duo's misunderstanding of the economic conditions confronting eighteenth-century Peru, especially its elites. On the ground, things looked very different in Lima in the 1770s.

The European image of Mexico City during Carrió's residence in Lima was not that of a viceregal capital vanquished by another. The compilers of *The American Gazetteer* offered a flattering portrait of Mexico City in 1762 that highlighted its natural and acquired resources:

Mexico, a royal city, archiepiscopal see, and the capital of the province of the same name, and of the whole kingdom of Mexico in N. America. It stands on an island in the middle of a spacious lake, and is accessible onle by causeways of a considerable length. It is of a square form, and about seven miles in circuit; some reckon the number of inhabitants to be about 70[,000] or 80,000. It is greatly admired for straight and spacious streets and squares, its cool situation in such a hot climate, and its natural strength. It contains 29 convents, 22 nunneries, and a great number of parish-churches, besides the cathedral.

It is the residence of the Viceroy, the seat of the first Audience, and one of the richest and most splendid cities in the world. And tho' it has no seaport, nor any communication with the sea by navigable rivers, it enjoys a prodigious commerce, and is itself the centre of all that is carried on between America and Europe on one hand, and between America and the East Indies on the other. The goods from Acapulco to La Vera Cruz, or from La Vera Cruz to Acapulco, for the use of the Philippines, and, in a great measure, for the use of Peru and Lima, pass through this city, and employ an incredible number of horses and mules. Hither all the gold and silver is brought to be coined; here the King's fifth is deposited; and all that immense quantity of plate wrought, which is annually sent into Europe. The shops glitter on all sides with gold, silver, and jewels, besides great chests piled up to the ceilings, waiting for an opportunity of being sent to Old Spain, &c. The city itself is regularly built, and the houses handsome, though not lofty. The ornaments of the churches are extravagantly rich. (Anonymous 1762, 2:n.p.)

From *Reforma del Perú,* a detailed critique and reform proposal that Carrió left unfinished at his death, it is clear that he viewed New Spain as a well-governed viceroyalty in contrast to Peru. Although New Spain was the Babylon of Spanish America, he wrote, at least the Indians and the Spaniards there respected their ministers and loved their king. There was order (1966, 46). The presence of trade and textiles even in the rural areas spelled civilization and marked the difference between a faltering Viceroyalty of Peru and that of New Spain (82). Spaniards in Peru, he argued, should imitate those in Queretaro and Cholula by working their lands and producing cotton (86). *Pila, Puente, Pan,* and *Peines,* the first solution to the riddle of Lima's 4Ps, anticipates in vivid detail why an infirm Carrió would still be calling for change after roughly seven decades of Bourbon reforms.

CHAPTER 2

Defacing a Bourbon Legend:
Pedro, Pardo, Paulino, and Perulero

In the witty anecdote that wraps up *El lazarillo de ciegos caminantes,* the inspector sets the scene for the mock trial by explaining that a Spaniard from Guatemala played a practical joke on several Spaniards from Peru at the archbishop
of Guatemala's palace, back when "two most illustrious lords, Araújo and Pardo,
peruleros, were governing that Kingdom." He then clarifies the meaning of *peruleros,* before he takes his readers into the trial of wits, and the *peruleros* present the
first solution to the riddle of the 4Ps from Lima. At this point, the Spaniard from
Guatemala politely rejects the solution offered by the *peruleros.* He recounts that
it was he who tacked the riddle to the doors of the archbishop's palace and argues
that his riddle must be given the solution that befits Guatemala, not Lima:

> No puedo negar que los Señores Limeños se explicaron en todo el sentido que
> se da en su Patria a mis quatro P.P.P.P. pero quisiera preguntar a estos Señores,
> si me tienen por tan fatuo para preguntarles una cosa tan notoria? No hay por
> ventura otras quatro P.P.P.P. en el mundo? Yo hablo en Guatemala, y en esta
> Ciudad debian estos Caballeros buscarlas, y sobretodo, en la misma Casa del
> Señor Arzobispo, a cuya principal Puerta las fixe. Los Chapetones se volbieron
> a alvorotar, y Segunda vez sonó la Campanilla el Sr. Arzobispo, y el Gachupín
> dixo que las quatro P.P.P.P. de su Enigma significaban: Pedro, Pardo, Paulino y
> Perulero que eran los quatro connotados del Sr. Arzobispo. (1775, n.p.)

> [I do not deny that the Liman Gentlemen fully explained the meaning that is
> given to my four Ps in their Homeland, but I would like to ask these Sires if
> they think I am foolish enough to ask them something so obvious? Are there
> not, by chance, other 4Ps in the world? I speak in Guatemala, and in this City
> these Gentlemen should search for them, and first and foremost at the very
> House of the Distinguished Archbishop, on whose front Door I posted them.
> The *Chapetones* got all riled again, and the Archbishop rang his Bell a Second
> time, and the *Gachupín* said that the 4Ps in his Riddle stood for *Pedro, Pardo,*

Paulino and *Perulero,* which were the four nicknames/associates/relatives of the Distinguished Archbishop.]

This second solution to the riddle transforms apparent details of the anecdote—that not just men born in Peru but all men who resided there were treated as *peruleros,* that two *peruleros* named Pardo and Araújo were governing the Kingdom of Guatemala—into the moral of the story: Lima's social networks in the first half of the eighteenth century created the conditions necessary for popular chicanery and official malfeasance to flourish in the second. The formation of hybrid elite clans (or *roscas*) in the viceregal capitals goes a long way toward explaining the persistence of old regime social practices in ostensibly modern, or enlightened, urban cultures. Correctly deciphered, *Pedro, Pardo, Paulino,* and *Perulero* alludes to historical continuities between the first half of the eighteenth century and the second, which analyses that are rooted in the *middle period* model fail to address.

The witty Guatemalan tale is a confabulation in which verisimilitude (or probability) is achieved so completely that Alonso Carrió de Lavandera has had critics over an interpretative barrel for more than two centuries. Competing interpretations abound. Emilio Carilla's edition of *El lazarillo de ciegos caminantes* suggested that "Pedro, Pardo, Paulino y Perulero" (Carrió 1973, 473) referred to known and unknown postal officials whose last names began with the letter P, whereas Antonio Lorente Medina's edition deformed Carrió's original text, changing "Pedro, Pardo, Paulino y Perulero" into "Pedro, Paulo, Paulino y Perulero" (Carrió 1985, 227). More recently, Mónica Klien-Samanez has suggested that the second solution was a pun on "Padre Pasante Presentado Predicador," the title by which Franciscan preachers and instructors of native languages were known within that religious community (2000, 143).

I am convinced that the four terms of the second solution stand for Archbishop *Pedro Pardo* de Figueroa, member of the Order of Minims of St. Francis de Paul (*Mínimo* + *San Francisco de Paula* = *Paulino*) and longtime resident of Peru (*Perulero*). It is entirely possible that Carrió wished to make fun of Pedro Pardo de Figueroa (1700/1701–1751) by demoting the archbishop, who was famous for his thousands of Indian converts, to the status of preacher. Or perhaps the second solution is a red herring, and Carrió truly wished to express disgust for an indigenous opponent of the *repartimiento* system, Calixto de San José Tupac Inga, a Franciscan friar who was in Santiago in late 1744 to 1745 working for subordinates of the archbishop as part of the archbishop's evangelization campaign. It is not impossible that Carrió actually met this friar and others at the archbishop's palace, as Klien-Samanez speculates (2000, 143–50).

Yet I think that we need to do all we can to separate the possible from the probable. In asserting that Archbishop Pardo de Figueroa, rather than the indigenous friar (a softer target), was the focus of Carrió's jocose *exemplum,* I am also making a commitment to answer some basic questions in the pages that follow:

What had the archbishop done, or allegedly done, that would merit Carrió's contempt (and that of his contemporaries)? How did public perceptions of Pedro Pardo de Figueroa's conduct link *Pila, Puente, Pan,* and *Peines* as I have explained them in Chapter 1 and *Pedro, Pardo, Paulino,* and *Perulero?* Where does Pedro's far more famous brother, José, fit into this equation? My answers begin with a review of the archbishop of Guatemala's family and career histories.

The Pardo de Figueroa Clan and the Favorite Son's Ascent

There was no family in New Spain or Peru whose members were regarded more highly than the Pardo de Figueroa clan, which included titled noblemen, business magnates, and government officials on both sides of the Atlantic. Pedro and his brothers José and Baltasar were descendants of the Houses of Pardo de Cela and Figueroa in Galicia, Carrió's native province.

Many Pardo de Figueroa men had served as judges on high courts or as governors of kingdoms in Spanish America during the sixteenth and seventeenth centuries. Pedro's father, Bernardo, was the son of Juana de Sotomayor Manrique and Baltasar Pardo de Figueroa, marquis de Figueroa and general of the Southern Sea Fleet. Pedro's paternal uncle was the marquis de Figueroa, and his paternal aunt, Juana Pardo de Figueroa, was the grandmother of brother José's future wife. Bernardo Pardo de Figueroa, like his wife, Margarita de Luján y Acuña, was a native of Lima. A distinguished general, he was appointed governor of two provincial towns in Peru in 1700 (Lohmann Villena 1947, 1:313–15, 2:412; Cagiga y Rada 1739).

Pardo de Figueroa relatives included two viceroys of the Spanish Indies. One was José de Mendoza Sotomayor y Camaño, marquis de Villagarcía, who served as viceroy of Peru (1736–1745). On his mother's side, Pedro Pardo de Figueroa was related to the House of Mendoza (Cagiga y Rada 1739, n.p.; Rubio Mañé 1955, 167–68). The other was Pedro Pardo de Figueroa's great-uncle, Juan Vázquez de Acuña y Bejarano, marquis de Casa Fuerte, who was born and reared in Lima. At age sixty-four, after forty-five years of service to the Crown, Vázquez became viceroy of New Spain and initiated the Bourbon reforms and customs profiled in Chapter 1.[1] Near the end of his life, in 1733, he founded the royal mint in Mexico City. Eleven years later, Baltasar Pardo de Figueroa, the brother of then-Bishop Pedro Pardo de Figueroa, was appointed treasurer of the royal mint in Mexico City, a post that he held until his death in 1756 (González Gutiérrez 1997, 151).[2]

As a merchant and the son of a Crown official, Carrió must have been well acquainted with the descendants of two illustrious dynasties in his native Galicia, Pardo de Cela and Figueroa. The Pardo de Figueroa clan figured prominently in Spanish government and merchant circles as participants in local and regional councils and players in the lucrative Indies trade. Francisco Agustín Pardo de Figueroa, probably the future archbishop's paternal uncle, was an alderman and the chief constable of Madrid in 1697. Juan Pardo y Figueroa, a native of Oviedo, joined the merchants' guild of Cádiz in 1751. The affluent merchant Antonio Pardo de Figueroa, quite possibly another paternal uncle of Pedro Pardo de Figueroa's, figured in the tax records of secular estate owners in 1713 as a member of the Order of Santiago. In 1760 he entailed his estate, which passed to one of the heavyweights of Spanish commerce, Francisco Antonio Pardo y Gago, the fourth wealthiest man in Cádiz. Captain Martín Pardo y Figueroa also entailed his estate (Bustos Rodríguez 1995, 243).

El pastor de ocho talentos que multiplicó como ninguno todos los talentos de Dios con los del mundo (*The Shepherd with Eight Talents Who Multiplied All Divine and Worldly Talents Like No One Else*), a eulogy delivered by the Jesuit Miguel de Benjumea and published after the archbishop of Guatemala's death in February 1751, offers us numerous insights into Pedro Pardo de Figueroa's career and travels. Pedro was born to the "noblest of parents," Bernardo Pardo de Figueroa and Margarita Luján y Acuña, in Lima. At the age of fifteen, he decided to join the Order of the Minims of St. Francis de Paul. The prelates elected him as their counsel general,

> sending him with the broadest of powers to the court in Madrid and that of Rome, causing such a sunburst with his talents in Europe that, after having served already as secretary general for the entire Order, father provincial for the Order in both Castiles and theologian for the nunciature of Spain, he became living proof that the wise man lives more in an instant than an ignorant man lives in a century, for at thirty-five years of age and thirty-five years of merit, he was already bishop of this very illustrious, most noble city of [Santiago de] Guatemala. (1751, n.p.)

According to modern sources, after completing his studies at the Monastery of the Minims of St. Francis de Paul, Pedro Pardo de Figueroa became a professor of theology and philosophy. Thereafter he became secretary general of the Franciscan Minors and the order's delegate in Madrid. He became known to Philip V, who nominated him as bishop of Guatemala, a post that he assumed in 1737 (Díez de Arriba n.d., 1:93).

The February 1736 issue of *Gaceta de México* recorded that a fleet from Spain carrying "Illmo. y Rvmo. Sr. Mró. D. Fr. Pedro Pardo de Figueroa, Obispo de Goathemala" had reached the port of Vera Cruz (1986, 2:318). Later that same month, the former viceroy of Peru, José de Armendáriz Perurena, was received at the viceregal palace in Mexico City by the viceroy and archbishop of New Spain (2:320–21). The *Gaceta de México* for April 1736 reported that Pardo de Figueroa, bishop-elect of Guatemala, had traveled to Mexico City on April 26 (2:329), and the issue for July recorded that on July 12, 1736, he received the bulls for his consecration (2:347). On September 9, the archbishop and viceroy of New Spain consecrated Bishop Pardo de Figueroa in the royal chapel of the palace in Mexico City (2:361–62). In October, he was still in Mexico City; the *Gaceta de México* reported that he had ordained a great number of secular and regular clergy on October 21 (2:368). In February 1737, he left Mexico City for Puebla, stopping at the sanctuary of Our Lady of Guadalupe on the way (3:11). On March 12, "the most important persons" in Puebla accompanied Pardo on the first leg of his journey to Santiago, Guatemala (3:18). On September 22, he arrived in the provincial capital, where he was received by the city council, the president and judges of the high court, and the nobility (3:88).

The cosmopolitan *perulero* began to fill his church with expensive art and lavish altars soon after he arrived in Santiago de Guatemala (Chinchilla 1953, 250). He also labored to wrest control of his bishopric from the archbishop of Mexico City. With a bull from Benedict XIV (1742), the permission of Philip V (1744), and the approval of the high court in Santiago (1745), his bishopric became an archdiocese and he became archbishop of Guatemala in 1746 (Córdova y Urritia 1875, 7:116). That very same year, as one historian sums it up, "drought, grain shortages, and a typhus epidemic dealt Santiago a serious blow" (Lutz 1994, 301 n. 18). Notwithstanding these hardships, celebrations at the archbishop of Guatemala's palace and country estate and in the downtown streets went ahead as scheduled: plays, caroling, banquets, fireworks, dances, and parades filled the days and nights.

Antonio de Paz y Salgado, a lawyer for the city council and the high court, recorded the festivities surrounding Pardo de Figueroa's consecration in *Las luces del Cielo de la Iglesia difundidas en el hemisferio de Guathemala* (*The Lights of the Church's Heaven Spread across Guatemala's Hemisphere*) (1747), which also contains several panegyrics preached in his honor.[3] In Friar Nicolás Paniagua's "Congratulatory Sermon," the public celebrations became expressions of the archbishop's own gratitude: "I can only admire and celebrate his most generous gratitude, which he demonstrates in commendable jubilations which that most noble heart must not ever dispense with (nor could they be passed over without grave censure), because seeing himself exalted with the sacred adornment of the pallium obliges, insists, prompts rejoicings and happiness, jubilations and mirth with which to give thanks to God that will be to His greater glory" (in Paz y Salgado 1747, 42). However, while Paniagua and other preachers praised Pardo de Figueroa, the cathedral, and the provincial capital to the heavens, others were chagrined by the festivities. In Cagiga y Rada's sermon, he employed a common rhetorical figure known as *occupatio* in hopes of diminishing the protests; he dwelled on them, after promising not to: "I am not going to speak now of impediments and objections that on a certain occasion malice, never prudent, put forth in order to cloud the glory of this promotion" (in Paz y Salgado 1747, 4).

Paz y Salgado described how the archbishop invited the leading citizens of Guatemala to his palace to enjoy soft music and rich food—the food ordered and served in the new fashion (French style)—and, of course, fine conversation, masquerade balls, and dances (1747, 34–35). The celebrations in the town of Milpandueñas, where Pardo de Figueroa owned a well-appointed estate, included bullfights, plays, dances, and Indian parades (40–46). More than twenty pages of the attorney's narration were devoted to a defense of all this Bourbon finery and an attack on the unnamed persons who objected to the expenditures. In inventing the feigned speech (*sermocinatio*) of detractors, Paz y Salgado most likely relied on conversations that he had overheard at the city council and high court, the grumblings of subordinates and the razor-sharp satires of the lower orders. The following passage sets the tone for an extended harangue that is representative of Hispanic lawyering in the eighteenth century insofar as Paz y Salgado suggests that his opponents are heretics—because they wished that the money had been spent on the poor rather than on the archbishop—and that they do not understand the (French) customs of modern courtiers:

> There is nothing so sacredly defended that the audacity of sacrilege will not attempt to profane it. By this I mean that these festive demonstrations may have appeared, to certain austere and triflingly mean spirts, to have bordered on excess, either because they do not understand the language of gallantries or because they wish to extend or to limit, becoming tyrants like Procustes, everything according to their fancy, and in judging it an excess they have taken the liberty of reformers [*la libertad de reformantes*] under color of custodianship. Going through the motions of detractors, they must have sighed for past moderation; they will mourn the privations of the discipline now past; they must have said, sunken in their circumspection, "*Ad quid perditio hac?*" They must have muttered, "Would it not be better to distribute these extravagances in relief to the suffering poor?" "The needy crying out loud," they will say, "and the festivities muffling grandeeships [*las fiestas rebozando grandezas*]." "The poor *cholas* overwhelmed by miseries and the banquets overflowing with luxuries. Pity the wretched ones!" And in this key they must have rung to the heavens, believing that with such invectives, which sound good but are of little substance, they do a great service to God. And in truth, theirs might very well be a heartfelt commitment of zeal, but what the latter inspires is not always rooted in the solid ground of reason. (47)

Paz y Salgado eventually concedes defeat, it would seem, by acknowledging that all of his "proofs" will not be enough to make the "stubbornness of pseudocritics yield" (1747, 64), but then he gets right back on his rhetorical horse and rides for another piece, finally winding down with a finger-wagging peroration on "the liberty of the reformers" who wish to take the path to "the country of detractions" (66).

In the succeeding section, Paz y Salgado defended the celebrations by stacking up the preeminences of archbishops within the hierarchy of the Roman Church and the qualities of Pedro Pardo de Figueroa (1747, 67–88). In a comparison that would have delighted the archbishop's deceased great-uncle, Viceroy Vázquez de Acuña (also known as *Gran Dux*), the Crown attorney recalled an encomium on King Louis XIV that he had read in *La manière de bien penser dans les ouvrages d'esprit* (1687), a series of dialogues by the Cartesian neoclassicist Dominique Bouhours, and he promptly redirected the praise to the archbishop of Guatemala (80).

What are we to make of the opposition to the archbishop? Maybe all of the arguments that Paz y Salgado attributed to elderly party poopers and the downtrodden were groundless, but at least one allusion in the lengthy passage previously quoted was probably more than the high scuttlebutt of courtiers or the low blows of plebs. I refer to the complaint about hidden quid por quo transactions: "'The needy crying out loud,' they will say, 'and the festivities muffling grandeeships.'" Here the Crown attorney has the detractors condemning a common social practice of the eighteenth century: the celebration sponsorships assumed by the wealthy in exchange for titles—that is, the archbishop's support during the application process. Pedro Pardo de Figueroa, a member of one of the wealthiest and most politically powerful families in Spain and Spanish America, had managed to have a backwoods bishopric elevated into an archdiocese. It was not, then, at all unreasonable for wealthy men in Guatemala to think it a good deal to hand over the Crown's money, and their own, in exchange for the archbishop's good word. It was the sort of investment that was made over and over in viceregal Spanish America, before and after the Spanish Bourbons came to power.

Personal Problem, Public Person: The Trials of Pedro, Pardo, Paulino, and Perulero

Whether the archbishop's actions were or were not criminal, detractors placed them alongside other actions to form a pattern of behavior and a public profile for the archbishop that Carrió need not have witnessed personally in order to ridicule. Before his promotion, Bishop Pardo de Figueroa was denounced several times to officials of the Inquisition. What is truly fascinating here is not the legal disposition of the cases—he or his lawyers won all of them—but the nature of the complaints and the investigations. In 1744 one complainant alleged that Pardo de Figueroa had "propitiated the death of the *fiscal* on the high court. . . . At which instant he tucked the dead man's wife into his cloak and carried her off to his palace around midnight and thereafter [he carried off] all that the man left behind, which was more than 100,000 pesos, without paying even the parish duties" (qtd. in Chinchilla 1953, 251). Essentially, Pardo de Figueroa was reported to the Inquisition because someone believed that the transfer of the *fiscal's* estate (and his widow) had been made to the bishop. Another complainant accused Pedro Pardo de Figueroa of consorting with nuns, dancing, drinking, gambling, and "notorious simony":

> Its *provisor* has held a notorious *fandango* in this city's convent of the Santa Catalina, with a great many seculars in his company going inside the cloister, the dance being in very profane dress, it getting to the point that they had a nun of righteous ways removed from the confessionary, once and then twice, for this purpose. . . . All of these things that I have put in here, along with notorious simony, even greater scandals in his palaces with plays, concerts, card games in which there is a canon who has lost five years' worth of income. (qtd. in Chinchilla 1953, 251–52)

The public profile of Pedro Pardo de Figueroa continued to deteriorate after his promotion to archbishop. For residents of Santiago, 1746 was a bad year, but it was even worse for the resident of the archbishop's palace. Oddly enough, the eulogies published after Archbishop Pardo de Figueroa's death in 1751 confirm his loss of face, his public shaming. At first blush they appear to be an unlikely venue for such revelations, but upon closer inspection, an epideictic assault takes shape before our very eyes, as their authors mount an offensive against the notoriety that was damning the archbishop even in death.

Dr. Miguel de Cilieza Velasco, canon of the cathedral and attorney at the high court in Santiago, dedicated to Baltasar Pardo de Figueroa a book containing a description of his brother's funeral and a sermon from the ceremony, *Los talentos mejor multiplicados en las gloriosas hazañas de un príncipe religioso y pastor caballero* (*The Talents Best Multiplied in the Glorious Feats of a Religious Prince and Gentleman-Shepherd*). He packed his unnumbered dedication with poetic conceits tied to mining, commerce, and accounting. He described how the archbishop bargained better than anyone "to end his negotiation with so much profit"—that is, eternal life. We encounter a pun on the archbishop's accounts being audited by his administrator and his facing the Final Judgment of God. His talents "were given in silver or gold not yet reduced to coin, doubtless because as ore is shaped into coin, it becomes more quantitative and of more value by communicating its worth to other, inferior metals." "So then," Cilieza Velasco preached on, "all who happily multiply the talents that God has put in their care can be called officials of the Lord's Mint. And the Archbishop who, with all of his talents combined, negotiated like all do, and like no one does (which was the same as making a treasure of all of his wealth), can very well be called Treasurer of this so very opulent, spiritual Mint." Baltasar had received no less silver and gold than his brother: gold in his "generous spirit, well known in both worlds," and silver in his "shining nobility, which descending from King Alonso the Eleventh, through the Infante Don Fadrique, follows a straight line until the Illustrious Houses of Pardo and

Figueroa." The only hint of discord was expressed in the description of the Tumulus. In one of the allegorical paintings that adorned it, the archbishop appeared bedridden, observing mass, with an Angel detaining death until mass has finished. While not even dogs dared to bark at Scipius Africanus, who got up every morning before dawn to adore Jove, the author implied, some Catholics in Guatemala were not at all shy about barking at the archbishop (1751, n.p.).[4]

Jesuit Father Benjumea adopted a different tack in *Sermón panegírico y fúnebre* (*Panegyric and Mournful Sermon*). Without ignoring the supposed talents of the deceased, he made the prodigal Pedro's legal and social troubles explicit in order to declaw detractors. The negatives became positives; the archbishop's vices were the archbishop's virtues:

> Everybody is familiar with that extraordinary, most singular prudence of his, so that in the many and most arduous litigations that confronted him he behaved in such a way that when they reached the Supreme Council of the Indies, all of those lords in agreement and in one voice could not stop praising to the heavens the singular moderation of his soul, his unbelievable and unheard-of gentleness, and his prudence. . . . And the heart of our Prince was so human and therefore so divine that, although they had paid him the most grievous insults, and although they had in every possible way dishonored him [*aunque le hubieran hecho los mayores agravios y aunque le hubieran de todos los modos posibles deshonrado*], by just asking his forgiveness the lawsuits ended and they went back to being friends as before. . . . But I misspeak, since by just asking his forgiveness they became closer friends than they had been before, and this truth was so great that the fact that they had been before his most stubborn enemies was his greatest motivation for doing them favors. Nor did he wait for them to ask his forgiveness before he forgave them like that, as the following—among other cases—proves so well: having received some papers in the town of Esquipulas right before he was to celebrate mass, and seeing that they advised him of all of the unbelievable calumnies [*todas las increíbles calumnias*] that his most declared enemies had written against him, he forgave them. (1751, n.p.)

The confessional canon Miguel Montúfar gave more details about the archbishop's trials and tribulations in his approbation to Benjumea's *Sermón*. He praised the Liman's capacity to suffer "the contumelies, the outrages, the disgraces with which his enemies sought to denigrate the shining innate splendor of his authority" (in Benjumea 1751, n.p.). Moreover, Montúfar revealed that the "papers" to which Benjumea referred in his funeral sermon had actually been sent to Pedro Pardo de Figueroa by the treasurer of Mexico City's royal mint, his brother Baltasar, in November 1746:

A faithful witness to this truth is that letter to which the orator refers in his *Sermón* and which his brother, Don Baltasar, wrote to His Most Illustrious on November 9, 1746, and in it he recounts that certain characters were giving an account of the life of His Most Illustrious to the high court in Mexico City, and this happened when [His Most Illustrious] was in seclusion at the Sanctuary of Esquipulas. He told him that they were declaring things unworthy of even the most shamed man [*del hombre más infame*], mounting an offensive against the reputation of His Most Illustrious. And [His Most Illustrious] received the letter when he was getting ready to go celebrate mass, and after he had read it what he did was, as he says in his letter of reply, place himself in the presence of that Almighty Lord and compare his pain with the torments that His Majesty suffered for His Most Illustrious, so that next to them, his would appear to be no pain at all. (n.p.)

This passage represents the archbishop as a soul tormented by his persecutors rather than his passions. What is just as important, however, is the revelation that the alleged calumnies and contumelies were first aired in suits filed with the high court in Mexico City and that they were substantiated enough to be forwarded to the Council of the Indies in Madrid. The passage quoted next, which immediately follows the passage just quoted, contains excerpts from the archbishop's reply to his brother in Mexico City (dated January 24, 1747) that allow us to ascertain that at least some allegations were, following the pattern he established when he was bishop, of a sexual nature:

I would copy the entire letter *verbatim,* as a wonder for saints and an example for sinners, if I did not foresee grave objections, but I must relate at least the closing sentences. The letter was written on January 24, 1747. "I do not deny"—these are the exact words of His Most Illustrious to his brother Don Baltasar—"I do not deny my many defects, or that I am capable, as long as I am in this mortal flesh of a man, and if God lets go of my hand, of committing even greater atrocities, if there are any that these miserable creatures have not convicted me of. And yet, I would be abominably ungrateful were I to fail to acknowledge the most singular presence that I continually owe to the infinite mercy of the divine Lord, in order not only to feel free from the countless conspirings with which they have tried to destroy my reputation [*de las innumerables sindicaciones con que han intentado destruir mi honor*], but to support with humble resignation His most sublime permissions. And so I ask you, bathing your heart with consolation, to help me give Him infinite thanks." O spirit worthy of eternal memory! That is how he suffered and that is how he endured the greatest defamations of his character [*los mayores descréditos de su persona*] by submitting to God's will. To endure with patience, to suffer with equanimity not one but many conspirings, I know cannot be rewarded with anything less than the crown of life that God has promised time and time again to those who truly love Him. (n.p.)

From the perspective of both Benjumea and Montúfar, what was at stake was the deceased archbishop's reputation. Unnamed enemies had accused him of acts "unworthy of even the most shamed man" in his lifetime, and although the archbishop had already died, this discomfiting litigation was not going to die. A vigorous public defense of Pedro Pardo de Figueroa's good name was, legally and socially, a matter of life or death for him and his illustrious family, but not for the psychologistic reasons that are commonly adduced in scholarly discussions of law and society in the Spanish world.

Shame, the Archbishop, and the Guatemalan Tale

Spaniards in Spain and Spanish America were not suit-happy: they were not "law-yering up" because of any particularly Spanish obsession with blood in the sixteenth, seventeeth, and eighteenth centuries. This common assumption is wrong on two accounts. First, it confuses cause and effect: even if we assume for argument's sake that the Spanish *were* obsessed with blood, we have to recognize that legal studies—especially canon law—occupied a privileged position within Spanish university studies from the middle of the sixteenth century forward (Muldoon 2000b, 18) and that the Spanish obsession with blood, no matter how pervasive, could not create this reality. Second, the Spanish discourse of religious and professional purity (*limpieza*) that has fascinated so many historians and historians of literature is better understood within the framework of *infamia* than within that of pop psychology.[5] Shame—the Latin *infamia* and the Spanish *enfamamiento* or *defamamiento*—meant social death and was firmly ensconced in the Spanish legal tradition.

According to the late medieval *Siete partidas,* honor and shame were diametrical opposites: "Honor is the good standing of a man who lives properly according to law and good morals, without a smear or moral concern. And shaming means bringing an end to a man's honor, which they call *infamia* in Latin" (Real Academia de la Historia 1807, *partida* 7, tit. 6, law 1, 3:555). The juridical disabilities incurred by a shamed man were devastating: "*Infames* in Latin means the same thing as shamed men [*homes enfamados*] in the vernacular [*romance*], and shaming [*enfamamiento*] has such a great power that such men as these can never again hold any of those offices or honors for which men of good standing [*buena fama*] must be chosen, and even those that they have earned previously they must give up after they are proved to be such men. And in addition to this, we declare that none of the shamed men can be a royal judge or councillor, or member or representative of any council, nor shall he live or work in any respectable lord's court" (*partida* 7, tit. 6, law 7, 3:559). It was not just respectable lords who banished shamed men. Shamed men became social outcasts, for shame was like leprosy in the body public:

> For just as that sickness is a disease that attacks the entire body and, after it is caught, it cannot be taken away or softened in a way that alleviates the man who has it, and it causes the man, after he is a leper, to be separated and cast away from all others, and besides all this, it is such a powerful malady that it does not harm only the man who has it, but even the line that descends directly from him and those who live with him, so unfaithfulness [*traición*] acts in that very same way upon the reputation [*fama*] of a man, for unfaithfulness [*traición*] damages it and corrodes it in such a way that it can never be made right, and it drives him to a great distancing and estrangement from those who know what is proper and true, and it blackens and stains the reputation [*fama*] of those who descend from that line, even if it was not their fault, so that they still become infamous because of it. (*partida* 7, tit. 2, 3:537)

The acts allegedly committed by Archbishop Pedro Pardo de Figueroa threatened his social standing and that of his clan, above and beyond any legal fact-finding. In what follows I do not intend to present the history of *infamia,* or shame, in the Spanish legal and popular imaginary. Neither do I address the broad topic of honor, which has generated thousands of essays and articles since the nineteenth century. Instead, I offer a thumbnail sketch of the legal and social questions in which the archbishop's conduct was imbricated and how Carrió's Guatemalan anecdote signals them.

Alphonso the Wise's *Siete partidas* reflected the elaboration and systemization of laws concerning *infamia* that European jurists and canonists had achieved in the twelfth and thirteenth centuries; it addressed both de facto shame (*infamia facti*) and juridical shame (*infamia iuris*): "And there are two ways of shaming [*enfamamiento*]: one is that which is born of the act [*fecho*] alone; the other is born of the law that considers them shamed because of the acts that they commit" (Real Academia de la Historia 1807, *partida* 7, tít. 6, law 1, 3:555). Edward Peters[6] has explained how shame was treated by the twelfth-century Italian monk Gratian, who authored the first compilation of papal decrees:

> Declared infamous in Gratian's *Decretum* were those who had violated the belief and unity of the church: heretics, apostates and schismatics. Those were infamous who acted against the precepts of religion: grave-robbers, those who consulted fortune-tellers and wise-women, those who practiced magic, those who committed sacrilege, and perjurors. A third class consisted of those who committed offenses against the ecclesiastical hierarchy; the disobedient, those

who joined conspiracies against prelates, those who incited others to riot or re-bellion against the hierarchy, and those who brought false accusations against the hierarchy. A fourth category included those who wrote satires or scurrilous defamations against the clergy. A fifth condemned robbery or alienation of the property of churches. A sixth made infamous those who committed crimes against life: murder and poisoning, and a seventh those who committed of-fenses against liberty: abduction. An eighth category infamed those who of-fended against morals: adulterers and those guilty of incest. A ninth infamed those guilty of crimes against property: thieves, usurers and robbers. A tenth condemned those guilty of bringing false witness or false accusations. An elev-enth condemned simoniacs. A twelfth condemned those who intruded into another's ecclesiastical office. A thirteenth condemned those who fled from battle, and a fourteenth infamed those who practiced infamous occupations, especially actors. A fifteenth category infamed those who committed such sins as to lose hope of salvation. A final umbrella clause condemned all those who for any other reason had been declared infamous, especially those excommu-nicated or anathematized. (1990, 69)

It is clear from this summation that the archbishop's alleged acts fell under many categories of infamy as formulated in Gratian's *Decretum.* What was truly unique in Gratian, according to Peters, was not his understanding of *infamia iuris* but his elaboration of *infamia facti*—that is, "infamy incurred not through a stat-utory offense, the declaration of a judge, or the performance of an infamous act, but *infamia* created by certain public knowledge that is widespread, so widespread as to constitute in effect the testimony of an eyewitness" (Peters 1990, 69). Both means of incurring shame are captured in the phrase quoted from the *Siete parti-das*: "And there are two ways of shaming [*enfamamiento*]: one is that which is born of the act [*fecho*] alone; the other is born of the law that considers them shamed [*enfamados*] because of the acts that they commit." The second law from *partida 7*, title 6, explains how *infamia facti* is incurred:

That man who is not born from a righteous marriage as the Holy Church orders is shamed by the act [*enfamado es de fecho*]. It would be the same thing if a father shamed his son in his last will and testament, by saying something bad about him, or if a king or a judge publicly told someone to find a better way of life than the life he was leading, not convicting him but chastising him, or if [a king or a judge] told some lawyer or any other man, chastising him, to take care not to wrongly accuse anyone, for it appeared [to the king or the judge] that he was doing this by setting men [in the case] to it. It would be the same thing if some man who was worthy of belief went around sham-ing another man and revealing in many places some evils that he was doing or had done, if the people believed him and said that it was so, afterwards [*si las gentes lo creyesen et lo dixiesen despues asi*]. Likewise, we say, that if someone were convicted and ordered by a judge's sentence to return or repair something that he had taken by force or by theft from another, that he is shamed de facto because of it [*es enfamado por ello de fecho*]. (Real Academia de la Historia 1807, 3:555–56)

As Peters has suggested, when a respectable man spread rumors about a man that were believed and transmitted across time and place by others, the talk of the town became infamous; no legal fact finding or verdict was required for him to lose his social standing. Similarly, when a man was born out of wedlock, or when a dying man disowned his son, or when enough people said this or that was so, a man's reputation became tarnished. In the Spanish context, however, *infamia facti* did not always occur in a legal vacuum. For instance, the man to whom the last sentence from law 2 refers did not have the rights and privileges of a morally upright man taken from him through a judge's determination of *infamia*, but neither did public opinion act alone to strip him of his good name: he was first found guilty of robbery or theft, and that caused people in his community to lose respect for him. The *Siete partidas* also detailed the "errors" that caused shame (adultery, theft, treachery, deception, and so on), discussed how bribing or coercing witnesses or accusers gave birth to shame, and explained that public punishments (e.g., being branded) incurred shame (Real Academia de la Historia 1807, *partida* 7, tit. 6, law 5, 3:557–58).

Trying to understand precisely how *infamia facti* was different from *infamia iuris* is not an easy task. Indeed, reading the *Partidas,* one senses that *infamia facti* relied on written law and the justice system as much as it relied on public notions of morality or notoriety. Law 4 of *partida* 7, title 6, deals with *defamamiento* that results from the law and the act—that is, how a man is "by law shamed by doing something that he must not" (Real Academia de la Historia 1807, 3:556). It begins with men who force female slaves or free women to sell their bodies. It then lists a series of persons and activities that are, by law, infamous because they constitute a public selling of oneself: "Likewise are shamed the jesters, and the imitators and the directors of the burlesques that they publicly sing before the people, or who dance or play games for the price that people will pay them, and this is because they debase themselves [*se envilecen*] in front of all in exchange for that which they the people give them" (*partida* 7, tit. 6, law 4, 3:556). However, singers and actors who performed for kings and lords, or for friends, were exempted (3:556–57). Also shamed were those men who fought with wild beasts, or with other men, for money. Since they risked their bodies for money, it was clear that "they would easily do another evil" for money (3:557). If men fought only to show their bravery, however, they were not shamed. "Likewise usurers are shamed, and all of those who break contracts or agreements that they were sworn to uphold, and all those who commit sin against nature [for example, sodomy], because for any one of these aforementioned reasons a man is shamed by the act alone, even if a sentence is not rendered against him, because the law and the justice system shame them [*porque la ley et el derecho los enfama*]" (3:557). Law 5 of the same title and *partida* begins with the following declaration: "A sentence that is handed down against another by one of the ordinary judges, convicting him of faithlessness [*traición*], or perjury, or adultery or some other error that he has committed, such a sentence as this shames the convicted" (3:557).

Shame remained part of the Spanish legal tradition for centuries, and the understanding of it differed from glossator to glossator. In Jesuit Juan de Alloza's *Summarum,* a widely disseminated manual for confessors, *infamia* was treated systematically. Alloza's bulky manual incorporated not only canon law and Spanish law but also canonical glosses and commentaries on common law and Spanish law. He explained that there were two kinds of *infamia,* one known as *infamia facti,* the other as *infamia iuris* (1666, 383). The first type was born of a grave and public crime, and the second was given by law and criminal penalty (383). *Infamia iuris* was a *definitive legal finding* about a public crime, whether it was robbery, usury, sacrilege, incest, homicide, adultery, or perjury. Alloza stressed that it required a legal sentence and noted that it could be lifted by the king (384).

The crime that incurred *infamia facti* not only had to be public, or notorious, but had to have actually occurred and carried infamy as a legal injunction and sentence (Alloza 1666, 383). Otherwise, *infamia facti* did not constitute a "legal and canonical impediment" (383), or *irregularity.* Irregularities (*irregularidades* or *defectos* in Spanish) were bodily and mental defects, acquired or innate, that either disqualified men from obtaining benefices and prelacies or circumscribed the ones for which they were eligible. A short list of persons who were not eligible for Catholic offices included hunchbacks, giants, dwarfs, adulterers, bigamists, bastards, perpetrators of honor killings, neophytes, men with only one eye or only one arm, heretics and apostates and their children and grandchildren, soldiers, attorneys, judges, and administrators of public affairs.[7] Unlike Peters's understanding of infamy in the *Decretum* and unlike the nod to public opinion in the *Siete partidas,* Alloza's gloss of the laws and commentaries on shame made it very clear that a public accusation, public opinion, or even a confession did not alone constitute *infamia facti* (383–84).

Spanish laws and canon laws on *infamia* did not speak with one voice, and commentaries on those laws only multiplied the plasticity inherent in a justice system operated by humans. The hidden (or silenced) failures of that system of justice in eighteenth-century Spanish America are a circumlocuted leitmotif of *El lazarillo de ciegos caminantes,* and the seriocomic case of the archbishop serves as an allegory of blind(ed) justice that his readers readily grasped. Although the archbishop was subject to ecclesiastical courts as much as Crown courts, Carrió did not invent the mock trial in Guatemala for inquisitors or judges on the high court: he was weaving a jocose tale that could be understood by persons without legal training.

Bilingual dictionaries confirm that the basic concept of *infamia* was known by all who could read. Shame and shaming appeared in Cesar Oudin's *Thrésor des deux langues françoise et espagnolle*: "Infamar, *diffamer, rendre infame*"; "Infamado, *diffamé, rendu infame, descrié*"; "Infamia, *infamie, diffame, mauvais bruit & renommee.*" The same author also recorded the most frequently employed terms for shame, which demonstrate the preference for metaphors of social standing rather than legal definitions of the same: "Macular, *maculer, tacher, blasmer, reprocher, diffamer, taxer la renommee*"; "Macula, *macule, tache, blasme, infamie*"; "Maculado, *maculé, taché, blasmé, diffamé*" (1607, n.p.). In *Vocabulario de las dos lenguas toscana y castellana*, Cristóbal de las Casas interpreted the Italian *nota* as a synonym of the Spanish *mancha* (the English "smear" or "stain") and as a metaphor for shame, the equivalent of the Spanish *infamia*: "*Nota*. Nota, mancha, infamia" (97). The Italian *macchia, macula*, and *magagna* were defined in Spanish as "stain" (*mancha*), "injury," and "defect" (*daño, defecto*) (1570, 89), whereas the Spanish *mancha* was defined as "pollution," "stain," "blackmark," and so on in Italian: "Mancha. *Contaminatione, macchia, macula, magagna, nota, tacca*" (212). In John Minsheu's *Dictionarie in Spanish and English*, both types of shame were implied: "Infamia, *f. infamie, evill report, an ill name, disgrace*" (1599, 151). He, too, understood the Spanish *macula* and its variants as metaphors for social hierarchy in the Hispanic world: "* Macula, *f. a spot, a blot, a blemish, an infamie, reproch, discredit, or shame*" (161); "* Maculado, *m. spotted, blotted, defamed, reproched, blemished, discredited*" (162); "* Macular, *to spot, to blemish, to reproach, to discredit*" (162). San Joseph Giral del Pino's *Diccionario Español e Inglés* provided a metaphor for shame that we have seen already: "NOTA, s.f. a note, a mark. *Latin.* Metaph. taken for infamy" (1763, n.p.). He did not ignore the publicity factor in his definitions of shame and its variants: "INFAMAR, v.a. to defame, to censure publickly"; "INFAME, adj. one term. infamous"; "INFAMIA, s.f. infamy. *Latin*" (n.p.). Giral del Pino's understanding of shame clearly entailed both *infamia iuris* and *infamia facti*.

It has already been established that Carrió's brother Antonio was a Carmelite in New Spain and that the Spanish merchant passed through Guatemala when he moved from New Spain to the Viceroyalty of Peru in 1746. Both of these facts constitute probable evidence that the Guatemalan anecdote at the close of *El lazarillo de ciegos caminantes* was a joke inspired by the public shaming of the archbishop of Guatemala. Beyond this biographical evidence, however, a wealth of circumstantial and textual evidence supports my claim that Carrió framed the second solution around the archbishop's very public fall.

First, the Spaniard from Guatemala's solution to the riddle of the 4Ps from Lima deliberately plays off the archbishop's name. In other words, "*Pedro, Pardo, Paulino*, and *Perulero*" directed the attention of Carrió's readers to a specific person through the four elements related to him ("connotados"). It is not insignificant that Carrió's tale emphasizes the different names, or "associates," of the archbishop in 1746, a bad year for Santiago de Guatemala, for the archbishop, and for his hometown of Lima. By doing so, the author signals the distinction between *infamia facti* and *infamia iuris* still current in his times.

In the late medieval period, tongue wagging was not enough to ruin one's chances at attending school, joining a military or religious order, and so forth: Alphonso distinguished between *mala nombradia* ("ill report", or "bad name") and *desfamamiento* ("loss of social standing," or "bad reputation") in terms of causes and effects. Yet the effects of "getting a bad name," in my assessment, were precisely those associated with *infamia facti:*

> *Nombradia mala* and *enfamamiento* are two words that are different from each other although it might appear that they are the same, for a man deservedly acquires a bad reputation [*mala fama*] for any of the reasons that we stated above, while men sometimes acquire a bad name and profile [*la nombradia et el precio del mal*] rightfully, and other times, without blame, and it is of a nature such that once the tongues of men have put a bad name [*mala nombradia*] on someone, he can never lose it, even if he did not deserve it, whereas in the case of a bad reputation, as we stated above, all that which pertains to the penalty that must be given for it, according to the law, can readily be struck down. (Real Academia de la Historia 1807, *partida* 7, tit. 6, law 6; 3:558)

Although it was distinct from *infamia* in the *Siete partidas,* this getting a bad name, or *mala nombradia,* became conflated with *infamia* over time, I suspect. Elio Antonio de Nebrija's work, for example, attested to the relationship between infamy and ill report, which was essentially the power of *infamia facti* as elaborated by Gratian and explicated by Peters.[8] It was precisely because words alone could wound one's name, to paraphrase Peters—could give a club or a school a reason to deny one or one's relatives admission—that Spaniards litigated their name and lineage incessantly (and libelers and rumormongers were severely punished) until infamy laws were repealed in the early nineteenth century.

In the 1740s, the archbishop's alleged crimes were reported to the Inquisition in Santiago de Guatemala, the high court in Mexico City, and the Council of the Indies, which ensured that not only residents in his adopted city but residents and officials in many other cities too would hear of his troubles. The effects of being badmouthed, or given a bad name (*mala nombradia*), as we have seen them, clarify why the archbishop's supporters were laboring to clear his name, despite the fact that he had cleared the legal hurdles of shame. His social standing was legally intact; but in the court of public opinion he had been tried and convicted. This is proved not only by the statements of his apologists or eulogists but by the very fact that Carrió chose to use the riddle of the 4Ps from Lima to organize his narration from start to finish: some thirty years after the archbishop's shaming, Carrió could count on the fact that his readers would get the Spaniard from Guatemala's "practical joke" on the *peruleros*.

In addition, Carrió opted to put highly charged words in the mouth of the Spaniard from Guatemala, specific terms that would have resonated with his readers because they connoted public disgrace at best and a legal finding of *infamia* at worst. I return to the challenge issued by the Spaniard from Guatemala:

> El Gachupín Guatemalteco reparó en los muchos elogios que hacian de Lima los Chapetones, pero al mismo tiempo advirtió que no habian hecho mencion de las quatro principales P.P.P.P. y una Noche las mandó poner con Almagre en la Puerta principal del Señor Arzobispo, con un Cartel de Desafio a los Chapetones, para que descifrasen su significacion. (1775, n.p.)

> [The Guatemalan *Gachupín* noted the many praises that the *Chapetones* sang of Lima, but at the same time he noticed that they had not made mention of the four illustrious Ps, and one Night he had them painted in Red Lead on the Distinguished archbishop's front Door along with a Letter of Public Challenge to the *Chapetones* to decipher their meaning.]

This challenge contains traces of the shaming suffered by "*Pedro, Pardo, Paulino, and Perulero.*" Carrió's use of the term *cartel de desafío* spoke directly to his contemporaries, and we too can hear its resonances by consulting some widely distributed dictionaries from the late sixteenth century through the early eighteenth century. In Minsheu's *Dictionarie in Spanish and English,* there are two definitions that pertain to my interpretation of the second solution, *Pedro, Pardo, Paulino* and *Perulero:* "Cartel de desafio, a letter of challenge or defiance"; "Cartel, m. a challenge, a cartell, a defiance, a libell" (1599, 59). The semantic field of *cartel,* which included *cartel de desafío,* overlapped, in the early eighteenth century, with the anonymous and public dressing-down orchestrated by the *pasquín* or *pasquinada* in viceregal Spanish America. According to the *Diccionario de la lengua castellana,* the meanings of *cartel* included the following: "CARTEL. It also means the defamatory libel that is anonymously circulated and posted at corners and in other public places in order to denigrate someone or to besmirch and defame something or operation of the government" (Real Academia Española 1979, 1:203). In a passage from his account of the Kingdom of Quito, the Jesuit Mario Cicala captured both the meaning and the impact of the *cartel* or *pasquinada* in Carrió's times:

Another unusual talent that people in Quito have is the invention of the most clever and concise satires and *pasquinadas*. In this area they are formidable and renowned throughout South America. They use them in drawings with laconic devices and also in cartels that are merely satirical. Royal ministers, bishops, high court presidents and other public persons invested with civil authority quake at the pasquinades of the people in Quito. Do not believe that only educated and erudite men invent them, but rather, most frequently it is some men there known as *capirotes* (which means that their cape or shawl is red, old and falling apart), and they are *mestizos*. The Marquis de Selva Alegre, Governor and President Montúfar of the High Court in Quito, told me many times: "My friend, I fear and I tremble at the vicious pasquinades by *mestizos*. I will have you know (and I knew much better than he did), I will have you know that *mestizos* in Quito are possessed when they invent their mordant and piquant pasquinades. One is forced to admit that they have a pact with the devil, since they can perfectly size up anybody in a few short words." (1994, 213)

Considering the accusations lodged against Pedro Pardo de Figueroa when he was bishop of Guatemala and the notorious charges lodged against him after he became archbishop, it is highly probable that anonymous satires not unlike those in Quito added insult to injury, further humiliating the order's favorite son, who had counted Philip V among his protectors. It is significant, in this regard, that Carrió chose to solve the riddle of the 4Ps from Lima by having an unnamed Spaniard from Guatemala post a *cartel* on the archbishop's door. Well after Carrió left New Spain for Peru, pasquinades rained down on secular and religious figures in Santiago de Guatemala, over whether fasting allowed one to drink broth, if it was licit for a mother to hope for the death of her daughters if they were ugly or too poor for her to marry off, and so on. A full century before Pardo de Figueroa's troubles began, the inquisitor general in Santiago de Guatemala had reiterated edicts that threatened with excommunication the authors of such satires, or "libelos infamatorios" (Chinchilla 1953, 254–55).

Another term used by the Spaniard from Guatemala, *almagre*, indicates to me that Carrió knew of the public drubbing suffered by the archbishop. At his entry for *almagre* (the English "red lead"), Sebastián de Covarrubias Orozco wrote of the red-leadeds: "*Enalmagrados*, they used to call those who were ill marked [*los señalados por mal*], such as people banished as outlaws, people marked by infamy [*los encartados, los notados de infamia*]; and at one time to throw a pan of red lead [*almagre*] or paint on someone's door was taken to mean the same" (1943, 94). As he defined *judío* ("Jew"), he explained that in fourteenth-century Spain Jews had earned the nickname of *red-leadeds* because the sign of their infamy was a piece of red cloth in the form of a circle, which resembled the brand, or red-leading, that owners put on their cattle:

In the time of King Henry, around the 1360s, in the courts that were held at Toro, it was ordered that the Jews who were living in the kingdom intermingled with Christians wear a certain mark by which they might be identified and distinguished from the rest. These were called *marked Jews*. And in 1405 it was ordered and executed that Jews wear as a sign a piece of red cloth, in the shape of a circle, on their right shoulder. And from this I understand they came to be called *red-leadeds* [*enalmagrados*], because it looked like the mark of red lead [*almagre*] that is put on livestock to distinguish one herd from another. (719–20)

Covarrubias opens up Carrió's choice of *almagre* to further readings, all of which are associated with infamy. In his *Tesoro* there also appeared the verb, "to red-lead": "ENALMAGRAR. To mark with red lead. Proverb: "Red-lead and send out to pasture" ["*Enalmagrar y echar a estremo*"], taken from cattlemen who red-lead their herds. They apply it wrongly to the man who, after taking advantage of some woman, casts her aside and looks for another. A saying of rakes" (1943, 510). The adjective also appeared: "RED-LEADED. He who is marked as base or part of a harmful faction [*señalado por ruín o por de vando contrario*]; and that is what they used to call those who were considered base [*ruines*] in times past. See *almagra*" (510).

It might seem odd in the twenty-first century that the term *almagre* (or *almagra*, as it appears in medieval texts and in eighteenth-century dictionaries) was associated with Jews in fourteenth-century Spain and with the archbishop of Guatemala, of illustrious Christian heritage, in the eighteenth. However, medieval infamy laws and glosses, like the religious and professional purity statutes that they inspired in fifteenth-century Spain, were not applicable only to the descendants of Jews and Moors in the Old World and to Africans and Indians in the New.[9] Anyone accused of having aided and abetted the death of the *fiscal* on Guatemala's high court, enjoyed a sexual romp with his widow, and appropriated the good man's estate was a candidate for shaming. By the same account, anyone accused of the sins that Pardo de Figueroa was rumored to have committed would have found the investigation required by the purity statutes in Spain and Spanish America to be very tough sledding indeed.

Carrió placed in the mouth of the Spanish challenger from Guatemala terms that rang bells in the heads of his contemporary readers; specific words that red-flagged Pardo's troubles with the Inquisition, the high court in Mexico City, and the Council of the Indies in Madrid. A popular expression recorded in the *Diccionario de la Lengua Castellana* confirms that the legal and social disabilities associated with the *almagrado* since medieval times were still embedded in the eighteenth century's sense of humor, although the compilers misunderstood the origins of the expression: "*ALMAGRADO*. It is said jocosely and mockingly of one who has come out injured or the loser in some brawl or other misfortune, and it arises from red lead's likeness in color to blood" (Real Academia Española 1979, 3:225). The fact that Pardo de Figueroa was a man of the cloth and belonged to one of the most venerated and powerful families on either side of the Atlantic probably explains the legal disposition of the cases brought against him. However, as I have made clear, shame (*infamia*) did not result from a legal finding alone: *infamia facti* was shame born of a heinous and notorious act, and the court of public opinion frequently decided such cases. Thus, although the archbishop beat back the legal challenges, he did not come out of his public trials—or the mock trial in Carrió's exposé—unscathed. Just as *limpieza de sangre* was not the result of blood tests, but instead a trope that expressed and enforced cultural values, the *almagrado* was a person whose wounds were profoundly social. As we have seen, *de facto* shame (*infamia facti*) was every bit as disabling, socially, as juridical shame (*infamia iuris*). As King Alphonso noted, a man's rights could be restored in a court of law, but a court of law could not restore a man's good name (*nombradía*) in the court of public opinion.

José Pardo de Figueroa: Riddles, Learning, and Lima as a Locus Amoenus

A dimension of the "Pedro, Pardo, Paulino, and Perulero" solution has been hidden for centuries: the relationship between the bucolic portrait of Lima, which is eclipsed by both solutions to the 4Ps from Lima riddle, and one of the troubled archbishop's brothers. Two basic questions need answers here: How was the archbishop's brother José associated with the newspaper riddles mentioned in the Introduction herein, and what was the connection between José and the riddle of the 4Ps from Lima?

A lawyer by trade, José Pardo de Figueroa (1695?–1747) was easily the most famous man to come out of Lima in the first half of the eighteenth century, and his fame was to last well into the second half of the century. Through blood and through marriage, he was related to one of the viceroyalty's most aristocratic and affluent families, the Esquivel clan of Cuzco, whose members were wholeheartedly devoted to commerce and politics. José's wife, Petronila Ignacia de Esquivel Espinola Pardo de Figueroa, was the daughter of Diego de Esquivel, marquis de Valleumbroso and former governor of Cuzco, and Josefa de Espinola Villavicencio y Pardo de Figueroa, the niece of Bernardo Pardo de Figueroa (father of José and Pedro). Petronila's half-brother was the chronicler of Cuzco Diego de Esquivel y Navia, an illegitimate son of the marquis. Her grandmother, Juana Pardo de Figueroa, was José and Pedro's paternal aunt, which meant that José and his wife were also cousins.[10]

José Pardo de Figueroa had been plugged into elite social networks in the Old and New Worlds since birth. In 1708 he began his studies at St. Martin's College, where he later became a professor of law. He received his doctorate in jurisprudence from the University of San Marcos and became a practicing lawyer. In 1720 he moved to Spain. Two years later, when his great-uncle the marquis de Casa Fuerte was appointed viceroy of New Spain, both men left Spain together for Mexico City, where José was to be designated infantry captain of the company that guarded the viceregal palace. In 1728 José returned to Spain, spending some time in Betanzos before he took up residence at the house of the duke de Solferino on Calle de Jácome Trezzo in Madrid.[11] There he would often introduce newly arrived Peruvians to the Benedictine friar Martín Sarmiento, friend and apologist of the internationally anointed cultural critic Father Benito Jerónimo Feijoo y Montenegro (Lohmann Villena 1944, 57–58).

José must have traveled extensively, for the French Jesuit and neoclassicist Jacques Vanière met him in Paris. It was an encounter that impressed Vanière. In his *Praedium rusticum,* which was inspired by Virgil and became the most widely circulated poem of its type in eighteenth-century Europe and America, he transformed Lima into a *locus amoenus* by praising its flowers, trees, gardens, fruits, and waters (1750, 117). He noted not only its abundance of precious metals but also a precious human resource, José Pardo de Figueroa, whose vast erudition made him a citizen of the world, at home in any city. José was a most noble citizen of Lima, Vanière observed, head of the palace guards in Mexico City under "the *Dux,*" and a man distinguished in all fields of knowledge (117 and n. 1). The success of Vanière's poem defined José's reputation for European literati and their Spanish American readers.

Pedro de Peralta Barnuevo praised *Praedium rusticum* in his prologue to *Lima fundada,* and he echoed the Latin poet's exaltation of his friend and fellow Liman José: "Ilustre Pardo, a quien injusta fuera,/Si su nombre omitiese ingrata Lima;/ Cuando aun le cantará musa estrangera,/Cuando aun pluma elegante le sublima:/ Que de libros á la docta esfera/La carga Atlante, espíritu la anima;/Y hará á la Europa con valor profundo/Descubrir otra vez el Nuevo Mundo" ("Shining Pardo, to whom it would be unjust/if Lima, ungrateful, left out your name/While even foreign muse will celebrate you/While even elegant pen elevates you/For unto the scholarly sphere of books/Atlantis carries it, mind animates it/And with profound valor it will make Europe/Discover the New World Again"). It was José who had corrected the common myth that Spaniards in the New World were intellectually inferior to those in the Old World, Peralta Barnuevo observed in a lengthy historical footnote to these verses (1732, can. 7, st. 291, and n.) (Hill 1994a; Williams 1998, 239). At this time, José was not in Paris or Mexico City; he was in Madrid. Peralta Barnuevo wrote to Pardo de Figueroa in April 1733, requesting that he try to get King Philip V to underwrite the remaining volumes of *Historia de España vindicada* (Williams 1994, 116 n. 12). That same year, Diego de Esquivel y Navia, the marquis de Valleumbroso's illegitimate son and José's future brother-in-law, conferred upon José power of attorney in hopes that the wealthy courtier from Lima could secure him an ecclesiastical promotion. José did just that: then prebendary of the cathedral in Cuzco, Esquivel y Navia was named canon of the same by Philip V in 1736 (Villanueva Urteaga in Esquivel y Navia 1980, 1:lxiii).

Feijoo y Montenegro met José Pardo de Figueroa in Madrid. As the nephew of Baltasar Pardo de Figueroa, marquis de Figueroa and lord of the houses of Pardo de Cela and Figueroa (Lohmann Villena 1947, 1:313), José belonged to the wealthiest and most aristocratic family in the Benedictine's native region of Galicia. In *Españoles americanos* (*American Spaniards*) (1944, 9–25), Feijoo y Montenegro portrayed the Peruvian court hopper as no less enlightened than another of his faithful and erudite correspondents from Lima, Peralta Barnuevo:

> I was about to omit another shining example because he is alive and he is nearby; circumstances that in those who read with unfavorable disposition my writings prompt a sinister interpretation of the praises that they find in them. But, in the end, I was persuaded by a reason that I decided must outweigh that nuisance. A shameful thing it is for the Spanish people [*nuestra nación*] that those of its sons who are celebrated by other peoples for their shining talents are not known to our own. This thought spurred me to extend my praise for Don Pedro de Peralta above and this same thought compels me now to make known another enlightened gentleman, not inferior to the former in his intellectual gifts. The latter is Don José Pardo de Figueroa, a native of the city of Lima, nephew of the Most Excellent Lord, Marquis de Figueroa. (21)

Here again, this time in the words of a Spaniard from Galicia who, unlike Carrió, had remained in Spain, an American Spaniard (*español americano*) is at once a native of Lima and a native son. Moreover, in the case of José Pardo de Figueroa, neither geographical nor professional elements of his identity affectively dissuaded him from seeking the rights and privileges accorded to members of his family who, it would seem, by chance had been born in Spain. In sum, neither was he rejected by educated European Spaniards nor did he reject them: as I made clear in the Introduction herein, they were members of one and the same people or stock (*nación*), irrespective of geography or profession.

I speculate that Feijoo y Montenegro's essay was prompted by Sletu Le Gentil's travelogue from 1728, in which he had offered a different view of Lima's wits. Without mentioning names, Le Gentil blasted the University of San Marcos, ridiculing its professors and administration, its ceremonies, its competitions for posts (1:112–13). Le Gentil left Lima for Pisco in January 1716, which means that he had been in Lima when Peralta Barnuevo was heavily involved with the administration of the University of San Marcos and José Pardo de Figueroa was a law student there. His dismissive attitude impinged on the intellectual and moral reputation of Feijoo y Montenegro's two Peruvian friends: "One finds, in effect, few talented people in this Kingdom, and those who have the reputation of being so do not find it so dear. It is not that the country does not produce handsome wits, but rather, the horrible upbringing, debauchery, the very method of studying render all the talents that nature gives them, useless" (1:113–14). By vindicating Peralta Barnuevo and Pardo de Figueroa, Feijoo y Montenegro was countering Le Gentil's attacks on two friends from Peru and vindicating the intellectual and moral capacities of *españoles americanos,* who were, as he described the two Peruvians, sons of Spain.

Feijoo y Montenegro first came across the name of José Pardo de Figueroa while reading Vanière's *Praedium rusticum.* Later he met José and began to correspond with him: "My first notice of this gentleman I owe to Father Jacques Vanière, who celebrates him in the poem quoted above, which sparked my curiosity to get to know more fully his person and qualities; an effort that produced the good fortune of striking up a friendship and correspondence with him" (1944, 22). Feijoo y Montenegro deployed the Jesuit's bucolic portrait of Lima and its precious intellectual metals, like José Pardo de Figueroa, as an external authority that buttressed the authority of his own experience with Peruvians in Spain. Feijoo y Montenegro's readers were to be persuaded that a best-selling Latin poet—and a French one at that—would never lie; therefore, Feijoo y Montenegro himself could not be exaggerating in the slightest: "Father Vanière's poem, *Praedium rusticum,* circulates with the greatest applause throughout Europe. A shameful thing, I say again, it would be if other peoples [*las demás naciones*] saw the gentleman praised in that book and he were ignored by our own. The esteem in which the wise Jesuit holds him is so high that he presents him as a model sufficient in his own right to qualify the wits of Lima as being most excellent" (22). According to the Spanish savant, José's many letters to him illustrated the virtues of the Peruvian's mind and pen:

> Having communicated with him, I cannot only subscribe to that praise but give it greater length, due to the wonderful breath of information that his letters show me about every sort of subject, accompanied by subtle reasoning, eloquent style, exacting critique, thorough judgment; gifts which, while so very worthy in and of themselves, are elevated to the highest value by a most singular modesty that shines through all he writes, and I do not doubt that the same is true of all he says and does. The letters with which he has favored me, which are many and quite lengthy, I guard as a great treasure of every sort of erudition, and as public testimony of my gratitude I hereby confess and swear that they have enlightened me with respect to certain subjects that I touch on in this volume, so that even dispensing with the tugs of friendship, the noble interest in learning is enough to compel me to continue our correspondence. (23)

Such was the international acclaim of the Spanish Benedictine that he was able to intervene decisively in the New World brains versus Old World brains controversy, creating the impression that men born in the New World were actually *smarter* than men born in the Old.[12] As a result, Carrió got pinned back on his heels trying to strike a balance between his *criollo* and European selves. Near the end of *El lazarillo de ciegos caminantes,* Carrió dismisses notions of *criollo* superiority and peninsular inferiority, implicitly rejecting the paradigm held aloft by Feijoo y Montenegro decades before. In the passage that follows, the inspector speaks as a European subject, trying to disabuse Concolorcorvo of the prevailing notion that American Spaniards are more intelligent and learned than European Spaniards:

> El cotejo que hasta el presente se hizo de los criollos de Lima con los que se avecindan aquí de España es injusto. Aquí raro es el mozo blanco que no se aplique a las letras desde su tierna edad, siendo muy raro el que viene de España con una escasa tintura, a excepción de los empleados para las letras. Bien notorio es que no siempre se eligen los más sobresalientes, porque además de que éstos, fiados en sus méritos, no les puede faltar allá acomodo, no quieren arriesgar sus vidas en una dilatada navegación y mudanza de temperamentos, o no tienen protectores para colocarse aquí a su satisfacción. Si se mudara el teatro, esto es, que se proveyesen en Lima todos los empleados, se vería claramente que había en la península tantos sabios a proporción, y cualquiera ciudad de las de España comparable a ésta la igualaba en ingenios, juicio y literatura, sin traer a consideración a varios monstruos de aquellos, tan raros que apenas en un siglo se ven dos, como el gran Peralta, limeño bien conocido en toda la Europa, a quien celebró tanto la más hermosa y crítica pluma que produjo Galicia en el presente siglo. (447)

> [The comparison that has been made up until now between the *criollos* of Lima and the men from Spain who reside here is unfair. Here, the young white man who does not devote himself to letters at a tender age is rare, while rarely does the man coming from Spain have the slightest trace of them, except those employed as scriveners. It is public knowledge that the ones chosen are not always the most capable because, besides the fact that the latter, relying on their merits, will never be without a job there, they do not want to bet their lives on an extended journey and change of climate, or they do not have protectors to set them up here as they would like. Were there a change of scene, that is, if all the employees in Lima were appointed (from Spain), it would become evident that there were learned men in the Peninsula in the same proportion, and that any of the cities in Spain comparable (in size) to this one would equal it in wits, judgment and erudition, leaving aside the

various monsters among those (*criollos*), so rare that hardly two are seen in a century, like the great Peralta, a Liman well-known in all of Europe, who was highly praised by the most handsome and critical feather pen that Galicia produced in the present century.]

The inspector facetiously concedes here that the intellectual "monsters" born in Lima were, in fact, so rare that the cultural critic could find only two, Peralta Barnuevo (named in the passage just quoted) and Pardo de Figueroa (not named in the passage), in the entire century. Moreover, by suggesting that European Spaniards were not permitted to compete for jobs that would allow them to prove their equality, Carrió was pointing out that the most influential posts in Lima were bought by *criollos* or arranged for them by protectors.

When José Pardo de Figueroa applied to become a knight of Santiago, his name was listed as José Pardo de Figueroa y Luján, age 38, and his father was listed as Bernardo Pardo de Figueroa y Sotomayor (Cadenas y Vicent 1978–1979 3:37–38). Like his father, his grandfather Baltasar, and a dozen of his paternal and maternal uncles, José was admitted into the Order of Santiago, supported by numerous Peruvians of influence at the court in Madrid, in 1734. Witnesses deposed there on his behalf included his uncle, Joaquín de Acuña, marquis de Escalona, a native of Lima; the *fiscal* on the high court in Santiago, Chile; Pedro Bravo del Ribero, who already had purchased a judgeship on the high court in his native Lima; Felipe de Zabala, a native of Lima and a future in-law of both Pedro Bravo del Ribero and Pedro José Bravo de Lagunas y Castilla, another native and future judge on the high court in Lima; Pedro de Oquendo, a native of Cuzco; José de Araújo y Río, a native of Lima who had been in Spain since 1730 and was to become the governor and president of the high court in Quito (1736–1743) and of Santiago, Guatemala, years later, as Carrió's Guatemalan tale makes clear. At this time, Pedro Pardo de Figueroa was also in Europe, and Bravo del Ribero and Araújo y Río, who would later travel with the future bishop and archbishop of Guatemala to New Spain, were neighbors in Madrid (Lohmann Villena 1947, 1:316). In late 1734, it is likely that José was making preparations for his return to Peru, pleased with his impending governorship and membership in Cuzco's *rosca*.[13]

In 1735 José was appointed governor (*corregidor*) of Abancay,[14] a provincial district that shared its eastern border with Cuzco and that had been the site of Francisco Pizarro's defeat of Almagro two hundred years earlier. Abancay was connected to Lima by the *royal road* (*camino real*), "a stone road four yards wide and three leagues long," which passed through Abancay's prosperous Jaquihuana Valley, where the Incas had battled the Spaniards (Bueno 1996, 260). Cuzco had long been famous throughout Europe and Spanish America, having been singled out—along with Mexico City, not Lima—for its "astounding magnificence" by none other than Michel Montaigne (1988, 398v.). A religious father in Santiago de

Guatemala called it "the most noble portion of Southern America, due to its illustrious residents, abundance of minerals and fertility of soil; it was the first and last court of those enlightened Incas" (in Cagiga y Rada 1739, n.p.). In Cuzco, in 1736, José married his wealthy cousin Petronila Ignacia (Mendiburu 1874–1890, 6:238), but the marriage was short-lived: Petronila Ignacia died in Cuzco on May 14, 1738, leaving José a considerable chunk of the Esquivel family fortune to supplement his own.

The pedigree and the reputation of José Pardo de Figueroa come into focus upon reading the week's worth of eulogies delivered for his wife at the cathedral in Santiago, Guatemala, in 1738. Tomás Alvarado de Guzmán edited Cagiga y Rada's description of the ceremonies, along with the sermons, in *Fúnebre pompa y Exequial aparato* (*Mournful Pomp and Machine of Obsequies*) (1739). He dedicated it to José Pardo de Figueroa and provided an exhaustive treatment of "the lustre [of the Pardo de Figueroa clan], which is well-known in that and this America" (n.p.). He acknowledged the praises heaped on José by Vanière, Feijoo y Montenegro, and Peralta Barnuevo. Even the renowned detractor of American Spaniards Manuel de Martí y Valenzuela admired José Pardo de Figueroa. What inspired "that incomparable wonder of erudition in our times, Dr. Don Manuel Martín [*sic*]," was the Peruvian's *Brief Dissertation on the Founding, Name and Antiquity of the Cities of Seville, Hispalis, and Italica* (n.p.). Martí y Valenzuela "built him an intellectual temple for worshiping, as if a divine oracle" (n.p.).

Diego Esquivel y Navia referred to his in-laws numerous times in *Noticias cronológicas del Cuzco* (*Annals of Cuzco*). In the post (*chasqui*) of April 26, 1742, there were ten mules and a decree from the viceroy of Lima, a relative of the Pardo de Figueroa clan, in which José Pardo de Figueroa was designated *corregidor* of Cuzco (Esquivel y Navia 1980, 2:435). The *Gazeta de Lima* also contributed to José's fame. In the issue for May 1 to June 30, 1744, Pardo de Figueroa landed on the front page:

> In the Cuzco post it became known that an aurora borealis was visible in that city on the night of April 20, which caused great consternation among the common folk and would have been greater if the paternal love of His Illustrious Pedro Morcillo, Bishop of that Holy Church, along with the corregidor, José Pardo de Figueroa, knight of Santiago, Marquis de Valleumbroso [and] an individual of universal learning, had not gone out and calmed the clamorings of the folk, remaining there until midnight to explain to them the natural causes of that phenomenon, which always appears in the northern sky in the form of an arch like a rainbow, of a bright though opaque light, and in which the exhalations that catch fire make different shapes visible, ones that fear makes out to be evil omens. By virtue of an energetic, eloquent argument and the respect that high learning commands, they managed to calm that fury, leaving to mathematicians and [natural] philosophers their predictions,

which never go beyond drought or sterility, as experience has demonstrated on like occasions. (n.p.)

Pedro Morcillo Rubio y Auñón, ordained as bishop of Cuzco on September 26, 1743 (Esquivel y Navia 1980, 2:282), was the nephew of the former archbishop and viceroy of Lima, Diego Morcillo Rubio de Auñón.[15] On April 23, 1746, according to Esquivel y Navia, "at three in the morning, the Honorable Bishop and a host of attendants left this city for the Marquis de Valleumbroso's *Glorieta* in Quispicanche, to spend a few days of fun and relaxation from the constant fatigue of managing and keeping zealous watch over his flock" (2:346). La Glorieta was the grandest *casa quinta,* or country estate, in the Viceroyalty of Peru (2:346 and n.), to which Pardo de Figueroa had retired after his governorship in 1744. He also owned a clothing factory (*obraje*) in Quispicanche and a *cañaveral* in Tambobamba (2:378).[16] With his wealth, his relatives, and his international fame, José was no stranger to Carrió even when Carrió maintained a residence in Lima (1746–1752, 1757–1783). Carrió was the governor of Chilques and Masques (or Paruro), a district that shared its northeastern border with Cuzco (Bueno 1996, 265–66) from 1752 to 1757. On the western border of this district was Abancay, where José Pardo de Figueroa had been governor in 1735 before he became governor of Cuzco (1742–1744). On the eastern side of Carrió's district was the famed Quispicanchi to which José had retired.

Another of José's hobbies in retirement was noncommercial and well-known to readers of the *Gaceta de Lima,* including Carrió: he composed riddles that echoed the *problems* posed by shepherds in Virgil's *Eclogues.* In "On the Conceits of Questions," a section of Gracián's *Arte de ingenio* where we find the sorts of riddles published in newspapers in eighteenth-century Mexico and Lima, he explained, "The moral and political Problems are also a branch that is born of this root of wit" (1998, 322). Several collections of these problems, which date back to Aristotle, were published in the Spanish renaissance and republished over and over in the baroque and the Enlightenment. Esquivel y Navia recorded in his *Noticias* that the postman from Lima left Cuzco to return to the viceregal capital on June 27, 1744, adding: "In response to the riddles that came in issues of the *Gaceta de Lima,* there went out in this post the one that the Marquis de Valleumbroso submitted" (1980, 2:309).

In 1746 Carrió arrived in Lima, and José Pardo de Figueroa challenged readers of the *Gaceta de Lima* to solve two riddles. On December 30, 1746, wrote Esquivel y Navia, "at 6 p.m., the postman arrived from Lima." He added, "The riddles that were sent to Lima in this post, written by the Marquis de Valleumbroso, are the following; the first ancient, the second modern: 1. Rubida curua, capax, alienis humida guttis,/Luminibus falsis auri mentita colorem,/Dedita sudori, modice succumbo labori./2. Die quibus in terris fuerit vir lumine captus,/Qui nec luscus, nec lumine captus, utroque" (1980, 2:336). The Spanish translation is as follows: "1. Rubia, curva, húmeda de gotas ajenas,/simulando el color del oro con falsas luces,/entregada al sudor, me rindo al trabajo. 2. Dí, en qué tierra hubo un hombre ciego,/el cual ni era tuerto ni ciego, a una y otra parte" (2:336 n.) ("1. Blond, curved, wet from foreign drops/Feigning the color of gold with fake lights/delivered to sweat, I surrender to work. 2. Say in which land there was a blind man/who was neither one-eyed nor blind to either side"). This "modern" riddle mimicked the problems posed by Virgil—though Lima's steamy *gauderios* were nothing like Virgil's fair-haired shepherds—and it would make Carrió's Guatemalan tale, and Secretary Concolorcorvo's appropriation of one of Virgil's problems, even more laughable.

The Inca Secretary poses a riddle, or "Virgilian Problem," as he describes the route from Huamanga to the Villa of Huancavelica, rich in mercury mines and in the social problems associated with the mining industry: gambling, theft, murder, and prostitution. First he describes a famous gorge outside of Huamanga: "A media legua de Huamanga se presenta un profundo barranco, que llaman la Quebrada Honda, que tiene media legua de bajada perpendicular y otro tanto de subida, con veredas estrechas, pero el visitador me dijo que jamás se había visto agua en su fondo" (415) ("A half-league from Huamanga one comes upon a deep ravine that they call the Quebrada Honda [Deep Gorge], which has a straight drop of a half-league and about that high of a rise, with narrow paths, but the inspector told me that he had never seen water at the bottom of it").[17] Next, Concolorcorvo claims that Virgil's riddle revealed his ignorance and lack of experience. Were he Virgil's shepherd, he would laugh at the challenge:

Puesto cualquiera en él y mirando al cielo daría solución al *Problema de Virgilio,* pues apenas se divisan las tres varas de cielo de su pensamiento. Voy a copiar los dos dísticos, con el mismo derecho que lo hicieron otros muchos:

*Dic quibus in terris, et
eris mihi magnus Apollo,
tres pateat Coeli spatium, non
amplius, ulnas.*

Muy poco sabía Virgilio de problemas cuando propuso éste por tal, o en su Mantua o en toda la Italia no habrá quebradas hondas y estrechas, que son tan comunes en toda la América; pero supongamos que no las hay, o que fuese una sola, de que tuvo noticia. ¿Es posible que no había elevadas chimeneas? A fe que si yo fuera su pastorcillo me reiría bastante de su pregunta, aunque le consta a Vm. muy bien que los indios apenas nos reímos tres veces en la vida. (415–16)[18]

[Anyone standing in it and looking at the sky could solve *Virgil's Problem*, because one can hardly make out the three yards of sky in his expression. I am going to copy the distics, with the same right that many others did before me:

*Dic quibus in terris, et
eris mihi magnus Apollo,
tres pateat Coeli spatium, non
amplius, ulnas.*

Virgil knew precious little about problems when he presented this one as such, or else there must not be, in Mantua or in all of Italy, deep and narrow ravines, which are so very common throughout Spanish America. But let us suppose that there are not any (in Italy), or there was only one that he knew about. Is it possible that there were not towering chimneys? Honestly, if I were his little shepherd, I would really laugh at his problem, although you will well recall that we Indians laugh maybe three times in our entire lives.]

What does a ravine near Huamanga, or anywhere else in Spanish America, have to do with chimneys in Mantua? Nothing, apparently, but that does not stop Concolorcorvo from engaging in his own brand of deep interpretation. Ancient and modern theorists of the risible had recommended the appropriation and alteration of verses and sayings to create humor,[19] but there is more to the passage just quoted than that.

The Inca secretary's stab at Virgil is, in fact, part of Carrió's radical subversion of the *locus amoenus* topos that had been created around Mexico City and Lima by Bernardo de Balbuena, Vanière, Peralta Barnuevo, and others. This subversion occurs on two levels. On the first level, as Concolorcorvo allegorizes Virgil willy-nilly, Carrió ridicules modern poets and historians who imitated Virgil's *Eclogues* or *Georgics* and implicitly or explicitly paralleled imperial Rome and Lima or Mexico City. Concolorcorvo's application of Virgil's riddle to Huamanga, of all places, represents Carrió's negative appraisal of the bucolic portrait of Peru and its wits created in neoclassical poems such as *Praedium rusticum.* Remember: an amplification of Lima as *locus amoenus,* in Vanière's poem, was the precious intellectual metal of José Pardo de Figueroa, who publicly imitated Virgil's problems in the *Gaceta de Lima.* As we saw earlier, the inspector's comments near the end of *El lazarillo de ciegos caminantes* imply that Carrió had read Feijoo y Montenegro's *Españoles americanos* and taken umbrage at the Benedictine's claim that American Spaniards, judging by the likes of Peralta Barnuevo and Pardo de Figueroa, were smarter than European Spaniards.

On the second level, Carrió exploits the equivocal nature and potential obscenity of "quebradas" and "chimeneas" to remind readers of the sexual commerce that was occurring in the region and the witticisms that had been told and published about prostitutes and riddles. Two facts should be taken into account here. First, what I will call "commercial gallantries"—pickup and payment lines exchanged between prostitutes and clients—were called *requiebros*. Second, the inspector tells Concolorcorvo that water has never been seen in the ravine, or *quebrada*. Taken together, both facts imply that Carrió intentionally left the door of interpretation ajar so that his readers could walk through it with their own conscience (or imagination) as their *lazarillo*. Those who were familiar with prostitutes and the tales about them would interpret "ravines" and "chimneys" in a metaphorical sense. Among the apothegms, riddles, and jocose tales that originated in the Italian collections of *facezie*, found their way into Spanish bestsellers like Joan Timoneda's *Buen aviso y Portacuentos*, and became proverbial expressions in the Spanish world, there was an anecdote about some quick-witted prostitutes. In Timoneda's collection, the story goes like this:

> Several ladies were chatting as they went from lodging to lodging, when they saw written on a scaffolding this verse that said, "Stay away from deep shafts [*pozos*]." Upon seeing it, one of them started to laugh, which made the others say, "What are you laughing at?" When they figured out why, the boldest one replied, "With your permission, ladies, I will answer for all of us." Since they were courtesans, she took a piece of charcoal, and below where it read, "Stay away from deep shafts," she wrote, "No, just stay away from short ropes [*sogas*]." (1990, 150–151)

Carrió substituted "quebradas" for "pozos" and "chimeneas" for "sogas," further unraveling the bucolic tapestries of Spanish America woven by literati at home and abroad.

José's death in 1747 was a major event in the political and intellectual lives of the viceroyalty, and it must have been a tremendous blow to his brothers in New Spain, especially the archbishop of Guatemala, who was covered in shame. Esquivel y Navia's eulogy in June 1747 did not report that José Pardo de Figueroa was the wealthiest man in Cuzco and the son-in-law of the second marquis de Valleumbroso, the chronicler's biological father. Esquivel y Navia portrayed him instead as the noblest and most learned man in Cuzco:

> Thursday, June 22, at 8 p.m., the Marquis de Valleumbroso, Don José Agustín Pardo de Figueroa, died suddenly while seated in his chair, after a long illness, on his *quinta* or farm called La Glorieta, next to his textile factory in Quispicanchi, where he had been living for the past three years. There was widespread sorrow because he was the most illustrious man in this city and the most learned in all letters, in addition to his expertise in both civil and canon law (which was his profession). Likewise, he was a most handsome encyclopedia of the fields of philosophy; scholastic, expositive and moral theology;

mathematics; poetry; mythology; sacred and civil history; and many others, plus the polish of eight languages: Latin, Castilian, Quichua, Nahuatl, Portuguese, Italian, French and Greek, in the latter with the greatest talent. He was a knight of Santiago, a native of Lima. He was buried in the town of Oropesa, on Monday, June 26. (1980, 2:394–95)

José's reputation was even greater in death than it had been in life, thanks in great part to French savants. He had sided with the French scientist Charles Marie de la Condamine in a well-ventilated dispute with the two Spanish scientists Juan and Ulloa over the inscription to be placed on the pyramids in Quito. La Condamine's respect and affection for José warmed José's *Histoire des Pyramides de Quito* (*History of the Pyramids in Quito*) (1751a) and *Journal du Voyage fait par ordre du Roi a l'Equateur* (*Diary of the Voyage to the Equator Taken by King's Order*) (1751b). In the first of these works, La Condamine stated that he could name any number of enlightened Spaniards and American Spaniards who granted his requests and supported the mission of the scientists, but he did not want to compromise anyone:

> However, without compromising anyone, I can at least produce the testimony of an illustrious deceased, Don José Pardo y Figueroa, Marquis de Valleumbroso, *corregidor* of Cuzco, nephew of a Viceroy of Mexico and brother of the Bishop of Guatemala. I cite an individual distinguished by birth and even more by his great knowledge and his vast reading, and one of the most suited to give honor to the Spanish people [*la nation Espagnole*]. Father Vanière, in his poem, [and] Father Feijoo y Montenegro, whose very name inspires praise, have rightly placed him in the category of illustrious *criollos*. (50)

Immediately thereafter he revealed the influence of José Pardo de Figueroa at the court in Madrid. The Peruvian had played a consultant's role with the Council of Indies, and it had been his idea to send the Spanish scientists on the trip with La Condamine and his French colleagues:

> He had traveled in Europe; he lived in the Court of Madrid. In 1734, when the Council of Indies was deliberating our petition to go and measure the degrees of the Earth in Quito, the Marquis de Valleumbroso himself had been consulted. It was he who had the suggestion of appointing two young navy men, trained in mathematics, to learn the methods of astronomy and trigonometry by assisting us in our work, tasks for which Don Jorge Juan and Don Antonio de Ulloa were later chosen. (50)

Extracts from two letters (dated March 12, 1742, and November 7, 1742) were reproduced after the passage just quoted. The first is especially pungent, as José Pardo de Figueroa wrote that the dispute over the inscription on the pyramids was an embarrassment to him and his fellow Spaniards:

> The manner in which your inscription has been challenged is worthy of laughter, and I am ashamed to show my face knowing that among my people [*nación*] someone would stoop to the sort of nonsense that has been directed at the inscription. I will request from Lima the papers filed in this matter, which would be a better subject for Molière, were he alive, to write a comedy than to be presented in the courts. And in Spain such fussbudgeting will be regretted because of the stigma it will place on the Spanish people [*nación*]. (51–52)

José also appeared in the *Voto consultivo* penned by Judge Bravo de Lagunas y Castilla. To prove the abundance of wheat and other grains, the Francophile jurist borrowed from the *Praedium rusticum,* writing of "Father Vanière, who got the most detailed and accurate data about this city of Lima from one of its most illustrious and learned sons, Don José Pardo de Figueroa, later Marquis de Valleumbroso, of whom this sage in France and the Most Illustrious (Father) Feijoo in Spain make due mention" (1755, 169). A year later, the renowned Jesuit historian Pierre François-Xavier de Charlevoix introduced José Pardo de Figueroa to an even broader audience through his *Histoire du Paraguay (History of Paraguay)*. He noted José's friendship with Francisco Javier Palacios, a judge on the high court in Charcas, who was commissioned by Philip V in 1745 to place the Chiquitos people under the same status as the Guarani. On June 14, 1746, Palacios received a letter from José, "who gave him all the insight he needed to carry out the commission with which he was charged" (3:217). Before reproducing the letter (1756, 3:218–19), Charlevoix launched this encomium:

> Nobody knew Spanish America better than this gentleman, who had been born in Lima, had traveled all the provinces that make up Peru and served with great distinction in New Spain. He was later seen in Europe, expressing himself in every language with the same ease and conversing about everything, a man to whom no field of knowledge was a stranger. That is the image of him that the Benedictine savant, Father Feijoo, gives us in several places in his works, and especially in the fourth volume of his *Teatro crítico.* Father Vanière, who had seen him in France, also paid him a most beautiful tribute in the sixteenth chapter of his *Praedium rusticum.* (3:218)[20]

It was probably due to Father Vanière in Paris, or Dean Martí in Rome, that the Jesuit Giandomenico Coleti included José in his *Dizionario.* At the entry for *Lima,* he observed: "Lima has produced in every period great figures in saintliness and letters, like Saint Rose, . . . and among the *literati,* the celebrated Peralta, the renowned Pardo de Figueroa, Marquis de Valleumbroso, . . . and others still living, who are the ornament and the splendor of their native land" (1771, 1:187–88). At the very time, then, that Carrió was beginning his inspection of the posts, still another author in Europe was keeping Pardo de Figueroa's legacy alive, in spite of the fact that he had published only a minor treatise on the name of Seville, which was quickly lost.

José and Pedro Pardo de Figueroa had been born at the turn of the eighteenth century and had grown up in Bourbon Peru and Spain. The Pardo de Figueroas were descendants of the most illustrious houses in Carrió's native province of Galicia, Pardo de Cela and Figueroa, which included wealthy owners of large estates and trading ventures as well as men who were well placed within the hierarchies of Crown and church on both sides of the Atlantic. They were men who enjoyed the finer things in life, like the king of Spain, and the finer things in Spanish life quite often were French, like the king of Spain. Their associates were men like themselves: members of illustrious families who had attended the best schools and universities, powerful men well versed in the ways of power and in the latest intellectual and cultural trends coming from France and Italy or from Spain by way of France and Italy. They gained Philip V's confidence at an early age, and they never lost it.

Carrió, in contrast, did not belong to a family of grandees, shipping magnates, and lords, and he was not a fan of French literature or Italian opera. Neither envy nor a generation gap alone, but profound ideological differences, separated Carrió from the ostensibly enlightened circles of power in Madrid and the viceregal capitals of Spanish America. He could not embrace the Pardo de Figueroas and their like-minded cohorts as shining examples of the new *Monarquía* that the Spanish Bourbons were laboring to create and sell not only to Spaniards but to everyone in Europe and America. Beneath the modern veneer of officials such as the Pardo de Figueroas, his exposé implied, there lurked talents as old as the world itself.

PART II

CHAPTER 3

En Route and in the Loops: Trade, Metals, and Elites, circa 1700–1750

In a manuscript titled *Reflections on the Decline of the Spanish* Monarquía *Due to the Expenditure of Treasures and Depopulation That Wars in the Seventeenth Century and This One Caused,* an anonymous writer noted that because foreigners could not rob Spain of its treasures by force, they resorted to "artful inventions." He detailed the complicity of Spaniards on both sides of the Atlantic in the illegal trade conducted by foreign merchants:

> Engaged in this, foreigners achieved their purpose first in Spain, draining it of the gold and silver that was arriving from the Indies, because extravagance is the child of abundance. This pestilence later passed to the Indies, through the hands of the Spaniards themselves, who bought products from foreigners, lured by the profits gained from transporting [and reselling] them, and even being content to be their agents in exchange for a percentage of the profits. All the measures of our government to ban foreigners from the Indies were undercut, thinking that if the oil passed through our hands at least our palms would be greased. (Anonymous, *Reflexiones* 63v.)

During the War of the Spanish Succession, European powers that had been friends became implacable enemies, and the French and the English fought over who would control illegal trade and the smuggling of gold and silver in Spanish America:

> And amidst these upheavals the French merchants, by taking the long route of Cape Horn, sought to transport many goods to Peru, and also, in registered ships, following the usual route to Mexico, and though it might be out of place, I will tell Your Majesty what is going on in Paris, and it just so happens that while Your Majesty's grandfather was desiring to deny his subjects the Indies trade, one of his ministers told him that the English would do the same trade and with what it earned them they would wage war on both Crowns, and for this reason he lifted the ban. (64r.)

During his reign of nearly half a century (1700–1724, 1724–1746), the first Spanish Bourbon, Philip V, signaled an interest in halting illegal trade between European powers and the Spanish Indies. Even before he triumphed in the War of the Spanish Succession (1700–1713), it appears that he had a handle on what our anonymous author wished to explain in his treatise. Philip V issued twelve decrees between 1703 and 1715 aimed at quashing illegal trade between the French and merchants in the Viceroyalty of Peru (Villalobos 1965, 32). Illegal trading in foreign goods and the smuggling of untaxed gold, silver, and mercury were to be persistent, interrelated practices in the viceroyalties of New Spain, New Granada, and Peru throughout the eighteenth century.[1] Both kinds of fraud relied not only on *caminantes,* or traders, who often traveled the postal routes, but also on the collaboration of Crown and church officials at the highest levels. *El lazarillo de ciegos caminantes* insinuates these commercial continuities between the first and second halves of the eighteenth century, which analyses attached to the *middle period* model underestimate.

The following pages examine how these illicit practices in the first half of the eighteenth century contributed to the economic rivalry between Lima and Buenos Aires and to the formation of elites in each city, both of which were important to the gestation of Alonso Carrió de Lavandera's exposé. As we shall see, mules, traders, and the post were often linked in the Crown's efforts to put a lid on the smuggling of precious metals out of the Spanish Indies and the trade in contraband goods. The following also suggests an allegorical interpretation of *Pedro, Pardo, Paulino,* and *Perulero* that links the posts on the inspector's itinerary to the Kingdom of Guatemala in New Spain, revealing that the latter was part of the trading and smuggling loop that connected the viceroyalties of New Spain, New Granada, and Peru to Asia and to each other.

Smuggling and the Economic Rivalry between Lima and Buenos Aires

In 1705, after the death of the count de la Monclova, the last Habsburg viceroy of Peru, the interim president of the high court in Lima called its judges into session; together they issued a decree, dated September 28 of that year, aimed at stemming the illegal exportation of gold and silver (Real Audiencia de Lima 1705). It was posted in Lima and Port Callao and directed to provincial governors, lower-ranking bureaucrats, and judges on the high courts in Chuquisaca, Santiago, Quito, and Panama. The decree barred everyone from removing silver ore, nuggets, gold, or any other metals without first declaring them in the nearest foundry and paying the royal fifth. Persons could not transport these metals by land or by sea, and those caught with nuggets, plates and bars of gold, silver ore, or bars of silver found to be untaxed or proven to have been skimmed off the top would be fined and would lose not only the metals but also their mule trains and wagons. The post played an essential role in the smuggling of foreign goods and in the diversion of precious metals, and the high court in Lima was attuned to this fact. Governors of kingdoms, provincial governors, various other Crown officials, and military officers were authorized to inspect the mule trains, postmen, mailbags, and packages as they left their districts whenever these officials received a secret or notorious report that untaxed silver or gold was being carried, but they were to conduct their inspections without touching the letters the postmen carried. The governors of Tucumán and Buenos Aires were charged with exercising the necessary caution and vigilance in those areas characterized by the decree as especially prone to the diversion of silver nuggets, bars, and untaxed gold.

Yet smuggling did not end either in 1705 or after the arrival of Manuel de Oms y de Santa-Pau Olim de Sentmanat y de Lanuza, marquis de Castell-dos-Rius, viceroy of Peru from 1707 to 1710. The marquis de Castell-dos-Rius had served as Spanish ambassador to France and had delivered the last will and testament of the Habsburg Charles II to his successor, Philip the Bourbon, an event that triggered the War of the Spanish Succession. In Lima, he was to earn the nickname of *Royal treasury robber* (*Ladrón del tesoro real*) for his unpopular war taxes, illegal trading with French ships, and other nefarious activities (Sánchez 1967, 58–76, 121–27; Williams 1994, 20–21). In 1707, Lima's merchants' guild (*consulado de comercio*) complained that by docking illegally in ports along the continental coastline, including Port Callao, and selling their abundant supply of cloth articles from Asia, ships bound for the Viceroyalty of New Spain were ruining merchants in Lima (Villalobos 1965, 61–62). A year later, Pedro de Peralta Barnuevo wrote of the problem of keeping trade going in Lima, given the difficulties posed by the lengthy War: "And therefore controlling it [trade] is the most difficult act of a government, especially in Lima. . . . And there being no doubt that the continuation of Spain's trade depends on that of this trade, it is clear how important the dispatch of this *armada* becomes in the present configuration of things" (1708, pt. 1, 3rd glory, n.p.). During the war, the institution of register ships (*registros* or *navíos de permiso*) allowed Spanish and French merchants to purchase the right to sell Spanish foodstuffs and clothing during a limited period of time in less-traveled ports. Both Spanish and French *registros* came to the viceroyalty through Cape Horn. Their stops in the ports of Chile transformed the architecture of cities such as Concepción and Santiago, allowing wealthy residents to adorn their homes with glass windows, iron bars, pianos, and fine crystal. French ships traveled between Port Callao and Asia during the first two decades of the eighteenth century, unloading Asian goods in the ports of Pisco, Arica, and Concepción (Benavides 1988, 175; Villalobos 1965, 61–62).

Diego Ladrón de Guevara, bishop of Quito (1706–1717), succeeded the marquis de Castell-dos-Rius, serving until 1716.[2] In 1714 Peralta Barnuevo wrote a brief panegyric, *Imagen política del gobierno del Excelentísimo Señor Don Diego Ladrón de Guevara* (*Political Image of the Administration of the Most Excellent Lord Don Diego Ladrón de Guevara*) (in Williams 1996, 39–74). Peralta Barnuevo claimed that the viceroy's government would have surpassed those of his predecessors had he been living "in that Golden Age of Peru" during which "the condition of the *Monarquía* left no room for enrichment, the provision of provincial governorships was a reward for the nobility, the *encomiendas* were nontransferable, the royal fifths were not diverted, commerce had not been disrupted and destroyed, and the cultivation of the fields was not impeded by the soil" (1996a, 69). In this apology for Ladrón de Guevara's misadministration, the *criollo* savant beat about for subordinates on whom to cast aspersions, blaming their humanity and their ability to use discourse as a substitute for material reality in the "vast Empire" of Peru.[3] He made no direct mention of the charges that were piling up against the viceroy: election tampering, providing family members with jobs and with unpaid Indian workers, misappropriating royal treasury funds, abetting illegal trade with French ships in the Pacific, aiding in the nonpayment of the royal fifth on gold and silver, diverting gold and silver, and refusing to prosecute officials who allowed such activities.[4] In what was to become common practice during the first century of Bourbon rule, Ladrón de Guevara was exonerated of all of these charges, and he officially quit his posts in 1716.[5]

Diego Morcillo Rubio Auñón, the archbishop of Charcas (and the uncle of Pedro Morcillo Rubio Auñón, José Pardo de Figueroa's friend and Cuzco's future bishop), succeeded Ladrón de Guevara in 1716.[6] His tenure was decidedly brief— he served for under two months. Again, Peralta Barnuevo employed his legal and oratorical acumen in defense of a viceroy of Peru (1996b). Again, the charges that had prompted public outcry and Crown intervention included illegal trade and the misappropriation of funds (Williams 1996, 109–15). Viceroy Morcillo Rubio Auñón gave the reins to a political veteran of Spanish Naples, Nicolá Caracciolo, prince de Santo Buono, who was to attempt numerous reforms during his tenure (1716–1720). He took an interest in reforming the *repartimiento* system (i.e., the sale of mules, agricultural tools, and other supplies to the Indian population by governors in rural areas), along with communications between Spain and the Viceroyalty of Peru. Caracciolo's proposal to reform the post (Tinagero n.d.) was an important albeit unsuccessful one, and it is safe to assume that Carrió would not have initiated his inspection without first having acquainted himself with prior recommendations and proposals to make the post operate more effectively. The viceroy wished to make the mail ships more frequent so that there would be less delay in the delivery of mail from Madrid to the viceroyalty. His proposal was rejected by the Crown, according to the royal consultant Bernardo Tinagero; it would, however, influence the century's first significant reform of the post, which came out of Peru during Caracciolo's tenure, thanks to the aforementioned Alcedo y Herrera (1915, introd.)

In 1719, under orders from the Ministry of the Navy, Alcedo put together a report on the need to establish communications between America and Spain by increasing the *avisos*—ferries that transported mail and supplies for the Crown—

that accompanied registered ships. Alcedo wanted to make the *avisos* more frequent and orderly. The merchants' guild of Cádiz would take over, charging 0.5 percent of the gold that came from the New World (González Palencia in Alcedo y Herrera 1915, v–viii). The *Royal Project* from 1720 was an attempt to standardize the number of fleets and galleons to New Spain and Peru and increase the *avisos* and *registros,* taking into account American demand. However, because of the lack of structural reforms—and the lack of cooperation from the merchants' guilds in Cádiz, Mexico City, and Lima—this Bourbon reform did not succeed in fixing the post or systematizing the legal and illegal trade that traveled the postal routes in Peru (García-Mauriño 1999, 113–15). The failures were many and diverse:

> On one hand, the schedules for departures and arrivals of *flotas* and *galeones* were not met, due mostly to the Cádiz merchants' interest in preserving the scarcity of products in the colonial markets not only for the purpose of selling all of the shipments, but of doing so at the highest possible price. On the other hand, business conditions in the Viceroyalties of New Spain and Peru had not experienced any change after the promulgation of the *Royal Project,* because the oversupply of external goods continued to upset the market balance envisaged by that legislation. In New Spain, the entry of goods from the Orient combined with the penetration of English products via registered ships (*navíos de permiso*) plus very diversified smuggling operations, contributing to a saturation of the markets and a sharp decline in prices. The same thing happened in Peru, where its markets continued to be supplied by illegal trade with Mexico City and Buenos Aires, but mostly by the smuggling in which the French and the Dutch engaged by way of the Pacific Ocean, and the English, via the South Sea Company, by way of the Atlantic. As a result, the products that arrived in Spanish America carried by fleets and galleons had little if any outlet in the Spanish American markets. (115)

The venerable tradition of smuggling foreign goods into Peru is one that cannot be studied in isolation from the smuggling of silver and gold out of Peru. In 1720 Morcillo Rubio Auñón became archbishop of Lima and again viceroy of Peru (1720–1724), and straightaway he began to issue a spate of decrees targeting both illegal trade with the French and the diversion of silver and gold. In a decree dated March 11, 1720, he explained that a French ship had been frequenting the ports of Arica and unloading cloth articles, thereby creating "a considerable diversion of bullion." Since "the greed of some merchants might move them to break the laws," he ordered that no one do business with the French or any other smugglers who reached the coastlands of Peru. Transgressors would be imprisoned and their assets confiscated. The owners of mule trains would be imprisoned, losing their mules and gear. Because governors (*corregidores*) in the coastal provinces had neglected to guard against the diversion of metals and trade in foreign goods, "an omission due to which the royal treasury suffered great setbacks," he directed this decree to them in particular.

The flow of decrees concerning trade in contraband goods and the diversion of precious metals, like the illegal practices themselves, continued unabated with José de Armendáriz Perurena, marquis de Castelfuerte, Morcillo Rubio Auñón's successor (1724–1736). A decree dated June 19, 1724, mentions that Philip V had issued a decree in 1720 ordering the confiscation of assets and the death of anyone found guilty of participating in illegal trade with foreign ships and another decree in 1723 that reiterated the previous one. As the king reminded his ministers and subjects, and Armendáriz repeated, smuggling relied on the complicity of "viceroys, governors and ministers" who allowed "the defrauders" to hawk their wares "openly and with free rein" during this period. It was not plausible, the marquis added, that the smugglers were doing business at gunpoint. Diverted gold and silver could not make their way to the coasts without passing first through the inland districts, "where they must be seen and could be seized with little effort." Similarly, smugglers required the dissimulation or tolerance of ministers in order to bring their cloth articles inland and make their fortune. He again pleaded that no smuggling whatsoever be permitted and that "particular attention" be paid to the South Sea, especially the ports and coastlines of Valdivia, Concepción, and Valparaíso. Crown officials, including viceroys, who feigned ignorance in such cases would not be given "the formalities of due process": they would be put to death, and their assets would revert to the Crown. He promised informants a reward equal to one-third of the smuggled goods if they reported the mule train owners who lent or leased their wagons for the transportation of smuggled cloth articles, gold, silver, and coins. Indian informants would be exempted from personal service and taxes for life; African informants would become freedmen in addition to receiving a monetary reward.

Sletu Le Gentil claimed that illegal trade and diversion of precious metals during this period were rampant. His countrymen—and Crown officials in the Viceroyalty of Peru—had made a fortune from smuggled silver:

> Prodigious amounts of silver are taken from the mines of this kingdom, and while the royal fifth should increase, it decreases every year because the governors, instead of devoting themselves to enforcing the King's laws, make a studied effort to flout them. The French have taken out of Peru several millions in unminted silver, which is called *piña*. I cannot understand why the Court of Spain does not make a better choice of ministers, and the result is that she gets so very little out of a colony so very rich. The officers keep everything for themselves, right up to the soldiers' pay and the silver designated for the repair of the towns and the servicing of the galleons that dock at Port Callao. (1728, 1:110–11)

The passage of merchandise, gold, and silver through the port of Buenos Aires had been prohibited since the founding of cities in the region, because gold
and silver originated in Potosí, Chile, and Peru and were supposed to be taken to
Portobelo during the trade fair.[7] While merchants in Lima had engaged in smuggling goods from Portugal, Spain, and New Spain into the Tierra Firme market
and in illegal trade with foreigners in order to break Seville's trade monopoly in
the seventeenth century (Suárez 1995, 41), the merchants' guild in Lima ardently
protested against similar practices adopted by merchants in Buenos Aires in order
to break Lima's trade monopoly in the eighteenth century. In a lengthy *Memorial
informativo (Informative Brief)* filed on behalf of Lima's merchants' guild, Alcedo
y Herrera described South America as "the same as a house with two exits, one
through Buenos Aires and the other through Tierra-Firme" (1726?). Both should
not be operable at the same time, because Buenos Aires made the dispatch of fleets
from Tierra Firme impossible. In addition, he wrote on behalf of his colleagues,
the port of Buenos Aires drained Peru of its silver:

> The aformentioned door of Buenos Aires is open only to injuries to the public
> utility and preservation of commercial activities, and to the sacred royal pre-
> rogatives of Your Majesty through evasions from the royal treasury, because
> with the greedy desire to buy goods more cheaply in that Port, they bring
> down from Potosí and the nearby mineral deposits all the *piñas* of virgin sil-
> ver that their lodes produce and all that the diligence of the interested parties
> can get; because, since this *especie* is the most desired by all the kingdoms on
> earth, the one who offers his goods for *piñas* sells to the buyer's greater advan-
> tage, and a silver mark [made] of this silver is worth more than its value in
> [minted] *reales,* due to the most lofty price it reaches among foreigners. (116)

Another vexing problem during the tenure of Viceroys Morcillo Rubio Auñón
and Armendáriz was mercury smuggling. The marquis de Casa Concha, José de
Santiago Concha, superintendent of the mercury mine and governor of Huancavélica, explained to his successor in 1726 that miners were assessed the royal fifth
on silver and gold according to the amount of mercury they had been given to extract them. Mercury smugglers defrauded the royal treasury of not only the royal
fifth assessed to mercury, he underscored, but also the royal fifth for the gold and
silver that was extracted illegally using unreported mercury. Penalties for convicted
mercury smugglers were stiff, ranging from the confiscation of their assets to permanent exile, even public execution (1726, f. 128v.). Nevertheless, the practice
was so widespread and resistant to reform efforts that the count hatched a series
of undercover operations in the provinces through which mercury traveled, ap-
pointing judges to patrol and seize unreported mercury and writing the provincial
governors and other royal officials to alert them (f. 130r.). Officials were ordered

to question the mule train owners who transported mercury to the treasury offices, compare their mercury manifest with the mercury being transported, and
arrest the carrier and his muleteers when discrepancies were found. Undercover
agents would be keeping the foundries under constant surveillance (f. 131v.). Yet
the smuggling of mercury, gold, and silver was to prove resistant even to these
comprehensive and innovative attempts at restraint.

In 1735 a poetic competition was held at the University of San Marcos to
honor a distant relative of the Pardo de Figueroa clan: José de Mendoza Sotomayor y Camaño, marquis de Villagarcía, the incoming viceroy of Peru (1736–
1745). Published later as *El cielo en el Parnaso* (*Heaven in Parnassus*), the compilation of poems included a lengthy discourse titled "State of the *Monarquía* and of
Peru," authored by the lawyer and poet of viceroys in distress, Peralta Barnuevo.
The discourse asseverated that two policy changes adopted by Philip V were going
to put aright his long-suffering Empire of Peru:

> The colony is finally being treated as an Empire and inheritance as a patri-
> mony. Finally it is being endowed with the faculty to entail affluence. And in
> just two decisions it has been given two eternities. The indulgence of the royal
> fifth has added another Peru to wealth: a generosity at interest of grandeur
> and a gift offered to remunerations of power. . . . This is to transform all of
> the hills into ore and to make a royal treasury out of the whole kingdom. To
> offer mercury on credit is to have abundance in cash. It should be an element,
> not a treasure; an air that metal breathes to give life to wealth. Both decrees
> are keys that will open the door to abundance and shut it to smuggling. (1736,
> ff. 60–61)

As stated at the beginning of this chapter, two fraudulent practices—trading in illegal goods and the diversion of metals—were persistent and interrelated.
As we have seen, the Empire of Peru was still infested with mercury smugglers
some ten years after the marquis de Casa Concha began his campaign to snuff out
smuggling. Peralta Barnuevo concluded the same section of his discourse with a
rhetorical flourish on trade and the smuggling of gold and silver:

> Only commerce has yet to participate in this good fortune, because its oper-
> ations are not separate parts, but the outcomes of links in which the one that
> went missing carried the chain down with it. Its government is a harmony
> of dealings in which, when time is not kept, it is only logical that the entire
> concert be off. The Kingdom today produces what it did before, according to
> what the stamp and the controls clearly indicate, and in spite of this, the fail-
> ure of the *armadas* to supply what they used to—for the harvest to remain the
> same and the profit to be so different—is a mystery (*misterio*) whose solution

is known to all. If the dike breaks, how can one blame the water that fills it? (1736, f. 63)

These mechanical and musical figurings of fraud, along with the politically sensitive metaphor of "mystery" (or "riddle"), are ready-made examples of the comingling of the literary and the political in Bourbon Spanish America,[8] which often allowed discourse to displace material reality in analyses of who and what were in need of reform. And make no mistake: Peralta Barnuevo's statements were nothing if not an unabashed rationalization of smuggling in precious metals and minerals and nonpayment of taxes, which in turn confirms the incentives for fraud stated earlier—the exorbitant price of mercury and the royal fifth.

As we have seen, the *Royal Project* of 1720 attempted to make the register ships, along with the fleets and mail ferries that regularly sailed to the viceroyalties of New Spain and Peru, more efficient (Gutiérrez de Rubalcava 1750, 266–80; Arazola Corvera 1998, 81–85). Nevertheless, that very project—Alcedo y Herrera's brainchild—had an unintended consequence: the *registros* that sailed between Spain and the Viceroyalty of Peru participated in the diversion of silver and gold through the port of Buenos Aires. A 1725 royal ordinance that sought to make the fleets and galleons annual, rather than biennial, had little positive effect. In 1735 another royal decree suspended galleons to Tierra Firme and replaced them with on-demand register ships to Cartagena and Portobelo. It also significantly reduced the number of galleons to New Spain (García-Mauriño 1999, 115–17). One year later, in his *Relación del Gobierno*, Viceroy Armendáriz expounded upon the problems of smuggling and diversion (2000, 524–36). After detailing the measures he took to curtail foreign smuggling (524–30), he claimed that slave-holding companies and register ships en route to Buenos Aires had caused the decline of Spanish and Peruvian commerce. Part of this problem was not new, of course: illegal foreign trade through the ports of the Riverplate region (Figure 10) had confounded the Spanish Crown for centuries, and Carrió certainly was aware of this situation, since the majority of Spanish register ships that participated in the Cádiz–Buenos Aires trade were from Carrió's own region of Northern Spain.

It was no secret to anyone, however, that the signing of the Treaty of Utrecht had exacerbated trade in illegal goods and the diversion of precious metals, for it allowed the South Sea Company to set up a slave-holding company in Buenos Aires that transformed the city into a smuggling center (Arazola Corvera 1998, 76). The South Sea Company purchased and exported hundreds of thousands of skins from the Riverplate. In the 1720s, the company purchased the right to transport slaves who had gone unsold in Buenos Aires for sale as far away as Santiago and Lima, under which pretext the English managed to smuggle all kinds of goods (Villalobos 1965, 34–35). In 1728 the Crown was informed that nearly one-third of illegal trading in the Viceroyalty of Peru could be attributed to the

South Sea Company, which smuggled goods in through the port of Buenos Aires and sold them there and as far north as Lima.[9] Again, trade in illegal goods cannot be understood in isolation from the smuggling of gold, silver, and mercury: according to the viceroy, both the inspector of the royal treasury office in Potosí and the provincial governor reported the "excessive disorder" with which the minerals of that office were handled as far back as 1721. Of note were the "repeated diversions [*extravíos*] of unminted silver that they executed in order to transport it to Buenos Aires where, [because the silver] sold at a price higher than it had in those parts, the enormity of their profit was the incentive for fraud" (532). Of concern were the bordering provinces, in particular Jujuy, "as the throat through which that run-off had to pass" (532). Another way to cheat the Crown of its fifth was to smuggle silver lacework along the same route (532). In 1728 the new inspector of Potosí and judge who investigated diversion cases asked that more clothing and food be allowed to pass between the Kingdom of Peru and Tucumán, Paraguay, and Buenos Aires. He suggested that "so that fraud does not find its way into the bundles, making them accomplices of diverted silver, it be ordered that they be inspected and transported by the guides [*guías*] of the minister appointed" (533).

Further into his *Relación del Gobierno*, Viceroy Armendáriz recounted that in 1728 the owners of two register ships en route to the port of Buenos Aires asked to be allowed to take the leftover merchandise from another register ship, along with their own goods from Spain, to Tucumán and Buenos Aires.[10] In 1727 the Crown had authorized them to take on any number of passengers and two million in taxed gold or silver from Tucumán, Paraguay, and Buenos Aires. A year later, the two ship owners were requesting to take that sum not only from those three cities but from the surrounding areas as well. One of the means for doing so was to sell the other register ship's leftover goods—among them, contraband. Armendáriz reported that he refused to allow the captains to sell any goods other than those carried on their own ships and denied them permission to take taxed gold and silver from provinces other than Tucumán, Paraguay, and Buenos Aires (2000, 534–35). He then identified the register ships that sailed to the port of Buenos Aires as the source of Lima's ruin:

> Buenos Aires is the ruin of merchants, the door through which wealth escapes them and the window that Peru is thrown out of. It is a land of enchantment in which a royal permission is transformed into a disloyal usurpation, and, if even the innocent silver cannot go about without blame, what should we think of the criminal silver that escapes? Merchants in Lima have always protested this fatal injury, judges have opposed it, and royal decrees have been exhausted to fight it, but the protests, the patrols and the decrees have always been useless, this evil being so much greater than that of illegal trade nowadays, given that the latter is foreign and the former, native, and in it license is the mother of transgression. It goes right to the heart of Peru, which are its

minerals, and the provinces that hold them, so that when their spirits do not drift down to this city, its opulence perforce peters out. (530)

It was the royal permission itself, according to Viceroy Armendáriz, that aggravated, rather than alleviated, the diversion of silver and gold: "There is no greater opposition than that between self-interest and public interest, for, as if it were created in order to destroy itself, the republic is the enemy of the republic. An experience that is seen more in this Kingdom than in any other part of the world, where silver and gold, since they are the only product of dominion, are the only target of usurpation; where the government must be in a never-ending war against fraud; where survival must always combat ruin, the latter turning even what is permissible into what is illegal, and the pretext of royal concessions into the reality of overreaches, by which means it turns royal dispatches against themselves" (2000, 534). The marquis de Castelfuerte concluded his treatment of smuggling with a fatalistic observation and a proposal, both concerning the port of Buenos Aires: "Thus there has been an effort to guard against this evil communication, but just as there is not a hand that can wholly support a structure that was born in ruins, the ruin that the entry of goods through Buenos Aires causes the Kingdom and both bodies of merchants becomes unavoidable. There is no art that can close off regions with decrees or separate, for one kind of trade, regions that are joined together for all kinds. The shots of fraud dismantle all the batteries of the Empire [of Peru], and against the royal permission itself prohibition is dashed. And thus, as long as there is Buenos Aires, one can never mind Peru" (536).

The marquis de Castelfuerte suggested an alternative, and legal, trading route—the transport of Castilian textiles from Lima to Tucumán, Paraguay, and Buenos Aires through Chile instead of the port of Buenos Aires—and lamented that a place established as the "bulwark of this America" was "more invaded by its own than defended against foreigners" because of the Pacific Ocean (2000, 536). Because gold and silver from Chile were to be taken to the mint in Lima and neither was to be carried from Lima to Chile following his 1724 decree, money was scarce in Chile in the 1730s (Villalobos 1990, 229–30). Viceroy Armendáriz also singled out royal officials along the northern coast of the viceroyalty, in a confidential letter addressed to his appointed successor, the marquis de Villagarcía ("Memoria reservada," in Moreno Cebrián 1977, 619–26). He made it clear that he was keenly aware of smuggling routes beyond Buenos Aires:

Illegal trade can be conducted through Buenos Aires or through Mexico, or by foreign ships or through Panama, in the interval of the galleons, along the coast to Paita. . . . With respect to the illegal trade through Mexico, I have not given permission to any freighter in nearly six years, thereby pulling out at the roots the illegal trade that could be conducted. . . . And insofar as this illegal trading can never take place without the consent and cooperation of royal officials in Guayaquil or Paita, it is necessary to subject these ministers to a law that makes them obedient and fearful of punishment, just as I have executed with respect to such trade and the illegal trade through Panama also, declaring that all goods transported after the armada be confiscated. (622)

A year earlier, King Philip V had instructed the incoming viceroy, José Mendoza Sotomayor y Camaño, not to allow trading between New Spain and Peru under any circumstances. In February 1736, the marquis de Villagarcía forwarded the order to the appropriate officials in Piura, the capital of the northwestern province that bordered the Kingdom of Quito and included the coastal cities of Paita and Tumbes. During the War of Jenkin's Ear between Great Britain and Spain (1739–1748), register ships crossed between Spain and Spanish America only sporadically, but Mexicans and Peruvians found other ways to supply their markets (Arazola Corvera 1998, 86; García-Mauriño 1999, 117). In his 1745 report to his successor, the marquis de Villagarcía wrote bitterly of the illegal commerce permitted by local governors and high-ranking royal officials in the Kingdom of Quito. "The grave threats by which . . . I reminded [my subordinates] of their obligations were not enough to prevent this age-old crime, in which the litigation pursued in other times against those ministers appears to have served only to embolden them and give them shameless license, showing them the paths [*los caminos*] to securing their impunity" (Mendoza Sotomayor y Camaño 1859, 372).

Had the *corregidor* and other royal officials in Paita not permitted illegal trading, the viceroy continued, the English pirate George Anson would not have succeeded in his attack and his attack would not have been so profitable. He offered his own analysis of *los caminos* that the *guía* (or *lazarillo*) Carrió would later lead his readers down in *El lazarillo de ciegos caminantes*: "The occasion on which cloth articles were being brought from Cartagena, legally and with guides from the royal accounting office in Quito, was the cover for the illegal dealings [*los fraudes*], but this is a strange kind of guilt in which the one who condemns it refuses to prove it with a sworn statement and the ones who break the law for their own profit grumble about the lack of enforcement, and what results is a public rumor [*pública voz*] without a witness to prove it legally and a complaint in which the very complainants impede their remedy with their silence" (Mendoza Sotomayor y Camaño 1859, 372). The frazzled viceroy appointed a special prosecutor who jailed the *corregidor* and two other officials in Piura, one of them the governor and president of the high court in Quito who appears as a judge of Carrió's mock trial in Santiago de Guatemala in 1746.

The tenor of the viceroy's complaints communicates his frustration with the duplicitous Bourbon technocrats charged with upholding the laws against smuggling and with the citizens who feared these Bourbon reformers as much as they resented them. That frustration was undeniably compounded by the circumstances of the marquis de Villagarcía's departure. From October 1741 to 1743, during the

War of Jenkin's Ear and the indigenous rebellions in Tarma and Jauja, the Crown received no correspondence from the viceroy of Peru, although a letter dated November 1742 arrived in Madrid in June 1744. Philip V responded by coercing the marquis into early retirement (Ramos Gómez in Ulloa and Juan 1985, 1:307–9). In retrospect, Lima began to lose its grip on South American trade once and for all during Viceroy Mendoza Sotomayor y Camaño's troubled administration.

The tenure of his successor, Viceroy José Antonio Manso de Velasco (1745–1761), was marked by natural disasters and reform measures that, because of continuous violations by the reformers themselves, sealed the respective economic fates of Buenos Aires and Lima.[11] His efforts to rebuild Lima and Port Callao after the 1746 earthquake earned him the title of count de Superunda and were immortalized in verse by a friend of José Pardo de Figueroa's and Pedro de Peralta Barnuevo's.[12] Asian goods came indirectly into the viceroyalty through Acapulco or directly through Callao, Realejo, Sonsonante, or Panama. In 1750 the legal representative of the merchants' guild in Buenos Aires wrote to Ferdinand VI that at times it appeared that the Peking Fair was being held in Lima. A common ruse was to deliver smuggled goods to a fall guy, accuse him of smuggling, and then buy the smuggled goods at auction, sometimes using the Crown's reward money (Céspedes 1946, 677). That same year, the building of the royal mint in Santiago (Figure 11), which had been approved in 1743 by Manso de Velasco's predecessor, became a reality (Villalobos 1990, 230). Although it had appeared to Viceroy Arméndariz that there would be fewer opportunities for trading in illegal goods and the diversion of metals in the Kingdom of Chile, royal officials there, including relatives of the Pardo de Figueroa brothers, were implicated in the smuggling of foreign goods and the diversion of metals.

Isabel, a sister of the Pardo de Figueroa brothers who lived in Santiago, Chile, was married to Martín de Recavarren (1679–1767), a native of Lima who graduated from the university in Mexico City and worked as a lawyer for the high court there. In 1717 José de Santiago Concha (later, marquis de Casa Concha), interim governor of Chile and judge on Lima's high court, made him a *corregidor,* an accountant for defense and the superintendent of the royal treasury in Santiago. His principal assignment was to stop the flow of goods from French ships docking in the port of Concepción. He was later assigned a judgeship on Panama's high court, and in 1723 he became a judge on Santiago's high court. In that capacity, he illegally purchased lands and engaged in smuggling European goods through Port Callao, but these infractions did not harm his career. In 1738 Manso de Velasco, then governor of Chile and president of its high court, relied on Recavarren as the two negotiated with *caciques* who were fiercely battling Spaniards in the region. Judge Recavarren organized the royal tobacco monopoly for the Kingdom of Chile and later became superintendent of the royal mint in Santiago (1749–1767).[13] Thus, Bernardo Pardo de Figueroa's tenure as treasurer of the royal mint in Mexico City (1744–1756) overlapped with his brother-in-law's tenure as superintendent of the royal mint in Santiago, Chile. The diversion of metals from the Kingdom of Peru to the Kingdom of Chile continued under Superintendent Recavarren, but a famed jurist in Lima argued (incredibly enough) that foreigners and Chilean farmers were to blame. By ceasing imports of Chilean wheat, "treasure would go . . . with more security straight to the Kingdoms of Spain, without the wanderings [*extravíos*] in which it is prone to be diverted [*a divertirse*] at the hands of foreigners, and even enemies" (Bravo de Lagunas y Castilla 1755, 223).

It was during Manso de Velasco's tenure that Lima was definitively displaced by Buenos Aires as the trading capital of the Viceroyalty of Peru.[14] The war between Spain and Great Britain (1753–1763) interrupted royal designs for transatlantic trade. In 1754 the convoy system was reestablished with New Spain by royal order, as a result of the complaints of the merchants' guilds in Cádiz, Mexico City, and Lima, while the register-ship system with Tierra Firme would be allowed to continue until Portobelo was rebuilt. Nevertheless, the superiority of the *registro* system contributed to the demise of the fleets and trade fairs and, with it, the position of the merchants in Lima as middlemen (García-Mauriño 1999, 117–118; Arazola Corvera 1998, 86–87). "Thus the entire south of the American continent," concludes María Jesús Arazola Corvera, "fell permanently under the sway of the efficient activity of the occasional registered ships, when these proved that they could cover better and more rapidly this vast territory previously reserved for the Liman merchants" (1998, 86). By 1754, Lima was no longer the center of distribution for the Viceroyalty of Peru: Buenos Aires was. The consolidation of commercial ties between Tucumán and Buenos Aires served as a trampoline to Charcas, where merchants from Buenos Aires got Peruvian gold and silver for their goods. Merchants in Lima thus lost that market to their counterparts in Buenos Aires before they lost the market in Chile to the same merchants (Céspedes 1946, 697–701).

The Elites of Lima and Buenos Aires

The relationship heretofore established between trade and political and religious influence in the viceroyalties invites several reflections on the formation of elites in viceregal Spanish America, especially in the eighteenth century. It has been established that pedigree, wealth, and social standing were inseparable for *peruleros* such as the Pardo de Figueroa brothers. Trade was the key to wealth, and it was the loss of Lima's commercial monopoly over the Viceroyalty of Peru that threatened the wealth and influence of Lima's *criollo*-peninsular elite in the first half of the eighteenth century. Elites in strong social networks were able to survive, and even thrive, while a great many noble families in Lima continued on a downward slope that had begun with the War of the Spanish Succession.

As a mathematician, lawyer, and Crown accountant whose writings were often underwritten by noblemen and political and religious figures, Peralta Barnuevo knew who was who in Lima, who had and who had not. In *Lima triumphante,* he lauded the marquis de Castell-dos-Rius for coming to the aid of Lima's nobility, "whose decline would be capable of saddening the fortune of even the most fortunate *monarquías*" (1708, pt. 1, 3rd glory, n.p.), and although nearly two decades separated *Imagen política* and *Lima fundada,* the nobility's travails were common to both of these works too. In *Imagen política,* he argued that the loyalty of Peru's nobility during the War of the Spanish Succession entitled its members to royal support: "The nobility loyal and obedient to the prince, and just and tempered with the people, is the power of the one and the refuge of the other. The nobility that shows itself to be loyal and zealous in times of civil disturbances is an illustrious one deserving of the favor of the monarch to whom rewards fairly distributed mean more than the most precious resources" (1996a, 66). Among Viceroy Ladrón de Guevara's virtues was his benevolence toward Lima's nobility: he had done all he could do to alleviate the sorry state of so many noble houses.[15] A monarch should assist impoverished noblemen, Peralta Barnuevo moralized, even when they had come to ruin through every fault of their own: "Noblemen are made by virtue and they are preserved by riches. A monarch must halt the ruin of those who by their own doing have fallen into necessity because to come to the aid of the impoverished nobility is a noble burden of majesty" (66). Later, however, he argued that the Peruvian nobility was in decline because the Empire of Peru was in decline, and the Empire of Peru was in decline because the entire *Monarquía* was in decline. The root cause was the War of the Spanish Succession—specifically, Barcelona and Valencia, or Sinon and the Trojan horse.[16] In this earlier assessment, then, either their own foolishness or the disruption of normal trade and the financial obligations of wartime had reduced many noblemen to poverty. In *Lima fundada,* he again lauded the nobility and lamented their decline. In an apostrophe to the city of Lima, he posed a somewhat threatening rhetorical question: "La nobleza que fiel te hubo fundado,/¿No es la que hasta ahora fiel te ha mantenido?" (1732, can. 10, st. 116, vv. 1–2). ("Is the nobility that founded you loyally/Not that which has kept you loyal?"). The poet explained in a footnote that Lima's nobility and its trade had always served the Crown loyally and generously, but the nobility could no longer afford to sponsor royal wedding celebrations and such as they would wish.[17]

In December 1740, Antonio de Ulloa and Jorge Juan stopped in Lima, but they did not penetrate the facade of the capital's most prominent houses. As a result, Lima's nobility appeared to be the picture of health in their travelogue:

The families of Spaniards are a great many, for it is thought that there must be between 16[,000] and 18,000 white persons, according to the most prudent estimate. Among them there is a third or a fourth who are the nobility, the most distinguished in all of Peru and descended from the most renowned and outstanding in these kingdoms. A large part of them have been elevated with ancient or modern titles from Castile, among which there are forty-five who hold the title of count or marquis, among whom there is a high number of knights, and beyond these are others of the same group who are not inferior in distinction and quality, among which there are twenty-four entailed estates without title, and the majority of them have ancient origins that prove sufficiently the antiquity of the families. . . . They all live with great decorum, and along with it, their opulence shines too. Just as they have at their domestic service a large number of free servants and slaves, the nobles of greatest distinction or means use carriages for their public image and convenience, and those who need not make such an expenditure use covered wagons. (1748, 3:67–68)

Ulloa and Juan did get one thing right, though: they understood the significance of commerce to many of Lima's elites. For noble families who did not have titles or entailed estates, trade was their lifeblood:

To those who do not obtain income from entailed estates or *haciendas,* trade adds the same advantages as it does to the others, to which commerce they dedicate themselves without qualms, even if they belong to the noblest and most distinguished families, for one's standing is not at all diminished by this occupation. However, it should not be understood that the trade in which they engage is the low sort of buying and selling retail or in stores, but instead each trades in keeping with his character and possibilities. With this assistance, families manage to survive without experiencing so often the insolvencies that befall families in Spain who do not enjoy the comfort of excellent entailed estates. There, not only is it not dishonoring to trade: the most select fortunes are derived from it, while those who either do not have the ready cash to trade or, due to carelessness, do not do so, lose out on it. This measure, decision or recourse that was instituted there without forethought or a set purpose (for it was only started by that first wish to get rich with which the Spaniards went there), is that which currently preserves the grandeur in which those Houses stand, and the royal proclamation that being a wholesaler or a merchant in the Indies would not hinder nobility or entry into orders of knights perhaps assisted from the very beginning in deflecting the fear of commerce; a resolution of such wisdom that Spain would experience its advantages were it common in all of its kingdoms. (1748, 3:69–70)

Another tourist in Lima, Courte de la Blanchardiere, must have listened to the same sources as Juan and Ulloa, for his statements about the titled and merchant elites in Lima were similar. The titles of marquis and count were commonplace, he stated. A merchant carried his suitcase for a short period of time, got rich, opened a store and then bought one of the titles that the king of Spain sold for a dear sum. Notwithstanding a prodigious amount of gold, silver, and precious stones, the majority of the inhabitants were very poor. Indeed, the amount of misery there was greater than all of Peru's gold, silver, and stones combined (1751, 127). This very sort of chauvinistic hyperbole is consistently derided in *El lazarillo de ciegos caminantes,* and exaggerations aside, Carrió knew more than any Spanish or French tourist about the disparity between Lima's resources and its output: he knew its economic profile from the inside out. He encoded explanations for that disparity throughout his exposé; explanations that range from excess expenditures on fashion to illegal dealings spearheaded by church and state officials. Moreover, Carrió was keenly aware of the ironies and contradictions inherent in the respective economic situations of Lima and Buenos Aires in the late 1740s.

The triumph of Buenos Aires was not inevitable, perhaps not even likely. In the first half of the eighteenth century, the city was neither densely populated nor filled with blacks and *mulatos* like Lima.[18] According to a 1738 census of Buenos Aires, there were just under 4,500 Spanish residents, and the rest of the population was as follows: 33 *mulatos,* 70 *pardos,* 14 Indians, 12 blacks, 16 *mestizos,* and 310 slaves. The hinterlands of Buenos Aires had just over 1,200 Spanish residents and 109 slaves in 1738. In the 1744 census, Buenos Aires had just over 10,000 Spanish residents, 188 Indians, 330 *mulatos,* 1,510 blacks, 99 *mestizos,* and 221 *pardos.* The surrounding countryside had just over 6,000 Spanish residents, 431 Indians, 180 *mulatos,* 327 blacks, 123 *pardos,* and 40 *mestizos* (Asdrúbal 1969, 473–74). Still, trade brought the residents of Buenos Aires into contact with people from France, Holland, Portugal, and England. At the same time, Basques, Catalonians, Canarians, and Italians (mostly Neapolitans and Sicilians) emigrated to the Riverplate, becoming part of a nascent mercantile bourgeoisie. Increasingly, "the acquisition of fortune was the means of ascent on the social platform"(Arazola Corvera 1998, 77) and acted as a spur to demographic growth.

During the first half of the eighteenth century, Buenos Aires got rich from trade, especially illegal trade. If the *criollo*-peninsular *rosca* in Lima was impenetrable or morally unacceptable to an *hidalgo* merchant and military man like Carrió who did not wish to play the game of Bourbon reformer, in Buenos Aires he fit right in. At the top of the social pyramid in Buenos Aires were the men who controlled wholesale imports and exports—the *registreros,* or wealthy Spanish merchants, who had a monopoly on foreign trade. Directly below them were the *criollo* wholesalers. The owners of shops and the owners of warehouses and shops of imported goods were also well positioned. "For all of them, trade was mostly illegal trade, because it was the easiest and the most lucrative, and by relying on it they wound up forming an important urban bourgeoisie" (Arazola Corvera 1998, 78).

This explosion of trade and capital investment demanded a regular means of sending and receiving not only letters but also goods. The royal administration of the posts in Buenos Aires dates back to 1748. The four postal routes covered by carriers from Buenos Aires led to Peru, Chile, Paraguay, and Montevideo (Bose 1933, 375–97; 1934, 349). Carrió began to establish friendships with postal adminis-trators and merchants in Buenos Aires during the 1740s. This gave him an insider's view of the Riverplate region in general and of Buenos Aires in particular that most merchants–civil servants in Lima lacked. Similarly, his decade-long residence in New Biscayne and Mexico City in New Spain and his travels throughout the Viceroyalty of Peru brought into relief the particular challenges that *caminantes—* merchants and travelers—faced in either viceroyalty at a time when Lima's *crio-llo*-peninsular oligarchy had its tentacles stretched north and south.

In view of the economic rivalry between Lima and Buenos Aires and the cul-tural rivalry between Mexico City and Lima, why would Carrió choose Santiago de Guatemala as the setting for the inspector's closing anecdote? Although they may appear to be petty details, some important clues to this mystery are embed-ded in the Guatemalan tale itself.

A Tale from "the Other Coast"

At the mock trial, the gold, silver, and Asian clothing worn by the senior *perulero* become an emblem of Francophilia and Orientalism decades before the *petime-tre* became legion in Spain. The inspector dwells on the appearance of the Liman lord, itemizing his articles of clothing and accessories, which readers in Bourbon Spanish America would immediately recognize as ill-gotten. Before the Liman spokesman presents their solution to the riddle, the inspector remarks, "Este buen hombre tendría como cincuenta años. Su fisionomía manifestaba una continua abstinencia, pero su traje indicaba cosa muy distinta" (470) ("This good man must have been about fifty years old. His physique signaled a continued abstinence, but his outfit suggested something else entirely"). He then goes on to describe the lord's outfit in lavish detail, beginning with his hat, collar, and cape:

> En el sombrero traía una toquilla de cinta de la china con una escuadra de paraos, bajeles mercantes a la chinesca, y para asegurarla en el canto una gran heblilla de oro, guarnecida de brillantes. Abrigaba su cuello con un pañuelo de clarín bordado de seda negra, con unos cortados a trechos, y al aire un finísimo encaje. La capa, aunque algo raída, era de paño azul finísimo, de Car-casona, con bordados de oro, que por la injuria de los tiempos se había con-vertido en plata. (470)

> [On his hat he wore a scarf made of Oriental ribbon with a squadron of *paraos*, (or) Asian-style merchant vessels, and to fasten it to the rim a large buckle of gold set off by diamonds. He wrapped around his neck a crepe scarf embroidered with black silk, with intermittent cuts, and a most delicate lace lift. His cape, though somewhat worn, was of the finest blue fabric, from

Carcasona, with gold embroidery that, with the ravages of time, had become silver.]

Silk and Chinese ribbon along with the squadron of *paraos* (vessels) together provide the provenance of the clothing described: Asia. Just as the representative of the merchants' guild in Buenos Aires had complained in 1750, the description of this Liman gentleman's clothing insinuates that the Peking Trade Fair was being held in Lima. Significantly, the previous allusion to gold embroidery that had become silver has criminal undertones that will be insinuated again. The inspector's eye pans downward:

La jaquetilla o valenciana, que le cubría las rodillas, era de terciopelo azul, con más de dos mil ojales y otros tantos botones de hilo de oro, que también tocaba en plata, según afirmó el contraste o ensayador. La chupa no llegaba al tamaño de la casqueta, pero tenía unos bolsillos que en cada uno cabían holgadamente mil piezas regulares de encajes manchegos. Era de lampazo matizado de colores, pero no se puede decir a punto fijo su fondo. (470)

[His short jacket, or Valencian, which covered his knees, was made of blue velvet and had over two thousand loops and as many buttons embroidered with gold thread, which also bordered on silver according to the stamp or assayer. His undercoat was not as big as his dress coat, but it had such pockets that each could easily accommodate one thousand standard pieces of lace from La Mancha. It was in variegated burdock, but one cannot say exactly what its lining was made of.]

The French influence is evident in this description, as is the Asian. Moreover, there is the inkling of impurity in the gold thread that borders on silver, as if the Liman lord (or the assayer for the royal mint) had been passing silver off as gold. Viceroy Armendáriz had listed lacework done in silver as one of the means and ends of diverting silver in the Viceroyalty of Peru. It was nearly impossible to prove whether the royal fifth had been paid on the silver used for this purpose because the hammer had deformed the silver that was used, or the silver lacing was too worn—it had become what was called *de chafalonía*—or it had been resilvered, or it had been burned (491). Moreover, Philip V ordered the viceroys of New Spain and Peru to investigate and punish officials in charge of the royal mints who were coining silver and gold with weights that did not correspond to their denominations, and Viceroy Armendáriz enforced that royal order in Potosí and Lima between 1728 and 1730 (466–77). As indicated earlier, in that fateful year of 1746, when Bernardo Pardo de Figueroa was the treasurer of the royal mint in Mexico City and his brother-in-law Recavarren was superintendent of the royal mint in Santiago, Chile, King Ferdinand VI sent a technocrat to Mexico City to serve as superintendent of the royal mint, ordering him to then proceed to Lima and put its mint in order too (Manso de Velasco 1983, 372). The allusion to gold that time was allegedly converting to silver was no rhetorical accident on Carrió's part.

The inspector arrives at the Liman lord's pants, socks, and shoes: "Los calzones eran de terciopelo carmesí, muy ajustados, y remataban sobre la rodilla con una charretela de tres dedos de ancho, de galón de oro, con tres botones de lo mismo, en lugar de los catorce que hoy se usan. Las medias eran carmesíes, de las mejores que se trabajaban en La Laguna, y los zapatos de cordobán de lustre, a doble suela" (470) ("His trousers, very tight-fighting, were made of crimson velvet, and they capped off at his knees with a garter, three inches wide, of gold braid, and three buttons of the same instead of the fourteen that are used today. His stockings were crimson, the best that were being made then in La Laguna [capital of the Canary Islands], and his shoes were made of polished cordovan and with double soles"). Next the gentleman's accessories, dress shirt, and cap are detailed:

> Las heblillas eran de oro, como la caja del tabaco, que pesaría, uno y otro, un par de libras. En los dedos de la mano derecha traía continuamente seis o siete tumbagas finísimas, y en un ojal de la chupa una cadena de oro con un limpiadientes y orejas, con otras guarniciones, que pudieran competir con las cadenas de los relojes que actualmente usan las damas. La camisa exterior, por su extremada blancura manifestaba ser de finísimo elefante, o socorrán, y el gorro, que descubría las orejas, de holán baptista, con tres andanas de trencillas de Quito, bordaduras con costosos cortados, y por remate un encarrujado encaje de Flandes, de dos dedos de ancho, que hoy día pareciera a los modernos una hermosa y costosa coroza. (470–71)

> [His cuff links were made of gold, like his snuff tin, and either one of them must have weighed a couple of pounds. On the fingers of his right hand he always wore six or seven of the finest gold-and-copper braided rings, and in the buttonhole of his undershirt a gold chain with a toothpick and handles, with other accoutrements that could compete with the watch chains that ladies currently use. His outer shirt, owing to its extreme whiteness, clearly showed that it was (made) of the most delicate elephant skin, or *socorrán,* and his cap, which exposed his ears, (was made) of Anabaptist linen with three rows of plaits from Quito, embroiderings with expensive cuts and, to top it off, a pleated lacework from Flanders, roughly two inches in width, which nowadays would seem like a gorgeous and costly cornet to the modern set.]

The inspector concludes his description by noting that all members of the Peruvian contingent were dressed in the same manner as the senior member: "Los compañeros se presentaron vestidos del mismo modo, que era el uso entonces de su patria, y así eran tan conocidos en la Nueva España como los húngaros en Francia" (471) ("His companions showed up dressed in the same way, which was then the style in their hometown, and thus they stood out in New Spain as much as Hungarians did in France"). To be sure, the general take-away point here was true not only of elites in Lima but of Limans in general: they were fastidious and exceedingly vain about their appearance. In Viceroy Armendáriz's *Relación,* male and female fashion plates among Lima's elites were strongly censured. He attended to "the reform of dress" by issuing a decree that detailed the fines to be paid by persons whose dress was too risqué or too costly, because "excess had become fashion" (546). This was motivated by his desire "to limit the immodesty and the excessive expenditure that ha[d] taken hold among the nobles" (425).

It would be a mistake to attribute those assertions to prudishness or circumspection: in 1740, when Ulloa and Juan passed through Lima, members of all cultural communities, or *castas,* and all orders were preening themselves.[19] Moreover, when La Blanchardiere visited Lima in 1747, he observed that men and women were extremely well dressed in the latest fashions; indeed, even their courtesies were paid in the French manner. Spanish women, *mulatas,* and black women were wearing diamonds and pearls, and their dress represented a considerable fortune for an individual in Europe. There was, he concluded, scarcely a place in the world where luxury and debauchery reigned as they did in Peru (1751, 123–25). Carrió's patient description of the Lima delegation redoubles Peralta Barnuevo's and Viceroy Armendáriz's complaints and La Blanchardiere's assertions about the lavish dress of persons in Lima.

However, the inspector's minute description of the Asian clothing, gold, and silver worn by the *peruleros* goes much further—gets much more personal—than any of the previous statements on fashion in Peru, becoming an emblem of smuggling, tax evasion, and other illegal practices aided and abetted by social networks in Carrió's Spanish America. The very deliberate sketch of only one party at the Guatemalan mock trial can be seen as an ironic eulogy: while the archbishop of Guatemala had been buried in a discourse of silver and gold by Miguel de Cilieza Velasco's eulogy, the Liman competitors are first dressed in silver and gold and then buried standing up by Carrió's jocose *exemplum.* This gives us the *what,* one could still argue, but not the *why.* Why Santiago de Guatemala? After all, the archbishop of Guatemala and the president of the high court there, both *peruleros,* had served the Crown in other capacities, in other locales. Why not conclude the inspection report in, say, Mexico City, or in Quito, or in Santiago, Chile, for that matter?

Although the historical record suggests that Guatemala in 1746 did not have the same burden of guilt as Lima or Buenos Aires, it was—like the 4Ps from Lima—guilty by association. Since 1566, Santiago de Guatemala flaunted the privileged title of *Very Noble and Very Loyal* granted by King Philip II, and the regents and aldermen of the city council flaunted their titles of *Very Illustrious Lords* and *Very Noble and Very Loyal Lords* (Chinchilla 1961, 172–78). To safeguard the privileges and responsibilities of the council, members were banned from trading (132). In the seventeenth century, many council seats were occupied by Spanish merchants and moneylenders who had recently emigrated to Santiago de Guatemala. The regents and aldermen were paid in currency, which was very scarce in Guatemala and increased their buying power. Wealthy families relied on the council to adjudicate not only the sale of goods to the Indian population by provincial governors but also compulsory Indian labor issues. Moreover, wealthy and distinguished businessmen had frequent contact with council members or worked on the tax commission within the council; they were therefore easily elected regents (Lutz 1994, 301 n. 16). In the last quarter of the seventeenth century, the governor of Guatemala and the judges on the high court in the capital city attempted to pare down the privileges of the regents who alternated the post of inspector of commerce. However, their idea of a cure turned out to be worse than the disease: middlemen, who would buy goods cheaply from the Indian population and resell them at higher prices, sprang up all over; the bread and beef markets showed the effects of price gouging and collusion; and at least one weaver began making and selling goods whose production and sale were legally restricted to trained and certified blacksmiths (Chinchilla 1961, 137–39).

The case of Fernando Álvarez de Castro, who had been born in Spain, reflects the difficult balancing act performed by entrepreneurial judges on the high court in Santiago de Guatemala. Appointed in 1739, Álvarez de Castro was secretly commissioned by the Crown in 1744 to investigate smuggling and other illegal business practices. In 1745 he was himself charged with smuggling and removed from his post, along with several other judges (Burkholder and Chandler 1977, 11). Elections ensured that *criollos* would control the city council until the last third of the eighteenth century, and they often wrangled over commercial issues with the peninsular judges on the high court. However, business opportunities were not denied the judges who, like their council counterparts, were legally prohibited from engaging in commercial activities, and birth in Spain did not prevent a judge from inserting himself into social networks with men born in Santiago de Guatemala. In this climate, Fernando de Echeverz, a member of one of Santiago de Guatemala's most influential families with links to the viceroyalties of New Granada and Peru, extolled the advantages of setting up a trading company in the capital in his *Ensayos mercantiles (Mercantile Essays)*. Once established, the company would regulate production and trade, inserting the Kingdom of Guatemala into the commercial network that linked Mexico City to Lima. If my historical analysis of the situation is correct, this would have required the disassembly of the informal system that already existed, or at least curtailment of illegal trade from Peru, Mexico, and Manila. Echeverz raised this issue rather gently, after complaints about the lack of interest in the shipyard and shipbuilding in Guatemala, which he considered paramount to increasing and regulating trade:

It is truly tragic that such a profitable sector of this Kingdom be subject to the ugly lawlessness in which it is presently conducted in off-course vessels that sneak out of Peru with some merchants of the lowest sort, who show up in this city to solicit goods on credit, twice as much of them as they have brought in, and the worst thing is that they usually manage to get them from some merchants in this city, and both groups are equally pleased: the latter because they have sold at good prices, and the former because of the profit they make from manipulating the great sum [owed to creditor merchants in Santiago de Guatemala] by making up various excuses that support their holding onto it. (1742, I, art. 55)

In the subsequent article, Echeverz warned that the present tolerance of such trading would soon abate: "During the past few years, because of the War [of Jenkin's Ear] and the shortage of cloth articles, the business community in Peru has tolerated illegal imports with outrageous dissimulation, [but] when the Portobelo trade is reopened in peacetime, it will no longer look the other way, and at the slightest infraction it commits against Spain's trade, and that both Guatemala and Peru commit against the King, who could prevent a strict prohibition?" (1742, art. 56).

Given the city council's role in the regulation and expansion of trade, it is hardly surprising that Echeverz chose to dedicate his *Ensayos mercantiles* to council members or that he neglected to mention its unhealthy recurrence of *criollo* surnames or the names of merchants and civil servants dedicated to smuggling, tax evasion, and the like. Carrió, on the other hand, would get very personal in his jocose *exemplum*. His decade of travel and trade in New Spain and three decades in the Viceroyalty of Peru had schooled him in the economic and political realities of both viceroyalties and had taught him who was who among Lima's *criollo*-peninsular oligarchy as it fanned out to the north and the south.

When Carrió arrived in Santiago de Guatemala in 1746, the capital was still reeling from the Crown's first methodical attempt to reorganize the high court that was charged with keeping the city council in order. Moreover, during that same year, Manso de Velasco gave royal permission to merchants from the Guatemalan Company to sail between Guatemala and Callao, although the regulations of the Guatemalan trading company that Echeverz had requested in 1742 were published in 1743 and the company already had several ships on the coast of the Pacific Ocean. In 1754, ignoring the objections of the shipping community and merchants' guild in Lima, Manso de Velasco ordered that the Guatemalan company's ships go undisturbed (1983, 360).[20]

It is not difficult to imagine the tenor of their complaints, if we keep the image of Carrió's natty Liman lord in mind. In his *Memorial informativo,* Alcedo y

Herrera not only attacked merchants in Buenos Aires; he also charged that the register ships that traveled between the coastal ports of Peru and New Spain facilitated the smuggling of articles from the Orient into Peru as well as the diversion of gold and silver: "The [royal] dispensation of Peru's trade with the Port of Acapulco in New Spain is not of less consequence . . . because with their contact it is imponderable and impossible to impede the diversion of silver and of gold and the [illegal] entry of cloth articles from China and the delays in the fleets that are committed through this route" (1726? 119). He also quoted the pertinent law from the legal code for the Spanish Indies (*Recopilación de las leyes de Indias*), which reads in part: "In the freighters that are permitted by us to go from Peru to New Spain and the Port of Acalpulco, or from New Spain to Peru and its ports, cloth articles from China shall not be loaded, sold, bought or exchanged in any quantity, even if it is said that it is free, as a donation, good work, service to the Church or some other stipulation or manner, in order that the prohibition not be violated by such pretexts" (1756, bk. 9, chap. 45, law 69, qtd. in Alcedo y Herrera 1726? 120).

Setting aside our astonishment that a wholesaler or a muleteer would collude with customs officials to declare that his silk and porcelain were meant for widows and orphans, and remembering the Liman fashion plate from Carrió's Guatemalan *exemplum*, one particular accusation in *Memorial informativo* goes a long way toward answering my initial question: why Santiago de Guatemala? Alcedo y Herrera complained that the greed of merchants led them to abuse the royal permission for limited trade with the province of Guatemala and the ports of Sonsonante and Realejo. Many merchants in Lima went broke after the abundance of smuggled cloth articles from the Orient had depressed the prices of similar items from Spain. A judge with exclusive jurisdiction was appointed by the Crown to "guard against the entries of articles from China" and to take measures that included the imprisonment of smugglers and the public burning of such articles. The public and the merchants' guild were happy with his job performance until Philip V ordered the viceroy of Peru to send two warships loaded with cacao from Guayaquil to Acapulco every year, "because with this the door swung wide open again to the diversion of silver and of considerably more gold " (1726? 120–21). When the cost of this proved too much for the royal treasury to bear, the viceroy was compelled to turn to the private sector, which paid for the right to take cacao and passengers, "which was the same as revoking the prohibition against entries of goods from China and the fleet and against the diversion of silver and of gold" (122). Such activities were rampant when the merchant Carrió was living in New Spain and preparing to leave for the Viceroyalty of Peru, where he would become a provincial governor (*corregidor*), a post that permitted legal trade in mules and agricultural items and facilitated illegal trade in other goods, locally and regionally, throughout the Spanish Indies.[21] In truth, Carrió's mercantile experience gave him a solid introduction to the mule trade well before he left for Peru, because mules and muleteers were absolutely essential to the post and to economic development and reform in viceregal Spanish America.

A variety of goods were transported by mule in New Spain: for example, mercury, barrels of domestic and Spanish liquor, imported steel, iron, clothing articles from Castile and the Orient, gold and silver bars that were driven to the royal mint in Mexico City to be taxed and stamped or to Veracruz to be shipped to Spain (Suárez Argüello 1997, 63–64). The transporting of silver in New Spain was just as hazardous as it was in Peru. To stem the tide of losses and diversions, new ordinances were issued in 1759. Henceforth, the Crown issued a printed and numbered invoice (*guía*) to the muleteer (*arriero*), which included the names of the owner or miner, the carrier (*conductor*), and the consignee and declared the weight, origins, and date of the silver. This *guía* had its corresponding *tornaguía,* or delivery confirmation. In time, this system covered all goods transported, and it served to regulate the payment of taxes. Customs officials maintained a register of goods to be transported, which included all of the information contained in the *guía,* and they received the *tornaguía* after the products had reached their destination (where they were inspected) and the *arrieros* had returned to their home base (82–83). These stricter controls were necessary, to judge from the statements of Crown authorities in New Spain. Viceroy Francisco de Güemes y Horcasitas made it clear that there was, indeed, smuggling going on in South America. Yes, trade between New Spain and Peru was prohibited by the laws of the Indies, he admitted, but it was also necessary. Again, the Kingdom of Guatemala, part of New Spain, makes an appearance in a Crown official's discussion of commerce and fraud:

Trade between this Kingdom and Peru is totally prohibited but continually acclaimed due to the mutual advantages that the older generations attribute to it, in benefit of not only individuals but also the royal treasury, for they say that it produced the wave of factories in this city [Mexico City] and Puebla that employed a lot of people and generated tax revenues, and they lament that foreigners conduct their smuggling along the vast coast of the North of that Kingdom in detriment to the Crown and traders in both New Spain and Peru.

On the southern coast of this Kingdom, from Acapulco to Guatemala, the Viceroy is the port authority with exclusive jurisdiction over the confiscations incurred by vessels that come in illegally from Peru with goods and the traders from this Kingdom take them, and during my tenure not one of these smuggling operations has occurred. Trade is also prohibited with foreigners who can introduce [goods] along the seacoasts of the North, and with the French through Tierra Firme, which is difficult to ascertain due to the distance and flight of the guilty parties, concerning which there have been some cases in the offices of the government. (1867, 17)[22]

That smuggling of both kinds had occurred during his tenure is not difficult to ascertain. An unpublished *Description of the Kingdom and Provinces of Guatemala,* written by the engineer Luis Díez Navarro, detailed the commercial life of this region that included the provinces of Nicaragua and Costa Rica and the towns that bordered the Kingdom of Tierra Firme. Although the title page dates his inspection and surveyal to 1744, Díez Navarro stated in his narration that he had worked from 1744 to 1747 on the Castle of the Immaculate Conception in the San Juan River region where years earlier, in the town of Carthage, two pirates (one Spanish and the other English) had attacked merchants and buyers who were holding a market (f. 332). In Nicoya, which Díez Navarro wished to submit to the jurisdiction of Granada in Nicaragua, "the vessels that come from the Kingdom of Tierra Firme" regularly dock and unload their merchandise without paying taxes, he wrote, and provincial governors "find themselves forced to acquiesce in these illegal dealings" (f. 333). Like Echeverz's *Ensayos mercantiles* and Viceroy Güemes y Horcasitas's report to his successor, Díez Navarro's account confirmed the steady trading patterns between the American viceroyalties, which were fostered by cities like Santiago de Guatemala and Nicaragua (in New Spain), Panama (in New Granada), and Guayaquil (in Peru).

Guayaquil was of major importance to trade between the Spanish American viceroyalties and the Spanish Orient. Ulloa neatly captured Guayaquil's role as a nexus between New Spain and Peru in *Relación histórica:*

> There are two ways in which the trade enjoyed by Guayaquil should be examined. One is the reciprocal trade of fruits and goods from its jurisdiction; the other is transitory, in which its port serves all the provinces of Peru, Tierra Firme and Guatemala as a port of call where they unload goods that, having crossed the Sea, will make their way to the Sierra; and in reverse, there are dispatched the goods that come down from the provinces of the Sierra to meet the opportune arrival of vessels that will transport them to ports on one or the other coast. (Ulloa and Juan 1748, 1:274)

The same Spanish scientist explained that the president of the high court in Panama had control over trade between Tierra Firme and New Spain. It was within his power to dispatch one or two ships per year "to the ports of Sonsonante, El Realejo and others belonging to the Province of Guatemala and the Kingdom of New Spain" (Ulloa and Juan 1748, 1:171–72). In 1741 Alcedo y Herrera was named captain general and president of the high court in Panama, and in July 1743 he assumed his duties. He remained in office until December 1749, the year in which judges there leveled a series of charges against him (González Palencia in Alcedo y Herrera 1915, xv–xvii; Mendiburu 1874–1890, 1:86). According to the Jesuit historian Mario Cicala, who had arrived in Panama in 1747, a military official with judicial powers came to Panama in 1751 to investigate and "first stripped the title of president and the staff of captain-general from the man who held them" (1994, 232). The Italian missionary continued:

> At the same time four judges were stripped of their judicial robes, one by one. . . . Only the senior judge managed to hang onto his robes. . . . [The investigating official] ordered the same thing done with the three royal officials of the royal accounting office, so that in the brief span of two hours he stripped them all of their dignity, put them in jail and extinguished the high court in Panama, abolished the presidency and brought down the royal accounting office, and established a different system, other courts, following the instructions and orders of the King. (232)

Some forty years after he published his *Memorial informativo,* and nearly fifteen years after leaving Panama, Alcedo y Herrera described the advantages of the Port of Guayaquil and its importance to the region, in his geographical report of the district under the jurisdiction of Quito's high court. The following passage makes it clear that Guayaquil played a significant part in the trade between New Spain, New Granada, and New Peru, and again the Kingdom of Guatemala is singled out:

> The maritime trade that they conduct through their port [of Guayaquil] with the ports of Peru and those in the valleys that they call *intermediaries,* in the southern zone, and in the zone of the North, with those [ports] in Barbacoas, El Chocó, Panama and the ones under its jurisdiction in Tierra Firme, and those [ports] in Realejo and Sonsonante in the Province of Guatemala that they call *on the other coast,* is most conducive to the prosperity and well-being of this province and its towns, and of the remaining provinces in this district. (1915, 37)[23]

Established here are the commercial links between the Kingdom of Quito and Tierra Firme and between the Viceroyalty of New Granada and the Viceroyalty of New Spain. Clothing, furniture, household items, jewelry, and other articles from the Orient arrived in Acapulco and were transferred to other ports of New Spain and New Granada. These goods traveled to the Viceroyalty of Peru, oftentimes disembarking in Piura, Guayaquil, Callao, and Buenos Aires, where they were carried across land by oxen or mule and resold.[24] Of course, these are some of the same articles that the lords from Lima are wearing at the mock trial at Archbishop Pardo de Figueroa's palace, *on the other coast,* in 1746. Carrió knew how to make his jocose *exemplum* not only funny but also realistic: he imitated material reality down to the last ruffle and cuff link.

Remember the words used by the senior member of the Lima delegation to belittle the challenger from Guatemala's experience and opinion of the *peruleros:*

"the riddle that the *gachupín,* our countryman, posed, and the challenge that he issued, confirm the little knowledge that he has about things that happen yonder the sea and that he assumes us *chapetones* to be a bunch of men who only look out for our particular interests, without thinking about the particulars of the country. Although outsiders, we are very well connected to everything." Now the suggestion that Spanish elites in Lima were interested only in their particular affairs was a charged one that collapsed the *criollo*-peninsular dichotomy: it attacked Spaniards from Peru, no matter where they had been born. Hence, the inspector's deliberation in defining clearly what *perulero* meant. What comes after is even more damaging: "the things that happen," a phrase that can be interpreted literally as the things that pass, or travel ("las cosas que pasan" in the Spanish original), meant illegal goods or diverted silver and gold, I am convinced, and "yonder the sea" ("allende el mar" in the original) referred to the Viceroyalty of Peru as it was viewed from the perspective of Guatemala, itself *on the other coast,* when viewed from Peru. These were illegal goods from foreign ships and Asian ports that crossed the sea or passed between the Viceroyalty of New Spain and the viceroyalties of New Granada and Peru.

Chapter 2 reconstructed the lives and careers of the Pardo de Figueroa clan in order to support my historical, or literal, interpretation of the second solution to Carrió's riddle of the 4Ps from Lima, *Pedro, Pardo, Paulino,* and *Perulero.* Immediately following, I propose an allegorical interpretation of this solution that is rooted in the preceding evidence of trade in illegal goods and diversion of precious metals.

Pedro Pardo de Figueroa's "Associates": Pedro, Pardo, Paulino, *and* Perulero

In *Pedro, Pardo, Paulino,* and *Perulero,* or "the four *connotados* of the Archbishop," *connotados* could be translated as "nicknames" or "monikers" but also as "associates" or "relatives." Read allegorically, *Pedro, Pardo, Paulino,* and *Perulero* identifies Archbishop Pedro Pardo de Figueroa's four associates or relatives who were principals in the Spanish American smuggling routes that included Guatemala: Pedro Bravo del Ribero (*Pedro*), José Pardo de Figueroa (*Pardo*), Pablo de Olavide (*Paulino*), and José de Araújo y Río (*Perulero*). All four of these men, like the archbishop, had attended such prestigious Lima schools as St. Martin's College and the University of San Marcos. St. Martin's was a college that brought future elites together at a young age. Upon graduation, these men held the values common to a group that was expected to achieve positions of leadership in the civil and religious spheres: they formed a social network in which members introduced one another to the right people in the right place at the right time.[25]

According to the February 1736 issue of *Gaceta de México,* two of the four men just named had traveled with Bishop Pedro Pardo de Figueroa of Guatemala from Spain to Mexico City. The fleet that arrived in the port of Vera Cruz was carrying Araújo y Río, governor and president of the high court in Quito (Fig. 12, no. 8), and Bravo del Ribero, a judge on the high court in Lima (1986, 2:318). Both, it is worth remembering, had been neighbors in Madrid, and each had been deposed for José Pardo de Figueroa's successful trial to become a knight of Santiago in 1734 (Lohmann Villena 1947, 1:316). Later in February 1736, the former viceroy of Peru, Armendáriz, was received at the viceregal palace in Mexico City by the viceroy and archbishop of New Spain (2:320–21). That same issue of the *Gaceta de México* recorded the entrance in Mexico City of Araújo y Río and Bravo del Ribero: "During this month Mr. Don José de Araújo y Río, a graduate of St. Martin's Royal College, a member of His Majesty's Council and president-elect of the high court in Quito, and Mr. Don Pedro Bravo del Ribero, a graduate of the same St. Martin's College, from which he rose to St. Philip's College in Lima, a member of His Majesty's Council and judge-elect in that same capital, arrived in this Court in order to travel to that of Lima" (2:321).

In Madrid, in 1733, Bravo del Ribero purchased a judgeship on the high court in Lima, where he was to serve for more than three decades.[26] Two years later he purchased the royal dispensation that allowed him to marry a woman from Lima, Petronila de Zabala Vázquez de Velasco Esquivel y Tello, daughter of José de Zabala y Esquivel, chief accountant for the Inquisition in Lima. The Zabalas were among the richest families in all of Peru,[27] and Bravo del Ribero's marrying into this family also made him a relative of the Pardo de Figueroa brothers[28] and of Pedro José Bravo de Lagunas y Castilla, judge, author, and art collector.[29] Under Viceroy Manso de Velasco, Bravo del Ribero often determined the legal boundaries between Crown and church.[30] In 1751 Manso de Velasco began to limit the archbishop's investigations into the Inquisition's accounts and church officials, and the archbishop Pedro Antonio de Barroeta fired off numerous legal briefs and motions to denounce Francisco de Herbosa y Figueroa,[31] Bravo del Ribero, and Bravo de Lagunas y Castilla, whom he qualified as "a gang of thugs." The rifts between the archbishop, the viceroy, and the judges on the high court and the Inquisition court were public knowledge (Manso de Velasco 1983, 171; Barroeta n.d.; Lohmann Villena 1959), and Carrió was in Lima at that time. Two decades later, when Carrió was inspecting the posts, *Pedro* Bravo del Ribero was one of the richest landowners in Peru: he owned a *chacra* in Ate Valley, two *haciendas* in Pisco, seven *haciendas* in Cuzco and Puno, and one *hacienda* in Chile (Lohmann Villena 1974, xxxix, lxxix, 1, 18–19).

We have seen enough of the archbishop's riddling brother José *Pardo* de Figueroa, but it remains to review briefly the lives and careers of the archbishop's two other *connotados*.

Archbishop Pardo de Figueroa's third associate or relative, *Paulino,* was Pablo de Olavide. Olavide's father, Martín de Olavide y Arbizu, was one of the richest merchants in Lima. Pablo's uncle, Domingo Antonio de Jáuregui, was the president of the high court in Charcas and governor of Huancavélica. Olavide was the nephew of García Lasso de la Vega e Híjar y Mendoza, count de Villanueva del Soto, who was the attorney assigned to Indian matters on the high court in Lima in 1744. After a young Olavide lost the battle for a chair in theology at the University of San Marcos to an older, more prominent figure, some faculty urged Viceroy Mendoza Sotomayor y Camaño—a descendant of the same dynasty as the paternal grandmother of the Pardo de Figueroa brothers, Juana de Sotomayor Manrique—to recommend Olavide for a judgeship. The *Gaceta de Lima,* monitored and used by Lima's viceroys and elites to shape public opinion, touted young Pablo's "merits" and "distinguished talents."[32] In truth, Olavide became a judge at the age of twenty because of his family's political and commercial ties and because he, like Bravo del Ribero, had purchased the post. As the editor of the *Gaceta de Lima* insinuated, Olavide required a royal dispensation in order to become a judge in his native city, and, again like Bravo del Ribero, he paid extra for that privilege (Mendiburu 1874–1890, 6:136; Lohmann Villena 1974, xxxix).

Paulino was tied to a man who was very powerful in Lima during Carrió's inspection of the posts, Miguel Feijoo de Sosa, born in Arequipa in 1718.[33] Feijoo de Sosa began his studies at St. Martin's College in 1733. One year later, Pablo de Olavide joined him, and the two teens became fast friends. After graduation, Feijoo de Sosa, like Olavide, attended the University of San Marcos. Miguel's father, Manuel Feijoo de Sosa, was a knight of Santiago and an accountant at the royal treasury court in Lima, but in the 1730s he became actively involved in the smuggling business, and in the following decade he purchased a provincial governorship.[34] In 1744 two events changed Miguel Feijoo de Sosa's life. First, he married María Micaela Josefa Antonia de Olavide y Jáuregui, the sister of his friend and former classmate Pablo de Olavide, and Pablo's father transferred the post of chief accountant on Lima's royal treasury court to Feijoo de Sosa as part of his daughter's dowry. Second, Miguel became the governor of Quispicanchi, a province bordering the town of Paruro, which later fell under Carrió's jurisdiction. Located in this province were the grandest country estate in all of the viceroyalty, La Glorieta, and a textile factory, both of which belonged to José Pardo de Figueroa, then governor of Cuzco. It is very likely that Feijoo de Sosa frequented La Glorieta, as other Crown and church officials commonly did, until his term ended in February 1750.[35] His brother-in-law was not as lucky.

After the devastating earthquake of 1746, Olavide became active in salvage efforts. He searched estates for deeds, jewels, and other valuables. He notified relatives of the deceased. He raised funds for the rebuilding of the theater in Lima, which he supervised. Carrió could not have ignored this heroic youth who was assuming very adult responsibilities in the public's eye, but fairly or unfairly, some in Lima did not view Olavide's deeds as precocious. The Jesuits accused him of impiety for having rebuilt the theater before the Church of Our Lady of Succour and for having used funds from an unknown source. He was also investigated for keeping more than he distributed to the relatives of persons killed in the earthquake. King Ferdinand VI ordered Olavide to stand trial in Madrid—a fact that suggests the influence of his family and friends—where he arrived in 1749 and turned himself in to authorities. Olavide lost the case, his judgeship, and his possessions, and he was forced to pay court costs as well. He went on to marry a wealthy widow, several years his senior, and to write novels and design Enlightenment projects in Spain. He later became infamous for his religious ideas and fled to France where he took the name Jean-Paul (Mendiburu 1874–1890, 6:136–37).

The fourth of Archbishop Pardo de Figueroa's associates or relatives was mentioned alongside Bravo del Ribero in that February 1736 issue of the *Gaceta de México:* Araújo y Río, governor and president of the high court in Quito. Araújo y Río was born in Lima. His father, born in Spain, was Francisco Araújo; his mother was Cándida del Río. Francisco was a merchant with a considerable fortune, according to the report on Peru's nobility that Viceroy Caracciolo prepared for King Philip V in 1721 (Balzo 1965, 112). He had made his fortune in trade and was for many years a member of Lima's merchants' guild; José's brother remained active in the same organization. In Madrid, José purchased the *corregidor*ship of Huarochiri in 1731, and a year later he purchased the twin posts of president of the high court and governor of Quito, where his wife's relatives lived. (Juan de Larrea, his father-in-law, had been a judge on the high court in Quito.) Araújo y Río purchased these Quito posts, which he would officially assume in 1736, with an eye to controlling trade routes during the Portobelo trade fair (Ramos Gómez in Ulloa and Juan 1985, 1:55–57, 74; Andrien 1995, 173–80).

At that time, Quito was the major center of consumption and redistribution of local and imported goods in the region, like Mexico City and Lima in their respective regions. The city of Quito exported and imported goods without using Lima as an intermediary, because it had direct access to the Portobelo trade fairs, Nombre de Dios and Panama via the port of Guayaquil, and contacts with Cartagena (Estupiñán 1997, 118). Araújo y Río's brother-in-law and business partner, Victorino Montero, was the *corregidor* of Paita (Piura). Through the port of Paita, whose importance was second only to Callao, Piura became an important hub of political and economic development in the Andean region (Glave 1997, 101–25). Piura was, as the marquis de Villagarcía reported in those exasperated passages from his *Relación,* the nexus of the Tierra Firme–Peru smuggling that roused his indignation and the imprisonment of the brothers-in-law Araújo y Río and Montero.

Before governor-president Araújo y Río's tenure, between 1723 and 1733, the local production of textiles in the Kingdom of Quito was greater than the level of imports. During his governorship, however, production levels and the balance of imports and exports changed dramatically. In 1743, for example, the level of imports, exports, and re-exports reached the highest level recorded, while local output fell off dramatically. The notarial registers of goods bought and sold indicate that foreign textiles came into the Kingdom of Quito in "bundles and large crates," without specification. In the 1740s, French and English textiles inundated the Quito market, although most of the imports were declared and recorded as "Merchandise from Castile." Nonspecified sales in 1743, for example, constituted the highest sum of money recorded for that year (Estupiñán 1997, 119, 135 n. 31).

Araújo y Río knew a thing or two about bundles and crates, and he took that knowledge from Spain to New Spain and from New Spain to what would soon be known as the Viceroyalty of New Granada. In 1736 the *San Fermín* transported Araújo y Río from Acapulco to Quito with trunks of Asian and Spanish goods in tow (Ramos Gómez in Ulloa and Juan 1985, 1:59). On December 31, 1736, Alcedo y Herrera, the departing governor of Quito, charged that under the supervision of Pedro Bravo del Ribero, the *San Fermín* had arrived in Paita and unloaded Governor Araújo y Río's trunks into the waiting arms of Victorino Montero (the *corregidor* of Piura and the governor's brother-in-law), while Araújo y Río himself set off for Lima to pick up his family. Upon his return to Paita, the governor took charge of 130 trunks of merchandise, dispatching most of it to Guayaquil, and took his family to Riobamba. Among the merchandise were cloth articles, spirits, and 130 *planchas* (which can mean either irons or sheets of silver). On December 26, Alcedo y Herrera witnessed the docking of the merchandise in Paita, and a notary later testified that the muleteers had been so overwhelmed that they had been forced to leave many boxes behind in Paita. The bishop of Quito, Andrés Paredes de Polanco y Armendáriz,[36] and a Crown official, Juan de Luján y Vedía,[37] met with Governor Araújo y Río in Riobamba, where he was holding another 66 boxes of goods.[38]

Araújo y Río's governorship was punctuated by these same sorts of dealings and others even more damaging to citizens and the Crown. He faced twenty-two charges, of which fifteen pertained to the period after he had been sworn in as governor of Quito. The accusations included the smuggling of cloth articles from Asia, manipulation of the sales of spirits to favor his brother-in-law's stock, misappropriation of Crown funds and personnel, illegal land deals, election tampering, false imprisonment of opponents, the sale of construction contracts, and the disruption of postal operations (Andrien 1995, 173–80; Ramos Gómez in Ulloa and Juan 1985, 1:333–35; Hill 1996b, *passim*).[39] Araújo y Río replied to the charges brought against him in *Manifiesto verídico y legal* (*Truthful and Legal Manifesto*) (1745), in which he petitioned to be heard by the Council of the Indies in Madrid. Araújo y Río wrote the king that flight was evidence of guilt and that he had been exiled without supervision in Tumbez for a year and was presently living, unsupervised, in his house in Quito, awaiting the outcome of his trial (f. 9r.). However, evidence does not support the claim that Araújo y Río had simply moved from Tumbez to Quito.

Enter St. Martin's alumni and relatives. When Araújo y Río's case was being tried in Quito, he violated the terms of his exile in Tumbez by fleeing to Lima in 1745 and then to Chile. Because of the influence of two judges on the high court in Lima, Pedro Bravo del Ribero and Alvaro de Navia Bolaño y Moscoso, Viceroy Manso de Velasco did not arrest the former president of Quito in Lima. It has already been shown that Bravo del Ribero was related by marriage to the Pardo de Figueroa brothers. Navia Bolaño y Moscoso, for his part, was related by marriage to Araújo y Río, but he was also married to the sister-in-law of Pedro and José Pardo de Figueroa.[40] Both judges in Lima had advised Manso de Velasco on the case and had testified on Araújo y Río's behalf during the trial that convicted him in Quito. (That the governor's brother-in-law, Victorino Montero, was Manso de Velasco's captain of the palace guard at the time also encouraged the viceroy to look the other way.) The viceroy gave Araújo y Río authorization to embark for Spain in December 1745. In Madrid, he lost his appeal with the Council of the Indies in November 1746, but he somehow managed to reverse that decision in August 1747. The governorship of Guatemala was one of the compensations that the Council of Indies awarded him (Ramos Gómez in Ulloa and Juan 1985, 1:59–61, 260–61, 333–35; Andrien 1995, 173–80).

Were all of this not enough, Carrió had another reason to ridicule Araújo y Río in his exposé: the rehabilitated and reincarnated governor and president of the high court in Santiago de Guatemala attempted to manipulate the postal system there as he had done in Quito. The job of postmaster general in Santiago was the most expensive to purchase and was hereditary, until it was incorporated by the Crown in 1767 (Palma Murga 1986, 248). In October 1748, Araújo y Río demanded that the postmaster general, Pedro Ortiz de Letona, embrace a new system of monthly postal runs between Guatemala and Oaxaca (which the postmaster refused to do) or resign in exchange for other posts. The governor persuaded the high court to remove the postmaster and install one of Araújo y Río's friends as supervisory judge of the postal system in Santiago, events that Araújo y Río reported to the Council of Indies in January 1749. In December of that year, King Ferdinand VI reprimanded President Araújo y Río and the judges and ordered that the directorship of the postal service in Guatemala be returned to its rightful owner. The Spanish monarch also requested that Archbishop Pardo de Figueroa conduct a secret investigation of the post and postmaster and report his findings directly to him. Archbishop Pedro Pardo de Figueroa's confidential report arrived in Madrid in July 1751 (Bose 1939, 261–74). Throughout his career, Araújo y Río's hide was spared by the St. Martin's network and by his family ties to Navia Bolaño y Moscoso and the Pardo de Figueroa brothers. From Carrió's perspective, Araújo y Río was the quintessential *Perulero*.[41]

In the pursuit of sexual and/or financial gratification, the excesses committed by Archbishop Pardo de Figueroa and his *connotados,* like those that would be committed by Viceroy Manuel de Amat y Junient and his cronies later in the same century, undercut their own moral and legal authority and, by extension, that of other Crown and church officials. All four of Archbishop Pardo de Figueroa's associates or relatives from Lima had attended schools such as St. Martin's College and the University of San Marcos. Friendships forged at St. Martin's and other schools for Lima's elites plugged graduates into social networks throughout the Hispanic world.

Many of these men had been trained in canon and civil law, and they maintained family contacts and friendships on both sides of the Atlantic, a fact that not only elucidates the failure of Bourbon reform measures throughout the eighteenth century but also challenges prevailing interpretations of the *criollo*-peninsular rivalry. These four men, like the archbishop himself, had gained their posts through inheritance, favors, or direct purchase. Their posts, along with strategic marriages and their reputations as loyal Bourbon bureaucrats, allowed them to shape legal and illegal trade and the diversion of silver and gold in an area that stretched from New Spain to Buenos Aires.

The eighteenth century spelled the triumph of Buenos Aires and the fall of Lima as the preeminent capital in South America, despite the Bourbon reforms taken since the beginning of the eighteenth century to curb trade in illegal goods and the diversion of gold, silver, and mercury. Decades before Carrió began his inspection of the posts, the writing was on the economic wall for Lima: merchants in Buenos Aires had broken the trade patterns and commercial monopolies long enjoyed by the merchants in Lima and had shown themselves to be every bit as good as Lima's merchants at illegal trade and the diversion of precious metals.

CHAPTER 4

Of Gods and Men: Bourbon Blindness and the Post, circa 1750–1800

We have already seen evidence of the intense economic rivalry between Lima and Buenos Aires during the first half of the eighteenth century and the harmonious relationship between Alonso Carrió de Lavandera and postal officials in Buenos Aires. Neither the rivalry nor Carrió's respect for the Riverplate faded in the second half of the century. Carrió had been charged with inspecting the posts from Lima to the Riverplate; however, the inspector's general itinerary, which begins in Montevideo and Buenos Aires, does not include Lima. The posts in Lima were being managed by Crown officials who disliked Carrió's charge and his ideas about changing postal rates, routes, and regulations. The following pages examine the disparity between the scope of Carrió's commission and the scope of his report in light of the rivalry between Lima and Buenos Aires and the disputes between Carrió and officials in Lima.

Carrió's career as a merchant, provincial governor, and soldier had schooled him in "informal" trading and accounting practices and in the silver, gold, and mercury that was "passing," or traveling, between the viceroyalties of New Spain, New Granada, and Peru. His subsequent stint as inspector of the posts from Lima to Buenos Aires/Montevideo expanded his knowledge base considerably. As inspector of the posts, Carrió gained firsthand knowledge of smugglers' use of the postal system to achieve their ends. This chapter presents numerous examples of trade in illegal goods and the diversion of precious metals and explores the post's role in these activities.

To be in the dark—to be ignorant—is to be blind, and blindness is a perfect example of semantic variegation in *El lazarillo de ciegos caminantes*. The contours of blindness, which was central to the representations of Error and Ignorance in iconographic and emblematic literature from the renaissance to the Enlightenment, are both epistemological and moral. From the title page to the closing Guatemalan tale, the immoral and illegal behaviors exhibited by church and Crown officials in Bourbon Spanish America are figured either as blindness, or its opposite, clairvoyance. From the renaissance forward, literature and the arts depicted Mercury as exercising a blinding, or immoral, influence on government officials. His legendary support of commerce, theft, witty discourse, and travel made him a logical presence in Carrió's exposé. Furthermore, Carrió's title and account entail another, more strictly epistemological, sense of blindness that captures the disjunction of material reality and discursive reality in the arena of historiography and in a myriad of cultural attitudes and practices that we associate today with the Enlightenment.

In the second half of the eighteenth century, many of the men who had come to power under Philip V were still controlling Lima's system of justice, which is to say that the officials charged with enacting the Bourbon reforms were the very individuals who often thwarted them. Carrió's skepticism toward Bourbon policy reform in the Indies and his scorn for Bourbon technocrats who were undermining that reform movement are conveyed by textual winks and nods, inside jokes, and ironic praise. Both the inspector and Concolorcorvo "speak mysteriously," or in riddles: a specific gesture performed by each of them at different points in the narration indicates that both know more than they are saying.[1] Mercury's influence on Crown and church in Bourbon Spanish America gave the god of Silence an accessory role in *El lazarillo de ciegos caminantes* that is profiled at the end of this chapter.

"In Reverse Order": Lima Vanquished, or the Triumph of Buenos Aires

Much of what men like Carrió knew, the Bourbon monarchs of Spain and Spanish America appear not to have known or to have chosen to ignore. In spite of the Riverplate's notoriety as a haven for smugglers, King Ferdinand VI, who ruled Spain from 1746 to 1759, granted a small group of Spanish merchants exclusive trading rights with Buenos Aires in 1754, provided that they also transport slaves. The resident merchants of Buenos Aires blamed the group, known as the Buenos Aires Company, for the decline in leather prices, and the city council worked actively to have it suppressed. In 1765 the Crown finally agreed, and the Buenos Aires Company was dissolved (Arazola Corvera 1998, 52–53). The will of elites in Buenos Aires, many of whom owed their fortune and social status to trade, was clearly behind the decision.

In Francisco Millau y Marabal's *Descripción de la Provincia del Río de la Plata y de sus Poblaciones* (*Description of Riverplate Province and Its Inhabitants*)—which the navy lieutenant presented to Julián de Arriaga, lieutenant general of the Royal Armada and secretary of the Indies and the navy—he qualified the city of Buenos Aires as one of the most populated by Spaniards in all of South America, estimating its population to be thirty thousand. One-fourth of the city's population was Portuguese or Portuguese American. The population of the surrounding countryside, divided into districts called *pagos,* was roughly twenty thousand (1772, 144r.–v.). Carrió's combined population estimate for Buenos Aires and Trinidad was more than twenty-two thousand,[2] considerably less than Millau's estimate for Bue-

nos Aires alone, but the different scopes of the estimates make comparison difficult. What the analyses here and in Chapter 3 indicate, in any case, is an upward
trend: in the second half of the century, Buenos Aires and the hinterlands experienced substantial demographic growth that we cannot measure with exactitude.

Moreover, Millau's account confirms that the elites in Buenos Aires differed
from those in Lima. There was no titled nobility among the city's most distinguished families, who were descended either from Spanish officials who had
served the Crown there or from ancestors who were born in Buenos Aires and
who had made their fortunes in ranching or trade or trips to the interior of the
Viceroyalty of Peru (1772, 145r.). These two groups, considered the most distinguished, intermarried as abundant trade, which had been growing since the previous decade, was increasing the number of new families descended from foreigners or from people born in Buenos Aires (145r.). Although there were no "massive
fortunes," there were many "sizeable ones," and there was a greater distribution
of wealth in Buenos Aires than in any other city: among the poor, for example,
there was no "wretchedness" because food was so cheap (145r.). Unlike the population of Lima, which Carrió compared unfavorably to that of Mexico City, the
population of Buenos Aires included very few Indians and *mestizos*. They worked
on brick-making operations, ranches, and mule trains. Millau drew a distinction
between peons, who were either Spaniards or members of the mixed *castas* who
worked in the countryside, and slaves, who were *negros* and *mulatos* in the city.
Nearly three-quarters of the city's families had a slave or a slave family living with
them. Still, the number of *negros* and *mulatos* in Buenos Aires was small relative to
other cities in South America, and with very few exceptions they were slaves (144r.
and v.).

It is undeniable that the increasing economic influence of Buenos Aires, which
continued to be a magnet for entrepreneurial Europeans in the second half of the
eighteenth century, was at least partially responsible for the restructuring and expansion of the postal system in the Riverplate region of the Viceroyalty of Peru. In
1767 Carrió's friend Domingo de Basavilbaso was named director of the maritime
post; in 1769 this office was joined to the ground post, to which he was named
the head. In September 1771 Basavilbaso hired an official to run the main office in
Buenos Aires. Carrió did an inventory of the office in the capital in October 1771
and May 1772 (Bose 1933; 1934, 349). Through Concolorcorvo and the textual inspector, Carrió would turn the narrowing of his commission as postal inspector—
that is, the elimination of Lima from his official itinerary—into a snub against the
extratextual lords from Lima who resented their mercantile (and postal) superiors
in Buenos Aires.

Carrió not only omitted Lima from his inspection report in 1775, under Viceroy Manuel de Amat y Junient's orders, but also elected to begin his report in
the Riverplate. Thus he taunted Lima's elites with the very real possibility that

his readers—Crown officials, merchants, and muleteers alike—would be interested primarily in postal routes and offices in the thriving Riverplate region, where they would be doing most of their traveling and trading, and would look to the Andean region only as an afterthought.[3] Ostensibly to smooth over this obvious snub, Carrió inverted this order in the summary of the postal routes that follows the narration proper, and he placed this editorial commentary in Concolorcorvo's mouth: "Después de concluido este itinerario histórico, le pareció muy del caso al visitador dar a sus lectores una sucinta idea de las provincias de su comisión, para que se dirijan las correspondencias con algún acierto. Estas advertencias se harán de modo retrógrado, para que los señores limeños no tengan la molestia que les causará el itinerario general" (433) ("After this historiographical itinerary was finished, it seemed to the inspector most fitting to give his readers a succinct notion of the provinces within his charge so that correspondence might be managed with some precision. These observations will be made in reverse order, so that they will not annoy the Liman sires as the general itinerary will"). This olive branch that Concolorcorvo extends to Lima's elites notwithstanding, Carrió adds insult to their injury, after the general itinerary and the summary (or "succinct notion") of the postal routes is presented "in reverse order," by ridiculing Lima under the guise of comparing it to Mexico City. This less-than-friendly insult should not distract our attention from the injury received by elites in Lima—from the wounding of their pride as they perceived that their city had been relegated not to second place, behind the older Mexico City, but to third place, behind the upstart Buenos Aires.[4]

In the second half of the eighteenth century, European authors continued to depict Lima as the crown jewel of South America. However, Buenos Aires came to be recognized by encyclopedists and compilers as a formidable competitor. *The American Gazetteer,* for example, underscored the influence of the merchants in Buenos Aires, who traded as they wished (Anonymous 1762, 1:n.p.). Giandomenico Coleti, too, recognized the aesthetic and economic pleasures of Buenos Aires: " Its climate is pleasant, healthy and mild, the neighboring countryside spacious, amenable and fertile. The gardens that are planted in the city and areas around it supply it with flowers, fruits and the most flavorful greens. Birds, wild game and meats are found in abundance and are dirt cheap. The inhabitants are of a most courteous nature, and almost all of them are engaged in trade, so the Indians trade and are affable, well-built and agile" (1771, 1:51). He conceded the lack of a mining industry in the province of Buenos Aires, although there was no lack of trade: "However, there are no minerals, and the gold and the silver that there are come from Chile and Peru in exchange for the cattle, horses and mules that exit this Province. Little money circulates, because it leaves on the ships that return to Spain" (1:52).[5]

Residents of Lima also understood that Buenos Aires was a significant population and economic center in the second half of the eighteenth century. Cosme Bueno, who wrote his descriptions of areas he had not visited from reports he received from religious and Crown officials and residents in those areas, published his description of the bishopric of Buenos Aires in 1776 (1996, 129–37). His portrayal, too, painted a pretty picture of Buenos Aires:

> The position of the City is such that some beautiful and stretching fields, always covered in green, can be seen from almost anywhere. On the outskirts there are many summer estates that provide recreation and relaxation to the landowning residents [of Buenos Aires]. The climate is healthy, the air clean. . . . The fertility of the area matches the gentleness of the air that one breathes [there]. And so it produces an abundance of grains and all [kinds of] seeds, vegetables and fruits. . . . The river that surrounds one-half of this city offers a gorgeous view, for in the North it resembles an expansive sea and its opposing shore cannot be seen. (133)

Bueno detailed the importance of Buenos Aires again in 1776, shortly before the creation of the new viceroyalty: "In the present century, particularly in the past few years, . . . it has grown so much in buildings and residents due to the increase in trade that it has become one of the most opulent and beautiful cities in this America, being the key and center of trade for all the neighboring provinces. . . . Its residents number nearly thirty thousand souls" (1996, 132). As one scholar puts it, "The administrative reorganization that created the viceroyalty of Río de la Plata in 1776, confirmed the victory of Buenos Aires over the pretensions of the Lima *consulado* [merchants' guild] to dominate the fate of the trade in the Río de la Plata basin" (Lugar 1986, 62).

A great deal of that trade was illegal, just as it had been during the first half of the eighteenth century. The anonymous compilers of *The American Gazetteer* wrote matter-of-factly, "The trade carried on between this place and Europe should be only by the register-ships from Spain, but besides this there is carried a contraband trade to England and Spain; but there is another with the Portuguese, who possess the opposite shore of Rio de la Plata, by means of little vessels under cover of sending their own commodities, but really European goods" (1762, 1:n.p.). Coleti, unlike the anonymous authors of *The American Gazetteer,* made no mention of the illegal trading and diversion of silver and gold in Buenos Aires, but the influx of Neapolitans and Sicilians into the Riverplate since the start of the eighteenth century suggests that word had reached Spanish Italy too.

Millau, for his part, wrote in vivid detail of smuggling in Montevideo, Maldonado, and Buenos Aires. The Portuguese colony of Sacramento, forty leagues from Montevideo, legally traded with Rio de Janeiro and Santa Catalina. It illegally traded with Montevideo and Buenos Aires by sailing from the port of Sacramento and docking in the mouths of two rivers between Maldonado and Montevideo. People from nearby farms loaded up their wagons with leather goods, wheat, oil, and meat to sell to the Portuguese; in return they purchased Portuguese spirits, Brazilian tobacco, and sundry items [1772, 194r. and v.].

Trade between Sacramento and Buenos Aires had changed, Millau observed: it used to be that the Portuguese came in fortified ships to Buenos Aires; then the merchants of Buenos Aires began taking their goods to the port of Sacramento, where the goods sold at prices up to three times greater than in Buenos Aires [1772, 195r. and v.]. The numerous islands covered by thick forests that dotted the River Paraná also aided smugglers from Buenos Aires, who dropped off their goods in the many canals or on the little islands, where they were retrieved by the Portuguese. Portuguese merchants from the ranches that lined the western bank of the Paraná took their goods in canoes to the arranged drop-off spot. The medium-sized boats that left Buenos Aires to pick up timber from the islands of the Paraná also became involved in this illegal trade [196r. and v.]. Once the smuggler, or *contrabandista,* left Sacramento, he had to get his goods into Buenos Aires. He did so under cover of darkness, little by little, from ranch to ranch, on wagons or horses, mixing the illegal goods with legal goods, and often using the same personnel charged with preventing illegal trade (197r.). The guard major received a salary, but his subordinates received only a commission on the confiscated goods. As a result, they turned a blind eye to smuggling or moonlighted as transporters of smuggled goods, making up stories to cover their actions when they ran into acquaintances along the way (197v.).

Residents of the Riverplate region trumpeted their economic triumph over their counterparts in Lima while perpetuating the fiction that smuggling played no role in their success. In an anonymous report written for the first viceroy of the Riverplate, a proud resident of Buenos Aires claimed that the thirty-three provinces in the Riverplate equaled, if they did not exceed, the fifty-seven in the Viceroyalty of Peru, in size, fertility, and riches, stating that "in all of the Kingdom they are the worthiest of favor because they are the principal key to all of Peru and Chile, and the magnet for all foreign powers" ("Informe Tercero," in *Cuatro informes* 1776, 33v.). In another report by the same author, he inveighed against merchants in Lima for engaging in unfair trading practices that were aimed at shutting down their counterparts in Buenos Aires. Buenos Aires, he stated, is "the most useful due to its fertility and all of its circumstances, the most rewarding of merit, and in all of this Kingdom the city with the most potential for abundant trade, and it would be [abundant] already if *Merchants* in the capital of Lima, with insatiable greed and tyranny, had not choked off its circulation and impeded the entry of its products throughout Peru, with their surreptitious filings" ("Informe Cuarto," in *Cuatro informes* 49r.). In still another report, as preposterous as it may sound, the same author directly accused *perulero* merchants of lying about smuggling between Buenos Aires and the Portuguese city of Sacramento ("Segundo informe," in *Cuatro informes* ff. 16v.–33r., at 28v.–29r.). He portrayed landowning residents in Lima as undeserving of the special treatment the Crown had assigned them and inferior to their counterparts in Buenos Aires:

> To this must be added that, in weighing the merits of one side and the other, it seems that the landowning residents of Buenos Aires should be granted what is not appropriate for those in Lima, and even less so for the singular preference [granted the latter] in detriment to so many and so loyal subjects, who know how to conquer the object that motivates their misfortune, since the natives and the landowning residents in this Province are the people with the most wherewithal, determination and fortitude that this Continent possesses, much to the contrary of the sons of Lima and its neighboring Provinces, notwithstanding all of the Europeans who live there, for both at an early age are stricken with several chronic ailments such that they are left completely disabled and weak-spirited, and they are [*sic*] not able to withstand a normal task and setback if wars were to break out in their homeland, and it is doubtful that they could head to another front, given their emaciated constitution, which stems from the poor diet that they follow and the obscene entertainments in which they engage. [29v.–30r.]

The hostility that existed between residents of Buenos Aires and Lima, evident in this anonymous report, also marks *El lazarillo de ciegos caminantes:* the reference to "obscene entertainments" brings to mind the first solution (*Pila, Puente, Pan,* and *Peines*) to the riddle of the 4Ps from Lima, and, as we saw earlier, Lima's negative superiority to Mexico City is both a defeat for Lima in the Lima versus Mexico City trial and an implicit verdict in favor of traders and landowning residents of Buenos Aires in the Lima versus Buenos Aires contest.[6] Nevertheless, Carrió did not portray the Riverplate region as an idyllic one. We have already seen how the inspector and Concolorcorvo describe sexual romps in the Riverplate *gauderios* before they slyly deflect them toward churchmen and statesmen in Lima. There were, however, graver sins being committed against the common good. Millau and a number of foreigners came right out and said this, whereas *El lazarillo de ciegos caminantes* gingerly insinuates it.

Carrió winks at the reader who knows something about trade in the Riverplate as he lets an example of smuggling drop: "El [carretero] que tuviere carga doble solicitará arriero de Escara, de la provincia de Chichas, que comúnmente bajan a Jujuy, y alg[u]nos hasta Salta, en solicitud de cargas de cera y otros efectos del Tucumán con *algo más,* que entenderá muy bien el lector sabio en materias de comercio" (239) ("The [wagoneer] who has a double load will send for a muleteer from Escara, in the province of Chichas, for [muleteers] often go down to Jujuy, and some go as far down as Salta, in search of loads of wax and other goods from Tucumán, along with *something else,* which the reader knowledgeable in matters of commerce will understand very well"). This "something else" could be any number of things—alcohol, leather, even precious metals. Concolorcorvo's description of the *gauderios* (or *gauchos*) in Montevideo includes a tale of thievery. A man was traveling the royal road between Luján and Buenos Aires with mules loaded down with silver coins. Several *gauchos* scared one of the mules, which ran off and was later found and picked clean by the *gauchos* (265–66). Repeated references such as these drive home the point that the Riverplate region had built its economic profile on trade, especially illegal trade, and on the diversion of Crown gold and silver. Carrió knew it, and he expected that readers with a local or regional business background would know it too.

For roughly thirty years it has been accepted without question that the second solution to the riddle of the 4Ps from Lima (*Pedro, Pardo, Paulino,* and *Perulero*) was an attack on postal authorities in Lima who were defrauding the Crown. I have already made my case for a literal interpretation and a complementary, allegorical, reading of that second solution; however, in a strange, roundabout way, my interpretations, too, lead us to the post, for commerce and fraud were equally dependent on it.

Traveling the Posts: Contraband Bundles and Untaxed Silver and Gold

Let us set one thing straight from the onset: the post was a smuggler's best friend in Bourbon Spanish America. In his satirical *quaestione* on lying in Lima, Friar Francisco del Castillo singled out the postal system as the greatest source of fraud, but the shipowners and merchants who relied on the post to do business also became the butt of the blind poet's jokes. When one of the competitors mentions that bureaucrats sell lies as truths, the other's reply is swift and severe: "Dijo otro: esas mentirillas/no son del mayor aplauso,/las Armadas del comercio/pueden abarrotar fardos./Aquí forman paz y guerra/los que no son soberanos,/con arribos de bajeles,/por ir ellos arribando./Pues que como no les cuesta/el mentir, sino barato,/a sus géneros los hacen/más amables por más caros" (1948, 89) ("The other said: those fibs/do not take the cake,/[For] the merchants' *armadas*/can really pack in the bundles./Here peace and war are waged/by those who are not sovereigns,/with the arrivals of vessels,/as they set to arriving./Since to them/lying comes cheap,/they make their goods/more desirable by making them costlier"). Such merchandise—legal or illegal bundles (of goods or lies)—was unloaded and then transported across land in the same way that private and official government and church correspondence was, by horse or mule, along the postal routes (*correos*). Traveling in the opposite direction on those postal routes and back roads were the gold and silver that smugglers "mailed" out of the viceroyalty and their carriers loaded onto foreign or Spanish ships.

Illegal merchandise—such as the Asian clothes that the Liman delegation was wearing, according to the inspector's anecdote—and untaxed silver, gold, and mercury traveled the same royal roads (*caminos reales*) and other postal routes that private and commercial correspondence did. However, they did so under the guise of "Cases that said *King's Tobacco* [registered royal monopoly tobacco]," as Veterano told Bisoño in the anonymous *Drama de los palanganas Veterano y Bisoño* (*Drama of the Two Blowhards, Veteran and Rookie*) (1938, 102), one of many social satirical dialogues that circulated in Bourbon Lima despite repeated attempts to curtail them in the second half of the eighteenth century.[7] If we think back to the inspector's description of the senior spokesman for the *peruleros* at the mock trial in Guatemala, this diversion scheme illuminates one of the inspector's seemingly hyperbolic observations: "His cufflinks were made of gold, like his snuff tin, and either one of them must have weighed a couple of pounds." Also, one of the judges at that mock trial, José de Araújo y Río, had manipulated the post when he was president of Quito, as he would later do as governor of Guatemala, and it is not hard to imagine that gold and other items traveled the posts disguised as Crown tobacco or that Crown tobacco itself was being diverted where he ruled. *Drama de los palanganas* explicitly mentioned post offices, or *Correos* (117), and Carrió's boss, Viceroy Amat, directly addressed the dangers of transporting massive amounts of Crown gold and silver by post in his *Memoria del Gobierno*. Such shipments tended to fall down steep inclines or into rivers so dangerous that retrieval by governors and postal administrators was impossible. (I suspect that something other than the force of gravity was at work there.) Amat's solution was to set up a special commission to decide such cases for the post (1947, 609). In addition, he proposed a system of money orders and treasury bonds to replace the transport of gold and silver via the posts, claiming that it was extremely difficult and dangerous and also slowed down the delivery of ordinary correspondence (607). Finally, in 1774 he set up a committee to handle postal reforms in Lima, after Carrió's run-ins with the postmaster general there, instructing committee members to observe the ten ordinances of the Royal Project of 1720 that directly concerned the administration of the posts (609–10).

Carrió alludes to fraud by members of the lower orders, merchants, churchmen, and postal officials throughout his exposé. All of these cases involved traveling, and the surest routes to travel were the so-called "royal roads" (*caminos reales*) and postal routes maintained by the Crown. In the description of Potosí, for instance, there is the suggestion of thievery by the postmaster and a suggestion that the same was occurring in Popayán:

> Administra los correos don Pedro de la Revilla, mozo instruído y fecundo en proyectos. Se divulgó en Potosí que había sido tiritero en Espana, porque le vieron hacer algunos juegos de manos. Por otro tanto, dijo el visitador, denunciaron en Popayán, y fue llamado a la Inquisición, don Pedro Sánchez Villalba, sujeto más conocido en este reino que Revilla, pero entre los dos Pedros hay la diferencia que los potosinos lo hicieron por malicia, y los popayanes con sencillez. (280)

[Don Pedro de la Revilla, an educated lad and (one) full of projects, administers the posts. Word got out in Potosí that he had been a puppet master in Spain because they saw him doing some sleight of hand. For the same sort of thing in Popayán, the inspector said, they denounced Don Pedro Sánchez Villalba, an individual better known in this Kingdom than Revilla is, and he was called to appear before the Inquisition, but there is this difference between the two Pedros: the Potosians did it out of malice and the Popayans out of naiveté.]

Nearly all men are light fingered, the inspector tells Concolorcorvo, before mentioning once again the riddle of the 4Ps from Lima: "Lo cierto es, señor Concolorcorvo, que de cien hombres apenas se hallará uno que no sea tiritero, y así ríase usted de los potosinos y popayanes con los dos Pedros y celebre cuatro PPPP tan memorables como las de Lima" (280) ("The truth is, Mr. Concolorcorvo, that you will hardly find one man in a hundred who is *not* a puppet master, and so laugh at the Potosians and the Popayans with their two Pedros, and applaud 4Ps as memorable as those from Lima"). The resignation or acquiescence in fraud that the inspector recommends to his secretary is as ironic as his praise for the "memorable" 4Ps from Lima: no matter which of the three solutions to the riddle Carrió had in mind here, there was hardly anything or anyone in them worthy of sincere applause.

Just as illegal trade cannot be separated from the diversion of precious metals in the Viceroyalty of Peru, the posts cannot be separated from the mercury and silver mines in *El lazarillo de ciegos caminantes*. Ventura de Santelices y Venero, a former judge at the royal trading house (*Casa de Contratación*) in Cádiz, had been appointed provincial governor (*corregidor*), supervisor of Indian compulsory labor (*la mita*), accountant and superintendent of the royal mint in Potosí. Shortly after Carrió arrived in Lima, Viceroy José Antonio Manso de Velasco issued a package of mining reforms, because two aspects of Santelices y Venero's regime had incensed miners and merchants. The first was the shortage of forced Indian laborers (*mitayos*), which miners asked the viceroy to remedy. However, his reform efforts in this area were unsuccessful, and he blamed Superintendent Santelices. The second was the *kajcheo*, which permitted Indians to work for themselves on weekends—to take minerals out of the mines and have them processed at privately owned mills instead of taking them to the Crown's receiving house set up by Santelices.[8] Workers engaged in this practice were known as *kajchas* (or *calcas*). "The *kajchas* as well as the millers were frowned upon by mine owners because they considered them to be thieves of metals that by law belonged to the mine owners." In 1751 a group of miners banded together to halt the practice, and "the results were protests, strikes and deaths." The practice was allowed to continue (Galaor et al. 1999, 66).

And continue it did, right up to the period of Carrió's inspection of the posts. In the Cerro of Potosí, the inspector complains, Indians "se emplean en el honrado ejercicio de Calcas, que son unos ladrones de metales que acometen de noche las minas, y como prácticos en ellas, sacan los más preciosos, que benefician y llevan al banco que el rey tiene de rescate, siendo cierto que estos permitidos piratas sacan más plata que los propietarios mineros" (279) ("are engaged in the honorable profession of *Calcas* [*kajchas*], who are certain thieves of metals that go into the mines at night and, since they know their way around them, they make off with the most valuable ones, which they process and take to the king's receiving house, and it is certain that these legal pirates get more silver out of the mines than the mine owners do"). In Oruro, he singles out the individual citizens who take silver nuggets out of the mines illegally ("los particulares . . . que rescatan piñas") (303). Scholars have ignored such observations, which place Carrió squarely in the camp of the mine owners who felt they were being wronged by Manso de Velasco and Santelices. Carrió most likely had no respect for the superintendent, who had made life difficult for the postmaster general of Buenos Aires, Juan Martín Mena y Mascarúa (1754–1761). The two tangled over several issues, including the rights and privileges of Mena's subordinates—postal officials and their lieutenants—to transport bundles of letters and packages by mule without interference or inspection (Bose 1934, 348). Carrió first visited Buenos Aires in 1749, two years after Basavilbaso proposed to Viceroy Manso the establishment of mail service in Buenos Aires and one year after the service was established under Mena's predecessor.

Another allusion to fraud involving silver and the church is so clever that scholars have completely passed it by. In the Cathedral of La Plata (or Charcas), there is a "mystery" and a "special feature," according to the inspector, and he challenges his fellow travelers to discover what they are. As Concolorcorvo writes, "Uno dijo que los muchos espejos con cantoneras de plata que adornaban el altar mayor. Otro dijo que eran muy hermosos los blandones de plata, y así fue diciendo cada uno su dictamen, pero el visitador nos dijo que todos éramos unos ciegos, pues no habíamos observado una maravilla patente y una particularidad que no se veía en iglesia alguna de los dominios de España" (291) ("One said that it was the many mirrors with silver corner bands that adorned the main altar. Another one said that the silver torches were most handsome, and so everybody went on to offer his own opinion, but the inspector told us that we were a bunch of blindmen, because we had not noticed an obvious marvel and a particular feature that could not be seen in a single church in Spain's dominions").

The inspector finally says what he finds amazing about the cathedral: "La maravilla es, que siendo los blandones de un metal tan sólido como la plata, y de dos varas de alto, con su grueso correspondiente, los maneja y suspende sin artificio alguno un monacillo como del codo a la mano. En esto hay un gran misterio; pero dejando aparte este prodigio, porque nada me importa su averiguación, voy a declarar a Vmds. la particularidad de esta iglesia" (291) ("The amazing thing is that, although the torches are made of a very solid metal like silver, and they are roughly three feet high, with a corresponding thickness, an acolyte about the size of my forearm carries them aloft without any device whatsoever. There is a great mystery in this, but leaving aside this marvel, because an inquiry into it does not concern me, I am going to explain to all of you a particular feature of this church"). The implication here is that the hefty silver torches (*blandones*) cannot be made of pure silver because a little acolyte, or server, manages to hold them aloft. Like the inspector's portrait of the Liman senior representative, this brief description compels us to remember that Philip V had instructed the viceroys of New Spain and Peru to surveil and bring to justice officials at the royal mint who manipulated the weights and denominations of silver and gold coinage.[9] The inspector declines to investigate the "mystery" that his companions are too "blind" to see, because such an investigation would point to the manipulation of silver ore and grades engineered by whoever donated, financed, or executed the cathedral's silverworks. The cathedral's "particular feature," which the inspector explains after he has pointed out the "mystery" of the silver torches, is that it does not have ceiling chandeliers like the churches in Spain. The subsequent description of ceiling lighting in Spanish churches (291–92) distracts attention from the fraud he has just intimated and indirectly supports the defense that Carrió was to offer of *El lazarillo de ciegos caminantes:* he had not defamed anyone; he had even silenced many truths in order to protect the guilty in positions of authority.

My final example of the fraud encoded in *El lazarillo de ciegos caminantes* again has Concolorcorvo leading the charge. The inspector's secretary writes of the *two* risks involved in moving loads across the land through the posts but makes only one explicit:

> Regularmente ha visto el visitador que todas las desgracias que han sucedido en estos tránsitos las ocasionaron las violencias de los dueños de las cargas. La seguridad de sus efectos por su asistencia es fantástica, porque en el caso, que es muy raro, de que un mal peón quiera hacer un robo, abriendo un fardo o un cajón, lo ejecuta en una noche tenebrosa y tempestuosa, en que los dueños de las cargas están recogidos en sus toldos, y hasta el dueño de la recua procura abrigarse bien, fiado en que el dueño está presente y que respecto de haberse fiado de él, no tiene otra responsabilidad que la de entregar fardos cerrados. Distinta vigilancia tuviera si, como sucede en todo el mundo, se les hiciera entrega formal de la hacienda; pero, dejando aparte estos dos riesgos, de bastante consideración, voy a poner delante las incomodidades del pasajero que camina con arrieros. (105–6)

[The inspector has often seen that outrages committed by the owners of loads triggered all of the misfortunes that have occurred in these routes. The security of their goods due to their presence is a myth, because in the event—which is most unusual—that a bad peon wants to commit a robbery, by breaking into a bundle or case of freight, he does so on a dark and stormy night when the owners of the loads have retired to their tents and even the owner of the mule train seeks to take proper shelter, counting on the fact that the owner (of the load) is present, and because he is counting on the owner he has no responsibility other than to deliver unopened bundles. He would maintain a different level of security if, as they do in the rest of the world, the property were formally signed over to his care, but leaving aside these two quite considerable risks, I am going to present the inconveniences (borne by) a passenger who travels by mule train.]

Here the owner of the mule train does not open and inspect the bundles, which he would do, as is done everywhere else, if the goods were formally assigned to his care. Although transporting goods by mule train is risky, it would be even riskier for owners to turn over their goods to the transporters, since the loads contain undeclared merchandise.

This interpretation is indirectly supported by historical evidence. In 1773, the year in which Carrió finished his inspection itinerary, Viceroy Amat issued new laws aimed at reforming operations at the customs houses and the collection of different taxes on goods and services. Merchants reacted with alarm at the publication and enforcement of these laws. The repeal of royal privileges that had been granted to businessmen in Lima angered the merchants' guild; they were especially piqued by a law that required merchants to open their bundles or cases while declaring their goods and paying their taxes (Lohmann Villena 1976, 250–51 n. 292).

Traveling Blind: The Iconology of Ignorance and Error

The semantic variegation exemplified by *blindness* in Carrió's exposé cannot be duly appreciated until we grasp the many semantic layers of *traveling*, beyond what is set down in the Introduction herein regarding genre and audience. Travelers, in Carrió's *Guide for Blind Travelers/ Traders,* are not only traders, muleteers, and foreign explorers; they are also travelers on the road of life. I focus first on two well-known and related symbols, or emblems, from the renaissance that connected travel and blindness: *Error* and *Ignorance.*

According to Cesare Ripa, *Ignorance* (*IGNORANZA*) was to be represented in the following manner:

Woman with a flabby face, deformed and blind, on her head she will have a garland of poppy, walking barefooted in a field full of brambles and limestones, off the road, dressed lavishly in gold and gems, and flying next to her there will be a bat or a noctule [a brown bat native to Europe].

The mere lack of knowledge is not represented by this figure here, but rather the vice of Ignorance, which is borne of the contempt for knowledge of those things that man is supposed to learn; and that is why she is depicted as barefooted, she walks freely off the road and among thorns; she is made without eyes because ignorance is a stupor and a blindness of the mind in which man forms an opinion of himself and he believes himself to be that which he is not, in everything, or perhaps because of the many difficulties that the ignorant man, straying from the straight path of virtue due to the faulty perceptions of his intellect, encounters in life.

The bat or the noctule is depicted close to her because, as Pierio Valeriano says in book 25, wisdom is similar to light and Ignorance to darkness, from which the noctule never emerges.

. . . Pompous dress is the trophy of Ignorance, and many labor to dress well, perhaps because underneath the beautiful habits of the body one has buried as best one can the stinking smell of ignorance of the soul. (1669, 270)

Note that Carrió's description of the senior spokesman for the *peruleros* at the Guatemalan trial of wits and the moral and legal censure of lavish dress in Peru that preceded Carrió's exposé are linked to blindness and travel in *El lazarillo de ciegos caminantes* just as Ripa joined them together in his depiction of *Ignorance*.

Another of Ripa's icons was called *Ignorance of All Things* (*Ignoranza di tutte le cose*). He described it as follows: "The ancient Egyptians, to represent one who was ignorant of all things, used to make an image with the head of an ass that was looking down at the ground, because the eye of ignorant people—who in their love for themselves and their own things are far more indulgent than others, like this animal loves its own more tenderly than do others, as Piero Valeriano says, in bk. 2, ch. 35—is never raised to the sun of virtue" (1669, 271). Carrió's allusions to Amat as the "Great Lord" of the mules, or an ass, resonate fully when we keep this icon in mind.

For Carrió, the blind traveler was a trope for the rookie (or ignorant) journeyman, trader, or other traveler of the posts (*caminante bisoño*), who was like a babe in the woods, or a child riding the posts. Still another of Ripa's icons of *Ignorance*, one that is similar to the previous in its intellectual and moral entailments and in its symbol, reads as follows:

Ignorance depicted by the Greeks, as Tomaso Garzoni says: a nude boy riding an ass, he has his eyes blindfolded and he has a cane in his hand. He is depicted as a boy and nude to show that the ignorant person is simple and of a childish mind and devoid of all good. He mounts an ass because this animal is deprived of reason, indocile and very similar to him, as it pleases Pierio Valeriano, in bk. 12 of his *Hieroglyphs*. The blindfold that covers his eyes denotes that he is completely blind in his intellect and he does not know what he is doing, and that is why Isidore [of Seville], *Soliloquiorum,* bk. 2, ch. 17, says, "Summa miseria est nescire quo tendas." (1669, 271)

This representation of *Ignorance,* like many of Ripa's icons, outlived the renaissance and the baroque: we find it in France, in a collection published the very year in which Carrió left New Spain, passing through Santiago de Guatemala on his way to Lima. In Daniel de La Feuille's *Science hiéroglyphique* (*The Science of Hieroglyphics*) (Figure 13), the emblem of *Ignorance* carried the following motto: "Le siècle est éclairé, chacun le represente,/comme le siècle des sçavants./Cependant chose surprenante,/On n'a jamais tant veu d'Escrivains ignorans" (1746, 81) ("The century is enlightened, everyone depicts it/as the century of the savants/However, what a surprise,/One has never seen so many ignorant Writers"). In his explanation of his motto and symbol, he did not depart substantially from previous authorities: "The Greeks portrayed it as you see it here, with the figure of a totally nude Child, symbol of Ignorance, along with his blindfolded eyes; he is mounted on an ass and has the reins in one hand and a stick in the other" (81). La Feuille's rejection of the optimistic representations of his times and his laconic rebuke of falsely enlightened authors were consonant with Carrió's values.[10]

In his *Iconologia,* Ripa represented *Error* (*Errore*) (Figure 14) in a way that again compels us to recognize Carrió's connections to emblematic literature and the visual culture of the renaissance:

A man basically wearing traveler's clothes, who has his eyes blindfolded and pokes with a walking stick, groping about, in the act of looking for the way by inching himself along, and this almost always comes with Ignorance. Error, according to the Stoics, is straying from the road, or deviating from the line, just as not erring is walking straight ahead without drifting to one side or the other, so that all works of our body or mind constitute, one could say, a journey or pilgrimage at the end of which, if we do not stray, we expect to arrive at happiness. (1669, 180)

Error, as symbolized in the blind traveler, had both epistemological and moral contours, although almanacs and guides for foreigners that employed the term blind traveler/trader appealed almost exclusively to their readers' thirst for knowledge. Stoic philosophy was not Ripa's only inspiration for representing *Error;* he ultimately derived his symbol from the Christian Bible:

This, Christ Our Lord showed us, whose actions were all for our instruction, when he appeared to his Disciples in pilgrim's clothes, and God in the Leviticus commanding the people of Israel not to stray to one side or the other on their journey. For this reason *Error* should be depicted in pilgrim's clothes, or rather in traveler's clothes, for error cannot occur without the course of our actions or thoughts, as it has been stated. (1669, 180)

Thereafter Ripa detailed the iconological values of the traveler's blindfolded eyes and walking cane:

> The blindfolded eyes signify that one readily falls into errors when the light of one's intellect is darkened by the veil of worldly pursuits.
> The walking stick with which he is looking for the street is put there to represent sense, like eye represents intellect, since just as the former is more corporeal, so the act of the latter is less sensitive and more spiritual, and, in short, it is indicated that the person who proceeds by way of sense can easily err at every turn, without the discourse of the intellect and without the true reason for wanting something, all of which (and more clearly) is shown by *Ignorance,* which is depicted nearby. (1669, 180)

Baltasar de Gracián's own Catholicized stoicism in *El criticón* approximated his representation of Error as traveling blind to Ripa's iconic scheme (1967, 559), but the emblem closest in spirit to Ripa's—or the most derivative—was La Feuille's. The Enlightenment iconographer's *Erreur* (Figure 15, no. 1) carried the following motto: "On doit mettre tout en usage,/Pour s'éclairer, mais par malheur,/On aime à voir ses yeux tout couverts d'un nuage;/Nous nous plaisons dans nostre Erreur" (1746, 107) ("One should put everything to use/In order to enlighten oneself, but unfortunately,/One loves to see one's eyes completely covered by a cloud;/We revel in our Error"). His explanation too tracked the Italian humanist's: "This Man who goes groping about, his eyes blindfolded and a walking stick in his hand, is a symbol of Error. The Stoics defined it as a straying from the road, just as, to the contrary, to stay the course without wavering in the slightest is what is called to go straight and not look around" (108).

The figurative contours of blindness, as we have seen in the iconographic and emblematic literature, were not limited to mere ignorance of facts; they included moral error, or waywardness—the blind traveler should have the will, according to Christianity, to choose the right path when it is shown to him or her. One of Carrió's contemporaries in Lima, the salty Friar Castillo, even rendered into Spanish verse Cicero's famous "O tempora! O mores!" to drive home this point with residents of Lima.[11] This understanding of blindness—blindness as moral corruption, not mere ignorance of facts, on the road of life—leads us to the convergence of blindness and government in *El lazarillo de ciegos caminantes.*

Mercury versus Argos: Blindness and Government in Lima

It has already been established that Carrió was an avid reader of newspapers (*mercurios* and *gacetas*). He was familiar with their language and their riddles, and he was well aware that newspapers (like Mercury himself) transformed events and shaped public opinion and taste. However, Mercury is present in *El lazarillo de ciegos caminantes* for multiple reasons and in different ways.

In medieval and renaissance treatises on Roman and Greek myths, Jupiter's son Mercury was portrayed as stepping on the head of Argos, the clairvoyant monster who appears in emblematic literature as the eyes of the republic.[12] Gracián was greatly influenced by mythology collections and emblematic literature, and the eyes of the republic in *El criticón* represented the king's ministers (1967, 508–600). In *El político, Don Fernando el Católico,* we read that "a prudent monarch [is a] royal Argus" (Gracián 1985, 124). Fraud, blindness, and government converged in Ferrante Pallavicino's sequel to *Il corriero svaligiato,* which circulated in eighteenth-century Lima. His message was clear: fraudulent Arguses, under the sway of Mercury, deceived their princes.[13] The judges on the high court in Lima were, of course, attorneys, and it is worth remembering that in the same sequel, lawyers were judged guilty by association with Mercury, god of learning and of thieves.[14] That Carrió was indebted to baroque authors—satirists, in particular—is a staple of scholarship on his work since Carilla's edition of *El lazarillo de ciegos caminantes;* however, as postmodern readers, we must reconnect with the culture of Carrió's time, remembering that Carrió's experiences and readings were broader than scholars have acknowledged.

Well before Gracián and Pallavicino, Stephen Batman described Mercury in *The Golden Booke of the Leaden Gods*: "Mercurie was portraicted with winges at head and feete, wearing an Hat of white & blacke colloures: A Fawlchon by his side, in one hande a Scepter & in the other a Pype, on the one side stode a Cocke and a Ramme, and close by his side a Fylcher or Cutpurse and headless Argus" (1976, 4). Batman tied this emblem to trade, travel, and theft. He specifically mentioned merchants, the posts, and trickery and how Argus was vigilant against fraud.[15] A slightly different representation of Mercury was to appear in Richard Lynche's 1599 *The Fountaine of Ancient Fiction,* an abridgement and translation of Vicenzo Cartari's *Imagini de gli dei delli antichi* (*Images of the Gods of the Ancients*):

> It has already been spoken that Mercurie was depictured & drawn forth with two wings on the top of his eares, and also . . . two lesser infixed in his heeles, & with his white rod or wand in his hand. . . . And indeed generally of all writers hee was described in that forme: unto those feathers or wings so placed upon Mercurie (who as I have said is sometimes taken for learning and eloquence) is compared and alluded the nature of speech, discourse and

words; in that they are no sooner pronounced and delivered from the pris-
on-like mansion of the mouth, but they doe as it were flie away, and are so
sudainely vanished and departed, as if they had wings . . . to carrie them away
bouth out of sight and hearing. . . . And for this and other causes the Ancients
worshipped and adored as a god, Mercurie, unto whom also, they attribute
the first devising and finding out of Letters, Musicke and Geometrie. Hee was
taken also for the god of Trafficke & Marchandises, as that unto those kind of
professores it is fit and necessarie to have eloquence, knowledge, and subtile-
tie of wit for the better managing & handling of their deceitfull affaires. . . .
And therefore Mercurie was often taken for that light of knowledge & spirit
of understanding, which guides men to the true conceavement of darke and
enigmaticall sentences. (1976, n.p.)

Note that Mercury aided merchants who used their wits to deceive, but he
also aided men who used their wits to solve riddles, or cryptic messages, as Carrió
asks his readers to do.

Finally, we should remember that Natale Conti explained in his *Mythology*
that interlocutors in Lucian of Samosata's *Dialogues of the Dead* described Mercury
as "a prodigious thief" (1976, n.p.), not unlike the "prodigious 4Ps from Lima" in
Carrió's Menippean exposé.

A playful, conniving Mercury became a courtier on Lima's stage, thanks to
Peralta Barnuevo's satirical operetta, *El Mercurio galante* (*The Gallant Mercury*)[16]
However, other workings of Mercury were necessary to government and society.
"The opulence of trade and the cultivation of letters," Peralta Barnuevo explained,
"are the two poles of a government's sphere, and an intellectual acuity [*agudeza*],
divided into two perspicacities, must rule over both. One makes the state rich,
and the other makes it wise" (1736, ff. 175–76). Mercury could influence government and society in still another way: he was, as Lucian had shown, the perfect
partner in satire. In his defense of Archbishop and Viceroy Pedro Morcillo Rubio
Auñón, *El templo de la Fama vindicado*, Peralta Barnuevo included a lengthy *proso-
popeia* in which the gods of Mt. Olympus judge the author who wrote a satire of
the viceroy's abbreviated first reign. Mercury instructed the unnamed author in
the true art of satire:

Satire, a true and lawful lady, is a graceful enemy of vices and a severe lover
of men. She is a shot of light-in-disguise that wounds and heals with clarity
because she does not roast with the fire of insult. She is the sword of truth
wielded with the skill that prudence teaches, to point out [defects], but not to
slash one's dignity. She is rigor dressed up as wit. Reason's postboy that brings
news of error's invasions. A judge who, the less she reveals about the culprits,
the better she punishes the crimes. A sniper who, the less she aims, the more
she hits, and who hits the target without looking because she never identifies

it. She is only useful when everybody receives her and she addresses herself to no one. (in Williams 1996, 126)

There are striking parallels between Mercury's explication of satire here and Carrió's account. The metaphors for satire— "a shot of light-in-disguise," "rigor dressed up as wit" and "reason's postboy"—voiced by Peralta Barnuevo's Mercury are not at odds with the intentions, topic, and methodology of *El lazarillo de ciegos caminantes*. Furthermore, Carrió's exposé respects the "do not name names" policy of Mercury here: Concolorcorvo claims that the inspector has instructed him not to reveal the names of officials who are violating Crown law.[17]

As a merchant, Carrió knew the tricks of his trade, and as an avid reader he was familiar with classical mythology: the numerous allusions to Greek and Roman gods, and to Virgil and Ovid, leave no doubt that he knew of Mercury's purported influence on trade, theft, witty discourse, and travel. Moreover, the role of Mercury in classical Menippean satire, combined with Peralta Barnuevo's appropriation of Mercury, made the volatile and witty Mercury a hidden icon of the dialogues and mock trial of Carrió's inspection report. Like quicksilver, which was commonly called mercury, Carrió transformed himself into the inspector and secretary who deliver his harsh truths wrapped in tomfoolery and a slippery riddle.[18]

The name of Mercury's father, Jupiter, was a common epithet for a monarch or a viceroy. In his *Júpiter Olímpico* (*Olympic Jupiter*), Peralta Barnuevo explained, "Astrology celebrates that God as a planet, as the greatest fortune for human influence, and Peru venerates our prince as the greatest felicity for the government of these kingdoms" (2001). He portrayed Viceroy and Archbishop Morcillo Rubio as "the copy of the Jupiter of Spain," the Bourbon Philip V (in Williams 2001, 48). Later, Viceroy José Antonio de Mendoza was "a Christian Jupiter," or a "Simulacrum of the Hispanic Jupiter" (1736, ff. 149, 150). In his exposé, Carrió does not offer his readers in eighteenth-century Spain and Spanish America an explicit identification between Viceroy Amat and Mercury's father, Jupiter.[19] Instead, he describes Jupiter in terms that insinuate Amat's conflict of interests: "Juno y Venus, rivales desde la decisión del pastor de Ida, siguen opuesto partido, procurando cada una traer al suyo al altisonante Júpiter que, como riguroso republicano, apetece la neutralidad; pero deseando complacer a las dos coquetas, arroja rayos ya a la derecha, ya a la izquierda, en la fuerza del combate, para que quede indecisa la victoria" (125) ("Juno and Venus, rivals ever since the pastor of Ide's decision [the judgment of Paris], take opposite sides, each trying to bring over to her side the booming Jupiter, who, being the strict statesman that he is, prefers neutrality; however, wishing to please both coquettes, he sends out lightning strikes to the left and to the right, in the heat of battle, so that victory will remain uncertain").[20] Carrió's Jupiter is torn between love and war, just as General and Viceroy

Amat in Lima was torn between love (of money and of women) and war (against foreign enemies and sexual rivals).

This inner conflict was, paradoxically, public knowledge. The anonymous *Drama de los palanganas Veterano y Bisoño* explicitly addressed many of General Amat's moral failings. Veterano and Bisoño were the two characters in this "drama de los caminantes Trujillano y Limeños" (1938, 327) ("drama of the travelers [or merchants], *Trujillano* and *Limeños*"). *Trujillano* represented one of Carrió's harshest critics, Miguel Feijoo de Sosa, former governor of Trujillo, Peru.[21] *Limeños* were the royal officials in Lima who, like their counterparts in the first half of the eighteenth century, were stealing the Crown blind. After accusing the viceroy of malfeasance and smuggling, Veterano drew from the Book of Isaiah to place Amat in his proper genus: "Traitorous Princes, companions of Thieves" (103). The venerable truth teller excoriated Amat's ministers who were struck by "glaucoma," or had their moral compass clouded by Mercury, this time turning to Ecclesiastes: "then come the renumerations, those renumerations that are bouts of glaucoma, rather than Cataracts, which harden and thicken the liquid (this simile is put in the language of Optics), neither the liquid between the cornea and the lens, nor the liquid behind the lens but, rather, the glacial liquid or liquid that covers the lens of the eyes of Ministers according to that short and sharp saying found in *Eccles[iastes]*, ch. 20, 'presents and offerings blind the eyes of Judges'" (103). Notwithstanding such underground attacks, Viceroy Amat did not admit his failings or those of the men whom he supervised. To the contrary, he ensured his commercial dominance in the same way that he preserved his sexual dominance—by eliminating his rivals.

In a secret report that he wrote to Charles III in 1762, Viceroy Amat claimed that even before he arrived in Lima he knew who controlled the high court and commerce there, because it was "notorious" throughout the Viceroyalty of Peru. In Chile, he wrote, "I knew . . . everything that was happening in this capital [of Lima], and that ministers were the accomplices and agents in the negotiations and sales of government posts." General Amat substantiated charges against senior judge Pedro Bravo del Ribero (among them, that he and another judge robbed the royal estate court of 120,000 pesos) that were to force him out of office for several years. Certain judges in Lima "abandoned themselves to their whims and their own interests," were "banded together and unified with such scandal that the senior judge [Bravo del Ribero] is the only voice in which the majority speak." Incompetent judges could be moved to another court, Amat advised, but Bravo del Ribero and his cronies, "individuals who are the first ones . . . to promote the very things that they should prevent," had to be removed from office (1942, 347–48). As we saw in my allegorical interpretation of the second solution to the 4Ps from Lima riddle, Carrió knew very well what Bravo del Ribero, who had interrogated him and other *corregidores* in the districts surrounding Cuzco in the early 1750s, was doing in the 1760s and 1770s.[22] Unlike the viceroy, however, Carrió condemned corrupt ministers in general, instead of restricting his attacks to those who were competing with him for ill-gotten gains.

Blindness in *El lazarillo de ciegos caminantes* is a metaphor for the unbridled influence of sexual and material goods and gains on ministers—from viceroys and jurists to postal workers and treasurers—who placed private interest above public interest to a degree that undermined Crown authority and the *Monarquía* as a whole. In brief, Mercury was defeating Argus.

Blindspots and Storytellers: Myth, Travel, and History

Carrió's exposé has numerous epistemological sites where rationalism and empiricism do battle and where he suggests that ostensibly enlightened types cannot be trusted to make decisions or policies about anything that they have not seen firsthand. In his *Diccionario,* San Joseph Giral del Pino defined a proverbial expression: "*El ciego no distingue de colores,* the blind cannot distinguish colours; that is, an ignorant person cannot be a proper judge to distinguish anything" (1763, n.p.). Blindness as an epistemological quandary or quagmire is always tied to a lack of experience and/or judgment in *El lazarillo de ciegos caminantes.* Carrió makes explicit and implicit reference to previous histories, poems, travelogues, newspaper stories, and critical essays about the New World empires of New Spain and Peru, their place within Spain as a *Monarquía,* and the vices and virtues of the Spanish people (*Nación*). As recent studies have ably demonstrated, his goal was to amend and, in some instances, discredit entirely previous discourses (Stolley 1993; Klien Samanez 2000; Meléndez 1999).

Carrió's thirty-five years of experience in New Spain and Peru invested him with confidence and skepticism: he was certain that he knew Spanish America better than European Spaniards and most American Spaniards who had written about it; he was also wary of the continued efforts to reform policy in Spanish America that were rooted in rationalism more often than empiricism, in theory more often than experience. We have already seen that Carrió was no admirer of Benito Jerónimo Feijoo y Montenegro, who enjoyed the royal protection of Ferdinand VI. The famed cultural critic's *Españoles americanos* was one of several essays that Carrió mocked in his exposé. Carrió found it exasperatingly ironic that a man so self-abrogatingly empiricist and rationalist—a man identified, at home and abroad, with the Spanish Bourbons and their political and cultural program for modernizing Spain and their New World Empires—could get it so wrong so often. After dispensing with the popular myth that *criollos* became mentally impaired in middle age, Feijoo y Montenegro wrote of his ardent faith in the human intellect, or "lights," which theoretically should be enough to keep us from making mistakes:

There are always the brightest of lights to undeceive men of a thousand inveterate errors; all that is missing is the reflection to make use of them. Prejudice throws I-do-not-know-what-clouds over the eyes of the intellect so that it cannot see, no matter how close it is, undeception. Doubtless it is sometimes a mere lack of occurrence of the object or information that would offer evidence of the truth. However, experience has shown me that a faulty intellectual disposition rules in most men, because of which common opinions are like a veil that hides the most evident truths from them (1944, 15).

Just as Charles Montesquieu had suggested, in his *Lettres Persanes*, that moderns had become their own gods, working miracles from their throne of Reason (1986, *Lettre* 97), so Carrió rebuked the self-styled experts on Spanish America who had been hoodwinked by travelers:

Así como los *monsiures* se jactan del honor de su idioma, por ser el que más se extendió en este siglo en toda la Europa y se escribieron en él tantas obras excelentes, deben tolerar la crítica y agravio que hacen a los españoles los viajeros que en su idioma pretenden denigrar a unos vecinos tan inmediatos como los españoles, que no hacen memoria de ellos sino para el elogio y que [los] reciben en sus países sin repugnancia, y muchas veces con una condescendencia más que común; pero estos *monsiures,* o sean *milords* o ilustrísimos a la francesa, inglesa o italiana, sólo piensan en abatir a los españoles, publicando primeramente en sus brochuras, que pasan después a sus historias generales, ignorancias y defectos que quasi hacen creer a los españoles poco advertidos, y dar motivo a los sabios a un concepto injusto por falta de práctica de los ingenios americanos, que aquéllos generalmente están reducidos a sus libros y particulares meditaciones. (349–50)

[Just as the *mon-sewers* brag about the dignity of their language because it is the one that has spread the most throughout Europe in this century and so many excellent works have been written in it, it is only right that they tolerate the criticism and insulting of Spaniards by travelers who in their language intend to smear a group of neighbors so close to them as the Spanish, who do not write of them but in praise and who welcome them in their homelands without disgust and often with uncommon deference. But these *mon-sewers,* or *milords,* or *most illustriouses,* à la France, England or Italy, only think about ways to put Spaniards down, publishing first in their brochures and later in their general histories, ignorant statements and errors that could almost make people believe that Spaniards are a little slow and give savants the wrong idea about American minds, due to their lack of experience with them, since savants are for the most part confined to their books and particular studies.]

Among these "savants" who had been misled was Feijoo y Montenegro, who condemned the Spanish Conquest and even claimed that Spaniards had become the "Indians" of Europe as a result of the conquistadors' abuses of the indigenous population in the New World (Hill 1998). My sense is that his energetic condemnation, or "declamation," as he labeled it, and his gushing over José Pardo de Figueroa and Peralta Barnuevo were enough to convince Carrió that the Spanish critic, like many of his brethren outside of Spain, needed schooling in New World reality.

The epigraphs that open and close Carrió's account signal his debts to Menippean satire in which Mercury often played the leading role.[23] The first appears after the prologue and at the head of his description of Montevideo: "Canendo et ludendo refero vera" (123). The second appears at the very end of his account: "Canendo et ludendo retuli vera" (473). Both of these evince the mercurial spirit of wit, travel, song, and theft that imbues the narration, and both suggest more than they say. Immediately after introducing his readers into the natural history of the realm and having given us a sketch of the Spanish character vis-à-vis that of other Europeans, the narrator begins his account with an exordium. The exordium is headed by the epigraph *Canendo et ludendo refero vera,* which prepares readers to accept the form and content of Carrió's skepticism toward the existing histories of Spain, New Spain, and Peru. The first sentence of the exordium is written in the conditional mood: "Si fuera cierta la opinión común, o llámese vulgar, que viajero y embustero son sinónimos, se debía preferir la lectura de la fábula a la de la historia" (123) ("Were the common, or let us call it *vulgar,* opinion true that traveler and storyteller are synonymous, one should prefer the reading of myth to that of history"). It suggests that the mob (*el vulgo*) sees traveler and scamp as synonymous and the relationship between travelers and historiography as one of cause and effect. Were this true, he writes, the reading of myth should be preferred to the reading of history. This sentence in the conditional mood and the preceding epigraph together hint that Carrió is going to take a different route: that of using experience to substantiate or to discredit his reasoning.

Carrió's skepticism toward historians is truly a condemnation of the poor judgment and self-interest exhibited by some historians rather than a Pyrrhonist assault on historiography. The narrator acknowledges that the medieval *General Istoria (General History)* of Spain, commissioned by Alphonso the Wise, was written largely from travelers' accounts, the veracity of which has been debated: "No se puede dudar, con razón, que la general extractó su principal fondo de los viajeros, y que algunas particulares se han escrito sobre la fe de sus relaciones" (123) ("One cannot doubt, and rightfully so, that the *General [History]* extracted its main substance from travelers, and that some individual histories have been written about the fidelity of their accounts"). Carrió claims that Spanish historiography and indigenous historiography, notwithstanding differences in age or media, are equally susceptible to corruption:

Las cifras de los peruleros, en quipus, o nudos de varios colores, los jeroglíficos o pinturas de los mexicanos, la tradición de unos y otros, vertida en cuentos y cantares y otros monumentos, corresponden (acaso con más pureza) a nuestros roídos pergaminos, carcomidos papeles, inscripciones sepulcrales, pirámides, estatuas, medallas y monedas, que por su antigüedad no merecen más crédito, porque así como no estorban las barbas para llorar, no impiden las canas para mentir. Con estos aparatos y otros casi infinitos se escribieron todas las historias antiguas y modernas. (124)[24]

[The codes of the Peruvians in their quipus, or knots of various colors, the hieroglyphics, or paintings, of the Mexicans, the tradition of the former and the latter, expressed in stories and songs and other monuments, correspond (perhaps more purely) to our worn parchments, worm-eaten papers, tomb inscriptions, pyramids, statues, medallions and coins, which are not worthier of belief because of their antiquity, for just as whiskers will not keep you from crying, grey hairs will not keep you from lying. With these instruments and others nearly infinite, all ancient and modern histories were written.]

Advanced age ("las canas") is not always wisdom, and it does not guarantee the fidelity of historians. In other words, ancient authority is no greater than modern authority. At the same time, modern authority was not, due to its modernity, greater than ancient authority. Unlike Guillaume-Thomas Raynal, for example, Carrió did not dismiss quipus because they did not employ a European writing system.[25]

It has already been established that in the eighteenth century almanacs that were not authored by astrologers often attributed their authors' predictions to astrologers and that on the very title page these astrologers were frequently described as blind seers (see the Introduction herein). This resonated with Carrió, who writes that ancient histories are categorized as myths ("fábulas"), whereas modern histories are compared to astrological predictions: "Los eruditos ponen las primeras en la clase de las fábulas, y a las segundas las comparan a las predicciones de los astrólogos, con la diferencia de que éstos, como conferencian con los dioses, anuncian lo futuro, y aquéllos, no pudiendo consultar más que con los mortales, sólo hacen presentes los sucesos pasados" (124) ("The erudite place the first in the class of myths, and the second they compare to the predictions of astrologers, the only difference being that the latter, since they conference with the gods, announce the future, and the former [i.e., modern historians], able to consult only mortals, merely make present past events"). Here one could argue that it is impossible to say if the joke was on astrologers and almanac authors or on the supposedly enlightened critics of historiography. I would suggest that the joke was on both sets of "erudites": the lowbrow and the highbrow authors.

On one hand, many almanacs were useless, in Carrió's view, and although he chose a title that was already being used by the authors of almanacs in Spain and Spanish America, the veteran bureaucrat did not intend his report to be used merely for "joy reading." On the other hand, I am convinced that Carrió was wielding his irony against Feijoo y Montenegro and the French authors who filled his essay titled *Reflexiones sobre la historia* ("Reflections on Historiography").[26] There Feijoo y Montenegro devoted several pages to modern French historians and their respective accounts of a French mathematician's astrological prediction of Henry IV's death (1773–1774, 4:179–81).[27] Later in Carrió's exposé, we read a facetiously skeptical embrace of the uncertainty of historiography and the superiority of myth: "Supuesta, pues, la incertidumbre de la historia, vuelvo a decir, se debe preferir la lectura y estudio de la fábula, porque siendo ella parto de una imaginación libre y desembarazada, instruye y deleita más" (124) ("Given, then, the uncertainty of history, I repeat, one should prefer the reading and study of myth, because it instructs and pleases more, being that it is the child of a free and unrestrained imagination"). In *Reflexiones sobre la historia,* Feijoo y Montenegro translated and abridged the marquis de San Aubin's "so pleasant and curious" discourse "about the uncertainty of History" (1773–1774, 4:220–41 n. 2).[28] Carrió parodies Feijoo y Montenegro to poke fun at his critical method and authorities. Carrió did not sincerely hold that myth was superior to, or should be substituted for, history, because he had not given up on historiography as many Enlightenment critics had under the pressures of empiricism and Cartesian rationalism (Hill 1994b, chap. 1; 2000b, *passim*).

Although some medieval mythmakers told some tall tales, not all historians were flatterers and liars, we read in the exordium to Carrió's exposé: "Sin embargo de los prodigios que cuentan los fabulistas, vemos que en todas edades y naciones se han aplicado a la historia los hombres más sabios. No se duda que algunos han sido notados de lisonjeros, y aun de venales, pero no faltaron otros tan ingenuos que no perdonaron a sus parientes y amigos, haciendo manifiestos sus defectos y publicando las buenas prendas de sus más acérrimos enemigos" (126) ("In spite of the marvels that mythmakers tell, we observe that in all ages and countries the wisest of men have applied themselves to history. One cannot deny that some have been vilified as flatterers, and even mercenaries, but there were others so honest that they did not spare their relatives and friends, making public their faults, and advertising the good qualities of their fiercest enemies"). Immediately thereafter, the inspector suggests that we all fall back on the alleged uncertainty of history when we wish to dismiss certain truths about ourselves: "Todos concurrimos a la incertidumbre de la historia, porque no hay quien no lea con gusto los aplausos que se hacen a su nación y que no vitupere al que habla de ella con desprecio o con indiferencia. En toda la Europa tiene gran crédito nuestro historiador Mariana por su exactitud e ingenuidad, y con todo eso, muchos de los nuestros le tienen por sospechoso, y desafecto a la nación" (127) ("We all go in for the uncertainty of history, because there is no one who can read without pleasure the praises that are sung of his people and no one who cannot vituperate someone who speaks of his people with disrespect or indifference. Throughout Europe, our historian Mariana has a great reputation for accuracy and honesty, and many of our own nonetheless view him as suspect and ill-disposed toward the Spanish people").[29]

In both *Divorcio de la Historia y de la Fábula* ("The Divorce of History and Myth") and *Fábulas de las Batuecas y países imaginarios* ("Myths about Batuecas and Imaginary Lands") (in *Teatro crítico* 1773–1774, 4:270–88), Feijoo y Montenegro pretended to delineate the frontier that separated fact from fiction. In the second of these essays, in order "to give greater length and amenity to this discourse," Feijoo y Montenegro added sections that treat myths of the riches of China, the Philippines, and Spanish America (Souza Penha 1978, 89–90; Hill 1998). The longest of these sections deals with St. Borondon Island (Isla de San Borondón), which he dismisses as "a mere illusion" (275). In the exordium to *El lazarillo de ciegos caminantes*, Carrió reports that he pulled aside the "salty" boatswain (*contramaestre*) of the mail ferry in which he was sailing from the Canary Islands to Montevideo in 1771 and asked him under solemn oath what he knew about St. Borondon. The witty boatswain replied "que no había visto el nombre de tal santo en el calendario español, ni conocía isleño alguno con tal nombre, ni tampoco a ninguno de los extranjeros con quienes había navegado, y que, desde luego, se persuadía que aquel nombre era una borondanga, o morondanga" (129) ("that he had not seen the name of such a saint in the Spanish calendar nor did he know a single isle by that name or any of the foreigners with whom he had traveled by that name, and so naturally he was convinced that that name was a *boron's tale* or a *moron's tale*"). Carrió included his trip from the Canary Islands to Montevideo in his inspection report in order to parody both travel literature and Feijoo y Montenegro's essay in which such myths appeared. To dispel the myth of San Borondon, Carrió implied, did not require a prolonged spell of critical thinking, a sheaf of authorities ancient and modern, and dozens of folios: common sense dictated that one ask an experienced and trustworthy seaman and then go from there.

In a passage from the prologue, we find a comparison that links *lazarillos* and blindmen to travelers and historians: "Los viajeros (aquí entro yo), respecto de los historiadores, son lo mismo que los lazarillos, en comparación de los ciegos. Éstos solicitan siempre unos hábiles zagales para que dirijan sus pasos y les den aquellas noticias precisas para componer sus canciones, con que deleitan al público y aseguran su subsistencia. Aquéllos, como de superior orden, recogen las memorias de los viajeros más distinguidos en la veracidad y talento" (127) ("Travelers [here is where I come in], in relation to historians, are the same as guides in relation to blindmen. The latter always seek out some skilled lads to direct their movements and give them all the information necessary to write their songs, with which they delight the public and guarantee their own survival. The former, belonging to a higher category, assemble reports from the travelers best known for their veracity and skill").[30] This passage does not refer to discursive realities alone. Blindmen, in the popular imaginary and in literature, were resourceful, dishonest, even greedy.[31] They hawked gazettes, magazines, almanacs, newsletters, and oral stories in verse or prose. Sebastián de Covarrubias's definition of *carta* ("letter") included the following variant: "*Carta-nova,* in the Valencian tongue, [means] the couplets or reports in prose of some new and important happening, which blindmen, charlatans and mountebanks sell in streets and squares" (1943, 312).[32] Throughout Spain, blindmen distributed sheets containing stories and news in prose or verse (*romance de ciegos*), or they recited them aloud for money like panhandlers.

A cultural practice that had originated in a social policy of charity was something quite different in the renaissance. Félix Lope de Vega complained that not only were blindmen reciting their verses in the streets and squares but also respectable people (including royal officials) were using them as agents or spokespersons in order to profit from their lies:

> It was an ancient remedy, and permitted [by law], for blindmen to learn songs and recite them door-to-door . . . so that they could make a living and feed themselves, taking this road to beg for alms . . . , but their being towncriers of lies and treacherous defamers of our people is a new invention of certain men who use [blindmen] as well as ministers and civil servants to make a living, while being themselves rich and holding posts in the republic, and even in the royal palace, from which they deserve to be removed. (qtd. in Marco 1977, 1:57)

In Miguel de Cervantes's *Don Quijote,* one of Sancho Panza's measures as governor was taken against blindmen: "He decreed that no blindman could sing a miracle in couplets if he did not carry sworn testimony that it was true, because he felt that most of the ones that blindmen sing are made up in detriment to the true ones" (1983, 2:441). Many times blindmen were authors of their poems and stories; other times they were agents for the true authors, just as Lope de Vega had complained (Marco 1977, 1:119). Several decades after Cervantes, in *Oráculo manual y arte de prudencia,* Gracián made it clear that blindmen took advantage of ignorant people. His advice titled "Open Your Eyes before It Is Too Late" (*Abrir los ojos con tiempo*) reads in part, "It is hard to give understanding (*entendimiento*) to someone who has no will (*voluntad*), and even more so to give will to someone who has no understanding; those who rove around them, like blindmen, toy with them to the delight of others" (1984, 212).

Spanish comedy from the same period abounds in references to the ingeniousness of *ciegos.*[33] According to playwright Alonso Jerónimo de Salas Barbadillo, women of ill repute paid blindmen to utter prayers for the souls in purgatory. Among scamps, blindmen were in a league of their own: "The other republic is that of the blind reciters and singers of couplets; this one I call the unilluminated [republic], because they are deprived of corporeal sight, as they say, and thereby [deprived] of the enjoyment of this most beautiful planet, the source of light, and because of the serious *disenlightenments* and errors that they utter in their couplets." These blindmen "have greater power than an eclipse, for when they want there to be a pestilence in the kingdom of Persia, they make it up, and we really ought to be grateful that they do their killing far from us and do not wish to include us even in that plot" (1911, 256).

In contesting the historiographical record on the relationship between Spanish governor (*corregidor*) and plebeian Indian,[34] Carrió implicitly reiterated the relationship between travelers and blind rovers by characterizing the former as *charlatanes*. The authors of travelogues, we read, are no better than blind minstrels in search of a story that will sell:

> Muchos ejemplares podía traer de estas providencias, dadas por algunos prudentes corregidores, pero las omito por no hacer dilatado este diario, que ya me tiene fastidiado, por lo que paso a defender a los buenos españoles de las injurias que publican los extranjeros de sus tiranías con los indios, en que convienen muchos de los nuestros por ignorancia, falta de práctica y conocimiento del reino. Para su clara inteligencia dividiré las acusaciones, sin otro fin que el de esclarecer a los españoles poco ilustrados en estas materias, y no den tanto crédito a los charlatanes extranjeros, y en particular a ciertos viajeros, que para hacer apacibles sus diarios andan a caza de extravagancias, fábulas y cuentos, que algunos españoles les inspiran para ridiculizar sus memorias entre los hombres serios. (343)

> [I could provide many copies of these measures issued by some prudent governors, but I choose to omit them because I do not want to drag out this itinerary, which is already annoying me, for which reason I now turn to defending the good Spaniards from the outrages that foreigners publish about their alleged abuses of the Indians, with which many of our own people are in agreement due to their ignorance, lack of experience and (lack of) knowledge of the kingdom. For clarity's sake I shall address the accusations by groups, with no other purpose than to illuminate those Spaniards who are poorly lit in these subjects and (teach them) not to give so much credence to foreign charlatans, and to certain travelers in particular who are always on the hunt for myths, tales and the bizarre to make their diaries more pleasing to read, with which some Spaniards provide them so as to render those reports absurd to serious people.]

Carrió probably was attacking the credulity and the credibility of scientists such as the Minim Father Louis Feuillée, whose *Journal des Observations Physiques, Mathematiques et Botaniques* included a bizarre depiction of a hybrid monster born in Buenos Aires (Figure 16) (1714–1725, 1:242–43). Works such as Feuillée's were read by Feijoo y Montenegro and other icons of Spanish modernity whom Carrió considered "poorly lit."

In sum, Carrió drew explicit or implicit comparisons between travelers and *lazarillos;* incredulous historians and blindmen; disingenuous historians and disingenuous foreigners; ostensibly enlightened Spaniards and blindmen; authors of travelogues and blindmen. Beyond the question of truth in historiographical discourse, and beyond the role that travelers' reports played in the construction of the historiographical record during the Enlightenment, Carrió's comparisons embedded a moral equation in epistemology. It was an equation popular in Hispanic societies from the sixteenth through eighteenth centuries: blind rovers are not men whose disability leads them into error and ignorance; they are *charlatanes* and *infames,* notorious storytellers and story sellers.

Blindness, Silence, and the Paradox of Clairvoyance

It is rather curious that both Concolorcorvo and the inspector use the term *clairvoyant* to describe Crown officials from the first and second halves of the eighteenth century. What did this term mean, and how is it linked to Carrió's silences, voiced alternately by the secretary and the inspector? The easy answer is that the popularity of the occult, as a result of French influence, as well as the wealth of astrologers in Spain and Peru, made his use of "clairvoyant" corrosively parodic. From this angle, it was a slap in the face to Francophile elites in Bourbon Peru and New Spain that assumed they were just as delirious as the people whom they assailed or patronized in their quest for modernity at all costs. The image that Montesquieu drew of the critics who live in the dream of Reason again comes to mind. However, the frequent appearance of *clairvoyant* in *El lazarillo de ciegos caminantes* has criminal undertones in addition to those Menippean and antirationalist intertexts.

Before leaving for Huamanga, the inspector tells Concolorcorvo to say a discreet goodbye to the administrator of the posts in Cuzco. The Inca secretary creates a grotesque image of the administrator. Then he offers insincere praise for him and for his boss, Viceroy Amat:

> Su talento no se puede comparar con el mío, porque no tengo alguno, y don Ignacio es muy clarivoyante; y, finalmente, es persona de entereza, tesón para vencer dificultades y exponerse a fatigas y pesadumbres por llevar a debido efecto las leyes y ordenanzas de la renta de correos, como se experimentó en los principios de su ingreso a la administración; ésta es la principal de las agregadas a este virreinato, porque recibe y despacha a un mismo tiempo, en sólo tres días, los correos de la ruta general de Lima a Buenos Aires, con el gravamen de las encomiendas de oro, plata y de bulto, de que se necesita mucho

cuidado, por lo que don Ignacio gana bien el sueldo de mil doscientos pesos anuales, que le señaló provisionalmente el excelentísimo señor don Manuel de Amat, actual virrey de los reinos y subdelegado de la renta de correos. Estas últimas expresiones, me dijo el visitador, libran a Vm. del lamprado, porque procedió Vm. al contrario de los cirujanos, que limpian y suavizan el casco o piel antes de aplicar la lanceta o tijera. (396–97)

[His talent cannot be compared to mine, because I do not have any, and Don Ignacio is very clairvoyant; and, in short, he is a person of integrity, tenacity for overcoming difficulties and laying himself open to hardships and grief to effectively enforce the laws and ordinances of the post's revenue, as was shown at the very beginning of his entry into the administration; this revenue is the principal among the revenues added to this viceroyalty, because it receives and dispatches at the very same time, in only three days, the correspondence of the general route from Lima to Buenos Aires, with the burden of the commissions of gold, silver and packages that require great care, for which Don Ignacio well deserves the salary of twelve hundred pesos per year that the Most Excellent Señor Manuel de Amat, current viceroy of the kingdoms and undersecretary of postal revenue, provisionally assigned him. These last expressions, the inspector told me, save you from a whipping, because you adopted a tack contrary to that of surgeons, who clean and strop the hide or skin before applying the lancet or scalpel.]

In this passage, it is the dishonest postal administrator in Cuzco whom Concolorcorvo describes as "clairvoyant." On another occasion, Concolorcorvo warns the inspector to be careful, labeling the men in Lima "clairvoyant": "No se fíe Vm. mucho Señor Don Alonso, . . . por que estos genios son muy Clarivoyantes, y espiritus muy vellacos, que no perdonan el mas leve descuydo" (1775, n.p.) ("Do not be so sure, Sir Don Alonso, . . . because these types are very clairvoyant and very feisty spirits who do not forgive the most innocent slip of the tongue"). Something else happens at the end of *El lazarillo de ciegos caminantes:* In the Guatemalan mock trial, after both delegations have accepted the terms of the *cartel,* Governor José de Araújo y Río attempts to paper over his anxiety, the inspector states, because he is more "clairvoyant"—that is, he can see what is coming: "El Señor Presidente, como mas Clarivoyante, manifestaba con una falsa risa alguna desconfianza de la Victoria de sus Compatriotas" (1775, n.p.) ("The president of the high court, since he was more clairvoyant, expressed with a forced laugh some uncertainty about the victory of his compatriots").

In all of these supposed cases of clairvoyance, the facetiousness on display conveys that these officials, who should have been the king's Arguses in order to better serve him and their fellow subjects, had their sights set on their own particular affairs—the very notion rejected by the senior spokesman from Lima at the Guatemalan mock trial. To be clairvoyant, then, was to look out for oneself at the expense of others and to turn a blind eye to the laws of Spain and the Indies in doing so, all of which brings us to a less obvious, but no less important, link between sight and hearing in Carrió's account: the emblem of the god of Silence, Harpocrates.

According to Carrió's exposé, the rural folks between Luján and Buenos Aires, like those in Tucumán, are not inclined to thievery, and in no part of the Viceroyalty of Peru has there even been an organized attack on silver shipments. Such shipments have been known to disappear, however, and just when it appears that Carrió's readers might be given an explanation, the dialogue between the inspector and the secretary is interrupted by silence:

> Verdaderamente que así esta gente campestre como la del Tucumán no es inclinada al robo, ni en todo el Perú se ha visto invasión formal a las muchas recuas de plata, así en barras como en oro, que atraviesan todo el reino con tan débil custodia que pudiera ponerla en fuga o sacrificarla un solo hombre, pues muchas veces sucede que dos arrieros solos caminan dilatadas distancias con diez cargas de plata. No conviene hablar más sobre este asunto, pero advierto a los conductores de los situados, que pasan de Potosí a Buenos Aires, tengan más cautela cuando se camina entre los espesos y dilatados montes del Tucumán. (266–67).

> [Truthfully, these country folks like those in Tucumán are not given to theft, nor in all of Peru has there been an organized attack on any of the many mule trains carrying silver, in bars or in ore, which cross the entire kingdom with such light security that one man alone could have them on the run or string them up, for it quite often happens that two muleteers by themselves travel lengthy distances with ten loads of silver. It is not a good idea to say any more on this subject, but I caution the drivers of the posts who go from Potosí to Buenos Aires to take greater care when they are traveling through the thick and numerous hills of Tucumán.]

Gold and silver traveled the same routes from Potosí to Buenos Aires as correspondence, parcels, and commercial merchandise, and the former were subject to the same dangers, natural or human-made, as the latter. Again, the interlocutors in *El lazarillo de ciegos caminantes* know much more than they are willing to say, or much more than Carrió's prudence would allow them to say.

While describing Huancavélica, Concolorcorvo expresses a desire to include a lengthy description of mining in his itinerary. The inspector tells him that such a description would be useless, and again, the dialogue is interrupted:

Muy ociosa sería, señor Concolorcorvo, esa descripción, que ya tienen hecha tantos hombres sabios. Me consta que el señor Sola presentó al Rey en plata maciza la mina de Huancavélica, con todas las obras hasta su tiempo, y cada gobernador ha dirigido a Espana y a este superior gobierno una delineación de la mina y haciendas por los sujetos que las trabajan, con los estados de aumento y disminución de leyes y sus causas. Eso no puede ser, le repliqué, porque más depende de la casualidad que del discurso humano. Está Vm. errado, me replicó, y no se hable más sobre el asunto. (418–19)

[Most useless, Mr. Concolorcorvo, would be that description, which so many learned men have already done. I am certain that Mr. Sola gave the King an introduction to the Huancavélica mine in the form of an immense chunk of silver, along with all of the activities up until his tenure, and every governor [of Huancavélica] has sent to Spain and to the viceroy of Peru a detailed breakdown of the mine and estates and the names of the individuals who work them, with the levels of increase and decrease in grades and their causes. That cannot be true, I answered him, because it depends more on chance than on human discourse. You are mistaken, he replied, and let us say no more on the subject.]

Not all of the best metals, or the highest-grade silvers, were being taken out of the mines by the *kajchas,* it seems: some of these metals were being taken out of Peru altogether. This problem was certainly not new: it had plagued the Crown during the first half of the eighteenth century, as we have seen (Chapter 3). This very human diversion of metal explains, far better than Concolorcorvo's "chance" can, the increase or drop in the production of certain grades. We should recall here some of the prescriptions for lawful satire set down by Peralta Barnuevo's Mercury, which Carrió followed: "[Satire is a] judge who, the less she reveals about the culprits, the better she punishes the crimes. A sniper who, the less she aims, the more she hits, and who hits the target without looking because she never identifies it" (1996b, 126).

Despite Concolorcorvo's penchant for amplifying his own accomplishments and those of the Incas and his incessant questioning of the inspector, his textual presence resembles well-known iconographic descriptions of Silence. In the third book of *Iconologia,* Ripa described several representations of the god Silence:

> *Silence.* A man without a face, with a little cap on his head, nude with a wolf's skin around him, and all of his body will be full of eyes and ears. . . .
> *Silence.* A young man who holds his index finger to his mouth in the act of giving the sign to be quiet, and who has a peach tree with leaves in his left hand. The peach tree was dedicated to Harpocrates, the God of Silence, because it has leaves similar to the human tongue. . . . He is portrayed

as a young man because in the young, especially, Silence is a sign of modesty & a token of virtue, following the custom of the Ancients, who painted Harpocrates as a young man with wings, and with his face a black color, because Silence is a friend of the night, as Poets say. (1669, 569)

In his *Imagini de gli dei delli antichi,* Cartari linked the god of Silence to the Eyptians and the Greeks (Figure 17):

Likewise those of Egypt worshipped the god of Silence, and they counted him among their principal gods. His name among them was Harpocrates, and Sigalione to the Greeks, and his statue was that of a young man who had his finger to his mouth, as one does when one gives a signal to others to be quiet. Sometimes the god of Silence was also made to be a figure without a face, with a little cap on his head and with a wolf's skin draped around him, and he was almost completely covered with eyes and ears, because he needs to see and hear a great deal, but speak little. And everybody can keep quiet when he feels like it, but he cannot always say what he wants to, which is shown by the cap, which is a sign of freedom. (1626, 309)

This was the infant Horus who, according to Seznec's research, was misidentified by the Greeks as Harpocrates, god of Silence (1995, 296). In the prologue of Carrió's account, it is the younger, dark and winged secretary, Concolorcorvo, or "Crow-with-Color," who plays Harpocrates, "poniendo el dedo en la boca" (121) ("putting his finger on his mouth"). His simple gesture is rife with meaning: he is seeing all and hearing all, but he is not telling all.

Nevertheless, the inspector frequently puts a stopper in the mouth of his secretary, who wishes to write like a swan,[35] and this textual muzzling is understandable in light of other iconographic representations of the god of Silence. Indeed, another of Ripa's icons of *Silence* is precisely that of an old man: "*Silence.* An old man who holds a finger to his lips, and next to him there will be a swan with a stopper in its mouth. Because old age easily reconciles itself to silence, as that age which puts more faith in men of experience and reputation earned than in words, Silence is made to be of this age by some" (1669, 569–70). In *The Golden Booke of the Leaden Gods,* Batman described the emblem in slightly different form: "Harpocrates and Angerona were figured in comely Apparell, holdinge their Fingers uppon theyr Mouth" (1976, 15). He then provided the "Signification" of this portrait, which bears on the prudence that is common to good government and silence: "They both resemble Taciturnitie, and in beinge comely Apparelled signifieth the grave modesty of prudent Governors. By the holding of theire Forefingers on their Mouthes, sheweth also the heedefulnes that Men ought to have, in speakinge" (15). In Concolorcorvo's description of the *gauderios,* it is the inspector who plays Harpocrates: "de cuya extravagancia nos reímos todos y no quisimos desengañarlos, porque el visitador hizo una cruz perfecta de su boca, atravesándola con el índice" (252) ("whose nonsense made us all laugh and we did not try to disabuse them of it, because the inspector made a perfect cross with his mouth by putting his index finger to it").

There were significant continuities, between the first half and the second half of the eighteenth century, in the Viceroyalty of Peru. The economic and social profiles of Buenos Aires and Lima, the former on the way up and the latter on the way down, are laid bare by Carrió's exposé, which tells the story of how Buenos Aires came to surpass Lima, as elites in the City of Kings knew only too well in spite of their pretensions. The men who held power in Carrió's times were many of the same men who had bought their jobs during the reign of Philip V: *peruleros,* they had been born or had taken up residence in Peru. As Michel Bertrand and others have shown, personal gain and Crown service were not at all incompatible, and some of the means used by the *roscas* were perfectly legal—for example, the purchase of governorships, judgeships, and marriage dispensations. The interest of the Crown did not lie in the integrity of its ministers but in their ability, as local representatives of their king, to control his subjects. Reform measures were designed to curtail *excesses* committed by ministers that could possibly undermine the Crown's authority and control; they did not pretend to eliminate personal gain altogether (Bertrand 1999b, 316).

Through my analysis of the key continuities between the first and second halves of the eighteenth century, an alternative to the *middle period* model has emerged. Instead of focusing exclusively on events that were supposed to have paved the way for modernity in Latin America, we should examine the eighteenth century as a bridge between the conquest and independence periods with more survivals than disappearances.

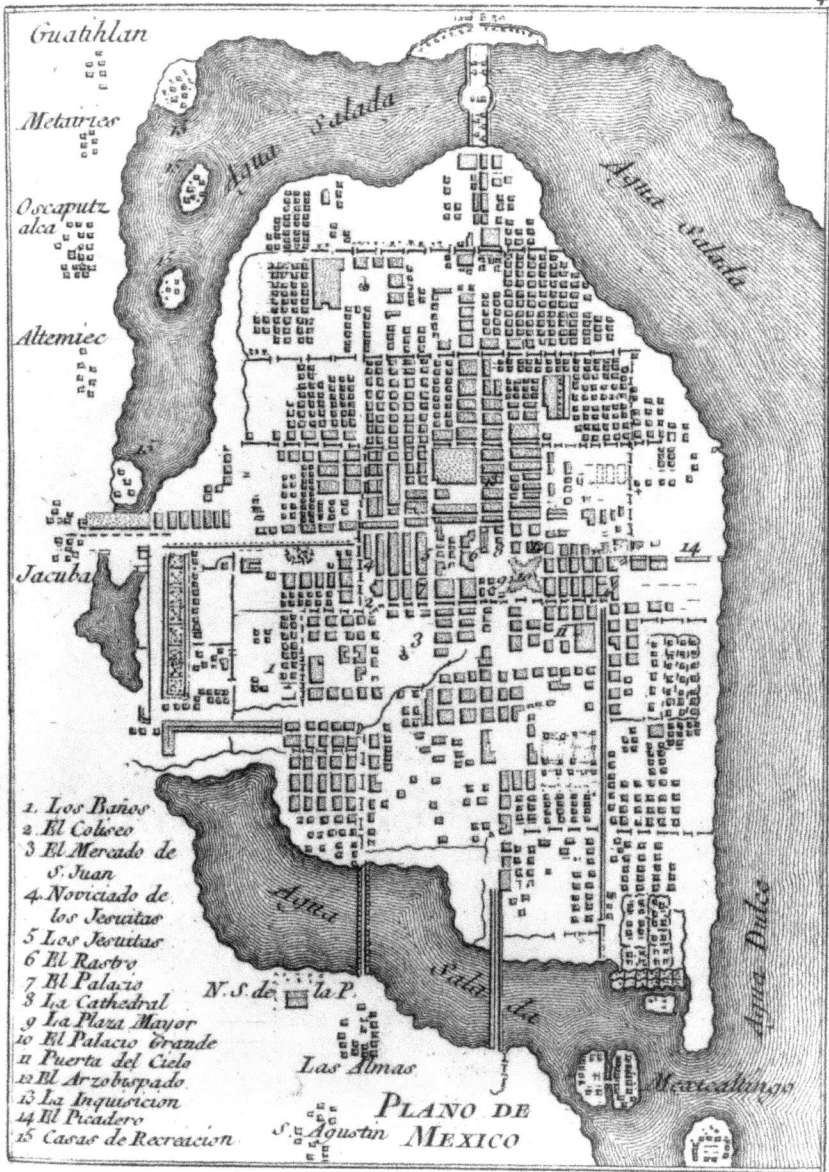

Figure 1. Map of Mexico City, 1758.

Plano de México. Tomás López, *Atlas Geográphico de la América* (1758).
Courtesy of the John Carter Brown Library at Brown University.

Figure 2. Map of Kingdom of Guatemala, 1758.

Plano de Provincias de Guatemala, Soconusco, Chiapa, y Vera Paz.
Tomás López, *Atlas Geográphico de la América* (1758).
Courtesy of the John Carter Brown Library at Brown University.

GAZETA

DE LIMA

QUE CONTIENE LAS NOTI-

cias de esta Capital, desde 20. de Enero hasta
20. de Abril de 1746.

EL VEINTE Y TRES DE ENERO SE CELEBRO EL
fausto Recibimiento del Excmo. Señor Virrey en la Real Universidad de San Marcos de esta Ciudad, con la Pompa, y Con-
curso debido á tan plausible Funccion. Dióle principio en nombre de
la Real Universidad, El Doctor Don Miguel Valdivieso Torrejon,
Abogado de esta Real Audiencia, con una Docta Eloquente Oracion
Panegyrica, que está ya impressa. Repartieronse luego las propinas

A   de

Figure 3. Mercury on the front page of the *Gaceta de Lima,* 1746.

Mercurio on the front page of the *Gaceta de Lima,* 1746.
Courtesy of the John Carter Brown Library at Brown University.

DECIMA.

Quando fin excufa alguna
el que vive ha de morir,
yo muero para vivir,
y es el fepulchro mi cuna.
Viva no foi mas de vna;
muerta, mi fer fe dilata;
por effo aunque me maltrata,
como mejoro defuerte,
agradecida à la muerte,
doi la vida á quien me mata.

Con Privilegío, del Real y Superior Govierno, en la
Imprenta de la Calle de S. Ildephonfo. *Por Antonio Gutierrez de Zevallos.* Año de 1744.

Figure 4. Riddle from the *Gaceta de Lima,* 1744.

Enigma from the *Gazeta de Lima,* 1744.
Courtesy of the John Carter Brown Library at Brown University.

Su Mageſtad ha concedido ſeis Titulos de Caſtilla de Marqués, óConde, para que el Preſidente de Chile los beneficie en 20ɉ. peſos cadavno libres de Media Anata, y Lanzas, á beneficio de aquel Reyno, y para ſus Poblaciones.

El Mote del Enigma de la antecedente Gazeta es, EL ESPEJO, Otro ſe propone en el ſiguiente

SONETO.

Mi principio es principio de la vida,
    que á la naturaleza preſta aliento,
    y mi fin es principio de vn portento,
    que en gran parte la tiene commovida.
Mi cabeza, riqueza apetecida
    engendra para amor del avariento,
    mas mi pie, vn prodigioſo movimiento,
    á lo inſenſible, y lo ſenſible embidia;
En mis partes, ſoy vtil, bueno, y ſano,
    pero entero, tan cruel, tan inclemente,
    que en tal qual gran Señor prive tyrano,
De vida, y libertad â muchas gentes.
    y en daño general ſoy inhumano
    aſſaſino de todo lo viviente.

Con Privilegio, del Real, y Superior Govierno: En la Imprenta de la Calle de San Ildephonſo, *Por Franciſco Sobrino, y Bados,* Año de 1745,
Y ſe halla Calle de San Diego, cerca de Santa Thereſa.

Figure 5. Riddle from the *Gaceta de Lima,* 1745.

Enigma from the *Gaceta de Lima,* 1745.
Courtesy of the John Carter Brown Library at Brown University.

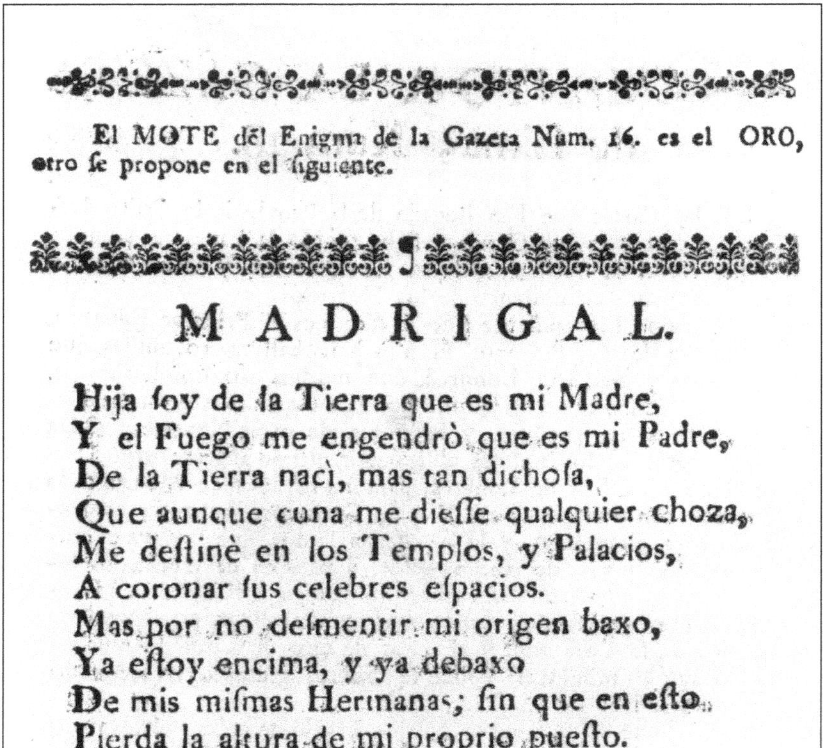

El MOTE del Enigma de la Gazeta Num. 16. es el ORO, otro se propone en el siguiente.

MADRIGAL.

Hija soy de la Tierra que es mi Madre,
Y el Fuego me engendró que es mi Padre,
De la Tierra nací, mas tan dichosa,
Que aunque cuna me diesse qualquier choza,
Me destiné en los Templos, y Palacios,
A coronar sus celebres espacios.
Mas por no desmentir mi origen baxo,
Ya estoy encima, y ya debaxo
De mis mismas Hermanas; sin que en esto
Pierda la altura de mi proprio puesto.
De la comodidad quieren las Leyes,
Que todos aun los Principes, y Reyes,
Me pongan a pesar de mis baxezas,
Sobre Thronos, Coronas, y Cabezas.
Sin embargo, ay ossado otro Elemento,
Que embidioso de mí, Padrino el Viento,
Mas alto sube, sobre mi se hospeda;
Yo le recibo afable, él no se queda,
Pues por su natural, ó por mi ultrage,
Se hospeda, y luego dexa el hospedage.

Figure 6. Riddle from the *Gaceta de Lima*, 1749.

Enigma from the *Gazeta de Lima*, 1749.
Courtesy of the John Carter Brown Library at Brown University.

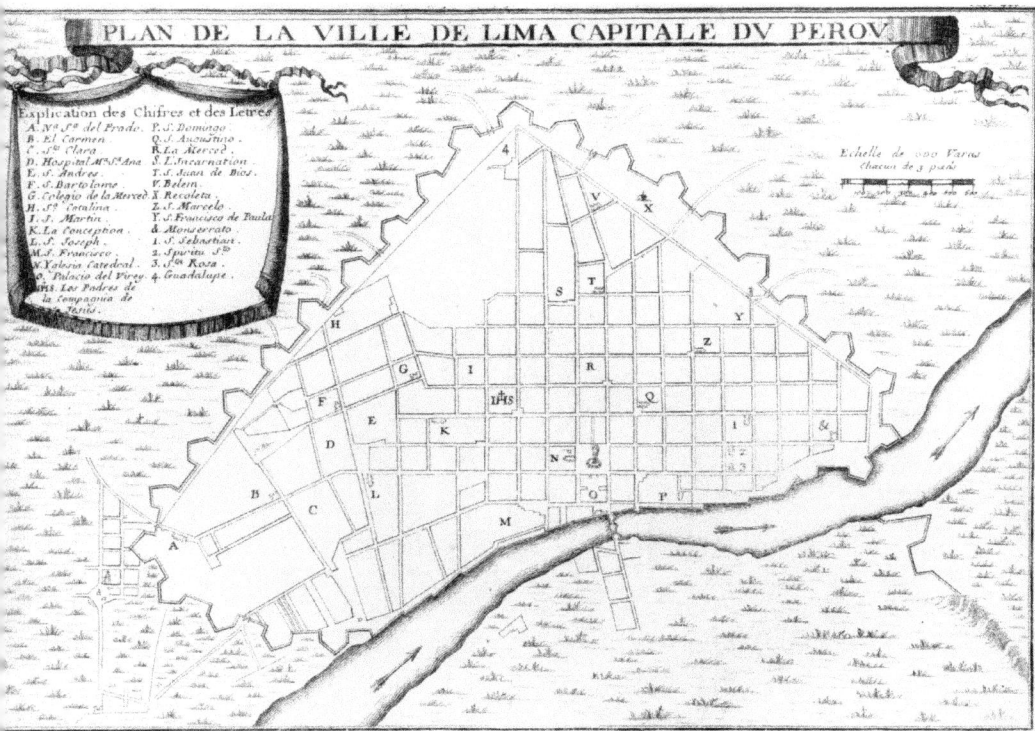

Figure 7. Map of Lima, 1714.

Plan de la Ville de Lima, Capitale du Perou. Louis Feuillée, *Journal des Observations Physiques, Mathematiques et Botaniques faites par ordre du Roi sur les Côtes Orientales de l'Amerique Meridionale, et dans les Indes Occidentales* (1714).

Courtesy of the John Carter Brown Library at Brown University.

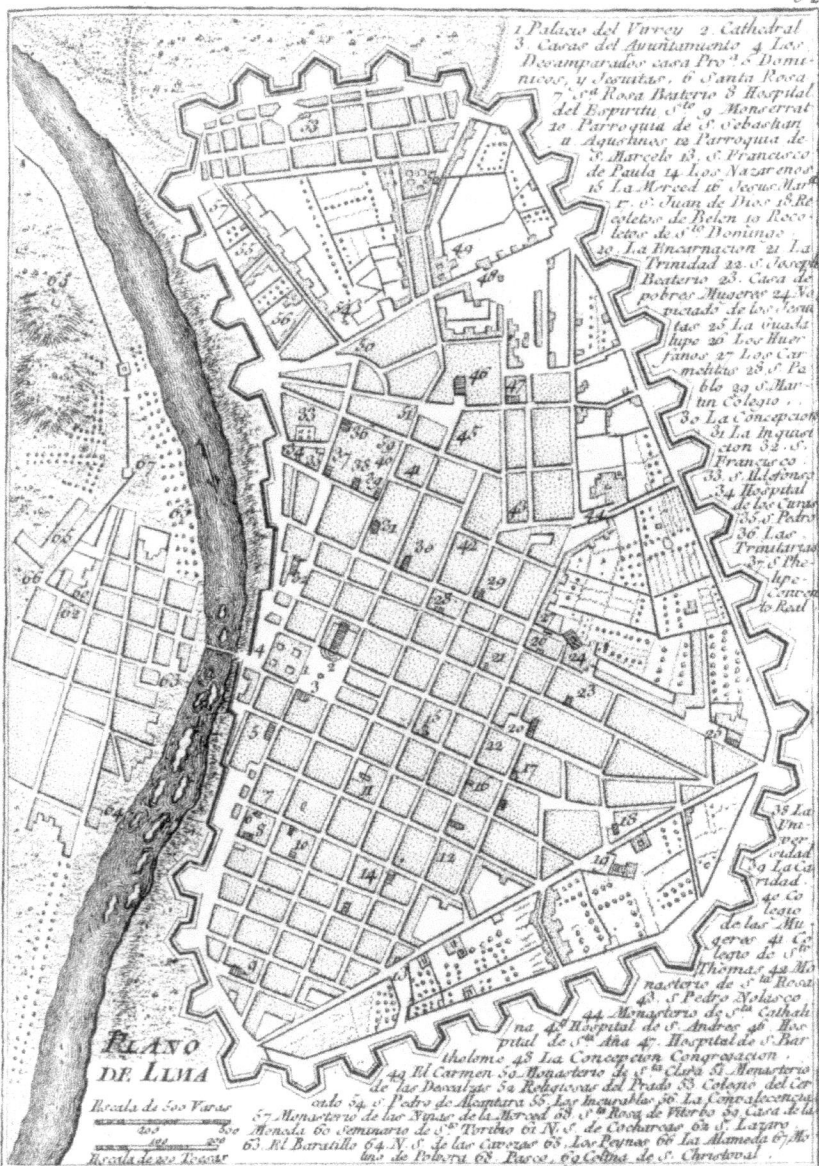

Figure 8. Map of Lima, 1758.

Plano de Lima. Tomás López, *Atlas Geográphico de la América* (1758).
Courtesy of the John Carter Brown Library at Brown University.

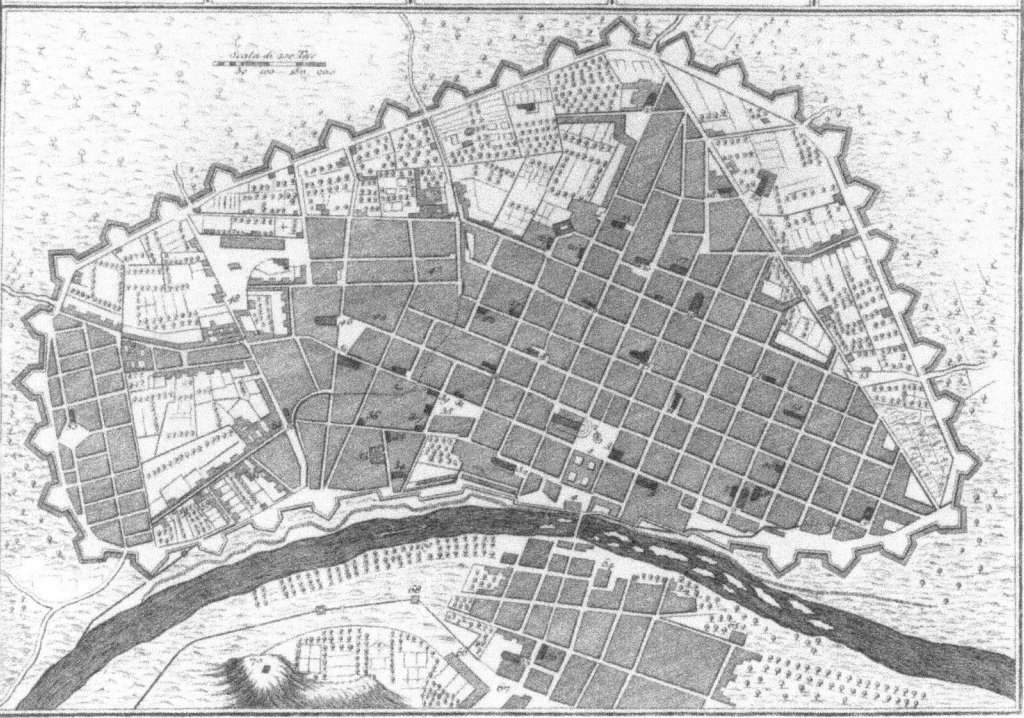

Figure 9. Map of Lima, 1763.

Plano Scenografico della Città dei Re, ò sia di Lima, Capitale del Regno
del Perù, tal quale era prima che fosse distrutta dall' ultimo Terremoto.
Il Gazzattiere Americano (1763).
Courtesy of the John Carter Brown Library at Brown University.

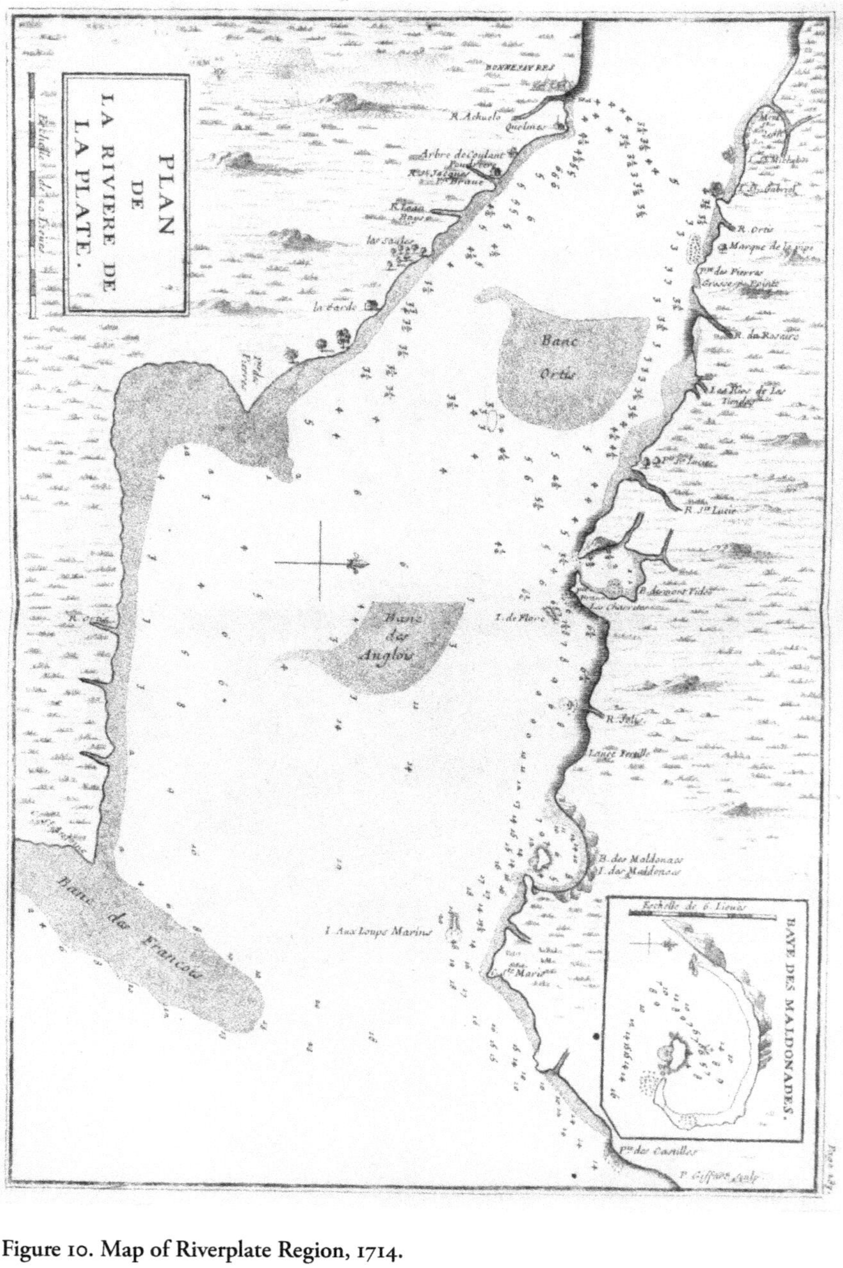

Figure 10. Map of Riverplate Region, 1714.

Plan de La Riviere de la Plate. Louis Feuillée, *Journal des Observations Physiques,
Mathematiques et Botaniques faites par ordre du Roi sur les Côtes Orientales
de l'Amerique Meridionale, et dans les Indes Occidentales* (1714).
Courtesy of the John Carter Brown Library at Brown University.

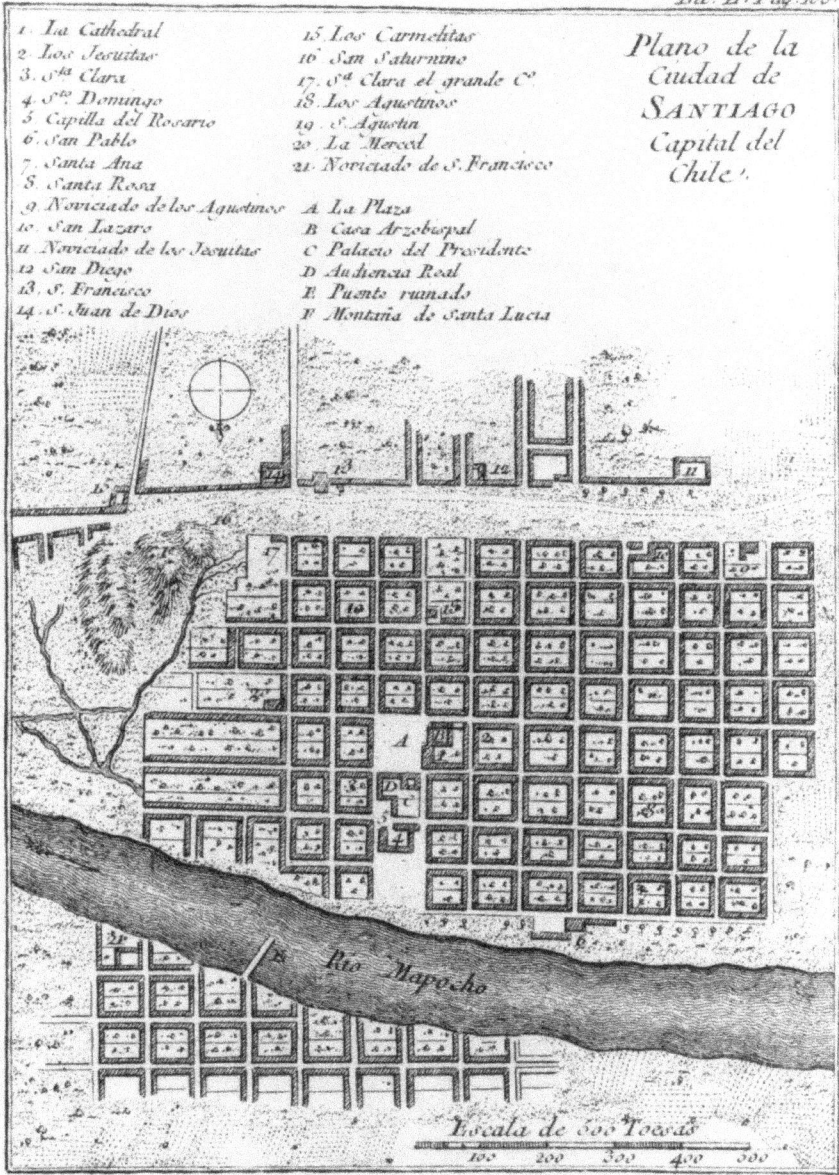

Figure 11. Map of Santiago, Chile, 1758.

Plano de la Ciudad de Santiago, Capital del Chile. Tomás López,
Atlas Geográphico de la América (1758).
Courtesy of the John Carter Brown Library at Brown University.

1. La Iglesia Mayor
2. El Sagrario
3. Parroquia de Sª Barbara
4. Parroquia de S. Roque
5. Parroquia de S. Sebastian
6. Parroquia de S. Marcos
7. Parroquia de S. Blas
   La Parroquia de Sª Prisca
   esta fuera de la Ciudad
8. Palacio de la Real Audiencia
9. Casa del Cavildo
10. Palacio Episcopal
11. Capilla Real
12. Carcel de Corte
13. Carcel comun
14. Sª Marta Carcel de Mugeres
15. Igl. y Co. R. o S. Fernando
16. Colegio de S. Luis
17. Santo Domingo
18. S. Francisco
19. S. Agustin

20. La Merced
21. La Com. de Jesus
    S. Dieg. esta fuera de la Ciudad
    los Recˢ estan fuera de la Ciudad
22. Recoletos de la Merced
23. Monjas de la Concepcion
24. Monjas de Sª Cathalina
25.
26. Carmelitas de Quito
27. Carmelitas de la Tacunga
28. Igl. N de las mesmas
29. Beaterio de Mercenarias
30. Hospital de Belermitas
31. Capilla de Jerusalem
32. Cap. de la R. de los Angeles
33. Igle. de S. Buenaventura
34. C. de N. S. de Cantuña
35. Cap. de los Indios
36. C. de N. S. de Desampˢ
37. Her. del Sᵗᵒ Christo
38. Ca. de S. Juan de Letran

Plano de la Ciudad de QUITO Por Lopez

39. Her. de N. Sᵒ de la Conso
    lacion
40. El Sᵗᵒ Christo de la Paz
41. Casa donde se hicieron
    las primeras observacion
    de Latitud, y de obliqui-
    dad de la Ecliptica

Toesas
50 100 200

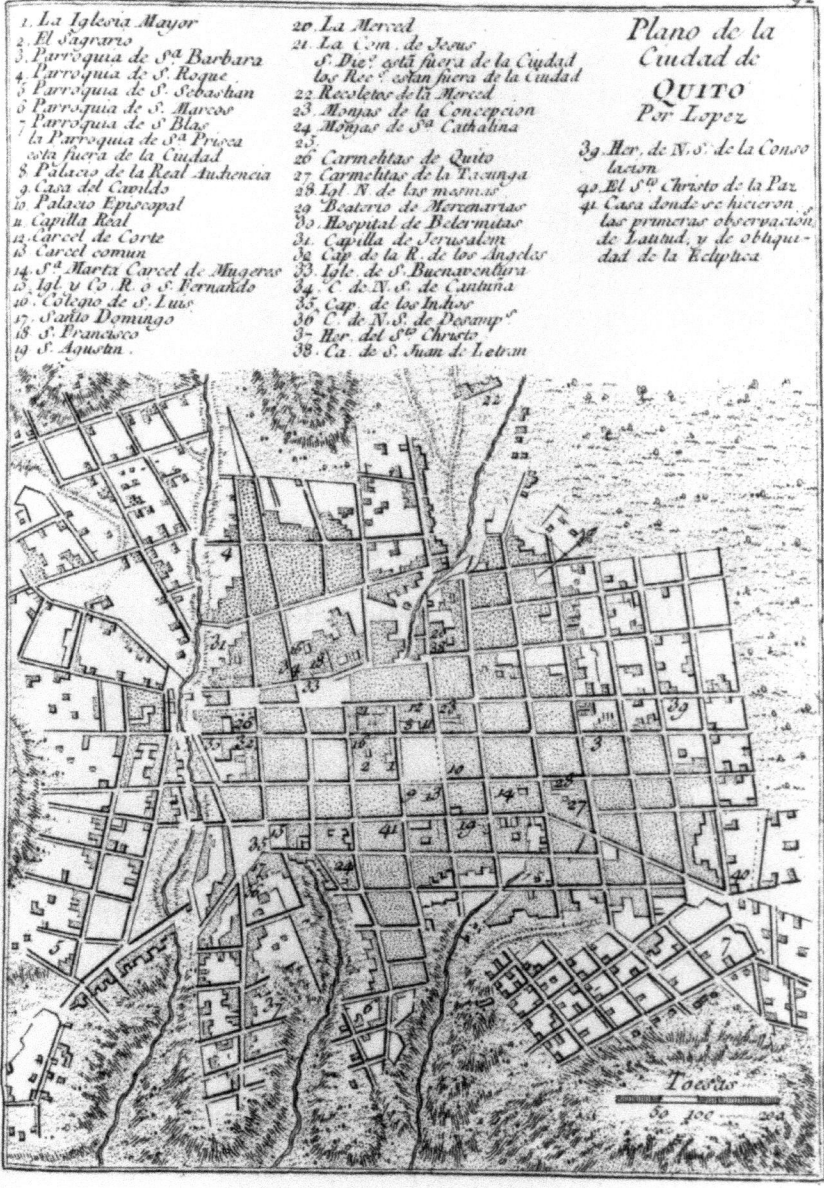

Figure 12. Map of City of Quito, *Kingdom of Quito*, 1758.

Plano de la Ciudad de Quito. Tomás López, *Atlas Geográphico de la América* (1758). Courtesy of the John Carter Brown Library at Brown University.

Figure 13. Emblems of *Shame* and *Ignorance,* 1746.

Infamie (no. 8) and *Ignorance* (no. 10). Daniel de La Feuille, *Science hiéroglyphique, ou Explication des Figures symboliques des anciens avec différentes devises historiques* (1746). Courtesy of Special Collections, Milton S. Eisenhower Library, The Johns Hopkins University.

Figure 14. Emblem of *Error*, 1669.

Errore. Cesare Ripa, *Iconologia* (1669).
Courtesy of Special Collections, Milton S. Eisenhower Library,
The Johns Hopkins University.

Figure 15. Emblem of *Error*, 1746.

Erreur (no. 1). Daniel de La Feuille, *Science hiéroglyphique, ou Explication des Figures symboliques des anciens avec différentes devises historiques* (1746). Courtesy of Special Collections, Milton S. Eisenhower Library, The Johns Hopkins University.

Figure 16. Monster born in Buenos Aires, 1714.

Louis Feuillée, *Journal des Observations Physiques, Mathematiques et Botaniques faites par ordre du Roi sur les Côtes Orientales de l'Amerique Meridionale, et dans les Indes Occidentales* (1714).
Courtesy of the John Carter Brown Library at Brown University.

Figure 17. Emblem of *Silence,* 1626.

Imagini del Dio del Silentio detto Harpocrate o Sigalione.
Vincenzo Cartari, *Imagini de gli Dei delli Antichi* (1626).
Courtesy of Special Collections, Milton S. Eisenhower Library,
The Johns Hopkins University.

Figure 18. Pre-Conquest Rulers of New Granada, 1688.

Title page, Lucas Fernández Piedrahita, *Historia general
de las conquistas del Nuevo Reyno de Granada* (1688).
Courtesy of the John Carter Brown Library at Brown University.

Figure 19. Pre-Conquest Rulers of New Granada, 1688.

Part I title page, Lucas Fernández Piedrahita, *Historia general de las conquistas del Nuevo Reyno de Granada* (1688).
Courtesy of the John Carter Brown Library at Brown University.

Figure 20. Map of Cape of Good Hope, 1692.

Carta del Paese et de Popoli del Capo di Bona Speranza.
Aurelio degli Anzi, *Genio vagante* (1692).
Courtesy of the John Carter Brown Library at Brown University.

PART III

CHAPTER 5

Before Race: Hierarchy in Bourbon Spanish America

I want to clarify from the outset what this chapter is and what it is not. By *hierarchy*, I do *not* mean "racial thinking" or "racism"; these are modern, postcolonial forms of hierarchy, which do not enter into this study of Carrió's Spanish America.[1] My approach to hierarchy is both limited in scope and experimental. It is not intended to replace Albert Sicroff's still important 1985 study of what are commonly known as blood purity statutes (*estatutos de limpieza de sangre*) or José Antonio Maravall's (1979) work on estates (*estamentos* or *estados*), and it does not address the immense literature on honor and gender. In order to make sense of Carrió's material reality—Bourbon Spanish America— and his inspection report, this study analyzes what I consider to be three overlapping principles of hierarchy in the Hispanic world: *casta, limpieza,* and *estado.* The main objectives of this chapter are two, one broad and the other narrow: On one hand, it aims to spark a scholarly dialogue about hierarchy and its generative base in the Hispanic world before the nineteenth century—not *race* but infamy as it was codified and interpreted since the twelfth century. On the other hand, it attempts to broaden the critical revision of Carrió's hierarchical values and attitudes in *El lazarillo de ciegos caminantes* that were presented in the Introduction and in Chapter 2 and that extend into Chapter 6 herein.

Spurred by the social anthropologist Louis Dumont's (1961, 1980) work on hierarchy, I postulate here that viceregal Spanish American societies had a norm of *inequality:* a written and unwritten hierarchy that *ostensibly* mirrored nature and its laws but was in fact a social construct. That written hierarchy was constituted by constitutions, edicts, rules, bylaws, glosses, and the like. However, it is not helpful to oppose this written hierarchy to the unwritten hierarchy of values (customs, assumptions, stereotypes, and so forth) as if the legal could be detached from the social. I therefore caution my readers not to dismiss legal analysis as top-down analysis or to oppose legal history to social history in studies of viceregal Spanish America. This is to give the rule of law an existence independent of social actors, be they judges, glossators, defendants, witnesses, or plaintiffs—an existence it did not have. Elizabeth Anne Kuznesof, for example, argues that "the race of individuals in Colonial Latin America [was] a subjective and malleable category which could be influenced and changed during a person's life," unlike gender (1995, 155–56). If we substitute for her "race" the phrase "*casta, limpieza,* and *estado,*" I agree with this affirmation. However, Kuznesof proceeds to oppose the written to the unwritten as if the legal were not social, a view that effectively legitimates the naturalizing ideology of written legal codes and protocols.[2] R. Douglas Cope (1994), on the other hand, has shown convincingly that social negotiation relied heavily on the legal system: *interpretation,* both written and unwritten, of the rule of law was key to establishing one's identity (i.e., one's duties and privileges within the social hierarchy).[3]

Skillful negotiation of the rule of law in viceregal Spanish America, I am convinced, offers at least a partial explanation for what Kuznesof has characterized as "the constant and minute legislation related to race in every aspect of colonial life, in every community and within every guild," which she feels is a demonstration of "the extreme level of social anxiety related to race-related privilege and discrimination" (1995, 156). Another partial explanation for the oversized load of legal literature related to *casta, limpieza,* and *estado* lies in the fact that infamy legislation and glosses were central to negotiations of one's place in local and regional hierarchies well before the religious and occupational purity bylaws, constitutions, rules, and definitions—the so-called *blood purity statutes*—that they engendered began to appear in viceregal Spanish America.

An important step toward the two main goals of this chapter is the recovery of *casta* through historical, or situational, semantics. To take that step, we must learn to distinguish *casta* from *raza* and from the Anglo concept of *race,* a differentiation that requires that we revisit the birth of both *raza* and *race* in the nineteenth century. The chapter then analyzes what *raza* and *estado* meant before the nineteenth century, initial spadework that provides a clear picture of the legal and social interdependence of *casta, limpieza,* and *estado.* Finally, this chapter demonstrates that *extralegal* movement between *castas*—passing—as well as *legal* maneuvers within the social hierarchy were rooted in that interdependence, which was a material reality for Carrió. The implications of such movements include the volatile demographics of Lima that are central to *El lazarillo de ciegos caminantes* and that scholars would do well to take into account when they analyze censuses and population estimates from viceregal Spanish America.

Raza *versus* Casta: *Historical Forms of Hierarchy*

Most historians, sociologists, and literary historians have assumed that *castas* in Spanish America were legal racial categories of persons or even mixed-race persons ("half-breeds" or "mixed bloods") without examining its meaning or its usage in Spain or Spanish America.[4] This scholarly racialization of cultural categories and scales from the Hispanic Middle Ages and viceregal Spanish America participates in an ideologized reductionism that chooses to locate in the "ancient" past what is of recent vintage, as if our own cultural norms and theirs were identical or our social inequalities were someone else's doing.[5] In fact, viceregal Spanish American societies are consistently studied and explained by using *race, racial,* and *racist,* whereas *hybrid* and *casta* are used interchangeably, as if they had once been equivalents.[6] Such terms undeniably reveal a great deal about the triumph of polygenetic thinking in the nineteenth century and its significance to our own times but very little about social hierarchy in viceregal Spanish America in general or *El lazarillo de ciegos caminantes* in particular.

Sociologists of India and the United States made a similar error in the 1930s, when they applied the term *castes* to North American blacks and whites and held that caste in India and the United States was an extreme form of class. This error, as Dumont observed in the 1960s, "appears to be rooted in the fact that, once equality is accepted as the norm, any form of inequality appears to be the same as any other because of their common deviation from the norm" (1961, 25). A lack of attendance to the historical forms of hierarchy appears in scholarship on both Spain and Spanish America. Richard C. Hoffman, for example, asserts the following with respect to medieval Spain: "When medieval writers and men of action chose words and images like 'birth,' 'blood,' 'inheritance,' and 'lineage' to refer to large social groups, they exhibited a fundamentally biological explanation of how the groups came to be. In modern biology the term 'race' correctly denotes an endogamous gene pool, a population separate from others of the same species and persisting over time in that genetic isolation. Hence racist or genetic thinking classifies groups and their attributes in terms of such distinctive descent up to the extreme of a fully differentiated species" (1983, 3–4). The problem is that Hoffman mistakes *metaphors* of social hierarchy *for the hierarchy itself:* he interprets "blood" and "bloody purity" *literally,* as if pre-nineteenth century discussions of human origins and religious difference had taken place in the same social milieu that harnessed natural science to social science for the invention of biological determinism (i.e., racial inferiority and superiority) or in his very own milieu.[7]

Hoffman's approach leaves him some room to maneuver. "Of course," he tells us, "medieval Europeans knew from their creation myth of Adam and Eve that all humans shared a common ancestry, so few medieval writers seriously argued for the wholly distinct origin of any human groups with which they were familiar" (1983, 4). Still, this caveat does not prevent him from again accepting as true the ideologized metaphors of social hierarchy in Iberia or from reducing that social hierarchy to a set of symbols or metaphors that interest him: "The Iberian peninsula had known in early and high medieval times as great and as recognized a cultural pluralism as ever existed in post-twelfth century Ireland or late medieval Scotland. Initially cast in cultural terms, the residue of pluralism came in the fifteenth century to be understood as a matter of descent, thus giving rise to the infamous Castilian preoccupation with *limpieza de sangre,* a Christian's 'purity of blood' from the pollution of Muslim or especially Jewish ancestry" (10). Hoffman unwittingly chooses a term that expresses precisely what he overlooks: *infamia* and its shaping of the concept of *limpieza de sangre,* a social norm that was not met simply by negotiating with the law to establish that one had no Jewish or Muslim ancestry.

A conceptual analysis of hierarchy in viceregal Spanish America reveals that *casta* was not biology: it was a cluster of somatic, economic, linguistic, geographical, and other circumstances that varied from parish to parish, from town to town, and from person to person.[8] Academic attempts from within Hispanism to circumvent this material reality by inventing the oxymoronic *social race,* or *not race but racial identity,* or even *racism without race* have distorted the material differences between traditional (cultural) and modern (biological) categories by collapsing them into each other.[9] Even outside of Hispanism, it is often the case that "race connotes both categories"—the social and the biological—as one scholar puts it, although "the idea of race implies a permanent biological entity" (Barkan 2003, 693). The carelessness that marks such usage ignores the fact that *race,* a cornerstone of biological determinism, was an invention of nineteenth-century scientists, social scientists, poets, and historians.[10] *Race* replaced, or at least came to outweigh, cultural explanations and rationales for difference: it was, by definition, a genetic or biological fiction, and therein lay its power.

The sociologist Gabriel Tarde's theories circulated throughout Spanish America, and he opposed the racial and the cultural (or social) in his understanding of why a relationship of shared duties and privileges had failed to develop between the Indians in the New World and their English and Spanish conquerors.[11] Gustave Le Bon, another sociologist whose theories were well-known to Spanish American intellectuals in the late nineteenth and early twentieth centuries,[12] was a social Darwinist for whom hereditary and selective aptitudes, along with adaptation in the social environment (through education, government, and economic policy), explained the rise and fall of nations. In *The Psychology of Socialism,* he wrote, "At the bottom of all our social questions lies always this dominant question of race, which is indeed the supreme arbiter of the destinies of nations" (1982, 260). The malaise of his century he attributed to a conflict between biology and society: "a general opposition between the sentiments fixed by hereditary [*sic*] and the conditions of existence and ideas created by modern necessities" (281).

Further evidence of the social Darwinist milieu in which *race* was born can be gleaned from the European intellectuals who wished to use *race* as a cultural (or "historical," in the language of the nineteenth century) category: I am speaking here of the forebears of contemporary Hispanists who write of *social race, racism without race,* and the like. Some of these nineteenth-century Europeans felt pressed to alert their readers that they were in fact redefining *race,* wresting it from the minds and pens of their contemporaries for whom *race* was a biological (or "anthropological") construction; others offered cultural categories in opposition to *race.* Ludwig Gumplowicz, an Austrian political scientist, is a good example. He became well-known in Spanish America after the translation and publication of

La lucha de razas (*The Struggle of the Races*) in Madrid at the end of the nineteenth century. Although he espoused polygenetic thinking, he nonetheless contended that *races* did not even exist, at least not in the sense that *race* was used in the natural sciences. As he understood it, *race* was a social construct—"a process of history."[13] Certain groups dominated others through language and religion, and the heterogeneous groups fused culturally and, thereafter, physically. *Race* was not a community within natural history "but, rather, a *historical community.*"[14] What united human *races,* in Gumplowicz's sense of the term, was not the cluster of physical characteristics that monogenetic thinkers proposed but *intellectual* ones.[15]

Latin American intellectuals, such as Víctor Arreguine in Argentina and Manuel González Prada in Peru, clearly agreed. In 1904 González Prada justified his cultural understanding of the *raza indígena* ("indigenous race"), one primarily based in economics, by quoting both J. A. Novicow's study (1897) in which he upbraided European thinkers who had turned sociological issues into biological ones and Arreguine's (1900) response to Edmond Demolins's (1898) treatise on the coming extinction of the "Latin race" (i.e., the French, Italians, Spanish, and Spanish Americans).[16] When Hispanists and other scholars use the word *race* to mean *culture,* they get little in return for the convenience of jettisoning history: intellectuals and scholars in nineteenth-century Europe and Spanish America who opposed the racialization of humanity by discursively converting *race* into a cultural category did not at all eliminate *race* as a biological fiction or mitigate the material effects of racism. Moreover, postmodern (or cultural) definitions of *race* tend to essentialize groups of people no less than the original invention of *race* in the nineteenth century. "As racism assumes more subtle and elusive forms in the contemporary world," one anthropologist observes, "it is being reconfigured without 'race' as a classificatory device. . . . The once largely biologized notion of race is now commonly being recoded as 'culture.'"[17] In other words, postmodern appropriations of *race,* while altering its valence, have not discharged its hierarchical freight.

In the viceregal period, culture meant culture. In a sermon from *Tratado de los Evangelios* (*Tract on the Gospels*), Francisco Dávila, the famed extirpator of idolatries in Cuzco, used culturally specific analogies to convince Indian converts that they shared the same ancestors as Spaniards and all of humanity:

Hold on, I left this out before. Have I not told all of you that Indian and Spaniard are of the same stock [*cepa*]? So, how is it that the Indian's color is brown and the Spaniard's white? Look here: you see here this ear of corn whose kernels are all white; is that not so? The seed of this ear was a white kernel, and therefore all of the kernels are white. Look here again: now then, how can it have other kernels through here that are black and gray? Do you not see them?

Now then, shall we say that these have a different origin? No. Well then, why are they not white like the others? Because, due to some unknown cause, they get that black shell from the dirt itself. The same thing happens to us.

Besides, does a female guinea-pig, all white, not give birth to black, brown, and white and rust-colored guinea-pigs? (1648, 299)

Dávila rejected outright the polygenetic thinking that was to underpin *race* and racism in the nineteenth century, insisting that all peoples had a common origin and should therefore have a common way of life: "And therefore, since we all have one and the same origin, our way of life [*modo de vivir*] should be one and the same, and to lead people astray on this point the Devil, father of falsity, said that every faction had a different origin" (1648, 301).[18] In terms of biology, or the nineteenth-century understanding of *race,* Indians and Spaniards were not different: they shared the same origin, or *cepa.*

The theological dimensions of the extirpator Dávila's arguments should not be disfigured in the manner that certain nineteenth-century Spanish American élites, mimicking their "Latin" (i.e., French) counterparts, reduced the Spanish Inquisition to a Gothic dungeon and underestimated the theological underpinnings of the Catholic way of life in viceregal Spanish America.[19] There were questions of religious purity in play before the nineteenth century that might withstand comparisons to postmodern Christian, Jewish, or Islamic fundamentalism but not to the laws of North American eugenicists, Mussolini, or Hitler. Religion was a way of life, or "modo de vivir," and in traditional societies it was embedded in the social hierarchy.

I do not at all suggest that there was no transition between hierarchical forms in Spanish America from the fifteenth century to the twentieth. To the contrary, I am convinced that *race* in the social evolutionary sense did not "always already" exist. Even in late nineteenth-century Spanish America, well after the repeal of infamy laws and the virtual abandonment of *castas* to refer to human groups, *raza* continued to be used in the modern sense, as a transnational kinship group (*la raza blanca, la raza anglosajona, la raza latina, la raza negra,* and so on), and in the older sense, as a cultural community marker that appealed to a common geography and/or history (e.g., *la raza inglesa* or *la raza americana*).[20] The transition, then, was from a traditional society to a modern one, from a hierarchy rooted in culture (primarily, religion) to one rooted in biology, or *race.* That shift did not occur until well after the legal separation of church and state, which permitted the abandonment of the infamy laws and the norm of inequality that they buttressed in Spanish America and in Spain, and the shift occurred in fits and starts, as we have seen.

Other scholars have assumed an earlier date for that transition or have implicitly denied it by racializing all forms of hierarchy, traditional or modern. Hoffman has a narrow racializing focus, positing the transition in Iberia from cultural to genetic hierarchies around the first *Sentencia-Estatuto* of Toledo in 1449 (1983, 12). Kuznesof also has noted the transition from religious hierarchy to racial hierarchy, claiming that the source for blood purity concerns in Spanish America was fifteenth-century Spain (1995, 160). Ann Twinam, for her part, devotes a paragraph to the existence of blood purity requirements in medieval Italy, which she views as a *religious* issue (without tackling the issues of infamy that are elucidated by Francesco Migliorino's 1985 study of Italy), in contrast to the blood purity statutes in Spain, which she views as a *racial* issue.[21] More recently, Morgan has expressed this view succinctly: "The resulting social and legal distinctions between the 'New Christians' and the so-called 'Old Christians' discriminated against members of the former group based not on the individual's actual religious beliefs and practices, but rather on the religious and ethnic identity of his or her ancestors. Thus, what had begun in late-medieval Iberia as religious discrimination took on the character of racial policy, reflecting a concern not simply with religious unity, but also with social and ethnic origins" (2002, 10). Like Sicroff (1985), Morgan focuses on Jewish converts to Christianity, artificially narrowing the scope of the so-called *blood purity statutes* (which were more often "constitutions," "definitions," or "rules" for admission) and ignoring links between the codification of infamy beginning in the twelfth century and the codification of *limpieza* (*de sangre* and *de oficio*) beginning in the fifteenth. In my view, there were no "social or ethnic origins" before the nineteenth century for us to study independently of questions of "religious unity."[22]

To make sense of hierarchy in *El lazarillo de ciegos caminantes,* we need to turn our backs on modernity. Although metaphors for hierarchy—such as clean blood (*sangre limpia*), service job (*vil oficio* or *oficio bajo* or *mecánico*), and dirty job (*oficio sórdido* or *infame*)—have the ring of modernity, the hierachical patterns that they represent are not modern. Dumont's differentiation between racial and caste societies reminds us that "particular features must be seen *in their relations* with the other particular features" of a social hierarchy and that "a particular feature, if taken not in itself but in its concrete position within a system (what is sometimes called its 'function'), can have a totally different meaning according to the position it occupies. That is to say, from a sociological standpoint it is *actually different*" (1961, 28). The *one-drop rule* in the United States (which arose in the nineteenth century and survived well into the twentieth) and the admission guidelines and club rules in the Hispanic world that became known as *blood purity statutes* (which appeared in the fifteenth century and were abolished in the nineteenth century wherever the separation of Catholic church and state was respected) were symptoms and tools of *different social hierarchies,* even though they shared the trope of *blood.* The hierarchies that existed before the nineteenth century must be analyzed with respect to the norms and values of the societies that constructed them, not with respect to modern and postmodern norms and values. Biology, or blood, occupied a different position—had a different function—in the social hierarchy of

viceregal Spanish America than it would occupy in modern societies with their
discourse of equality and their material reality of inequality.

Rescuing Difference, or the Recovery of Casta

Some thirty years ago, the sociologist Julian Pitt-Rivers authored an essay in which
he reinscribed *casta* within a modern and postmodern semantics, tearing asunder
its local roots. The term as he redefined it made immediate sense to a generation
of scholars, many of them Anglos, who were living through the civil rights and
black power movements, César Chávez's organizational triumphs, and the cultural
movement built around *La Raza:*

> The term [*casta*] became elaborated in the Spanish empire, moreover, in a
> sense yet more antithetical to that of India: it came to mean all those who were
> neither purely Spanish nor Indian. In the seventeenth and eighteenth centu-
> ries it signified above all, not the pure, but the *im*pure, the half-breeds. . . .
> The castas were people of mixed ancestry and a pseudo-biological vocabulary
> was elaborated from popular zoology and the slang of the day to accord a
> distinct social identity to each combination of White, Indian or Negro. (1973,
> 23)[23]

In my view, the Spanish and Portuguese referred to religious groups in India
as *castas* because this term meant something similar in their own societies. Religious purity, while a fiction to many, is a different fiction than racial purity, and it
is not an oxymoronic *distinction without a difference*.[24] It is, I repeat, a "modo de
vivir"; it is *culture*. Up to this point, I have asserted, but not proven, that *casta* was
beyond biology. I now turn to the historical evidence that backs my claim.

In the Spanish renaissance, *casta* meant a noble lineage, as Elio Antonio de
Nebrija's *Vocabulario Español-Latino* attests: "Casta buen linage. genus.eris" (1951,
n.p.). This meaning was to remain stable into the early seventeenth century. The
contours of *casta* are clear in Italian-Spanish and French-Spanish dictionaries that
were published before Sebastián de Covarrubias's *Tesoro de la lengua castellana*.
From Cristóbal de las Casas's *Vocabulario de las dos lenguas toscana y castellana*,
two definitions are significant: "Casta o generacion. *Prole, razza*" (1570, 1731.) and
"*Razza*. Casta o generacion" (114v.). In Cesar Oudin's *Tesoro de las dos lenguas francesa y española*, *casta* and its many synonyms abound: "Casta o generacion, *race,
generation, lignee, lignage*"; "Linage, *lignage, race, parentage, genre, sorte, espece*";
"Generacion, *generation, race, lignee, engendrement, engeance*"; "Genero, *genre,
sorte, maniere, race, lignee, parenté, lignage*"; "Raça, *race, lignee, generation*"; "Ralea,
une sorte de gibier: race, lignage"; "*Une race*, raça, casta, cepa, linage, alcuña"; "*De
bonne race*, castizo, de buen linaje" (1607, n.p.). In *Tesoro de la lengua castellana*,
I find: "CASTA means noble and pure lineage, one that is of a good line and de-

scent, notwithstanding the fact that we say, "it is of a good *casta*" and "bad *casta*" (1943, 316). From Covarrubias's definition, I surmise that popular usage of *casta* flattened out its original meaning, so that *casta* came to mean *linaje, ralea, cepa, raza, generación, parentela, cría,* and so on. In other words, it meant "breed, descent, kind, parentage, lineage," and so forth, rather than "pure breed" (i.e., thoroughbred) or "noble lineage."[25]

Gabriel Alonso de Herrera frequently employed *casta* in this sense in his influential treatise on husbandry, *Obra de Agricultura,* originally published in 1513. In "How a Rooster Should Be," for example, he advised: "One should always look for a rooster of a very select *casta,* for a rooster of good *casta* plants his *casta* in all of the hens, and all of the hens and roosters come from him, and this is a better bet than having hens of such a *casta,* for it multiplies more from the male than from the female" (1970, bk. 5, chap. 17, 297).[26] Historians used *casta* in the same way.[27] Friar Agustín Salucio's *Discurso sobre los estatutos de limpieza de sangre* (*Discourse on the Blood Purity Statutes*), in which he proposed limiting the perpetual infamy that was attached to descendants of heretics, non-Catholics, and Catholic converts (or *new Christians*), also provides compelling evidence that *casta* did not mean "race," much less "half-breed," at the end of the sixteenth century. He wrote, "It also seems a sort of iniquity for a man who has fifteen noteworthy and distinguished great-great-grandparents, and only one from the *casta* of Moors or of Jews, to lose more because of the one than what he gains because of the fifteen" (1975, 30v).[28] What is clear from both the dictionaries published between 1570 and 1611, and from the textual examples, is that *casta* commonly meant the English "breed, lineage, species, vine, ancestry, descent." It meant neither "mixed-blood" nor "half-breed" nor precisely the English "race" or "ethnicity," for plants and horses in English do not constitute a race or an ethnic group in common parlance.

Two other texts from this period that were authored by Crown officials with years of experience in the Spanish Indies are worth mentioning. The first is from New Spain: Viceroy Ortega Montañés's 1697 *Instrucción reservada al Conde de Moctezuma* (*Confidential Directive to the Count de Moctezuma*), in which he frequently employed the terms *mestizo, mulato, chino,* and *negro.* The viceroy used *casta* to mean "group" (mixed or unmixed) in this document: "As the order of nobility [*el estado de la nobleza*] and officials, though sizeable, does not come close to the number of blacks, *mulatos, mestizos,* Indians and other *castas,* it needs to be attended to" (1965, 58–59). Two points are in order here: (1) had *casta* meant only "mixed-blood," or "half-breed," neither the viceroy nor other officials and historians would have bothered to use the other lexicon and (2) *casta* was not a surrogate for *class* because *casta*—to echo Dumont—*occupied a position,* or *had a function,* within the viceregal hierarchies that was *actually different* from that of *class* in modern and postmodern Anglo social hierarchies.[29]

The second text is the 1681 Spanish legal code for the Indies, *Recopilación de leyes de los Reynos de las Indias.* The term *casta* had been used in two sixteenth-century laws (1756, bk. 9, tit. 26). Law 17, first enacted in 1530, reads in part: "If the slave who comes over thusly without permission is a Christian Berber [*ber-berisco*], or belongs to the *casta* of Moors or Jews [*de casta de Moros o Judíos*], or a *mulato,* the general or head of the armada or fleet shall return him, at the expense of whoever sent him, to the Casa de Contratación and deliver him to its judges as our own" (4:41r.). The wording here makes it clear that *casta* meant a religious or kinship group. In the phrase "de casta de Moros o Judíos," *casta* is certainly not the equivalent of mixed-blood. Law 19, based on laws issued in 1526, 1532, and 1550, employed *casta* in the same way. However, the reference was no longer to Jews and Moors: "In the Casa de Contratación great care shall be taken to ensure that no black slaves called *gelofes* nor those from the Middle East, nor those who have been brought from over there, nor any others reared among Moors even if they belong to the *casta* of Guinean blacks, go over to the Indies" (4:4v.). The term *casta* did not signify mixture in either of these two laws. Moreover, in the many laws of the *Recopilación* that pertain to *mestizos, zambos,* and *mulatos,* the term *casta* does not even appear. In sum, to consider that *castas* were legal categories of mixed-bloods (Jackson 1999, 4) is to misread a principal source on which educated Spaniards and Spanish Americans relied in legal, commercial, and political matters of the Indies.

To carry this analytical review of *casta* and its synonyms into Carrió's century, I turn to Francisco Sobrino's *Dicionario nuevo de las lenguas española y francesa,* in which the following entries appeared: "Casta, f. *Race, lignée, f. lignange, m*" (1721, 119); "Casta perruna, f. *Race de chien,* f" (399); "Raza, o Casta, f. *Race, f*" (430); "Decendencia, f. *Genealogie, posterité, race, origine, lignée, f*" (169). The *Diccionario de la lengua castellana* provides us with several similar definitions of *casta:* "Generation and descent from noted Parents" (Real Academia Española 1979, 1:218); "The lineage of horses, bulls and other animals is also called [*casta*], because they come from parents noted for their loyalty, fierceness or other characteristic that makes them distinguished and singular" (1:218); "Metaphorically, all things that descend or proceed from some origin are called [*casta*], for example, *casta* of bergamots, *casta* of apricots, and of other inanimate things" (1:220). In the same *Diccionario,* another entry made it clear that *casta* did not denote only a mixed origin, or a mixed-blood: "MESTIZO, ZA. adjective that is applied to an animal from a mother and a father of different *castas*" (2:556). Were we to assume that *castas* meant mixed, or impure, individuals or groups, this definition would make no sense whatsoever.

When we examine Spanish-English dictionaries from the eighteenth century, we must remember that *race,* in English, did not transcend familial and national ties and did not refer to members of an endogamous gene pool until the nineteenth and twentieth centuries. In Pedro Pineda's monumental *New Dictionary, Spanish and English and English and Spanish,* numerous words, definitions and even adages convey what *casta* meant to this teacher of Latin and Spanish in

London: "*Casta,* a Race, a Breed, a Progeny, a Stock." "PROV. *De Casta le viene al galgo ser rabilargo,* it is natural, or proper to his Breed for a Greyhound to have a long Tail. This is the same as, Cat after kind"; "*Genero,* s.m. a Kind, a Sort, a Manner, a Stock, a Lineage; also a Gender. Latin *Genus*"; "*Cepa,* s.f. the Body of the Vine, whence the Branches shoot out; the Bottom or Foot of any Tree, the Foundation of a House; also a Hedge"; "*Ralea,* s.f. a Race, Stock, Kind, or Breed"; "*De buena Cepa,* of a good Stock or Race"; "*Generación,* s.f. a Generation, a Family, or Lineage. Latin *Generatio*"; "PROV. *No ay Generación, donde no aya ramera o ladrón,* there is no Race without a Whore or a Thief"; and, finally, "*A Race or Stock,* f. raça, casta, abolorio, abolengo, linage" (1740, n.p.). The English *race* to render *generación* made sense in the eighteenth century, but it fails to communicate to us today what *generación* or *race* once meant: the equivalent expression today would be "there's one in every family," for *generación* meant something much more local and familial than *race* means today. Nearly two decades later, San Joseph Giral del Pino did not contradict Pineda's understanding of *casta* in his own *Diccionario Español e Inglés, e Inglés y Español*: "CASTA, s.f. a race, a breed, a progeny, a stock" (1763, n.p.); "RALEA, s.f. a race, stock, kind or breed" (n.p.); "RAZA, s.f. a race, breed" (n.p.). Here *casta* and *ralea* are more semantically flexible than *raza,* which appears to be applicable only to beasts.

In an account of an *auto de fe* in eighteenth-century Lima, Pedro de Peralta Barnuevo used *casta* in the sense that it is found in these dictionaries from the same century. The seventh *penitenciado* was the slave Manuel de Jesus, "Black from Guinea, belonging to the Congo *casta*" (Causa Séptima, in *Relación del auto de fe,* 1733, n.p.). In an anonymous report on mining reforms in Peru, which dates from circa 1740, *castas* appeared several times, as in the following example: "It is asked that by other measures they revive the advantageous results of the *repartimiento,* i.e., that Indians and the rest of the *castas* with the same properties and habits be compelled to go to work" (qtd. in Colin 1966, 61 n. 2). In the first issue of the *Gazeta de Lima* (1744), we read of the fugitive Lucas de Valladolid "of the *mestizo casta*" (1982–1983, n.p.), a phrase that would have been redundant if *casta* had meant to the editor what scholars today want it to mean: a mixed-blood or a group of mixed-bloods. It is only reasonable to assume that the editor of the *Gazeta de Lima* was addressing the paper's readership in a shared language and that *españoles, indios, negros, mestizos,* and *mulatos*—every group, mixed or unmixed—constituted a *casta* in that language.

In the *Instrucción* that Viceroy Francisco de Güemes y Horcasitas of New Spain left his successor, the Marquis de las Amarillas, he first employed *casta* to include at least one unmixed group:

> The majority of inhabitants in this kingdom is composed of reduced Indians, gathered together into pueblos, under ecclesiastical and royal jurisdiction of priests and mayors; of blacks, *mulatos, mestizos* and other *castas* spread about

in cities, pueblos and working farms; and the least number [is composed] of those whom they call Spaniards, a generic name common to those who come from Europe and to those who were born or who descend from them in these parts, to whom they give the particular designation of *criollos*. (1867, 6)

Here it appears that *all groups other than* Indians and Spaniards were *castas,* which means that *negros,* an unmixed group, formed a *casta.* Immediately thereafter, however, it seems that even unmixed peoples other than *negros* were conceived of as *castas:*

The diversity of these *castas* can be seen in this capital, which is populated by all of them, with some foreigners mixed in with them, and though the plebes are base and depraved, they are also cowardly, so in the largest public gatherings a few soldiers are enough to contain their disturbances and excesses, and in my tenure, neither among the plebes nor among the white and distinguished people, has there been an uprising or conspiracy that has disturbed the public peace or caused suspicions of disloyalty. (Güemes y Horcasitas 1867, 6)

The viceroy of New Spain's opposition directly concerns estate (*estado/calidad/condición*). He clearly distinguished between the lower estate that drew from all *castas*—including some foreigners, presumably Europeans—and the high estate comprising "the white and distinguished."

Given the sense in which contemporary scholarship employs *casta,* the entry on Lima in *The American Gazetteer* would confound readers: "The inhabitants of Lima are composed of whites or Spaniards, negroes, Indians, Mestizoes, and other casts proceeding from the mixture of these three." (Anonymous 1762, 2:n.p.). Two interpretations are possible here: (1) that Spaniards and Negroes and Indians gave rise to "Mestizoes and other casts" and (2) that "other casts" implied that "these three," too, were *castas,* or "casts." What was meant by "these three"—that is, "these three" *castas*—and therefore what was meant by "other casts" and "cast," becomes clear forthright: "The negroes, mulattoes, and their descendants, form the greater number of the inhabitants. . . . The third and last class are the Indians and Mestizos; but these are very small in proportion to the multitudes of the second class, and the magnitude of the city" (2:n.p.). Clearly, "cast" and "class"—meaning group or kind—were interchangeable for these authors. At the entry on Guayaquil, their use of "other" conveys that even Europeans and *criollos* constituted "casts": "This city is computed to contain 20,000 inhabitants, Europeans, Creols, and other Casts, besides a great number of strangers drawn hither by commercial interests" (2:n.p.). The summary of the population of Trujillo, Peru, confirms my reading: "The inhabitants consist of Spaniards, Indians, and all the other Casts" (3:n.p.).

Viceroy José Antonio Manso de Velasco used *castas* to mean "kinds" or "kin groups": "many Indians and individuals of other *castas*" (1983, 262). Indians constitute a *casta* in this example. In the 1764 edition of his annual almanac, Cosme Bueno included a description of the provinces within the archdiocese of Lima, in which *casta* designated a mixed group or an unmixed group (1951, 20). In the 1766 edition, Bueno included a description of the provinces belonging to the bishopric of Trujillo (49–68). Again, *casta* appeared in a sense that confounds current scholarship on viceregal Spanish America, as Bueno described Lambayeque, capital of Saña Province: "There are many respectable and noble people, and more than 7,000 souls, between Spaniards, Indians and other *castas,* who along with the other souls in the Province come to 9,000" (1951, 53). In 1768, Bueno included a description of the provinces within the bishopric of Cuzco (92–115), where he wrote, "It has nearly 26,000 inhabitants from all *castas,* among whom the number of Indians is twice that of Spaniards" (1951, 94).

In *El lazarillo de ciegos caminantes,* Carrió writes of the population of Cordoba, Argentina: "En mi concepto, habrá en el casco de la ciudad y estrecho ejido, de quinientos a seiscientos vecinos, pero en las casas principales es crecidísimo el número de esclavos, la mayor parte criollos, de cuantas castas se pueden discurrir, porque en esta ciudad y en todo el Tucumán no hay la fragilidad de dar libertad a ninguno . . ." (167) ("In my estimation, within the confines of this city and its narrow environs, there must be 500 to 600 landowning residents, but in distinguished houses the number of slaves is very high, the majority of them born in the Indies from as many *castas* as you can think of, because in this city and in all of Tucumán there is not the weakness of granting freedom to a single one . . .").[30] In the subsequent paragraph, he details a slave auction in which religious schools were selling slaves from their farms, and his use of *mezcla* reveals that this term and *casta* were not identical to him:

> A mi tránsito se estaban vendiendo en Córdoba dos mil negros, todos criollos de las Temporalidades, sólo de las dos haciendas de los colegios de esta ciudad. He visto las listas, porque cada uno tiene la suya aparte, y se procede por familias, que las hay desde dos hasta once, todos negros puros, sin mezcla alguna, y criollos hasta la cuarta generación, porque los regulares vendían todas aquellas criaturas que salían con mezcla de español, mulato o indio. (168)

> [On my way, two thousand blacks were being sold in Cordoba, all of them born in the Indies and from the temporalities, just from the two farms that belong to the colleges in this city. I have seen the inventories, because each one has its own inventory, and it goes by families, for there are families with two to eleven members, all of them pure blacks without any mixture and the fourth generation to be born in the Indies, because the regular clergy would always sell all of those creatures that came out with a mixture of Spaniard, *mulato* or Indian.]

Together these examples suggest that *casta* and *mezcla* were not interchangeable for Carrió: *casta* was the more inclusive term and *mezcla* the more restrictive term.

To confirm this we need only refer to a few other statements contained in the inspector's exposé. Carrió writes of the population of Salta, "No se pudo averiguar el número de vecinos de la ciudad y su ejido, pero el cura rector, que así llaman al más antiguo, me aseguró y puso de su letra que el año d[e] 1771 se habían bautizado 278 párvulos. Los 97 españoles; y los 181 indios, mulatos y negros; que en el mismo habían fallecido de todas estas castas 186, por lo que resulta que en dicha ciudad y su ejido se aumentaron los vivientes hasta el número de 92" (201) ("The number of residents in the city and its environs could not be determined, but the priest rector, which is what they call the oldest priest, assured me and put into writing that in 1771, 278 were baptized. Ninety-seven of them Spaniards, and 181 of them Indians, *mulatos* and blacks; and that in the same year, from all of these *castas,* 186 had died, which means that in the aforementioned city and its environs the living increased by 92"). On another occasion, he observes, "Todos saben que en este reino, y en particular en los valles desde Piura hasta La Nasca, están entrando, de más de ciento cincuenta años a esta parte, considerables partidas de negros puros, de ambos sexos, y, sin embargo de que los hacendados los casan, no vemos que se aumenta esta casta, no obstante de su fecundidad, y esto nace de que muchos españoles se mezclan con las negras, de que nacen unos mulatillos que procuran sus padres libertar" (390) ("Everybody knows that for more than 150 years now considerable consignments of pure blacks of both sexes have been coming into this kingdom, and into the valleys from Piura to La Nasca, in particular, and although farm owners make them marry, we do not see this *casta* increasing, despite its fertility, and this stems from the fact that many Spaniards get together with the black women, from which are born some little *mulatos* whom their fathers set about to free"). Spaniards, Indians, *mestizos, mulatos,* and blacks: each of these groups constituted a *casta* for Carrió.

Even at the end of the eighteenth century, *casta* was applied to all groups in Spanish America. Economic historians of New Spain and Peru are familiar with the censuses tucked away in archives, and "General census of all persons of either sex and of all estates, *castas* and ages registered in the city of Queretaro, 1778" ("Padrón general de todas las personas de ambos sexos y de todos los estados, castas y edades empadronados en la ciudad de Querétaro, 1778") (see Moreno Toscano 1998, 93) is representative of the genre. Clearly, *castas* here does not mean only persons of mixed ancestry; it covers all groups. In 1796 a chart was drawn up in Lima to represent tributes, the salaries of corregidores, the partidos of the viceroyalty, and so on. Under the heading of "Castas," the chart lists "Spaniards," "Indians," "Mestizos," "Free People of Color," and "Slaves" (see Moreno Cebrián 1977, 730–31). Finally, in his monumental *Diccionario Geográfico de las Indias Occidentales o América* (1786–1789), Colonel Antonio de Alcedo launched a passionate abolitionist's plea at the definition of *negro* (1967, 3:18–19), in which he used *casta* to refer to lineages or tribes of Africans (3:18).

It is in the work of two Spanish travelers to South America that I find *casta* used in the sense that modern scholars use it and in the other senses of the word that it properly had for residents of the Spanish Indies. Jorge Juan and Antonio de Ulloa were at least partly responsible for the current misreading of the term *casta*, which has been an impetus for the scholarly racialization of hierarchy in viceregal Spanish America. In the opening description of Cartagena, Ulloa and Juan wrote, "The communities, and especially that of San Francisco [de Quito], comprise a good number of subjects, Europeans and white criollos as well as *castas* like the ones from that region" (1748, 1:33). Here *casta* denotes all groups that do not belong to "European" or "white criollos," just as scholars of viceregal Spanish America (who, it should be duly noted, have been avid readers of Juan and Ulloa's travels), use it today. Again, as Ulloa and Juan described Cartagena's savannahs, *casta* had this meaning: "In them there are many large population centers and small towns, composed of European and American Spaniards, as well as people from *castas*" (1:35). Later they said of the city's population, "It can be divided into various *Castas* produced by the union of Whites, Blacks and Indians" (1:40). Here it is not at all clear how restrictive *casta* was, for the descriptor "produced by the union of Whites, Blacks and Indians" would have been redundant had "Castas" meant "mixed groups" or "mixed-bloods" or "half-breeds."

The preceding examples suggest to me that *castas*, in their estimation, could be applied not only to groups of people of mixed ancestry or mixed culture but also to unmixed groups that were not made up of European or American Spaniards. In fact, a few more pages into the account of their travels, the traveling scientists Juan and Ulloa applied *casta* to a nonmixed group of people in Cartagena—blacks: "Among all of the *Castas*, that of Blacks is not the smallest in number. These are divided into two estates, which are *Freedmen* and *Slaves*, and the one and the other into another two, which are American borns [*criollos*] and Foreign borns [*bozales*]. A part of these latter are employed in the cultivation of the Estates or Ranches. The ones who live in the city are engaged in the tough jobs by which they earn their daily pay, and from that they give to their Masters a certain sum everyday and they live off what they have left" (1748, 1:43). Even in their *Relación*, then, *casta* was not restricted to groups of mixed ancestry or mixed culture.

Casta's *Counterparts:* Raza *and* Estado *before the Nineteenth Century*

The scholarly racialization of social hierarchy in premodern Spanish America has foregone any conceptual analysis of *raza*. Similarly, the semantics of *estado* (or *condición*) has been assumed more often than analyzed. Because a thorough examination of *raza* and *estado* is not possible within the confines of this study, I offer an abbreviated analysis to clarify what scholars must begin to address in *El lazarillo de ciegos caminantes* and other pre-Romantic texts to which they have transferred their own racial thinking: the failure of anachronistic, reductionist approaches to hierarchy in pre-Romantic Spain and Spanish America.

Several dictionaries and glossaries of Spanish before the seventeenth century suggest the semantic variegation of *raza*. Alfonso XI's *Libro de la Montería* (*Book of Hunting*) employed *raza* as a synonym of the Spanish *almagre* ("red lead") or *minio* ("minium"). In English, minium is more commonly known as cinnabar or another oxide of a metal other than iron, such as red ochre or vermilion.[31] As Chapter 2 of this study shows, *almagre* was used to mark livestock and to mark infamy, so it is not surprising to find its synonym, *raza,* used in a medieval hunter's guide. According to Alonso's research on medieval Spanish, *raza* had widely different meanings. It meant *casta,* or the quality of origins or lineage but also a disease that caused cracks in the upper part of the hoof.[32] In the raucous *Libro de buen amor* (*Book of Good Love*), *raza* carried a physical or a moral charge. In the singular, it signified a flaw in a woven fabric; in the plural, it signified moral flaws, or defects.[33]

In Minsheu's *Dictionarie in Spanish and English,* several entries confirm a variety of usages for the term, which he believed was taken from Arabic (+): "+ Raça, *f. a ray or beame shining through a hole. Also a race, stocke, kinde or breede*"; "Raça de sol, *the sunne-beame*"; "Raça de paño, *the place where cloath is seare or thin, a bracke in cloth*"; "Raçado, *full of bracks in cloath. Speckled or spotted as a horse or beast*" (1599, 202); "*a Race or stocke, v.* Raça, casta, Abolorio, Abolengo" (344). In his Spanish-Italian dictionary, Casas did not equate the Italian *razza* with the Spanish *raza* but instead with *casta*: "*Razza.* Casta o generacion" (1570, 114) and "Casta o generacion. *Prole, razza*" (173). This suggests that he did not think of *raza* as a group, or kind, of humans.

At the beginning of the seventeenth century, Oudin's *Tresor* captured several senses of the Spanish term: "Raça*, race, lignee, generation*"; "Raça del paño, *une raye au drap*"; "*Une race,* raça, casta, cepa, linage, alcuña"; "*Desguiser sa race,* disfraçar, negar su familia"; "*Faire race,* hazer casta"; "*Il tient cela de race,* viene, tiene lo de casta"; "*De bonne race,* castizo, de buen linaje" (1675, n.p.). Covarrubias defined *raza* as follows: "RAZA. The *casta* of purebred horses, which they brand so that they will be recognized [as such]. . . . *Raza* in lineages is taken in a bad way, like to have some *raza* of a Moor or a Jew" (1943, 897). Several other entries from his *Tesoro* give us a sense of the usage of *raza* in contexts ranging from religion and weaving to husbandry and child welfare legislation: "CRISTIANO VIEJO. The clean man [*hombre limpio*] who has no *raza* of a Moor or a Jew. New Christian, the opposite" (371); "ENECHADO. . . . Given all of these trials and risks of theirs, they [i.e., babies abandoned at churches or orphanages] have many legal privileges; among others, they are presumed to be clean [*limpios*], without *raza* of Moors or Jews" (518); "IEGUADA. The breeding group of mares,

... and princes and lords usually have outstanding *razas* of them" (727); "LIM-PIO. ... commonly means an Old Christian man, without *raza* of a Moor or a Jew" (767); "PAÑO. ... 'Even in the best cloth there's a *raza*' ['En el mejor paño cae la raza']: To show one's true colors [*Descubrir la hilaza*, literally, 'to show one's coarse thread'], as a bad cloth does" (851). In *A Most Copious Spanish Dictionary,* Minsheu recorded, "Raça, *vt* Casta, Raça del paño" (1617, n.p.). Finally, the 1675 expanded edition of Oudin's *Tresor* included this: "Raza, f. *Race*" (1675, 1:801); "*Race, f.* Casta, raça, cepa, linage, alcuña, familia" (2:557); "*de bonne Race,* Castizo" (2:557); "*Race d'animal,* Casta, raça" (2:557).

Many of the previously cited definitions from the sixteenth and seventeenth centuries suggest that *raza* and *casta* were nearly indistinguishable. However, Salucio's use of *raza,* which was even more frequent than his use of *casta,* leaves no doubt that they were not synonymous in their legal and social applications to human beings. He began his *Discurso* with the following declaration:

> The Office of the Holy Inquisition in Spain, colleges, military orders and some of the monastic orders, the Church of Toledo and some other churches, certain convents and confraternities exclude by their statutes any person, even if he has all the qualities of nobility and bravery and Christianity and letters imaginable, who on some side [of his family] has the *raza* of a Moor, Jew, heretic or religious convict, and this disability extends to all of the descendants of those who are now excluded, without any limitations whatsoever. (1975, IV.–2r.)

Dozens of other examples confirm the true meaning of *raza* (or *raça,* which I amend to *raza*), including the following three: "It is not astonishing that honorable people who are affected by some *raza* view their being excluded from some privileges as a terrible disgrace" (Salucio 1975,23v.); "To begin with, it should be noted that the people who have some *raza* of Moors or Jews or heretics are of two types" (17v.); "because the sole aim is to encourage those who are in charge of the republic to consider whether it might suit the service of God and the public good that an ancient *raza* not be cause for making countless noble and honorable people, of whose Christianity there is all the proof that one could ask for, ineligible for [religious] habits and colleges and similar things" (18v.). The term *casta* cannot be substituted for *raza* in these examples.

On the other hand, *raza* and *hilaza* and two terms analyzed in Chapter 2 herein, *nota* and *mancha,* were synonymous: they were different metaphors for hierarchy so tightly intertwined with *infamia* that the effect became a semantic substitute for the cause. In Covarrubias's *Tesoro,* we encounter the following: "NOTA. The sign [or mark] of something, from the Latin noun *nota.* ... It also means infamy in someone" (1943, 831). Another example, this one taken from Salucio, is of *hilaza:* "For, how could there be a family who, being unfaithful and living among such faithful people, does not reveal the *hilaza* in parents, or in children or in grandchildren or in great-grandchildren, for a period of 100 or 150 years straight? Certainly, those who never give a sign of infidelity during such a long time rightly deserve that the republic trust them and honor them" (1975, 37r.–37v.). This metaphorical usage of *hilaza* is similar to one of the previous metaphorical usages of *raza*.[34] Yet another example included *nota* and *raza,* the latter being the cause of the former:

> The more distinguished, or more noble, one is, the more the *nota* on one's lineage is perpetuated if one has one, but in the low people [i.e., plebs] the memory of their parents' infidelity rarely goes back 50 years, because no one knows a little or a lot about who their grandparents were, and so if [the latter] have been Moors or Jews or heretics or religious convicts, it does not hinder them, because they are easily concealed wherever. The powerful and noble people are the ones who cannot hide anything or make the *nota* of some *raza* be forgotten. (5v.)

While descent from a Jew, Moor, heretic, or person guilty of religious crimes was the *raza* (or *hilaza*) to which the *nota* of infamy attached in this context, *nota* (or *mancha* or *señal*) was often used in place of *raza* or *hilaza,* perhaps because the effect—the legal and social disability of perpetual shame—was the same for a host of defects. Salucio argued that shame (*infamia*) was brought on all of Spain by the high number of marked people (*gente notada*) and that the black mark (*nota*), or stain (*mancha*), had rendered half of the population incapable of legally holding public office, attending school, or being knighted (1975, 28v.–29r.).

The *nota, mancha,* or *señal* of shame in seventeenth-century Spain was alive and well in seventeenth-century Peru as well. The laws of the Indies demanded that qualified *mestizos, zambos, mulatos,* and black quadroons be allowed to attend the University of San Marcos in Lima, provided they did not violate the university's *Constitution* 238, contained in *Constituciones y Ordenanças de la Universidad y Studio General de la ciudad de los Reyes del Piru.*[35] This *Constitution* 238 was, for all intents and purposes, an admissions statute, and in it we do not find the term *raza:* "Item. Any person who has been punished by the Holy Office, or whose parents or grandparents [have been punished by the Holy Office], or who has some *nota* of shame [*infamia*], shall not be admitted to any rank [*grado*] nor be examined for any rank nor given any rank" (*Constituciones y Ordenanças de la Universidad y Studio General de la ciudad de los Reyes del Piru* 1602, 41 v.). At the end of the seventeenth century, the count de la Monclova reiterated Constitution 238 and ordered the degrees of many graduates rescinded on the grounds that they had been obtained through fraud (Laschober 1979, 123).

Carrió's century presents several definitions and usages of *raza.* In John Stevens's *A New Spanish and English Dictionary,* there were three entries: "*Raça,* a Race, Stock, Kind or Breed. Absolutely spoken it is understood of one of a *Jewish* Breed. Goth[ic]"; "*Raça en paño,* a thin place ill wove in Cloth"; "*a Race or stock,* Raça, Casta, Abolorio, Abolengo, Linage" (1706, n.p.). In Sobrino's Spanish-French dictionary, there appeared the following: "Raza, o Casta, f. *Race, f*" (1721, 430). In Pineda's work, which borrows here and elsewhere from Stevens's (1706) pioneering work, we find the term several times: "*Raça,* s.f. a Race, a Stock, Kind, or Breed; absolutely spoken, it is understood of one of a *Jewish* Breed. *Goth.*"; "*Raça de sol,* a Ray or Beam of the Sun"; "*Raça en paño,* a thin place ill wove in Cloth"; "*Raçado,* that has many thin Places, ill wove"; "*A Race or Stock,* f. raça, casta, abolorio, abolengo, linage" (1740, n.p.). In Giral del Pino, there appeared the following entry: "RAZA, s.f. a race, breed" (1763, n.p.), but it is not clear whether the term was applied to beasts, to humans, or to both.

In Bourbon Spanish America, however, *raza* was applied to humans but not in the social Darwinist sense of the English *race.* Viceroy Diego Ladrón de Guevara of Peru supported a petitioner's claim of innocence in 1713, noting: "The petitioner is supported in his possession and public reputation of Old Christian, notorious *hidalgo,* free of all bad *raza* of Jews, Moors and recent converts to the Catholic faith, and in order that the privileges and honors to which he is entitled, because of his distinction and *hidalguía,* be respected" (qtd. in Lavallé 1987, 56). Ladrón de Guevara clearly believed that not only Jews and Moors but also "recent converts to the Catholic faith" were marked, or tainted, and he determined that the petitioner was *limpio,* or clean, of those bad marks, or *razas.* It would make no sense whatsoever to interpret *raza* here as the equivalent of the English "homogeneous gene pool": recent converts to the Catholic faith do not constitute a *race* in this modern sense.

Casta and *raza* are two of the three intersecting principles of hierarchy that interest us, but to get a more distinct picture of the differences between the social hierarchy of Spanish America in the viceregal period and the racial hierarchy that developed after independence from the Spanish Crown, a third principle requires exploration. The terms *condición, calidad,* and *estado* referred to orders, or estates. This is clear in several entries from Nebrija's *Vocabulario Español-Latino:* "Condicion por estado. conditio.onis"; "Condicion por lei o partido. conditio.onis"; "Estado grado en que esta cada cosa. status.us"; "Estado grande. su~mus status. conditio"; "Estado mediano. mediocris status. conditio"; "Estado baxo. infimus status. conditio" (1951, n.p.). Here again I underscore the fact that the rule of law was the rule of interpretation; it was not a transcendent superstructure that existed independently of social agents. To understand how estate was negotiated, we must look to the estate that was subjected to the most interpretation or litigation: the nobility.

Some sixty years after the publication of Nebrija's work, Juan Arce de Otálora published a treatise on nobility and its privileges that circulated throughout the Spanish world and would be published in several editions. *De nobilitatis & immunitatis hispaniae causis (quas hidalguia appellant)* was in the personal libraries of several high-ranking church and Crown officials in the Spanish Indies, from bishops to governors of cities and judges on high courts.[36] His treatise glossed common law as well as the particular Spanish laws that were independent of Roman laws, for, according to Arce de Otálora, nobility cases and trial procedures could not be properly understood or tried in terms of common law (1553, 37v.).

Reading this lengthy tract written in Spanish and Latin, it becomes evident that a recodification of nobility had occurred in Spain by the early sixteenth century. In the twenty years prior to Arce de Otálora's writing, the legal process of proving one's nobility, and the terms in which the legal finding was rendered, had been reformed: the court's legal finding thereafter distinguished between *senorío,* or having nobility as an inherent property, and *possession* of nobility; between *ser hombre hijo dalgo* and *haber estado y estar en posesión de hombre hijo dalgo.* This distinction was not new, he stated, but its incorporation into the legal instrument—into a court's decision—was (1553, 52r.–54v.). In other words, in the 1530s the Spanish courts where Arce de Otálora was working began to respond to calls to formalize this distinction between *ser* and *estar,* which is worth examining in detail.

Much of Arce de Otálora's treatise is not devoted to the distinction found in the *Siete partidas* between nobility by lineage (*linaje*) and nobility by virtue (*bondad*), in which the latter trumps the former: *E nobles son llamados en dos maneras, o por linage, o por bondad, e como quier que el linage es noble cosa, la bondad passa e vence* (Real Academia de la Historia 1807, *partida* 2, tit. 9, law 6). He was aware of these two definitions of nobility, and he adduced another: "nobility of letters," or intellectual nobility. Yet it is clear that the *Siete partidas* did not hold sway when Arce de Otálora determined that nobility *por bondad* was not the superior type of nobility (1553, 40r.). In his treatise the two types of nobility set down by Alphonso the Wise are reformulated: it is now a distinction between *ser* and *estar,* between *hidalguía nativa,* or nobility as invisible substance/property/essence (38v.–40v.), and *hidalguía postdativa,* or nobility as possession/accident/privilege (88v., 111r.). Proving possession was not enough to be judged to be a nobleman: *possession,* local or general (in one's homeland or throughout the kingdoms of Spain), was based on *common opinion and reputation* of nobility, *not* on the *substance of nobility* (88v.–90r.). Moreover, it was not sufficient to prove that one was a nobleman (i.e., had nobility as an essence) with a *carta executoria de propriedad:* one could have nobility as a property but lose *dominium,* or legal exercise, of nobility by losing the common opinion of nobility (e.g., by being a slave, by exercising a mechanical or sordid trade, by committing a crime, and so forth) (41 r.).

One can imagine some of the applications of Arce de Otálora's interpretation of nobility in the Spanish Indies. A man who legally proved his legitimate descent from an Aztec or Inca belonged to the *casta* of españoles and to the noble order, and he was superior to a Spaniard who had possession of nobility only through royal privilege or public reputation. Similarly, a Spaniard who had legally both the substance and the possession of nobility was superior to a black man who descended from slaves and was granted a *privilegio de hidalguía* by the Crown. The king, Arce de Otálora observed, cannot change blood (1553, IIIr.). His distinction between local and general possession, too, is significant. It suggests that future research into legal cases involving estate, *casta,* and *limpieza de sangre* must be done locally, for possession of nobility in, say, Cuzco did not necessarily obtain in Lima. Or one could be a noble and hold possession of nobility in Lima but lose one's reputation and hence possession of nobility in Mexico City and Santiago de Guatemala, which was the situation that threatened Archbishop Pedro Pardo de Figueroa in 1746. Finally, the distinction between local and general possession helps us to understand how so many Spanish "nothings" became New World "somethings" and then chose to remain in the New World, where they received the social esteem that they had attained there.

Arce de Otálora recognized the Alfonsine distinction between nobility *por linaje* and nobility *por bondad,* but he denied the superiority of the latter and affirmed its inferiority by distinguishing between property and possession: *bondad,* according to his interpretation, was no longer superior to *linaje.* This might also explain why, in Carrió's century, there was little room for *bondad* in a popular scheme of the estates. In 1733 the anonymous author who rewrote Cristóbal Suárez de Figueroa's sixteenth-century *Plaza universal* makes it clear that there are three estates (*estados*) in Spain: the *nobles,* the *ignobles* but honorables, and the *ignobles* and dishonorables. In the second category were *ignobles* whose lineage was pure but not illustrious; in the third category were *ignobles* whose lineage was impure or "infected."[37] Goodness had nothing to do with it. Another eighteenth-century text also picked lineage over goodness, but in a circular way, and while directly acknowledging Arce de Otálora's treatise. Suárez de Figueroa, a censor for the Holy Inquisition and honorary chaplain of Philip V, edited a Spanish version of Sousa de Macedo's 1631 Portuguese treatise on the Virgin Mary, *Eva y Ave.* Nobility was acquired in many ways, but the "inherent nobility of blood" according to Aristotle and the law of Castile was his topic: "It is an inherited quality that inclines [one] to all virtues" (1882, 231). At the same time, however, he asserted that "it usually starts with wealth, and it is perpetuated and perfected with the very same continued wealth" (231). He then reasoned that "a rich man makes use of better foods, which, according to Galen, make for a better temperament, [one] more skilled and suited to good habits" (231). "He has more authority," the Spaniard explained, "and so he converses and is in contact with wise men and virtuous men, in whose company he can learn" (231). According to this scheme, wealth was passed down to his children, along with the same dealings and effects, and the same results followed:

And so by force of habit it happens, and a transmutation of the coporeal origin injects itself little by little, and a most powerful custom is transfused from fathers to sons that in a sense strips nature of all that was base [*vil*] and dresses it in generosity, and the more this transmutation transfuses itself in the branches from the oldest roots the more the inclination to virtue gets hard and strong and becomes inseparable, so that what was found in those who engendered them will be found in their children. (231)

The "continued wealth" segment of this circular equation was paramount, for it allowed Suárez de Figueroa to argue that without wealth men were not noble: "if they are poor they decline from that good origin and incur contrary inclinations, just as we see many grandchildren of well-known grandfathers [fallen] into baseness [*vileza*], and so only continued wealth goes along continuing the antecedents from which, in the future years, out of the habit of good customs, natural nobility results" (Sousa de Macedo 1882, 232).

Although Arce de Otálora is adduced as an authority in *Eva y Ave,* the very circularity of its author's arguments in fact undercut the sixteenth-century glossator's assertions. Neither money nor monarch could make one noble, Arce de Otálora had claimed, because nobility was a natural property, an essence. The "natural nobility starts with wealth . . . and it continues as long as wealth continues" proposition is a labyrinthine defiance of logic in which the social is "explained" as natural and the natural as social, and the poor—whether they were born that way or, instead, fell into poverty—need not apply. One could lose the *legal exercise* of one's native nobility, according to Arce de Otálora, as a result of slavery or having to perform menial labor, for example, but that was not the same as saying that one ceased to be noble when one ceased to be wealthy. On the other hand, Suárez de Figueroa claimed that exercising a base profession did *not* cause the *naturally noble* to lose their nobility but affirmed that "without a doubt [it] strips the nobility acquired by privilege." Exceptions to this rule were certain provinces in Spain like Vizcaya (Sousa de Macedo 1882, 233). From the evidence presented earlier (Chapter 3 herein), it is evident that the nobility in Lima and other cities in Bourbon Spanish America did not all have sufficient funds and networking opportunities to be considered elites, but I have not found any indication that impoverished nobles simply fell out of the noble estate when they fell into the poverty in which Peralta Barnuevo found them. Once again, glosses were every bit as contradictory and intricate as the rule of law itself, and they played a significant role in negotiations of identity at the local and regional levels.

Casta, Limpieza, *and* Estado

We have seen that in viceregal Spanish America, *estado* (or *condición*) was distinct from *casta* and *raza,* although it was joined to these two in the legal and social hierarchy. In book 2, chapter 30, of perhaps the most famous legal gloss of all, *Política indiana,* Juan de Solórzano y Pereira objected to the compulsory labor of Indians in the mines: "For it does not seem fair that this work requiring so rough and tough shoulders, as it requires and as Georgius Agricola points out, is all left to those miserable creatures, while they remain at their leisure and pleasures the *mestizos* and *mulatos,* who are of such bad *castas, razas* and *condiciones,* contradicting the rule that teaches us that lechery must not be preferred to chastity, but, to the contrary, those who are born of legitimate matrimony [must be] more favored and preferred than illegitimates and bastards, as St. Thomas Aquinas and other grave authorities teach" (219). Solórzano assumed that one's place in the social hierarchy was determined by three social facts: a group assignment rooted in social perceptions about religion, hair type, color, language, residence, and profession ("castas"); the legal presence or absence of religious, or "blood," defects ("razas"), that is, the range from *limpio* to *manchando* or *notado* or *infame;* and membership in one of the estates ("condiciones") ranging from noble to plebeian. The interplay of these three hierarchical principles allowed for elastic interpretations of law and custom and for plastic constructions of identity in viceregal Spanish America.

In Bourbon Spanish America, *estado* often overlapped with *casta.* In *Relación,* the marquis de Castelfuerte described the mob in Lima in the most unflattering of terms:

> The mob [*vulgo*] in Lima are many mobs, because it holds as many mobs as the communities [*naciones*] and *castas* who constitute it; and among the latter, the lowest are the most impetuous because they are the most barbarous, and the ones with a mixture of Spanish, although they boast of their orderliness to [advance] the presumption, have barbarity in their haughtiness. Thus, the plebs in Lima is all extremes—comprising the highest and the lowest, of servile communities and of Spaniards—in which the most plebeians consider themselves noblemen, because upon comparison, color alone is their lineage. And so, this variety and disorder, although usually all of the mob is totally loyal and manageable, causes it to be subject to unusual motions. (Armendáriz Perurena 2000, 578)

This ominous mixture of *castas* and *estados* was blamed for the thefts, assaults, and murders that were common in the viceregal capital. By keeping the common people (plebs) away from certain public spaces, the viceroy hoped to improve the quality of life for the higher orders:

> All of the robberies and murders that occur generally stem from the *castas* and communities [*naciones*] of which the city is full, and who are so barbarous that their badness does not shrink from punishment, so that those who do not fear the threat [of punishment] hardly learn by example, and therefore, consider-

ing prevention a better solution than punishment, I have made the greatest vigilance be applied to achieve it, by prohibiting the common people, with the most severe threats, from being in the city streets after 10 p.m. and from using arms and knives, and by having the patrols and troops from both guards constantly on the move, in addition to the rounds that the police make. (545)

Enforcement, it is safe to assume, was not based on a legal finding but relied on what could be called *casta* and *estado* profiling. However, limited access to public spaces in Lima was not the only restriction placed on the plebs and on the distinct *castas* that constituted this order.

The *mala nombradía* of the *Partidas,* which I believe became conflated with *infamia facti* at some point in the fifteenth century, affected possession of nobility, especially on the local level, in Bourbon Spanish America. Spaniards who did not belong to a higher order stayed away from certain trades because they feared *infamia facti.* This fear was rooted in medieval Europe but had parallels in Muslim culture. In countries that had infamy legislation, numerous professions and trades were associated with *vilitas;* they were "dirty jobs" that rendered their practitioners ineligible to join military orders, attend university, take public baths, or even testify in a trial.[38] In Germany, for example, fear of being seen with or even touching certain workers—policemen, actors, skinners, janitors, executioners, and many others—reflected what Kathy Stuart calls "the polluting quality of dishonor" (1999, 3). In the *Diccionario de la Lengua Castellana,* the Spanish Royal Academy referred to *limpieza de oficio* in their definition of *raza;* one of its usages was in fact exemplified by the *Definición,* or blood purity statute, of the knights of Calatrava:

> RAZA. s.f. Casta or quality of origin or lineage. Spoken of men, it is very often taken in a bad way. It is from the Latin *Radix.* Lat. *Genus. Stirps. Etiam generis macula, vel ignominia.* DEFINIC. DE CALATR. title 6, chap. 1: "We order and demand that no one, whatever his quality and *condición,* shall be admitted into said Order, or be awarded the Habit, if he is not an *hidalgo* according to the legal code of Spain, on both his father's and mother's sides, and on both sets of grandparents' sides, and born of legitimate matrimony, and that *raza* of a Jew, a Moor, a Heretic or a Plebeian [*Villano*] must not touch him." (Real Academia Española 1979, 3:500)

In Spain and Spanish America, *limpieza de oficio* (occupational purity) was covered by bylaws, rules, and constitutions that required nobility in addition to purity, and it too had originated in the laws regarding infamy, as Chapter 2 suggested. Arce de Otálora's treatise touched on dirty jobs, or "occupations base and contrary to nobility" (*officios baxos y contrarios de hidalguia*), "as are lessors or merchants and others that the law stipulates . . . , tailors, skinners, carpenters, stonemasons, excavators, shearers, barbers, apothecaries, peddlers, cobblers, etc."

(1553, 73 r.). Those persons who lacked *limpieza de oficio* were *villanos;* this *raza,* or defect, greatly restricted their social space and life choices. The result was that mechanical, or impure, professions were often the domain of members of the lower *castas* and orders. This was especially true of Spanish America, where Spaniards involved in the Indies trade were legally exempt from the shame associated with merchants shown previously but where manual, or mechanical, labor was incompatible with nobility, according to common opinion.

The Inca Garcilaso reported that Beatriz Coya, the daughter of Huaina Cápac, rejected marriage to a well-to-do Spanish man because it was rumored that he had been a tailor. She relented only after much coercion from her family, who feared that strained feelings between the Spanish nobility and the Incan would result if she did not accept the marriage offer (Pérez de Barradas 1976, 149–50). The conviction that occupational purity, or *limpieza de oficio,* was intertwined with estate and *casta* was still very much alive in the eighteenth century. After his discussion of noble Spaniards in Lima, the Marquis de Castelfuerte added, "As for the rest of the people here who, being Spaniards, do not consider themselves plebs, some crafts and manufactures could be assigned to them. . . . Which could be met by prohibiting those who were not Spaniards from exercising certain mechanical trades, which have to such a degree been handed over to those of the lower *castas* that, out of disdain for being equal to the latter, there is no one who will practice the former" (Armendáriz Perurena 2000, 425).[39] Despite royal attempts in the seventeenth and eighteenth centuries to change the de facto shame that was associated with certain trades or callings, these continued to be considered indicators of estate, *casta,* and *limpieza* in common opinion (Rípodas 1977, 29–30). If not merit but instead blood determined one's estate, if trades were often handed down from father to son like blood, if a decision by the king altered not a man's essence (substance) but only his legal exercise (possession), then the well-documented efforts of the Spanish Crown to rehabilitate mechanical trades were doomed to failure (Jacobs 2001, 61–70). As one mulatto complained in the anonymous *Drama de los palanganas,* Viceroy Amat encouraged women of the higher orders to shame themselves when he insisted that they dance with his girlfriend, *La Perricholi,* in the 1770s. That she belonged to a mixed *casta* was not the cause; it was her shameful profession: "for an actress, by her trade (*por su oficio*), becomes shamed (*infame*) and unworthy of having contact with ladies (*señoras*)" (in Lohmann Villena 1976, 200).

The interface of *casta* and *estado* is evident in *El lazarillo de ciegos caminantes,* as the inspector reports that Spaniards in Peru respect Indians who are not noblemen and not members of the *casta* of Spaniards but merchants: "El raro indio que se hace de algunas conveniencias es estimado de los españoles, que le ofrecen sus efectos y se los fían con generosidad, y no desdenan tratar con ellos y ponerlos a sus mesas" (382) ("The uncommon Indian who dabbles in trade is esteemed by Spaniards, who offer him their goods and do not hesitate to sell them to him on credit, and they do not frown upon associating with them or seating them at their dinner table"). Moreover, although Carrió ridiculed the panhandling Indians who represented themselves as skilled painters, sculptors, and embroiderers, he underlined that the Indians who had settled down in Lima and were devoted to manual trades (*oficios mecánicos*) were exceptions to this general rule (388). On this score, Carrió was less rigid and fearful than many of his contemporaries in Peru, who feared being "polluted" (as Stuart terms it in her 1999 study on Germany) by association with certain trades and tradesmen.

Wherever Carrió lived and traveled in eighteenth-century Spanish America, local hierarchies were built from interpretations of the intersecting principles of *casta, estado,* and *limpieza* (*de sangre* and *de oficio*), which are irreducible to *race*.[40] Viceroy Francisco de Güemes y Horcasitas of New Spain titled a section of his report as follows: "Mob of diverse *castas,* poor, prone to vice, and inevitably in a state of idleness due to the lack of something productive for them to do." In the body of the text, he wrote, "The second group, comprising plebeians, is a monster of as many species as the *castas* are diverse, its number being increased by Spaniards lowered by poverty and sloth, the roots from which base habits, ignorance and irremediable vices in general arise" (1867, 7). Evidence from La Plata, another stop on Carrió's inspection tour, suggests that plebeian Indians (*indios*) could hardly feel their honor or reputation (*honra, fama,* or *crédito*) offended by another person because they were entitled to so little. In his *Practica de la Doctrina Christiana* (*The Practice of Christian Doctrine*), Juan Antonio Dávila Morales explained how gossips violated the Ninth Commandment: "Gossips who ruin a reputation [*quitan fama*], which is usually called honor [*honra*], with their bad tongue, are really bad people, and they sin mortally. Besides the great sin that they commit, they have the obligation to make restitution for the reputation and name that they ruined and for all of the damages that they have caused with their bad tongue" (1730, 47). But not all transgressors ruined someone else's reputation, he noted, for "it is necessary that [what is said] be very bad and very ugly with respect to the person of whom it is spoken" (48). The examples he gave prove that estate was every bit as powerful, socially speaking, as *casta* in Bourbon Spanish America:

> Getting drunk is very bad and very ugly, because it is a mortal sin, and yet, to say of some Indian that he gets drunk is not to ruin his reputation, but to say it of a respectable Spaniard would be to ruin his reputation; the reason is, because for the respectable Spaniard, this offense is very ugly, and for the Indian it is not, in the eyes of men [*al parezer de los hombres* (sic)], nor does the Indian lose his reputation because of it like the Spaniard would. Likewise, if it were said of a spirited and wanton young man that he goes with a lot of women, or of a woman who lives wrongly and is viewed by all as a hooker it were said that she was shacking up, neither the man's nor the woman's reputation would be ruined by this, either because they had already lost it in this

area or because these offenses do not seem as ugly in such individuals as they do in a respectable man or woman. (48)

Two things are evident in this passage. First, neither *casta* nor *limpieza de sangre* is invoked, although drunkenness was often associated with members of the *casta* of *indios* (who should not be confused with the documented descendants of the pre-Columbian nobility and royalty who were members of the noble estate and belonged to the *casta* of Spaniards, as I explain later) and although the behavior of the young man and the woman would have made the people around them treat them as outcasts, or shamed persons. Second, precious little respect was afforded persons who had the denomination of *indios* because, like the prostitute and the womanizer, they belonged to the lower estate, or behaved as if they did, which was the same thing, *al parezer de los hombres* (*sic*).

Dávila implicitly confirmed that *indios,* or plebeian Indians, had no shame.[41] They had not assimilated the Spanish cultural paradigm that made one's reputation or name (*honra* or *fama*) a matter of life or death, in terms of its legal and social implications: "From what has been said I infer that, among the Indians, rarely do they ruin each other's reputations (*pocas vezes se quitan la honra*), because they care very little about moral failings and offenses (*faltas y delitos*), and [therefore] they lose none of their name or public standing [*de credito ni de estimacion*], and when they do lose some, what they lose is not much. However, by this I am not denying that it could happen" (1730, 40). Dávila's statements about *indios* reveal how this *casta* assignment was inextricably intertwined with an *estado* assignment: no one could write such things about men who belonged to the *estado* of noblemen without being charged with libel or defamation of character. Just as Arce de Otálora's treatise revealed that by the early sixteenth century, the *probatio* (or legal test) of nobility relied on social actors (from judges and lawyers to members of one's community), Dávila's comments demonstrate that de facto *casta* and *estado* assignments were made *al parecer de los hombres*—in the court of public opinion.

Biology Vanquished, or the Legal Contradictions of Casta Membership

We cannot forget that laws as well as their glosses, in addition to local practices themselves, maintained the social hierarchy in which a *casta* did not exist independently of the persons who belonged to it: a biological *mestizo* whom the Crown made a member of the *casta* of Spaniards was a Spaniard, not a *mestizo*. In other words, the Spanish legal tradition itself reflected (and reinforced) a social hierarchy in which *casta* was not synonymous with common descent or *race* as we understand it today. This is abundantly clear from a letter to the Council of the Indies written by the count de la Monclova, viceroy of Peru, in 1698: "The *mestizos* . . . although in truth they are [*mestizos*] with this name because they are the sons of Spanish men and Indian women, must not be called that way generally, since none of them rates himself as anything but a Spaniard, and in the King's paid ranks, and in the ranks of the militia in this city and in the entire Kingdom, they are enlisted as such" (qtd. in Lavallé 1987, 43). Biological *mestizos* whose Spanish parent acknowledged them and who served in the military or the local militias belonged to the *casta* of Spaniards and to the same *estado* as Spanish militiamen—that is, they were plebeians. Like militia men who belonged to the *casta* of Spaniards through their parents, half-Spanish militia men who legally possessed the privileges and responsibilities of the *casta* of Spaniards did not qualify for marriages and positions that required nobility in addition to membership in the *casta* of Spaniards.

Similarly, appointments that could be bought or assumed only by members of the *casta* of Spaniards who did not belong to the lower estate were legally held by men who were, in strictly biological terms, not Spaniards. For example, even in Carrió's times it was not unusual for *mestizos* to serve as scribes or scriveners (*escribanos* or *escribientes*), posts restricted to Spaniards in good social standing (i.e., those without *razas,* or defects, that incurred shame). According to the reporter for the Council of Indies who glossed Solórzano y Pereira's *Política indiana* for re-publication in the eighteenth century, many applications were filed by biological *mestizos* and approved by the Council of Indies.[42]

In Ulloa and Juan's discussion of the ancient nobility who constituted a third or a fourth of Lima's white population of sixteen thousand to eighteen thousand people, they took for granted that *casta* and *estado* could be legally and socially independent of biological or genetic notions of descent:

> Among these there can be found one that traces its origins to the Inca Kings, and that is the Ampuero family, the last name of one of the Spanish captains who participated in the Conquest and who married a *coya* (that is what the Incas called their princesses of royal blood). The Kings of Spain have conferred various graces and distinguished privileges on this family, who hold them as proof of their high quality, and many of the most illustrious families are related to this family in that city, in which the families make of every House a village. (1748, 3:67–68).

Carrió himself implicitly acknowledged that Spanish laws from the early seventeenth century, reiterated in 1697 and in 1725, defined Indian governors, *caciques,* militia leaders, and even their legitimate, biologically *mestizo* descendants, not only as Spaniards but as *hidalgos* as well. In *El lazarillo de ciegos caminantes,* we read that the inspector nominated "an honorable landowning resident" ("un vecino honrado") to be in charge of the posts in Oruro: Don Manuel de Campo Verde y Choquetilla, "a Spaniard, and a descendant on his mother's side of legitimate *caciques,* and a governor of Indians" ("español, y descendiente por línea materna de legítimos caciques, y gobernador de indios") (301). Carrió does not call Campo a *mestizo,* although his father was Spanish and his mother indigenous, because his mother was the descendant of legitimate *caciques* (members of the pre-Columbian nobility), and we can assume that she married her equal: a *legitimate* Spanish nobleman. Campo, then, did not belong to the *casta* of *indios* or to the *casta* of *mestizos,* and his *casta* and *estado* memberships support a claim already made about viceregal Spanish America: "Indian lineage, in fact, was not necessarily a handicap, and if noble or royal, could be used to advantage" (Schwartz 1995, 189). In brief, royal or noble *Indian* lineage *was not Indian at all* within the viceregal hierarchy: it occupied the position reserved for noble *Spanish* lineage.

However, I contend that as the definitions, constitutions, rules, and bylaws that required religious and professional purity, or *limpieza,* gained strength in Spain and crossed the Atlantic and as the treatises and commentaries on nobility and purity proliferated, the absence of Catholic roots became a source of de facto infamy (what Alphonso the Wise had called *mala nombradía*) that was not always compensated by membership in the *casta* of *españoles* and the noble estate. The possession of *infamia,* like that of nobility (*fama* or *honra*), had general as well as local dimensions. New Granada is a good example. The Spaniards who founded and settled the New Kingdom of Granada in the first half of the sixteenth century had lived the social hierarchy in Iberia. Proof of its ability to discourage Spanish-Indian marriages is obliquely suggested in Lucas Fernández de Piedrahita's *Historia general de las conquistas del Nuevo Reyno de Granada* (*General History of the Conquests of the New Kingdom of Granada*), whose illustrations highlighted the pre-Conquest rulers in a quasi-retable format (Figures 18 and 19). He closed his chronicle by noting the last of the kingdom's three singularities:

> The third and last singularity may be, no matter how reason tries to attribute it to the great arrogance of its conquerors, that although there were in the New Kingdom so many noble women, daughters and sisters of Kings, *Caciques* and *Uzaques,* whom the noblest men who set out on its Conquest might, without detriment to their splendor, have taken as their wives, as was the practice everywhere else in Spanish America, one cannot establish that a single one among all of them married an Indian no matter how distinguished she was, and not, in my opinion, because they faulted an inequality of blood, but rather, because upon seeing them—gentiles and in the subjection of prisoners—the Castilian point of honor disdained receiving in matrimony someone who did not assent to it with a lady's liberty and a Catholic woman's upbringing, and as a result, married men sent for their wives in Castile, and those who were not married resorted to choosing, from among their own community [*nación*], the daughters or relatives of those married men, or women who by some seemly accident had gone over to the Indies, upon whom the many Houses of Lords that distinguish the New Kingdom of Granada were founded. (1688, 599)

It is explained here that the conquerors of New Granada, unlike those earlier conquerors of New Spain and Peru, did not feel comfortable marrying a member of the pre-Columbian nobility or royalty. I would suggest that their discomfort was not caused by her ignorance of Catholicism but by *what people would say* about her lack of a Catholic upbringing. The problem was not biological—a lack of noble blood that would make her inferior to a Spanish nobleman—but social: de facto infamy, or the loss of good name, was probably their fear.

Yet their fear appears to have been unfounded in light of other bits of historical evidence. The *Constituciones,* or bylaws, of Santa Fe de Bogotá's Colegio Mayor de Nuestra Señora del Rosario (1666), for instance, treated young men who were related to the pre-Columbian nobility or royalty deferentially, just as Carrió was to treat them a century later in the Viceroyalty of Peru. The pertinent *Constitution,* or blood purity statute, reads as follows: "First of all, all the students shall be legitimate, without the contrary being dispensable, and we even wish that their parents be legitimate and that the contrary be dispensed with only for the gravest of reasons. Second, their parents shall not exercise lowly trades, and much less ones that are shamed [*infames*] according to the laws of the Kingdom, without there being any dispensation for this, either. Third, they shall not have blood of the land [*sangre de la tierra*], and if their ancestors had it, it shall have come out in a way that the students are eligible for knighthood, and not any other way" (Torres 1666, 10v.). How are we to reconcile these two historical documents from the New Kingdom of Granada?

Tracing the origins of religious and professional purity (*limpieza de sangre* and *de oficio*) in Spain back to the laws and opinions about shame (*infamia*) is only the first step to understanding hierarchy in viceregal Spanish America. As we have seen, the lack of a Catholic upbringing was one of the numerous "defects" defined by theologians and glossators as *irregularities,* and neophytes and their descendants were shamed according to Gratian's *Decretum* (see Chapter 2). The second step consists of understanding and articulating how the debates over nobility and *limpieza* in Spain shaped the ways in which bylaws, constitutions, rules, and statutes on *limpieza* operated in the Spanish Indies.[43] These controversies were every bit as heated as those that arose from the Indian Privileges legislation, and, in fact, the two controversies did not lead wholly separate lives.[44] To take this second step, we must first comprehend that two main camps existed. One held that religious and occupational purity bylaws, constitutions, and so forth could not be applied to groups for whom they had not been designed; the other argued that they could and should be applied outside the original groups. The first camp was led by Crown authorities; the second was led by church authorities.

In *Política indiana,* the eminent jurist Solórzano y Pereira upheld the opinion that the religious and professional purity statutes did not apply outside the groups that they targeted, stating that the long-converted Indians, though they descend from parents and grandparents who were infidels, must be admitted to the priesthood and to all benefices and ecclesiastical dignities, public posts and offices, in which neither God nor the law normally wishes that there be exclusion or preference of persons, and he finds no law that includes them in the Statutes of Churches, Orders and Colleges that deny admission to Jews and Moors and those who in any way descend from them. . . . Which doctrine I consider to be most correct, because these Statutes must be interpreted and applied strictly, and only in the cases and persons of whom they speak, and with particular attention to the causes in which they are founded, which are the heart and mind that gives the Statutes life and sustains them, and where it is absent or ceases, its disposition likewise ceases, according to the Rules of Law. . . . In which [Law], or in other Books or Histories, we never find that descent from Gentiles or Infidels who were not Jews or Moors, and who voluntarily received the Faith of Christ, has been blackmarked or considered to be tainted and excluded. To the contrary, those today who boast the most of the splendor and glory of their Ancestors trace their origins to them, and they are proud of this, as Juan de Arce Otálora, in terms of such Statutes, and Antonio Riciulo, about the member of the Neophytes, point out. (1:213–14)

Arce de Otálora did, indeed, express this opinion (1553, pt. 2, chap. 7, 76r.). Still, it was a stretch for the former judge on Lima's high court to adduce this as a foundation for his interpretation of the letter and spirit of the purity statutes. Arce de Otálora recognized that such statutes violated Holy Scripture, common law, and the *Siete partidas* (76v.). However, popes supported them, as did the Spanish laws against treason and divine treason (which rendered the guilty and their descendants perpetually shamed, or *infames*), so he argued that they were both just and holy (77v., 79r.). He acknowledged doubts only about the applications of statutes to *Muslims and Sarracens* (79v.). His discussion of the statutes did not broach the issue of the applicability of purity statutes to Africans, Indians, and their descendants in Spain or Spanish America. For Judge Solórzano y Pereira, the rule of law was the rule of interpretation, and the written interpretations (or glosses) themselves were subject to interpretation.

The second camp was represented by Ildefonso Pérez de Lara, a native of Toledo, Spain, who was a chancellor at the Lima Cathedral and a member of His Majesty's Council in Madrid. Like Arce de Otálora's treatise, Pérez de Lara's *De anniversariis et capellaniis* (*On Anniversaries and Chaplaincies*), first published in 1608, was often aired in Spanish discussions of *estado* and litigation around nobility.[45] Pérez de Lara's opinion on the application of purity statutes to groups for whom they had not been designed turned on the foundation that Indians, blacks, and their descendants were neophytes, or *cristianos nuevos,* just like *moriscos* and *conversos.* He adduced numerous authorities to argue that noblemen must be preferred in ecclesiastical appointments and admissions, memberships in confraternities, military orders, and so forth, and the *Constitutions* from the Bogotá college legislated the same. Santa María del Rosario's admissions constitution, however, allowed men who had "sangre de la tierra," or some indigenous ancestry, to attend as long as they belonged to the noble estate. This was consonant with Solórzano y Pereira's legal opinion in *Política indiana,* in which he argued that Indian and African nobles should be treated as the Spanish nobility were:

> Where there would rightfully be objections is if we were in a case of Statutes that required not only purity, or purity of blood, but also nobility, as in those of military orders, and then I would not admit plebeian or tributary Indians and Blacks, and even less so if they had been slaves or the descendants of them, for it cannot be said that the nobility that such illustrious insignias require is found in the latter. But if they were to prove that they possess or have possessed it in themselves, or in their ancestors, because they descend from the Kings or ancient Caciques of those lands—from Incas or Montezumas, let us say, or from others in those lands who in their own way were held and commonly known to be Nobles and like Little Kings and Bosses to the others—I would not hesitate to admit them and consider them worthy of them [military orders], just as the King's Council of Orders has acted in some cases. . . . Because, although formal findings of Nobility in those Provinces and peoples cannot be discovered and proven like those of Castile, everybody in his own way has his rules and customs with which he measures and distinguishes it [nobility] . . . , and we must utilize and be contented with that [nobility] when those from other Kingdoms wish to be admitted to the Illustrious Knighthoods and Communities in ours, as the Council of Orders itself acts and observes in assaying and weighing the Nobility of Frenchmen, Italians, Germans, Venetians, Genovans and other Foreigners. (1:214)

The *probatio,* or trial, commonly called *información* or *interrogatorio* in the constitutions or statutes of Spain and Spanish America, could not prove the nobility, or *fama,* of Africans and Indians by resorting to written documents, but the means and customs used in a particular land by a particular people were admissible in such a trial, according to the Spanish judge.

Pérez de Lara, in contrast, contended that purity statutes applied not only to Jews, Moors, and their descendants but to *all* neophytes and their descendants (1767–1768, 185). Solórzano y Pereira was thoroughly familiar with Pérez de Lara's moral authority and with his blanket application of the purity statutes to Indians, Africans, and all of their descendants, which was similar to the blanket application of the statutes to Jews, Moors, and all of their descendants in Spain that had been repudiated by Pérez de Lara's contemporary, Salucio:

Noting, as is proper, the opposing opinion regarding this matter that Pérez de Lara (a Man worth praising and following in all other matters) appears to hold, for after debating both sides of it he concludes that in our Spain it has been the practice that neither Indians nor Blacks nor those who descend from them shall be admitted where such Statutes exist, for it cannot be verified that they are Old Christians. . . . But I cannot fathom the law on which this practice could have been founded, nor have I heard of any individual cases that have been brought to trial and decided, which are the ones that could introduce it, and if neither Indians nor Blacks have been admitted, it must be because, as Riciulo says, they have never applied, or where there are Statutes that exclude all Infidels and their descendants. . . . In which opinion I find that the learned and prudent man, Don Juan de Escobar del Corro, who is today Most Worthy Councillor of the Supreme and General Inquisition, agrees with me, in the erudite and copious Treatise that he wrote on the purity of blood that these Statutes require, in which he considers and answers, one by one, all of Pérez de Lara's arguments, and he deduces the great equity that exists for the descendants of Indians and Africans to be treated favorably. . . . So then, at the same time we shall resolve the matter that Pérez de Lara himself promises to treat elsewhere—to wit, what are we to think and to say of the children of the noble and ancient Spaniards who got married to Indian, *mestizo* and *mulato* women in those Provinces?[46] Because if, as it has been said here, these Statutes do not properly apply to the already converted Indians themselves, much less will they apply to their descendants. We neither can nor should practice or apply here the doctrine of Simancas and Calderón, which requires at least two hundred years of conversion in the ancestors of one that wishes to prove that he is an Old Christian, and be considered and admitted as such, because they speak of those who descend from Jews and Moors, who are subject to other rules and conditions specific to them, as it has been said. (1:214)

Solórzano y Pereira's narrow application of the religious and professional purity statutes came nearly a century after Arce de Otálora's demonstration of nobility as a cultural construct. The College of Santa María del Rosario's *Constitutions* had been based on the *Constitutions* of a school in Granada, the city where Arce de Otálora was serving the Crown when he published his treatise, and it is not unlikely that his opinion, either directly or by way of Solórzano y Pereira's *Política indiana,* shaped the college's admissions constitution.

The hierarchical cluster of *casta, estado,* and *limpieza* permitted a biological *mestizo* with a noble indigenous mother like Carrió's "honrado vecino" and "español" to attend a college for the Spanish nobility: this is the opening acknowledged by the third requirement of the Bogotá college's admissions constitution. Yet other colleges in the American viceroyalties operated according to a different interpretation. Another member of Arce de Otálora's family, Father Francisco de Otálora, was a Franciscan minim and commissar for all of the provinces of Peru in 1601, when the order's *Constitutions* for the Province of the Twelve Apostles were published. These *Constitutions* followed the general statutes of Toledo, and the order did not admit a man whose parents were not Spaniards, a man who was physically deformed, or a man who was clearly stained or shamed (*señalado*) (*Constituciones de los F. menores desta Provincia de los Doze Apostoles del Piru* 1601, chap. 1, 2v.). In their 1631 *Constitutions,* which claimed to uphold the general statutes of Barcelona as reformed in Segovia, the admissions ban (*Constituciones desta Provincia de los Doze Apostoles del Piru* 1631, chap. 1, 4) was even more explicit. The *Constitutions* for the Province of the Holy Gospel in New Spain denied admission to Indians, *mestizos,* and men who had an Indian grandparent (*Constituciones de la Provincia del Santo Evangelio* 1640, 2r.). In none of these cases was *estado* (or *condición*) invoked. However, we do know that in 1728 the Corpus Christi convent for Indian noblewomen (*cacicas*) was founded in New Spain, which later belonged to the Franciscan order.[47] It is not surprising to find schools whose constitutions or monasteries and convents whose rules did not concord with those of the college in Bogotá: whether canon law or common law or Spanish law was invoked, glosses as much as the laws themselves shaped purity constitutions, bylaws, and statutes at the local level. The glossators adroitly contradicted one another as often as the laws themselves did, and the authority of the glossators in different circles suggests why the purity rules varied so widely and how the conflicting interpretations of these rules carved out a person's space within the social hierarchy.

Passing, or Vertical Movement within the Social Hierarchy

If the ideological foundation of the social hierarchy in Carrió's times had not acknowledged, implicitly and explicitly, that *casta, estado,* and *limpieza* were socially constructed; if it had had the scientific pretensions of, say, nineteenth-century biological determinisim; if it had acted to exterminate non-Spaniards, rather than attempt to convert them to the great extirpator Dávila's "[Spanish] way of life"; then *passing,* or extralegal end arounds, would have been more difficult. As it was, the ideological foundation of the social hierarchy—laws and glosses in particular—facilitated extralegal vertical movements between *castas* and *estados* by showing men and women that the supposedly immutable laws of nature could be overturned. It was a short step from hiring a lawyer to litigate or negotiate possession, or membership in a certain *casta* or *estado,* to simply performing socially—taking possession of—a desired *casta* or *estado* until someone questioned it.

While the legal system and tradition provided the means and the incentives to change *castas,* the norms and values of Peruvian society in Carrió's times also encouraged de facto movement between *castas.*[48] Rebellions organized by *mestizos* and Indians, along with negative assessments of *cholos* (the offspring of *mestizo* men and Indian women), encouraged members of these different *castas* to switch *castas* whenever it was convenient and possible to do so. In 1750, after three Indian actors had conspired against the Crown in Lima, Viceroy Manso de Velasco banned Indians from acting in dramas that recreated episodes from the Inca period and the Spanish Conquest.[49] In 1756, shortly after the indigenous rebellion in Huarochiri, the theologian and official chronicler of the Order of Mercy, Father Diego Mondragón, wrote a report to King Ferdinand VI.[50] He viewed the rebellion as one in a series that had begun in Tarma in 1744, and he accused the Indians of treason and apostasy:

> The crimes of the Indians who have revolted in the mountains of these Kingdoms and principally of those within the Provinces of Tarma, Guanuco and Guamalíes, are enormous; they are guilty of lese majesty for their uprising and revolt against their legitimate King and Lord, by coming down from the mountains to commit hostilities against the Indian Christians here outside, inciting in them disobedience and revolt, as experience has shown in these years. They are blasphemous, uttering execrable propositions about Christ, his saints and the Church. With their rhetoric and support they have induced many Christian Indians to abandon their faith and return to their infidel beliefs, giving them a home among them and in the mountains. They have committed sacrilegious persecutions of missionaries and preachers of the faith, the converted apostates taking their lives with the help of the gentiles from the mountains, where these good Samaritan Indian murderers, Christians in name and apostate Judases [in deed], took refuge during these past few years. His Majesty will know all about this already from the details that the Viceroys must have provided you. (1756, f. 338r. and v.)

Mondragón claimed that Indians in all of the kingdoms of Peru delivered themselves, body and soul, to laziness, the "mother of all vices." "They are ungrateful, deceitful, timid, inconstant, of servile nature, lazy on their own and great workers by force and fear" (1756 ff. 324v.–325r.). After being charged, rebellious Indians and *mestizos* falsely accused their shepherds: "Many are the false testimonies that arraigned Indians and *mestizos* are now giving against their priests and lay clergy" (f. 325r. and v.). However, the Indians "in the lowlands and in the highlands," and others who lived in towns, were exceptions: they were in constant contact with priests and Spaniards, they attended church and they were docile. Mondragón even complained that Spaniards and *mestizos* had converted these long-suffering innocents into slaves: "Many Indians live in various factories, cattle, horse and mule or sheep and goat ranches, working farms and silver and gold refineries. In these places live the Indians, enslaved by Spaniards and *mestizos*" (f. 327r.).

Neither the *casta* of *cholos* nor the *casta* of *mestizos* was looked upon favorably in eighteenth-century Peru. Father Mondragón explained how *mestizos* came to be, and he repudiated their ill treatment of their "uncles":

> From the incontinence of Spaniards and the weakness of Indian women, about whom Father José Acosta says discreetly and sententiously that their modesty or womanly shame is rare and their willingness is common or abundant, *rarus pudor nimia facilitas,* there were born the *mestizos* whom Mr. Solórzano calls *h* [i.e., hybrids], which in the Latin language is *quid progenitum ex Apro et suc,* which is not translated into Castilian [here] due to the indecency of its meanings. They are nephews of the Indians, and *mestizos* are now lords of their uncles, and they hold them enslaved on the farms inherited from their [Spanish] fathers: their morals are dissolute, and they are seditious. Because of these and other vices, the Second Liman Council orders that neither blacks nor *mestizos* live among the Indians, and the laws and royal ordinances stipulate it, because by their bad example they are the ruin of the Indians in Christian and civic matters. (1756 f. 327r. and v.)

The *cholos,* a *casta* formed by the offspring of Indian mothers and *mestizo* fathers, were even worse:

> From these *mestizos* a third kind of persons has been engendered in these parts, whom they call *cholos,* the children of *mestizo* men and Indian women. These people are worse than their fathers: they do not pay a tribute to Your Majesty, nor are they subject to the labor obligations of the wretched Indians. With respect to the *mestizos,* Mr. Solórzano [y Pereira], in his *Política indiana,* advises Your Majesty to make them pay tributes for the incontinence of their fathers, and that upon committing crimes they be condemned to labor in the mines following the example of the Romans, which would be a great help to the Indians who are wasting away by the day, if this adjudication, punishment or politically sound, lawful and Christian resolution could be achieved without a disturbance. (1756 f. 327v.)

We have already seen others advocate for this position—a legal shifting of the labor burden from the *indios* to *mestizos* and/or *mulatos.* Father Mondragón's defense of Indians provides us with at least one motive for the vertical climb that many of them took, which was recorded in the viceroy's memoir: the Spanish compulsory labor and tax laws, which favored the members of mixed *castas* in Spanish America. Under the Habsburgs, Indians had stayed on the move to evade compulsory labor (*la mita*), often relying on the incompetence or indolence of Crown officials who were supposed to administer the royal census in their jurisdictions.[51] Clearheaded Indians in eighteenth-century Peru were not banking on the laws to change anytime soon; they were changing themselves to fit the laws that favored *mestizos.*

According to a 1726 broadside attached to an *auto de gobierno* and signed by the Marquis de Castelfuerte, the *corregidor* of Guamanga should be vigilant about the problem addressed by the priest in the San Juan de Ica parish: the propensity of officials to recognize Indian claims to *mestizo* status without examination.[52] This was not an isolated phenomenon in the Viceroyalty of Peru: ten years later, in *Relación,* Viceroy José de Armendáriz Perurena detailed a new head count that he had ordered. "It is a new comprehensive census," he wrote, "on which a true idea of the Indians that said provinces presently contain—especially the provinces subject to the *mitas* of Huancavélica and Potosí—and the dissolving of the fraudulent schemes that were being committed in their hiding depended, requiring that inspections of their *pueblos* be conducted throughout the Kingdom, with the most exacting scrupulousness that ought to be applied and selecting for them [i.e., the inspections] the judges who seemed to me most fit" (2000, 423). This "Measure so that Indians cannot exempt themselves in the census with the pretext that they are *mestizos*" conveyed that the decline in the number of Indians who were subject to forced labor was due to their ingenuity, not their mortality: "And because the [Indian] *pueblos* themselves are all mingled with *mestizos* (persons who are more a hindrance than an abundance because they neither respect the ones nor love the others, and who neither obey nor contribute with tribute), [and] in order to prevent the fraudulent schemes in which many Indians alleged that they were such *mestizos* for the purpose of exempting themselves from this obligation, I demanded that those who thusly pretended to steal their bodies from their patrons present proof that they were *mestizos*" (423). The viceroy claimed that tributes and participants in the *mita* had greatly increased, adding that either disease had not killed as many Indians as people thought, or the ones killed had been replaced by children who had reached legal age, "(or what is closer to the truth) that they had been hiding" (424).

In *Noticias americanas* (*American News*), a 1772 work with which Carrió was familiar, Antonio de Ulloa conveyed explicitly that the exemption from tribute enjoyed by the offspring of Spanish males and Indian females (but not by the offspring of Spanish females and Indian males), by some *mulatos,* and by the offspring of *zambos,* had the unintended consequence of shrinking the Indian population and favoring "the mixed progeny" (*las generaciones mixtas*) (1772, 293).[53] As we shall see, the inspector in *El lazarillo de ciegos caminantes* confirms that legal and extralegal forms of social mobility were rampant among certain *castas,* confirming what Gerald D. Berreman suggested nearly forty years ago in his work on India: mobility is inherent to caste societies and, although punished, can never be wholly suppressed.[54]

What I have set down in the preceding pages compels us to rethink how we approach demographics in Bourbon Spanish America. The very baseline of identity—the position or positions that one occupied within a local hierarchy—was different from our own, racial, baseline. If scholars continue to racialize the groups and categories of the pre-nineteenth-century Hispanic world, they will also continue to skew the demographic reality of that world. Carrió's exposé points the way out of this quandary; it compels us to approach population "statistics" with caution by underlining that *castas* were not at all biological, genetic, or fixed. Before we turn to that demonstration, however, let us review the eighteenth-century numbers on Lima and Peru.

In *Relation du Voyage de la Mer du Sud aux côtes du Chily et du Perou (Account of a Trip to the South Sea Along the Coast of Chile and Peru,* Amédée François Frezier estimated Lima's population at between twenty-three thousand and twenty-eight thousand people, of which eight thousand or nine thousand were Spaniards and the rest were blacks, *mestizos, mulatos,* and Indians (1716, 195). In a travelogue published four years later, Durret claimed that there were more than twelve thousand Africans and Indians enslaved in Lima, in addition to Lima's population of five thousand Spaniards and forty thousand blacks (1720, 249). In *A New Dictionary, Spanish and English and English and Spanish,* Pineda, a Spanish and Latin teacher in London, pegged Lima's population at "about 5000 *Spaniards,* 40000 *Blacks,* and many thousands of *Indians*" (1740, n.p.) These were the same figures that Captain Stevens had given in his *New Spanish and English Dictionary* thirty-four years before (1706, n.p.). Based on their brief stint in Lima in 1740, Ulloa and Juan (1748) estimated that there were between sixteen thousand and eighteen thousand Spaniards in Lima, one-fourth of whom were titled noblemen, including descendants of the Incas. Although they observed that blacks and *mulatos* greatly outnumbered the *casta* of Spaniards, whereas Indians and *mestizos* were the smallest populations, the Spanish scientists did not put a number on any of them. Courte de la Blanchardiere did not offer figures for Lima's population in 1747; he merely noted that "the majority of the inhabitants are blacks, *mulatos* or Indians; there are few whites" (1751, 128).

Important information about Lima's population was provided by *Voto consultivo,* which I have mentioned repeatedly. Judge Pedro José Bravo de Lagunas y Castilla's rarely studied opinion from 1755 is compelling because it brought together chronicles and censuses of Lima from the period between 1600 and 1754. The judge noted that Lima's population under Viceroy Luis de Velasco in 1600 was 14,262 *vecinos* (landowning residents), which did not include slaves or service workers. Under Viceroy Marquis de Montes Claros, Lima had 25,454 inhabitants in 1614. Sixteen years later, a friar claimed that the viceregal capital had 40,000 inhabitants. In 1637 another friar wrote that Lima had thousands of *negros, mulatos, mestizos, indios,* and other *castas;* 6,000 Spanish men; and 20,000 women from all *castas.* Fifty years later, a historian recorded that Lima had more than 10,000 Spaniards and more than 70,000 Indians and blacks. Under Viceroy Count de la Monclova in 1700, the capital city had 37,234 inhabitants in total. In the same period, a French geographer asserted that Lima had between 50,000 and 60,000 inhabitants. An account of the earthquake in Lima (1746) put its population at 60,000 before the earthquake, whereas the judge himself claimed that in 1750 Lima had between 52,000 and 54,000 inhabitants and that at his present (1754), it had between 54,000 and 55,000 people (Bravo de Lagunas y Castilla 1755, 129–46).

In the 1764 edition of his annual almanac, Bueno wrote that the population under the jurisdiction of the archbishop in Lima "amounts to almost 54,000 persons, of whom an estimated 16[,000] to 18,000 are Spaniards, among whom there are families of shining nobility, founding families from illustrious Houses in Spain; a little over 2,000 Indians; and the rest [are] *mestizos, mulatos* and blacks, these last two *castas* being the ones that are most abundant" (1951, 20). Bueno's estimate from 1764 suggested a preponderance of persons whose language, dress, residence, occupation, and appearance associated them with an African or partially African community. In his *Memoria de gobierno,* Viceroy Manuel de Amat y Junient cautioned that in Lima and the outskirts of Lima lived "many blacks, *mulatos* and makers of mischief," who, because they were not slaves, easily "deliver[ed] themselves to every sort of vice and criminality" (1947, 166).

According to all of the preceding population "statistics" and estimates, Spaniards born in America or Europe were outnumbered by other *castas.* However, because *casta* assignment was a very subjective business, and it could not be made without a concomitant *estado* assignment and a social or legal judgment about a person's *limpieza,* we should not treat these figures as if they were scientific.[55] Another discernible pattern in these "statistics" is the penchant for generalities, or the refusal to talk numbers. Carrió also adopted this tack in *El lazarillo de ciegos caminantes.*

He faulted Spanish and other men for the decline in the Indian population. The union of *indias* (plebeian Indian women) and non-Indian males (especially blacks and Europeans) increased the number of *mezclas,* or persons who belonged to mixed *castas,* and decreased the number of *indios*: "Estas mezclas inevitables son las que disminuyen más el número de indios netos, por tener un color muy cercano a blanco y las facciones sin deformidad, principalmente en narices y labios" (390) ("These inevitable mixtures are the ones who most diminish the number of pure Indians, because they have a color very close to white and features without deformity, principally in the nose and lips"). The inspector tells Concolorcorvo some of the differences between Peru and New Spain. There were far more Indians in the latter than in the former to begin with, and since the Conquest, very few Spaniards and very few blacks had mixed with Indians. In New Spain, there were very few blacks as a general rule, and they were particularly scant in the interior, or rural areas. Because of its proximity to Europe, there was an abundance of Spanish women in New Spain. As a result, Spanish men did not need to turn to Indian women for sex, and more *indios* existed there:

En México, además de estar infinitamente más poblado aquel imperio de indios, no ha tenido los motivos que éste para que se corrompiese esta nación con la entrada de europeos, y mucho menos con la de negros. Esta nación solamente se conoce en poco número de Veracruz a México, porque es muy raro el que pasa a las provincias interiores, en donde no los necesitan y son inútiles para el cultivo de los campos y obrajes, por la abundancia de indios coyotes y mestizos, y algunos españoles que la necesidad los obliga a aplicarse a estos ejercicios. La proximidad de Europa convida a muchas mujeres a pasar al imperio de México, de que proceden muchas españolas, y la abundancia hace barato el género para el abasto común de la sensualidad y proporción de casamientos. (389–90)

[Mexico, beyond that Empire's being infinitely more populated by Indians, has not had the reasons that this one (i.e., the Empire of Peru) (has had) for this community to become corrupted by the entry of Europeans, and much less by that of blacks. This community (i.e., blacks) is seen only in small numbers from Veracruz to Mexico City, because it is rare for a black to move into the interior provinces where they do not need blacks, and they are useless for the cultivation of the fields and textile works due to the abundance of mountain Indians and mestizos, and some Spaniards who are compelled by necessity to apply themselves to these labors. The proximity of Europe invites many women to go over to the Empire of Mexico, from which spring many Spanish women, and abundance makes the product cheap for the common supply of sensuality and proportion of marriages.]

The Viceroyalty of Peru was a different story, of course. From Lima to Jujuy, and in Huamanga, Cuzco, La Paz, Oruro, Huancavélica, and Chuquisaca, Spanish women were basically nowhere to be found. And in these areas and throughout the viceroyalty, "hacen sus conquistas españoles, negros, mestizos y otras castas entre las indias, como lo hicieron los primeros españoles, de que procedieron los mestizos" (390) ("Spaniards, blacks, *mestizos* and other *castas* make their conquests among the Indian women, like the first Spaniards did, from which sprang the *mestizos*"). One of the reasons, then, for the decline in the Indian population was that men other than Indians had sexual relations, and children, with Indian women. Furthermore, many Spanish men had sexual relations with black women, which was the reason for the decline in the black population (390).

As Berreman long ago observed about India, it is impossible to stop the members of different caste groups from interacting with each other, and from their interaction spring cultural sharings and mobility.[56] However, Carrió was confident that something very basic could be done to stem the decline in the black and the Indian populations of Peru: all offspring should be given back to their respective mothers (black and Indian). As he put it, "Yo creo que si se restituyeran todos los vivientes a sus madres, ni el indio padeciera decadencia ni el negro. *Intelligenti pauca*" (390) ("I think that if all newborn babies were returned to their mothers, neither the Indian nor the black would suffer decline. *Intelligenti pauca*"). Knowing what we do about caste systems in general and about the Spanish American *sociedades de castas* in particular it is unlikely that Carrió's strategy would have worked. Still, it is important that we understand the nature of the social dream that Carrió was chasing. What he proposed was the eventual elimination of mixed *castas,* not by killing them but by keeping *mulatos* and *mestizos* and other mixed *castas* from assimilating to Spanish culture. His demographic engineering scheme assumed that *mulatos* were *mulatos* not because their fathers were Spaniards and their mothers blacks but because they were not *reared* as blacks. Similarly, *mestizos* were *mestizos* not because their fathers were Spaniards and their mothers Indians but because they were not *reared* as Indians. If all *mestizos* and *mulatos* were returned to their respective mothers and *reared* as Indians and blacks, Carrió argued, they would *be* Indians and blacks.

Indians who work for Spaniards, the inspector tells Concolorcorvo, cut their nails, wash up, do their hair, and "pass for *cholos,* which is the same thing as having a mingling of *mestizo*" ("pasan por cholos, que es lo mismo que tener mezcla de mestizo") (386). A *cholo* in eighteenth-century Peru was, legally and socially, between an Indian and a *mestizo.* The inspector states rather casually here that (biologically) plebeian Indians were able to pass out of the *casta* of *indios* and into that of *cholos,* a vertical ascent within the social hierarchy of Peru. If the same Indian exchanges his native dress for Spanish dress and puts on a pair of shoes, "a los dos meses es un mestizo en el nombre" (386) ("he's a *mestizo* in name, two months later"). On another occasion, the inspector corrects Concolorcorvo's assertion that the men and women who worked as sculptors, painters, and embroiderers were not Indians because they were too light skinned: "No piense Vm. sacar de la esfera de indios a muchos hombres y mujeres porque los ve Vm. de color más claro, porque éste proviene de la limpieza y mejor trato, ayudado de la benignidad del clima, y así sus descendientes pasan por mestizos finos, y mucho número por españoles" (388) ("Don't think of removing many men and women from the sphere of Indians because you see that they are of a lighter color, for the latter comes from hygiene and better dealings, helped along by the benign climate, and thus their descendants pass for refined *mestizos*—and a good number [of them] for Spaniards").

Viceregal identities, as we are prone to label them today, were always to some degree both consensual and positional, not assigned by blood. The latter was simply shorthand, or code, for the negotiations themselves: hence, the incessant desire to establish one's religious and occupational purity. It was not really "pure blood" that was at stake; rather, it was the privileges or disadvantages associated with this trope—what "clean blood" or "dirty blood," derived from certain ancestors or certain jobs, allowed or disallowed people. In retrospect, Arce de Otálora's observation that it was not *really* possible to change one's blood was largely irrelevant in the face of material reality: in sixteenth-century Spain and in eighteenth-century Spanish America, people could, and did, manipulate their *casta* and *estado* and hide a *raza* here or there.

When we handle population counts or demographic observations from Carrió's Peru, we should always acknowledge that *casta* was not a biological artifice: it was not the equivalent of the nineteenth-century *raza* (or *race*). The inescapable implication of this acknowledgment, which is long overdue, is that we do not truly know the descent of persons listed in censuses as *negros, mulatos, españoles,* and so forth, and quite often neither did they. By the same token, it would not necessarily have told us anything relevant about those unnamed persons: as Carrió knew very well, a "modo de vivir," or *culture*—not biology or *race*—generated local and regional hierarchies.

CHAPTER 6

The Inca Impostor Unmasked: Culture, Controversy, and Concolorcorvo

Alonso Carrió de Lavandera's views of the Inca descendants who belonged to the same *casta* and *estado* as he did and of the *indios, mestizos,* and *cholos* who did not are the subtext of many of the dialogues between the inspector and Secretary Concolorcorvo examined in the following pages. The oscillating subjectivity of Concolorcorvo—the metamorphosis that he undergoes in their sometimes feisty, sometimes ridiculous dialogues—has been the subject of competing critical interpretations (Stolley 1993, 105–7; Meléndez 1999, 80–84). However, previous scholarly assessments have not ontologically assessed this demasking, which reflects debates about identity, responsibilities, and privileges that were raging *outside* of the text.

The fictional intertexts and historical inspirations for Carrió's invention of Concolorcorvo cannot be ignored. As explored herein, they range from newspapers and literary magazines to historiography, geography, and satirical poetry and prose. In addition, the interface of the fictional scribe Concolorcorvo and the historical Calixto Bustamante and the extratextual relationship between the latter and Alonso Carrió de Lavandera are two issues that I plumb in depth. Both of these issues entail others already raised in this study: for example, the personal relationship between postal officials in Buenos Aires and Carrió (see Chapters 3 and 4) and the ideological and structural affinities between *El lazarillo de ciegos caminantes* and *Don Quijote de la Mancha* (see the Introduction herein)

What follows explores still another problem: the postmodern notion of *hybridity,* which must be set aside if we are to grasp why Concolorcorvo is defaced in *El lazarillo de ciegos caminantes.* To this end, I explain (1) the meaning of *hybris* and (2) how Catholic norms and the legal system of the Hispanic world shamed not only many persons who belonged to mixed *castas* but also, and relentlessly, persons related to anyone who had been born out of wedlock.

Finally, we have already considered Carrió's stint as a *corregidor* and his opinions of some high court judges and other officials in Lima who supervised provincial governors. It remains to be seen how the figure of Concolorcorvo is related to Carrió's experience as a governor and to the controversy around a viceregal institution known as the *repartimiento* ("distribution"), in which Indians were forced to purchase mules, agricultural tools, and sundry supplies from their governor.[1] The discussion of the *repartimiento* controversy also reveals an ideological and personal overlap with Carrió's inspection of the posts, his exposé, and his eventual imprisonment.

Concolorcorvo: A Dialogue with Journalists, Satirists, Historians, and Critics

Carrió's construction of Concolorcorvo was, at least in part, a reaction by a long-time Lima resident, or *perulero,* to what he viewed as the delusions of grandeur suffered by residents of rival Cuzco. In both *El lazarillo de ciegos caminantes* and *Reforma del Perú,* it is evident that Carrió felt that authors had greatly exaggerated Cuzco's grandeur.[2] Inca ruins were just that—ruins. Spaniards who told otherwise were like the man from La Mancha, Carrió wrote:

> It is true that there are some Spaniards who appear to have been transported here from Toboso by the art of enchantment to see the temples and palaces of the Incas, and that some idol makes them see what is not really there. Many other fragments are spread throughout the Kingdom, which testify to the barbarism of the Indians, and this is what the Spaniards inherited from the Incas and caciques (1966, 47)

Whether it was precipitated by a Baconian idol, as Carrió suggests in this passage, or by Michel Montaigne's lofty praise for the royal roads built by the Incas and later frequented by travelers, merchants, and postmen (1988, 402), the image of Cuzco in the Old and New Worlds was as imperial in Carrió's times as it had been during José Pardo de Figueroa's lifetime. According to Cosme Bueno, whom Carrió admired:

> This is the largest City in our South America, after Lima. . . . This City has very good buildings that can compete with those in Europe, wide streets and roomy squares. It has a good amount of water, brought in by water mains from nearly a league away that supply the City, distributed in various fountains, though it is not very clean. . . . Among its ancient monuments the most significant is the fortress that, although worn and torn from neglect by its inhabitants and the toll of time, nonetheless exhibits the grandeur of its owners, the Incas. . . . . Cuzco is a place of great commerce and full of the finest provisions that the neighboring Provinces supply. It has nearly 26,000 inhabitants of all *Castas,* of which the number of Indians is twice that of Spaniards. Among the latter there are some families of distinguished and ancient nobility. (1996, 93–94)

In *El lazarillo de ciegos caminantes,* the inspector will hear none of this. When Concolorcorvo wishes to praise the ancient Incas and the Spaniards, the inspector cuts him off:

Iba a insertar, o como dicen los vulgares españoles, a ensartar, en compendio, todo lo sustancial sobre las conquistas de los españoles en las Américas, pero el visitador, que tenía ya conocido mi genio difuso, me atajó más de setecientos pliegos que había escrito en defensa de los españoles y honor de los indios cozqueños, por parecerle asunto impertinente a un diarista, y asimismo me previno no me excediese en los elogios de mi patria, por hallarme incapaz de desempeñarlo con todo el aire y energía que merece un lugar que fue corte principal de los Incas, mis antepasados, y el más estimado de los españoles conquistadores y principales pobladores. A éstos, que desde sus principios ennoblecieron la ciudad con suntuosos edificios de iglesias y conventos, en que resplandeció su piedad y culto al verdadero Dios, y en sus palacios y obras públicas su magnanimidad, se les acusa alguna soberbia. (334)

[I was going to insert, or, as the Spanish plebs say, in*sort,* in abridged form the significant stuff of the Spaniards' conquests in the Americas, but the inspector, who had already experienced my diffuse nature, cut out more than seven hundred of the pages that I had written in defense of the Spaniards and in honor of the Cuzcan Indians, because he thought the subject was impertinent for a diarist/journalist, and likewise he warned me not to go too far in the praises of my homeland because I was incapable of performing the task with all of the elegance and force that a place that was the principal court of the Incas, my ancestors, and the most prized by the conquering Spaniards and the distinguished settlers, deserves. In the latter, who, from their very beginnings (here), ennobled the city with sumptuous buildings of churches and monasteries in which their piety and worship of the one true God glittered, and their magnanimity in their palaces and public works, some haughtiness is clearly visible.]

An apparent detail in this passage brings us to another stark imprint on *El lazarillo de ciegos caminantes.* Here and elsewhere there are explicit references to *diario* and *extracto* that might suggest that Concolorcorvo is keeping a diary or even a travelogue. Yet we should not miss an important link between the invention of Concolorcorvo and newspapers: *diario* was a synonym for "newspaper" or "literary magazine." The eighteenth-century understanding of *diario* makes it clear to me why Carrió placed this term in Concolorcorvo's mouth (or feather pen):

DIARIO. Used as a noun it means the historical report of what has been occurring for days, or day by day, on an expedition, trip, etc., like those that come off the press today in France, England and Holland with the title of

Journals of the Wisemen [*Jornales de los Sabios*], which contain the progress that the Sciences and Arts are making by the day. It comes from the Latin *Diarium, ii,* which means just that. (Real Academia Española 1979, 1:265)

The *Journal des Savants* (or *Jornal de los Sabios,* Spanish singular) was a *diario* dear to Bourbon elites in Spain and the Spanish Indies. Moreover, *Gaceta de Lima* issues from 1756 through 1758 usually had a section of international news followed by a section of local news titled DIARIO DE LIMA. Its news was called *memorias,*[3] just as literary news in Paris appeared in *Memoires de Trévoux,* also followed by elites in Lima, and just as we find several times in Carrió's exposé.[4]

There are still other parallels that suggest to me that the culture of the newspaper and the magazine left a deep imprint on Carrió's exposé. First, in *The Post-Man Robb'd of his Mail. Or the Packet broke open* (1717), Charles Gildon wrote that British periodicals such as *The Tattler* and *The Spectator* were essentially letters written to the public and that he was adopting the same format because of the short attention span of modern readers.[5] Moreover, Secretary Concolorcorvo's *diario* is ostensibly an extract of the inspector's full inspection report, just as the political or literary extract—or letter—was a common feature of newspapers and literary journals. Furthermore, the "Crow-with-Color" himself is visually linked to newspapers. The Spanish *gaceta* (*gazeta* with a "z" in the eighteenth century) came from the diminutive (*gazzetta*) of the Venetian *gazza,* which meant magpie (*urraca* in Spanish), and appeared at the top of many issues. The letter that opened the first report in some issues of *Gaceta de Madrid* included a magpie (Torrione 1998, 19–20). A magpie is a bird of prey that is similar to a crow, has black and white or gray plumage, and is known for chattering and for stealing various and sundry objects. In Carrió's times, and in the early nineteenth century, *urraca* was defined as similar to a *grajo* or a *corneja.*[6] The European magpie (*urraca*) was synonymous with the Spanish American mockingbird (*arrendajo* or *cercio*).[7] An *arrendajo* is similar to a crow, but it has black and white and gray plumage and a blue spot on each wing: it is a *crow with color,* or *Concolorcorvo.*[8]

Not only journalism but also Menippean satire can be related to Carrió's invention of Concolorcorvo. In Baltasar de Gracián's *El criticón,* the allegorical character Historia remarks that every golden feather pen errs. Sugarcoated history "while it will be laughed at now, will be believed 100 years from now" (1967, 716). Historia tells a soldier prince to cut his own feather pen with his sword. If the sword cuts well, the pen will write better (718). Another prince wished to have the best feather pen of all so that he could be immortalized. Historia could see that he deserved it, so he gave the prince a feather pen taken from the wings of a crow: "He was not happy about it, but instead grumbled that while he thought that [History] would give him the feather of some royal eagle to fly to the sun, he was giving him that so very unlucky one. 'Hey, Mister, you don't get it!' History said, 'these are crow's feathers for pecking, for making out motives, for uncovering the deepest of secrets'" (718).[9] Carrió's invention of Concolorcorvo, then, is at least in part an indication of how he is often to be used by the inspector in the text (Carrió outside of the text): to tell the truth—pecking away; getting to the bottom of motives; uncovering the deepest secrets about hierarchy, commerce, and fraud in Bourbon Spanish America.

Lucian of Samosata's *Icaromenippus* (1961) is a satire that could have inspired Carrió's transformation of the historical Calixto Bustamante into Concolorcorvo—an *Inca Menippus,* if you will. Carrió's *Inca Menippus* rides not the majestic sun chariot (*Carro del Sol*) of Ovid's *Metamorphoses* but, instead, a mule.[10] Icarus Menippus is given wings and an eagle's eye, and he flies over the world so that the protagonist can ridicule pedantics and other fools. Europeans and Americans knew that the Incas had worshipped the Sun. They could read Carrió's jocose parallel of the proud Icarus, who flew too close to the sun and went down in flames and the proud Calixto Bustamante who flaunted his relationship to the Incas, whose worship of the sun had not safeguarded them from invading Spaniards. Just as Lucian had fashioned of the mythical Icarus a satirical Icarus, Icarus Menippus, Carrió fashioned of Calixto Bustamante (whose relationship to the Incas, Carrió considered mythical) a mercurial Inca, Concolorcorvo. This invention allowed Carrió a safe way to express his anger and humor on topics of philosophy, history, and politics and toward the Bourbon technocrats who were claiming to reform and transform Spanish America.

The relationship between the inspector and Concolorcorvo is also similar, as a rhetorical device, to that which is established in a satirical poem by Carrió's blind contemporary, Friar Fancisco del Castillo Andraca y Tamayo, who aimed to correct social vices by poking fun at them.[11] The poet is walking toward Merchants Street (*Calle de los Mercaderes*), which formed one side of the Plaza Mayor (see Figures 8 and 9) and which was so named not only because it is the site of the merchants' guild but also because whorehouses do good business there (905–6). Accompanying him is a *lazarillo* (906, 907, 909), who laughs at the disorder and moral decay of the downtown district: "Aquí, mi buen Lazarillo,/riéndose a boca llena,/celebra en alegres burlas/las que juzgó tristes veras" (909) ("Here, my dear guide,/by laughing right out loud,/celebrates in merry jests/those that he deemed sad truths"). Just as Friar Castillo had a scribe who wrote down his poetry and plays, Carrió had a secretary who accompanied him during a piece of his inspection of the posts, and the textual representation of that secretary, Concolorcorvo, charges himself with writing down the itinerary of the inspector's commission (and then some).

On one metaphorical level, the nickname *Concolorcorvo* plays off the rhetorical and poetical sense of the term *color*—that is, embellishment, trope, or figure—for the Inca secretary fancies himself what he is not. During the Italian renaissance, Cesare Ripa highlighted *colors* and wings similar to those of Mercury in his representation of the imagination.[12] Appearances and the imagination came together in Gracián's understanding of *color* in *El criticón*. Seer (*Veedor*) tells Crit-ilo that our perception, or conceptualization, of objects and events corresponds to our emotions rather than the objects and events themselves:

> So be aware that it is the plain truth, and thus every day you will see that one says white and another says black about the very same thing. From what each conceives, or from what each perceives, one gives a thing the color that he wishes, according to affect, not effect. Things are nothing more than how they are taken, thus what Rome admired, Greece laughed at. Most people in life are dyers and they give to the deal, the feat, the project and the event the color that suits them. Everybody reports in his own way, because as is his affection, so is his affectation. Everybody speaks of the market according to how it went for him. Painting is like wishing. So it is necessary to examine the thing praised or scorned as well as the person who praises or scorns. (904–5).[13]

Decades before Gracián, Traiano Boccalini said much the same, but he un-derlined the connections between princes and their lying erudite mouthpieces and how the latter controlled the mob.[14] Clearly, the semantics of *color* included sim-ulation, or feigning,[15] and the *Diccionario de la lengua castellana* in Carrió's times associated *color* with dissimulation: "*Color*. Means also pretext, motive and appar-ent reason to undertake and execute something undercover and underhandedly" (Real Academia Española 1979, 1:420).

In *Reflexiones sobre la historia,* Benito Jerónimo Feijoo y Montenegro had criticized the Greek historian Xenophon for being less determined to write his-tory than to "paint a perfect Prince in false colors" (1773–1774, 4:164). He had de-manded that rhetorical adornments be natural, not artificial: "The same colors of a face that are pleasing to the eye when they are natural, become repulsive when one senses that they are imitated with added ingredients" (4:168). Feijoo y Montenegro there had also created an opposition of importance to Carrió's exposé, praising historians who "are accustomed to a middle style that rubs shoulders neither with the plebs nor with the Muses, equally distant from the squawkings of crows and the song of swans" (4:167). Carrió slightly altered this opposition to suggest that the inspector's secretary was a failed historian. Near the end of *El lazarillo de ciegos caminantes,* when Concolorcorvo wishes to extend even further his extract by de-scribing Lima, the inspector denies him: "Los señores don Jorge Juan, . . . don Antonio de Ulloa y el cosmógrafo mayor del reino, doctor don Cosme Bueno, escribieron con plumas de *cisne* todo lo más particular que hay en esta capital, a que no puede Vm. añadir nada sustancial con la suya, que es de *ganso*" (441–42) ("Lords Don Jorge Juan, . . . Don Antonio de Ulloa and the royal cosmographer, Doctor Don Cosme Bueno, wrote with *swan's* feathers [plumes] everything that is most particular in this capital, to which you cannot add anything substantial with your own, which is a *goose's*").[16] In addition, in the passage on Cuzco quoted earlier, Carrió obliquely insinuated a parallel between Concolorcorvo and Feijoo y Montenegro, based on his reading of the Benedictine's *Reflexiones sobre la Historia:* the Inca Concolorcorvo uses a term of "common Spaniards," *ensartar,* which was similar to the language of Feijoo y Montenegro's earnest description of the process of writing history.[17]

In sum, Carrió both debunked Feijoo y Montenegro's discourse and appropriated it to invent the posturing Inca secretary. The latter is an inarticulate man who has flights of fancy, wishing to adopt the sublime style of epic in his description of Cuzco and the Incas. In his dialogues with the inspector, Concolorcorvo exhibits the very same characteristics that Antonio de Ulloa, three years before the clandestine publication of Carrió's exposé, had attributed to Indian plebs. In North and South America alike, they were garrulous, and they suffered from delusions of grandeur.[18] *Concolorcorvo* is a crow-with-embellishment, or a crow-in–swan's disguise: a prolific scribbler who fancies himself a historian. Carrió valued experience above all else, and on this score neither Concolorcorvo nor Feijoo y Montenegro had the experience necessary to judge the New World or to write a history of it.

In Sebastián de Covarrubias Orozco's 1610 *Emblemas morales,* there is an emblem on the value of experience that illuminates Carrió's desire to instruct rookies, or *bisoños* (1978, cent. 2, emb. 69, f. 169). The renaissance humanist found his motto ("Nec frena remittit, nec retinere valet") in Ovid's *Metamorphoses* and described his symbol as "Phaeton disguised as a coachman." Part of his poem reads, "No basta la teorica, o la ciencia,/Ni leyes de Partida, o del Quaderno,/Si no pratica un tiempo y se exercita,/En qualquiera ocasión se precipita" (f. 169), which roughly translates as "Theory, or study, is not enough,/nor are Spanish or Roman laws/If he does not practice for a while and gain experience/At any moment he will hasten his end." By proclaiming himself the author of the inspector's report, Concolorcorvo fashions himself the guide to blind travelers or blind traders—the driver of the coach. Near the end of Carrió's account, Concolorcorvo asks if Lima can be compared to Mexico City. The inspector replies dryly, "*Alta petis Phaeton,*" in an Ovidian reminiscence (467 and n. 4) that becomes a jocose conceit. Concolorcorvo wants to drive the inspection, to be the author, but he flies too high when he writes of the Incas and other topics.

On this metaphorical level, then, *Concolorcorvo* is a metaphor for the scribbler with delusions of historiographical grandeur, and Carrió chose this nickname because it created a disproportion between the person who is revealed to the reader and the person the secretary claims to be. In *Treatise on the Ridiculous* (Il *Cannocchiale Aristotelico,* chap. 12), Tesauro noted that much material could be found in *comparative deformity*—that is, the disproportion between two joined objects: "As an example, if the NAME does not fit the person . . ." (1968, 587). Under the heading of *simple metaphor,* he dealt with *antiphrasis*—giving the name of *Gi-*

ants, for example, to midgets (294). Both of these examples fit under the single rubric of "contrary dissimulation" in Baldassare Castiglione's treatment of humor, according to Juan de Boscán (1994, 304).

As for Feijoo y Montenegro, he aspired to eliminate errors, introducing empiricism and Cartesian rationalism into the Hispanic republic of letters. However, in Carrió's opinion, the Benedictine *savant* failed to judge properly the minds and territory of the New World: his declamation against the Spanish conquerors, coming in the middle of his *Fábulas de las Batuecas y países imaginarios,* was just as out of place as Montaigne's criticism of the Spanish conquerors in his essay on coaches (Hill 1998, *passim;* Montaigne 1988, *passim*).

Both Concolorcorvo and Feijoo y Montenegro are failed authors because they are ignorant: they lack the experience necessary to discharge the responsibilities that they have abrogated for themselves.

Carrió's Dialogue with Cervantes: Entrée into the Debate on Origins

Far too many comparisons between the Incas and the Moors are drawn in *El lazarillo de ciegos caminantes* for readers to ignore the African (specifically, Muslim) dimension of the Incas as Carrió portrays them. The dimension is both historical and fictional. The implicit and explicit comparsion of Concolorcorvo and his alleged Inca ancestors to the Moors is one of the contexts in which I find an ideological affinity between Cervantes's satire and Carrió's exposé. Recall my assertion in the Introduction that the alleged authors of both (Cide Hamete Benengeli and Concolorcorvo, respectively) expressed the desire of the material authors to vanquish certain genres of literature: chivalric romances in Cide Hamete's case, geographical and historiographical romances in Concolorcorvo's. The discursive tensions between Concolorcorvo and the inspector, no less than the narratorial hybridity of the text itself, reenact *Don Quijote de la Mancha* as a jocose diatribe against geographical and historiographical romances.[19]

Like Sancho Panza and Don Quijote, Concolorcorvo and the inspector dialogue and debate, and the voice of reason is sometimes ventriloquized by the inspector's secretary as it was by Don Quijote's social inferior, Sancho. (Both Sancho and Concolorcorvo aspire to be what each text reveals that they are not.) For example, the implicit author of *Don Quijote* claims that he purchased some notebooks or piles of papers in the merchant district of Toledo. According to the *morisco* translator, the notebooks contained the *Historia de don Quijote de la Mancha, escrita por Cide Hamete Benegeli, historiador arábigo* (Cervantes 1983, 1:141–43). Concolorcorvo claims to have extracted the inspector's original report, just as the implicit author of Don Quijote claims to have relied in part on the *morisco's* translation of Cide Hamete's *Historia.*[20]

Another parallel can be found in the prologues to both works. The implicit author of Cervantes's Menippean satire frets about his prologue. A friend advises him to inject poets and historians, moralizing tidbits and the like in this invective against books of chivalry. The prologue of Carrió's exposé, its epigraph taken from Ovid's *Tristium,* mocks the Inca Concolorcorvo's gravity and authority.[21] Concolorcorvo admits that he extracted his itinerary of the postal inspection from the inspector's report, aided by "neighbors who . . . blew into my ear, and a certain friar from San Juan de Dios who came up with the introduction and Latin bits" (116–17). These bits of Latin Concolorcorvo does not understand, because they are not his own. Statements and admissions of this ilk belittle Concolorcorvo's pretensions and undercut his truth claims. With respect to Cide (or *Señor*) Hamete's history (*historia*), the implicit author of *Don Quijote* notes that if its veracity is questionable, Arabs are liars, and if there is something good lacking, it is the fault of the greyhound (*galgo*), or Cide Hamete (Cervantes 1983, 1:143–44).[22] In Carrió's exposé, we read that if all men were compared to dogs, Indians would be greyhounds (*galgos*) not because of their legendary speed as postboys (*chasquis*) but because they are able to handle hills well (313). Greyhound (*galgo*) was still used in seventeenth-century Peru to refer to a person judged to have at least some African ancestry.[23] Concolorcorvo's *casta* renders him no more trustwothy in Carrió's Peru than Cide Hamete's *casta* in Cervantes's Spain. The invention of Concolorcorvo confirms Carrió's dialogue with Cervantes. Carrió redirected his model not only to lambast the distortions and misreporting of a very successful New World travel literature but also to poke fun of highbrow historical debates on the origins of the Indians. He wanted to get out his own opinions about the Crown and church policies of integration and assimilation of non-Spaniards from the reconquest period to the late eighteenth century, both of which were well-treaded subjects for travelogues and histories.

Near the beginning of Carrió's exposé, Concolorcorvo states that he wishes to apply for the position of *perrero* of the Cathedral in Cuzco so that he can enjoy ecclesiastical immunity and that his having written this itinerary will help his candidacy (116). Dog (*perro*), not dog catcher (*perrero*), was still used in late eighteenth-century Peru to refer to persons believed to be of indigenous descent. In Spain it meant a person of Jewish or Moorish descent.[24] The inspector explicitly compares the *aymará* spoken in La Paz to the language of the Moors (371). In the main, Carrió's invention of Concolorcorvo inserts the secretary and his ancestors within a cultural, predominantly religious, hierarchy in which the inferior is the Moor—who might specifically be an Egyptian (or gypsy)—or the non-Muslim African.

It was common knowledge in the Hispanic world that crows removed the eyes of their prey, and people of African origins in Spain were associated with crows, especially if they were mean-spirited. In *Buen aviso y Portacuentos,* Joan Timoneda tells of a brown-skinned woman who gets testy with her one-eyed suitor who does not suit her: "A lady who was very brown skinned was looking out her blinds, when she saw her unbeloved suitor who had a cataract on his eye and was looking at her through a monocle, and she said, 'Good Lord, what a cloudy day!' Seeing that she had addressed him as one-eyed, the suitor responded by addressing her as brown skinned: 'It is true, dear lady, but you belong to the crow category, for you always go straight for the eye'" (1990, 166).[25]

The textual references to Concolorcorvo's physique cut any number of ways. The inspector notes that all Indians look alike in New Spain and Peru, but he adds, "Reparé en las pinturas de sus antepasados los Incas, y aun en Vm. y otros que dicen descender de casa real, más deformidad, y que sus rostros se acercan a los de los moros en narices y boca, aunque aquéllos tienen el color ceniciento y Vms. de ala de cuervo" (364) ("I noticed in the paintings of your descendants, the Incas, and even in you and others who say they descend from royalty, more deformity, and that your faces resemble those of the Moors in the nose and mouth, although they are the color of ash and you all the color of a crow's wing"). The supposed descendants of the Incas resemble the Moors, although the latter are ashy, whereas the former are darker. In Higher Ethiopia, which was Christian, inhabitants were also ashy (*atezados*) (Fernández de Medrano 1686, 234). Concolorcorvo compares his own physique and that of the administrator of the posts in Cuzco, comparing his face to that of the king of Monicongo: "En el color somos opuestos, porque el mío es de cuervo y el suyo es de cisne. . . . Su boca es rasgada de oreja a oreja, y la mía, aunque no es tan dilatada, se adorna en ambos labios de una jeta tan buena, que puede competir con la del rey de Monicongo" (396) ("We are opposites in color, because mine is that of a crow and his is that of a swan. . . . His mouth stretches from ear to ear, and mine, while it is not as wide, is adorned on both lips with such a good mug that it can compete with the King of Monicongo's").[26] This comparison situates Concolorcorvo in two of the four kingdoms (Congo, Monomotapa, Zanzibar, and Ayana) that constituted Lower Ethiopia (*Etiopía Inferior*) according to the Spanish geographical imaginary. In Congo and Monomotapa, the majority of the inhabitants were either idolatrous or followed Islam, and they were black in color, not ashy (Fernández de Medrano 1686, 239–41). On his highly exoticized "Map of the Country and the Peoples of the Cape of Good Hope," Anzi, an Italian geographer, explained that "Kaffirs from Monomotapa inhabit these countries" (Figure 20).

The totality of textual references in Carrió's exposé situates Concolorcorvo precariously between Northern Africa in general, Higher Ethiopia, and Lower Ethiopia, which might simply have been the unbridled expression of Carrió's cultural color wheel, or his somatic preferences, or even the compromise that he struck between what he was seeing and what he was reading (e.g., his debts to *Don Quijote de la Mancha*). But I think there was more to it: I am convinced that the observations, put-downs, jocose comparisons, and contradictions reviewed here also parody the debates and theories about the origins of the Indians.

Many Europeans associated Shem with the settlement of Asia, Japhet with the settlement of Europe, and Ham with the settlement of Africa, but this settlement theory was one of several theories known to Spaniards, and it cannot be adduced as a Spanish justification for African slavery or evidence of Spanish racism before the nineteenth century.[27] According to some Spaniards, Noah's son Ham settled in Africa and the East. His descendants settled in the New World and were the ancestors of the Amerindians.[28] According to other Spaniards, these same Indians were the lost tribes of Israel.[29] According to the French author Durret, the Indians considered themselves the carrier of Ham's curse of eternal servitude. Many Indians were like Arabs, he claimed. With a tale about the origins of the groups, they justified not only the tricks they played on Europeans, especially merchants, but also their hatred of blacks (1720, 167).[30] They claimed that the first man had three sons—one white, one brown, and one black. The father fell asleep, and the white son woke up and stole all of the riches and settled in Europe. The brown son woke up next and took all of the beasts and settled in Barbary. The Indians descended from the black son, who woke up last, found nothing but a pipe and tobacco, and went to live in a warm climate (the New World) because he was nude (167–68). That was how the armchair tourist Durret had put it. As we have seen, the inspector in *El lazarillo de ciegos caminantes* consistently derides French travelers and their travelogues, blaming the former for their incredulity and malice and the latter for being *brochures* and distributors of anti-Spanish propaganda and tall tales. Durret's confabulations might have made Carrió howl with laughter had French travelogues not already become the materials for many histories of the Spanish Indies (just as newspapers had)—a fount of disinformation with worldwide distribution.

There is also a gypsy dimension to Carrió's portrait of the Indian plebs. According to the inspector, Indians who worked as painters or embroiderers or held other lowly occupations were professional thieves, capable of teaching the gypsies in Spain a thing or two. This was especially true of Cuzco and Huamanga and was even truer of Quito and Mexico City, "the two greatest universities founded by Cacus" (387).[31] Carrió compared the Indian plebs in Peru, New Granada, and New Spain to a segment of the lower order in Spain and Spanish America: Roms, or gypsies. Carrió was well versed in the laws of Spain and the Spanish Indies, and since the late sixteenth century, the Crown had been insisting that gypsies and their imitators be returned from Spanish America to Spain. In the Spanish Indies legal code, for example, gypsies were prohibited from traveling to Spanish America, as were itinerant Spaniards who lived like gypsies, that is, "vagrants who use their dress, language, manners and disorderly way of life among the Indians." That Gypsy, or Gypsy-like, lifestyle included tricks, robberies, and lies (*Recopilación de leyes de los Reynos de las Indias* 1756, bk. 6, tit. 4, 1aw 5, 2:284v.).

These comparisons of the Indian plebs to gypsies and of the Incas to Moors are related discourses. Gypsies (*gitanos*) were commonly called Egyptians (*egipcios*).[32] Undoubtedly, part of the conflation was a result of the Spanish name for the part of Northern Africa that contained Fez and Morocco, *Mauritania Tingitana*.[33] Its inhabitants were famous horsemen and notorious thieves, as were gypsies.[34] Moreover, like the legal code for the Spanish Indies, Carrió compared even Spaniards in Peru in this fashion, because such analogies concerned geography and culture, not *race* as it is understood today. The following passage—which follows the mention of the dishonest postmaster in Potosí, Pedro de la Revilla, and another dishonest Pedro, this one from Popayán (see Chapter 4)—exemplifies how Carrió's text hitches even a distinguished Spaniard to a code of cultural alterity:

> Cierto bufón probó en Arequipa que don José Gorosabel era descendiente de judíos, porque leyó en el libro de la generación del mayor Hombre que hubo y habrá en el mundo las siguientes palabras: *Salathiel autem genuit Zorobabel.* Lo cierto es, señor Concolorcorvo, que de cien hombres apenas se hallará uno que no sea tiritero, y así ríase usted de los potosinos y popayanes con los dos Pedros y celebre cuatro PPPP tan memorables como las de Lima, y a Gorosabel dele el parabién de que Matorras le haya emparentado con los *Romaníes,* y Vm. siga su discurso sin hacer juicio de bagatelas. (280)

> [A certain buffoon in Arequipa established that José Gorosabel was a descendant of Jews, because he read in the book about the lineage of the greatest Man there ever was and will ever be in the world, the following words: *Salathiel autem genuit Zorobabel.* The truth is, Mr. Concolorcorvo, you will hardly find one man out of a hundred who is not a puppet master, and so laugh at the Potosians and the Popayans with the two Pedros, and applaud four Ps as memorable as those from Lima, and congratulate Gorosabel for Matorras's having made him a relative of the Romanies, and continue your discourse without considering such trifles.]

The "buffoon" Matorras had crafted a jocose equation between Zorobabel (*Gorosabel*), a prince descended from David who made the Jews return to their country after Cyrus's edict, and Zarathustra (*Zoroastres* or *Zoroastro* in Spanish), the inventor of magic and astrology from the East, who was reputed to be Noah's son Ham. It was said that he, unlike most mortals, laughed when he was born (Covarrubias 1943, 1018). I have already established that Ham, according to many Spaniards, settled in Africa and the East. The buffoon from Popayán had truly compared Gorosabel to thieves—to Roms, or Romanies (*Romaníes*), or Egyptians. The same way of life—stealing, lying, moving from place to place—was associated with North Africans, gypsies, and dishonest Spanish officials in Bourbon Spanish America.

Social Privileges, Duties, and Taxonomies:
The Metamorphoses of Concolorcorvo

In the most important study of Carrió's work published in the twentieth century, the encounter between "Spaniard" and "Indian" takes center stage, because "it defines *El lazarillo de ciegos caminantes*" and "is realized on various historical and textual levels" (Stolley 1993, 103). Earlier we saw how the positional hybridity that exists within the inspector—that is, his oscillating subjectivity—calls into question the alleged *criollo*-peninsular rivalry and makes it difficult even to describe Carrió as a Spaniard (see the Introduction herein). Here I shed light on Concolorcorvo's unstable positioning in the text, which unfolds through ever-changing genealogical claims and makes it difficult to categorize him as an Indian.

Chapter 5's discussion of hierarchy showed that being *indio* was not a matter of blood but of *casta* and *estado,* and Concolorcorvo's negotiations of these two hierarchical principles in Carrió's exposé prove that he understood which side his bread was buttered on. The metamorphoses, or vertical movements, accommodated by the social hierarchy are figuratively embodied in Concolorcorvo's. Concolorcorvo is a self-fashioned Inca when he initiates the narration; he is masquerading. Masquerades, according to Tesauro, are "metaphors representative of a concept through diverse habits and appearances" (1968, 732). Some are grave, such as the masquerades of heroes, whereas "others are whimsical and ridiculous, which bizarrely imitate [someone's] looks or represent disproportionate or imaginary things" (732). The dialogues between Concolorcorvo and the inspector gradually expose Concolorcorvo's ridiculous masquerade as the self-proclaimed Inca secretary is stripped of his costume, or borrowed feathers, *layer by layer.* I emphasize this point because I believe that Concolorcorvo's metamorphosis, rather than being a transformation from white to black (Stolley 1993, 5), begins at a state of nobility and Spanishness (according to the hierarchy of Bourbon Spanish America) and unfolds through several *castas* and *estados.* Significantly, this ontological transformation often contradicts the transformations of others judged to be of indigenous ancestry whom the inspector mentions in their dialogues or those addressed in viceregal decrees, church documents, and the like: while they move up the social ladder, the masquerading Concolorcorvo drops in rights and responsibilities like a man disgraced.

Spaniards in Peru feared the *casta* of *mestizos* because they considered them too clever by half and unafraid of authority. Let us remember here that *mestizos* meant *mestizos* and plebeians; the *casta de mestizos* did not include noble biological *mestizos* such as the Inca Garcilaso de la Vega. Placing some of his most biting commentary in Concolorcorvo's mouth was not just Carrió's way of protecting himself, then, but a question of verisimilitude and the expectations of his readership. As a *cholo,* which the self-fashioned Inca claims to be on another occasion, Concolorcorvo's father was a *mestizo,* and we saw earlier that members of this *casta* were renowned for their wicked wit. Remember, too, that *mestizos* were regularly blamed for the uprisings that exasperated viceroys of Peru throughout most of the eighteenth century. However, Concolorcorvo's genealogical claims and the inspector's genealogical assessments of Concolorcorvo do not end there: the inspector progressively transforms his interlocutor's *casta* and *estado* until he pronounces the incredibly self-inventive Concolorcorvo a plebeian Spaniard. Let us examine this transformation layer by layer.

Carrió invented Concolorcorvo as the king of confabulation: Concolorcorvo claims that he is a descendant of the Incas, although he occasionally identifies himself as a *cholo*. It is well known in Peru "que los cholos respetamos a los españoles, como a hijos del Sol, y así no tengo valor (aunque descendiente de sangre real, por línea tan recta como la del arco iris) a tratar a mis lectores con la llaneza que acostumbran los más despreciables escribientes" (100) ("that we *cholos* respect the Spaniards like they were children of the Sun, and thus I [although descended from royal blood, by a line as straight as a rainbow] do not dare to address my readers with the familiarity that most despicable scribes are in the habit of "). Here two classical rhetorical techniques signaled to Carrió's eighteenth-century readers a cleft in the alignment of Concolorcorvo's discursive and material realities.

The first is irony. As Cicero explained in *On the Ideal Orator,* "Remarks that are rather absurd, but often humorous for that very reason" create irony when "someone who is really no fool says something as if he were, in a humorous way" (2001, 199–200). Although Concolorcorvo is often outsmarted by the inspector, his noble savage impersonation is simply not convincing. He is rather too shrewd and manipulative here, ironically suggesting that his interlocutor is one of those superior "children of the Sun" and that he, like all of the Inca royals, worships Spaniards. Carrió also makes use of a second technique, which Cicero calls *insinuation,* "in which a small detail, often a single word, throws light on an unclear and hidden situation" (197). At the very same time that Concolorcorvo ironically praises the inspector, trying to flatter him into recognizing the alleged Inca's claim to be an Inca, Carrió inserts in the secretary's speech the word *cholos.* This single word makes both the genealogical claim and the attempt to soft-soap the inspector futile. The net result is that Concolorcorvo is outwitted by the inspector, or perhaps it is better to say that Concolorcorvo outwits himself.

A similar exchange between the two causes readers to fall again into that fissure that cannot be bridged by the narrator Concolorcorvo's authority: "Yo soy indio neto, salvo las trampas de mi madre, de que no salgo por fiador. Dos primas mías coyas conservan la virginidad, a su pesar, en un convento del Cuzco, en donde las mantiene el rey nuestro señor" (116) ("I am a pure-blooded Indian, barring the schemes of my mother, whom I cannot vouch for. Two *coya* cousins of mine preserve their virginity, to their dismay, in a convent in Cuzco, where the King Our Lord supports them"). In Cuzco there was, in fact, a convent for the daughters of *caciques* that was supported by the Spanish monarchy.[35] However,

Concolorcorvo banties his cousins' virginity and his mother's chastity about as if he were swatting at flies: irony and insinuation signal to readers that Concolorcorvo's word is not his bond. Thus far, Concolorcorvo has gone from being an Inca (who belongs to the noble order and to the *casta* of Spaniards) to being a *cholo* with royal pretensions and from being the latter to being a plebeian Indian (*indio*) with royal cousins of dubious virtue.

Further into Carrió's exposé, the inspector tells Secretary Concolorcorvo that he and *the other* "little *mestizos*" (*mesticillos*) say and write *llovia* instead of *lluvia* ("rain") and *lluver* instead of *llover* ("to rain") (371). Here Carrió's readers have reached another stage in the metamorphosis of Concolorcorvo: he has gone from Indian commoner (*indio*) with two royal cousins ("dos primas coyas"), in his own words, to *mestizo* in the inspector's words. Still, the transformation continues, as Concolorcorvo claims that he is of unmixed ancestry to answer the inspector's charge: "No es mucho esto, señor don Alonso, porque yo soy indio neto" (371) ("This does not mean much, Mr. Don Alonso, because I am a pure-blooded Indian"). The inspector rejects outright this biological explanantion and adds still another wrinkle to our discussion of metamorphosis: "Dejemos lo neto para que lo declare la madre que lo parió, que esto no es del caso, porque Vm. tuvo la misma crianza fuera de casa que el resto de los españoles comunes serranos, y siempre sirvió a europeos y no lee otros libros que los que están escritos en castellano" (371) ("Let us leave the pure-blooded bit for the mother who bore you to decide, since it is neither here nor there, because you had the same upbringing outside of the home as the rest of the common highlander Spaniards, and you always worked for Europeans, and you do not read any books other than those that are written in Castilian"). The inspector here tells his secretary that he had the same education outside of the home *as the rest of the common Spaniards* from the Peruvian highlands. Concolorcorvo is, because of his culture or "modo de vivir, " a plebeian Spaniard from the *sierra,* or highlands, according to this latest statement by the inspector. That Concolorcorvo claims to be a legitimate descendant of the Incas or an Indian commoner holds no explicative power for the inspector: "esto no es del caso."

Cultural practices (experience), not nature (or natural reason), determine language: "porque si siguiera Vm. ésta [natural reason], dijera de *llover, llovía,* y de *lluvia, llúver*" (371) ("because if you were to follow natural reason, you would say *llovía* from *llover,* and *llúver* from *lluvia*"). In other words, there is an arbitrariness in this identity business that has nothing to do with blood, or nature, and everything to do with how and where a person is reared. Let us situate the inspector's foray into linguistics within a broader frame, since the inspector effectively roots identity in a cultural mechanism, that of language, in order to conclude that Concolorcorvo belongs to the lower *estado* (the mob, or *el vulgo*) and to the *casta* of *españoles*. This argument, in turn, participates in a vigorous debate from the seventeenth and eighteenth centuries that centered on these questions: For how long should special protections be afforded to Indian plebeians (*indios*)? Do partially indigenous members of the *casta* of *españoles,* or even of the *casta* of *mestizos,* and of the lower estate deserve these same protections? Do the Indian Privileges apply to the *casta* of *negros* and the *casta* of *mulatos* as well?

The special protections were primarily religious in nature. A handy source for understanding the debate over them is Miguel Olabarrieta Medrano's *Recuerdo de las obligaciones del Ministerio Apostolico en la cura de las almas* (*Reminder of the Apostolic Ministry's Obligations in Caring for Souls*), a manual for priests. A native of Lima, Olabarrieta Medrano graduated from St. Martin's College and the University of San Marcos. He worked as an attorney for the high court in Lima and was also a priest and vicar in Soraya, Cuzco. At length he discussed whether the special privileges and dispensations were to be enjoyed by New Christians ("Christianos nuevos") alone or by all *indios,* as the term *Privilegios Indicos* suggested (1717, art. 143, 95). The distinguished theologians and church dignitaries whom he quoted are numerous. Bishop Montenegro, for instance, adduced papal bulls and briefs to support his opinion that the Indian Privileges were granted to neophytes and that it was not legal to extend them to Indians whose parents were Christians and baptized their children when they were babies, which was the case of the majority of the *indios* in the Viceroyalty of Peru. The Indian Privileges applied only to recent converts and only up to ten years after their baptism (art. 143, 95). Father Diego de Avendaño disagreed, holding that the use of all the Indian Privileges was lawful even for Indians who already braided their hair and spoke Spanish and lived with Spaniards. "The fact that these such Indians are more capable than the other Indians [who] live wildly in the mountains and smell like dirt" should not lessen their rights or place them in an inferior position to the "incompetent Indians or the more rigorous neophytes" (art. 143, 95).[36]

Bishop Montenegro also argued, against the opinion of many doctors, that the bulk of the *Privilegios Indicos* could not be extended to *mestizos.* However, he supported extending the exemption from the limits on marriage between relatives to *mestizos, cuarterones de mestizo* (persons who were legally one-fourth Indian), and *puchuelas* (persons who were legally one-eighth Indian), which contradicted recent papal briefs on the interpretation of the Indian Privileges regarding marriage. Moreover, Olabarrieta argued, the bishop's inclusion of the last two groups, based on the claim that persons who were legally one-fourth or one-eighth Indian were commonly called *mestizos,* was false reasoning: Father Avendaño had correctly affirmed that this was not the case. Besides, only children with Spanish fathers and *mulata* mothers are commonly called *cuarterones* in Peru (1717, art. 144, 96). Avendaño believed, according to Olabarrieta, that it was reasonable that *mestizos* not be eligible to enjoy the Indian Privileges without any limitation or distinction whatsoever but that it also was reasonable to extend the privileges to "those *mestizos* and *mestizas* who live among the Indians with their common dress and lifestyle, as if they were *indios* or *indias* in reality, although they are not fully such (*como si fuera en la realidad Indios o Indias, aunque no lo son enteramente*)" (art. 144, 96). The analogy that Avendaño posed is striking: novices in the various religious orders are not "fully," or "in reality," *religiosos,* but in their common dress and bearing they behave like and live like *religiosos* and among *religiosos,* so they enjoy the same privileges as *religiosos.* This is not, let us be clear, at all distant from what Carrió was arguing about identity—that it is social not individual, cultural not biological. The "racial laws" and "racial categories" that scholars insist on seeing in viceregal Spanish America were simply not there: *race* would come later, as a postcolonial category central to modern forms of hierarchy.

Another analogy involved acculturated *mestizos* and acculturated Indians. According to Olabarrieta, mountain-dwelling, dirty-smelling Indians and Spanish-speaking, capital-dwelling Indians (*Indios cortesanos ladinos*) alike enjoyed the same *Privilegios Indicos,* because there was no reason to punish the latter for being "more competent, kempt, fluent in Spanish or for living among Spaniards, whose dress they uniformly wear, just as we all see in this court of Lima." So, Olabarrieta asks, "for what reason can the same not be said of the *mestizos* . . . more competent due to their interaction with Spaniards . . . than the less competent mountain-dwelling *mestizos* with their manners and dress of Indians, among whom they live?" (1717, art. 144, 96–97). It is clear here, as it is in the inspector's statements that opened this discussion, that when social taxonomies are rooted in cultural expectations—dress, language, manners, or behavior—we cannot speak of *race,* and we cannot ignore geography.[37] As much as Olabarrieta, Carrió distinguished between the *sierra* and the city, between the wild (mountain people) and the tame (city dwellers).

To the first two questions that were posed by men such as Bishop Montenegro, Avendaño, and Olabarrieta Medrano, Carrió's exposé adds a rhetorical one: Why do many partially indigenous members of the *casta* of *españoles,* or even the *casta* of *mestizos,* continue to identify themselves as *indios* (a *casta* for unacculturated Indians and one that implied commoner status) when they are not *indios,* socially or legally speaking? In his estimation, they did so in order to claim the special Indian Privileges *under the law,* just as members of the *casta de indios* metamorphosed, slipping into the *casta de mestizos* when tax time rolled around.[38] Remember what is most significant about Concolorcorvo's overarching genealogical claim and the legal and social purchase that claims such as his possessed within the hierarchy of Bourbon Spanish America: by claiming to be a full-blooded Indian and a descendant of the Incas, he is claiming to be a *legitimate descendant* of the Incas. In the material world outside of Carrió's discourse, such a claim, when legally substantiated, obtained the privileges of a member of the *casta de españoles* and of the noble estate. If Concolorcorvo were, legally and socially, a member of the Spanish gentry, he would be the equal of the real-life inspector: Carrió was a Spaniard and a certified *hidalgo.* Were Concolorcorvo's genealogical claim certified by the Crown, it would fundamentally transform the hierarchical relationship between author (inspector) and scribe (Secretary Concolorcorvo), and the account would not read as it does, for no member of the Spanish gentry would treat a peer with such disdain in print.

Not to worry: we know (as did some of Carrió's contemporaries) that the real Calixto Bustamante forged the signature of a Spaniard on a letter of recommendation sent to Carrió's friend Domingo de Basavilbaso, the postal administrator in Buenos Aires. The letter asked Basavilbaso to give Calixto a job.[39] He was, like the False-Galloper's twin brother in the sequel to *The Compleat Tradesman,* "bringing counterfeit letters of commendation."[40] The Inca impostor in the text inspired by the historical Calixto has even graver faults to overcome.

Deception, Mixture, and Slander: Sources of Concolorcorvo's Shame

It is often noted that Concolorcorvo's authority as a reliable narrator is undercut by disparaging references to his color (Stolley 1993, 162), and color does indeed overlap with issues of hygiene (Meléndez 1999, 147–51, 214–18) in many of the inspector's references to persons who did not belong to the *casta* of Spaniards. However, the fact that color has come to constitute the folk concept of *race* in the modern West should not be confused with the symbolic dimensions of color in traditional and modern societies. For example, in Carrió's times, *pardo* did not mean what it means today (*brown*); it meant *gray.* Freedmen of at least partial African descent were not called *grays* because they were "ashy" in appearance but because they were neither black slaves (*negros*) nor Spaniards (the majority of whom were *blancos* by comparison). Another example is the tarnishing or blackening mentioned repeatedly in this study. Because it is well documented that certain colors are *universally* associated with specific affective states, the fact that Spaniards associated the color black with sadness or bad luck and the color white with purity is not at all indicative of "Iberian racism."[41] Shame (*infamia*) was intertwined with the principles of social hierarchy in the Hispanic world, and both were frequently expressed in symbolic terms: not only the "stain" or "blot" but also "polluted blood" and "dirty jobs" (the second, which Kathy Stuart [1999] associates with "ritual pollution," firmly rooted in Germany as well) and "crack," "hoof disease," "run," and "snag" (the various meanings of *raza*). That Carrió attacks on the basis of color, in a manner reminiscent of Francisco de Quevedo Villegas, is undeniable, and the folk concept of *race* in the modern and postmodern periods has turned primarily on color. However, we need to restrain ourselves when we are tempted to collapse historical forms of hierachy into a single form—our own. Just like blood, color must be examined from within the hierachy to which it belonged. Authority in Carrió's exposé does not turn on color (or *race*) but on something very different, which takes us into the second metaphorical level of Carrió's invention of Concolorcorvo.

Concolorcorvo does not square with the name of the secretary who accompanied Carrió on part of his inspection and whose name appears on the cover of the first edition of *El lazarillo de ciegos caminantes:* Don Calixto Bustamante Carlos Inga.[42] The historical Calixto Bustamante identified himself as a legitimate descendant of the Incas, which would have placed him in the *casta* of Spaniards and in the order of nobility. A legitimate descendant of the Incas would neither be flattered by a "booming" nickname nor wish to use it as a last name as the Secretary Concolorcorvo claims:

> Pues juro por la batalla de Almansa y por la paz de Nimega, que he de perpetuar en mi casa este apellido, como lo hicieron mis antepasados con el de Carlos, que no es tan sonoro y significativo: ¡*Concolorcorvo*!, es un término retumbante y capaz de atronar un ejército numeroso y de competir con el de Manco-Cápac, que siempre me chocó tanto como el de Miramamolín de Marruecos. (364–65)

> [Well, I swear on the battle of Almansa and the peace of Nimega that I shall perpetuate this last name in my house, as my ancestors did with *Carlos,* which is not nearly as sonorous and meaningful. *Concolorcorvo*! is a rousing term and capable of thunderstriking a numerous army and of competing with *Manco Capac,* which always grated my nerves as much as *Miramolín* of Morocco.]

The nickname directly contradicts the noble surname Inga. *Concolorcorvo* is a laconic, or enthymeme, in the sense supplied by Tesauro: it is an argument in part vocal and in part mental (1968, 40). In one or a few words, we see an image of customs, the witticism remaining in our ears and the image in our mind. Carrió's readers could immediately get a sense of what kind of person Concolorcorvo was (an impostor), and the ridiculous name itself would ring in their ears. Further, the self-fashioned Inca diminishes his own authority in the previous example because Carrió chose to employ what Cicero had defined as an example of humor achieved through words: "the interpretation of a name has cleverness in it, when you make a joke out of the reason someone bears the name that he does" (2001, 193). At the very same time, Carrió makes use of irony, one kind of which consisted in "calling something disgraceful by an honorable name," according to Cicero (199). As strange as it may sound, Concolorcorvo's drubbing here is not wholly unlike that of Archbishop Pedro Pardo de Figueroa at the end of Carrió's exposé. Concolorcorvo's "something disgraceful" had historical and legal roots that must be explained in order to understand the second metaphorical level of Carrió's invention of Concolorcorvo.

To begin with, Concolorcorvo's genealogical striving was illegal. According to the *Siete partidas,* a man who pretended to be a gentleman (*caballero*) when he was not was committing fraud (*falsedad*). Similarly, a man who changed his name to that of another and claimed to be the son of a king or some other distinguished person when he knew that he was not was guilty of fraud (Real Academia de la Historia 1807, *partida* 7, tit. 7, 3:561). Fraud incurred *infamia,* as we saw in Chapter 2, but Concolorcorvo's social profile reminds us that some of his reasons for committing fraud were themselves carriers of perpetual shame.

A person born out of wedlock or who had a parent who was illegitimate did not have *limpieza de sangre.*[43] In the admissions constitutions or bylaws of military orders and selective colleges, this veritable *birth defect* generally appeared before the phrase that attached a *raza* to being, descending from, or associating with a heretic, a Jew, a Moor, or a plebeian (*villano*). This birth defect carried *infamia* in its train, and its centrality to the relationship between the inspector and Concolorcorvo—a relationship of social inequality—has gone unnoticed. In Cuzco, Concolorcorvo reports the following exchange:

> Luego que llegamos a divisar los techos y torres de la mayor ciudad que en los principios y medios tuvo el gran imperio peruano, se detuvo el visitador y me dijo: "Ahi está la capital de sus antepasados, señor Concolorcorvo, muy mejorada por los españoles"; pero como yo había salido de ella muy niño, no tenía idea fija de sus edificios, entradas y salidas, y solamente me acordé que mi padre vivía en unos cuartos bajos bien estrechos y con un dilatado corralón. (326)

> [As soon as we began to make out the roofs and towers of the largest city that the great Peruvian Empire had in its beginnings and middles, the inspector stopped and told me, "There's the capital of your ancestors, Mr. Concolorcorvo, very much improved by the Spaniards." But, since I left there when I was very little, I did not have a clear idea of its buildings, entries and exits, and I only remembered that my father used to live in some ground-level rooms, really small, and with a long hallway.]

The sordid bit of local history insinuated here is that Concolorcorvo's father lived among prostitutes and that his mother was a prostitute. The casual description of his father's quarters in Cuzco actually fits that of bordellos in Lima: "cylinders" (*cilindros*), "syringes" (*jeringes*), "flutes" (*flautas*), and "narrow streets" or "alleys" (*callejones*) are ubiquitous tropes in Friar Castillo's "Conversations" on the nocturnal commerce waged by members of different *castas* and *estados,* backroom abortions, prostitutes ravaged by disease, and newborns abandoned on church steps.[44] The interface of bastardy and mixture, which makes the foregoing admission so damaging, has also gone unnoticed, probably because of the postmodern sense in which *hybridity* is used in discussions of Anglo and French colonial situations in general and of viceregal Spanish America in particular.[45] Again, however, Louis Dumont's principle should be foremost in our minds: "A particular feature, if taken not in itself but in its concrete position within a system (what is sometimes called its 'function'), can have a totally different meaning according to the position it occupies" (1961, 28).

A variety of learned discourses suggest that mixture in the Spanish world was layered and far more intricate than postmodern notions of miscegenation or *hybridity*. In husbandry, for example, it cut both ways. On one hand, Gabriel Alonso de Herrera looked favorably on the *mestizo* when it meant a mixed breed of dogs;[46] on the other, he used a term of *infamia* when the half-breed was a honeybee. After declaring that "some are wild [*monteses*] and fierce, others domestic and gentle," he notes that certain bees "are not naturally disposed to the making of good honey for they are like half-breeds [*bastardos*] and mountain dwellers [*monteses*]" (1970, 275). The term *bastardo* was associated with beasts of mixed species and with people who should not, morally, be having sex, according to Covarrubias. Such mixtures were degenerate with respect to their parents.[47] Mountain dwellers (*monteses*) were wild: like certain *indios* and *mestizos* in viceregal society, these bees had a "modo de vivir"—to borrow the extirpator Francisco Dávila's (1648) phrase—that was not right, as Spaniards saw it.[48]As we saw earlier, Concolorcorvo undergoes an ontological metamorphosis in his dialogues with the inspector. He belongs to mixed *castas* (*los cholos, los mestizos*), or perhaps a nonmixed *casta* (*los españoles*). Sometimes he is a member of the lower order (a mountain-dwelling Spaniard, or *español serrano*); other times, he is a nobleman. Hybridity and bastardy, then, were overlapping notions to which *infamia* often attached itself.[49]

That *persons* of mixed faith or mixed ancestry should be social outcasts was not only stipulated in the European infamy laws and the Hispanic purity statutes that they informed; mixture had been associated with promiscuity, or sexual shamelessness, since ancient times. The Latin verb *promiscere* meant to mix a lot, and the noun *promiscuus* meant a mixed thing, as Elio Antonio de Nebrija recorded in his *Diccionario Latino-Español:* "Promisceo.es.cui. por mezclar mucho.a.i." (1979, n.p.); "Promiscuus.a.um. por cosa mezclada" (n.p.). The Greeks also associated mixture with promiscuity: an animal that had sex outside of its family was an animal that mixed, and the offspring was a mixed animal, an object of reproach. Three related entries in Nebrija's *Diccionario Latino-Español* are worth examining here. The first indicated that hybrid (derived from the Greek *hybris*) was a term of defamation, an insult: "Hybris. interpretatur contumelia" (n.p.). The second defined hybridity as the offspring of a citizen and an outsider, or traveler: "Hybris. hijo de peregrino y ciudadano" (n.p.).[50] Nebrija's third entry was consonant with Herrera's use of the term *bastardo:* "Hybrida.e. por hijo de fiero y manso" (n.p.). In a Latin-Portuguese dictionary published in the sixteenth century, both *mestiço* and *mulato* were defined as *hybrida,* and in a Latin-Portuguese dictionary from 1646, *hybrida* was defined as a child of adultery, a mixed breed of sow or dog, a *mulato,* or a child whose parents came from different countries (Forbes 1988, 101). Two years later, Judge Solórzano y Pereira's *Política indiana* equated *mestizo* and *mulato* and *hybrida:* "But setting aside now the *Criollos,* and turning to the ones whom they call *Mestizos* and *Mulatos,* of whom there is a great abundance in the provinces of these Indies, what I have to say is that they got the name of *Mestizos* from the mixture of blood and Communities [*Naciones*] who were joined when they were engendered, whereby the Latins called them *Varios* and *Hibridas*" (217).[51] In seventeenth-century Spanish Naples, Della Porta wrote about breeding animals. He explained that mixtures in the field of husbandry were "half-wilds," or "hybrides," a Greek concept but one that he had probably taken from Pliny, who applied it to beasts and men alike.[52]

If mixture was semantically entangled with promiscuity, bastardy was associated with both. It has been pointed out that *mulato* was defined in Portuguese-Latin dictionaries from the sixteenth and seventeenth centuries not only as *hybrida* but also as *burdo* (Forbes 1988, 134–35). The term *burdo* was, like *hybris* or *hybrida,* a term of reproach when applied to humans. Well into the eighteenth century, Pineda recorded, "*Burdo,* adj. coarse; metaph. degenerate, worthless" and its derivation, "*Borde,* the Edge, the Brim, the Side of a Ship; also a bastard Son" (1740, n.p.). Unlike animals and birds, human *bordes* (or *burdos*) were born in whorehouses, according to Covarrubias: "BURDEL. The public house of bad women; in French it is called *bordeau,* but it comes from the Latin noun, *burdus,* which means mule, which is engendered by parents from different species, to wit, from a horse and a donkey or she-ass. And because the couplings that are made in such a place are unlawful [*ilegítimos*] it was called *burdel,* and the one engendered by them, *burdo* or *borde*" (1943, 245). Prostitutes were unlawful and shamed sexual partners; they were akin to she-asses, and their clients were akin to stallions.[53]

The offspring of such sexual commerce—illegitimate men like Concolorcorvo in Carrió's satirical narration—were "mixed" persons, or hybrids, *regardless of the ancestry of the father or mother.* This would explain why Solórzano y Pereira argued in *Política indiana* that for religious or public honors, *mestizos* and *mulatos* without the shame of illegitimacy should be treated as citizens and considered candidates (provided they carried no other "stain") (217–18). In other words, *race* (or color) had nothing to do with it; Catholic norms of wholeness, or wholesomeness, had everything to do with it.[54] However, according to Solórzano y Pereira, *mestizos* and *mulatos* were born of unlawful couplings more often than not—respectable Spanish men rarely married Indian or black women—and their resulting bastardy incurred de facto infamy. Moreover, their mixed color was another source of shame (*infamia*), for it signaled that they had the vices of half-wilds or adulterous offspring that we saw in Herrera's treatment of wild and domestic honeybees.[55] Illegitimacy had many forms and was so very grave, among Spaniards as well as members of other *castas,* that the Crown found a way to profit from the sins of the fathers and mothers. The legal foundation of the social hierarchy allowed many persons born out of wedlock to "cleanse" their blood by negotiating their legitimacy from the local bishop and, in Carrió's times, purchasing it from the Spanish Crown (Twinam 1999, *passim*).

On this second level, then, Concolorcorvo is a metaphor for a man with several manifestations of hybridity and, consequently, several *razas* (his mother was shamed by her profession, he was born in a brothel, and so on), who nonetheless impersonates a lord—that is, a legitimate descendant of the Incas, a Spanish nobleman. There was, indeed, some historical inspiration to be found along these lines in the real-life Calixto Bustamante. Bustamante's mother or father was most likely an illegitimate child fathered by Juan de Bustamante Carlos Inga's father (Dunbar Temple 1947, 300–301), and Calixto falsified records to hide this fact. Deception was not just a sin, we must remember. The *Siete partidas* explicitly addressed cases of men who committed fraud by altering or forging documents. Punishment was tied to the social status of the guilty man: if he was a servant, the punishment was death; if he was a free man, his fate was permanent exile to an island (Real Academia de la Historia 1807, *partida* 7, tit. 7, 3:562–63). In either case, *infamia facti* resulted from a legal finding of deception, or fraud, and although that might not matter to a dead man, his family certainly would suffer because of it. The historical Calixto Bustamante was therefore not eligible for any honors, much less that of holding public office, and Concolorcorvo, the Inca impostor inspired by his life, is just as guilty of deception, or misrepresentation, in *El lazarillo de ciegos caminantes*.

In Carrió's invention of a deceitful and loquacious secretary, legal and literary history come together. One of the most important scholarly discoveries about Carrió's text is the relationship between Ovid and Concolorcorvo. According to *Metamorphoses*, the white crow prattled so much, speaking out of turn about the sexual indiscretions of others, that Apollo transformed him into a black crow (Stolley 1993, 3–5). In effect, that black-marked, or *notado*, crow illustrates *infamia facti;* the act of gossiping, or slandering, alone marked the crow, or made him infamous. Throughout the renaissance, baroque, and Enlightenment periods, representations of shame overlapped with representations of the maligner or gossiper: the crow, or a member of the same family, was common to them both. In the 1669 revised edition of Ripa's *Iconologia*, two different representations of Shame (*Infamia*) appeared. The first is the following:

> Ugly woman with black wings on her shoulders and covered to her waist with feathers of the ardiolo bird, and from the waist down she will be wearing a yellow sash striped with the color *verdigris* green, but torn, and she will be holding the *ibis* bird.
>
> Shame [*infamia*] is the ill opinion that one has of people who lead immoral lives [*mala vita*], but it is depicted with black wings to denote that its flight is ill and of unfortunate fame.
>
> The feathers of the aforementioned bird show that shame is born for the most part of inconstancy, because this is a sign of madness, and it is seen in

this bird, which is most inconstant. However, Martial called the person who went from one action to another, without doing anything good, *ardiolo.*

The color yellow and the *verdigris* green are used universally to represent fraud and shame, and also the *ibis* bird, which is most sordid, as some write, and is used to a similar end; and as torn clothing shames men according to the mob, so the vices of the soul wound the reputation according to wisemen, and render a man displeasing to God, in whom our good reputation principally resides. (1669, 279)

Ripa's second representation of Shame (*Infamia*), which certainly overlaps with this first one, is no less important to my interpretation of Concolorcorvo's shaming in *El lazarillo de ciegos caminantes:*

Woman nude and leprous for her entire life, with black wings, with little hair, in the act of blowing a horn, she has written on her forehead the word *Turpe,* and she bares one of her sides with her hand.

Leprosy in the Old Testament was a figure of sin, which principally engenders shame (*infamia*).
The horn that she blows indicates that her tidings are unfortunate among men, just as this is a rough and ignoble sound.

The motto written on her forehead declares that Shame (*infamia*) is seen clearly by everyone except those who parade it, thus she willingly bares her side, giving free rein to vices without seeing or thinking about the damaging event to her own reputation. (1669, 279)

Beyond Ripa's *Iconologia,* a Spanish renaissance manual, Covarrubias's *Emblemas morales,* included two emblems that pertain to our discussion. The first is of a raven that crows from sunup until sundown, representing the irresolute, or wavering, person whom Martial associated with the *ardiolo* bird (1978, cent. II, emb. 100, f. 200).[56] The second was inspired by Ovid's tale about Apollo and the crow in *Metamorphoses* and is set off by these lines: "Su credito y su fama denegrece,/El malsin, el parlero y el chismoso,/Que de su voluntad propia se ofrece,/A descubrir lo oculto y lo dudoso./Al negro cuervo en esto se parece,/Que siendo blanco, vuelve tenebroso,/Por haber descubierto al rojo Apolo,/Lo que otro no sabía sino él solo" (cent. III, emb. 20, f. 220r.). A faithful, if discordant, translation reads as follows: "He blackens his standing and good name/The tattler, the chatterbox or the gossiper/Who by his own choice steps forward/To reveal what is concealed and uncertain/In this he resembles the black crow/That once white, turned dark/For having revealed to red Apollo/That which no one but he knew"). The illustration is a crow on a branch looking from a distance at two naked people in the countryside, with the accompanying motto *"Hoc illi garrula lingua dedit."* [57] The Spanish humanist's explanation is straightforward:

Tattlers, big mouths and denouncers—shamed people [*gente infame*]—were always hated and even punished many times by Princes and their ministers, because they are always laying traps, digging around to find out secret things that are not cause for scandal and cannot be verified, neither has shame [*infamia*] preceded them nor [have] the other requirements [been met] in order to proceed to an inquiry and fact finding. Roman Emperors, upon finding out about the evils of these [tattlers, big mouths and denouncers], used to insult and whip them in public, or they made them slaves or exiled them to deserted islands. (220v.)

In Carrió's own century, Daniel de La Feuille included Shame in his *Science hiéroglyphique* (Figure 13, no. 8). The motto for *Infamie* read: "Aime l'honneur plus que la vie,/Plus que tous les tresors de ce vaste Univers;/L'indigence de tout, l'esclavage, les fers,/La mort même, est un mal plus doux que l'infamie" (1746, 80) ("Love your good name more than life itself,/More than all the treasures in this vast Universe;/Utter misery, slavery, shackles,/Even death itself is a lesser evil than shame"). His explanation was as follows: "It is the figure of a half-naked woman with Crow's wings, playing the trumpet, which signals that the ugliness of her actions blackens her without her knowing. She has this word *Turpe* written on her forehead in order to show that shame [*l'infamie*] is felt by others more than by those who are covered in it" (80).

Finally, I note that the iconography of shame overlapped with that of comingling, or promiscuity, to a striking degree. Covarrubias explained at the entry for *cuervo* that one of the meanings of the Hebrew word for "raven" was to comingle, or mix (*commiscere*). The light of Apollo's swan and the dark of Apollo's raven mixed together in the early evening, which is why it was called *vespera* (1994, 380–81). Concolorcorvo, the "Crow-with-Color," Carrió named the textual inspector's secretary, whose mother was promiscuous, whose father lived in a bordello, and whose *casta* and *estado* remain unknown to Carrió's readers. Concolorcorvo was a hybrid, then, in more than one sense; legally and socially, *infamia* was written all over him.

False in One, False in All: Concolorcorvo and Other Royal Pretenders

Signaled throughout *El lazarillo de ciegos caminantes* is the fact that Concolorcorvo's failure to prove descent from legitimate caciques on at least one side placed him well outside the *casta* of Spaniards and the noble estate. The dialectics of genealogy and authority in *El lazarillo de ciegos caminantes* turns on the topos known in judicial oratory as "false in one, false in all." If the alleged author Concolorcorvo is lying about his own genealogy, he may well be lying about everything else, including the Incas he mentions in his dialogues with the inspector.

Many scholars have argued that Carrió's construction of Concolorcorvo undermines the authority of the renaissance humanist the Inca Garcilaso (Souza Penha 1978, 80–81, 84, 197–98; Hill 1994b, chap. 6; Meléndez 1994). Garcilaso's authority in the eighteenth century, among Spaniards such as Feijoo y Montenegro and Peruvians such as Pedro de Peralta Barnuevo, among French philosophers and historians such as Buffon and Guillaume-Thomas Raynal, would have made him a sitting duck for Carrió.[58] Yet I am not convinced that the Inca Garcilaso, long dead and gone, was Carrió's real target. I suspect that he was gunning for illegitimate Inca descendants and Inca impersonators—pretenders to Spanishness and gentryhood—who had rebelled against the Crown, inciting *indios, mestizos,* and *cholos.* Mixed in with these pretenders were Inca descendants who possessed special legal and social privileges. One was a friar from Tarma named Calixto de San José Tupac Inga, who protested the fraud and abuse heaped on the Indians by their governors in the 1730s. Unlike his namesake, Calixto Bustamante, Friar Calixto was implicated in the 1742 rebellion of the *chuncho* people in Jauja Valley, Tarma, led by Juan Santos Atahualpa. He traveled to Spain to litigate on behalf of Indians and then returned to Peru. In 1757, under suspicion by royal authorities, Friar Calixto was ordered to return to Spain, which he did in 1759.[59] A satirical "Conversation" that Friar Castillo wrote in the late 1760s alluded to Friar Calixto's public shaming. A beleaguered Indian tells his wealthy black friend that Spaniards will not give him a chance: "Emprendí meterme fraile/y en altas voces dijeron/que yo me iba a levantar/otro Frai Calixto siendo" ("I started down a friar's path,/and they shouted out loud/that, being another Friar Calixto,/I was going to rise up against them").[60]

The fictional Concolorcorvo, who masquerades as Calixto Bustamante in Carrió's exposé, leads us to another historic figure whom Carrió disprized: Juan de Bustamante Carlos Inga. Like Diego de Navia y Esquivel, who in his *Noticias cronológicas del Cuzco* (1980) praised his brother-in-law, José Pardo de Figueroa, Juan de Bustamante Carlos Inga was related to the Esquivel family in Cuzco. His great-great-great-great-grandfather, Carlos Inga (father of Melchor Carlos Inga), had married María de Esquivel, and his maternal grandmother was named Gabriel Mexía Carlos de Esquivel Coya (Dunbar Temple 1947, 285–89). He spent thirty years constructing genealogies of the Incas and writing legal petitions to viceroys, kings, bishops, and the Council of Indies to safeguard and enforce the privileges of Inca descendants in Abancay and Cuzco. In 1726, for example, he requested the attention of the viceroy of Peru to Philip V's decree, dated February 28, 1725, which confirmed Charles II's decree on March 12, 1697, which had itself reiterated Spanish laws that defined Indian governors and *caciques,* militia leaders, and their *mestizo* descendants not just as *Spaniards* but as *Spanish gentry (hidalgos)* (Dunbar Temple 1947, 287, 290–91, 301).

Some ten years later, Juan de Bustamante Carlos Inga was living at his mother's house in Cuzco, because his father had been murdered in Abancay (where José Pardo de Figueroa was governor) and his wife had engaged in an extramarital affair that ended their union. From 1734 to 1735, he wrote several petitions to prove his direct descent from Cristóbal Paullu Inga and to claim the assets of his great-great-great-grandfather, Melchor Carlos Inga, Paullu Inga's grandson (Dunbar Temple 1947, 285, 287–89). Juan and his wayward wife became locked in a bitter divorce dispute that landed him in prison sometime in 1735. To get out, he vindicated his rights as an *hidalgo,* which, as we have seen, every *legitimate* descendant of the Incas enjoyed. However, Juan was the descendant of a woman who had sex and children out of wedlock with Melchor Carlos Inga—a birth defect, as I have explained, that should have made him ineligible for membership in the *casta* of *españoles* and the noble order. He was released from prison in September 1736 (Dunbar Temple 1947, 287, 290–91, 301). Juan de Bustamante Carlos Inga's deft legal maneuvers were the bane of a provincial governor's existence, and his successful appeal to privileges held by *legitimate* descendants of the Incas must have still roiled Carrió well after he left his governorship of Chilques and Mesques.

In January 1737, Juan wrote Juan Vélez de Córdoba, a *mestizo* who was plotting to overthrow the Crown. He tried to talk Vélez out of his plans; Vélez claimed that Juan supported his efforts to reestablish the Inca Empire, efforts that failed and resulted in Vélez's execution in 1739. In late 1742 or early 1743, Juan left Cuzco for Madrid, writing several genealogies and petitions to King Philip V and the viceroy of Peru during his voyage (Dunbar Temple 1947, 291–92). The governor of Cuzco during those years was José Pardo de Figueroa (see Chapter 2). Given his Esquivel in-laws, his previous service as governor of Abancay, where many of Juan's relatives lived, his distant kinship with the viceroy of Peru (José Caamano y Sotomayor, count de Villagarcía), and his connections with the court in Madrid, it is almost certain that José knew Juan and used his personal and family connections to the Spanish Bourbons to help Juan get established in Madrid.

In June and July 1746, Juan wrote dozens of letters and petitions documenting his genealogical claims and requesting royal favors. In September 1747, Juan was a *gentilhombre de boca* and the Council of Indies denied his claim to the title and lands of the marquis de Oropesa because he was an illegitimate descendant of Melchor Carlos Inga. Even so, members of the council recognized that he was a descendant of the family to whom the title (and lands) had been granted centuries earlier. In February 1748, King Ferdinand VI issued a royal decree to the viceroy of Peru, instructing him to investigate the descendants of the Incas in the viceroyalty and Juan's land claims, which were still pending in the high court in Lima as a result of the petitions that Juan had made to the Council of the Indies. This royal decree from February 18, 1748, reveals Juan's claim that in 1603 eleven Ingas gave powers of attorney to the Inca Garcilaso and to Melchor Carlos Inga in Spain to litigate their exemption from tribute and other causes. The Ingas sent a painted family tree of the Inga emperors along with documents that supported their genealogical claims to the Inca Garcilaso, who thereafter sent these materials to Melchor Carlos Inga, who was then living in Valladolid. Ferdinand VI instructed the viceroy to investigate whether tax exemptions had been granted in 1603 and whether they were being observed at present (Dunbar Temple 1947, 293–95).

Juan de Bustamante Carlos Inga had opposed the *repartimiento*, and Carrió knew it. In 1753 the viceroy of Peru informed the king of Spain that Juan had written to him and to the former governor of Calaca and Lares about various legal petitions he was preparing on behalf of *caciques* in the province of Cuzco. Writing from Madrid, Juan assured the viceroy in Lima that the former governor, who had risen to the post of president of the high court in La Plata, would be ruined once the king found out. The Council of the Indies reviewed the viceroy's report in 1754. The *fiscal* of the Council of the Indies advised that Juan de Bustamante Carlos Inga be prohibited from returning to Peru under any circumstances and that he be instructed to limit his contacts with Peru to family members and family matters. The other members of the council agreed with the *fiscal* and decided that they would not admit letters or reports written by Juan, a determination that had been communicated to him as early as 1747. In November 1759, Juan de Bustamante Carlos Inga was still a *gentilhombre* at the court in Madrid (Moreno Cebrián 1977, 426–27 n. 106; Dunbar Temple 1947, 296).

Carrió was aware of Juan's biography and activities for several reasons. Recall that between 1752 and 1757 Carrió was *corregidor* of Chilques and Mesques, two towns near Cuzco. He had to have been in contact with the governor of Calaca and Lares during that period. Further, Carrió had already been to Buenos Aires in 1749. He returned to the Riverplate region during his inspection of the posts, so he could have met up with former colleagues in La Plata with whom he discussed events from fifteen or twenty years before. Finally, Carrió could easily have learned about Juan de Bustamante Carlos Inga through his own brief association with the deceptive Calixto Bustamante, whom Concolorcorvo impersonates in *El lazarillo de ciegos caminantes*. Calixto Bustamante's mother or father was probably an illegitimate child fathered by Juan's father, making Juan a half-brother to her or him. Juan was Calixto's uncle, and Calixto had female *coya* cousins who enjoyed royal pensions (Dunbar Temple 1947, 287, 290–91, 300–301), probably in a convent like Juan's cheating wife and like the fictional Concolorcorvo's cousins of dubious virtue. This is only one of many allusions to Juan de Bustamante Carlos Inga in *El lazarillo de ciegos caminantes*.

In an exchange between the inspector and the secretary analyzed earlier, the inspector compares the Incas to the Moors and Concolorcorvo assumes the role of the buffoon as he delights in his nickname. He refers to the last name of his ancestors, Carlos (364–65). Later, in the most importance reference to Juan de Bustamante Carlos Inga, Concolorcorvo proudly claims that he is his nephew and that he had planned to go to Madrid to be with his famous uncle:

> Estoy pronto, le dije, a seguir a Vm. hasta Lima, a donde hice mi primero y único viaje cuando salí del Cuzco con ánimo de pasar a España, en solicitud

de mi tío, que aunque indio logró la dicha de morir en el honorífico empleo de gentilhombre de cámara del actual señor Carlos III, que Dios eternice, por merced del señor Fernando el VI, que goza de gloria inmortal, porque los católicos Reyes de España jamás han olvidado a los descendientes de los Incas, aunque por línea transversal y dudosa; y si yo, en la realidad, no seguí desde Buenos Aires mi idea de ponerme a los pies del Rey, fue por haber tenido la noticia de la muerte de mi tío, y porque muchos españoles de juicio me dijeron que mis papeles estaban tan mojados y llenos de borrones que no se podrían leer en la corte, aunque en la realidad eran tan buenos como los de mi buen tío. (394)[61]

[I am ready, I said to him, to follow you as far as Lima, where I made my first and only trip when I left Cuzco in hopes of traveling to Spain, in the care of my uncle, who though an Indian was lucky enough to die in the honored employment of chamber gentleman to the present King Charles III, may God grant him eternal life, by favor of King Ferdinand VI, who enjoys immortal glory, because the Catholic kings of Spain never have forgotten the descendants of the Incas, although of transversal and doubtful lines; and if I did not actually go ahead, from Buenos Aires, with my plan to kneel at the feet of the King, it was because I received news of my uncle's death, and because many Spaniards with sense told me that my papers were so wet and full of stains that they could not be read at court, although they were actually as good as my uncle's.]

Two things are important here. First, the notion that Concolorcorvo's plans were halted in Buenos Aires is an allusion to Basavilbaso's discovery that a recommendation for employment written on behalf of Calixto Bustamante was a forgery. News of his uncle's death is a pretext. Similarly, the fact that Concolorcorvo's papers were not valid is an allusion to Calixto's papers. Second, through Concolorcorvo, Carrió undermines the genealogy and the authority of Juan de Bustamante Carlos Inga. Calixto's "papers" were as "wet and full of stains" as Juan's *memoriales* to the viceroy of Peru and the king of Spain. Carrió's attack on Juan de Bustamante Carlos Inga's credibility through the fictional Concolorcorvo leads us back to the *repartimiento* controversy and to Bourbon elites whom Carrió neither trusted nor admired.

The Repartimiento *Controversy and the Facade of Reform*

It is clear that (as we might expect from someone who had served as a provincial governor) Carrió was well versed in the *repartimiento* reforms from the first half of the eighteenth century. In his exposé, we read that the commerce in which *corregidores* engaged to stave off poverty generated "endless lawsuits and charges" ("infinitos pleitos y capítulos") (346). In a 1744 letter to the secretary of the Council of the Indies, José Pardo de Figueroa's friend Bishop Pedro Morcillo Rubio Auñón of Cuzco had criticized the mistreatment of Indians at the hands of governors in some provinces under his jurisdiction. This stoked the embers of the forced-sales fire that Viceroy José de Mendoza Sotomayor y Camaño in Lima had tried unsuccessfully to extinguish. By 1746, the year Carrió arrived in Peru, the *repartimiento* issue had really heated up. As we have just seen, the unsuccessful petitions and accusations filed by Juan Bustamante de Carlos Inga began thereafter. In 1747 the Council of the Indies reported to King Ferdinand VI that Viceroy José Antonio Manso de Velasco should examine the *repartimiento* system and punish provincial governors who continued to abuse and extort Indians (Moreno Cebrián 1977, 298–305). Carrió picks up the story from there:

> Estas turbaciones dieron motivo a los señores virreyes y tribunales para consultar al supremo oráculo el medio que se debía de tomar para libertar a sus vasallos de unos pleitos interminables, en que se arruinaban unos a otros. . . . La corte de Madrid, con los informes que se dieron de Lima y otras partes, y a consulta de juristas y teólogos, declaró que en lo sucesivo fuesen lícitos los comercios de los corregidores en todos aquellos efectos necesarios para la subsistencia de las provincias, y en particular útiles a los indios, y que se hiciesen aranceles de los efectos que se debían repartir, y sus precios. (346–47)

> [These disturbances motivated the Lords Viceroy and the courts to inquire of the supreme oracle the means that needed to be taken in order to free their vassals from some endless litigations in which they were financially ruining each other. . . . The Court in Madrid, based on the investigations conducted in Lima and other parts, and on consultations with jurists and theologians, ruled that the governors' sales of all those goods necessary for the subsistence of the provinces, and useful to the Indians in particular, would be allowed by law, and that controls on the goods that should be distributed, and their prices, would be set up.]

It appears here that the *repartimiento* firestorm had been a dustup: a handful of contumacious governors had been given a slap on the wrist, there had been a cooling-off period, new laws had been drawn up, and then the whole matter had been put to rest. This was not the case. The *repartimiento* controversy is a fine illustration of how tightly political and religious factions in late viceregal Peru were enmeshed with disparate cultural schema. Several of the Bourbon officials involved in the debates and deliberations were crusaders for causes that Carrió did not believe in, a handful of them were to tangle with him over the post, and he considered all of them to be enlightened criminals masquerading as reformers.

Important information on the *repartimiento* battles and their actors can be gleaned from four manuscripted reports written for Viceroy Pedro Ceballos of the Riverplate region in 1776. In a section of the *Primer Informe*, the anonymous author recounts that in April 1752 Viceroy Manso de Velasco invited Pedro Bravo de Lagunas y Castilla, Pedro Bravo del Ribero (whom Carrió derides as 'the supreme oracle' in the previous passage), Manuel de Goxena, and Manuel Yidro (all judges on the high court in Lima), and Diego Holgado de Guzmán (*fiscal* on the same) (Anonymous 1776, 3v.) to investigate the provincial governors and their distribution of goods to the Indians.[62] Bravo del Ribero was charged with analyzing the *repartimiento* in the bishoprics of Cuzco (which included Governor Carrió's two towns), Arequipa (where Bravo del Ribero's own brother served as bishop), and Huamanga. His brother-in-law, Bravo de Lagunas y Castilla, was charged with studying the bishoprics of Lima and Trujillo (Moreno Cebrián 1977, 314–15). In 1756 Ceballos, then governor of Buenos Aires and president of the high court in La Plata (1756–1766), informed the *fiscal* of the high court in Charcas of the Lima committee's findings and ordered that these be implemented in his district. Enter Antonio Porlier, who was to galvanize opposition to Carrió's inspection report and other postal interventions in the 1770s. Porlier played a key role in the campaign to reform the *repartimiento* in the Viceroyalty of Peru, spearheaded by Bravo del Ribero. In 1760, from his post as *fiscal* on the high court in La Plata, Porlier wrote a report to Charles III that would prompt the king's overhaul of the *repartimiento* system four years later:

> The *Fiscal*, Don Antonio Porlier, was consulted, who requested testimony in order to inform His Majesty, which he executed on 14 April 1760, [and] as a result His Majesty saw fit to issue the following Royal Decree: "In San Lorenzo, on the 27th day of October of the year 1764. In view of the findings of the Committee on *Corregidores* established by my Royal Decree on the 19th of June in the year 1751, with the report from the *Fiscal* of my High Court in La Plata, I order and command that the aforementioned Committee must concern itself only with the quality, quantity and prices of the products, fruits and goods that shall be sent to each province according to its particular circumstances, and with setting down all of those provisions and rules that it deems appropriate in order to prevent all of the fraudulent schemes and coercions that can be effected against the Indians in the *corregidores'* distributions [*repartimientos*], while the hearing and resolution of the complaints, appeals and suits that arise in their respective Jurisdictions remains in the charge and care of my high courts." (Anonymous 1776, 4v.–5r.)

Enter another of Carrió's enemies, Miguel Feijoo de Sosa (see Chapters 3 and 4). In 1757 Feijoo de Sosa, then a chief accountant for the royal treasury court in Lima, was appointed *corregidor* of Trujillo (1757–1760). He rewarded the largesse of his patron, Viceroy Manso de Velasco, by portraying him in his 1763 *Relación descriptiva de la Ciudad y Provincia de Trujillo del Perú* (*Descriptive Account of the City and Province of Trujillo, Peru*) as an economic genius who had reformed trade and taxes.[63] Unlike Carrió, Feijoo de Sosa highly valued Peralta Barnuevo as a historian (1984, 1:20), and, like many ardently Bourbon bureaucrats in the Spanish Indies, he embraced the Spanish cultural critic Feijoo y Montenegro. Obviously, Feijoo de Sosa and Carrió had very different literary tastes, but their differences were not limited to literature: these men took divergent paths once they had finished their stints as provincial governors.

In 1763 Feijoo de Sosa, son of a Crown power broker and notorious smuggler from the first half of the eighteenth century, became comptroller at the royal tobacco monopoly (whose connection to the smuggling of gold and silver through the posts came to light in Chapter 4). A year later, he began what was to be a decade-long tenure as director of the same monopoly. In 1765 Viceroy Manuel de Amat y Junient's secretary and Feijoo de Sosa's former law professor had the former governor of Trujillo appointed to the royal treasury court, alongside José Herboso y Figueroa (a member of the Navia y Esquivel clan into which José Pardo de Figueroa had married and a fixture of the upper echelons of the church in the Viceroyalty of Peru).[64] In September 1767, Feijoo de Sosa and a handful of other Crown officials personally delivered to the Jesuits the news of their expulsion, and Carrió was charged with accompanying them on their voyage to Europe. By 1769, Feijoo de Sosa headed a commission set up by the viceroy to expedite the privatization of the Jesuit properties. That same year he also began a review and personal inspection of the royal treasury, metals receiving center, and mint in Potosí. In 1771, the year Carrió began his inspection of the posts, Amat approved Feijoo de Sosa's proposal to tax slave owners who freed their elderly and disabled slaves and to direct the revenues to a hospital for indigents in Lima. Pushing the proposal was the *fiscal* on Lima's high court, Porlier, a man who had played a pivotal role in the overhaul of the *repartimiento* system. After serving as the *fiscal* for Indian affairs on the high court in La Plata (1757–1765), Porlier became a judge on that court (1765–1769) and then a *fiscal* on the high court in Lima (1769–1775) (Lohmann Villena 1974, 103–4).

In 1772 Viceroy Amat charged Porlier with reviewing the postal regulations (*Reglamento General de Correos*) proposed by José Antonio Pando, the postmaster general in Lima, with whom Carrió had locked horns from the very beginning of his inspection of the posts (Carilla in Carrió 1973, 79). It was because of Pando, in fact, that Carrió did not inspect the posts in Lima, although they were included in his original commission. Pando's accounting records for 1773 to 1774, which Feijoo de Sosa was to include in Amat's *Memoria de gobierno* (1947, 606), sparked Carrió's ire. In 1777, after being appointed an auditing accountant for the postal administration in Lima, Carrió published a *Manifiesto* to set the record straight. Carrió was briefly imprisoned and then released and forced to retire (Carilla in Carrió 1973, 12–13; Bataillon 1960, 206). Undoubtedly, Porlier played a role in

Carrió's forced retirement: he had left his post as *fiscal* on the high court in Lima to accept the same post on the Council of the Indies in 1775 and became a full-fledged member of the council in 1780 (Lohmann Villena 1974, 103–4).

Like Porlier, Feijoo de Sosa opposed provincial governors at every turn. He condemned them and the *repartimiento* in the prologue he wrote for Viceroy Amat's *Memoria de gobierno* and again in a treatise he wrote for the succeeding viceroy of Peru, Manuel de Guirior.[65] Carrió, on the other hand, argued that it was impossible for a Spaniard to deceive an Indian: Indians were too clever. This sentiment was shared by some of his contemporaries.[66] Still, we should not mistake the inspector's rebuttal of many of the accusations lodged against *corregidores,* or his acknowledgment of the Indian business sense, for a ringing endorsement of the distribution system. Carrió's overall assessment of provincial governors was not encouraging. After Concolorcorvo reports how the governor of Oruro opposed the inspector's appointment of Manuel de Campo Verde y Choquetilla (the *cacique* and Spaniard mentioned in Chapter 5), the inspector explains, "Lo que puedo asegurar a Vmds. es que a excepción de un corto número de racionales corregidores, que comuniqué por más de veinte anhos en todas estas provincias, todos los demás me han parecido unos locos, por lo que creo cualquiera extravagancia que se refiera de ellos" (302) ("What I can assure you of is that with the exception of a small number of sound-minded *corregidores* with whom I have come in contact during my more than twenty years in all of these provinces, the rest have struck me as madmen, which is why I believe whatever nonsense they are said to have done").[67] How, then, do we make sense of the fact that Carrió discursively breaks out in hives every time he discusses Bourbon reforms in this area?

What Carrió found objectionable in the condemnations of the provincial governors and the *repartimiento* system was the hyperbole and the hypocrisy of Bourbon officials in Lima. Viceroy Amat, for instance, complained that Bravo del Ribero and other judges on the high court in Lima were the most active and successful merchants in town, without whom the *repartimiento* could not harm as it did (Lohmann Villena 1976, 205–8 and n. 177; Moreno Cebrián 1977, 169).[68] The viceroy even had Feijoo de Sosa file charges against Holgado de Guzmán, who had been Bravo del Ribero's colleague on the *repartimiento* reform committee in the 1750s.[69] Yet Feijoo de Sosa's boss was famous for selling governorships and for removing governors before their terms had expired in order to resell their posts at a higher price. These dealings involved Amat's chief of staff, Jaime Palmer, and his nephew, José de Amat y Rocabertí (Lohmann Villena 1976, 205–8 and n. 177).[70] Carrió had every reason to believe that Amat was saying one thing—wishing to reform the forced sales system—and doing another. The same could have been said of the former governor, Feijoo de Sosa, who found religion regarding his own wrongs against the Indians some fifteen years after his governorship of Trujillo ended (Hill 1996b).

In his *Plan* to reform the Viceroyalty of Peru, left unfinished at his death,

Carrió alluded to Feijoo de Sosa as the "supreme oracle" (1966, 153) and "rigid censor" (202). Later the Bourbon administrator's negative appraisal of governors and their forced sales to the Indians is hinted at and then ridiculed:

> This, in spite of the fact that in a report on the *corregidores'* distributions that he wrote for [Viceroy] Mr. Guirior, a certain critic of great renown in this city said that the Thebans did not admit any merchant to the Magistracy until he had been in quarantine, if you will pardon the expression, for at least ten years. The laws of the Seven Sages of Greece are summarized in less than ten cuarto folios, and the densest merchant could gloss them in less than a week, and he would spend the remaining nine years and fifty-one weeks at the baths of the Athenians, where the mob used to debate the fate of the conquerors, the miscalculations of the Areopagus, and used to qualify Demosthenes' speeches as too fiery. On another occasion, he gives his word—meaning he gives no proof—that *corregidores* were all usurers because they were selling their goods to the poor, with a [profit] margin of 100%. (232)

In his *Plan,* Carrió defended *El lazarillo de ciegos caminantes* against his Crown critics:

> The chief Cosmographer of the Kingdom—I mean, Doctor Cosme Bueno, senior professor of Mathematics—adorned his annual predictions [i.e., almanacs] by geographically describing the provinces of the Kingdom by Bishoprics. His reports are full of very useful information for ecclesiastical, Natural and Civil history. If the critics of Lima qualified a work of this character as astrological hallucinations, why should we be surprised that the oracle of critics has treated *El lazarillo* [*de ciegos caminantes*] as a bunch of simplisms [*simplezas*]? Nonetheless, I do not believe that the Archcritic used *simpleza* in the common sense of the word, which is aired with such scorn among all groups of men. He really meant to say that *El lazarillo* [*de ciegos caminantes*] was a simple account of what [the author] had observed on the Royal Postal Roads from Montevideo to Lima to which he was assigned by the Court. This expression, "simple," a certain sage did not consider an insult when he was speaking of a simple, truthful and sincere writer, for he praises him by calling him a man of most distinguished simplicity, *eminentissimes simplicitatis virum.* From these cavils, which are truly minor at the start, divisions are born, and these often become implacable hatreds and factions. (1966, 106)

This virulent reaction to Feijoo de Sosa's belittling of *El lazarillo de ciegos caminantes* was also, I suspect, a reaction to his integration of Postmaster General Pando's fraudulent accounting records into Amat's *Memoria de gobierno,* which had prompted Carrió's *Manifiesto* and earned him jail time.

Earlier we saw that Feijoo de Sosa and his cronies in Lima were allegorized as *Trujillano* and *Limeños* in the satirical *Drama de los palanganas* (see Chapter 4). All of these men were Crown officials and ostensible "moderns," or Bourbon reformers. A handful, as I have demonstrated, had been involved in the *repartimiento* controversy *and* the debates and decisions about the posts. Moribund, Carrió still resented Amat's minions who had made life difficult for him since the clandestine publication of his exposé.

Critical assumptions about the relationship between the inspector and the alleged Inca secretary in Carrió's narration are often rooted in a postmodern sensibility that blinds us to Carrió's material reality. Shame, or *infamia,* is an important part of *El lazarillo de ciegos caminantes* that has been neglected by modern readers, but it was certainly not unknown to his contemporaries, as we saw in Chapters 2 and 5. The storied past and shame of the historical Calixto Bustamante partly shaped the figure of Concolorcorvo as an Inca impostor and a hybrid who carried shame. In addition, we have seen a good number of other literary, historiographical, and iconographic influences on Carrió's invention of Concolorcorvo. The preceding analysis has taken us from Lucian to newspapers, from Cervantes to travelogues, and from debates about the origins of the Indians to the legal controversy about who was covered by the Indian Privileges legislation.

Finally, our analysis has brought us to the rows over the *repartimiento* institution and Carrió's opinions of provincial governors, as he expressed them in his exposé and in his *Plan.* Carrió resented the men who claimed to be legitimate descendants of the Incas as they defrauded, or even rebelled against, the Crown and the church, adding fuel to the *repartimiento* fire. My purpose here has been not to side with Carrió or his opponents but to trace the ideologized history of this controversy, whose importance to Carrió's account (although noted by a handful of historians from Latin America) has been disconnected from Carrió's invention of Concolorcorvo and from the personnel involved in the reform of the posts.

CHAPTER 7

Trial of the Century: Humor, Rhetoric, and the Law

There had been no firm boundary between popular and high cultures in the Spanish world before the eighteenth century, and Alonso Carrió de Lavandera's mixture of the practical and the jocose was truly a reflection of the cultural paradigm that supposedly enlightened literati and officials had been trying to overturn since the triumph of the Bourbon Philip V in the War of the Spanish Succession. Perhaps Carrió feared that he would soon be living in a humorless century: the apex of high culture in Spanish America during the second half of the century was the eloquence of Virgil, Ovid, and their French neoclassical followers and the critical spirit of Father Benito Jerónimo Feijoo y Montenegro, who did not suffer ribaldry or irony gladly. On the other hand, mock trials were not only a preferred resort of deadpan satirists in the eighteenth century; according to the European literary journals and newspapers that arrived in Lima, they were highbrow academic exercises for the ostensibly enlightened in Paris. We have seen the Francophilia of some elites, which constituted part of the material reality against which Carrió reacted in New Spain and, later, Peru. The pages that follow examine Carrió's anecdote about the Guatemalan mock trial as an *exemplum* that comments on not only Bourbon court culture—including the alliance of supposedly enlightened literati and Crown officials—but also the protocols of the courts of law.

This chapter begins by making the case that the public challenge to solve the 4Ps from Lima riddle and the Guatemalan mock trial at which it is solved did not spring from popular culture, or orality; they form a rhetorical construct. It goes on to demonstrate that the riddle itself closely tracks prescriptions for the invention of riddles. Both of these beginning sections present Carrió's dialogue with classical, medieval, renaissance, baroque and Enlightenment authorities on humor. In my view, the Spaniard from Guatemala's practical joke ("burla chistosa") on the *peruleros* should be approached as Carrió's manifestation of what was known to previous generations of intellectuals and politicians as *urbanity*. The discussion continues with an examination of a number of other witty stories and sayings found in *El lazarillo de ciegos caminantes*—stories and sayings that could have been written two hundred years earlier and that challenged the sense of humor that Bourbon elites were promoting for their "illuminated" century. A review of the potential literary and social stimuli for Carrió's invention of the trial of wits in Santiago de Guatemala follows, including rhetorical prescriptions, medieval jousts, and French academic and political culture. The chapter concludes by analyzing the Guatemalan tale in light of rhetorical and legal distinctions between friendly insult and defamation of character.

Crafting the Guatemalan Tale: The Rhetoric of the Risible and the Ridiculous

As befits an account that details the contradictions between hegemonic discourse and material reality in eighteenth-century Spanish America, Carrió mocks lawyers and judges in the Guatemalan tale. The jocose tale was neither historical in the modern sense nor fictional in the eighteenth-century sense. The challenge and the mock trial proceedings in Santiago de Guatemala never took place, but the activities censured by either solution to the 4Ps riddle are, indeed, part of the historical record. How, then, can we make sense of the tale as a rhetorical unit and of the larger rhetorical unit in which the tale is embedded, the exposé itself? Cicero's treatment of humor in *On the Ideal Orator* offers us several initial leads.

Cicero was an important source for Baldassare Castiglione, whose treatment of humor was influential in renaissance Spain through Juan de Boscán's translation, *Los cuatro libros de El cortesano* (1994). Castiglione's work, I am convinced, holds many of the interpretative keys to Carrió's sense of humor in his report and to the Guatemalan tale in particular. Antonius, one of Cicero's interlocutors, noted that Caesar, the expert on humor, warned, "We ought take account of the people, the case, and the circumstances, so that our joking should not detract from our authority" (2001, 184). If the inspector was to maintain his authority vis-à-vis his social inferior Concolorcorvo within the text, and Postal Inspector Carrió was to maintain his authority outside of the text, within Liman society, the author Carrió had to heed this advice, and he did. The Guatemalan tale and the witticisms aired by the elderly and praised in Carrió's narration are circumspect and spaced throughout the narration in a manner intended to keep his readers entertained while they were absorbing the practical information. The "jocosities," as he would call them in the defensive letter that he sent to the Crown, are not pervasive, so his readers could not dismiss the entire exposé as one big joke.

In Cicero's manual, Caesar divided and defined witty discourse for his interlocutors: "Every witty utterance derives its wit sometimes from the content, sometimes from the words; but people particularly enjoy it whenever a laugh is stirred up by a combination of contents and words" (2001, 190). Carrió's Guatemalan tale, or the narrative circle that contains two solutions to the riddle of the 4Ps from Lima, relies heavily (though not entirely) on humor through content. However, the riddle and its solutions—a circle within that larger circle—turn on humor drawn from words and from content. Caesar provided an example of humor through content that sheds light on Carrió's jocose story:

> For there are two types of witticisms, one of which works through content, the other through sayings. Through content, whenever something like an anecdote is told, such as you, Crassus, once used against Memmius. You said that he had swallowed Largus' arm when the two were in a fight over a mistress at Tarracina. A witty story, but just the same, you had entirely fabricated it yourself. To round it off, you added that the letters M M L L L were written on the walls all over Tarracina at that time, and that when you asked what they stood for, one of the old locals told you, "Mordacious Memmius lacerates Largus' limb." You can see how witty, how refined, and how fitting for the orator this type of humor is, whether you have a true story to tell—which should still be spiced with little lies—or whether you are fabricating one. The good thing about this type is that you describe the actions in such a way, that the character, the manner of speaking, and all the facial expressions of the person about whom you are telling the story are portrayed so that it seems to the audience that all actions and events are taking place right there and then. (187–88)

There are numerous parallels between Cicero's definition of humor achieved through content and Carrió's crafting of the Guatemalan tale. To begin with, Concolorcorvo states that the inspector told him an anecdote, which the inspector qualifies as a jest, funny trick, or practical joke ("burla chistosa"). In the previous example, Crassus's "entirely fabricated" "witty story" accused Memmius of beating up Largus, his alleged rival for the affections of a dame in Tarracina. This tale had to have resonated with Carrió, who was only too familiar with the violently amorous intrigues of Viceroy Manuel de Amat y Junient in Lima and of Archbishop Pedro Pardo de Figueroa in Santiago de Guatemala. The initials "written on the walls all over Tarracina at that time," according to Cicero's dialogue, have their correspondence in Carrió's fabricated anecdote: the Spaniard from Guatemala tacked his *cartel* containing the 4Ps from Lima riddle to the doors of the archbishop's residence in Santiago. Carrió had "a true story to tell"—at least one—but he "spiced [it] with little lies": he molded his true story, or what everyone considered to be true, into an *exemplum,* or brief allegorical tale. Classical rhetoric permitted fabricated *exempla* in demonstrative oratory, that is, the branch of rhetoric to which historiography belonged before the rationalist and empiricist decoupling of historiographical discourse and rhetoric in the seventeenth century.

Renaissance and baroque prescriptions for humor also sanctioned the embellishment of true stories as Cicero explains it. In Boscán's translation of Castiglione's *Il corteggiano,* there is a tale about a courtier who was in the Vatican palace when he remembered a Roman author's dialogue with a door that revealed the adultery committed by the woman who owned the house. The courtier at the Vatican cleverly transferred this story to the intrigues following Pope Alexander VI's death and the appointment of his successor, Pius III (1994, 274–75 and n. 5). The raconteur commented, "You know very well that this way of knowing how to poke fun can be good and sometimes it will fit with what is appropriate to any good man at court, whether what is told is true or feigned, because in such a case feigning is allowed, and while the foundation is built on truth, it can be spiced up by daring to lie a little, adding or taking away as is needed" (276). Carrió's tale was founded on truth—on the public shaming of *Pedro, Pardo, Paulino,* and *Perulero*—and then spiced up in a manner that would turn something grave into grave nonsense.

Emanuele Tesauro discussed *comparative deformity* and explained how laughter can be provoked when instruments do not match a task or when they are misused. What he wrote sheds light on Carrió's invention of the Guatemalan anecdote: "And with such pieces of nonsense [*spropositi*] there are performed many *Comic Skits,* or *Facetious Poems,* or *Mock Masquerades and Tournaments* that rework letters of public challenge [*Cartelli*], trophies, cryptic symbols [*Divise*] and ridiculous mottoes [*Imprese*] into the most ingenious plots. And also of this nature are certain *Oratorical Narrations* woven from inverisimilitudes made verisimilar through imitation, with no other wit [*acume*]" (1968, 588). The battle of wits in 1746 Guatemala never took place, I am certain. It is a rhetorical construct (or *Oratorical Narration*): a mock trial with lawyers and judges that turns on one of those *cartelli,* or public letters of challenge, mentioned by Tesauro. Just as justice becomes ridiculous when its instruments are used to decide a rivalry between two cities that is rooted in unseemly conduct, so the office of archbishop is worthy of ridicule when—in the face of widespread disease and famine and charges of immoral and illegal conduct—an archbishop attends comedies, banquets, dances, and concerts for two weeks running.

By supposedly reenacting the trial of wits from 1746, Carrió made it possible for his contemporary readership to fill the benches (so to speak) of the archbishop's court: they not only read the tale; they participated in the courtroom drama. Carrió's *exemplum* conforms with Cicero's prescriptions for humor and storytelling: "You must describe and place before the audience's eyes such things as are both plausible (one of the requirements of a story) and somewhat dishonorable (one of the requirements of humor)" (2001, 196). It has been sufficiently demonstrated that both solutions to the riddle of the 4Ps from Lima, and the "oratorical narration" in which they are embedded, refer to actual events that damaged the good name of powerful church and state officials, notwithstanding the final outcomes of the actual investigations or trials of those officials. That the judges of the trial of wits within the text and the eighteenth-century readers outside of the text found the solutions humorous does not discredit my historical interpretation of them; it confirms it: the Guatemalan tale meets at least one of Cicero's requirements for humor by dealing with events that are at least "somewhat dishonorable." Moreover, it must be judged to have met one of Cicero's requirements for a story: the very fact that literary historians have grappled with the genesis of this 1746 tale in the context of Carrió's biography, wondering how he heard it or whether he was actually there when it happened, confirms that this spiced up *exemplum* does not lack plausibility.[1] Both of Cicero's requirements for a witty anecdote, then, are fulfilled by the "burla chistosa" that ends *El lazarillo de ciegos caminantes*. Carrió knew how to tell a story, and he knew how to tell a joke.

Beyond the witty anecdote, another kind of humor worked through content: *imitation,* or *caricature.* These prescriptions, too, are central to my analysis of Carrió's tale as a rhetorical construct: "The orator should employ imitation slyly, so that the hearer imagines more than he actually sees. In addition, the orator must give proof of his own good manners and modesty by avoiding dishonorable words and obscene subjects" (Cicero 2001, 188–89). Not a dishonorable word is spoken by anyone in Carrió's hilarious *exemplum;* moreover, the arguments presented by both sides in the mock trial do not explicitly address the obscene and irreligious actions allegedly performed by the actual archbishop, Pardo de Figueroa, or the trials and machinations of the actual president-governor of Guatemala, José de Araújo y Río. Similarly, the inspector's description of the Liman orator dripping with Oriental silk, silver, and gold does not openly accuse the Peruvian fashion plate of illegal trading or the diversion of silver and gold: Carrió left it to the imagination of his readers, at least some of whom, according to both textual declarations and Carrió's extratextual declarations to postal administrators, were well-traveled muleteers and traders.

In his treatment of symbols of wit that work through content, Tesauro discussed mimicry and offered the ridiculous example of Nero, dressed as Homer, singing about the burning of Troy while Rome was in flames. That Pardo de Figueroa wished to celebrate the fact that he had been promoted to archbishop in 1746 was quite understandable. However, amidst the disease and natural disasters that were ravaging his city that year, the scale of his celebrations made some citizens indignant, as we saw in Chapter 2. In the Guatemalan tale, Carrió places the archbishop and his fellow Limans on a stage quite unlike the one constructed for the historical celebrations in Santiago de Guatemala. The trial of wits that the inspector situates in 1746 turns on mimicry every bit as ridiculous as the example given by Tesauro: the city is falling down around the archbishop and the governor, who are holding court at the archbishop's residence—that is, entertaining themselves with a riddle and refreshments. The participants in the mock trial give highly stylized performances, because Carrió's imitation exemplified *vivid description in action (Hipotipósi in Attione)*, which expressed "manners and heroic or servile actions" (Tesauro 1968, 616). The Guatemalan practical joke ("burla chistosa") embodies both types of humor through content (caricature and anecdote). It is not the sort of grave *exemplum* that one commonly finds in historiographical discourse; it is, instead, a jocose *exemplum* that simulates gravity.

As Caesar made clear, both types of humor through content "are peculiar to the witticisms of the continuous kind, in which the characters of individuals are described and molded in such a way that the telling of a story makes it clear what sort of people they are or the insertion of a brief imitation reveals that they have a conspicuous fault that will make the audience laugh" (Cicero 2001, 188–89). This "conspicuous fault" was later treated as a *moral deformity*—a vile and shameful extreme—that could be imitated directly or indirectly: "Ridiculous Objects are not only shameful Actions and things, but also the SIGNS, Traces and indications of them. The latter, rather, are a lot more ridiculous insofar as a certain figurative something comes in, while wit on its own travels from that trace to the Work itself" (Tesauro 1968, 586). Carrió's physical description of the debonair Liman orator insinuated that one of his "conspicuous faults" was vanity. This fault (or some other) led him into the illegal and immoral behaviors implied by the provenance of certain clothing articles and the abundance of silver and gold, these being "SIGNS" or "traces" of "shameful Actions and things."

Carrió's caricature of the orator's harangue begins, remember, with this phrase: "The senior member of the *peruleros* was a grave man and one of few words." The Liman lord then touches his cap, we read, before he begins his "harangue." Both of these descriptions allow us to visualize this gentleman as a vain and fastidious man: he is, given the circumstances, far too serious. The formality exhibited by the senior *perulero* in this trial of a riddle, when it is mentally combined with the prior physical description of him, suggests that he is out of touch with reality and perhaps the perfect exhibit of the earnest flakiness that Carrió associated with French academic and courtly culture. In addition, the haranguing *perulero* has at least one other "conspicuous fault"; a very irksome petulance is suggested by his *ad hominem* thrust at competing counsel: "The riddle that the *Gachupín,* our Countryman, posed, and the Challenge that he issued, confirm the little knowledge that he has about things that happen yonder the Sea" (1775, n.p.). This statement leads into another one, which is positively condescending: "It causes me no small embarrassment to solve a Riddle so obvious that even the kids in Lima know it" (1775, n.p.). Thus, Carrió's caricature of the Spaniard from Lima brings subtly to life what is contained in his description of the mindset of the Liman delegation as a whole: "Los *chapetones* estaban ciertos de su victoria" (469) ("The *chapetones* were convinced of their [impending] victory").

In contrast, Carrió's caricature of the Spaniard from Guatemala shows us a gentleman who is modest, affable, and patient in the face of his senior opponent's unbridled arrogance. There is no physical description of the challenger, but the inspector describes his actions as background to the trial: "The Guatemalan *Gachupín* noted the many praises that the *Chapetones* sang of Lima, but at the

same time he noticed that they had not made mention of the four illustrious Ps"
(1775, n.p.). His own harangue evinces the topic known as *humilitas auctorial,* as
he nearly begs to differ with his Liman opponent: "I do not deny that the Liman
Gentlemen fully explained the meaning that is given to my four Ps in their Homeland, but I would like to ask these Sires if they think I am foolish enough to ask
them something so obvious? Are there not, by chance, other 4Ps in the world?"
(1775, n.p.). The conspicuous absence of a physical description of the Spaniard
from Guatemala and the conspicuous presence of a generous and temperate bearing were consciously rhetorical choices by Carrió. The Guatemalan *exemplum* is,
in fact, full of what Tesauro called *moral deceptions:* "those that, not by praise or
blame, but through *imitation,* or some *narrative performance [Rappresentation Nar-
rativa],* make you see the ridiculous or grave customs of the person in such a way
that the listener's expectation gets betrayed and surprised" (1968, 477). The Guatemalan Spaniard gives a flawless performance as friendly foil to the well-appointed
Liman lord, who both embodies and performs ignorance—intellectual and moral
blindness—and is therefore outwitted in the end.

Another source of humor defined by Cicero appears in the Guatemalan tale
and throughout *El lazarillo de ciegos caminantes:* insinuation. In the anecdote,
both the Spaniard from Lima and the Spaniard from Guatemala employ it in their
respective arguments, but one of the most ingenious examples can be found in the
inspector's description of President-Governor Araújo y Río's gesture and state of
mind (see Chapter 4 herein): "The president of the high court, since he was more
clairvoyant, expressed with a forced laugh some uncertainty about the victory of
his compatriots" (1775, n.p.). The use of a single word, "clairvoyant," reminds the
exposé's readers of corrupt officials in the Viceroyalty of Peru who are very touchy
or vindictive and are qualified jocosely as "clairvoyant." The president is nervous
because he can see what is coming—and it is not a victory for his fellow Limans.

Numerous examples of insinuation can be found in the inspector's description
of the Guatemalan's actions prior to the trial proceedings (as we saw in Chapters
1 and 2): "The Guatemalan *Gachupín* noted the many praises that the *Chapetones*
sang of Lima, but at the same time he noticed that they had not made mention
of the four illustrious Ps, and one Night he had them painted in Red Lead [*almagre*] on the Distinguished Archbishop's front Door along with a Letter of Public Challenge [*cartel de desafío*] to the *Chapetones* to decipher their meaning" (1775,
n.p.). Both *almagre* and *cartel de desafío* conjured legal and social shame, and the
adjectival form of *red lead* was employed jokingly, as in the definition from the
Diccionario de la lengua castellana that we saw in Chapter 2: "ALMAGRADO. Is
said jocosely and mockingly of one who has come out injured or the loser in some
brawl or other misfortune, and it arises from red lead's likeness in color to blood"
(Real Academia Española 1979, 3:225). Another salient example can be found in
the Spaniard from Guatemala's exordium to his solution, where Carrió's use of
insinuation conveys to me that one of the archbishop's alleged indiscretions had

hit his satirical vein more bluntly than the others. Let us return to the Guatemalan tale at the point when the Spanish resident from Guatemala prefaces the triumphant solution to his own riddle:

No dudo Señores, que si me hallara en Athenas, adonde opinaban los Sabios, y resolvia la Plebe, se sentenciaria contra mi, y me tendrian todos por un animoso insensato, como me graduan los Señores Limeños; pero como me hallo en una Junta, en que han de decidir dos Hombres Sabios e Imparciales, sin embargo del Patriotismo, estoy cierto de alcanzar una Victoria, que mis Contrarios cantaron por suya con aplauso de todos los circunstantes. (1775, n.p.)

[I do not doubt, Sires, that if I were in Athens, where the Sages gave their opinions and the Mob settled things, the ruling would go against me and all would consider me a foolish brave heart as the Liman Sires assess me. But since I find myself in an Assembly in which two Wise and Impartial Men will render a decision, notwithstanding Hometown Loyalties, I am certain to secure a Victory that my Opponents claimed as theirs to the applause of all those present.]

The Imperial and Pontificate University of Mexico City considered itself the Athens of the New World. Lima's University of San Marcos was another Athens, according to alumni.[2] The Spanish resident's reference to Athens, his characterization of the archbishop and the president of Guatemala as "two Wise and Impartial Men," and his packaging of the riddle in four letters slyly insinuated a parallel between Archbishop Pardo de Figueroa's alleged crime and another that had occurred in ancient Athens.

One of Benito Remigio Noydens's additions to Sebastián de Covarrubias Orozco's *Tesoro de la lengua castellana* is found at the word *mujer* (*woman*): "In Athens, they posted these 4 Ms, [and] those shining wits came up with different solutions and various interpretations to no avail. Only Plato got it right, writing underneath the letters, *Mulier mala mors mariti* [*A bad woman is the death of her husband*]" (1943, 818). The preface to the second solution to the 4Ps from Lima riddle insinuated a historical precedent for the competition that had nothing to do with an earnest comparison of Lima and Mexico City. While Plato had blamed the widow, the orator from Guatemala implicated the archbishop as much as the widow, just as Archbishop Pardo de Figueroa's accusers had done in their complaints to the Inquisition, the high court in Mexico City, and the Council of the Indies between 1744 and 1747. Insinuation, in Carrió's Guatemalan tale, not only served to create humor; it also was a strategy for building community with an eighteenth-century readership: each insinuative detail or word was like a wink and a nod that confirmed their membership in an interpretative community formed around the inside joke.

Beyond insinuation, the Spaniard from Guatemala's speech demonstrates vividly the role of irony in the witty Guatemalan tale. Irony is so very central to Carrió's invention of the jocose *exemplum,* and to my interpretation of it on the material and discursive levels, that it merits a brief, but punctual, analysis. First, a general observation: Cicero's definition of irony and Castiglione's comments on irony (through Boscán's Spanish version of *The Courtier*) both were important in the genealogy of Carrió's mock trial. Cicero clarified:

> Irony, that is, saying something different from what you think, is also elegant and witty. I don't mean ... saying the exact opposite [*antithesis,* a type of humor drawn from words] ... , but being mock-serious in your whole manner of speaking, while thinking something different from what you are saying. ... I think that Socrates by his refined wit far excelled all others in this "irony," this dissembling. This is a thoroughly elegant type, combining wit with seriousness, and it is appropriate both for public speaking and for urbane conversation. (2001, 198–99)

In Boscán's translation, *Los cuatro libros de El cortesano,* too, irony—what he often labeled *dissimulation*—was highly praised: "What consists of a certain dissimulation, when one thing is said and another is understood underneath it, is also very funny and artful; ... such contraries are sneaky and crude when mocking, in a measured and earnest tone, a man says deliciously what he does not have in his heart" (Castiglione 1994, 304). This sort of irony was well suited to men of authority and practiced by the ancients as well as a modern Spanish monarch: "This way of saying witticisms that achieves this manner of irony or dissimulation appears very well suited to men of authority, because it is grave and has taste and it can be used in jests and in earnests. That is why many of the Ancients and of the most venerated used it, like Cato and Scipius Africanus the Younger, but Socrates is said to have been more distinguished by it than all others, and in our times, King Don Alphonso I of Aragon" (305–6). Through Carrió's use of dissimulation, the fictional Spaniard from Guatemala appears humble and uncertain about the merits of his case—a mark of his urbanity (and, ultimately, of course, Carrió's own). Rhetorically, that *humilitas auctorial* augments the impact of his case, as we see when his unexpected solution to the riddle (an instance of simulation) causes the archbishop of Guatemala and the president-governor of Guatemala to double over in laughter and issue a verdict in his favor.[3]

Irony permeates the rebuttal of the Spaniard from Guatemala, which reads in part, "I do not deny that the Liman Gentlemen fully explained the meaning which is given to my four Ps in their Homeland, but I would like to ask these Sires if they think I am foolish enough to ask them something so obvious? Are there not, by chance, other 4 Ps in the world? I speak in Guatemala, and in this City these Gentlemen should search for them." First, the Guatemalan challenger understands a lot more than he appears to understand when he speaks (Cicero 2001, 200; Castiglione 1994, 308). This is clear from a description of him given to readers before his speech begins: "El guatemalteco se hacía de pencas, fingiendo algún temor; pero por fin entró y tomó el inferior asiento, como reo convicto" (469) ("The Guatemalan made them coax him, feigning a degree of fear, but he finally went in and took the lower seat like a convicted criminal"). Second, the modesty of language and rhetorical questions that he exhibits is ironic, as Cicero makes it clear that it is "neat to criticize someone in a friendly way, pretending he is making a mistake" (2001, 201). According to Boscán, "It is likewise artful and funny, especially for grave persons of authority, to answer the opposite of what the person with whom one is speaking would wish; but this must be done gently, and almost with a certain doubting respect and a prudent falseness" (Castiglione 1994, 316). That ironic humility, or false modesty, is related to a third instance of irony: the geographical conjecture, or the Guatemalan's explanation that Spaniards in Lima have a solution to the riddle about Lima that is radically different from a solution dreamt up in Guatemala. "Laughter," Cicero explained, "is also provoked by conjectural explanations that are very different from the way the matter actually stands, but that are clever and elegant at the same time" (2001, 201). The truth is, the Guatemalan responds negatively to their solution because he is not truly interested in talking about the grandeur of Lima or Mexico City: his riddle has less to do with grandeur than with the *delusions* of grandeur exhibited by certain *peruleros*.

The Spaniard from Guatemala historicizes, or particularizes, the riddle the moment he tacks his *cartel* to the door of the archbishop's residence. Through their orator, the Limans deflect the riddle away from themselves and the other Limans—that is, the two who are presiding over this mock trial, attempting to turn a case that revolves around their actions into a universal case about their city's legendary grandeur vis-à-vis that of Mexico City. The senior *perulero* believes that he and his counterparts have come up with a witty solution to the Guatemalan's riddle, but in Carrió's fourth ironic maneuver, the Spaniard from Guatemala offers a solution that directs the riddle back to the Limans. "It is also neat," Cicero explained, "when the one who has made a joke is mocked by the same kind of joke that he made" (2001, 200), a point seconded by Castiglione in Boscán's Spanish translation of *Il corteggiano* (1994, 309).

Deception, or the unexpected turn, is a rhetorical choice that reveals an intimate relationship between Carrió's jocose *exemplum* and literary theory that dates back to the Greeks and Romans. Cicero claimed that of all the witticisms that work through content, "none provokes more laughter than the unexpected turn" (2001, 202). During the renaissance, Castiglione made the unexpected a requirement for jests based on words as well as jests based on content, as Boscán made clear: "In one genre and the other . . . the main thing is to deceive opinion and end up far removed from where those who are listening expect you [to end up]"

(Castiglione 1994, 317). Humor cannot truly be created without surprising the listeners or readers: "For the jest to be good, it needs to be mixed with this deception, either by dissimulating or mocking or reprimanding or using whatever other means" (317). In Carrió's anecdote, the Spaniard from Guatemala performs this required inflection by flipping the riddle to the surprise and delight of his competitors and judges—and of Carrió's eighteenth-century readers.

The classical and renaissance prescriptions on this point were continued in the baroque. As indicated earlier, Tesauro made a strong case for deception (*la decettione*) and the unexpected (*l'inaspettato*), observing that the "crossing over from deception to undeception is a sort of learning by a route not expected and therefore extremely pleasing" (1968, 460). "Of this nature are all of the jocose jests and the practical jokes by which one deceives another unexpectedly in urbane conversations" (460). There were two principal kinds of deception: one that relied on things (or content), *facetia,* and another that relied on words, *dicacita* (461). He was almost itemizing as he presented the relationship between the ridiculous and deception:

> And generally speaking, few are those ridiculous jests [*Ridicoli*], either through words or through deeds, that are *not* due to the *Unexpected,* which is this figure, *Deception.* Because all [ridiculous jests] make [us] laugh either because the *Object* is not *That* which one was expecting, or because it is not the *Quantity,* or not the *Kind,* or not at its *Time,* or not in its *Place* nor its proper *Spot,* or the *Relationship,* or the *Action,* or the *Emotion* or the *instruments* are contrary to the norm or beyond the norm, as has been said in the [prior] Theorem of the *Ridiculous.* (622)

Given that Carrió's exposé concerns his inspection of the posts from Lima to Buenos Aires/Montevideo between 1771 and 1773, a number of aspects of his tale were unexpected and heightened its ridiculous effect on his readers in Bourbon Spanish America and Spain. The site was unexpected: the archbishop's palace. The place was unexpected: Santiago de Guatemala. The time was unexpected: 1746. The object of the riddle was unexpected: Archbishop Pardo de Figueroa. The emotions were unexpected: the gravity with which the *peruleros* treat a riddle that they qualify as child's play, the cool placidity of the Spaniard from Guatemala, the laughter from the archbishop and the president-governor. The action and instruments were unexpected: the mock trial with its competing solutions to a riddle.

Finally, it is possible to understand Carrió's manipulation of the date (Governor Araújo y Río was still in legal hot water in Madrid in 1746, and he did not become governor of Guatemala until later) as purposefully humorous rather than accidentally anachronistic if Tesauro's treatment of the eighth species of metaphor of proportion is considered: "This is that which takes one TIME FOR ANOTHER TIME. . . . The first marvel is that it makes you see past events, or future ones, as present ones. And with similar *Anachronisms,* either tolerated or praised, *Spanish Dramas* are filled, which put on stage before you King *Ramirus,* and quicker than you can spit, as if you had been asleep for fifty years, they give you *Charles V*" (1968, 333).

Carrió did not, I am convinced, overhear the Guatemalan tale, much less participate in the trial of wits, because it never happened. It is a rhetorical construct that fulfills rhetorical prescriptions for witty discourse, or urbanity.

The Invention of the Riddle of the 4Ps from Lima: Theory and Praxis

Virgil's *Eclogues* contain more than one literary competition between shepherds, and Ernst Robert Curtius (1990) long ago explained how such literary challenges were answered in earnest and in jest during the European Latin middle ages and the baroque period. José Pardo de Figueroa and other literary moderns in Spanish America loved Virgil, and they loved riddles, at least riddles posed and answered in earnest. While Carrió's riddle of the 4Ps from Lima carries political and religious freight that is heavier than that of the riddles or "problems" posed by shepherds (or by neoclassical riddlers), it parodies the above-the-fray, highbrow posturing of some riddlers and their trivial, and sometimes trivializing, topics.[4] In a century in which many French and Francophile men fancied themselves the embodiment of Castiglione's *The Courtier,* and in view of the fact that the anecdote describes the competitors as "hac[iendo] la corte" at the archbishop's palace, it is important to remember the Italian humanist's comments on *burlas,* or *recaudos falsos,* in the version familiar to Spaniards, Boscán's *Los cuatro libros de El cortesano*:

> It seems to me that *recaudo falso* is nothing more than a trick that can be played on friends about things that do not offend or, at least, offend little. And, just as saying the opposite of what is expected causes laughter in witticisms, so too doing the opposite of what we expect causes it; and the edgier they are, on the one hand, and the more restrained they are, on the other, the more these practical jokes please. . . . Two sorts of *recaudos falsos* can be found, each of which could be divided into many parts. One is when a trick is played slyly and with relish, no matter who the duped is; the other, when one very underhandedly avails himself of something or makes something up in such a way that the man himself rushes into deception on his own. (1994, 319–20)

In *Arte de ingenio,* Baltasar de Gracián discussed mysteries (*misterios*), or riddles, in two different discourses. In "On the Conceits of Riddles" ("De los Conceptos de Misterio"), he wrote, "The name promises a lot, reality fulfills it. He who says Riddle, says pregnancy, hidden and recondite truth. Truths litigated cause more pleasure than [truths arrived at] by pacific cognition; they are like discourse's victories, [intellectual] curiosity's trophies" (1998, 166).[5] Later, in a discourse titled "On Clever Retorts" ("De las Respuestas prontas Ingeniosas"), I find something that linked Gracián to a discourse of the risible that stretched from Cicero to Castiglione/Boscán. Gracián began by noting that these "made the Seven Sages of Greece famous" and that "their humor lies in going beyond what is asked with so much subtlety" (325). Now, as we have seen, the Spaniard from Guatemala begins his rebuttal of the Liman litigant by casually mentioning Athens and the Seven Sages, which took the minds of his readers back to Athens and Plato's solution to the riddle of the 4Ms. When the Spaniard from Guatemala finally delivers the correct solution, my literal interpretation has shown, the situations that generated the 4Ps and the 4Ms are joined at the hip. It is, indeed, a clever retort.

Tesauro's explanation on this point was perhaps more accessible than Gracián's. The comeback, or facetious response, is achieved through deception: "With this salt are likewise sprinkled those FACETIOUS RESPONSES [*RISPOSTE FACETE*] that, while appearing to be on point, unexpectedly cross from one category into another and surprise you" (1968, 470). Through the two different solutions to the riddle of the 4Ps from Lima, Carrió makes this jump from the metaphorical to the literal: the first solution deals with the excesses figured in *Pila, Puente, Pan,* and *Peines* (in either 1746 or 1775), whereas the second deals with the historical (not metaphorical) excesses allegedly committed by the bishop and, later, Archbishop Pardo de Figueroa, or the corruption of his brother and cronies (Pedro Bravo del Ribero, José Pardo de Figueroa, Pablo de Olavide, and José Araújo y Río). By the same token, the Guatemalan's clever retort shifts the 4Ps away from the quality of the city of Lima to the quality of the archbishop of Guatemala and other Limans, thereby turning the subject into the object. All of these facetious shifts or twists were covered by Tesauro (471).

In Tesauro's treatment of ambiguities, he explained how they were jumping-off points for works of fiction: "because all of them are based on an equivocation [*Equivoco*], either of one person for another, or an *Action*, or *Time*, or *Place*, or one circumstance for another. And as a result of this *fundamental Equivocation* are born many other astonishing and extraordinary *episodic Equivocations, Complications* and *Reversals of Fortune,* which take credence away from what is true or lend it to what is false, and finally, the unexpected and delightful *Agnitions,* when the *Equivocation* is clarified and the *Conflict* is dissolved" (1968, 393). Ambiguities provided copious and rich "materials to make up all sorts of *Poems, Novels* and *Scenic Compositions,*" as well as "*Inscriptions, Riddles, Oracles* and *Mots*" (393). The function of the 4Ps from Lima riddle is similar to its function in drama, or "scenic compositions": it is an ambiguity introduced, then brought up again and again to build suspense, and then solved at the end. It is both serious and comic, and it lends dramatic tension to Carrió's inspection report.

Gracián did not offer instructions on how to put together riddles using ciphers or initials, but Tesauro did. He detailed the relationship between riddles and wit, including the ridiculous. Under instrumental causes of witticisms, or pointed jests, Tesauro treated what he called written witticisms, or acuities:

> WRITTEN WITTICISMS [*ARGUTIE SCRITTE*] are images of verbal ones, however . . . what is written is a sign of the voice, and to write is to sow words on the page. But this means is rather more varied, more pointed and bears more of the wittiest fruits than the verbal. Whence are born the Witty In-scriptions, Mots on Emblems, Cutting Maxims, Laconic Messages, Cryptic Characters, Epigrams, Hierograms, Logographs, Ciphers, Slang Words, which in a thousand pointed ways manifest concepts by covering them up. Many times you will see truncated words, which make you read the rest in the heart of whoever wrote them. . . . Other times you will see words contained inside their initial letters, like the motto of the Sabines, SPQR., that is, *Sabinis Populis Quis Resistet?* Here the witty Romans, in response to the SPQR, reverber-ated the writing and drummed on the writers, wiping out the Sabines and keeping their characters as a trophy. (1968, 20)

Under the heading of *Deceptions,* Tesauro observed that solutions to ciphers and initials have the power to amaze: "From the same source spring the amazing and unexpected *Interpretations* of *Ciphers & Initial Letters.* Like that one already mentioned of the four letters, AFPR, which Caninio so delightfully twists into a ridiculous jest. And the *Pointed & Pungent Corrections,* when in the course of the *Speech* you throw a Metaphor out there nonchalantly, through which later, by correcting it in the proper sense, you make understood the cutting point of the *Metaphor*" (1968, 297). This is what Carrió does through the Spanish resident of Guatemala, who poses the riddle, listens to the first solution offered by the Span-iards from Lima (*Pila, Puente, Pan,* and *Peines*) and then corrects it in his own triumphant solution (*Pedro, Pardo, Paulino,* and *Perulero*), whose equivocal nature was damaging to the archbishop and his four associates, or relatives, from Lima.

The interpretation of riddles built from initials was a favorite topic of Tesau-ro's, who returned to it again and again in *Cannocchiale Aristotelico.* The Italian explained that a laconic (*laconismo*) signified a concept by means of the conjoining circumstances and that its meaning was both hidden and malicious. He also noted that it cut more deeply than did other figures: "*Laconic* is the Figure most suited to Threats & to Satires, a veiled mot causing . . . a deeper wound than a glaring insult [*ingiuria*]" (1968, 434). Near the end of his treatment, he writes, "And all of these Laconics, when they are joined with Equivocation, the Sharper they are, and the more avidly they are listened to" (439). I have already qualified the solution of the Spaniard from Guatemala as equivocal, but it must be said that the solu-tion of the Spaniard from Lima is equally equivocal: it allowed readers who were unfamiliar with Mexico City and Lima to take it at face value, while readers who were in the know dismissed the literal meaning and focused on the "conjoining circumstances."

The last type of *laconismo* treated by Tesauro also goes to the heart of both solutions to the riddle of the 4Ps from Lima: "Finally, the WITTY INTERPRE-TATIONS of Words, or of mere letters, and of Ciphers can be placed in this category. Like the aforementioned Initial letters, S.P.Q.R., which were pointed, due more to fanciful interpretations than their own meaning" (1968, 441). The initials P.P.P.P. alone meant nothing, and if Carrió's readers expected them to be deciphered as *Padre Pasante Presentado Predicador*, the unflattering nickname popularly given to Franciscan preachers and instructors of native languages (Klien-Samanez 2000, 143), the two "fanciful interpretations" of them by the Spaniards from Lima and Guatemala, respectively, were what made these initials "pointed," or striking. Tesauro returned to the topic of witty solutions to riddles to explain the various modes of deception, one of which directly impinges on the two solutions to the 4Ps from Lima riddle and the expectations of Carrió's contemporary readers: "Even striking and unexpected INTERPRETATIONS acknowledge their Origins in this figure [of deception]. Which is done sometimes by giving *unthought-of and jocose explanations* of Ciphers or Letters, or by *spinning one Language into another*, with laughable and silly meanings according to art. . . . Of which means, because they are mixed together with Laconic and Equivocation, we have provided examples there. Whence, likewise, the *unexpected reflections* on the doings and sayings of others" (1968, 469). If readers in Lima were expecting to read what they had heard, *Padre Pasante Presentado Predicador*, they got the surprise of their lives when they read the two solutions to the riddle posed by the Spaniard from Guatemala. The practical joke ("burla chistosa") that the Spaniard from Guatemala played on the men from Lima was also played on Carrió's readers in Lima in 1775: he intended them to laugh at the "unthought-of and jocose explanations" of the 4Ps every bit as much as did the men at the trial of wits in his spiced-up tale.

Finally, Tesauro's explanation of laconic allusion lends itself to my synchronic and diachronic approaches to Carrió's riddle of the 4Ps from Lima: "If the *Laconic* causes the witty mind to fly to things past or very distant, it is called *Allusion*, which is as delightful in Symbols as it is in Verbal Expressions" (1968, 618). The two solutions to Carrió's riddle (*Pila, Puente, Pan,* and *Peines*) are laconic allusions that transported his contemporary readership between Lima in 1775 and Santiago de Guatemala in 1746. Laconic allusion is ever present in *El lazarillo de ciegos caminantes,* for it allowed him to insinuate what was truly happening in Lima when he was ostensibly writing about other locales, to indirectly indict officials and elites, in a few choice words. A different sort of insinuation manifests itself in the decidedly detailed physical description of the Spaniards from Lima and in the speech that prefaces their solution to the riddle posed by the Spaniard from Guatemala. That allusion moved his readers from the physical to the moral and intellectual qualities of Liman elites and between the first half of the eighteenth century and their own, as we saw in Chapters 3 and 4.

Carrió understood very well how to invent a merry riddle and tell it with panache. At the same time, however, he had plenty of practical examples to imitate, examples that were rooted in the renaissance and then grew into the baroque and the Enlightenment. In *Floresta española,* for example, a chapter titled "On Corrections and Interpretations of Letters" ("De enmiendas y declaraciones de letras") included a witty interpretation of SPQT, which was painted above the door of the slaughterhouse in Toledo (Santa Cruz 1997, 104 and n. 9). This renaissance collection of wit went through at least six editions in Carrió's times. Note that it contained a riddle whose formulation was similar to Carrió's riddle of the 4Ps from Lima: "A lady sent a message to a gentleman who was pursuing her that the man she would like must have these 4S's: sagacious, single, secretive, solicitous [*sabio, solo, secreto, solícito*]. The gentleman answered that the woman he liked must not have these 4Fs: neither foul looking nor flimsy nor frigid nor fickle [*que no sea fea, ni flaca, ni fría, ni floja*]" (279). Another renaissance collection of wit, *Miscelánea o varia historia,* borrowed heavily from *Los cuatro libros de El cortesano.* In a story titled "Mots Interpreted" ("Los motes interpretados"), Zapata de Chaves mentioned a "a very flimsy lady, who nearly had the 4Fs" (1999, 99). The woman's requirements in a male suitor, the 4S's, appeared in Félix Lope de Vega's *Arcadia* and were echoed in Miguel de Cervantes's *Don Quijote,* and Pedro Calderón de la Barca's *Lances de amor y fortuna* (*Strokes of Love and Fate*). The 4Fs were proverbial by the sixteenth century, appearing even in Gonzalo Fernández de Oviedo's *Historia general de las Indias* (*General History of the Spanish Indies*), in which he added a fifth F to laconically describe the man who loved this sort of woman: "flaco de seso," or "soft in the head." Echoes of the 4Fs formulation, as well as additions and subtractions, can be found in works by Francisco de Quevedo Villegas, Lope de Vega, Mateo Alemán, Tirso de Molina, Jacinto Polo, and Antonio Hurtado de Mendoza, and even in Baltasar de Gracián's *El criticón.*[6]

Both *Deleite de la discreción y fácil escuela de la agudeza* (which went through numerous editions in the eighteenth century) and *Tertulia de la aldea* (a periodical collection of short stories published between 1768 and 1777) contained riddles built from glyphs or initials. Also, both contained a tale about a painting of Pedro Pascual, president of a high court in the Indies or president of the Council of the Indies, which was adorned with 4Ps. In the tale, either a subordinate in Madrid or a Spanish resident of the Indies solves the riddle of the 4Ps in order to move up the ladder.[7] Readers of Carrió's Guatemalan anecdote who were familiar with other riddles containing 4Ps would have been even more struck by the solution of the Spaniard from Guatemala. In Tesauro's discussion of ambiguity, or equivocation, he included the witticisms that consist in the manipulation of someone's motto, or initials. Sayings that normally would not be funny, he argued, become very sharp when they are applied to another subject. This twist is most effective when it adds a serious sense to a ridiculous sense (1968, 41). For readers who were expecting a solution that they had read or heard before—one tied to Pascual, perhaps, or even to the motto of Franciscan missionaries that we saw in Chapter 2, *Padre Pasante Presentado Predicador*—and who were already familiar with Archbishop Pardo de Figueroa's trials and tribulations or with the unsavory activities of his "associates" or their successors in Lima, the second solution to the riddle of the 4Ps from Lima made the entire trial a piece of grave nonsense.

Strategic Silliness and Jocosity: Carrió's Response to Enlightenment Gravity

Although some today might be surprised to find riddles in authors such as Lope de Vega, Cervantes, and Tirso de Molina, we should remember that the literary establishment in Bourbon Spain labored throughout the eighteenth century to change Spanish taste and that baroque masters of today such as Gracián and Quevedo would not be rehabilitated until the advent of Romanticism (Hill 1994b, chap. 1; 2000b, introd.) The rambunctious, and sometimes challenging, wit of such authors was partly responsible for their consignment to the Spanish literary junkyard by many ministers, cultural critics, and censors in Bourbon Spain and Spanish America.

In *Impunidad de la mentira* (*The Impunity of Lying*), for example, Feijoo y Montenegro had insisted that practical jokes and officious lies, although venial sins, posed a grave threat to public welfare (in *Teatro crítico* 1773–1774, 6:314–30). He morally condemned the deceptive sales practices of authors and booksellers in *Nuevo caso de conciencia* (*A New Burden of Conscience*). Many times, he complained, a large font was used or pages were left blank to increase the weight and price of books. A seller or a gazetteer deceived a buyer when a book's title did not correspond to its subject. Books, he argued, should be priced according to their utility (4:292–303).[8] In the same essay, Feijoo y Montenegro condemned Lucian of Samosata's Menippean satire, although he recognized Lucian's wit in rationalist terms: "The *Dialogues* [*of the Dead*] by Lucian are not only useless for regulating morals, but can even be harmful. Nonetheless, they have a high intrinsic value with respect to their volume, because one does not seek spiritual benefit from them but instead the pleasure that repartee produces, which is supreme in that impious author" (293). To judge from Carrió's mockery of Feijoo y Montenegro in Spain and from his praise for some urbane seniors in Lima the so-called enlighteneds (*ilustrados*) needed to lighten up.

All of the *peruleros* whom the inspector praises in earnest are men and women loaded for bear with salty expressions and trenchant replies. Carrió chose to include in his account a handful of jests, witty sayings, and replies (*gracias* or *dichos prestos y agudos*) that demonstrated what the Romans had defined as *urbanity*. As one of Boscán's courtiers remarked, writing a witty tale was just as difficult as telling it: "And given that, in what is told, appropriate facial expressions and hand motions are required, as well as that energy that comes from a live voice, in what is written too one can recognize the skill and excellence of really knowing how to explain what is relevant" (in Castiglione 1994, 276). Carrió's ability to put down in writing the witty tales that he had heard in a way that preserved their spark was itself a mark of urbanity.

According to Tesauro, the materials of the ridiculous were physical or moral deformity, and the means of representing deformity were basically two, one appropriate (urbanity) and the other inappropriate (scurrility). There were two notable differences between these. First, the purpose of a *bomoloco* ("parasite" or "buffoon") is to please others out of a desire for vile gain, whereas an urbane man entertains others through the free exercise of his wit. Second, a buffoon stops at nothing in the obscenity of his words or the mordacity of his defamation (*maledicenza*), whereas an urbane man mixes the pungent and the sweet, modesty with *facetia*, truthfulness with wit. Tesauro noted that Aristotle was behind his own distinction between irony (urbanity), which was worthy of a free man, and *bomolochia* (buffoonery), proper only for the shameless and the servile (1968, 591). Carrió's thorough understanding of this classical distinction was at least one of his motives for publishing his exposé under the name of Concolorcorvo. It also compels us to acknowledge that the bulk of the inside jokes and takedowns of certain officials is, according to the text, the handiwork of Concolorcorvo, not the inspector, which safeguarded Carrió's authority (if we recall Cicero's advice to respectable people to go easy on the jokes lest they become one). Finally, Carrió was able to increase his exposé's humor quotient by letting urbane residents of Lima tell some of the jokes.

The inspector tells us that one prudent old gal in Lima was treated as if she had lost her mind. Not so, according to the inspector: "Esta ilustre señora, en edad tan avanzada, y así como muchas, mantiene su juicio, lee y escribe sin anteojos, con mucho acierto, y mantiene una conversación llena de sentencias chistosas; pero como éstas se dirigen al fin de alabar las costumbres antiguas y reprender las modernas, las gradúan las jóvenes por epidemias de viejas" (460) ("This illustrious lady, at such an advanced age, and just like many others, still has her mind, she reads and writes without spectacles, with great accuracy, and she carries on a conversation full of witty old sayings; but because these are aimed at praising the old ways and reprimanding modern ones, young women classify them as old bags' epidemics"). These "witty old sayings" were the mark of urbane conversation.

A clever comeback told by an American Spaniard, whom the inspector identifies only as Bermúdez, forms the heart of one tale. This *criollo* jester was almost certainly Pedro José Bermúdez de la Torre y Solier (1661–1746), minor poet and dramatist and member of the Academia Limense (1709–1710), a literary club hosted by Viceroy Manuel de Oms y de Santa-Pau Olim de Sentmanat y de Lanuza and attended by Pedro de Peralta Barnuevo. Throughout the first three decades of the eighteenth century, Bermúdez was active at the high court, the Inquisition, and the University of San Marcos (Williams 1994, 20–23). The following anecdote shows just how much Carrió admired the quick-witted, whether they had been born in Spain or in Spanish America:

> No ha muchos años que murió en esta capital un sujeto distinguido, y criollo de Lima, conocido por su antigua nobleza y literatura, y mucho más por su humor jocoso, y en el último período de su vida que discurro sería después de haber cumplido los noventa años, prorrumpió en la idea de vituperar todas las cosas del país y ensalzar las de la península, de tal suerte que un bisnieto le dijo un día que no le faltaba otra cosa que decir que la hostia consagrada de España era mejor que la que se consagraba aquí, a lo que respondió el longevo sin titubear: Sí, bisnieto, porque aquellas hostias son de mejor harina. Respuesta verdaderamente escandalosa si no se tomara en el estilo jocoso con que quiso reprender a su descendiente. (460–61)[9]

> [A distinguished subject and *criollo* from Lima, known for his ancient nobility and learning, and even more for his jocose humor, died in this capital not too many years ago, and during the last stage of his life, which I reckon would have been after he had reached the age of ninety, he seized upon the idea of condemning all things Peruvian and exalting all things Peninsular, so much so that one day a great-grandson told him that the only thing left to say was that the consecrated host from Spain was better than the one that was consecrated here, to which the aged man replied without faltering, "Yes, my great-grandson, because those hosts are made from better wheat." A truly scandalous reply were it not taken in the jocose style with which he wished to reprimand his great-grandson.]

Two explanations found in Boscán's translation of *Il corteggiano* directly impinge on this retort. The first is the following: "And because . . . there where jests that bite are based, earnest sayings that praise can also be based, a genteel and humorous means for both effects is when a man accepts or agrees with what another says, but interprets it in a different way than the latter means it" (Castiglione 1994, 295). Bermúdez's great-grandson used *host* as a symbol for the body of Christ, and Bermúdez appeared to agree with his great-grandson's charge, but then he proceeded to interpret *host* literally. The second explanation reads as follows: "For the humorous sayings to bite and for the earnest ones to praise, appropriate metaphors or figurative turns also work well, especially if they are retorts and if the one who answers stays within the same figurative turn used by the other who is speaking to him" (296). In his response, Bermúdez stayed within the same figurative turn as his great-grandson and then explained that the host in Spain was better than the host in Peru because the wheat in Spain was better. Given the storied history of wheat in Lima, his jocose reply to his great-grandson was even more clever.

According to Carrió's exposé, one of Bermúdez's contemporaries, a Spaniard named Mendoza, equaled the American Spaniard in wit:

> Coetáneo al señor Bermúdez, criollo, hubo otro igual caballero de apellido Mendoza, europeo que conservó hasta los últimos instantes de su vida su humor jocoso. Al tiempo de darle la Santa Unción reparó que uno de aquellos monigotillos, que regularmente asisten a los párrocos, miraba con asombro su pálido semblante, ojos hundidos y nariz afilada, y en el mismo instante le hizo un gesto tan formidable, que el muchacho, arrojando la vela sobre la cama, corrió dando gritos como si le hubiera querido tragar un espectro. El padre que le ayudaba a bien morir le preguntó poco después si sentía que se moría, y respondió con su voz trémula que, como no se había muerto otra vez, no podía darle razón con formalidad. La gente de poco juicio atribuye a falta de juicio, lo que en realidad es tenerlo muy despejado hasta los últimos instantes de la vida: necedad más o menos. (461)

[At the same time as Mr. Bermúdez, a *criollo,* there was another gentleman like him by the last name of Mendoza, a European who kept up his jocose humor until the day he died. When they were giving him last rites he noticed that one of the seminarians who regularly assist the parish priests was staring in shock at his pale appearance, sunken eyes and sharpened nose, and in that very instant he made an expression so tremendous that the young man threw the candle on the bed and ran away screaming as if a ghost had tried to swallow him. The priest who was attending to his death asked him shortly thereafter if he felt that he was going to die, and he replied in his quivering voice that, since he had not died before, he could not give him a definite answer. People with little minds put down to a loss of mind what is actually to possess a very lucid mind up until the moment of death: silliness, more or less.]

At the end of this anecdote, Carrió clearly signals his belief in Gracián's concept of strategic silliness (*necedad valida*). When Andrenio is passing through Mob's Square (*Plaza del Vulgo*) in Gracián's *El criticón,* Fortuna recommends that he invent some bats for his own belfry, so to speak, since he cannot remove silliness from the heads of others. In his *Oráculo manual,* too, there is an advice called *Know How to Use Silliness* (*Saber usar de la necedad*). Instead of trying to point out to the priest what a ridiculous question he had just asked, the moribund Spaniard played along with him, turning a grave situation into a humorous one. That exemplified strategic silliness, or the mixture of gravity and lightness in negotiations,

according to one of the political emblems of the Spanish humanist Diego Saavedra Fajardo.[10]

Among his many goals, Carrió aimed to eclipse geographical and historiographical romances as Cervantes had aimed to extinguish chivalric romances, and
both *El lazarillo de ciegos caminantes* and *Don Quijote de la Mancha* entail a ribbing of useless knowledge, or erudition for erudition's sake. A college student in
Don Quijote de la Mancha, who publishes books and dedicates them to princes, ir-
ritates Sancho Panza with his incessant academic questions, and Sancho's reply to
one stuns Don Quijote, who claims the answer cannot be his own. Sancho replies,
"Yes, it is, 'cause to ask foolish questions and give ridiculous answers, I do not
need to go asking the neighbors for help." Don Quijote, in a moment of lucidity,
answers, "You have said more than you know, Sancho . . . , for there are some men
who wear themselves out to learn and understand things that, once learned and
understood, are not worth a darned thing to one's intellect or memory" (Cervantes
1983, 2:198–99). The imprint of Cervantes's Menippean satire can be seen clearly
in the prologue to Carrió's exposé, in what I call the *Don Quijote de La Plata* tale.
To set up the tale, Carrió has Concolorcorvo praise the utility of the geographical
descriptions contained in Cosme Bueno's almanacs (117) and then contrast them
with Peralta Barnuevo's works:

> Si el tiempo y erudición que gastó el gran Peralta en su *Lima fundada* y *España
> vindicada,* lo hubiera aplicado a escribir la historia civil y natural de este reino,
> no dudo que hubiera adquirido más fama, dando lustre y esplendor a toda la
> monarquía; pero la mayor parte de los hombres se inclinan a saber con ante-
> lación los sucesos de los países más distantes, descuidándose enteramente de
> lo que pasa en los suyos. No por esto quiero decir que Peralta no supiese la
> historia de este reino, y sólo culpo su elección por lo que oí a hombres sabios.
> (117–18)

> [If the time and erudition that the great Peralta spent on his *Lima fundada*
> and (*Historia de*) *España vindicada* he had applied to writing the civil and
> natural history of this Kingdom, I do not doubt that he would have garnered
> more fame, thereby giving polish and splendor to the whole *Monarquía,* but
> the majority of men bend over backwards to discover the goings-on in the
> most distant lands, completely ignoring what goes on in their own. By this
> I do not mean to suggest that Peralta did not know the history of this King-
> dom, and I criticize his choice just because I heard it from learned men.]

Part I of this book clarified how and why *El lazarillo de ciegos caminantes* de-
constructs the image of Lima as a *locus amoenus* created by Jacques Vanière, José
Pardo de Figueroa, and Pedro Peralta Barnuevo, all of whom were either French
by birth or Francophile by choice. In these works, a veritable chasm opens up

between discourse and material reality as Carrió knew it. In Peralta Barnuevo's *Lima fundada o Conquista del Perú,* Lima is an extrapolation of that city praised in Vanière's Virgilian *Praedium rusticum.* It is an idea, or an abstraction, more than a real city with real people and real problems. Although he footnoted the economic troubles of the nobility and inserted modern scientific explanations of certain natural phenomena, his epic poem was not about Lima's quest to truly embody the City of Kings, or Caesars. Rather, it was about Peralta Barnuevo's quest to conquer the epic genre and ingratiate himself with churchmen, statesmen, and icons of modernity such as Father Feijoo y Montenegro. It must be said that even his "patriotism," or love of Lima, was platonic, for there is no emotional connection between the poetic self and Lima in the poem. There is merely a one-on-one between the poet and his ideal, or *Lima as an idea.* A similar lack of integration exists between discourse and material reality in *Historia de España vindicada,* although readers should not have expected to encounter real-world problems in this apology, and even Peralta Barnuevo himself admitted that it was risky for an American Spaniard to write a history of Spain (1730, x; Souza Penha 1978, 158). In *El lazarillo de ciegos caminantes,* immediately after Concolorcorvo's negative assessment of Peralta Barnuevo's epic poem and account of Spain, Carrió reiterates that book smarts are not street smarts, by constructing his own tale of *Don Quijote de la Plata.*

The Inca secretary reports that he and the inspector once visited the rural home of a gentleman (*caballero*) in Tucumán, an individual who spent his time studying a handful of travel accounts, chivalric romances, and allegorical histories. Among the *caballero's* books is the account of Portugal's Ferñao Mendes Pinto of his journey to China, notable because its veracity was attacked from all corners (Stolley 1993, 97). It was precisely the sort of geographical romance that Carrió despised. The inspector comments that he had read such books in his *jumentud* (or "assolescence"), rather than *juventud* ("adolescence").[11] The utterance of *jumentud,* in a region famous for its mule trade, was an ingeniously wry dismissal of the *caballero's* literary values. It should remind us of the renaissance and Enlightenment iconography of ignorance and of Gracián's chronology of prudence in *El criticón,* namely, his correlation of *jumento* (wiseass) and *sabio* (wise man) with youth and maturity, respectively. At the end of their visit, the inspector has the following exchange with the gentleman scholar:

> Observando el visitador la extravangia del buen hombre, le preguntó si sabía el nombre del actual rey de España y de las Indias, a que respondió que se llamaba Carlos III, porque así lo había oído nombrar en el título del gobernador, y que tenía noticia de que era un buen caballero de capa y espada. ¿Y su padre de ese caballero?, replicó el visitador, ¿cómo se llamó? A que respondió sin perplejidad, que por razón natural lo podían saber todos. El visitador, teniendo presente lo que respondió otro erudito de la Francia, le apuró para que

dijese su nombre, y sin titubear dijo que había sido el S. Carlos II. De su país no dio más noticia que de siete a ocho leguas en torno, y todas tan imperfectas y trastornadas, que parecían delirios o sueños de hombres despiertos. (118–19)

[Upon observing the good man's eccentricity, the inspector asked him if he knew the name of the current King of Spain and the Indies, to which he replied that he was called Charles III, because that is what he had heard him called in the Governor's title, and that he was informed that he was a good gentleman knight. "And the father of that gentleman," the inspector rejoined, "what was his name?" Upon which he responded confidently that anyone could figure it out by using natural reason. The inspector, remembering what another erudite in France had answered, pressured him to say his name, and without hesitation he said that it had been Charles II. About his homeland he could not tell us a thing beyond seven or eight leagues around, and all of his reports were so spotty and mixed-up that they sounded like ravings or the dreams of men awake.]

This Don Quijote of the Riverplate states matter-of-factly here that the Bourbon Charles III was the son of the Habsburg Charles II. Although Concolorcorvo sails past this exchange between the inspector and the gentleman scholar and headlong into an unfavorable review of the latter's knowledge about the region, there is an ideological stratum to this bit of grave nonsense. In point of fact, Charles III was the title assumed by the Habsburg Archduke Charles, later Emperor Charles VI of Austria, when he made his unsuccessful claim to the Spanish throne and occupied Catalonia and Valencia during the War of the Spanish Succession. The Riverplate anecdote, like the Guatemalan mock trial, is an *exemplum,* or brief allegorical tale, that illustrates the perils of mistaking discursive realities for material realities. The Riverplate tale's proximity to the dismissal of Peralta Barnuevo and the books in the *caballero's* library together imply something important about the nexus between literature and society and about the responsibilities and privileges of the literati who were often ad hoc advisors to viceroys and kings in the eighteenth century. Both groups had forged an intimate working relationship in France, under Louis XIV, and in Spain, under Philip V and his successors. Carrió viewed them as feverishly modern types who theorized about the uncertainty of history but unwittingly accepted myth as history, because they lacked experience with the subjects of their readings. The tale of the *caballero* from the Riverplate, like so much of Carrió's exposé, is a jab at the hegemonic culture of the urban centers of the *Monarquía* under the Spanish Bourbons.

Literary and Legal Challenges as Stimuli for Carrió's Trial of Wits

Many of the potential literary inspirations for Carrió's Guatemalan tale involved lawyers, orators, and trials of one sort or another. Peralta Barnuevo, who began his career as a lawyer with the high court in Lima and would later write Viceroy José de Armendáriz Perurena's *Relación del Gobierno*, admitted in *Historia de España vindicada* that distance and reliance on the testimonies of others could blind a historian to reality (Souza Penha 1978, 158). Carrió would have wished that Peralta Barnuevo and his influential friend Feijoo y Montenegro had taken this to heart, and to feather pen, in their published writings on Peru.

There are suggestive parallels between Carrió's tale and Mercury's ardent defense of Satire in Peralta Barnuevo's *Templo de la fama vindicado*. Mercury's harangue set down the laws for proper satire in a language and a spirit that *El lazarillo de ciegos caminantes* mimics. In addition, the Guatemalan mock trial is similar in *structure* to that Olympic trial of the satirical detractor of the archbish-op-viceroy of Peru. Thus, the spirit, language, and structure of Peralta Barnuevo's defense of a notorious viceroy and archbishop in Lima are echoed in Carrió's ex-posé, which ends with an indictment of a notorious archbishop and the *perulero* cronies who frequented his court in Santiago de Guatemala.

Another local inspiration for Carrió's mock trial was Judge Pedro José Bravo de Lagunas y Castilla's *Voto consultivo*, a legal opinion requested by the viceroy of Peru that I have referred to repeatedly. It was an important intertext for *El lazarillo de ciegos caminantes* for at least two reasons. First, in view of the explicit references to the *repartimiento* controversy and the indirect references to the high court judge in *El lazarillo de ciegos caminantes*, we can safely assume that Carrió had disliked Bravo de Lagunas y Castilla since his *corregidor* days. Second, Carrió did not believe in theoretical, one-size-fits-all solutions to local or regional prob-lems, whereas the jurist's hard-boiled analysis of Peru's economic and social pro-files mentions a plethora of economic and historiographical treatises produced in France (and in England) during the first half of the eighteenth century. Carrió, we already know, positively detested the influence of the French on Spanish poli-tics and customs, whereas the Liman judge's references to the June 1754 issue of *Memoires de Trévoux,* Buffon's *History of Man,* and Charles Montesquieu's *Spirit of the Laws* were indirect but powerful proof of his enthusiasm for the literary and political culture of France. Remember that the judge *published* this legal opinion commissioned by the count de Superunda, which allowed him to flaunt his mo-dernity to contemporaries.[12]

Near the end of his opinion, the Liman fawned over Viceroy José Antonio Manso de Velasco. In Paris, he emoted, the viceroy's rebuilding of Lima had made him the subject of a *quaestione* argued in Louis XIV's college in 1753:

It must be likewise owed to Your Excellency the glorious title of Wise Restorer of our fields as well as our walls. Of Second Founder of our capital, and of Illustrious Viceroy, whom it appears Providence has led to the New World in order to retrieve Lima from the abyss of her ruins. . . . This is the idea that the first orator presented while speaking of Your Excellency, adopting the voice and person of a citizen of Lima, in Paris, one of the greatest courts in the world, at the celebrated Louis the Great's College, during one of its numerous and illustrious assemblies and in a case argued as an exercise of rhetoricians, on the occasion of the earthquake suffered in the year 1746. For Fame, occasional announcer of Truth, has this way of spreading it where, in keeping with the character of the French people [*la nación*], one judges with free and exacting critique, and the purest eloquence expresses itself without the perils of flattery. (Bravo de Lagunas y Castilla 1755, 248–49)

There is no doubt that French critique and French eloquence were the yardsticks with which this Liman jurist and art collector measured critique and eloquence, but perhaps the last lines were also intended to legitimate the shameless gushing over his boss in a legal, and decidedly empirical, treatise on wheat exports and imports. By dialoguing with the judge's reporting and toadiness, Carrió was able to turn both against the modern-spirited Limans represented by Pardo de Figueroa and his associates in the 1740s and 1750s and by their successors in late eighteenth-century Lima. In the Guatemalan tale and elsewhere in *El lazarillo de ciegos caminantes,* Carrió inverts the respect given to all things French because they are French, interrogating the influence of French language, customs, and policies on Spain and the Spanish Indies. The mock trial in Guatemala turns that august rhetorical exercise in Paris on its head, questioning its praise for Viceroy Manso de Velasco and its appearance in *Voto consultivo.* At the very same time, of course, the Guatemalan trial of wits is conducted in earnest and in jest: judges and litigants argue over a ridiculous *quaestione* with utter seriousness, but then the rivalry between Mexico City and Lima is interpreted by the Spaniard from Guatemala in a manner that makes it a grave *quaestione,* which he solves to the applause and laughter of the *peruleros.*

I site another stimulus for Carrió's trial of wits in a staple of Hispanic court culture from the thirteenth century through the seventeenth. Beyond the definitions and resonances of *cartel* that were presented earlier, this term used by the Spaniard from Guatemala to describe his challenge had still another meaning, already archaic in Carrió's times: "The document [*el escrito*] that used to be posted in several spots on the occasion of solemn and public festivities [*festejos*] like jousts, tournaments and other games, by the sponsors of them, to make them known to all, and at the bottom of which the participants [*aventureros*] signed their names" (Real Academia Española 1979, 1:203). As Macpherson has shown, the tournament began in Spain in the late thirteenth century and flourished in the second half of the fifteenth century, "by which time the early emphasis on military training had declined, and jousts between individual knights on horseback . . . had largely given way to jousts *à plaisance,* displays of pageantry and wealth dominated by the theatrical and decorative aspects of the spectacle" (1998, 7). The *fiestas,* relatives of the tournaments, stretched over several days and nights. Archbishop Pardo de Figueroa's promotion celebrations, which only increased his notoriety and legal troubles in Santiago de Guatemala, were very much like the medieval *fiestas,* as Macpherson has described them:

> During the day *corridas de toros, juegos de tablas,* and *juegos de cañas* were organized, as were displays of riding at the ring and the quintain, and *entremeses,* pageants, and parades, characterized by fantastic and colourful costume. Troupes of jesters, mummers, dancers and singers contributed to the entertainment, and elaborate mechanical contrivances, floats, arches, bridges, towers, and mock castles, constructed of wood and richly ornamented with tapestries, silks, cloth of gold and French gold, decorated the field. Temporary pavilions were erected, and wooden scaffolding (*cadalsos*) provided grandstands to seat the ladies of the court, there to grant their tokens of favour to the knights, to award prizes to the successful, and to see and be seen. Although the jousting occasionally continued after dark, lit by torchlight, most commonly evenings were dedicated to banqueting, mimes, improvizations, dancing, poetry readings, and song recitals. (10)

Carrió's festive, or in-jest-and-in-earnest, tale flipped the archaic and the contemporary *fiestas.* Recall Tesauro's assertion that we can elicit laughter by using the wrong instruments for a task or by misusing the right instruments: "with such pieces of nonsense there are performed many . . . *Mock Masquerades and Tournaments* that rework letters of public challenge [*Cartelli*], trophies, cryptic symbols [*Divise*] and ridiculous mottoes [*Imprese*] into the most ingenious plots" (588). Carrió invented a mock tournament—an intellectual joust about moral indecency—at the archbishop's palace, where "hacían la corte los chapetones o gachupines." Lima's courtiers answered the challenge of the Spaniard from Guatemala (*cartel*) to decipher "cryptic" initials whose two "ridiculous" solutions versed on the dissolution of Lima's nobility, judges, and viceroy in Carrió's present and on the immorality of the archbishop and his *connotados* in Carrió's past. The jocose *exemplum* that wraps up the inspector and Concolorcorvo's inspection report was a deformation of the *fiestas* and tournaments of courtiers past; the riddle of the 4Ps from Lima was a subversive echo of the cryptic symbol (*divisa*) and verse (*letra*) in the often amorous *invenciones* composed for and deciphered on such occasions and later included in several *cancioneros* (Macpherson 1998, 11).

Carrió did not need to be a scholar of the *cancioneros* in order to be familiar with them, because these were still very much alive in the popular imaginary and in literary culture during Carrió's lifetime. There was, I reiterate, no hard-and-fast distinction between popular and learned discourses or cultures before ardently "modern" literati in the Spanish world attempted to set up and maintain such a distinction under the twin pressures of rationalism and empiricism. The importance of *cancioneros* to oral tradition, poetry, and collections of witticisms is well documented (Alberto Blecua in Rufo 1972, xxv–xlv; Macpherson 1998, 12). In the sixteenth century, more than half of the poetry belonged to the gloss category, a courtier's specialty, while a reliable source for the apothegms and practical jokes in Rufo's and other authors' works was the *Cancionero General*. In the seventeenth century, Gracián "analyzed with exactly the same standard an epigram by Martial and the first verses of a *canción* from the fifteenth and sixteenth centuries" (Blecua in Rufo 1972, xxv). Carrió knew the various meanings of *cartel*, and he knew that *cartel* had high and low cultural connotations, archaic and modern usages. Of course, he also knew that formal and informal *fiestas* had been Archbishop Pardo de Figueroa's—and later Viceroy Amat's—undoing in the honor department.

The Inflection of the Guatemalan Tale: Defamation or Friendly Insult?

What got Carrió in hot water after the publication of *El lazarillo de ciegos caminantes* was not simply its clandestine publication without permission. The truth is that the baseline of high culture, including humor, had shifted in the Spanish world. Erudites and ministers who were engaged in the Crown's attempts to make over the *Monarquía* were very serious about controlling the public face of culture: what went on stage, what was sold in bookstores, what was preached from pulpits, even what constituted practical jokes. Carrió was decidedly out of step with those enlightened types, to judge from their response to his inspection report. They got his jokes, all right, but they did not think they were funny. Finding out *why* they did not think they were funny could tell us a great deal about Carrió's time and place.

Carrió claimed that he was not defaming anyone; his exposé did not contain "satire" ("sátira"). Still, he chided the long-dead archbishop and his cronies, and the long-lived Viceroy Amat and his, so would that not be defamation? In *Siete partidas,* Spain's oldest comprehensive legal code, we read of defamation (*deshonra*) committed in writing "by making bad songs, or rhymes or written statements of the sort that have the flavor of defamation" (Real Academia de la Historia 1807, *partida* 7, tit. 9, law 3, 3:576). At times this was done openly, at times secretly, "posting those bad writings in the houses of great lords, or in churches, or in the public squares of cities or villages, so that everyone can read [them]" (3:576). King Alphonso's *Partidas* also provide the origins for the term *libelo,* or "libel": "And such writings as these are called in Latin *famosos libellos,* which means the same thing as small book that is written for the defamation of another" (3:576). If this (or a gloss of this) roughly constituted Carrió's understanding of the matter, he was being honest when he told postal officials in Madrid that his inspection report did not contain "sátira," as we saw earlier (see the Introduction herein). Had the Guatemalan mock trial actually occurred—had a Spaniard from Guatemala actually painted the 4Ps in red lead on the archbishop's door in 1746—it would have been a classic case of defamation. But that did not occur, and Carrió did not make unambiguous and specific charges against men who were living or dead, in the Guatemalan tale or anywhere else in *El lazarillo de ciegos caminantes.*

In *El lazarillo de ciegos caminantes,* a particular passage hints at the depth of his bitterness and communicates, in a roundabout way, that Carrió felt that *he* was being defamed—that *his* dignity and reputation were being unjustly tarnished. After claiming that a "rookie informant" ("informante bisoño") had exaggerated a sandpit six leagues from Lima, the inspector and Concolorcorvo have the following exchange: "Hay hombres que no saben otra cosa que contradecir y oponerse a todas las ideas que no son propias. A éstos, dijo el visitador, los llama el agudo Gracián *libros verdes.* ¿Qué quiere decir libros verdes?, le repliqué; a que me respondió que eran todos aquellos que piensan honrarse a sí mismos con desdoro y desprecio de otros" (427–28) ("There are men who know only how to contradict and go against ideas that are not their own. These, the inspector said, the witty Gracián calls *green books.* What does *green books* mean?, I answered him, to which he responded that they were all those who believe that they become honorable through the tarnish and scorn of others"). In Spain, *libros verdes* were the anonymous geneaological catalogues of the most distinguished families or individuals who had a *raza,* or mark of shame, such as *El libro verde de Aragón,* which circulated well into the seventeenth century. In Gracián's very Menippean *El criticón,* we read that a con artist goes only so far as to become a charlatan or mountebank. A despicable and shameless man [*infame*], on the other hand, dares even to write or read a *libro verde.*[13] In his *Oráculo manual y arte de prudencia,* the Spanish moralist offered the following advice, which played off *hilaza* (thread), then a synonym of *raza* (as we learned in Chapter 5):

> *Do not be a green book.* A sign of having one's own reputation worn thin is to look after another's shame [*infamia ajena*]. Some men would like to cover their own stains, if not wash them away, with those of others; or it makes them feel better, which is fools' consolation. Their mouths stink, for they are the sewers of society's rubbish. In these matters, the man who digs the deepest gets the muddiest; few men can avoid some sort of defective origin, either directly or indirectly. Defects do not become known in the little known. The careful man shall avoid being a register of shames [*registro de infamias*], which is to be a detested poll [or stain] [*padrón*], and although alive, soulless. (Gracián 1984, 181).

Gracián recommended that the people who wrote such books—people who defamed others—be shunned, for they were walking *green books* themselves. In fact, *libros verdes* might more properly be translated as "catalogues of shame," for this medieval term already put a color on the hierarchical trope of shame that was to appear in Cesare Ripa's 1669 *Iconologia: (verdigris)* green. Carrió's allusion to *green books* (or *shaming books*), like his defacing of the archbishop of Guatemala (see Chapter 2 herein) and his invention of Concolorcorvo (see Chapter 6 herein), underscores the towering nature of social and legal shame even in the late eighteenth century.

It also offers us some clues about Carrió's literary understanding of defamation—namely, the lines drawn between a vicious libel and an urbane slap down. The fleetest perusal of *Miscelánea o varia historia* is more than enough to make it clear that the humor practiced by Zapata de Chaves was a far cry from that of the mountebanks of popular culture. The renaissance humanist himself pressed this point as he distinguished between urbanity and buffoonery:

> But in witty sayings and mots and *recaudos falsos,* I conclude that these limits must be respected: that they not be filthy or morally dishonest, or disrespectful toward God or King; or hurtful or malicious, or against reputation, which in men consists of bravery and of chastity in women, [or] . . . against the poor man, or the afflicted, because it is cruel; or the powerful man, because it is not appropriate; or a friend, because it is not right and it means losing him; or an enemy, because it means provoking ; or against father, or son or brother or wife. . . . Also the time and place must be considered, that it be the right [time and place] for jokes, and also, do not tell them constantly, because the same meal over and over is annoying, and honey makes many sick of it; and just as they call witty sayings *salt,* salt must be little in order to be savory and not bitter. (1999, 106–7)

In another story, titled "On *Recados Falsos,*" Zapata de Chaves echoed Castiglione's warning: "*Recados falsos* are a great ornament, but it is necessary to obey their laws—that they not offend or injure or be heavy; the elegant ones are those that do not end when the tricked persons find out the truth" (1999, 198). Still another story versed on the wall between a friendly insult and defamation:

> Defamatory libels are so far from being mots and funny things and practical jokes that there is hardly an adequate comparison amidst such disproportion, like from heaven to hell . . . ; libel is a mortal sin that kills the soul of the man who does it, just as he kills the dignity and reputation of his fellow man, and it is forever, because things in writing and [things] said cuttingly have a long life, and restitution is nearly impossible, but witty sayings are the fun and games of gentlemen and courtiers. . . . Libels cut to the quick, defame houses

and successions and lineages, and the laws justly condemn [the authors of] such to death. (327–28)

Zapata de Chaves's observation here that the laws of Spain punished convicted libelers with death should remind us of Covarrubias's emblem of the tattler who delved into matters that were not officially under investigation in order to ruin reputations (see Chapter 6). When a joke went too far, it was no longer a joke. Rather, it constituted defamation that was as damaging as a false or unproven rumor.

In the seventeenth century, the distance between defamation and urbanity was still clearly marked. Comedy was different from satire, according to Tesauro: the former adopted the ridiculous, whereas the latter adopted defamation (*maledicenza*). A ridiculous subject matter could easily become satirical if it was not handled properly: the ridiculous must provoke laughter, he warned, not pain or injury to reputation. By the same token, a satirical and mordant subject matter could be turned into something ridiculous if one poked fun in a way that played rather than bit. Carrió's tale with the embedded riddle takes the historical and turns it into comedy, by adopting Tesauro's conceptualization of the *urbane ridiculous*:

The FORM of the Urbane Ridiculous consists in a manner of presenting it so that if the Mot is mordant, it appear innocent, and if it is obscene, it appear restrained, in such a way that it can truly be called DEFORMITAS MINIME NOXIA. And this is that which he reminds his great Disciple of: *that in the facetie one refrain from naming filthy things with filthy words, but instead allude to them as in Riddle*. . . . Now this artful skill consists in covering the wicked and obscene Mot in a modest veil, not sending it out nude on its own terms, but FIGURED & SHARPENED by Metaphor. (1968, 591)

This is precisely what occurs in the riddle of the 4Ps from Lima, which encodes, or covers up, unseemly and even criminal activities that were popularly believed to be occurring in Guatemala in 1746 and in other cities in the second half of the eighteenth century. Tesauro gave numerous examples to demonstrate how a defamation could be figured, or given the form of an urbane *ridicolo*: irony through a pointed laconic, through equivocation, through metaphor, hypotyposis, hyperbole, deception, enthymeme, and so on. "These are the Ridicoli," he summed up, "which cover base ideas [*concetti servili*] with proper & noble words" (1968, 594). Carrió's riddle and tale do the same.

Circumstances greatly alter the material, Tesauro noted. For example, a serious crime, once it was public knowledge or the guilty party was absent or convicted of infamy, could properly be the object of ridicule: "A grave crime, because it is shamed and notorious, will sooner become material for ridiculous plays-on-name. . . . Even more so if the Convicted were absent, or had legally forfeited his reputation, because then it will be a Deformity without pain" (1968, 590). The alleged crimes of the archbishop of Guatemala and his cronies were public knowledge in the 1740s and 1750s, and nearly all of the men were dead and/or gone by 1775. Moreover, the archbishop had for years suffered from *mala nombradía,* or de facto infamy, rightly or wrongly. For literary reasons, too, then, Carrió could reasonably claim that he had not defamed anyone, that he had not written a "satire."

Nonetheless, Carrió's placement and framing of the Guatemalan *exemplum* within his inspection report might convey to some that his protestations of innocence, while legally defensible, were not wholly in earnest. Here is why: the frame of the so-called *anecdote* that Concolorcorvo claims he heard from the inspector dissolves into the inspection itinerary and its frame (the report itself). This calculated dissolution discursively duplicates the material linkage between the activities of *peruleros* in 1746 and those of *peruleros* in the 1770s.

It works like this: Immediately *after* the Spaniard from Guatemala presents the second solution (*Pedro, Pardo, Paulino,* and *Perulero*), and right *before* the closing epigraph, *Canendo et ludendo retuli vera,* the following is written: "El presidente se tendió, con la fuerza de la risa, sobre el canapé, y el arzobispo se recostó sobre sus piernas sin poderse contener. Los chapetones se rieron igualmente y confesaron haber perdido su pleito, e hicieron homenaje de dar el refresco, con lo que se disolvió la junta y dio fin este cansado viaje histórico" (473) ("From the force of his laughter, the president stretched out on the canopy, and the archbishop was doubled over, unable to contain himself. The *chapetones* likewise laughed, and confessed to having lost their case, and paid their tribute in drink, upon which the session was adjourned and this tiresome historical journey came to an end"). There is no discursive pause or separation here to bracket off the mock trial of 1746 from the historical actions of 1771 to 1773 (the inspection) or 1775 (the writing of the inspection report). Indeed, "the session was adjourned and this tiresome historical journey came to an end" is so very porous that it becomes an implicit confirmation of the historical continuity between the first half of the eighteenth century and the second.

It also implicitly confirms Carrió's careful reading of Castiglione, probably through Boscán's *Los cuatro libros de El cortesano.* The Italian's lengthy treatment of humor awkwardly ends when one courtier tells another that he must feel like a weary traveler who has entered an inn of ill repute. He concludes, in Boscán's version: "Therefore you will do well, like the chatty postman [*correo plático*] who wants to get out of a despicable lodging house, to leave a little earlier than usual and get on down the road" (319). The postal inspector Carrió never entered the archbishop of Guatemala's palace, or despicable lodging house, but he had read Castiglione, and he knew how to use urbane wit to skewer political and cultural elites in Lima who misbehaved, like the archbishop and his cronies, wherever they worked or resided in Spanish America.

Epilogue

In this study, and on many other occasions, I have grappled with cultural practices, as well as religious and political institutions, that do not fit scholarly models of modernity. I hope that the Hispanists among us can, collectively, engage in a sustained and *historical* dialogue about the unevenness of modernity in the Hispanic world that surfaces when non-Hispanic models are applied to Hispanic cultures. Far too often we duplicate Anglocentric and Gallocentric theoretical biases when we decry the Eurocentrism of modernity studies in Latin America: we subconsciously reduce Europe to England and France, erasing Spain, Italy, and Portugal just as eighteenth-century English and French writers erased them. Rather than focus exclusively on the eighteenth or the nineteenth century, such a dialogue should begin by identifying particular practices or problems. Only by doing so will we be able to generate models that make sense.

The bulk of this book does not approach Alonso Carrió de Lavandera's exposé as a literary text; instead, it attempts to reinscribe *El lazarillo de ciegos caminantes* within a pre-nineteenth-century understanding of *literature* including almanacs, newspapers, business travel guides, literary magazines, and collections of wit. It does so with the expectation of not only raising the baroque ceiling on Carrió's borrowing and influences but also illuminating some of the seemingly innocuous, bizarre, and pedestrian passages of his exposé. Moreover, it has attempted to engage literary history scholars in a discussion about genre and audience, issues that are related not only to each other but to the main focus of this study: hierarchy, commerce, and fraud.

One of the many lessons that I learned while working on this book was that one social network can illuminate or, at the very least, challenge our assumptions about another. According to their senior spokesman, the *peruleros*, although they are outsiders, are well informed about the particulars of the Viceroyalty of New Spain. They are celebrating in the Viceroyalty of New Spain, at the archbishop's palace in Santiago de Guatemala, with two men born in Lima: the archbishop of Guatemala and the governor of Guatemala. These *peruleros* were members of a social network of all Spaniards (peninsulars or *criollos*) who were, or had been at one time, based in Lima: the designation transcended geography, place of origin, and profession. At the same time, they belonged to several other networks, which explains why they, and not all *peruleros*, were meeting with its archbishop and governor in Santiago de Guatemala (or so Carrió's "anecdote" goes).

Scholars have forgotten that Carrió's opinions about the societies of New Spain (especially Mexico City and Santiago de Guatemala) and Peru (especially

Lima and Buenos Aires) were shaped by his travels and the professions that he exercised. As we saw in Part I of this study, his experience in the Viceroyalty of New Spain, along with his lengthy residence in the Viceroyalty of Peru, allowed him to make the absurd comparisons between Mexico City and Lima that appear in the riddle of the 4Ps from Lima. Carrió's exposé insinuates, time and time again, that the activity that occurred at Los Peines was widespread in the Viceroyalty of Peru. Indeed, illicit sex is so very present in his account that he might just as well have written *Los Penes* as *Los Peines;* for his readers in eighteenth-century Lima, the sexual activities at *Los Peines* made its very name an obvious double entendre. Viceroy Amat's proclivity for parading his sexual prowess, like his penchant for selling government offices, was characteristic of so-called *reformers.*

The importance of the Pardo de Figueroa clan to eighteenth-century Spain and Spanish America is underscored. First, the study offers a portrait of the life and careers—palace guardsman, *corregidor,* riddler, humanist, royal consultant—of José Pardo de Figueroa. Then it details the conclusion that Archbishop Pedro Pardo de Figueroa's sexual and financial "missteps" (to be charitable) provide the missing link between the two solutions to the riddle of the 4Ps from Lima offered by the *peruleros* and the Spaniard from Guatemala, respectively. The book's approach to the archbishop's public drubbing allowed only a glimpse of the possible relationships between *infamia* and *limpieza de sangre.* It is my hope that other scholars with an interest in the Pardo de Figueroa family (which deserves a book-length study in its own right) will ask and attempt to answer some of the key questions outside the domain of this study.

The *peruleros* in Carrió's jocose *exemplum* can help us to rethink another group, another problematic. The historical evidence marshaled in the preceding pages suggests that *criollo* resentment did not come from members of the *criollo*-peninsular *roscas,* who were the disenfranchising, not the disenfranchised. I urge scholars in the United States to read what scholars in Latin America and other regions have been writing about the *criollo*-peninsular rivalry, in the hope that they will be inspired to entertain other sources and motivations for *criollo* resentment and protonationalism. How likely is it, for example, that *criollos* of the lower or middle estates used the specter of the *criollo*-peninsular dichotomy as a wedge issue in order to gain more of the resources that noble *criollos* controlled in tandem with peninsulars? Is it possible that, by painting themselves as the downtrodden victims of avaricious European Spaniards, wealthy *criollos* who were not plugged into all of the local networks attempted to deflect the resentment that was building up in poor American Spaniards, blacks, and others of the lower orders away from themselves and toward the faraway Crown? These and many other questions deserve deliberation.

Part II lays out the most significant of the economic and political continuities that *El lazarillo de ciegos caminantes* illustrates. Commerce and fraud have received considerable attention from scholars in many disciplines; Carrió's exposé helps us understand why: illegal trade in silk and other articles from the Orient and the diversion of gold, silver, and mercury often relied on the posts. Chapter 3 examines how associates or relatives of Archbishop Pardo de Figueroa were implicated in these very activities in the first half of the eighteenth century. Future research may clarify the degree to which specific social networks were responsible for the economic head winds that buffeted Lima in the first half of the eighteenth century and swept her into submission to Buenos Aires.

Chapter 3 also examines the formation of elites in both Lima and Buenos Aires during the first half of the century. In the Riverplate region, oligarchies were not ideologically based in descent from the aristocracy of Spain or the first conquerors of the Viceroyalty of Peru. Nevertheless, the economic triumph of Buenos Aires in the first half of the eighteenth century was largely due to the same types of activity in which the archbishop's cohorts were engaged: illegal trade and the diversion of silver and gold. Further research into the respective formations of elites in Lima and Buenos Aires may clarify (1) to what degree Bourbon reforms themselves, during the first half of the eighteenth century, made possible the economic irrelevance of Lima vis-à-vis Buenos Aires in Carrió's times and (2) why capitalism and globalization developed more rapidly in Argentina than in Peru after independence.

Chapter 4 demonstrates that trade in illegal goods and the diversion of precious metals on a massive scale continued into the 1770s, when Carrió became directly involved in the continuing Bourbon reforms of the post, and how such practices were related to the economic development of Buenos Aires and to its population during the second half of the eighteenth century. It also shows how and why blindness in Carrió's exposé impinges on different types of travelers and their literal or metaphorical freight. Blindness is a nexus of ideological and epistemological concerns in Carrió's text, but it is also an iconographic link between epistemological concerns and the cultural traditions of Italy, France, and England from the middle ages to the nineteenth century. The same may be said of the inspector's and Concolorcorvo's use of *clairvoyance* and the gesture of *silence* in the exposé.

Relying in part on the analyses produced by economic and social historians and in part on unpublished or forgotten sources, Chapter 3 demonstrates that many Bourbon reforms were attempted in the first half of the eighteenth century. If, as I have argued in Chapter 4, the presumably enlightened reforms of the second half failed as miserably as Carrió's account and others demonstrate, *the middle period* is not less inadequate than other historical models that we use in our approaches to the eighteenth century. When such a model obfuscates rather than illuminates history, when it encourages the intension rather than extension of scholarly research and teaching, when it contributes to the further marginalization of the first fifty years of one century by interpreting them from the perspective of the first fifty years of another, the model needs rethinking, and literary historians have a role to play in that critical enterprise.

The riddle of the 4Ps from Lima dented the facade of renovation and amelioration-through-education/coercion that was—and still is—associated with the Spanish Bourbons, whether they were kings or viceroys or censors. Like many historians and cultural critics in Spain, the kings were in the dark when it came to knowing what was truly happening in Spanish America during the eighteenth century, just as many ministers in Peru were in the dark when it came to serving their king and their fellow subjects properly. The Bourbon reform measures that were to be enacted in the last quarter of the eighteenth century, after the publication of *El lazarillo de ciegos caminantes,* would further confirm the failure of earlier reform efforts to contain the 4Ps from Lima and the merchants and Crown and church officials similar to them who used legal institutions and illegal stratagems for personal gain.

Chapter 5 begins by arguing that the critical approach to hierarchy in viceregal Spanish America needs to change course. Mistaking language for life, or for history, cannot reveal hierarchical principles and relations as they functioned in viceregal Spanish America. Indeed, in the case of such terms as *casta, limpieza (de sangre and de oficio)* and *estado,* the failure to engage them as social constructs—the unwillingness to recognize their metaphorical dimensions—has been aggravated by the critical tendency to isolate a specific feature of a social hierarchy (blood, for example) and thereafter conclude that it has the same function in all hierarchies, traditional or modern. This unfortunate coupling has led scholarship on viceregal Spanish America away from the material reality of those times and places and toward the material reality of contemporary North America. An implication of this critical tradition should now be sufficiently clear: Hispanists have told us a lot about the racial hierarchy of the United States in the nineteenth and twentieth centuries under the guise of analyzing viceregal Spanish America.

Down the road, scholars may also wish to re-examine some of the dictionaries that were published before the nineteenth century that are essential to the discussion of hierarchy in Chapter 5. Their integration of popular and learned registers may prove to be especially significant to the development and dissemination of the nomenclature of hierarchy in Europe and America. How, for example, did John Stevens know nearly a dozen *castas* when Spanish dictionaries from the same period record very few? Was he familiar with the paintings of *castas* commissioned by Europeans? How many Spaniards in Spain learned the names of *castas* by reading his *New Spanish and English Dictionary* or Pedro de Pineda's *New Dictionary,* which borrowed from Stevens's monumental work?

Carrió's invention of Secretary Concolorcorvo in *El lazarillo de ciegos caminantes* encrypts his views about noble Spaniards who were legitimate descendants of the Incas and about their social unequals (and his): *indios, mestizos,* and *cholos.* All four of these are unfortunately lumped together into one race, "the indigenous," by modern and postmodern paradigms. Chapter 6 details the intertexts and inspirations for Carrió's invention of Concolorcorvo and suggests that the legal and social travails of the "real-life" Calixto Bustamante were a subtext for Carrió's creation of Concolorcorvo. In addition, it frames the discursive tensions between Concolorcorvo and the inspector, and the narratorial hybridity of the text itself, as a reenactment of *Don Quijote de la Mancha,* whose playfulness belies the highbrow culture debates into which Carrió enters. It explains how the debates about the origins of the Indians, the competing interpretations of the *Privilegios Indicos* (rooted in cultural definitions, not biological ones), and the controversies swirling around the rights and responsibilities of *corregidores* played into *El lazarillo de ciegos caminantes.* It also addresses bastardy, perfidy, and other sources of *infamia* and how they, rather than *race,* informed the inspector's treatment of Concolorcorvo in the satirical report. In Carrió's times, hybridity was a broader and deeper concept than it is today, and numerous contexts in which hybridity (like *casta*) figured are presented: the vegetable kingdom, the animal kingdom, and others. It is important to neither discount the influence of folk beliefs and taxonomies on husbandry nor isolate such beliefs and taxonomies from other disciplines (e.g., anthropology, sociology, and social history). Future research may well uncover further links between husbandry and hierarchy in the pre-nineteenth-century Hispanic world.

On either side of 1750, the enlightened age in Spanish America was a mixture of the highbrow and the low-down, of the pious and the tawdry, and of so many in-between shades that are refracted through Carrió's exposé. Moreover, what appears trivial or slapdash or arid to us today was not necessarily so in Carrió's day: riddles and witty tales were good enough for the Greeks and the Romans, for the men and women of the European middle ages and renaissance, for the stoic and corrosive moralists of the baroque, and for middle-aged men who were disenchanted with the Enlightenment as Carrió was. It was not enough, in my view, to write of semantic variegation, to establish the presence of different registers and how different audiences are addressed in Carrió's exposé (see the Introduction herein). It was necessary to show that the humor and the literature that today might fall under the rubric of orality (or popular culture) had links to rhetoric (or high culture).

In examining the rhetorical pedigree of the Guatemalan tale, it is difficult to imagine why literary historians have been so quick to tie *El lazarillo de ciegos caminantes* to the Spanish baroque. Chapter 7 makes it clear that Emanuele Tesauro was a significant influence on Carrió's crafting of the tale, but as baroque as Tesauro was by today's cultural standards, he plainly acknowledged his debts to Aristotle in the title of his work and throughout the work itself. It is not at all difficult to see where Tesauro's theory of the risible overlapped with Cicero's prescriptions for humor or where Tesauro borrowed from Baldassare Castiglione, who had borrowed from Cicero. All of their prescriptions imply that humor was an art form, from the Greeks and Romans to the men and women of the seventeenth century, and Carrió's Guatemalan tale reflects their combined influence.

The salty sayings of the prudent old gal in Lima (whom the postal inspector admired and whom the fiercely modern young women avoided like the plague) were not the sayings of barmaids but the sententious saws of seniors who had been reared to express disdain or discuss distasteful matters in a veiled sort of way. The humorous reproach was considered urbane: prudent and clever. Humanists like Luis Zapata de Chaves and Joan Timoneda saw this urbanity even in some members of the lower orders or put it in the mouths of the lower orders in order to jolt their highbrow readers. Carrió was keenly aware of rhetorical prescriptions for jocose discourse, and he was so good at it that it is difficult to know where he was "spicing things up," as Cicero allowed for, and where he intended to be factual, to distinguish what he wrote from what he actually heard or saw personally. He was also cognizant of the laws and conventions governing retorts, accusations, riddles, and the like: he knew the difference between defamation (or "sátira") and friendly insult.

Finally, I am fully aware that this study repeatedly goes out on an intellectual limb and that some will find fault with both its facts and its interpretations. Hispanists have not successfully built out the eighteenth century under the rubric of *colonial* or *peninsular:* today thousands upon thousands of eighteenth-century works in Spanish are buried in archives, novels go unpublished or go out of print, and undergraduate and graduate students leave their colleges and universities with degrees in Spanish and no exposure to the eighteenth century. We do not get the field that we deserve, of course, but the field that we build, and we have not yet built models that truly capture the entanglements, nuances, and maddening contradictions of the first century of Bourbon rule in Spain and Spanish America. In my estimation, the conscious or subconscious assimilation of Hispanic regional and local cultures to Anglo and French Enlightenment models has so skewed approaches to *El lazarillo de ciegos caminantes* that Carrió's material reality has been made invisible. I hope that this study helps to make it visible and serves the reader as a "guide to the *Guide*."

Notes

INTRODUCTION

1. Note that although the title page of the exposé gives the publication date as 1773, the actual date was 1775 (see Chapter 1). Note too that in previous monographs on Carrió, and in the manuals of Latin American literature, Carrió's paternal surname is divided as follows: Carrió de la Vandera. I follow the spelling used by José Gómez-Tabanera (1984), who consulted the legal documents to which I refer subsequently.

2. I am greatly indebted to Bryan Palmer (1990) for his *Descent into Discourse,* a critique of cultural historians who ignore material reality, or history, in their discourse-analysis approach to social history.

3. Víctor Uribe-Urán's study is representative of this tendency. For a brief history of the *middle period* model, see his "Introduction—Beating a Dead Horse?" (2001, xi–xxi). For a succinct counterpoint, see Bertrand 1999b, 315 and n. 78. More recently, Voss 2000 has greatly extended the middle period to include part of the twentieth century.

4. The textbook on hybridity in Carrió is Meléndez 1999. Her approach is rooted in Young 1995 and McClintock 1995.

5. Rather than argue that Carrió's exposé has a "style and sensibility partially baroque" (O'Connor 1996, 342) or that it "entails basic coordinates of the literature of the Enlightenment" (Mathieu 1994–1995, 42), I let the terms *enlightened* and *baroque* emerge where they may, without focusing on them to the exclusion of other periods.

6. All references to *El lazarillo de ciegos caminantes* follow Carilla's 1973 edition unless otherwise indicated.

7. Peter Bakewell asks the right rhetorical question, "Eighteenth-Century Spanish America: Reformed or Deformed?" (2004, 271), but he is considerably more optimistic than Carrió and many of his contemporaries were. Assessments of the Bourbon reforms in New Spain tend to emphasize the economic gains of the second half of the eighteenth century, as in Vázquez 1992, Román Gutiérrez 1998, and Silva Riquer and López Martínez 1998.

8. The reluctance of Spanish American politicians to enfranchise, economically and culturally, peoples who did not identify themselves as the descendants of *criollos*— peoples who, in many instances, were on the front lines during the wars of independence—and the failure to distribute resources fairly even among peoples who did identify themselves as the descendants of *criollos* were commonly explained by the construction of Spanish rule and all its attendant circumstances as the Middle Ages (*Edad Media*) or childhood (*infancia*) of Spanish America. The development model at work there was European to the exclusion of Spain. See Vayssiere 1994, 204–5; Hill, "Inventing the Spanish-American Middle Ages," in *Sceptres* (2000, 251–57). Elites co-opted the indigenous and the African elements of Spanish American culture when

these could be used as a wedge to differentiate themselves from "tyrannical" Spaniards (their ancestors). On this, see Pagden 1992.

9. Tamar Herzog's finely crafted study of citizenship in the early modern Hispanic world was published in 2003 after I had completed this book.

10. After noting that "the most extensive period of imperial development was from the sixteenth to the nineteenth centuries," James Muldoon claims that only Charles V was labeled an emperor. He goes on to note, however, that *empire* and *emperor,* while not used "in the legal and constitutional sense . . . , nevertheless . . . were employed in discussions of governance from the sixteenth to the eighteenth centuries" (1999, 114). In the middle ages, emperor "clearly meant rule over a wide expanse of territory, a wide variety of peoples, and, above all, rule over other monarchs" (141). As I show in this study, Spaniards born in New Spain or Peru commonly referred to those viceroyalties as empires (*imperios*), and books published in Spain, Italy, and Portugal commonly referred to one Spanish Bourbon monarch or another as emperor of the Indies (*emperador de las Indias*). What is today commonly called the Spanish empire was in the eighteenth century called *Monarquía,* meaning Spain and the lands outside of Spain that were under the control of the Spanish Crown.

11. I wholeheartedly embrace J. Jorge Klor de Alva's (1992) objections to the use of colonial and postcolonial constructs developed from Anglo and French situations to analyze Spanish America. (On this question, see also Adorno 1993.) However, his objections concern the period from 1500 to 1750 or 1760, whereas I doubt that the modernity in which such constructs are imbricated can be found in Spanish America before 1830.

12. See Benita Parry's pointed critique of Homi Bhabha's notion of *hybridity* (1987, 39–43). Anthony Pagden has argued that by the middle of the seventeenth century, American Spaniards already viewed themselves as belonging to a culture different (although not wholly separate) from that of Spain (1987, 51). However, he has muddied the water by claiming that persons who belonged to the first families (the conqueror elites) were *criollos* (54), without specifying (1) at what point a European Spaniard became a *criollo,* (2) when a first-generation *criollo* began to have a culture different from his mother's or father's, or (3) why we do not speak of Spaniards who moved to the Philippines, or who were born there, as *criollos.* Walter Mignolo, for his part, writes in a nineteenth-century vein of momentous *moments,* increasing the fetishistic tinges of the *criollo:* "The Creole consciousness, as it was articulated in their history and literature, had two historical moments. The first was the awareness of being a nation without the state during the colonial period in both Americas. The second was the awareness of being Americans of European descent in the margin of the West (in both Americas). It was precisely this feeling of being Western but not quite like Europeans, that defined the Creole double consciousness in the Americas" (2002, 175). It is beyond the scope of this study to confront the *criollo* as scholarly fetish, but I hope to make it clear that the current critical enchantment with the *criollo*/Other and his or her *criollo-ness*/Other-ness in viceregal Spanish America is not justified by eighteenth-century material reality.

13. Susan Migden Socolow points out the same problem for Buenos Aires: "Even had it been willing to enforce its own legislation on marriage, the crown could not easily

dismiss or replace officials who had worked in government offices before the found-ing of the viceroyalty. Instead, bureaucrats already in Buenos Aires before 1776 were maintained in managerial positions while staff was also augmented at all levels. As a result of this policy, based on the perceived need to provide continuity and as a result of the lack of a policy that encouraged the retirement of older bureaucrats, men who came to head 'new' agencies were products of an older mentality. While Charles III was trying to lessen bureaucratic ties to the local elite, many of those heading the agencies of Buenos Aires were men who at an earlier date had carefully established just those ties" (1987, 196).

14. Artís is forceful on this point: "Social organization was what allowed the old families to remain in the privileged stratum of society. It also favored the constant incorpora-tion into the old families of individuals that acquired a fortune or power. This pro-cess of aggregation resulted in an ever increasing concentration of wealth and power" (1994, 21).

15. Whereas Benedict Anderson singles out the underrepresentation of *criollos* among the viceroys of Spanish America as proof of the lack of vertical mobility experienced by *criollos* (1983, 58), I suggest that the power truly lay with the judges on the high courts. Moreover, statistics do not support Anderson's claim that judges, too, suffered limits on their horizontal mobility because they were not allowed to occupy posts far away from their hometowns (58). True, the law required that *criollo* judges serve in posts outside of their hometowns, but the Crown often waived this requirement when *criollos* in Spain purchased their posts and provided the dispensation that permitted them to serve on their hometown high courts—a dispensation that *criollos* actively sought in order to reinforce their position within social networks.

16. See Lohmann Villena 1974, chap. 10; Brenot 1989, 307–9. On *criollo* representation on the high courts and other government bodies and the marriage patterns among *criollo* and peninsular officials in the eighteenth century, also see Campbell 1972, 1973 (Peru); Burkholder 1982 (Peru); Phelan 1972 (New Granada); Barbier 1972 (Chile). On the finance ministers, part of the "intermediary elite," see Bertrand 1994, 1999a, and 1999b. What was true of *criollo* participation in terms of judgeships and finance posts was true also of the ecclesiastical cabildo in both Mexico City and Lima: it was dominated by *criollos* in the eighteenth century, even after the royal decree of 1776 (Ganster 1991). Some of my ideas and statistics have appeared in Hill 1994b, 1996b, 2000a.

17. On sales and dispensations, see Burkholder and Chandler 1977, passim. This was true also of American Spaniards who traveled to Spain to purchase their posts and dispen-sations in the New World.

18. Larson 1994 makes similar arguments concerning India.

19. Juan de Solórzano y Pereira made this very clear in his *Política indiana*. Discussing how crucial roads were to trade, he noted: "Given that, and for the use and frequency of these commercial dealings, the men who pursue them are forced to leave their homes and lands, and, *with their persons, savings and merchandise, to journey and trans-port goods through someone else's* [*y con sus personas, haciendas, y mercaderias caminen, y traginen por las agenas*], because that is what merchants do, according to Marsilio Fi-cino's definition and the opinion of the Hebrews, who for that very reason gave them

the name of *Sahhar*, which means *he who travels or circles about*" (1972, 2:240, italics added. (Further references to *Política indiana* follow the 1736–1739 edition.) Mariselle Meléndez discusses the attention paid to roads (*caminos*) in Carrió's report, tying it to "colonial desire" for domination of the land, namely, through economic development (1999, 96–98). I disagree with Patrick O'Connor, who distinguishes between "a travelling reader" and "a curious reader" and holds that on one level "the travelling reader is a tourist" (1996, 336–37).

20. The armchair traveler is hilariously represented by the Spaniard José Cadalso in his Menippean satire *Eruditos a la violeta* (originally published in 1772), which may have influenced Carrió. See "Carta de un viajante a la violeta a su catedrático" (1967, 187).

21. See Outram 1995, 28–29, on the difficulties in distinguishing between high and low culture in the French and English Enlightenments.

22. Stolley 1994, 247–54. As she astutely points out, "If we accept without question the conventional wisdom that genre is the necessary first step in studying eighteenth-century texts, we will find ourselves obliged to conclude that *The Guide* is a failed text. But if we abandon the quixotic search for generic definition, it becomes possible to read *The Guide* as the hybrid work it is" (254).

23. See Palmer 1990. Parry makes a similar charge for a different purpose: "The significant differences in the critical practices of Spivak and Bhabha are submerged in a shared programme marked by the exorbitation of discourse and a related incuriosity about the enabling socio-economic and political institutions and other forms of social praxis" (1987, 43).

24. See Souza Penha 1978, especially chap. 5. Julie Greer Johnson has duly noted the "multiple intercalated parodies of Menippean tradition" (1993, 110) and the "Menippean structure" of the account (116). Her work was unavailable when I was writing my own study between 1992 and 1993, which I incorporate here. See Hill 1994b, chap. 6.

25. Souza Penha's treatment of the carnivalesque and elements of Menippean satire in Carrió's account do not allow him to consider it as belonging to any genre (1978, 213, 222); I view Menippean satire as a genre.

26. On the title page of the clandestine and unauthorized edition, we read the following attribution: "POR DON CALIXTO BUSTAMANTE CARLOS Inca, alias CON-COLORCORVO, Natural del Cuzco, que acompañó al referido Comisionado en dicho Viage y escribió sus Extractos" ("BY DON CALIXTO BUSTAMANTE CARLOS Inca, a.k.a. CONCOLORCORVO, Native of Cuzco, Who Accompanied Said Commissioner on Said Journey and Wrote His Extracts"). (Note that I have followed punctuation, spelling, and capitalization of original texts throughout.)

27. Lodovico Antonio Muratori (Lamindo Pritanio) compared the geographies of the ancients and the moderns, noting that one could not automatically give authority to modern travelers because—out of an exotic impulse, not out of ignorance—they filled their reports with myths (*favoli*), composing *geographic romances* to entertain, not to teach, their readers (Pritanio 1766, 2:63). In *Don Quijote,* the implicit author states the same intention as Cide Hamete does. In *El lazarillo de ciegos caminantes,* the inspector voices the same complaint as the secretary in his Prologue: "y no den tanto crédito a los charlatanes extranjeros, y en particular a ciertos viajeros, que para hacer

apacibles sus diarios andan a caza de extravagancias, fábulas y cuentos, que algunos españoles les inspiran para ridiculizar sus memorias entre los hombres serios" (343) ("not to give so much credence to foreign charlatans, and to certain travelers in particular who are always on the hunt for myths, tales and the bizarre to make their diaries more pleasing to read, with which some Spaniards provide them so as to render those reports absurd to serious people").

28. See Rodrigo 2000; Malverde Disselkoen 1992. This approach is also adopted by Mary Louise Pratt: "This grueling overland trek from Lima to Buenos Aires is the subject of the most famous travel book written within colonial Spanish America, the sardonically titled *Lazarillo de ciegos caminantes* (*Guide for the Walking Blind*, 1771) [*sic*]" (1992, 148). Greer Johnson first suggested that Carrió's exposé was indeed a travelogue: "To thwart the trickery of these deceitful individuals, the author penned this instructive guide book with the intention of giving needed direction to the unwary traveler, just as the young boy Lazarillo de Tormes led his blind master, to avoid the inconveniences and unpleasantries in transit to their appointed destinations" (1980, 11–12). She qualified it as a "remarkable travelogue" (12). More recently, however, she has offered a nuanced view of the relationship between travel literature and Carrió's account, stating that "Carrió de la Vandera uses the travelogue as a vehicle as well as a target of his satire" (1993, 111). Stolley has cautioned, "*Caveat viator.* Let us not be deceived by appearances: *The Guide of Roving Blindmen* is by no means a mere travel journal characterized by a descriptive and reformist intent. Concolorcorvo conceives his narrative enterprise in terms that go beyond and ultimately subvert the conventions of the genre" (1994, 250).

29. Souza Penha presents affinities between several of Cervantes's works and Carrió's account (1978, 169–97).

30. I am indebted here to a distinction found in Reyes 1944, pt. 2, chap. 3.

31. The title in Spanish is *Itinerarios y derroteros de las Provincias del Perú, en que se manifiestan las leguas y mansiones que generalmente se hacen en los Viajes desde Buenos Ayres a Lima; de esta Ciudad a la de Potosí; a esta desde Payta; de la de la Plata a las de Buenos Ayres y Chile; de Lima a Arequipa; y Carrera que siguen las Mulas desde el Tucumán a las Tabladas del Perú. Y en que igualmente se nota la distancia que hay de unas Ciudades y Pueblos principales a otras, con algunas advertencias útiles para los que hubiesen de viajar por dichas Provincias.*

32. The 1772 synodal constitutions from Lima banned business travel on holidays under the rubric "Muleteers and wagoneers shall not prepare nor start a trip on holidays." It is clear from this constitution that the trips made by such men were about traffic and business deals (*tráfico y negociaciones*) stretching from Chile to Port Callao (Vargas Ugarte 1952, tit. 2, bk. 2, chap. 4, 2:64).

33. See the poem written by the mailman who was in the galleys when the Captain General of Castile was attacked by English ships, in Rufo 1972, 212. Zapata de Chaves writes with astonishment of a blindman who used to guide the postmen on their routes (1999, 97–98).

34. On Concolorcorvo as *bufón* see Souza Penha 1978, 215; Stolley 1993, 164–66; and Hill, "Literary Absolutism" chap. 6, passim. On the links between the closing epitaph and

Peruvian opera, see Hill 1996b, 102. On the satirical drama that resembles Carrió's account, see Hill 1994b, chap. 6, passim, and Hill 1996b, 112–13.

35. Joaquín Marco has vividly demonstrated the "constant" overlapping of theater and *literatura de cordel* (1977, 2:619).

36. Souza Penha discusses the rustic cowboys or *gauchos* (*los gauderios*) (1978, 99–108), noting that Carrió's second treatment of them parodies the *novela pastoril* (218). For a detailed treatment of *los gauderios,* see Chapter 1 of this study.

37. *Diccionario de la lengua castellana* recorded this as a popular expression, explaining that gazettes were usually sold by blindmen (Real Academia Española 1979, 2:37).

38. See Botello de Moraes 1987, 139, 237. Feijoo y Montenegro found many myths in the gazettes published in England, Holland, even Zaragoza and Barcelona. But he claimed that the Spanish were less credulous than other peoples, and he swore by the gazettes of Madrid. See *Fábulas gazetales,* in Feijoo y Montenegro 1773–1774, 8:55.

39. Important studies on Spanish-language journalism during this period have been published. On Spain, see Urzainqui 1995 and Sáiz 1996. On Spanish America, see Agüeros de la Portilla 1911, Díaz 1929, Vela 1960, and Clement 1987. Also see the introductions to the modern editions of Mexico City's and Lima's respective newspapers from the eighteenth century.

40. In 1765 alone, more than 15,000 issues of the *Gaceta de Madrid* were mailed to Spanish America; in 1768 nearly 14,500; in 1769 more than 10,000; in 1770 more than 54,000; in 1771 nearly 30,000; in 1772 and 1773 more than 23,000 each; in 1774, more than 24,000; and in 1775 almost 25,000. The circulation of *Mercurio histórico y político* throughout Spanish America was much more limited. In 1768 about 1,200 issues were mailed to Spanish America; in 1769 roughly 2,250; in 1770 almost 2,800; in 1771, 1772, and 1773 nearly 3,600 each; in 1774 almost 3,300; and in 1775 about 3,700. The postmaster generals in Havana and in Buenos Aires were responsible for the sale and delivery of both newspapers. The monies collected, a delivery charge (*flete*), and other charges stipulated by the postal service were to be duly recorded in the accounting ledger, and the last was to accompany the payment to the office of the royal publishing house. However, the postmaster generals were negligent: records were not kept or were lost, money was not sent or was sent to Spain years late, and both the postal service and the royal publishing house lost revenues as a result (Enciso Recio 1957, 84–87 and app.).

41. Other, lesser known, Spanish periodicals may have interested Carrió. In 1758, Francisco Mariano Nipho y Cagigal began publishing his *Diario noticioso, curioso-e-rudito y comercial, público y económico* in Madrid. This daily was later called *Diario Noticioso* and *Diario Noticioso Universal* (Enciso Recio 1956, 159–69). Much of this newspaper was devoted to business activities and notices, from rentals to robberies; employment opportunities; consumer advice; real estate; and bids and offers concerning mules, coaches, and household goods (177–81). Nipho wished to rid commerce of its *chalanes,* a significant "corruption of commerce" (Nipho qtd. in Enciso Recio 1956, 182). The *chalán* was the middleman who profited by buying mules, horses, or goods and reselling them at a higher price or simply by stealing goods and selling them. Beyond "arrangements and consignments" that were both illegal and bad for the economy, dealing in stolen goods was a favorite practice of the *chalanes* and a

favorite target of Nipho's *Diario.* In 1763 Nipho began publishing another newspaper, *Diario Estrangero: Noticias importantes y gustosas para los verdaderos apasionados de artes y ciencias que ofrecen en el dia los reinos civilizados de Europa. Añadidos muchos secretos para las artes, agricultura y mecánica aprovechadora* (Enciso Recio 1956, 217 n. 70). See Chapter 6 herein on the potential relationship between Carrió's invention of Concolorcorvo and *diarios* published in France and Spain.

42. Such differences are stark in Valle y Caviedes 1984, "Coloquio entre una vieja y Periquillo a una procesión celebrada en esta Ciudad" (205–13, verses 313–28).

43. On riddles (*enigmas*) in general, see Serra 1991, 78–83.

44. Moureau 1982, 37–38. Also see Vincent 1998. A Spanish translation of the French collection of Dufresny's *Amusements serieux et comiques* (1699) was published in 1751. Enrique Rodrigo (2000) believes that Carrió was familiar with the Spanish translation of *Amusements,* although he does not address the issue of riddles in either author's work or discuss *Mercure galant.* I believe it is more likely that Carrió, like Pedro de Peralta Barnuevo, was familiar with the news magazine run by Dufresny.

45. In some issues the riddle appeared directly after the news section, whereas in others it followed the news section and the culture section (i.e., the section that recorded recent works by local and European authors, household hints, and health advances). For examples of riddles from the 1750s, see *Gaceta de Lima* 1982–1983, 2:8, 16.

46. Strict laws prohibited mail theft, the interruption of mail delivery, and the like in Spain and the Spanish Indies. Juan de Solórzano y Pereira treated these laws in rich detail (bk. 2, chap. 14).

47. I have also consulted the French translation, *Le Courrier desvalisé,* published in 1644.

48. "Lettera metaforica d'un pedante vitioso," in *Continuazione del Corriero svaligiato* (Pallavicino 1660a, 236–44), contains a reference to a popular witticism, "the 4 Hs" (244).

49. Greer Johnson has underscored the picaresque schemes of men who prey on travelers: "The emblem of the postal system is the robber, Carrió insists in *El lazarillo,* as he ironically demonstrates the high degree of professionalism encountered along the route from Buenos Aires to Lima. Although these confidence operators appear to have a wide range of occupations from *corregidor* ("Indian agent") to mule driver, they all display a common talent, which is their competence at fraud and thievery" (1993, 112).

CHAPTER 1

1. The fame of Lima's promenade was not spread by only one French traveler. Like Durret before him, Sletu Le Gentil de la Barbinais praised La Alameda (1728, 1:96).

2. In "Algunos episodios de Miquita Villegas—El Real Coliseo de Comedias" (in *Leyendas* 1945, 216–21), Luis Antonio Eguiguren refers to "Paseo Militar" and "Paseo de Aguas," two of La Alameda's three streets (217).

3. I quote from "En Persona de la Alameda a quien han dexado decierta los Ciudadanos de Lima, por la facilidad con que se pasa al Pueblo de Lurigancho, se quexa el Autor en las siguientes Endechas Reales," in an undated manuscript, Fondo Varios, vol. 805.

4. Luis Alberto Sánchez believed that Paseo de los Descalzos and Paseo de Aguas dated from 1773 (1971, 100), although Bueno had clearly established 1762 as the date of Amat's renovation of La Alameda. Eguiguren observed that "Amat felt like a real King

with his Versailles, or Paseo de Aguas" (1945, 216). See also Lohmann Villena 1976, 193–94 and n. 151.

5. Castillo writes, "Los dos deven su ser a una alta mano/puesto que a Su Exelencia/cada uno da en su tiempo complacencia./Y asi el que errar no quiere/donde el Principe fuere/alla deve ir porque es naturaleza/que siga todo el Cuerpo a la Cabeza" ("Both owe their existence to a hand on high/Since it is to His Excellency/That each gives its pleasure in its season,/And so he who to err wishes not/Wherever the Prince goes/ There he too must go, because it is only natural/ That the whole body follow the head") in "En vista de los Autos que han seguido por competencia el Lurigancho y la Alameda pronunció la Sentencia mas ajustada a razon el Author en los siguientes Pariados," in an undated manuscript, Fondo Varios, vol. 805.

6. "Responde el Lurigancho a la injusta quexa de la Alameda siguiendo las mismas ende-chas Reales," undated mansucript, Fondo Varios, vol. 805.

7. A copy of *L'inoculation* appeared in Spanish on an inventory of Gaspar Jovellanos's personal library. See Aguilar Piñal 1984, 93, no. 350. On the relationship between Selis and Carrió, see Hill 2000b, 20, 39, 40.

8. I am convinced that Selis's satire was incorporated into José Cadalso's very Menippean *Eruditos a la violeta* (mentioned in the Introduction herein). See the letter sent to the professor of the course by the good soldier *a la violeta* (1967, 203–17), who has deter-mined to subordinate all principles of military theory to the suave and useful empire of fashion (206).

9. Although modern Spanish defines *pardo* as "brown," the color was, according to Sebastián de Covarrubias, that of the sheep or lamb. Covarrubias also provided the popular expression "At night all cats are gray" ("De noche todos los gatos son pardos") and noted that gray clothing was worn by poor people (1943, 853).

10. For other interpretations of references to mules and breeding in Carrió's exposé, see Stolley 1993, 84, and Meléndez 1999, 195–98.

11. Eguiguren noted that, according to the Inca Garcilaso, the children of *mulatos* were called *cholos,* meaning "dogs" (*perros*), but Eguiguren claimed that *chulu* meant *mes-tizo* and *Perri choli* meant *chola-mestiza*—a mixture of *mulata* (*perra*) and *mestiza* (*ch-ula*) (1945, 217). Sánchez asserted that "Perricholi" was a term of endearment based on *chola* (1971, 92–93).

12. There is a relationship between Carrió's allusions to the Gran Señor, or "Great Lord," of the Mules, and Menippean satire. Carrió was probably familiar with Apuleius's *The Golden Ass.* Like the protagonist in that classic, Amat refused to recognize his own mortality and was, in popular opinion at least, transformed into a lustful and humil-iated ass. In Francisco Botello's eighteenth-century Menippean satire, the poet-nar-rator travels to the republic of asses where Alexander the Great houses a jackass in Darius's huge box, which is filled with gold, jewels, and tobacco to make the box smell good (1987, 137–38). Significantly, Carrió discusses the historical Darius's defeat by Alexander at length (377). On the transportation of tobacco through the posts as a pretext for smuggling precious metals during Amat's tenure, see Chapter 4 herein.

13. For a very different reading of the inspector's description and intent, see Meléndez 1999, 215–17.

14. In a poetic competition to celebrate the arrival of Viceroy José de Mendoza Soto-

mayor y Camaño, Pedro de Peralta Barnuevo recalled the spring or fountain near Jupiter's temple in Arcadia, which transformed men who had been turned into beasts
into men again (1736, ff. 147–48), which perhaps set up Carrió's treatment of Amat as
the great lord of the mules when he was with his harem and a man when he was in his
palace near the *Pila* in the main square of Lima, or "Arcadia." See my analysis of *Pila*
later in this chapter. For a detailed discussion of Carrió's subversion of Lima as *locus
amoenus,* see Chapter 2 herein.

15. "Conversación y disputa de Tío Huancho," undated manuscript, Fondo Varios, vol.
805.

16. After the viceroy's death in March 1734, the glowing newspaper reports that had
marked his reign were overshadowed by a macabre celebration of his demise. Prominent citizens and their slaves staged a reenactment of his funeral and burial: they led
a coffin containing an effigy through the streets, mimicking his final journey from the
church to the cemetery. These amateur actors played the roles of monks and nuns,
clergy, aldermen, judges, and the newly arrived viceroy (Rubio Mañé 1955, 173–82).
The episode and ensuing investigation became part of popular lore in Mexico City,
where Carrió was a merchant some ten years later.

17. For a full discussion of *preferentismo* and the opposition to it, see Ramos Pérez 1967,
111–16.

18. "MIXTURA. They call bread made from different grains. In Latin, *Panis mixtus*"
(Real Academia Española 1979, 2:580). A related word denoted a bird of mixed species: "MIXTO. The bird procreated from two species is usually called. In Latin, *Mixtus*" (2:580).

19. See, for example, Lobo Guerrero 1614, 19r., 21r. and v., 37r.

20. "*Pan de munición.* That which is given to Soldiers is called, and they make it from
wheat and chaff " (Real Academia Española 1979, 3:102). The inspector claims that
forced laborers in the textile factories of Cuzco are better treated than in Europe,
Asia, and Africa, where their ration, if they are lucky, consists of "pan, que llaman en
Espana de *munición,* que es de un trigo mal molido mezclado con las aristas, y muchas veces con paja, de cuya masa se podía hacer una fuerte *muralla* mejor que la del
tepín" (353) ("bread that is called *bullet bread,* which is made of a poorly ground wheat
mixed with chaff, and often with straw, from whose dough you could make a strong
wall better than that of China").

21. I examine the different *castas* in Chapter 5.

22. Castillo's use of *chicharronera* calls to mind simultaneously the loquaciousness, li-
centiousness, complexion, and occupation of the *negra,* a feat lost in translation. See
chicharrar, chicharro, chicharrón, and *chicharra,* in Real Academia Española 1979, 1:
315.

23. "Flautas de todas las casas,/donde el mal aire respira/como por las enflautadas/que
de aquesto se originan" ("Conversación de unas negras en la calle de los Borricos," in
Obras 1948, 42).

24. "Responde el Lurigancho . . . ," undated manuscript, Fondo Varios, vol. 805.

25. "BUBAS. The disease that they call French. . . . *Buba* is a French noun that means
pustula [in Latin], because roguish buboes cover the face and head with crusty little
scabs." Covarrubias believed the origin of the term was a Greek word that meant

"Swellings of the body . . . , and, specifically, the cause of them, *incordios* [or *encordios*], which got this name because they start in the groin area" (1943, 239). "ENCORDIO. Is a malignant bursting of the glands that starts in the groin area, and because many veins/strings [*cuerdas*] connect there, it was called *encordio,* quasi *in cordis,* in Latin. These strings make a really bad sound, and it is often composed of a lack of moderation; it is a filthy, disgusting disease, the French disease's ambassador . . . , in Latin, *bubo*" (515). Here Covarrubias equivocates with the term *cuerdas,* which means both "strings" and "veins": "*Cuerdas* we call the nerves that crisscross the body, of which some of them physicians call *tendons*" (378).

26. The interlocutor named Dark Shadow (*Sombra*) says, "There is nothing new; it is just that the [female] vegetable sellers and children of Lima are arming themselves with vegetable cuttings to congratulate the Author when the Verdict comes from down here below, and the *mulatas* already got him stuck on the strings of the Harps [*puesto sobre las cuerdas de las Harpas*]" (1994, 156).

27. The advertisement—or public service announcement—for Petit's cure appeared in the November 1, 1746–January 15, 1747, issue of *Gazeta de Lima,* after the section on European and American news ("Noticias de la Europa y la Costa"). On Petit, see Hill 2000b, 164, 185, and n. 92.

CHAPTER 2

1. At nineteen, Vázquez de Acuña y Bejarano moved to Spain, where he began to occupy a series of military posts: captain of the infantry regiment of Milan, captain assigned to the Royal Fleet of Sicily, artillery general of Catalonia, member of Charles II's Council of War. In 1679 he became a knight of Santiago, a family tradition. Under Philip V, he became governor of Messina and later governor and lieutenant general of Aragon and Mallorca. He was later the captain general of the royal armies and witness to the marriage of the Prince of Asturias (later King Luis I of Spain) and Princess Luisa-Isabel de Orléans. See Núñez y Domínguez 1927, 83–87.

2. On the royal mint in Mexico City, also see Soria Murillo 1994. During Baltasar's tenure as treasurer, there was close coordination between the royal mint in Mexico City and the royal mint in Lima. In the fateful year of 1746, the king of Spain sent Inspector Andrés de Morales to Mexico City as superintendent of the mint and ordered him to proceed to Lima to straighten out the mint there too. See Manso de Velasco 1983, 372.

3. The "lights of the Church's Heaven," or the "Church's heavenly lights" seems to play off an expression popular in Mexico City and remembered as the height of exaggeration by the inspector in *El lazarillo de ciegos caminantes:* "Los Mexicanos dicen que de Mexico al Cielo, y en el Cielo una ventanilla o Balcon para ver al Cielo, que es a quanto puede llegar la ponderacion e intusiasmo" [1775, n.p.] ("Mexicans say that from Mexico to Heaven, and in Heaven a little window or balcony in order to see Heaven, which is as far as exaggeration or enthusiasm can go"). This expression perhaps played off the Puerta del Cielo, or Heaven's Gate, in Mexico City (see Figure 1, no. 11).

4. I suspect that Velasco was responding to the attacks on Archbishop Pardo de Figueroa

and his activities at Esquipulas, where he had built the first neoclassical structure in Guatemala, the Templo de Santo Cristo (Chinchilla 1953, 250).

5. See Chapters 5 and 6 herein.

6. Peters, "Wounded Names" (1990). I thank Professor James Muldoon for bringing this article to my attention. The broadest and most detailed treatment of infamy remains Francesco Migliorino's *Fama e infamia* (1985). On the Spanish case, Julio Caro Baroja's "Honour and Shame" (1966) is still useful.

7. A detailed treatment of these Catholic irregularities and the canon law, papal decrees, and later Council of Trent decrees, in which they were based, is available in a set of bylaws from the Archdiocese of Bahia, Brazil, *Constituiçoens primeyras do Arcebispado da Bahia,* which issued from the synod in 1707. See bk. 5, tit. 69, const. 1285–89; bk. 5, tit. 70, const. 1290–1300; bk. 5, tit. 71, const. 1301–7; bk. 5, tit. 72, const. 1308–9 in Monteiro da Vide 1719. The purity (*limpeza de sangue*) required of priests and others was dwarfed in these constitutions by the treatment of "irregularities" (*irregularidades*). In bk 3, tit. 23, const. 521, we read, "In accordance with the disposition of Canon law, and the Holy Council of Trent and the very words of the Supreme Pontiffs, we order and decree that a public or a secret investigation (whichever seems most appropriate to us or our Provisor) be conducted of those who are going to be assigned [as parish priests], to verify their virtue and integrity, good habits, example and *limpeza de sangue* (as is ordered in the very decrees of Pope Sextus V, Clement VIII and Paul V), and that they are not Regulars, . . . nor are they excommunicated, suspended, prohibited or irregular candidates" (211–12). Bk. 3, tit. 16, const. 528, detailed the admissions requirements, including the "examination," and the certificate of purity that had to be presented (214).

8. In *Diccionario Latino-Español,* Nebrija revealed his awareness of shame in general: "Infamis.e. por cosa desenfamada" and "Infamia.e. por aquella mala fama" (1979, n.p.). In *Vocabulario Español-Latino,* he recorded: "Infamar. infamo.as.avi. defamo. as.avi"; "Infame cosa. infamis.e. ignominiosus.a.um"; "Infamia. infamia.e. ignominia.e"; "Infamado ser. male audio" (1951, n.p.). The last of these four suggests to me that Nebrija was aware of the court of public opinion, whose ill report, it appears, had the same power as *infamia facti* in Gratian's elaboration.

9. See Chapters 5 and 6 herein.

10. See Cagiga y Rada 1739, n.p.; Lavallé 1987, 64–65; Villanueva Urteaga in Esquivel y Navia 1980, 1:lxii.

11. Lohmann Villena 1947, 1:315.

12. Antonio de Ulloa and Jorge Juan discounted notions of American inferiority and praised Feijoo y Montenegro's essay for doing away with the myth (1748, 1:47–48). Feijoo y Montenegro's influence on this point is also visible in several Jesuit characterizations of Spaniards in the New World as ignorant and inferior written in the 1750s. See Hill 1994b, chap. 5.

13. I base my estimation on a letter written by Feijoo y Montenegro to Peralta Barnuevo, dated July 3, 1734. The letter is reproduced in Williams 1998. After praising the only published tome of Peralta Barnuevo's *Historia de Espana vindicada,* Feijoo y Montenegro stated that the sixth tome of his own *Teatro crítico* was in press and that he would

have a copy delivered to his (and Peralta Barnuevo's) friend José Pardo de Figueroa (243).

14. Alfredo Moreno Cebrián incorrectly reports that Pardo de Figueroa's profession was military and that he had been born in Spain (1977, 161).

15. Diego, a native of La Mancha (Spain) and a Trinitarian friar, was elected bishop of Nicaragua and Costa Rica in 1702 and became bishop of La Paz in 1709 (Blanco Segura 1984, 47). He later became archbishop of Charcas and Lima. See Chapter 3 herein.

16. For background on the families that dominated Cuzco and its importance to the Viceroyalty of Peru, see Colin 1966 and Lavallé 1987.

17. The inspector later describes the ravines in the viceroyalty in general: "Las quebradas son estrechas y cuasi reducidas a un barranco, por donde pasa el agua que desciende de las montañas, a cuyas faldas se siembra algún maíz y cebada, con algunas menestras de poca consideración" (392) ("The gorges are narrow and almost reduced to a small ravine through which water flows down from the mountains, along the base of which some corn and barley are planted, as well as an occasional legume").

18. Carilla has correctly identified these verses from Virgil's *Eclogue* 3 (Carrió 416 n. 1).

19. In Cicero's *On the Ideal Orator,* Caesar explained this type of humor drawn from words: "Also, a line of verse can often be humorously inserted (either as it is or altered a little), or part of a verse" (2001, 193). In the renaissance, Castiglione, too, recommended the technique, according to Boscán's *Cuatro libros de El cortesano* (1994, 290). In the baroque, Tesauro explained how verses and sayings of others could be twisted for comic effect and applied to disparate situations (1968, 390). Later, among the means of *deception* or *the unexpected,* he included a type that did not turn on words but on meaning (467). Gracián, too, addressed these means (1998, 313–18).

20. See also "Pieces Justificatives" (3:ccxii–ccxx), where Charlevoix reproduced a letter written by Pedro de Peralta Barnuevo's brother José, bishop of Buenos Aires, to King Philip V (January 8, 1743), included in a royal decree dated December 28, 1743, according to Charlevoix, who also reproduced part of José's letter (3:203–10).

CHAPTER 3

1. They had, of course, begun much earlier, and Judge Juan de Solórzano y Pereira devoted several pages to these problems (bk. 6, especially chaps. 10 and 11). See also Stein and Stein 2000.

2. On the bishops of Panama, Quito, and Trujillo, who were under the jurisdiction of the archbishop of Lima, see Vargas Ugarte 1961, 4:51–66, 203–7.

3. "Events hide in plain sight and disguise themselves in the reporting. The governor's understanding is a theater in which everyone shows up well appointed. If the men sent to correct irregularities are worthy themselves of correction, how far can the remedy, once executed, go? To pick the right people for the job in Peru is a crapshoot, because the man who is honest in the city is transformed, by a sort of spell, once he is in the provinces. Nobility, learning, not even authority exempt ministers from being men, and this fragility is a bold one that blends in with all of the qualities of a person. Every very vast empire is like the machines that are made up of many wheels, in which the precision of them all is not easy and in which it is logical that there be

more mistakes. What the governor is called to do is remedy the excesses once he discovers them and punish the vices once he becomes aware of them" (Peralta Barnuevo 1996a, 68). A detailed account of the state of the empire of Peru in the days of Ladrón de Guevara is found in Williams 1996, 21–37.

4. Williams details the twenty-three charges lodged against Ladrón de Guevara according to Ladrón's legal counsel in a defense written in 1718 (1996, 25–26).

5. Two years later, Dionisio de Alcedo y Herrera, for whom Peralta worked at Lima's royal treasury court, returned to his native Madrid to present Ladrón de Guevara's petition for a higher royal pension, but the former viceroy and bishop died in Mexico while en route to Spain. See González Palencia in Alcedo y Herrera 1915, vii.

6. On the events that led up to Morcillo Rubio Auñón's first stint as viceroy, see Torre 1716. The bulk of this work is a libretto of the operetta that celebrated his appointment.

7. On the illegal entry and exit of gold and silver through the port of Buenos Aires, see Gutiérrez de Rubalcava 1750, 209, 213–14, 218, which states that the "ancient splendor" of the viceroyalty's commerce through Portobelo in Tierra Firme would return if this "unlawful Commerce" through Buenos Aires were eradicated (227).

8. On the political connotations of *mystery* (or *riddle*) in Spanish, see the Introduction herein. It is no mystery, either, why New Spain's silver mining industry overcame Peru's at the turn of the eighteenth century and continued to outpace it throughout the eighteenth century (Bakewell 2004, 274).

9. The Crown's efforts to maintain the South Sea Company within its legal limits later contributed mightily to the War of Jenkin's Ear. The company's slaving operation in Buenos Aires was dissolved in 1750, after the end of the war between Spain and England (1739–1748) (Arazola Corvera 1998, 58–60).

10. The role of Buenos Aires in the trade between Spain and the Viceroyalty of Peru is still misunderstood by some scholars. In *Imperial Eyes*, Mary Louise Pratt writes, "Spanish trade restrictions forbade direct communication between Buenos Aires and Spain. Goods and letters headed for Argentina had first to be shipped through Lima then carried overland to the southeastern parts of the continent" (1992, 148).

11. On the policies of Manso de Velasco while José Pardo de Figueroa and José de Araújo y Río were archbishop and governor of Guatemala, respectively, see Moreno Cebrián in Manso de Velasco 1983, 110–11.

12. See the sonnet by Diego de Villegas y Quevedo, canon of the Cuzco Cathedral, in Manso de Velasco 1983, 151.

13. See his son's "Relación de la literatura, grados, méritos y servicios del doctor D. Estanislao de Recabarren Pardo de Figueroa" (in Secretaría del Supremo Consejo y Cámara de Indias 1784); Burkholder and Chandler 1977, 279–80; Villalobos 1990, 33.

14. Contrast the historical record on this point with literary and cultural criticism, both of which have misunderstood the chronological and economic dimensions of the Lima–Buenos Aires rivalry and its centrality to *El lazarillo de ciegos caminantes*. Souza Penha claimed that Carrió looked at Buenos Aires idealistically: "In reality, compared with the ones in Lima, the merchants of Buenos Aires were truly dirt-poor" (1978, 93); "His benevolence toward Buenos Aires is primarily due to the fact that this city was an excellent market for the Liman monopolists. And the possibility of a good deal

had the capacity to transform the indigenous themselves into rational beings" (94). More recently, Pratt has affirmed that "following independence, Buenos Aires and its environs rapidly overtook Lima as a point of entry and center of transatlantic entrepreneurial energies, which then flowed westward as they were doing in North America" (1992, 148). The truth is that Buenos Aires "overtook Lima as a point of entry," and in every other economic way, more than one hundred years earlier.

15. "The nobility of Peru and that of this city, after ancient Spain, is among the grandest and most illustrious of the *Monarquía*. In them shines the blood of conquering heroes of a New World for whom it was no meaner feat to discover than to conquer, and the blood of the oldest houses in Spain among which you can hardly find a trunk that does not have branches in Peru. Their splendor was as great as their wealth; they have always spent it in service to their kings, be it in the maintenance and defense of this kingdom or in donations to their majesties. But without the income from a good part of the *encomiendas,* without the rewards of public office, and without the profit from the lands, it is logical that they find themselves in utter decay, with many houses wiped out due to this and the majority of them in serious trouble. . . . His Excellency has treated them with a benevolence capable of compensating for their arrears, and he has offered to many those graces and betterments that the times have allowed. . . . All that has issued from his generosity has gone into consoling the noblemen" (66).

16. "It is no wonder that Peru's nobility is in the decline that it now suffers, when the entire ship of the empire is buffeted by such a cruel storm. With the *Monarquía* exhausted from conflicts so powerful, it is only logical that all of its parts be. The pounding given to the crown echoes along its entire circumference. An injury to the head of the state spells the paralysis of all the provinces; and the battle torch glows even in the areas farthest from where it is lit. War cannot be waged without money, nor can money be had in emptied coffers without negotiated means. This has been the cruelest war that Spain has suffered since its loss to the Moors. It has sent shudders through all of its kingdoms, the hinges of the *Monarquía* shaken: horrible, within Spain and without. . . . Twice the very throne has been occupied by the enemy and twice the invincible force of His Majesty has regained it, defeating the enemy in two famous battles. What would not be destroyed by a war that has lasted more than ten years, which has made Spain into a Troy due to the stubbornness of a province that has been at once the Sinon and the horse that has let in the ravages? What has Spain not endured, with its kingdoms the theater of war, its fields leveled and its cities oppressed by friends and enemies? Against this backdrop, what misfortune can there be in Peru that would appear considerable, and with what expression should a discouragement appear before a havoc?" (67).

17. "The most loyal nobility of Lima, who for the most part are descendants of the conquerors of this Kingdom and are an extraction of the grandest in Spain, and their most fervent trade have always served His Majesty with very large donations. They have contributed to the building of its walls and they have come to its defense and to that of the Kingdom at sea and on land on every occasion, and its knights have always supported the royal celebrations of canonizations, proclamations, births and marriages of kings and princes, arrivals of viceroys, military victories and other events with the greatest splendor that could fit their zeal, which today they cannot do be-

cause of the great decline in which they find themselves and which will snuff them out in a pitiful end if they are not restored, as they must hope, by royal kindness" (1732, can. 10, st. 116 and n. 67).

18. On Lima's demographics, see Chapter 5 herein.

19. "The wardrobe that men use there is not different from those which are customary in Spain, nor is there a sizeable difference among the different hierarchies of which it is composed, because all fabrics are common and are used by whoever can afford them, and therefore it is not at all unusual to see a mulatto or other craftsman in a lavish tissue while an individual of the greatest worth cannot find another, more splendid, with which to stand out from the crowd. Everyone dresses with the greatest flair, and one can say without exaggerating that the fabrics produced in countries where industry labors to achieve inventions sparkle in Lima more than any place else due to their widespread usage, this being the reason why there is such demand for the many fabrics that the armadas of *galeones* and registered ships transport. And though their cost is so high there that it cannot even be compared to the price that the same goods command in Europe, this does not affect them enough to make them stop wearing the best ones, and wearing them without inhibitions and with magnanimity" (1748, 3:71–72). On the dress of women, see Meléndez 1999, chap. 5.

20. See Moreno Cebrián in Manso de Velasco 1983, 110–11, although he errs in writing that "Pardo y Figueroa" and Araújo y Río were archbishop and president of Guatemala, respectively, in 1743.

21. On the provincial governors and the controversy surrounding their institution of forced sales (*el repartimiento*) to the Indians, see Chapter 6 herein.

22. On the benefits of allowing trade between New Spain and Peru, see Güemes y Horcasitas 1867, 26.

23. In opposition to "la otra costa," or New Spain, "la costa" was used throughout Peru. In the *Gaceta de Lima,* the section of news from Europe, New Granada, and Tierra Firme is often headlined by "Noticias de la Europa y la Costa." See, for example, the November 1, 1745–January 15, 1746, issue of *Gazeta de Lima.*

24. According to Luis J. Ramos Gómez, "This subject is treated at length in manuscript 2888 of the Biblioteca del Palacio in Madrid, and the kingdom of Mexico [in the Viceroyalty of New Spain] is characterized as the third port of entry into Peru for illegal merchandise; the goods that are identified are 'sizeable consignments of cloth articles from Asia and Castile of the sort that ships from Manila and register ships from Honduras convey to that Kingdom, and foreign sloops intermingle with them, and this [illegal] export is estimated at three million *pesos* a year'" (in Ulloa and Juan 1985, 1:59 n. 2).

25. A good example is Villegas y Quevedo, whose friendship with Peralta Barnuevo and José Pardo de Figueroa opened doors for him with the Spanish Royal Academy of Language in Madrid. In 1711 he began his studies at St. Martin's, where he met Pardo de Figueroa and Bravo del Ribero, four years his junior. In 1730 Villegas traveled to Madrid, where he settled in the same neighborhood in which his friends and former classmates Pardo de Figueroa, Bravo del Ribero, and Araújo y Río were living. In 1735 he left Cádiz for Portobelo on the same ship that carried the newly elected viceroy

of Peru, the marquis de Villagarcía, and the Spanish royal scientist Jorge Juan. See Lohmann Villena 1944, 48–49, 63, 71.

26. Early in his career, he also served as a judge of poetic competitions at the University of San Marcos. See Peralta Barnuevo 1736, f. 258.

27. Viceroy Caracciolo's report on the state of the nobility in Peru in 1721 included three Zabalas who were born in Spanish America, were knights, and had fortunes, as well as the father of Bravo del Ribero's wife, José de Zabala y Esquivel. The viceroy described these men for the Spanish Crown: "Don Francisco Zabala is a *criollo* married to Doña Rosa Esquivel, and a knight of Calatrava; he is well-to-do, he holds the post of accountant on the Holy Inquisition tribunal as inheritance, he owns a farm" (Balzo 1965, 112); "Don Felipe de Zabala is a *criollo,* he has a fortune, he is a knight of Santiago married to Doña de la Riva y Agüero" (113); "Don Antonio de Zabala, *criollo,* bachelor, knight of Santiago, he is the son of Don Felipe de Zavala" (113); "Don José Zabala [y Esquivel], *criollo,* bachelor, he is well-to-do, he will inherit the post of Inquisition accountant that his father possesses" (117).

28. José de Zabala y Esquivel was the son of José Zabala and the sister of Diego de Navia y Esquivel, second marquis de Valleumbroso. In addition to fathering an out-of-wedlock son, the chronicler Diego de Navia y Esquivel, the second marquis de Valleumbroso fathered a daughter named Petronila Ignacia de Esquivel Espinola Pardo de Figueroa, who married José Pardo de Figueroa. Through marriage, then, Bravo del Ribero became one of Archbishop Pardo de Figueroa's relatives.

29. A famed art collector whose private gallery held more than one hundred paintings, Bravo de Lagunas y Castilla served as a legal advisor to two viceroys of Peru (the marquis de Castelfuerte and the marquis de Villagarcía) and as a *fiscal* on the high court in Lima (1735–1736) before he purchased a supernumerary judgeship on the high court in Lima on June 25, 1746. Because he was a native of Lima and owned property there, this required a royal dispensation. He served in Lima for a decade (1747–1757), becoming an honorary councilor of the Indies in 1753. Bravo de Lagunas's brother José was married to Ana de Zabala y Vázquez de Velasco, the sister of Bravo del Ribero's wife. See Lohmann Villena 1974, xxxix, li, 17–19; Burkholder and Chandler 1977, 56–57, 394.

30. See Manso de Velasco 1983, 201. The church in fact employed several members of this family. In the May–June 1744 issue of the *Gazeta de Lima,* we read of another powerful Bravo del Ribero, Pedro's brother Juan. He had served as a judge on the high court in Charcas in 1708. In 1746, the year Carrió went to Peru, Juan Bravo del Ribero was the bishop of Arequipa. See Lohmann Villena 1974, 19. Another brother, Jesuit José Bravo del Ribero, was professor of philosophy and theology at the Royal University of St. Francis Xavier in La Plata and professor of theology at St. Peter's College in Lima. Reporting his death in September 1757, the editor of the *Gaceta de Lima* singled out his depth of knowledge as a theologian and his skills as an orator, his clear understanding of six languages (in all of which he wrote poetry), and his "incessant incubation in every sort of *belles lettres,*" especially the works of the Parisian Royal Academy of Sciences and the *Memoires de Trévoux* (1982–1983, 2:94).

31. Herbosa y Figueroa was a member of the Navia y Esquivel clan—and therefore related to Bravo del Ribero, Bravo de Lagunas y Castilla, and the Pardo de Figueroa

brothers—and he was Viceroy Manso de Velasco's personal secretary. He later served as precentor at Lima's cathedral, judge on the Inquisition court, provisor and vicar general of the archdiocese of Lima, and bishop of Santa Cruz de la Sierra (*Gaceta de Lima* 1982–1983, 2:25, 52, 71, 155, 168; 3:173). His brother José Herboso y Figueroa worked for the royal treasury court in Lima well into the 1760s (3:226).

32. The July–September 1745 issue of the *Gazeta de Lima* highlighted his precociousness: "His Majesty having seen fit to bestow one of the judgeships on this high court upon Doctor Don Pablo Antonio de Olavide y Jaúregui, attending to his merits and distinguished talents, [and] dispensing with his ties to the land and age, . . . [the doctor] was sworn in on 17 August." At age seventeen Olavide already held doctoral degrees in theology and law from the University of San Marcos, and he began a teaching career at St. Martin's and St. Philip's. The editor also singled out Olavide's application to other fields of study and *belles lettres* (n.p.).

33. On Feijoo de Sosa's biography and career, see Lohmann Villena in Feijoo de Sosa 1984, 1:23–49.

34. The elder Feijoo de Sosa became a key player in a smuggling ring that stretched from Lima to Panama. In 1740 he purchased the *corregidor* post in Quispicanchi, a province rich in cereals and active in textile production. In 1741 the Council of the Indies ordered the marquis de Villagarcía to arrest Manuel Feijoo de Sosa and his contrabanding cohorts in Lima, an order that the viceroy received in February 1742. He did not arrest these powerful men, in part because his own secretary was implicated in their smuggling ring. (The intervention of José Pardo de Figueroa, then governor of Cuzco and owner of the choicest real estate in Quispicanchi, cannot be proven, but it cannot be discounted either.) Further, in the case of Manuel Feijoo de Sosa, the viceroy noted in his reply to the king, in November 1742, that he had already died. On Manuel Feijoo de Sosa's career and illegal dealings, see Ramos Gómez in Ulloa and Juan 1985, 1:121–22; Moreno Cebrián 1977, 505.

35. On his subsequent career and how he locked horns with Carrió, see Chapter 6 herein.

36. The bishop of Quito (1734–1745) was born in Lima, the son of Andrés Paredes y Polanco and Catalina Armendáriz, a relative of Viceroy José Armendáriz. In a lengthy footnote to his *Lima fundada*, Peralta Barnuevo explained that Paredes y Polanco had held several religious offices before he became a *fiscal* on the high court in Quito and a judge on the same court. Nicolás Paredes de Polanco y Armendáriz, the bishop's brother, had been appointed to the high court in Lima in 1699. A plaintive eulogy of the bishop appeared in the July 15–September 1745 issue of the *Gazeta de Lima* (n.p.). Also see Mendiburu 1874–1890, 6:243–44.

37. Luján y Vedía was a native of Lima and a graduate of the University of San Marcos and the University of Paris. In September 1724 he was appointed the attorney on the high court charged with handling cases involving Indians in Quito. Although he was investigated for illegal activities in the 1730s, in September 1743 he was appointed a *fiscal* on the high court in Quito, a post that he held until his death in 1755 (Burkholder and Chandler 1977, 190–91). Charles Marie de La Condamine observed that Luján was one of the few residents in Elena who could speak French and that Luján had studied in Paris and shown the French scientist a thesis he had written on philosophy (1751b, 66 and n.). Given his last name, which he shared with the mother of

the Pardo de Figueroa brothers (Margarita Luján), and his academic career in Paris, where José Pardo de Figueroa had lived for a period, it is likely that this French-speaking native of Lima was related to the Pardo de Figueroa brothers by marriage if not by blood.

38. On Araújo y Río's entry into the Kingdom of Quito and Alcedo's accusations, see Ramos Gómez in Ulloa and Juan 1985, 1:60–61, and nn. 7–10.

39. On smuggling in New Granada during the first half of the eighteenth century, see the superb study by Lance Grahn (1997).

40. Navia Bolaño y Moscoso was a judge on the high court in Charcas (1705–1709) before he bought a supernumerary judgeship on the high court in Lima in 1709. In 1723, while serving on the high court in Lima, he purchased a royal dispensation that allowed him to marry Isabel María de Espínola Villavicencio Pardo de Figueroa, sister-in-law and second cousin of the Pardo de Figueroa brothers. Later he served as an appeals judge for the merchants' guild and supervisory judge for the royal mint. He became an honorary member of the Council of the Indies and a knight of Santiago in 1741. See Burkholder and Chandler 1977, 233–34; Lavallé 1987, 64–65; Lohmann Villena 1974, xxxix, 80–81.

41. From the historical evidence presented here, it is clear that Carrió could not have personally witnessed the events contained in his Guatemalan anecdote. Araújo y Río was not in Santiago de Guatemala in 1746: he was tied up in litigation in Madrid until late 1747.

CHAPTER 4

1. On the political implications of "mystery" (*misterio*) and "speaking mysteriously," or "speaking in riddles" (*hablar en misterio*), see the Introduction herein.

2. Carrió's population chart of Buenos Aires and Santísima Trinidad is reproduced in Meléndez 1999, 145.

3. Amat recorded the following in *Memoria del Gobierno:* "Don Alonso Carrió [de Lavandera] arrived via Buenos Aires, commissioned by the General Administration [of the Posts] in Madrid, with the purpose of straightening out the [postal] routes [from Buenos Aires] to this capital, Lima, in the capacity of inspector. He had his differences with the Postmaster General [here in Lima], about inspecting the main cashier's office, as well as the number of posts that should operate annually" (1947, 609–10).

4. On the Mexico City versus Lima rivalry, see Chapters 1 and 2 herein.

5. Mining was not the preferred route to enrichment for elites in Buenos Aires, though some speculated that the province held as much precious ore as the Kingdom of Peru. In a report on the role of mercury in the economy of the Viceroyalty of the Riverplate, an anonymous critic writes, "What surprises this Author the most is that, whereas His Catholic Majesty has so many Tribunals set up for all the Branches [of government], everyone lives in crass ignorance of the pure treasures that are in this Kingdom and little effort is expended in [the branch of] Minerals, due to a lack of incentive. . . . But, then again, how is it possible to pursue matters when every one of us Spaniards seems to attend only to our own business?" ("Informe Tercero," in Cuatro informes, 1776, 36r.). The similarity between the Liman lord's denial that they are "a bunch of men who only look after our particular interests" ("unos Hombres que solo

pensamos en nuestros particulares Intereses'), at the Guatemalan mock trial, and the last phrase here (in Spanish, "cada uno de los Españoles parece no entendemos a más que a nuestro negocio particular?") is uncanny.

6. Even in France, the assumed decadence of Spanish residents of Lima (and Mexico City) tended to leave Buenos Aires untarnished in the late eighteenth century. See, for example, Castilhon 1770, 1:61.

7. The *Gaceta de Lima* from January 10, 1759, noted that the Inquisition in Lima had published an edict that prohibited and suppressed *Títulos de comedias nuevas*. (1982–1983, 2:170). Kendall W. Brown (1992) has attributed the gains in the mining sector achieved in the early nineteenth century to the improved distribution of mercury.

8. On these receiving houses, see Méndez 1992.

9. See Chapter 3 herein.

10. I recall his agreement with another French author, the so-called innoculator of *bon sens*, Nicholas Josef Selis, in Chapter 1 herein.

11. "¡O tiempos! ¡O costumbres! ¿Quién pensara/que hay hombres de tan viles intenciones/que estando en posesión de vista clara/afectan ceguedad en sus acciones?/ Esta niebla común se disipara/si a la luz de prudentes reflexiones,/vieran que a Dios y al mundo son malquistos/los ciegos voluntarios por mal vistos./¡Ay de aquellos que tienen pies quebrados,/sólo para los vicios dirigidos,/del camino seguro separados/porque todos sus rumbos son torcidos!/Faetones serán precipitados/si van en sus caprichos sostenidos,/corriendo padecer tormento eterno/por sus pasos contados al infierno" (undated manuscript, Fondo Antiguo, vol. 6). A very rough translation is the following: "Oh the times! Oh the customs! Who could imagine/that there are men of such base intentions/who, while in possession of keen sight,/affect blindness in their actions?/This common cloud would vanish/if, in the light of prudent reflections,/they could see that willfully blind men,/because they are looked down on,/are estranged from God and men./Pity those who have unsteady feet,/pointed only toward vices,/ gone astray from the right road/because all of their paths are crooked!/They shall be fallen Phaetons/if they continue borne on their whims,/running in their numbered steps/to suffer eternal torment in Hell."

12. Jean Seznec's (1995) study remains the best introduction to this literature.

13. A marquis, a baron, a count, and a *cavaliere* voice their opinions about letters addressed to various persons, one of them being a "Letter from Someone Who Sends Two Dozen Pairs of Spectacles to the Viceroy of Naples" ("Lettera d'uno che invia due dozine d'occhiali al ViceRè di Napoli" in *Continuazione del Corriero* 1660a, 51–59). The *cavaliere* states that a prince will be supplied most often with those false spectacles that represent things as different from what they are, because the powerful with their rotten morals are only too content to be flattered with lies (56). The baron replies that there must be plenty of false spectacles on the flatterers who abound at the courts and that the Spanish viceroy of Naples uses spectacles that impede his sight, giving him false appearances, with which he convinces himself that they serve to make his sight clearer (56–57).

14. Directly after "Lettera d'un Avvocato," the count moralizes, "In short, . . . who made Mercury the god of sciences and, on the other hand, the god of theives, had his eye on these doctors, whom science helps to cheat and steal" (in *Continuazione del Cor-*

riero 1660a, 61). A reader of that work in eighteenth-century Lima, Pedro de Peralta Barnuevo, tied sight to good government and gold and silver to blindness in a discourse on the "State of the *Monarquía* and of Peru": "Lycurgus wound up forbidding Lacedemonians to have gold and silver coins, ordering instead that they be made of iron, by which he transformed theft into wealth and death into profanity. And because of this, a greedy man poked his eye out, and he preferred the loss of one eye to the disorder that was blinding both eyes of his city. He preferred to see his face without any sight than his government blind without his light" ("Estado de la Monarchia y del Perú" in *El Cielo en el Parnasso* 1736, ff. 45–46).

15. "By Mercurie Marchauntes be ment. His wynges at head & feete betoken the expedition of Marchantes, which to gett worldly pelse, post through all corners of the World: the whyte & blacke coloured Hat, signifieth their subtility, which for greediness of gaine, spare not to face white for blacke, & blacke for white. By his fawlchon is signified, goodes gotten by violence, when subtiltie cannot comprehend. . . . The figured cutpurse is a proofe that Mercurie was a theife, and headlesse Argus is a witnesse that one Plague bewrayes a thousand evilles. The Poets feigne that Argus . . . had an hundred eyes, of al which only two did sleepe by course, so that he was not to be taken with al asleepe. So subtil was Argus, that what fraude soever was imagined, hee had policie to defend it" (1976, 4).

16. Inspired by tales that were appearing in Charles Riviere Dufresny's *Mercure galant*, Peralta Barnuevo created this "dandy Mercury" to determine the fate of men and women who represent different provinces and kingdoms of the viceroyalty (1964, 83–96).

17. "Éste era un capitán de más de sesenta años de edad, cuyo nombre me mandó don Alonso que no expresase en mi itinerario por no exponerlo al desprecio de todo el mundo, como lo ejecutaré con todos los demás que desprecian las reales ordenanzas, ni tampoco diré los motivos que este corregidor y otros tienen para semejantes atentados, porque causa pudor expresarlos" (301) ("This guy was a captain more than sixty years of age, whose name Don Alonso told me not to reveal in my itinerary, so as not to expose him to public scorn, just as I will do with all of the others who flout the royal ordinances, nor shall I give the motives that this governor and others have for such violations because it is embarrassing to reveal them"). Carrió made a similar claim in defense of his account, as I indicated in the Introduction herein.

18. Carrió certainly knew that quicksilver (*azogue*) was vital to the mining sector in the viceroyalties of New Spain and Peru. Chemists had given it the name of the god Mercury, so convinced were they of its ability to transform itself into any metal (Real Academia Española 1979, 2:550).

19. Mercury was, however, depicted alongside the viceroy in a work that Carrió could easily have seen. In 1770 a Spanish translation of Nebrija 1951 had been dedicated to Viceroy Amat, which sported a "woodcut of Mercury flying with his caduceus in one hand and the shield of Lima in the other" (Mendiburu 1874–1890, 1:455).

20. Carilla has attributed this and other passages to the influence of *Les aventures de Télémaque* (1968) (Carrió 125 n. 3).

21. On Feijoo de Sosa, see Chapters 3 and 6 herein.

22. On those interrogations, see Chapter 6 herein.

23. On Carrió's debts to Menippean satire, see the Introduction and Chapters 6 and 7 herein.

24. On myths in medieval Spanish chronicles, see Gregorio de Mayans y Siscar, *Censura de la España primitiva* (in *Obras* 1983, 1:261–305). Also see his *Vida de Don Nicolás Antonio* and his edition of Antonio's *Censura de historias fabulosas* (in *Obras* 1:321–96). In his preface to Gaspar Ibáñez's *Advertencias a la Historia del P. Juan de Mariana* (in *Obras* 1:527–57), Mayans recognized that Mariana had included "mythical kings" and sundry fictions from the Moors because he trusted dubious medieval chronicles (*chronicones*) and "la *General* del Rei Don Alonso" (552) ("King Don Alonso's *General* [*History*]"). Feijoo y Montenegro, too, led the charge against lies in historiography. It is very likely that Feijoo y Montenegro had read Bernard Le Bovier Fontenelle's "Digression sur les Anciens et les Modernes" (in *Oeuvres* 1825, 1:235–54) and his "De l'Origine des Fables," where the French rationalist described fables as nothing other than the history of the errors of the human mind (in *Oeuvres* 1:302–7).

25. Carrió denied a cause-and-effect relationship for age and truth in the same sententious manner in which Juan Rufo had drawn a parallel between Ovid's tale of the chattering white crow that was transformed into a black crow and the elderly person who gives his last will and testament: "Upon hearing told one of Ovid's myths, in which it says that the feathers of the crow, which used to be white, turned black because it delivered bad news, he said 'that the same thing happens to gray hairs when they are giving their last testament'" (1972, 194–95). It is not advanced age but an impending death, then, that compels a mature person to reveal dark truths. On Raynal's attitude toward the quipus and the "fables" of the Incas in Spanish- and *mestizo*-authored histories, see Hill 1994b, ch. 5, especially 403–6. Recently, Jorge Cañizares Esguerra has echoed my point (2001, 37, 115).

26. Evaristo de Souza Penha correctly observed, "In reality, the exordium to Part One is a parody of the essays that Feijoo y Montenegro devotes to history" (1978, 159). At page 201, note 4, he provided the names of the six essays, but he did not discuss the passages discussed here. Throughout *Reflexiones sobre la historia*, Feijoo y Montenegro praised a speech given by François de Salignac de la Mothe Fénelon to the French Royal Academy, but to Carrió, the author of *Les aventures de Télémaque* (1968) was the last person to turn to for historiographical counsel.

27. "Carrió looks down on the ingenuousness of Feijoo y Montenegro, who, despite his lucid understanding of the factors that shape the writing of a historiographical text, does not get discouraged; [rather,] he keeps on believing in the necessity of writing a true history, while he acknowledges the difficulty of being sincere. . . . Without a doubt, Feijoo y Montenegro is among the Spanish savants who are repeatedly accused of being ingenuous in *El lazarillo* [*de ciegos caminantes*]" (Souza Penha 1978, 161). I am not convinced that Carrió adopted a "rational stance" or supported it seriously with "encyclopedic information . . . in the tradition of the eighteenth-century Spanish writer and philosopher Father Benito Jerónimo Feijoo y Montenegro," as Julie Greer Johnson has asserted (1993, 124).

28. The increasing popularity of this rationalist and empiricist brand of history—or history *theory*, to be precise—was ridiculed by Cadalso in *Eruditos a la violeta*. In this Menippean satire, which shares much with *El lazarillo de ciegos caminantes*, the *pe-*

timetre professor of the academy tells his students not to bother actually reading histories, ancient or modern, but instead to spout theoretical statements about historiography: "you will make yourselves much more famous by saying that it is a short step from the most ridiculous myth [*fábula*] to the most expansive history" (1967,113).

29. Mayans y Siscar defended Juan de Mariana and explained the motives for attacking him in similar terms, in his preface to *Advertencias* (in *Obras* 1983, 544). I detail these issues in Hill 1994b, especially chaps. 1 and 6, and in Hill 2000b, introduction. More recently, see Cañizares 2001, 155.

30. The inspector's parenthetical "(aquí entro yo)" recalls a Menippean satire authored by Francisco de Quevedo Villegas, *El mundo de por dentro* (in *Obras* 1945, 1:224–33): "Otros hay (y en éstos, que son los peores, entro yo) que no saben nada, ni quieren saber nada, ni creen que se sepa nada, y dicen de todos que no saben nada, y todos dicen dellos lo mismo, y nadie miente" ("Al letor" in *Obras* 224) ("There are others, and these are the worst—and here is where I come in—who do not know anything, do not want to know anything, nor believe that anyone can know anything, and they say of all people that they know nothing, and all say the same about them, and no one lies"). Emilio Carilla has tied *El lazarillo de ciegos caminantes* to other works by Quevedo (1976, *passim*).

31. The blindman who first comes to mind is the one in the picaresque novel *El lazarillo de Tormes*, which explains why *El lazarillo de ciegos caminantes* was initially approached as a picareque novel by eminent Hispanists. See the Introduction herein.

32. One of Rufo's pithy sayings (1972, 583) turned precisely on this Valencian sense of the term *carta* (203).

33. See Anonymous 1911. On the "most witty conversations" of blindmen, see pages 164–65. The editor notes, on page 162, note 1, that it was attributed to Cervantes.

34. See Chapter 6 herein for a full discussion of the *corregidor* controversy. On French criticism of the Spanish Conquest and government, see Hill 1994b, especially chaps. 5 and 6; 1998; 2000b, *passim*. More recently, see Cañizares 2001, 159–60.

35. See Chapter 6 herein.

CHAPTER 5

1. Carrió's alleged racial and racist attitudes in *El lazarillo de ciegos caminantes* have been the subject of numerous other studies, whose focus I do not intend to duplicate. The most comprehensive and most recent is Meléndez 1999. On some future occasion, I hope to present an account of the passage from *casta* to *raza* in Spanish America. This clearly stands outside the scope of a study of eighteenth-century Spanish America, however, even one that recognizes, as this study does, the importance of hierarchy to that century and to *El lazarillo de ciegos caminantes* in particular.

2. "Colonial legislation treated race as a crucial, but completely transparent category of social discrimination so that privilege based on race was an inevitable characteristic of colonial society, but the definition of specific racial identity was negotiated within the colonial context" (Kuznesof 1995, 156). Here she suggests, independently of Dumont, that viceregal Spanish America had a norm of inequality. However, I cannot agree that the norm was a "racial" one or that "colonial legislation" sanctioned "racial" hierarchies.

3. This strategy was used successfully in Spain before Spanish America, as Michael Gerli (1996) has recently shown.

4. The use of opposing definitions of *casta* by the same scholar tends to give way to the definition of *casta* as a "mixed-blood." Nicolás León wrote that "new things" required "new denominations," proceeded to observe that *castas* had already existed in Spain, and then defined *castas* as "hybrids" or "mixed-bloods" (1924, 4–5). Throughout *Race Mixture,* Magnus Mörner (1967) appears to understand that *castas* were descent groups that were either homogeneous (pure) or heterogeneous (impure, or mixed), but as he treats the "learned" taxonomies of *castas,* he omits all *castas* that are homogeneous, from which one could incorrectly infer that *castas* are, by definition, groups of people of mixed ancestry. Stuart B. Schwartz's use of *casta* appears to include homogeneous groups other than Spaniards: "Africans were another matter and as their presence in colonial population grew it tended to lower the status of all the castas" (1995, 191): "Indians, mestizos, and other castas" (192). The term *casta* means "mixed-blood" in R. Anderson 1988. David Cahill notes that the genealogies first studied seriously by Mörner were "known generically as 'castas' or 'genízaros.'" He discusses a "genealogy of the plebs," which appeared in a manuscripted "Description of all of the towns in the Viceroyalty of Peru," written in the second half of the eighteenth century (1994, 339 and n. 41). This genealogy, like Mörner's eighteenth-century lists, contains no homogenous group. However, the "genealogy of the plebs" employs *genízaros* rather than *castas* because (I am convinced) the categories were not racial but cultural: *genízaro* in Spain designated the man who had one parent who was not born in Spain or the man who had one parent who was not born a Christian. See Hill, "*Casta* as Culture" (2004). Cope writes of the "sociedad de castas," in which Spaniards compose the highest *casta,* but on the same page he writes that "all Spaniards ranked higher than all castas" and he writes of the "Spanish-casta boundary" (1994, 24). Susan Migden Socolow also imbricates *casta* in modernity: "Legal status was reflected in legislation which detailed disabilities that Indians, blacks, and *castas* (persons of mixed racial ancestry) incurred" (in Hoberman and Socolow 1986, Introduction, 7). The term *casta* means "mixed-blood" in Dueñas Vargas 1997, *passim.* Robert H. Jackson shares the misunderstanding of *casta:* "The Spanish government passed laws that prohibited Spaniards and *castas* (individuals legally defined as being of mixed European and/or African and indigenous ancestry) from living among Indians in their designated communities" (1999, 4). J. Jorge Klor de Alva too has defined *castas* as hybrids (1992, 7). More recently, Ronald J. Morgan writes of "nonwhite ethnic types or *castas*" (2002, 6) and "New World racial types" (10). Perhaps the only Latin Americanist who has consistently employed *casta* as it was used during the viceregal period is Gonzalo Aguirre Beltrán (1984, *passim*).

5. Like Dumont before him, Patrick Wolfe recognizes that racial hierarchy is only one type of hierarchy. He goes on to point out that the failure to engage with other forms is a sign of the omnipotence of the *race* construct in the modern period: "the unexamined assumption that other forms of collective differentiation necessarily presuppose racial awareness is a prime example of the ideological process whereby race has been naturalised and eternalised in Western culture" (2000, 52).

6. Recently, Magali M. Carrera (2003) has argued against using such terms in the con-

text of eighteenth-century New Spain. She proposes that *calidad* (what is also called *condición* or *estado*) was a social construct, an argument that we share. See Hill, "*Casta as Culture*" (2004).

7. More recently, philosophers Julie Ward and Tommy Lott have edited a volume of essays on philosophy and race, of which roughly half assume the existence of *race* before the nineteenth century. (I thank Ricardo Padrón for bringing this collection to my attention.) Their introduction contains the following claim: "a sharpened awareness of race is introduced into the modern period, as is illustrated in the classic debates about slavery and race between Bartolomé de Las Casas and Juan Gines de Sepúlveda in the sixteenth century" (2002, xi–xii). For a different view, see Muldoon 2000b.

8. There are no studies on the distinction between *casta* and *raza* in viceregal Spanish America. However, over half a century ago, Oliver C. Cox (1944–1945) attempted to outline the differences between *race* and *caste* in order to discourage the use of *caste* by sociologists and other scholars of North American race relations. More recently, Paul C. Taylor has tried to sort out the two concepts: "It is useful to have distinct vocabularies available to us to serve different purposes, to indicate the different realities that the core uses of these terms denote. Race is principally about appearance, and derivatively about the bloodlines that produce people who, in the general run of things, look a certain way. Caste is principally about hereditary hierarchies that are not indexed to the morphology of the body" (2004, 63). Although this may be true of caste in India or Japan, it is not a distinction that holds for *casta* and *raza* in viceregal Spanish America, as we shall see.

9. Eric Voeglin made the distinction between race as a political idea and race as a biological concept in 1940. In 1944 Hannah Arendt made a similar distinction between *race thinking* and *racism*. Taylor builds on K. Anthony Appiah's contention that "races do not exist but racial identities do" (1996, 123) and employs Arendt's *race thinking* over and over without attribution. Other scholars prefer a variant: *racial thinking*. See, for example, Dorinda Outram's 1995 work (75ss). However, the same author notes that "the Enlightenment devoted considerable attention to what we would now call issues of race, though it did so with significant differences to the way this issue was to be handled in the nineteenth and twentieth centuries" (74). An early approach to Latin America is found in Charles Wagley's "Concept of Social Race," originally published in 1959: "The term 'social race' is used because these groups or categories are socially, not biologically, defined in all of our American societies, although the terms by which they are labeled may have originally referred to biological characteristics" (in *Latin American Tradition*, 1968, 155). More recently, see Seed 1982. Kuznesof writes that "few modern scholars would deny that race in colonial Spanish America was 'socially constructed,' yet the 'Spanishness' (in both biological and social terms) of creole society is seldom questioned" (1995, 153). James H. Sweet claims that a "people's inferior culture implied a biologically inferior people," after establishing that "for the early modern period, race and culture cannot be easily separated" (1997, 144). He traces "the immediate foundations of racism in modern Western thought" (143) to medieval Iberia, contending that "the racist beliefs that Iberians and others would later refine to a 'science' were firmly entrenched before Christopher Columbus made landfall in the Americas" (144). However, he admits that "to use the term race in a fifteenth-

century Iberian context may be problematic" (144), a recognition that compels him to conclude his study by positing the oxymoronic "Racism without Race" (165–66), a formulation that Leon G. Campbell (1973) applied to Bourbon Spanish America. Paul Julian Smith clearly states that *race* is a social construct (1992, 1–3), but he does not acknowledge that his overlay of a modern concept and term (*race*) on a premodern hierarchy, in his earlier chapters, is itself a form of cultural imperialism and a signaling of the hierarchy to which he belongs. My general disagreement with this view is based in the fact that *race* as it is used today did not exist before the nineteenth century and that the very concept was invented in opposition to the cultural categories that existed before its invention. I have a particular problem, as I have stated on another occasion (2000b, "Conclusion"), with using theoretical concepts invented in cultures that treated Spaniards as objects of domination. On the French role in the invention of *race* in the nineteenth century, see Arendt 1944.

10. Audrey Smedley discusses the invention of the white race and other hierarchical fictions at the turn of the eighteenth century, and then notes, "By the mid-nineteenth century virtually all Americans had been conditioned to this arbitrary ranking of the American peoples, and racial ideology had diffused around much of the world, including to the colonized peoples of the Third World and among Europeans themselves. . . . 'Race' identity took priority over religion, ethnic origin, education and training, socioeconomic class, occupation, language, values, beliefs, morals, lifestyles, geographical location, and all other human attributes that hitherto provided all groups and individuals with a sense of who they were" (1998, 695). Michael Banton upholds the nineteenth-century thesis regarding the birth of *race* in the modern sense (1977, chap. 3). Colette Guillaumin has carefully explained how social relations were ideologized as natural, or racial, relations beginning in the nineteenth century (1995, 63–64). Kenan Malik, too, locates the invention of race in the nineteenth century: "The modern concept of race is not simply a continuation of age-old prejudices. It could only have risen in opposition to the Enlightenment view" (1996, 55). The Romantics led this opposition, according to Malik (73–79). Ivan Hannaford (1996, 63) has situated the birth of race after Carolus Linnaeus and Johann Friedrich Blumenbach. Wolfe traces *race* to the late eighteenth century: "Race, in short, is endemic to modernity" (2000, 53).

11. "But the recognition and assumption by two beings of mutual rights and obligations involves one indispensable condition, the possession of a common foundation of ideas and traditions, of a common language or interpreter. These close points of likeness are formed by education, which is one of the forms by which imitation spreads. For this reason the recognition of mutual responsibilities never arose between the Spanish or English conquerors of America and the conquered natives. In this case, racial dissimilarity either played a much smaller role than difference of language, custom, or religion; or it served merely as an added cause of incompatibility" (1903, 62).

12. The imprint of Le Bon's thinking was especially deep in Carlos Bunge's 1903 *Nuestra América* (see Helg 1990, 39). However, negative reactions to Le Bon's theories, especially his claims about miscegenation, were plentiful: I find them, for example, in González Prada 1986 and Arreguine 1900.

13. "Over the course of the development of humanity, we see heterogeneous groups, which we shall call simply *races,* springing forth always and everywhere from superior communities, which in turn present themselves as races in opposition to other heterogeneous communities and groups. Certainly, to be precise about things, there currently are no *races* in the sense that natural science uses this word, since there are no human trunks that find themselves in the homogeneous state of *primordial hordes.* Nor can one [properly] assign the name of *races* to heterogeneous, ethnic and even social communities and groups who, *in the struggles that they wage with one another, are the propagating agents of the process of history*" (italics textual) (1894, 211).

14. "The current nation of race, at no place or time could ever be simply the nation belonging to natural history, in the strict sense of the word; in effect, it is nothing other than a *historical nation.* Race is not the product of a simple natural process, in the sense that this word has had up until now: it is a product of the historical process, which is also, for its part, natural. Race is a unity that, over the course of history, has been produced within social development, and by it. Its initial factors are . . . intellectual: language, religion, custom, law, civilization, etc. It is only later that the physical factor arises—the unity of blood" (italics textual) (1894, 211–12).

15. "Can there not be a different base, in intellectual kinship, meaning, the *essential similarity of intelectual aptitudes?* No one has ever seriously tried to deny these aptitudes, this intellectual kinship, between all human races" (italics textual) (1894, 65–66).

16. See González Prada 1986, 196–97, 207. He rejected the theories of Tarde (González Prada 1986, 196), Le Bon (196–99), Demolins (197), and Gumplowicz (200). Though aware that Novicow had affirmed that *race* as scientists employed it in contemporary discussions was, to a degree, a subjective category of the mind rather than an external reality, González Prada never denied the existence of *race* outside of those discussions. *Civilization* was cultural, whereas *race* was physiological, or biological: "Civilization and race cannot be treated as identical, since the first is a notion of the psychological and social order, and the second, a notion of the physiological order" (González Prada 1986, 120). Significantly, however, he denied that mental faculties (certain ideas, emotions, and so forth that Europeans abrogated for themselves) were the sole property of one race or another (86). In theory, then, a black man reared in Europe could possess European culture (civilization) and still belong to the black race (120–21). Arreguine, too, noted that ideological imperatives had manipulated biology: the most notable example was the Anglo-Saxon use of *civilization*—an alleged cultural superiority that they tied to racial superiority—to justify imperial designs on Australia, India, Jamaica, Africa, Mexico, and the Philippines (1900, 11–14).

17. Harrison 1998, 610. Abandoning the nineteenth-century sense concept of *race,* then, and redefining the term did not undo the damage: "However revolutionary in conceptual terms, the dismantling of the race construct's biological validity was not immediately followed up by a sustained examination and theorizing of the ideological and material processes that engender the *social construction* of race under the historically specific circumstances and cultural logic found here in the United States" (611). See also Visweswaran (1998). What interests me, of course, are the "historically specific circumstances and cultural logic" found in pre-nineteenth-century Spain and

Spanish America. The racial hierarchy that stubbornly survives in the United States has played a significant role in the scholarly racialization of viceregal Spanish America, but it cannot be examined within the confines of this study.

18. This "modo de vivir" was Spanish, not German or Swedish or any other term that we today use for "Western" or "Western European." For this very reason, we would do well to forego such word forms as *Occidentalism* and *Occidentalization*. Despite the interesting work that employs such terms (for example, Gruzinski and Watchel 1997), the homogenization of cultures and ideologies that later were put under the Western umbrella should inspire scholarly trepidation.

19. As Benjamin Braude puts it, "The treatment of Jews, blacks, and Indians in the early modern world arose despite, not because of, theological acceptance of a shared genealogy. No matter how destructive European behavior was, it would have been even worse had the many conflicting visions of human origins—pre-Adamic, polygenetic, diabolic, or animal ancestry, for example—gained general acceptance. . . . The logic of common descent, once accepted, carried the assumption of a unified blood relation. This was consistent with the infinite capacity of people of the early modern era to connect and thereby explain everything. They still retained the traditional certainty, rooted in a belief in one god, that all were united and related through the single act of creation. As a result of Europe's explorations and the doubling of the known world, the sphere through which this unity could in theory then be traced was greater than it had ever been. This was a unique moment of opportunity for connecting and understanding all human experience, which subsequent skepticism and worse were to destroy. Thus it is anachronistic (as well as ethnocentric) to discuss one of the many ethnic-religious Others of this era without acknowledging their interconnectedness with all, both Self and Others. A case in point is the early modern theory that the New World Indians were the Ten Lost Tribes of Israel. More generally, peoples whom today we might regard as totally distinct could easily be linked in early modern speculation" (1997, 104–5). Braude's research indirectly confirms my assertion that *casta* as a hierarchical principle in the Spanish world always meant something other than *race*.

20. This is evident in the writings of José Martí (1978), José Enrique Rodó (2000), Eugenio de Hostos (1939), Víctor Arreguine (1900), and Manuel González Prada (1986) and in the writings of the European authors whom many of these men were contesting: Gumplowicz (1894), Le Bon (1982), Demolins (1898), Tarde (1903), and others.

21. Twinam explains the inclusion of legitimacy within the concept of blood purity (1999, 45), and she writes that "at some unknown point American colonists added 'mulatto' to the historical *limpieza de sangre* discrimination against 'commoner, Jew, Moor . . . [and] *converso*'" (43).

22. Their approach is reductionist in another way too: it ignores what Spain had in common with other cultures. In the French Indies, Jews were a principal target of the Black Code, or *Code Noir*, which banished them from French Islands in the Caribbean and from Louisiana. Jean-Baptiste Labat reproduced the *Code Noir* with some sixty articles that applied to the French Caribbean (1730, 4:535–58). Article I mentioned Louis XIII's edict (April 23, 1615) that had banished Jews (4:537). He also reproduced another *Code Noir* (4:558–83) with fifty-five articles that applied to Louisi-

ana. Article I banished Jews from that French territory (4:559–60). Similarly, until the 1820s, Jews could not hold public office in Maryland, the former colony established as a refuge for Catholics because they could not take the requisite Christian oath. A large-scale reproduction of the Jewish Relief Act passed in the 1820s is on display at the old town hall in Annapolis, Maryland.

23. In "Caste Theater," an essay that I wrote in 1998, I accepted Pitt-Rivers's affirmations but voiced reservations about the usage of *casta* and *raza* in the works of twentieth-century scholars vis-à-vis the usage of the terms in the eighteenth century. By the time the essay was published in 2000, I had become convinced that we must abandon Pitt-Rivers's definition of *casta,* as I clarified in my essay "*Casta* as Culture" (2004). Following Pitt-Rivers, Dumont, too, went astray in his understanding of *casta* in the Hispanic world: "The word [*casta*] seems to have been used in the sense of race by the Spaniards, and to have been applied to India by the Portuguese in the middle of the fifteenth century" (1980, 21). The note corresponding to this affirmation (at 347, 11b) reads in part, "Regarding the etymology of the word 'caste' in the Iberian languages, cf. J. Pitt-Rivers, 'On the Word Caste,' publication forthcoming, 1970." Quite possibly the article in question is the one that I cite here.

24. The term *casta* was not, as Josep María Fradera mistakenly suggests, born in the sixteenth century or in Spanish America (1999, 57–58). (I thank my colleague Professor Mané Lagos for bringing Fradera's book to my attention.) What the Spanish and the Portuguese with experience in Asia took to the New World is an inquiry that needs to be opened. Jack Forbes, for example, was surprised to learn that Portuguese missionaries had referred to indigenous people in Brazil as *negros,* but the experience of the Portuguese in Asia makes this usage understandable. In my view, he is wrong to equate the Portuguese *negro* and the English "nigger" (1988, 75). Moreover, the notion that Ham's descendants populated India and thereafter the New World was still circulating in the late seventeenth century, and the belief that some of the indigenous population or their ancestors were black can still be found in Bourbon Spanish America. See Chapter 6 herein.

25. In my view, although popular usage flattened out the meaning of *casta,* the term still retained traces of its earlier meaning: for example, the common phrase of Spanish husbandry, *hacer casta,* or Oudin's "*Faire race,* hazer casta" and "*Il tient cela de race, viene, tiene lo de casta.*" See also Herrera 1970, 306–7.

26. For similar examples that address sheep, turkeys, pigeons, and so on, see pages 307–8, 317, 320, and 332.

27. Luis del Mármol Carvajal, perhaps best known for his *Historia del rebelión y castigo de los moriscos del Reyno de Granada* (1600), first penned a monumental account of Africa, where he had been a captive and a soldier among warring Muslim and non-Muslim Africans. In *Descripción General de África,* the terms *casta* and *generación* were synonymous and applied equally to humans and animals. While describing the marvels of the Nile, for instance, he wrote of the three kingdoms and faiths in Isla de Meroe: "The second is of idolatrous opinion and *casta* of blacks" (1953, f. 21v.). In a chapter on the animals of Africa that differ from those in Europe, he explained, "Those that come from Barbary are called Wild Horses [*Cavallos barbaros*] in Europe, but there is a group of horses in Africa and Egypt and in the Arabias and throughout

Asia that they call Arabian horses, which belong to the *casta* of savage horses that are raised in the deserts of Arabia" (f. 23v.). And on the origins of the Azuagos of Africa, he observed, "These persons are right proud to say that they come from the *casta* of Christians" (34r.). Diego Hurtado de Mendoza, author of *Guerra de Granada*, another important account of the rebellion of the *moriscos*, once served as the Spanish ambassador to Lisbon. In a satirical gloss of a sermon on the Portuguese victory over the Spaniards published as "Sermón de Aljubarrota con las glosas de D. Diego Hurtado de Mendoza," he commented wryly, "As for what the Father preached to us that the Castilians were very discouraged and the Portuguese gentlemen brave, because they all were going without eating, it is true that both groups [*naciones*] have this quality, and they get it from their *casta*, taking the part for the whole, since [people in] Galicia, of which Portugal has a poor memory, are such hearty eaters because they have a lot of shit" (1964, 73). Later he feigned surprise at the preacher's claim that the archbishop was granting indulgences to his Spanish troops from Braga so that they would fight harder: "And I have been told that the reason that motivated this Archbishop was none other than the fact that the war was against Castilians, for they take them to be Jews and from the *casta* of Moors" (76).

28. The term appeared more than two dozen times, as in the following examples: "The vanity of lineage had not reached the point that it has today, because the ones who belonged to the *casta* of Jews were very distinctive and well-known, so there was no more honor in not being from the shamed [*notados*] than there is now in not being from the *moriscos*" (1975, 14v.); "And everything the Holy Scripture says against the Jews and Pharisees is not apposite for us to distrust those of that *casta* if they are good and reliable Christians" (18r.); "And when there is proof that a horse is excellent in appearance and in deeds, it would be sheer folly to cling to the presumption that its *casta* was base" (32v.); and so on.

29. Schwartz has affirmed that status and lineage "are surrogates for class" (1995, 189), but *casta* was other than a surrogate for class, in my assessment. Needless to say, I agree with his rejection of lineage as an ethnic or racial marker (189).

30. Mariselle Meléndez examines population statistics for Argentina (1999, 144–45).

31. Alfonso XI included "RAÇA, f. minium, red oxide of lead" ("Glossary," in *Libro de la Montería* 1983, 143). Nebrija recorded "Minium, ii. por el bermellon" (1979, n.p.) and "Almagra quemada. ochra.e" (1951, n.p.).

32. Martín Alonso recorded this entry: "RAZA (probablemente forma semiculta del l. *ratio, -onis*, cálculo, cuenta). f. s. XV. Casta o calidad del origen o linaje. Arcipreste de Talavera: *El Corbacho*, 1438, ed. Pérez Pastor (4890–4891), c. 18, p. 60–29.⬚ 2. s. XIII. Grieta que se forma a veces en la parte superior del casco de las caballerías: 'Una maletia que dizen *raza*. Et face se de sequedat et de la unna.' *Libro caballos* (c. 1275?), ed. Georg Sachs, 39, 16" (1986, 2:1544). See also the fifteenth-century work by Johan Alvares de Salamiellas, *Tratado de menescalcia*: "De la enfermedat quel dizen Raça" (1998, bk. 2, chap. 14, 39–40).

33. R. S. Boggs and colleagues included this definition: "RAÇA [¿] *s.* (1) lista de paño en que el tejido está más claro que en el resto, *Lba* 94c. (2) *pl.* defectos morales, *Lba* 504c" (1946, 2:424). Again, *raza* meant a physical flaw, or, in the plural, *moral* flaws, according to Julio Cejador y Frauca: "*RAZA, RAÇA, RASA,* como raja, desigualdad en

el tejido, falta. J. RUIZ, 94: non ay paño syn rraça. CABRERA, *Derm.*, p. 286: paño al parecer finísimo, y desdoblado tiene mil razas. J. RUIZ, 504: con el dinero cunplen sus menguas e sus raças. BAENA, p. 254: cortara doquier que falle rasa" (1983, 334).

34. At PAÑO, Covarrubias included several popular sayings about lineage and family that were all derived from textiles: "No ay mejor remiendo que del mismo paño." "En el mejor paño cae la raza." "Descubrir la hilaza, como mal paño" (1943, 851) (literally, "The best mend comes from the same cloth"; "Even the best cloth gets a snag"; "Spot the rough thread, as in a bad cloth"). At HILANDERA, he included "*Hilaza,* the thread that comes out thick and uneven" (690).

35. See *Recopilación de leyes de los Reynos de Indias* (1756, bk. 1, tit. 22, 1aw 57), "Sobre diferentes puntos que se han ofrecido acerca del govierno de la Universidad de Lima" (1:120r.). It was based on a royal decree by Charles II, December 10, 1678.

36. See Teodor Hampe Martínez's *Bibliotecas privadas* (1996a, app. 2, "Inventario de la biblioteca del doctor Agustín Valenciano de Quiñones [1576]," 217; app. 3, "Memoria de los libros del señor doctor Gregorio Gonçález de Cuenca, Presidente de Santo Domingo desta ysla Española (1581)," 234; app. 8, "Inventario y tasación de la biblioteca de Don Hernando Arias de Ugarte (1614)," 267). See also Hampe Martínez's *Cultura barroca* (1996b, 93).

37. The anonymous author also mentioned that there were further divisions and distinctions within these three basic estates ("De los Nobles y Nobleza," 1733, 295–311). He affirmed that inherited nobility was "of such powerful influence" that by law "for servants and even for beasts," sellers have to declare "the *casta* or *generación* from which they were produced, because of how much the price varies according to it" (307). This argument was old-hat: the archbishop of Toledo—the son of a shepherd—had codified purity for the Cathedral of Toledo, arguing that no breeder of horses would accept a horse without knowing its lineage (Sicroff 1985, 131) and no buyer of a slave could be refused a refund if he discovered that he had been deceived about the slave's *casta* (146).

38. On shameful and sordid professions or trades in medieval Western Europe, see Robert 1891; Jacques Le Goff's "Métiers" in Le Goff 1977, 91–107; and Stuart 1999. Robert Brunschvig's study of infamous professions and trades in the Islamic world complements the findings of scholars of medieval Western Europe. On the development of infamy in common law and canon law, see the excellent studies by Peters 1990 and Migliorino 1985. To become a knight, a nobleman had to possess both types of *limpieza,* as Elena Postigo Castellanos points out (1988,134–141).

39. It should be noted, however, that Ulloa and Juan contradicted the viceroy's blanket statement: "Blacks, *mulatos* and those descended from them . . . are the ones who shoulder all the work of the mechanical trades, while Europeans likewise devote themselves to them without the criticisms that impede them in Quito" (1748, 3:70–71). They explained this phenomenon by noting that the desire of Europeans in Lima was to get rich and "the fact that there are other masters in the same trade who are *mulatos* poses no obstacle to them, because self-gain is above all other considerations" (3:71). Lower-order Spaniards in Cartagena shared with their counterparts in Quito the fear of social contamination through contact with *mulatos* (1:41–44).

40. Sicroff correctly observed that purity, nobility, and *honor* were intertwined in some

treatises (1985, 346). Yet his interest lay in addressing how the purity statutes were used against Jews, or converted Jews, not in discovering the roots of the statutes and their applications beyond the Jewish community. As for America, Cahill has noted that "there were three distinct levels of nobility in Inca Cuzco, depending upon purity of lineage" (1994, 332) and claimed that "these Inca distinctions of blood were in certain measure precursors of the caste system that the Spaniards established in the Indies" (332). Clearly, my understanding of viceregal hierarchy and his are irreconcilable.

41. In this they were like the plebs in Spain, as Sousa de Macedo's statements about the nobility and the plebs reveal: "And when free will . . . [leads] them to commit crimes and be depraved, . . . they are more at fault and worthy of scorn than rustic plebs who are delinquent, because they act against the natural inclination of their blood and they abandon the custom inveterate in their elders" (1882, 231).

42. Gabriel Ramírez glossed *Política indiana* based on his personal experience with cases that had been debated and decided at the Council of Indies during the opening decades of the eighteenth century. At the conclusion of book 2, chapter 30, he observed that book 5, title 8, 1. 40 of the *Recopilación* forbid *mestizos* and *mulatos* from being *escribanos,* which contradicted Solórzano y Pereira's legal opinion. To make them agree, he argued, the prohibition should be understood as applying only to *mestizos* born out of wedlock, or *mestizo* should include *zambo* (half-Indian and half-black) within its semantic field (as *mestizo* originally did), for "these notaries are awarded to legitimate *mestizos* every day at the Chamber of Indies" (Solórzano y Pereira 1736–1739, 1:220).

43. As noted above, Twinam writes that "at some unknown point American colonists added 'mulatto' to the historical *limpieza de sangre* discrimination against 'commoner, Jew, Moor . . . [and] *converso*'" (1999, 43). Although I cannot put a precise date on this question, I am convinced that the debates summarized here are strong evidence that colonists did not dream up the inclusion of *mulatos;* it began in Spain. See Hill, "*Casta* as Culture" (2004) for a detailed and historical analysis of terms such as *mestizo* and *mulato* and how *limpieza* statutes intersected unmixed and mixed *castas.* To my knowledge, the first eighteenth-century dictionary to record the mixed *castas* accurately in viceregal Spanish America is not a Spanish dictionary; it is John Stevens's *New Spanish and English Dictionary.* See the entries for *grifo, zambo, tente en el ayre, cabra, castizo, mulato, mestizo,* and so forth (1706, n.p.). Pineda (1740) copied these entries directly from Stevens.

44. See Chapter 6 herein.

45. It, too, appears on the inventories of personal libraries from the viceregal period. See Hampe Martínez 1996a (174–75 and app. 8, "Inventario y tasación de la biblioteca de Don Hernando Arias de Ugarte [1614]," 267); 1996b (75).

46. Solórzano y Pereira referred to a specific passage in book 2, chapter 4, of Pérez de Lara's treatise. After listing the laws and glosses that support his view that the statutes that had been applied to the Christian descendants of Jews and Moors in Spain also must be applied to the Christian descendants of Africans and Indians, Pérez de Lara promised to address on another occasion whether the statutes should be applied to the descendants of Spanish noblemen who married non-Spaniards in the Indies (1767–1768, 195).

47. See Sampson Vera Tudela 2000 (chap. 5, "Cacique Nuns: From Saints' Lives to Indian Lives"). See Chapter 6 herein, where I refer to a similar institution for *cacicas* in eighteenth-century Cuzco that is mentioned in *El lazarillo de ciegos caminantes.*

48. This fluidity has marked societies other than the viceregal *sociedades de castas.* On caste mobility in India, see Berreman 1967, 66–67.

49. See Ramón 2002, 269–70. On these dramas, see Hill 2000a.

50. The title page of his *Informe histórico* bears the date 1750, but this cannot be correct. Mondragón wrote, "His Viceroy will inform His Majesty about the current apostasy and rebellion hatched this year of 1756 by Indians from this City and province of Huarochiri" (f. 325v.), and throughout the manuscript there are references to King Ferdinand VI (1746–1759).

51. See the classic study by Jeffrey Cole (1985), especially chapter 6.

52. See Armendáriz Perurena 1726.

53. On the other hand, the legal privileges held by Indians might have encouraged some of those "mixed progeny" to slide *into* the *casta* of Indians, instead of the reverse. See Chapter 6 herein, which discusses the debate over the applications of the so-called *Indian Privileges (Privilegios Indicos).*

54. "Mobility striving in a caste system, while intrinsic, is a constant threat to the status quo. As a consequence, it is suppressed whenever possible, but the process of suppression is difficult and never completely effective. Caste systems are always in disequilibrium, like pots of water on the fire, always threatening to boil over. They are characterized not by consensus but by conformity. They are maintained not by agreement but by sanctions. When change occurs it is quickly rationalized in order to maintain the system and the myth of its stability" (Berreman 1967, 67). On indigenous and *mestizo* women who used dress to move between *castas,* see Meléndez 1999, 182–85.

55. "In the 1700s," Peter Bakewell asserts, "mixed-blooded people multiplied fast almost everywhere" (2004, 273). If my analysis is correct, this statement cannot be proven or disproven, because it assumes the existence of a category (*race*) and a hierarchy (*race*-based, or modern) that did not yet exist in Spanish America, and it treats viceregal categories such as *indio, mestizo,* or *zambo* as if they were measurable, objective realities.

56. "The cultural differences and accompanying lack of consensus between groups creates the potential for emulation, acculturation, diffusion and conflict simply because different cultures are juxtaposed and inevitably impinge upon one another despite relative isolation. Caste mobility is now known to be endemic in India and needs no elaboration here, while individual or group mobility seem to be inherent in stratification systems" (Berreman 1967, 67).

CHAPTER 6

1. On the *repartimiento* in Carrió's times, see the unsurpassed study by Alfredo Moreno Cebrián, *Corregidor* (1977); see also Brenot 1989.

2. See, for example, Llano Zapata 1904, art. 20, chap. 7, 490.

3. See the first issue of 1757 and *Suplemento,* in *Gaceta de Lima* (1982–1983, 3:57, 61).

4. Another journalistic impetus for Carrió's invention of Concolorcorvo may have been

a raucous newspaper published weekly in Madrid beginning in 1767, Francisco Mariano Nipho y Cagigal's *El bufón de la Corte* (Enciso Recio 1956, 295–302). In the fourth week, Nipho jocosely claimed that because of illness he would have to step aside and let his gallant, blind, and drunk correspondent do the writing (296 n. 23). We know that blindmen sold newspapers and, according to Carrió, provided editors with their stories. Could this "simulation of substitution," as Luis Miguel Enciso Recio calls it (296 n. 23), have inspired Carrió's invention of Concolorcorvo? *El bufón de la Corte* was first published in Madrid in 1767, the same year in which Carrió took the Jesuits out of the viceroyalty. He was in Madrid in 1768. *El bufón de la Corte* was republished in Barcelona in 1775 (Enciso Recio 1956, 302), the year in which Carrió published his report.

5. "This being my Taste of Authors antient and modern, thou wilt not, gentle Reader, be surpriz'd, that when I write myself, I spin not out my Matter in Length, or that I chuse Subjects that may be kept within the narrow Bounds of a Letter: But that which determin'd me to this way of late Years, has been the Observation that I have made of the Gust of the Times. I find most Readers are of my Mind, and love not to dwell long on any thing. This gave Success to the *Tatlers,* the *Spectators,* the *Lay-Monk,* and the like, which are a Sort of Epistles to the Publick, such as I now present thee, tho' not in the same Form" (pref., xiv).

6. "HURRACA. s.f. A bird very similar to the *corneja* and the *grajo.* It is a prattler and a glutton, and it imitates the human voice like a parrot does. The word comes from the Latin *fur,* quasi *furraca* (as they used to say in the olden days), because it steals and then hides the things it finds. In Latin, *pica.*" (Real Academia Española 1979, 2:194); "CORNEJA. s.f. A female bird that is a species of crow, smaller in size than a panera crow and somewhat bigger than a graja, pitch black in color. Her beak is all black and made the same as a crow's, and at the top of it, right where it starts near her eyes, some very black whiskers grow like thick bristles, and along the bottom of them she has some black bumps like the heads of ants. In Latin, *corniz,* which is where corneja comes from. TORR. Philos[ophy], bk. 20, chap.10: 'The corneja back in those ancient myths dressed herself up in stolen feathers and, getting haughty off her borrowed beauty, she paid no mind to the others.'" (Real Academia Española 1979, 2:598); "GRAJO. s.m. A very big bird and as black as the crow. She makes her nest in tall trees and crags. She is very chatty, and her meat tastes good, but she must be skinned like a rabbit or a hare. It comes from the Latin *gracus,* which means the same thing" (Real Academia Española 1979, 2:70); "URRACA, *sf.* (Orn.) Magpie. Corvus pica *L*" (*Neuman and Baretti's Dictionary of the Spanish and English Languages* 1827, 2:690); "CORNEJA, *sf.* (Orn.) Crow. Corvus corone. *L.*" (*Neuman and Baretti's Dictionary of the Spanish and English Languages* 1827, 2:223); "GRAJO, *sm.* (Orn.) Jack-daw. Corvus monedula *L.*" (*Neuman and Baretti's Dictionary of the Spanish and English Languages* 1827, 2:384).

7. "ARRENDAJO, sm. 1. (Orn.) The mocking-bird, an American bird which imitates all the notes and sounds it hears. 2. Mimic, buffoon, a person who imitates the words and actions of others" (*Neuman and Baretti's Dictionary of the Spanish and English Languages* 1827, 1:72); "MOCKING-BIRD, MOCK-BIRD, *s.* (Orn.) Cercio, cercion" (*Neuman and Baretti's Dictionary of the Spanish and English Languages* 1827, 2:366);

"CERCIO O CERCION, *sm.* An Indian mocking-bird, belonging to the family of starlings, which imitates the human voice" (*Neuman and Baretti's Dictionary of the Spanish and English Languages* 1827, 2:172).

8. According to a tale by Luis Zapata de Chaves, there once was a magpie that could imitate human speech. "These birds, they call *picazas* in the wild, and *hurracas* if they are caged, like the Ancients [called] their false goddess *Minerva* in the sciences, and *Pallas* in battles, and it is also called *pega,* although this name is more Portuguese than Castilian" (1999, 148).

9. Julie Greer Johnson correctly generalizes the relationship between *El criticón* and *El lazarillo de ciegos caminantes:* "*El criticón* is particularly indicative of the character types and their relationship found in *El lazarillo,* as Gracián's literary figures, the sophisticated Critilo and the naive Andrenio, share their opinions as they travel throughout various European countries" (1993, 113). On the surveillance function of the raven, see also Meléndez 1999, 87.

10. Works by Ovid are mentioned repeatedly in Agustín de la Cagiga y Rada's description of the funeral exercises for José de Pardo Figueroa's wife in Guatemala. *Metamorphoses* is cited explicitly five times and quoted ten more times. He even writes of "the most pointed Poet Ovid . . . painting the majestic Sun Chariot" (1739, n.p.).

11. Francisco del Castillo, "Romance 10" (in *Obra completa,* 1996, 905–12).

12. Ripa, at *Imaginatione:* "Woman dressed in various colors, she will have her hair unkempt and, at her temples, a pair of wings similar to those of Mercury, and a crown of diverse figurines in *chiaroscuro,* she will have her eyes fixed on high, completely absorbed in thought, and she will have one hand on top of the other in the air" (1669, 271).

13. In Gracián's *Oráculo manual,* he distinguished between seeing events and relying on the testimony of others, singling out the colors, or passions, of the imagination (1984, 168).

14. In "The politicians' guild opens a shop on Parnassus in which diverse goods useful to the virtuous life of the *literati* are sold," feather brushes are for sale, which are useful to princes and flatterers who paint things out to be different from what they really are, trading in appearances: "In the same shop there are also sold a very great amount of feather brushes, most excellent for those princes who on pressing occasions are forced to paint black as white for the common folk; and although this is merchandise only for princes, those treacherous men who, being in the business of appearances, attend to nothing more than the infamous profession of laughing, deceiving and containing the simple mob with beautiful words and ugly deeds, also supply themselves with them" (Boccalini 1910–1948, 1:10).

15. As Emanuele Tesauro noted in his treatment of metaphors of proportion, "like color in paintings, and especially on the face of *Women,* gives them a *feigned appearance* [*simulata apparenza*], every *Simulation* is called *color*" (1968, 312).

16. See note 26.

17. See Feijoo y Montenegro's abridged translation of St. Aubin's *Treatise on Opinion,* which quotes Pierre Bayle as saying that history is cooked up almost like meals in the kitchen and that all peoples use the same ingredients but each dresses them differently, according to their particular taste (and prejudices) (1773–1774, 4:228 n. 29).

18. "This breed of people think themselves more alert and more clever than the European, . . . believing that there are not peoples who can be as knowledgeable as they are. This presumption is the child of malice and self-love, and also of their [limited] capacity; and when one confronts them in any of the many scams that they think up, they say that the Spaniards, or *Viracochas,* now pretend to know as much as they do. . . . When those who live freely among European peoples give their *monologues,* they give some—in their view—majestic speeches, but without order or method, talking in figures and comparisons that usually are based in the sun, because of its light, because of its heat and because of the orbit it follows, and this they accompany with actions and demonstrative signs. They are long-winded in their speeches, repeating the same thing many times, and they would go on all day without adding anything to what they said at the beginning if one did not manage to cut them off. They think a lot about what they are going to say, and in the end they do not produce more than what seems suited to convince others to give them what they want. In this sort of peroration with presumption they ground their science and the craftiness in which they surpass the other, European persons with whom they deal, believing that with their great eloquence they induce them to hand over what they want. The reservation Indians are the same in their speeches—long-winded, tiring and inopportune in the extreme, knowing no limits—so they are not any different from the others; and if the language were not different, one could believe that an Indian from Peru was speaking in the North, or vice versa" (Ulloa 1772, 281–83).

19. Some of these parallels are discussed briefly in Hill 1996b.

20. Evaristo de Souza Penha argues that, structurally, the inspector in Carrió's account is the equivalent of Cide Hamete in *Don Quijote de la Mancha;* Concolorcorvo is the equivalent of the narrator (what I call the implicit author) of Cervantes's novel (1978, 195). He does not discuss the similarities between the implicit author's prologue in *Don Quijote de la Mancha* and Concolorcorvo's prologue in *El lazarillo de ciegos caminantes,* which complicate his neat division between structure and content. I do not agree that the inspector (the structural equivalent of Cervantes's Cide Hamete) is responsible for all of the "assertive content"; similarly, the implicit author of *Don Quijote* (the structural equivalent of Concolorcorvo, according to Souza Penha) does not assign responsibility for all of the assertive content to Cide Hamete. Indeed, on numerous occasions Concolorcorvo reports that the inspector tells him to stop writing, which suggests to me that Concolorcorvo does not claim sole responsibility for the "definitive version" of the report or leave the "assertive content" entirely to the inspector, as Souza Penha asserts (195). Earlier in his study he admits as much: "It is impossible to mark where Concolorcorvo's diary begins and the extracts from the inspector's memoirs end" (106).

21. Ignacio de Luzán's discussion of jocose discourse (1991, 159–75) noted that the educated appreciated the intercalation of a celebrated author's verse, verbatim or altered, and that Gracián was adept at this, appropriating Ovid's fables for his own purposes (168–69).

22. In his sixteenth-century manuscript published as *Libro de chistes,* Luis de Pinedo included a joke in which "dog" (*perro*) and "greyhound" (*galgo*) are associated with a Moor (1964, 107). In *Vida de Miguel de Cervantes Saavedra* (in *Obras* 2:213–312), Gre-

gorio de Mayans y Siscar claimed that Cervantes had attributed his novel to an Arab because chivalric romances began to be written in Spain while the Moors were still there (1983, 236).

23. In Gonzalo Cano Señeo, "Redondillas," part of a manuscripted *Cancionero* owned by Judge Juan de Solórzano y Pereira, a procession by a black brotherhood is satirized, and hidalgo (*hijo de algo*) becomes higalgo (*hijo de galgo*). See *Cancionero peruano* 1983, 125–27. Raquel Chang-Rodriguez, who prepared the *Cancionero* for publication, writes that the poems were written between 1607 and 1626. In Juan de Valle y Caviedes's "Al casamiento de Pedro de Utrilla" (in *Obra completa* 1984, 141–42), *galgo, perro* and their variants are related to both the *zambo* surgeon Pedro de Utrilla and the *mulata* with whom he is having children.

24. "PERRO. Metaphorically, this name is used as an insult, affront or disparagement, especially against Moors and Jews. In Latin, *canis*" (Real Academia Española 1979, 3:232). Blacks in Spanish America enslaved indigenous people and called them dogs, according to Bartolomé de las Casas (Esteva Fabregat 1995, 176).

25. A similar, though abbreviated, tale appeared in Melchor de Santa Cruz's *Floresta española*: "A one-eyed gentleman was serving a very brown lady, who called him short-sighted. He replied, 'Don't act like a crow, which goes straight for the eye'" (1997, 228). Not only Northern Africans but also Northern Africa in general was imagined to be volatile and capable of ferocity. In the late seventeenth century, the Spanish geographer and military officer Sebastián Fernández de Medrano warned travelers to the abandoned regions of Higher Ethiopia to travel in groups or run the risk of being torn apart by beasts or of falling into the hands of legions of thieves (1686, 234). See also the animals adorning Aurelio degli Anzi's map (Figure 20).

26. The opposition between goose feather and swan feather, Covarrubias observed, had been consecrated in Virgil's *Ninth Eclogue* (Covarrubias 1994, 579). Carrió altered the opposition to further ridicule Concolorcorvo. Later in *El lazarillo de ciegos caminantes*, however, the inspector criticizes Concolorcorvo by preserving Virgil's opposition unaltered (441–42).

27. James H. Sweet (1997) argues that the Spaniards' belief in Ham's curse justified slavery. However, Benjamin Braude (1997) has shown that this notion was not widely accepted until the French embraced it in the nineteenth century. Moreover, Spaniards did not uniformly adopt Ham's curse as a corollary of the settlement of Africa by Ham, this particular settlement theory being one of several that Spaniards entertained. Ivan Hannaford (1996) summarizes the history of Ham's curse. Father Feijoo y Montenegro wholly rejected the notion that blacks were shouldering Ham's curse (Aldridge 1973, 265–66), as did Father José Gumilla, humanist and author of *El Orinoco ilustrado* (*The River Orinoco Illustrated*) (1944, 87–103).

28. Torquemada 1615, 2:bk. 11, chap. 8, and bk. 14, chap. 19; Núñez de la Vega 1702, 9–10. Also see Solórzano y Pereira's critical review of settlement theories (1:19).

29. See Solórzano y Pereira 1:18; Gregorio García 1607, *passim*; Braude 1997, 105. On the theories about the origins of the Indians, see Antonello Gerbi's seminal study (1955).

30. Fernández de Medrano applied *alarbes* ("Arabs") and *adarves de Moros* to Indians, not blacks, in the New World (specifically, to the Indians in New France, which for him included Virginia, New England, New Holland, and Canada). Clearly, these were un-

deniably cultural markers, for he also used them to describe Swedes (1686, III–12, 260).

31. See the Introduction to this study, which situates Carrió's biting remarks on thievery in a historical context.

32. After Covarrubias's definition of DAR, Benito Remigio Noydens conflated Egyptian (*egipcio*) and gypsy (*gitano*) (Covarrubias 1943, 443). Pedro Pineda recorded this entry: "*Gitano,* s.m. a Gipsey or an *Egyptian*" (1740, n.p.).

33. Fernández de Medrano wrote, "The *Mauritania Tingitana* is that which borders on the Atlantic Ocean, [and] includes the Kingdoms of Morocco and Fez" (1686, 217–18).

34. Pineda recorded this: "*Gitanería,* s.f. a cheating Trick, and particularly in Horse-Flesh, because the Gipsies are great Jockies, and consequently great Cheats in that Kind" (1740, n.p.). The inhabitants of Northern Africa were known for their prized horses, and it was widely believed that they were deceitful, thieving, and always on the move. Giambattista Della Porta wrote, "Arabs are thieves, of duplicitous spirit, fraudulent, of servile spirit, unstable and desirous of gain" (1637, 112).

35. See Bueno 1996. N. Ivette Malverde Disselkoen argues that the secretary's wit here indicates the Crown's attempt to use the church to control the sexuality of indigenous women (1992, 132). Yet the inspector's complaints about the decline in the indigenous population suggest that there were no efforts in the Viceroyalty of Peru to control Indian women's sexuality or the unbridled sexuality of non-Indian men who consorted with Indian women.

36. The cultural distinction that is being made in Spanish is important enough that I provide here Olabarrieta's text, along with the eighteenth-century definitions that I used to translate it: "es licito el uso de todos los privilegios Indicos aun a los Indios ya tresnados [*sic*] y ladinos, que viven entre los Españoles; pues el ser estos tales Indios mas capazes que los demas Indios montarazes y chontales, no les debe perjudicar a su derecho ni hazerlos de peor condicion, para gozar de los privilegios que gozan los Indios incapazes o los Neofitos mas rigorosos" (1717, art. 143, 95). "MONTARAZ. adj. . . . What roams, or is made to roam, the mountains, or has been reared in them" (Real Academia Española 1979, 2:600). "CHOTUNO, NA. adj. that Shepherds apply to thin, sickly and lifeless lambs"; "CHOTUNO. By extension it means the smell of dirt, which seems akin to that of a sick lamb or goat" (1:332).

37. When it came to blacks, it is worth noting, Olabarrieta claimed that they enjoyed the same privileges and dispensations as Indians, according to many authorities and his own interpretation of Urban the Eighth's bull (1717, art. 112, 72). He claimed that although blacks, like Indians, could legally work on religious holidays, they *chose* to observe the same holidays as Spaniards. They simply preferred a day of rest and could at any time claim the privilege of working on religious holidays, just as they could claim any of the other Indian Privileges (art. 112, 72). Further, he claimed that, according to the same papal bull's usage of *mixtim progenitis, mulatos* enjoyed the same privileges as *mestizos* (art. 113, 73).

38. Mariselle Melendez writes that "Concolorcorvo is represented as the epitome of the colonial subject who is capable of adopting different positions and ethnic identities due to his subtle manipulation of the system" (1999, 79). However, "the system," or social hierarchy, itself entailed mobility, as we saw in Chapter 5.

39. Walter Bose's analysis of the letter is summarized by José J. Real Díaz (1956, 19 and n. 53).

40. On the similarities between *El lazarillo de ciegos caminantes* and *The Pleasant Art of Money-Catching, Newly and Fully Discovered,* the sequel to *The Compleat Tradesman,* see the Introduction herein.

41. Sweet's tying of the Hispanic light/dark contrast to racial preference and prejudice flies in the face of structuralist anthropology. As Marshall Sahlins reconfirmed in 1977, quoting the findings of Radcliffe-Brown from the 1920s, "The association of light and dark with euphoric and dysphoric conditions respectively has a psychological basis, for it seems to be universal in human nature" (qtd. in Sahlins 1977, 179 n. 5).

42. I do not disagree with scholars who argue that the textual inspector undercuts Concolorcorvo's authority by deforming his name in the narration. See Stolley 1993, 163; Meléndez 1999, 86–87. However, I view Carrió's rhetorical manuevers in *El lazarillo de ciegos caminantes* within a different framework and his invention of Concolorcorvo in particular as circumscribed by the legal and social distinctions and contradictions inherent in Lima's social hierarchy.

43. Ann Twinam traces the legal inclusion of legitimacy within the concept of blood purity to 1411 (1999, 45), which pre-dates the Toledo Statute, uniformly assumed to be the first blood purity statute. However, she does not pursue the implications of her discovery: the links between the codification of infamy beginning in the twelfth century and the codification of *limpieza* (*de sangre* and *de oficio*) in the fifteenth.

44. See Hill 2000a and 2004. On illegitimacy in viceregal Spanish America, see the excellent studies by María Emma Mannarelli (1999), Twinam (1999), and Guiomar Dueñas Vargas (1997). Also see Seed 1988.

45. See, for example, Meléndez 1999, 29–33. Antonio Cornejo Polar (1997) warned Hispanists about the slippery metaphor of hybridity in cultural studies. I detail the nomenclature of Spanish American mixture and its genesis in Spain in "*Casta* as Culture," which I wrote for the American Society for Eighteenth Century Studies International Seminar at UCLA in June 2000. Some of the ideas and sources that I present in this section appear, in a primitive version, in that essay (2004). Caro Baroja 1965 established some of the similarities between people of mixed faith in Spain and people who belonged to the mixed *castas* in Spanish America.

46. One of the most popular treatises on alchemy, Della Porta's 1558 *Natural Magick* (*Magia Naturalis*), devoted an entire book to the breeding of different types of dogs, hogs, mules, birds, and other animals (1959, especially bk. 2, chaps. 5 to 9). Physiognomy, which deduced an individual human's moral and intellectual aptitudes from the animal that resembled him or her (as in Della Porta's treatises on physiognomy) was extremely popular in the Hispanic world until the nineteenth century. The materials were plagiarized and included in treatises on husbandry, almanacs, astronomy, and so forth. See Hill, "*Casta* as Culture" (2004). On physiognomy in eighteenth-century Spain, see Haidt 1998.

47. "*BASTARDO*. What is coarse and made without order, reason or rule. . . . And bastard [is] the person born of an unlawful coupling [*ayuntamiento ilegítimo*]. Bastardy [*Bastardía*] [is] descent from such a coupling. And it is said also of birds and animals when they are engendered by [parents] of two different species or breeds [*dos diferentes*

especies o raleas], and because [bastards] such as these degenerate from their nature, in Greek they are called *nothos*, . . . [meaning] *degeneratio* [in Latin], and by another name . . . , *lathremaeos*, [meaning] ones made in the dark and in corners. . . . They are also called *bordes*, from the Latin noun *burdus*, the offspring of a mare and an ass" (Covarrubias 1943, 199). This understanding of degeneration was not exclusively Spanish. Stuart C. Gilman's "Political Theory and Degeneration" (1985) culls examples of "degenerate" and "degeneracy" from seventeenth-century English texts and concludes that degeneracy was not biologically based—that is, it was not *racial* in the nineteenth-century sense.

48. Scott Atran (1990) firmly established the importance of folk, or popular, taxonomies to European botanists in the sixteenth and seventeeth centuries, and I am persuaded that future investigations will uncover links between husbandry and hierarchy in the pre-nineteenth-century Hispanic world. Henry Lowood makes it very clear that Atran's discoveries can significantly alter the way the development of natural history and science are traditionally analyzed: "Atran's important contribution is the notion that systematic taxonomy grew gradually out of local discoveries followed by the comparison and integration of empirical data. In other words, he recasts the usual opposition of folk knowledge and system, concluding that the goal of an overarching 'worldwide system' rose out of efforts to express local material more or less uniformly for the purposes of comparison and identification" (1995, 298).

49. In his *Natural History,* Pliny noted that the breeding of a jackass and a donkey produced a mule. When they were little, the jackass and the hinny were placed in the dark (*in tenebris*), and each babe would drink the milk of the other species so that they would not reject each other when they reached the breeding stage (1940, bk. 8, 82–83). This calls to mind Covarrubias's phrase, "ones made in the dark," with which he explained how *bastard* (*borde*) was derived from a Latin term for mule (*burdus*). Shortly after he explained how different breeds of mules were generated, Pliny claimed that all animals that were products of two diffferent species resembled neither their father nor their mother, and they were usually sterile. Covarrubias, as I have shown, understood that animals and birds that were engendered by animals of different species were degenerate with respect to their progenitors. It is this discussion of mules in Pliny, I am convinced, that Judge Solórzano y Pereira mentions in his discussion of mulattos: "And *mulatos,* though for the same reason also fall under the general name of *Mestizos,* were [*sic*] given this [name] in particular when they are the children of a Black woman and a white man, or vice versa, because this mixing is considered uglier and more unusual, and to make it understood that with such a name they compare it to the nature of the mule, as Don Sebastián de Covarrubias noted appropriately, about whose breeding and mixtures and differences what Pliny offers is worth reading" (217).

50. This definition allows us to see the conceptual breadth of mixture in Nebrija's times, and it also sheds light on the hierarchical implications of mixture in the eighteenth-century Spanish world. The merchants' guild in Cádiz argued time and time again that only "old Spaniards," or Spaniards without "mixture of foreignness" (*mezcla de extranjería*), could become members. The pretenders were *jenízaros*—first- or second-generation Spaniards, or Spaniards who had a parent who was not born in Spain.

In 1742 the president of the house of trade in Cádiz wrote the fiscal of the Council of Indies that *jenízaros* should not feel unduly excluded, since different privileges and inequalities existed among "old Spaniards" themselves. For example, everyone accepted the fact that not all "old Spaniards" could join military orders, which admitted only nobles (García-Mauriño 1999, 88).

51. Like *hibrida* and *bastardo, vario* was associated with a lack of order or a lack of adherence to natural or moral rules in the Spanish world, before and after Columbus. These entries from Nebrija's *Diccionario Latino-Español* substantiate the first half of my claim: "Varius.a.um. por cosa diversa en color" (1979, n.p.); "Varius.a.um. por cosa desvariada" (n.p.). Moreover, *vario* is similar to *remendado* and *quebrado,* both of which connotated inferior quality in beasts, according to Herrera 1970, 286, 290, 333. In Oudin's *Trésor* I find a definition of "broken" that recalls the metaphorical usage of *raza* in the religious and occupational purity constitutions, and in the works of Salucio and Solórzano y Pereira, it's "broken in color": "Quebrado de color, *blesme, decoloré, défait*" (1607, n.p.).

52. "The like is experienced in Swine: for we may bring forth *Of a wild and tame Swine, the beast called Hybrides,* For a Boar is exceeding hot in lust, and wonderfully desires coition; insomuch that if the female refuse to couple with him, either he will force her or kill her. And surely howsoever, some wilde beasts being made tame are thereby unfit for generation, as a Goose, a Hart brought up by hand from his birth; and a Boar is hardly fruitfull in such a case: yet there is no kind so apt for generation, the one being wilde and the other tame, as the kind of Swine is. And those which are thus gendred, these half-wilds, are called Hybrides, happily because they are generated in reproachful adultery: for *Hybris* signifies reproach" (Della Porta 1959, bk. 2, chap. 10, 40). Pliny observed that all domestic animals had savage counterparts, just as there were savage breeds of men. Swine were the easiest animals to cross breed—that is, to join a domestic and a wild breed—and crossbred offspring were called *hybrides,* or half-wilds, a denomination thereafter applied to men, for example, one of Cicero's colleagues in the consulate (1940, bk. 8, 98).

53. "BORDE. Sometimes means the son born to an illegitimate woman [*mujer no legítima*] and more often a woman who has had a horrible reputation because she has been with many men [*la que ha tenido ruin fama por aver sido común a muchos*]. The noun is French from *bordeau,* which we call *burdel;* it means what *lustrum, seu lupanar,* means in Latin, but its original etymology is from the Latin noun *burdo, burdonis,* meaning the animal [that is the] offspring of a horse and a she-ass, which is the mule" (Covarrubias 1943, 229).

54. At his entry for ANA, Covarrubias supported the orthodox exegesis of Genesis, chapter 6 and chapter 36, which compares the birth of mules to that of giants and attributes the birth of giants to the mixture of two *castas:* the "religious" sons of Seth and the "carnal" daughters of Cain (1943, 114–15).

55. "However, . . . the most common thing is that they are born from adultery or from other unlawful and punishable couplings [*ilícitos y punibles ayuntamientos*], for there are few Spaniards of good name [*de honra*] who will marry Indians or Black women, which defect in the newborns makes them shamed [*infames*], at least de facto shamed [*por lo menos infamia facti*], according to the weightiest and most common opinion

of grave authorities, [and] on top of it [i.e., this defect] falls the stain [*la mancha*] of mixed color [*color vario*] and other vices that usually are like innate and suckled in the breast milk. In these men I find that by many other decrees they are not allowed to enter any positions of authority and in the republic, even if they are guardianships, administrations or clerkships, without first declaring this defect when they applied [*sic*] for them and unless they are specifically exempted [*particularmente dispensados*] in them, and those that have got their jobs in some other fashion shall be stripped of their Titles" (218). To claim, then, as Emilio Carilla does, that Carrió shared Judge Solórzano y Pereira's negative opinion of *mestizos* (Carrió 116 n. 35) is to ignore the complexity of hierarchy in Bourbon Spanish America and Solórzano y Pereira's articulation of hybridity.

56. Covarrubias noted that the Egyptians had compared adulators to crows, and he lamented that a five-string guitar in the hands of a fool had more influence on princes than did all of the seven liberal arts contained in the mind of a prudent man (1994, 381).

57. Similar tales were told about the *corneja*, a type of crow, and Minerva, goddess of wisdom. In Vicenzo Cartari's emblem of the god of Silence, he noted, "Thus remaining silent at the right time is a virtue, as Minerva demonstrated by caging the crow [*cornacchia* is *corneja* in Spanish], a garrulous and loquacious bird, because it is not for the prudent man to waste time on a lot of vain words, but rather, by remaining silent, he will consider things very carefully before he gives an opinion about them and later say only that which is necessary" (1626, 311). In *El discreto*, Gracián followed Horace's tale of the trick that a *corneja* played on some birds that were choosing a king: she stole their feathers and afterward was picked clean of the borrowed feathers and her own ("Hombre de ostentación," 1997, 260 and n. 227). The story also appeared in Phaedrus, in St. Jerome, and in Desiderius Erasmus's *Praise of Folly* (1979, 11–12 and n. 6). In England, this tale informed the image of the False-Galloper, in the second part of *The Compleat Tradesman* attributed to Daniel Defoe: "And thus with the Feathers of other Birds is this Monster stuck, making wings of sundry fashions, with which he thus basely flies over a whole Kingdom" (Merchant 1684a; see the Introduction herein).

58. Moreover, Carrió's borrowings from Ovid, which are employed by Concolorcorvo, perhaps call into question the truthfulness of the Inca Garcilaso's two-part chronicle of Peru. Perhaps he grasped what Carrió and Garcilaso scholars alike have ignored: the imprint of Ovid's *Metamorphoses* on Garcilaso's *Comentarios reales de los Incas* (1943), of his *Tristium* on the Inca's *Historia general del Perú* (Part II of *Comentarios reales*).

59. See Luis J. Ramos Gómez in Ulloa and Juan 1985, 376, on the unnamed sources of their work. On Friar Calixto's activities, see Rubén Vargas Ugarte in Castillo 1948, 51 n. 2. On the rebellion in Jauja Valley, see Bueno's "Descripción de Tarma" (1764) in *Geografía* (1951, 46–47) and "Catálogo histórico de los Virreyes, Gobernadores, Presidentes y Capitanes Generales del Perú, con los sucesos más principales de sus tiempos" (1763) in *Geografía* (1951, 139). Souza Penha discusses several indigenous rebellions (1978, 48–54), and Klien-Samanez details Tupac Inga's missionary efforts in Guatemala that began in late 1744 and extended into 1746 (2000, 143–44).

60. "Conversación de un negro, mayordomo de chacra, con un Indio, alcalde de los Ca-
    maroneros, en la calle de los Borricos" in *Obras* (1948, 51).

61. Souza Penha quotes this passage and states that Carrió wished to correct the Crown's
    error of recognizing doubtful descendants of the Incas. He also claims that it was "less
    dangerous to ridicule Juan Bustamante Carlos Inca's nephew," which Calixto claimed
    to be (1978, 79).

62. Alfredo Moreno Cebrián lists these men as Pedro Bravo del Ribero, Pedro Bravo de
    Castilla, Manuel de Gorena y Beyria, Manuel Isidoro de Mirones y Benavente, and
    the *fiscal* Diego Holgado de Guzmán (1977, 314).

63. "With the excessive and extraordinary expenditures that he has suspended in various
    obligations pertaining to His Majesty's Service, the Kingdom has not been burdened;
    as a matter of fact, he has banished the impositions that were squeezing trade, on the
    grounds that they were contrary to public welfare: now a more just and exact distri-
    bution is noticeable, whereas before even the payment of ordinary taxes was not on
    schedule. Justice, which demands recognition and praise (and in which hyperbole has
    no role whatsoever), suspended my feather pen in this short digression" (Feijoo de
    Sosa 1984, 1:37). On Feijoo de Sosa's report, see Hill 1996a, *passim*.

64. See the May–July 1765 issue of *Gaceta de Lima* (1982–1983, 3:226). As noted earlier, his
    brother Francisco was Viceroy Manso de Velasco's secretary before he assumed numer-
    ous positions with the cathedral and Inquisition in Lima and became bishop of Santa
    Cruz de la Sierra in 1764.

65. Moreno Cebrián 1977 details Feijoo de Sosa's report and Carrió's opinions as expressed
    in *El lazarillo de ciegos caminantes*. Also see Hill 1996b.

66. According to Jesuit Father Mario Cicala, the educated Indians of Quito could out-
    smart the smartest European. It was patently false that the arguments and replies of
    the Indians were ridiculous and foolish: "I am just telling you: let the sharpest and
    swiftest European go there and see if he can swindle and con a single Indian (I am
    talking about the civilized and schooled Indians, in the city and country, throughout
    the Province), let him use every single one of his cleverest ploys and schemes to trip
    the Indian up, but you can be sure he will never manage to trick him. An Indian will
    throw out so many arguments, so many answers, all of them spot-on, he will handle
    himself and find his way out of difficult situations in such a way that he will not be
    swindled or convinced, and it is even harder to fool an Indian woman. And do not
    believe that an Indian's arguments and answers are all nonsense, just blowing smoke
    and being silly. They most certainly are not; rather, they are all plotted out well, linked
    together well and articulated well. I will just cite the case of the two *caciques* . . . who,
    in the weightiest of litigations, had the shrewdest and most famous of lawyers, as
    well as the judges, with their backs to the wall, as they presented their arguments
    "*non in scriptis,*" [as they said], but, rather, "*verbaliter,*" confounding the lawyers and
    judges so much that they compelled [the latter] to overturn their decisions, and every-
    body would tremble wherever they showed up to try a case" (1994, 211–12). Meléndez
    points out Carrió's opinion that the Indians were nobody's fools: many spoke *aymará*
    or *quechua* in public, when they were among Spanish speakers but Spanish at home
    (1999, 42 and n. 8). This is similar to Concolorcorvo's ploy to convince the inspector
    that his Spanish is lacking because he is a full-blooded Indian.

67. On the corruption of provincial governors, see Chapter 4 herein.

68. In 1779, however, Bravo del Ribero was still working for the Crown—at the royal tobacco monopoly where Feijoo de Sosa had served first as comptroller (1763) and then as director (1764–1775). See Bueno's "Guía de forasteros de Lima Año 1779" in *Geografía* (1951).

69. In 1768, King Charles III issued a decree ordering Amat to have *Fiscal* Holgado come up with ideas about how to get the provincial governors to submit prompt accounting records of the tributes collected in their districts (Moreno Cebrián 1977, 254). Holgado retired and returned that year to Spain. However, in 1770 Feijoo de Sosa, still chief accountant on the royal treasury court, lodged charges against him with the Council of the Indies. Holgado was absolved of wrongdoing in 1771 (Moreno Cebrián 1977, 506).

70. See Chapter 4 herein for Amat's complaints about governors and judges on the high court in Lima.

CHAPTER 7

1. See the discussion of previous solutions to the 4Ps from Lima riddle in Chapters 1 and 2 herein.

2. See Tomás de Cuevas Garcés de los Fallos's 1748 collection of occasional poems and addresses read in Mexico City to celebrate the crowning of Ferdinand VI, whose very title calls the University in Mexico "the Athens of the New World" (*la Imperial y Pontífica Universida Mexicana, Athenas del Nuevo Mundo*). Pedro de Peralta Barnuevo glorified Athens and then claimed that the Sages (los *Sabios*) had moved their Academy to Lima (1736, ff. 89, 97). Later, in the fifth section titled "Cartel del Certamen," he announced that the "Liman Athens" was calling on "the spirits of the River Rimac" who had "a Muse in every Feather pen" (f. 116).

3. A trademark of jocose discourse is the feigned gravity of the Spaniard from Guatemala. According to Ignacio de Luzán, these witty remarks made a conversation urbane. They were ridiculous because, as Marcus Fabius Quintilian knew, the more serious the speaker's bearing, the funnier the jokes (1991, 162).

4. Antonio Fernández Insuela asserts that the playful discourse exemplified by witty tales (or "bulls"), jokes, funny sayings, and the like, constituted "realidad popular" (1990, 851). For me, such discourse was not "popular reality" but part of *urbanity*, the learned man's repertoire before the model of the learned man was altered in the eighteenth century. See the Introduction and Chapter 2 herein.

5. These were "enigmatic deliberations" ("ponderaciones misteriosas") (Gracián 1998, 170), most of them written in verse, like the highbrow riddles published in Enlightenment newspapers and literary magazines. They were neither laughable challenges or *burlas* such as Carrió's riddle and witty anecdote nor problems like those posed by Virgil and José Pardo de Figueroa. In "On the Similarities That Are Based in a Riddle or Correction" ("De las Semejancas que se fundan en Misterio o Reparo") (184–86), there is nothing to suggest his interest in humor. Similarly, in "On the Acuity of Correction" ("De la Agudeza de Reparo"), he deals with corrections, or retorts, but again there is nothing playful or hilarious there (174–79).

6. See Maxime Chevalier's superb note to Melchor de Santa Cruz's tale in Santa Cruz 1997, 470–71. I owe this reference to Emilio Blanco in Gracián 1998, 328 n. 15.

7. On both works and the tale in each, see Fernández Insuela 1990, *passim*. I do not believe that this Pascual tale in either version fits the life trajectory of Carrió, as Fernández Insuela asserts (853). However, I share his view that Carrió was familiar with such tales.

8. His apologist, Martín Sarmiento, complained about the shoddy work that deceptive binders in Holland covered over with colored paper, explaining that the cause was the impurity or dishonor (*vileza*) associated with their lowly profession ("oficio mecánico, servil y vil") and that their shameful conduct spelled the ruin of the Republic of Letters (Antonio Valladares de Sotomayor in Sarmiento 1789, 20:229–99, at 267).

9. Emilio Carilla has pointed out that this joke was popular in Spain (in Carrió 461 n. 34).

10. "In negotiations, it is very helpful to mix sweetness with gravity and jests with earnest matters, as long as they are timely and do not offend propriety or the gravity of the matter at hand. . . . No one can stand a melancholy austerity, always up to his eyeballs in work, weighing every word and measuring every move. It is [the mark] of great prudence to inject some foolishness into proceedings at the right time, and then non-sense is [actually] wisdom. The playfulness of wit and a mot at the right time tends to win people over and to channel even the most unpleasant business to the desired end, and it sometimes can conceal true intentions, frustrate malice, soften a blow, and get one out of a serious reply in matters where it is not advisable" (1999, emblem 42, 518–23, at 522).

11. This sort of witticism was characteristic of "acute," or witty, discourse in the Spanish world since the Middle Ages, and it was recommended in Boscán's translation, *Los cuatro libros de El cortesano:* "There is also another sort of saying [*dicho*] that we commonly call *deriving,* and this consists in changing or subtracting or adding a letter or syllable" (Castiglione 1994, 289).

12. It is important to me, for a third reason: it undermines the common notion that the Latin American Enlightenment was some sort of retarded, or staggered, version of the Spanish Enlightenment. On this, see Hill 2000b, introd. In a marginal note, Bravo de Lagunas y Castilla placed the French announcement of the Parisian aca-demic trial, which was to be held on August 29, 1753, at 3:00 P.M., and it is likely that the announcement had originally appeared in *Memoires de Trévoux.* This leads me to believe that it took longer for erudites in Paris to react to events in the New World than for Peruvian elites to digest Old World news: nearly seven years separated the Pe-ruvian disaster and the Parisian mock trial, whereas roughly eleven months separated the June 1754 issue of *Memoires de Trévoux* and the Peruvian jurist's *Voto consultivo.*

13. Carilla has correctly identified this passage from *El criticón* (Carrió 427), but he does not acknowledge the parallel that Carrió draws between the infamous slanderer and his unnamed detractor, probably Miguel Feijoo de Sosa.

Bibliography

Adorno, Rolena. 1993. "Reconsidering Colonial Discourse for Sixteenth- and Seventeenth-Century Spanish America." *Latin American Research Review* 28.3:135–45.

Agüeros de la Portilla, Agustín. 1911. "El periodismo en México durante la dominación española." *Anales del Museo Nacional de Arqueología, Historia y Etnología* 2.9 (April): 385–465.

Aguilar Piñal, Francisco. 1978. *La prensa española en el siglo XVIII: Diarios, revistas y pronósticos.* Madrid: CSIC.

_____. 1984. *La biblioteca de Jovellanos (1778).* Madrid: CSIC–Instituto "Miguel de Cervantes."

Aguirre Beltrán, Gonzalo. 1984. *La población negra de México: Estudio etnohistórico.* Mexico City: Fondo de Cultura Económica.

Alcedo, Antonio de. 1967. *Diccionario geográfico de las Indias Occidentales o América.* Ed. and prol. Ciriaco Pérez-Bustamante. 4 vols. Madrid: Atlas.

Alcedo y Herrera, Dionisio de. 1726? *Memorial informativo que pusieron en las reales manos del Rey Nuestro Señor (que Dios guarde) el Tribunal del Consulado de la Ciudad de los Reyes y la Junta General del Comercio de las provincias del Perú, sobre diferentes puntos tocantes al estado de la Real Hacienda y del Comercio, justificando las causas de su descaecimiento y pidiendo todas las providencias que convienen para restablecer en su mayor aumento el Real Patrimonio y en su antigua comunicacion y prosperidad los Comercios de España y de las Indias.* Lima: Consulado del Comercio.

_____. 1915. *Descripción geográfica de la Real Audiencia de Quito.* Prol. and ed. C. A. González Palencia. New York: Hispanic Society of America.

Aldridge, A. Owen. 1973. "Feijoo and the Problem of Ethiopian Color." In *Racism in the Eighteenth Century,* ed. Harold E. Pagliaro, 263–77. Vol. 3 of *Studies in Eighteenth-Century Culture.* Cleveland: Case Western Reserve University Press.

Alfonso XI. 1983. *Libro de la Montería.* Ed. Dennis P. Seniff. Madison, Wis.: Hispanic Seminary of Medieval Studies.

Alloza, Juan de. 1666. *Flores Summarum, seu Alphabetum morale.* 3rd ed. Lyons, France: H. Boissat and G. Remeus.

Alonso, Martín. 1986. *Diccionario medieval español: Desde las Glosas Emilianenses y Silenses (s. X) hasta el siglo XV.* 2 vols. Salamanca, Spain: Universidad Pontifica de Salamanca

Amat y Junient, Manuel de. 1942. "El Virrey Amat da cuenta al Rey de los defectos y vicios de organización del Virreinato del Perú—1762." *Revista de la Biblioteca Nacional* 24:345–50.

_____. 1947. *Memoria de gobierno.* Ed. Vicente Rodríguez Casado and Florention Pérez Embid. Seville, Spain: Escuela de Estudios Hispano-Americanos.

Anderson, Benedict. 1983. *Imagined Communities: Reflections on the Origin and Spread of Nationalism.* London: Verso.

Anderson, Rodney D. 1988. "Race and Social Stratification: A Comparison of Working-Class Spaniards, Indians and Castas in Guadalajara, Mexico in 1821." *Hispanic American Historical Review* 68.2:209–43.

Andrien, Kenneth J. 1995. *The Kingdom of Quito, 1690–1830: The State and Regional Development.* New York: Cambridge University Press.

Anonymous. 1711. *The English Chapman's and Traveller's Almanack for the Year of Christ, 1711, Wherein All the Post-Roads, . . . the Marts, Fairs and Markets in England and Wales Are Alphabetically Disposed in Every Month.* London: Company of Stationers.

Anonymous. 1731. *Thesaurus aenigmaticus, or, A Collection of CXL of the Most Ingenious and Diverting Aenigmas or Riddles With Their Explanations, Being Designed for Universal Entertainment and for the Exercise of the Fancies of the Curious.* London: J. Wilford.

Anonymous. 1760. *The Polite Companion, or Wit a-la-Mode, Adapted to the Recreation of All Ranks and Degrees, from the Prince to the Peasant.* London: G. Kearsley.

Anonymous. 1762. *The American Gazetteer, containing a distinct account of all the Parts of the New World, their situation, climate, soil, produce, former and present condition; commodities, manufactures and commerce. Together with An accurate Account of the Cities, Towns, Ports, Bays, Rivers, Lakes, Mountains, Passes and Fortifications. The whole intended to exhibit The Present State of Things in that Part of the Globe and the Views and Interests of the several Powers who have Possessions in AMERICA.* 3 vols. London: Printed for A. Millar and J. and R. Tonson, in the Strand.

Anonymous. 1766. *The Book of Knowledge, or, The Trial of wit Containing Above An Hundred riddles for the Benefit of All That Desire to Try Their Wits.* Edinburgh: A. Robertson.

Anonymous. 1776. *Cuatro informes hechos al Excmo. Sr. Don Pedro Ceballos, Virrey de las provincias del Río de la Plata por un Apasionado.* Madrid: Biblioteca de Palacio, Colección Miscelánea de Ayala, XXX, ms. 2844.

Anonymous. 1911. *Entremés de los mirones.* Vol. 1, *Colección,* ed. Emilio Cotarelo y Mori, 162–72. Madrid: Casa Editorial Bailly-Bailliére.

Anonymous, 1938. *Drama de los palanganas Veterano y Bisoño tenido en las gradas de la Catedral, en las noches 17, 18 y 19 de Julio de este año de 1776.* Ed. Luis Alberto Sánchez. *Revista Chilena de Historia y Geografía* 92 (January–June): 78–130; 93 (July–December): 326–32.

Anonymous. 1983. *Cancionero peruano del siglo XVII.* Introd. and ed. Raquel Chang-Rodríguez. Lima: Pontificia Universidad Católica del Perú.

Anonymous. 2003. *El libro verde de Aragón.* Introd. and transcript. Monique Combescure Thiry. Pref. and prel. study Miguel Ángel Motis Dolader. Zaragoza, Spain: Libros Certeza.

Anonymous. n.d. *Itinerarios y derroteros de las Provincias del Perú, en que se manifiestan las leguas y mansiones que generalmente se hacen en los Viajes desde Buenos Ayres a Lima; de esta Ciudad a la de Potosí; a esta desde Payta; de la de la Plata a las de Buenos Ayres y Chile; de Lima a Arequipa; y Carrera que siguen las Mulas desde el Tucumán a las Tabladas del Perú. Y en que igualmente se nota la distancia que hay de unas Ciudades y Pueblos principales a otras, con algunas advertencias útiles para los que hubiesen de viajar por dichas Provincias.* Madrid: Biblioteca de Palacio, Colección Miscelánea de Ayala, XXI, ms. 2835.

Anonymous. n.d. *Reflexiones sobre la decadencia de la Monarquía Espanola por el dispendio de caudales y despoblación que causaron las guerras en el siglo XVII y presente. Medios de restablecer la paz y con ella el lustre y opulencia de sus Provincias.* Madrid: Biblioteca de Palacio, Colección Miscelánea de Ayala, IL, ms. 2862.

Appiah, K. Anthony. 1996. "Race, Culture, Identity: Misunderstood Connections." In *Color Conscious,* ed. K. Anthony Appiah and Amy Gutmann, 30–105. Princeton: Princeton University Press.

Araújo y Río, José. 1745. *Manifiesto verídico y legal que en hecho y derecho evidencia las tropelías y perjuicios que en el Juicio de Pesquisa está padeciendo Don Joseph Araújo y Río, del Consejo de su Magestad, Presidente, Governador y Capitán General de la Real Audiencia de Quito.* Madrid: n.p.

Arazola Corvera, María Jesús. 1998. *Hombres, barcos y comercio de la ruta Cádiz-Buenos Aires (1737–1757).* Seville, Spain: Diputación de Sevilla.

Arce Otálora, Juan. 1553. *De nobilitatis & immunitatis hispaniae causis (quas hidalguia appellant).* Granada, Spain: n.p.

Arendt, Hannah. 1944. "Race-Thinking before Racism." *Review of Politics* 6.1 (January): 36–73.

Armendáriz Perurena, José de, Marquis de Castelfuerte. 1724. *Vando contra los que comerciaren en el Comercio ilicito. Dado en Lima a diez y nueve de Junio de mil setecientos y veinte y quatro anos.* Lima, Peru, June 19.

———. 1726. Broadside directed to Gerónimo de Villares, corregidor of Guamanga. Lima, Peru, June 19.

———. 2000. *Relación de lo acaecido en las provincias del Perú durante el gobierno del excelentísimo señor don José de Armendáriz, y Relación del Gobierno de aquellos reinos.* Ed. and introd. Alfredo Moreno Cebrián, 351–618. *El virreinato del marqués de Castelfuerte 1724–1736: El primer intento borbónico por reformar el Perú.* Madrid: Catriel.

Arnold, Linda. 1991. *Burocracia y burócratas en México, 1742–1835.* Trans. Enrique Palos. Mexico City: Grijalbo.

Arreguine, Víctor. 1900. *En qué consiste la superioridad de los latinos sobre los anglosajones.* Buenos Aires, Argentina: Enseñanza Pública.

Arrelucea Barrantes, Maribel. 1996. "Conducta y control social: Estudio de las panadería limeñas en el siglo XVIII." *Revista del Archivo General de la Nación* 13:133–50.

Artís Espriu, Gloria. 1994. *Familia, riqueza y poder: Un estudio genealógico de la oligarquía novohispana.* Mexico City: Centro de Investigaciones y Estudios Superiores en Antropología Social.

Asdrúbal Silva, Hernán. 1969. "Pulperías, tendejones, sastres y zapateros: Buenos Aires en la primera mitad del s. XVIII." *Anuario de Estudios Americanos* 25:471–506.

Atran, Scott. 1990. *Cognitive Foundations of Natural History: Towards an Anthropology of Science.* New York: Cambridge University Press.

Avila, Dolores, Inés Herrera, and Rina Ortiz, eds. 1992. *Minería colonial latinoamericana: Primera Reunión de Historiadores de la Minería Latinoamericana.* Mexico City: Instituto Nacional de Antropología e Historia.

Ávila, Francisco de. 1911. *Entremés famoso del Mortero y chistes del Sacristán.* Vol. 1, *Colección,* ed. Emilio Cotarelo y Mori, 203–8. Madrid: Casa Editorial Bailly-Bailliére.

Bakewell, Peter. 2004. *A History of Latin America: C. 1450 to the Present.* 2nd ed. Oxford, England: Blackwell.

Balzo, Bertrando del. 1965. "Familias nobles y destacadas del Perú en los informes secretos de un Virrey napolitano (1715–1725)." *Revista del Instituto Peruano de Investigaciones Genealógicas* 14 (December): 107–33.

Banton, Michael. 1977. *The Idea of Race.* London: Tavistock Publications.

Barbier, Jacques A. 1972. "Elites and Cadres in Bourbon Chile." *Hispanic American Historical Review* 52:416–35.

Barkan, Elazar. 2003. "Race and the Social Sciences." In *The Modern Social Sciences,* ed. Theodore M. Porter and Dorothy Ross, 693–707. Vol. 7 of *The Cambridge History of Science.* Cambridge, England: Cambridge University Press.

Barroeta, Pedro Antonio. n.d. *Concordato celebrado entre el Ilustrissimo Senhor D. Pedro Antonio Barroeta, Arzobispo de Lima, y el Dean y Cabildo de aquella Santa Iglesia, sobre nueve puntos que se ofrecieron en la Visita que actuó dicho Metropolitano el anho de 1754, cerca del Tratamiento que devia darles en los Autos y edictos, y otras Materias de Goviero comunes a la Dignidad y Cabildo.* Madrid: Biblioteca de Palacio, Colección Miscelánea de Ayala, X, ms. 2824.

Bataillon, Marcel. 1960. "Introducción a Concolorcorvo y su itinerario de Buenos Aires a Lima." *Cuadernos Americanos* III, no. 4, 197–216.

Batman, Stephen. 1976. *The Golden Booke of the Leaden Gods.* Facs. ed. New York: Garland Publishing.

Benavides Rodríguez, Alfredo. 1988. *La arquitectura en el Virreinato del Perú y en la Capitanía General de Chile.* Rev. Juan Benavides Courtois. 3rd ed. Santiago, Chile: Editorial Andrés Bello.

Benjumea, Miguel de. 1751. *El pastor de ocho talentos que multiplicó como ninguno todos los talentos de Dios con los del mundo, el Illmo. y Rmo. Señor Mío, D. F. Pedro Pardo de Figueroa. Sermon panegirico y funebre.* Santiago de Guatemala: Sebastián de Arévalo.

Berreman, Gerald D. 1967. "Stratification, Pluralism and Interaction: A Comparative Analysis of Caste." In *Caste and Race: Comparative Approaches,* ed. Anthony de Reuck and Julie Knight, 45–73. Boston: Little, Brown and Company.

Bertrand, Michel. 1994. "Comment peut-on être créole? Sur les relations sociales en Nouvelle-Espagne au XVIIIe siècle." *Caravelle* 62:99–109.

———. 1999a. "La élite colonial en la Nueva España del siglo XVIII: Un planteamiento en términos de redes sociales." In *Beneméritos, aristócratas y empresarios: Identidades y estructuras sociales de las capas altas urbanas en América hispánica,* ed. Bernd Schröter and Christian Büschges, 35–52. Frankfurt, Germany: Vervuert-Iberoamericana.

———. 1999b. *Grandeur et misères de l'office: Les officiers de finances de Nouvelle-Espagne (XVIIe–XVIIIe siècles).* Paris: Publications de la Sorbonne.

Blanco Segura, Ricardo. 1984. *Obispos, arzobispos y representantes de la Santa Sede en Costa Rica.* San José, Costa Rica: Editorial Universidad Estatal a Distancia.

Boccalini, Traiano. 1910–1948. *Ragguagli di Parnaso e Pietra del paragone politico.* Ed. Giuseppe Rua and Luigi Firpo. 3 vols. Bari, Italy: Gius. Laterza & Figli.

Boggs, R. S., Lloyd Kasten, Hayward Keniston, and H. B. Richardson. 1946. *Tentative Dictionary of Medieval Spanish.* 2 vols. Chapel Hill, N.C.: n.p.

Bose, Walter B. L. 1933. "Expedición y recepción de correspondencia en la época del Virreynato del Río de la Plata." *Humanidades* 23:375–97.

———. 1934. "Los orígenes del correo terrestre en el Río de la Plata." *Boletín de la Universidad Nacional de La Plata* 18.6:331–50.

———. 1939. "Los orígenes del correo terrestre en Guatemala." *Revista Chilena de Historia y Geografía* 86.9 (January–June): 242–79.

Botello de Moraes e Vasconcelos, Francisco. 1987. *Historia de las cuevas de Salamanca.* Introd. Fernando R. de la Flor. Ed. Eugenio Cobo. Madrid: Tecnos.

Brading, David A. 1991. *The First America: The Spanish Monarchy, Creole Patriots, and the Liberal State 1492–1867*. Cambridge, England: Cambridge University Press.

Braude, Benjamin. 1997. "The Sons of Noah and the Construction of Ethnic and Geographical Identities in the Medieval and Early Modern Periods." *William and Mary Quarterly*, 3d. series, 54.1 (January): 103–42.

Bravo de Lagunas y Castilla, Pedro José. 1755. *Voto consultivo que ofrece al Excelentísimo Señor D. José Antonio Manso de Velasco*. Lima, Peru: Calle del Tigre.

Brenot, Anne-Marie. 1989. *Pouvoir et profits au Pérou colonial au XVIIIe siècle: Gouverneurs, clientèles et ventes forcées*. Paris: Editions L'Harmattan.

Brown, Kendall W. 1992. "La distribución del mercurio a finales del período colonial, y los trastornos provocados por la independencia hipanoamericana." In *Minería colonial latinoamericana: Primera Reunión de Historiadores de la Minería Latinoamericana*, ed. Dolores Avila, Inés Herrera, and Rina Ortiz, 155–66. Mexico City: Instituto Nacional de Antropología e Historia.

Brunschvig, Robert. 1962. "Métiers vils en Islam." *Studia Islamica* 16:4–60.

Bueno, Cosme. 1951. *Geografía virreinal (siglo XVIII)*. Ed. Daniel Valcárcel. Lima, Peru: Azángaro.

———. 1996. "Descripción del Obispado de Buenos Aires." In *El aragonés Cosme Bueno y la Descripción geográfica del Río de la Plata (1768–1776)*, ed. Ramón María Serrera Contreras, Luisa Vila Vilar, and Concepción Hernández-Díaz, 129–46. Huesca, Spain: Instituto de Estudios Altoaragoneses.

Burkholder, Mark A. 1982. *Biographical Dictionary of Audiencia Ministers in the Americas, 1687–1821*. Westport, Conn.: Greenwood Press.

Burkholder, Mark A., and D. S. Chandler. 1977. *From Impotence to Authority: The Spanish Crown and the American Audiencias, 1687–1808*. Columbia: University of Missouri Press.

Bustos Rodríguez, Manuel. 1995. *Los comerciantes en la carrera de Indias en el Cádiz del siglo XVIII (1713–1775)*. Cádiz, Spain: Universidad de Cádiz.

Cadalso, José. 1967. *Los eruditos a la violeta o Curso completo de todas las ciencias dividido en siete lecciones para los siete días de la semana*, Ed. José Luis Aguirre. Madrid: Aguilar.

Cadenas y Vicent, Vicente de. 1978–1979. *Caballeros de la Orden de Santiago, Siglo XVIII*. 5 vols. Madrid: Ediciones Hidalguía.

Cagiga y Rada, Augustín de la. 1739. *Fúnebre pompa y Exequial aparato que selebro en su Iglesia Cathedral, el Yllmo. y Rmo. Sr. Mro. D. Fr. Pedro Pardo de Figueroa de el Sagrado Orden de los Minimos de S. Francisco de Paula, dignissimo Obispo de Guathemala y Verapaz, de el Consejo de su Mag. &c, en las honras de la M. Ylustre Señora Doña Petronila Ygnacia de Esquibel, Espinola Villavicencio, Pardo de Figueroa, Marqueza de Valleumbroso*. Santiago de Guatemala: Imprenta de Sebastián de Arévalo.

Cahill, David. 1994. "Colour by Numbers: Racial and Ethnic Categories in the Viceroyalty of Peru, 1532–1824." *Journal of Latin American Studies* 26.2:325–46.

Campbell, Leon G. 1972. "A Colonial Establishment: Creole Domination of the Audiencia of Lima during the Late Eighteenth Century." *Hispanic American Historical Review* 52:1–25.

———. 1973. "Racism without Race: Ethnic Group Relations in Late Colonial Peru." In *Racism in the Eighteenth Century*, ed. Harold E. Pagliaro, 323–34. Vol. 3 of *Studies in Eighteenth-Century Culture*. Cleveland: Case Western Reserve University Press.

Cañizares Esguerra, Jorge. 2001. *How to Write the History of the New World: Histories,*

Epistemologies and Identities in the Eighteenth-Century Atlantic World. Stanford, Calif.: Stanford University Press.

Carilla, Emilio. 1976. *El libro de los misterios:* El lazarillo de ciegos caminantes. Madrid: Editorial Gredos.

Caro Baroja, Julio. 1965. "Antecedentes españoles de algunos problemas relativos al mestizaje." *Revista Histórica* 28:197–210.

_____. 1966. "Honour and Shame: A Historical Account of Several Conflicts." In *Honour and Shame: The Values of Mediterranean Society,* ed. J. G. Peristiany, 81–137. London: University of Chicago Press.

Carrera, Magali M. 2003. *Imagining Identity in New Spain: Race, Lineage, and the Colonial Body in Portraiture and Casta Paintings.* Austin: University of Texas Press.

Carrió de la Vandera [Carrió de Lavandera], Alonso. 1775. *EL LAZARILLO DE CIEGOS CAMINANTES desde Buenos-Ayres hasta Lima con sus Itinerarios segun la mas puntual observacion, con algunas noticias utiles a los Nuevos Comerciantes que tratan en Mulas; y otras Historicas. SACADO DE LAS MEMORIAS QUE hizo Don Alonso Carrió de la Vandera en este dilatado Viage y Comision que tubo por la Corte para el arreglo de Correos y Estafetas, Situacion y ajuste de Postas, desde Montevideo. POR DON CALIXTO BUSTAMANTE CARLOS Inca, alias CONCOLORCORVO, Natural del Cuzco, que acompañó al referido Comisionado en dicho Viage y escribió sus Extractos.* CON LICENCIA. Lima, Peru: Imprenta de la Rovada.

_____. 1966. *Reforma del Perú.* Ed. and introd. Pablo Macera. Lima, Peru: Universidad Mayor de San Marcos.

_____. 1973. *El lazarillo de ciegos caminantes.* Ed. and introd. Emilio Carilla. Barcelona, Spain: Labor.

_____. 1985. *El lazarillo de ciegos caminantes.* Ed. Antonio Lorente Medina. Caracas, Venezuela: Biblioteca Ayacucho.

Cartari, Vicenzo. 1626. *Imagini de gli dei delli antichi.* Padua, Italy: Pietro Paolo Tozzi.

Cartmill, Matt. 1998. "The Status of the Race Concept in Physical Anthropology." *American Anthropologist* 100.3 (September): 651–60.

Casas, Cristóbal de las. 1570. *Vocabulario de las dos lenguas toscana y castellana de Christoval de las Casas en que se contiene la declaracion de Toscano en Castellano, y de Castellano en Toscano. En dos partes, con una introduccion para leer y pronunciar bien entrambas lenguas.* Seville, Spain: Casa de Alonso Escrivano.

Castiglione, Baldassare. 1994. *Los cuatro libros de El cortesano.* Trans. Juan de Boscán. Ed. Mario Pozzi. Madrid: Cátedra.

Castilhon, M. L. 1770. *Considérations sure les causes physiques et morales de la diversité du genie, des moeurs, et du gouvernement des nations.* 2nd enlarged ed. 2 vols. Bouillon, Belgium: Société Typographique.

Castillo Andraca y Tamayo, Francisco del. 1948. *Obras de Fray Francisco del Castillo Andraca y Tamayo.* Introd. and ed. Rubén Vargas Ugarte. Lima, Peru: Editorial Studium.

_____. 1996. *Obra completa de Fray Francisco del Castillo, O.M., "El Ciego de la Merced," 1716–1770.* Introd. and ed. César A. Debarbieri. Lima, Peru: n.p.

_____. n.d. Microfilm of ms. Vol. 6, Fondo Antiguo, Archivo Nacional de Santiago de Chile.

_____. n.d. Microfilm. of ms. Vol. 805, Fondo Varios, Archivo Nacional de Santiago de Chile.

Cejador y Frauca, Julio. 1983. *Vocabulario medieval castellano.* Madrid: Visor Libros.

Cervantes Saavedra, Miguel de. 1983. *Don Quijote de la Mancha.* Ed. Juan Bautista Avalle-Arce. 2 vols. Madrid: Alhambra.

Céspedes del Castillo, Guillermo. 1946. "Lima y Buenos Aires: Repercusiones económicas y políticas de la creación del Virreinato del Plata." *Anuario de Estudios Americanos* 3:667–874.

Charlevoix, Pierre François-Xavier de. 1756. *Histoire du Paraguay.* 3 vols. Paris: Didot, Giffart and Nyon.

Chinchilla Aguilar. 1953. *La Inquisición en Guatemala.* Guatemala City: Editorial del Ministerio de Educación Pública.

———. 1961. *El ayuntamiento colonial de la Ciudad de Guatemala.* Guatemala City: Editorial Universitaria.

Cicala, Mario. 1994. *Descripción histórico-topográfica de la Provincia de Quito de la Compañía de Jesús.* Quito, Ecuador: Biblioteca Ecuatoriana "Aurelio Espinosa Pólit."

Cicero. 2001. *On the Ideal Orator (De Oratore).* Introd., trans., and notes James M. May and Jakob Wisse. New York: Oxford University Press.

Cilieza Velasco, Miguel de. 1751. *Los talentos mejor multiplicados en las gloriosas hazañas de un príncipe religioso y pastor caballero, el Illmo. y Rmo. Señor Mro. D. F. Pedro Pardo de Figueroa de el Sagrado Orden de los Minimos de San Francisco de Paula, Obispo de esta Santa Iglesia de San Tiago de Goathemala y su primero Dignissimo Arzobispo, de el Consejo de su Magestad &c. Descripcion de el Tumulo que erigio su Ilmo. y venerable Cabildo en las muy solemnes Exequias que hizo a su feliz memoria.* Santiago de Guatemala: Sebastián de Arévalo.

Clement, Jean-Pierre. 1987. "L'apparition de la presse periodique en Amerique Espagnole: Le cas du *Mercurio Peruano,*" In *L'Amérique Espagnole à l'Epoque des Lumières: Tradition-Innovation-Représentations,* ed. Groupe Interdisciplinaire de Recherche et de Documentation sur l'Amérique Latine, 273–86, pref. Bernard Lavalle. Paris: Editions du CNRS.

Cole, Jeffrey A. 1985. *The Potosí Mita 1573–1700: Compulsory Indian Labor in the Andes.* Stanford, Calif.: Stanford University Press.

Coleti, Giandomenico. 1771. *Dizionario storico-geografico dell'America Meridionale.* 2 vols. Venice, Italy: Stamperia Coleti.

Colin, Michèle. 1966. *Le Cuzco a la fin du XVIIe et au début du XVIIIe siècle.* Pref. Pierre Chaunu. Caen, France: Association des Publications de la Faculté des Lettres et Sciences Humaines, Université de Caen.

Constituciones de la Provincia del Santo Evangelio, Hechas y recopiladas en el Capitulo Provincial, celebrado en Xuchimilco a diez y ocho de Enero de mil y seiscientos y catorze. Y agora nuebamente reformadas en el Capitulo Provincial celebrado en la Ciudad de Mexico a quatro de Febrero de mil y seiscientos y quarenta Años. Por las quales se revocan las demas hasta el dicho dia en ella hechas. 1640. Mexico City: Bernardo Calderón.

Constituciones de los F. menores desta Provincia de los Doze Apostoles del Piru. 1601. Lima, Peru: Antonio Ricardo.

Constituciones desta Provincia de los Doze Apostoles del Piru. 1631. Lima, Peru: Jerónimo de Contreras.

Constituciones y Ordenanças de la Universidad y Studio General de la ciudad de los Reyes del Piru. 1602. Lima, Peru: Antonio Ricardo.

Conti, Natale. 1976. *Mythologie.* Trans. Jean Baudoin. Facs. ed. New York: Garland Publishing.

Cope, R. Douglas. 1994. *The Limits of Racial Domination: Plebeian Society in Colonial Mexico City, 1660–1720.* Madison: University of Wisconsin Press.

Córdova y Urrutia, José María. 1875. *Las tres épocas del Perú ó Compendio de su historia.* Vol. 7 of *Documentos literarios del Perú,* ed. Manuel de Odriozola. Lima, Peru: Imprenta del Estado.

Cornejo Polar, Antonio. 1997. *Mestizaje e hibridez: Los riesgos de las metáforas.* No. 6 of *Cuadernos de la Literatura.* La Paz, Bolivia: Universidad Mayor de San Andrés.

Cotarelo y Mori, Emilio. 1904. *Bibliografía de las controversias sobre la licitud del teatro en España.* Madrid: Est. Tip. de la *Revista de Archivos, Bibliotecas y Museos.*

———, ed. 1911. *Colección de entremeses, loas, bailes, jácaras y mojigangas desde fines del siglo XVI á mediados del XVIII.* 2 vols. Madrid: Casa Editorial Bailly-Baillière.

Covarrubias Orozco, Sebastián de. 1943. *Tesoro de la lengua castellana o española según la impresión de 1611, con las adiciones de Benito Remigio Noydens publicadas en la de 1674.* Ed. Martín de Riquer. Barcelona, Spain: S. A. Horta, I.E.

———. 1978. *Emblemas morales.* Facs. ed. and introd. Carmen Bravo-Villasante. Madrid: Fundación Universitaria Española.

———. 1979. *Tesoro de la lengua castellana o española.* Madrid: Ediciones Turner.

———. 1994. *Tesoro de la lengua castellana o española.* Ed. Felipe C. R. Maldonado. Rev. Manuel Camarero. Madrid: Castalia.

Cox, Oliver C. 1944–1945. "Race and Caste: A Distinction." *American Journal of Sociology* 50:360–68.

Crawford, Frederic M., Jr. "The *Mercure Historique et Politique* 1715–1781: A Critical Analysis." Ph.D. diss., University of Kentucky, 1969.

Crouch, Nathaniel. 1737. *Winter-Evening Entertainments in Two Parts.* 6th ed. London: A. Bettesworth and C. Hitch.

Cuevas Garcés de los Fallos, Tomás de. 1748. *Colosso eloquente que en la solemne aclamación del augusto Monarca de las Españas, D. Fernando VI (que Dios prospere), erigió sobre brillantes columnas la reconocida lealtad y fidelísima gratitud de la Imperial y Pontífica Universida Mexicana, Athenas del Nuevo Mundo.* Mexico City: Imprenta del Nuevo Rezado de Dona María de Ribera.

Curll, Edmund. 1736. *Post-Office Intelligence, or, Universal Gallantry, Being a Collection of Love-Letters.* London: Edmund Curll.

Curtius, Ernst Robert. 1990. *European Literature and the Latin Middle Ages.* Afterword Peter Godman. Trans. Willard R. Trask. 7th ed. Princeton: Princeton University Press.

Dávila, Francisco. 1648. *Tratado de los Evangelios.* Lima, Peru: n.p.

Dávila Morales, Juan Antonio. 1730. *Practica de la Doctrina Christiana.* Lima, Peru: Francisco Sobrino.

Della Porta, Giambattista. 1637. *Della Fisonomia di tutto il corpo humano.* Abridged ed. Francesco Stelluti. Rome: Vitale Mascardi.

———. 1959. *Natural Magick.* Trans. unknown. Ed. Derek J. Price. Facs. ed. New York: Basic Books.

Demolins, Edmond. 1898. *Anglo-Saxon Superiority: To What It Is Due [A quoi tient la supériorité des Anglo-Saxons].* Trans. Louis Bert Lavigne. London: Leadenhall Press; New York: Charles Scribner's Sons.

Díaz, Víctor Miguel. 1929. *Breve historia del periodismo en Guatemala desde la época colonial hasta los primeros años del presente siglo.* Guatemala City: n.p.

Díez de Arriba, Luis. n.d. *Historia de la Iglesia de Guatemala.* Vol. 1, *Período colonial.* Guatemala City: n.p.

Díez Navarro, Luis. n.d. *Descripción del Reyno y Provincias de Goathemala.* Madrid: Biblioteca de Palacio, Colección Miscelánea de Ayala, VI, ms. 2821.

Dueñas Vargas, Guiomar. 1997. *Los hijos del pecado: Ilegitimidad y vida familiar en la Santafé de Bogotá colonial.* Bogotá, Colombia: Editorial Universidad Nacional.

Dumont, Louis. 1961. "Caste, Racism and 'Stratification': Reflections of a Social Anthropologist." *Contributions to Indian Sociology* 5 (October): 20–43.

———. 1980. *Homo Hierarchicus: The Caste System and Its Implications.* Trans. Mark Sainsbury, Louis Dumont, and Basia Gulati. Rev. Eng. ed. Chicago: University of Chicago Press.

Dunbar Temple, Ella. 1947. "Los Bustamante Carlos Inca: La familia del autor del *Lazarillo de ciegos caminantes.*" *Mercurio Peruano: Revista Mensual de Ciencias Sociales y Letras* 243 (June): 283–305.

Durret. 1720. *Voyage de Marseille a Lima, et dans les autres lieux des Indes Occidentales. Avec une exacte Description de ce qu' il y a de plus remarquable tant pour la Geographie, que pour les Moeurs, les Coûtumes, le Commerce, le Gouvernement et la Religion des Peuples; avec des notes et des figures en taille-douce. Par le Sieur D***.* Paris: Jean-Baptiste Coignard.

Echeverz, Fernando de. 1742. *Ensayos mercantiles para adelantar por medio del establecimiento de una Compañía el Comercio de los frutos del Reino de Guathemala.* Santiago de Guatemala: Sebastián de Arévalo.

Eguiguren, Luis Antonio. 1945. *Leyendas y curiosidades de la Historia nacional.* Lima, Peru: n.p.

———. 1966. Lima inexpugnable: *Un libro desconocido del polígrafo Don Pedro Peralta Barnuevo.* Lima, Peru: n.p.

Enciso Recio, Luis Miguel. 1956. *Nipho y el periodismo español del siglo XVIII.* Prol. Vicente Palacio Atard. Valladolid, Spain: Universidad de Valladolid.

———. 1957. *La* Gaceta de Madrid *y el* Mercurio Histórico y Político. *Estudios y Documentos: Cuadernos de Historia Moderna,* no. 11. Valladolid, Spain: Universidad de Vallodolid-CSIC.

Erasmus, Desiderius. 1979. *The Praise of Folly.* Trans. and introd. Clarence H. Miller. New Haven, Conn.: Yale University Press.

Esquivel y Navia, Diego de. 1980. *Noticias cronológicas de la gran Ciudad del Cuzco.* Ed., prol., and notes Félix Denegri Luna, Horacio Villanueva Urteaga, and César Gutiérrez Muñoz. 2 vols. Lima, Peru: Fundación Augusto N. Wiese, Banco Qiese.

Esteva Fabregat, Claudio. 1995. *Mestizaje in Ibero-America.* Trans. John Wheat. Tucson: University of Arizona Press.

Estupiñán Viteri, Tamara. 1997. *El mercado interno en la Audiencia de Quito.* Quito: Ediciones del Banco Central del Ecuador.

Feijoo de Sosa, Miguel. 1984. *Relación descriptiva de la Ciudad y Provincia de Trujillo del Perú.* Ed. and introd. Guillermo Lohmann Villena. 2 vols. Lima: Fondo del Libro, Banco Industrial del Perú.

Feijoo y Montenegro, Benito Jerónimo. 1773–1774. *Teatro crítico universal, o Discursos varios en todo género de materias para desengaño de errores comunes. Cartas eruditas y curiosas en que por la mayor parte se continúa el designio del Theatro crítico universal,*

impugnando o reduciendo a dudosas, varias opiniones comunes. 15 vols. Madrid: Real
Compañía de Impresores.

_____. 1944. Españoles americanos y otros ensayos. 2nd ed. Buenos Aires, Argentina:
Emecé Editores.

Fénelon, François de Salignac de la Mothe. 1968. Les aventures de Télémaque. Ed. Jeanne-
Lydie Goré. Paris: Garnier-Flammarion.

Fernández de Medrano, Captain Sebastián. 1686. Breve descripcion del Mundo y sus partes, o
Guia Geographica y hydrographica dividida en tres libros. Brussels, Belgium: Herederos
de Francisco Foppens.

Fernández de Piedrahita, Lucas. 1688. Historia general de las conquistas del Nuevo Reyno de
Granada. Antwerp, Belgium: Juan Baptista Verdussen.

Fernández Insuela, Antonio. 1990. "Un dato sobre un enigma del Lazarillo de ciegos caminantes." Bulletin Hispanique 92.2 (July–December): 847–56.

Feuillée, Louis. 1714–1725. Journal des Observations Physiques, Mathematiques et Botaniques.
Faites par ordre du Roi sur les Côtes Orientales de l'Amerique Meridionale, et dans les
Indes Occidentales, depuis l'année 1707. Jusques en 1712. 3 vols. Paris: Pierre Giffart and
Jean Mariette.

Fontenelle, Bernard Le Bovier. 1825. Oeuvres de Fontenelle précédées d'une notice sur sa vie et
sus ouvrages. 3 vols. Paris: Salmon.

Forbes, Jack. 1988. Black Africans and Native Americans: Color, Race and Caste in the Evolution of Red-Black Peoples. Oxford, England: Blackwell.

Fradera, Josep María. 1999. Gobernar colonias. Barcelona, Spain: Ediciones Península.

Frezier, Amédée François. 1716. Relation du Voyage de la Mer du Sud aux côtes du Chily et
du Perou. Fait pendant les années 1712, 1713, & 1714. Paris: Jean-Geoffroy Nyon, Eti-
enne Ganeau, and Jacque Quillau.

Gaceta de Lima. 1982–1983. Ed. and prol. José Durand. 5 vols. Lima, Peru: Oficina de
Asuntos Culturales COFIDE.

Gacetas de México. 1986. Facs. ed. 3 vols. Mexico City: CONDUMEX.

Galaor, Isabel, Daniela Gloner, and Bernd Hasuberger. 1999. Las minas hispanoamericanas
a mediados del siglo XVIII: Informes enviados al Real Gabinete de Historia Natural de
Madrid. Introd. Bernd Hausberger. Frankfurt, Germany: Vervuert-Iberoamericana.

Ganster, Paul. 1991. "Miembros de cabildos eclesiásticos y sus familias en Lima." In Familias novohispanas Siglos XVI al XIX, ed. Pilar Gonzalbo Aizpuru, 149–62. Mexico City:
Colegio de México.

García, Gregorio. 1607. Origen de los indios del Nuevo Mundo e Indias Occidentales. Valencia, Spain: Pedro Patricio.

García Acosta, Virginia. 1989. Las panaderías, sus dueños y trabajadores: Ciudad de México,
siglo XVIII. Mexico City: Ediciones de la Casa Chata–CIESAS.

García-Mauriño Mundi, Margarita. 1999. La pugna entre el Consulado de Cádiz y los jenízaros por las exportaciones a Indias (1720–1765). Seville, Spain: Universidad de Sevilla.

Garcilaso de la Vega, El Inca. 1722. Historia general del Perú. Madrid: Oficina Real.

_____. 1943. Comentarios reales de los Incas. Prol. Ricardo Rojas. Ed. Angel Rosenblat.
Facs. ed. 2 vols. Buenos Aires, Argentina: Emecé Editores.

Gazeta de Lima. 1744. No. 4 (May 1–June 30).

Gazeta de Lima. 1745a. No. 10 (February 8–March 28).

Gazeta de Lima. 1745b. No. 13 (July 15–September 25).

Gazeta de Lima. 1745–1746. No. 15 (November 1–January 15).

Gerbi, Antonello. 1955. *La disputa del Nuovo Mondo.* Milan, Italy: R. Ricciardi.

Gerli, Michael. 1996. "Performing Nobility: Mosén Diego de Valera and the Poetics of Converso Identity." *La corónica* 25.1:19–36.

Gildon, Charles. 1717. *The Post-Man Robb'd of his Mail. Or, the Packet broke open. Being a Collection of Miscellaneous Letters, Serious and Comical, Amorous and Gallant.* London: A. Bettesworth and C. Rivington.

Gilman, Stuart C. 1985. "Political Theory and Degeneration: From Left to Right, from Up to Down." In *Degeneration: The Dark Side of Progress,* ed. J. Edward Chamberlin and Sander L. Gilman, 165–98. New York: Columbia University Press.

Giral del Pino, Hto San Joseph. 1763. *Diccionario Español e Inglés, e Inglés y Español que contiene la significación de las voces, su etymologia, sus varios sentidos y accepciones proprias y metaphóricas; los términos de las artes, ciencias y del comercio; las construcciones y modos de hablar, de ambos idiomas, millares de palabras mas que en otro Diccionario alguno; con su significacion propria, figurada, burlesca y Germanesca.* London: A. Millar, J. Nourse, and P. Vaillant.

Glave, Luis Miguel. 1997. "La puerta del Perú: Paita y el extremo norte peruano, 1600–1615." In *Comercio marítimo colonial: Nuevas interpretaciones y últimas fuentes,* 101–26. Mexico City: Instituto Nacional de Antropología e Historia.

Gómez-Tabanera, José. 1984. "Nueva luz sobre el gijonés Don Alonso Carrió de Lavandera, 'Concolorcorvo': Su estirpe, hidalguía, nacimiento y relaciones." *Boletín del Instituto de Estudios Asturianos* III (January–April): 227–36.

González Gutiérrez, Pilar. 1997. *Creación de Casas de Moneda en Nueva España.* Alcalá, Spain: Servicio de Publicaciones, Universidad de Alcalá.

González Prada, Manuel. 1986. "Nuestros indios." In vol. 3 of *Obras,* ed. Luis Alberto Sánchez, 195–210. Lima, Peru: Ediciones COPE.

Gracián, Baltasar de. 1967. *El criticón.* In *Obras completas,* ed. Arturo del Hoyo, 516–1011. Madrid: Aguilar.

_____. 1984. *Oráculo manual y arte de prudencia.* Ed. Luys Santa Marina. Introd. and ed. Raquel Asun. Barcelona, Spain: Planeta.

_____. 1985. *El Político Don Fernando el Católico.* Prol. Aurora Egido. Zaragoza, Spain: Institución "Fernando el Católico" and Diputación Provincial de Zaragoza.

_____. 1997. *El discreto.* Ed. and prol. Aurora Egido. Madrid: Alianza.

_____. 1998. *Arte de ingenio, Tratado de la Agudeza.* Ed. Emilio Blanco. Madrid: Cátedra.

Grahn, Lance. 1997. *The Political Economy of Smuggling: Regional Informal Economies in Early Bourbon New Granada.* Boulder, Colo.: Westview Press.

Greer Johnson, Julie. 1980. "Feminine Satire in Concolorcorvo's *El lazarillo de ciegos caminantes.*" *South Atlantic Bulletin* 45.1 (January): 11–20.

_____. 1993. *Satire in Colonial Spanish America: Turning the New World Upside Down.* Foreword Daniel R. Reedy. Austin: University of Texas Press.

Gruzinski, Serge, and Nathan Watchel. 1997. "Cultural Interbreedings: Constituting the Majority as a Minority." *Comparative Studies in Society and History* 39.2:231–50.

Güemes y Horcasitas, Francisco de, Viceroy of New Spain. 1867. *Instrucción del Sr. Conde de Revillagigedo al Sr. Marqués de las Amarillas. Instrucciones que los Vi[r]reyes de Nueva España dejaron a sus sucesores.* Mexico City: Imprenta Imperial.

Guillaumin, Colette. 1995. *Racism, Sexism, Power and Ideology.* London: Routledge.

Gumilla, José. 1944. *El Orinoco ilustrado.* Introd. and ed. Constantino Bayle. Madrid: Aguilar.

Gumplowicz, Ludwig. 1894. *La lucha de razas*. Trans. unknown. Madrid: *La España Moderna*.

Gutiérrez de Rubalcava, José. 1750. *Tratado histórico, político y legal de el comercio de las Indias Occidentales, pertenecientes a los Reyes Catholicos, conforme al tiempo de Paz y Guerra, en interpretación de las Leyes de la Nueva Recopilación a ellas, Primera parte: Compendio histórico del Comercio de las Indias, desde su principio hasta su actual Estado*. Cádiz, Spain: Imprenta Real de Marina.

Haidt, Rebecca. 1998. *Embodying Enlightenment: Knowing the Body in Eighteenth-Century Spanish Literature and Culture*. New York: St. Martin's Press.

Hampe Martínez, Teodor. 1996a. *Bibliotecas privadas en el mundo colonial: La difusión de libros e ideas en el virreinato del Perú (siglos XVI–XVII)*. Madrid: Iberoamericana.

———. 1996b. *Cultura barroca y extirpación de idolatrías: La biblioteca de Francisco de Avila—1648*. Cuzco, Peru: Centro de Estudios Regionales Andinos Bartolomé de las Casas.

Hannaford, Ivan. 1996. *Race: The History of an Idea in the West*. Baltimore: Johns Hopkins University Press.

Harrison, Faye V. 1998. "Introduction: Expanding the Discourse on 'Race.'" *American Anthropologist* 100.3 (September): 609–31.

Head, Richard. 1675. *Nugae Venales, or Complaisant Companion, Being New Jests, Domestick and Foreign, Bulls, Rhodomontados, Pleasant Novels and Miscellanies*. 2nd rev. and exp. ed. London: W.D.

Helg, Aline. 1990. "Race in Argentina and Cuba, 1880–1930: Theory, Policies, and Popular Reaction." In *The Idea of Race in Latin America, 1870–1940*, ed. Richard Graham, 37–69. Austin: University of Texas Press.

Herrera, Gabriel Alonso de. 1970. *Obra de Agricultura*. Vol. 235 of *Biblioteca de Autores Españoles*, ed. and introd. José Urbano Martínez Carreras. Madrid: Atlas.

Herzog, Tamar. 2003. *Defining Nations: Immigrants and Citizens in Early Modern Spain and Spanish America*. New Haven and London: Yale University Press.

Hill, Ruth. 1994a. "Between Reason and Piety: *Inventio* and Verisimilitude in Pedro de Peralta's Prologue to *Lima fundada* (1732)." *Dieciocho* 17.2 (Fall): 129–41.

———. 1994b. "Literary Absolutism: 'Fable' and 'History' in Spain and Peru, 1670–1900." 2 vols. Ph.D. diss., University of Michigan.

———. 1996a. "Arrate's *La Habana descripta* and the Modernization of the Geographical Report (ca. 1750–1769)." *Revista Hispánica Moderna* 49 (December): 329–40.

———. 1996b. "Churchmen, Statesmen, Smugglers *Extraordinaires:* The Prodigious 4 P's from Lima." *Indiana Journal of Hispanic Literatures* 8 (Spring): 95–125.

———. 1998. "A Transatlantic Rebuke of Rationalism: Text and Subtext in *El lazarillo de ciegos caminantes*." *Dieciocho* 21.2 (Fall): 167–80.

———. 2000a. "Caste Theater and Poetry in 18th-Century Spanish America." *Revista de Estudios Hispánicos* 34.1 (January): 3–26.

———. 2000b. *Sceptres and Sciences in the Spains: Four Humanists and the New Philosophy (ca. 1680–1740)*. Liverpool: Liverpool University Press.

———. 2004. "*Casta* as Culture and the *Sociedad de Castas* as Literature." In *Interpreting Colonialism*, ed. Byron Wells and Philip Stewart. Oxford, England: Voltaire Foundation.

Hoberman, Louisa, and Susan Socolow, eds. 1986. *City and Society in Colonial Latin America*. Albuquerque: University of New Mexico Press.

Hoffman, Richard C. 1983. "Outsiders by Birth and Blood: Racist Ideologies and Realities around the Periphery of Medieval European Culture." *Studies in Medieval and Renaissance History* 6:3–34.

Hostos, Eugenio M. de. 1939. *Obras completas.* Vol. 7, *Temas sudamericanos.* San Juan: Gobierno de Puerto Rico.

Hurtado de Mendoza, Diego. 1964. "Sermón de Aljubarrota con las glosas de D. Diego Hurtado de Mendoza." In *Sales Españolas o Agudezas del ingenio nacional,* ed. Antonio Paz y Melia and Ramón Paz, 45–81. 2nd rev. ed. Madrid: Atlas.

———. 1996. *Guerra de Granada.* Ed. and introd. Bernardo Blanco-González. Madrid: Castalia.

Jackson, Robert H. 1999. *Race, Caste, and Status: Indians in Colonial Spanish America.* Albuquerque: University of New Mexico Press.

Jacobs, Helmut C. 2001. *Belleza y buen gusto: Las teorías de las artes en la literatura española del siglo XVIII.* Trans. Beatriz Galán Echevarría. Madrid: Iberoamericana.

Johnson, Ben. 1760? *Ben Johnson's Jests, or, The Wit's Pocket Companion.* London: R. Baldwin and S. Crowder.

Klien-Samanez, Mónica. 2000. "El recorrido histórico de *El lazarillo de ciegos caminantes.*" Ph.D. diss., Boston University.

Klor de Alva, J. Jorge. 1992. "Colonialism and Postcolonialism as (Latin) American Mirages." *Colonial Latin American Review* 1.1–2:3–23.

Kuznesof, Elizabeth Anne. 1995. "Ethnic and Gender Influences on 'Spanish' Creole Society in Colonial Spanish America." *Colonial Latin American Review* 4.1:153–77.

Labat, Jean-Baptiste. 1730. *Voyage du Chevalier des Marches en Guinée, Isles Voisines, et a Cayénne, Fait en 1725, 1726 et 1727. Contenant une Description très exacte et très étendue de ces Païs, et du Commerce qui s'y fait. Enrichis d'un grand nombre de Cartes et de Figures en Tailles douces.* 4 vols. Paris: Guillaume Saugrain.

La Blanchardiere, Courte de. 1751. *Nouveau voyage fait au Pérou.* Paris: Imprimerie de Delaguette.

La Condamine, Charles Marie de. 1751a. *Histoire des Pyramides de Quito élevées par les Académiciens envoyés sous l'Equateur par ordre du Roi.* Paris: L'Imprimerie Royale.

———. 1751b. *Journal du Voyage fait par ordre du Roi a l'Equateur, servant d'introduction historique a la Mesure des Trois Premiers Degrés du Méridien.* Paris: L'Imprimerie Royale.

La Feuille, Daniel de. 1746. *Science hiéroglyphique, ou Explication des figures symboliques des anciens avec différentes devises historiques: Ouvrage utile aux peintres, aux amateurs des arts qui ont rapport au dessin.* The Hague: Jean Swart.

Larson, Neil. 1994. "National Consciousness and the Specificity of (Post) Colonial Intellectualism." In *Colonial Discourse/Postcolonial Theory,* ed. Francis Barker, Peter Hulme, and Margaret Iversen, 197–220. Manchester, England: Manchester University Press.

Laschober, Paula Jeanne. 1979. "Socio-economic Aspects of Juan del Valle y Caviedes' Satire of Colonial Afro-Peruvians." Ph.D. diss., University of Washington.

Lavallé, Bernard. 1987. *Le Marquis et le Marchand: Les luttes de pouvoir au Cuzco (1700–1730).* Paris: Editions du Centre National de la Recherche Scientifique.

Le Bon, Gustave. 1982. *The Psychology of Socialism.* Introd. John L. Stanley. New Brunswick, N.J.: Transaction Books.

Le Bovier Fontenelle, Bernard. 1825. *Oeuvres de Fontenelle précédées d'une notice sur sa vie et sus ouvrages.* 3 vols. Paris: Salmon.

Le Gentil de la Barbinais, Sletu. 1728. *Nouveau Voyage au tour du Monde par M. Le Gentil.* 3 vols. Amsterdam: Pierre Mortier.

Le Goff, Jacques, ed. 1977. *Pour un autre Moyen Age: Temps, travail et culture en Occident: 18 essais.* Paris: Gallimard.

León, Nicolás. 1924. *Las castas del México colonial o Nueva Espana: Noticias etno-antropológicas.* Mexico City: Talleres Gráficos del Museo Nacional de Arqueología, Historia y Etnografía.

Llano Zapata, José Eusebio de. 1904. *Memorias histórico-físicas-apologéticas de la América meridional.* Ed. Manuel de Mendiburu. Lima, Peru: Imprenta y Librería de San Pedro.

Lobo Guerrero, Bartolomé. 1614. *Constituciones synodales del Arçobispado de los Reyes en el Piru.* Lima, Peru: Francisco del Canto.

Lohmann Villena, Guillermo. 1944. "Don Diego de Villegas y Quevedo, individuo de la Real Academia Española (1696–1751)." *Revista de Indias* 5.15 (January–March): 41–88.

———. 1947. *Los americanos en las órdenes nobiliarias.* 2 vols. Madrid: CSIC.

———. 1959. "Las relaciones de los virreyes del Perú." *Anuario de Estudios Americanos* 16:315–532.

———. 1974. *Los ministros de la Audiencia de Lima en el reinado de los Borbones (1700–1821): Esquema de un estudio sobre un núcleo dirigente.* Seville, Spain: Escuela de Estudios Hispano-Americanos.

———, ed. 1976. *Un tríptico del Perú virreinal: El virrey Amat, el marqués de Soto Florido y la Perricholi. El* Drama de dos palanganas *y su circunstancia.* Chapel Hill: University of North Carolina Department of Romance Languages.

Lowood, Henry. 1995. "The New World and the European Catalog of Nature." In *America in European Consciousness 1493–1750,* ed. Karen Ordahl Kupperman, 295–323. Chapel Hill: University of North Carolina Press.

Lucian of Samosata. 1961. *Icaromenippus: Satirical Sketches.* Ed. Paul Turner. Baltimore: Penguin.

Lugar, Catherine. 1986. *Cities and Society in Colonial Latin America.* Ed. Louisa Schell Hoberman and Susan Migden Socolow. Albuquerque: University of New Mexico Press.

Lutz, Christopher. 1994. *Santiago de Guatemala, 1541–1773: City, Caste, and the Colonial Experience.* Norman: University of Oklahoma Press.

Luzán, Ignacio de. 1991. *Arte de hablar, o sea, retórica de las conversaciones.* Ed., introd., and notes Manuel Béjar Hurtado. Madrid: Editorial Gredos.

Lynche, Richard. 1976. *The Fountain of Ancient Fiction.* Facs. ed. New York: Garland Publishing.

Macpherson, Ian. 1998. *The* Invenciones y Letras *of the* Cancionero General. London: Department of Hispanic Studies, Queen Mary and Westfield College.

Malik, Kenan. 1996. *The Meaning of Race: Race, History and Culture in Western Society.* New York: New York University Press.

Malverde Disselkoen, N. Ivette. 1992. "La palabra mestiza en *El lazarillo de ciegos caminantes,*" *Acta Literaria* 17:127–35.

Mannarelli, María Emma. 1999. *Hechiceras, beatas y expósitas: Mujeres y poder inquisitorial en Lima.* Lima: Ediciones del Congreso del Perú.

Manso de Velasco, José Antonio, Count de Superunda. 1983. *Relación y documentos de gobierno del virrey del Perú, José A. Manso de Velasco, conde de Superunda (1745–1761).*

Introd., ed., and notes Alfredo Moreno Cebrián. Madrid: CSIC–Instituto "Gonzalo Fernández de Oviedo."

Maravall, José Antonio. 1979. *Poder, honor y élites en el siglo XVII.* Madrid: Siglo XXI.

Marco, Joaquín. 1977. *Literatura popular en España en los siglos XVIII y XIX (una aproximación a los pliegos de cordel).* 2 vols. Madrid: Taurus Ediciones.

Mármol Carvajal, Luis del. 1600. *Historia del rebelion y castigo de los moriscos del Reyno de Granada.* Malaga, Spain: Juan Rene.

———. 1953. *Descripción General de África.* Fac. ed. Prol. Agustín G. de Amezúa. Madrid: Instituo de Estudios Africanos del Patronato Diego Saavedra Fajardo del Consejo Superior de Investigaciones Científicas.

Márquez Villanueva, Francisco. 1979. "Un aspect de la littérature du 'fou.'" In *L'Humanisme dans les lettres espagnoles,* ed. Augustín Redondo, 233–50. Paris: Libraire Philosophique J. Vrin.

Martí, José. 1978. *Obras escogidas.* Vol. 3. Havana: Editora Política.

Mathieu, Colin S. 1994–1995. "El didactismo en *El lazarillo de ciegos caminantes.*" *Explicación de Textos Literarios* 23.1:33–42.

Mayans y Siscar, Gregorio de. 1983. *Obras completas.* Ed. Antonio Mestre Sanchis. 5 vols. Valencia, Spain: Ayuntamiento de Oliva–Diputación de Valencia.

McClintock, Anne. 1995. *Imperial Leather: Race, Gender and Sexuality in the Colonial Contest.* New York: Routledge.

Meléndez, Mariselle. 1994. "La lucha discursiva entre dos incas en *El lazarillo de ciegos caminantes:* El Inca Concolorcorvo ante su 'paysano' el Inca Garcilaso." *Revista de Estudios Hispánicos* 21:209–19.

———. 1999. *Raza, género e hibridez en* El lazarillo de ciegos caminantes. Chapel Hill: University of North Carolina, Department of Romance Languages.

Méndez, Luz María. 1992. "Los bancos de rescate en Hispanomérica (1747–1832). El proceso histórico y sus fundamentos ideológicos. Estudio comparado para México, Perú y Chile." In *Minería colonial latinoamericana: Primera Reunión de Historiadores de la Minería Latinoamericana,* ed. Dolores Avila, Inés Herrera, and Rina Ortiz, 87–119. Mexico City: Instituto Nacional de Antropología e Historia.

Mendiburu, Manuel de. 1874–1890. *Diccionario histórico-biográfico del Perú.* 8 vols. Lima, Peru: J. F. Solís.

Mendoza, Antonio de. 1911. *Famoso entremés de Getafe.* Vol. 1, *Colección,* ed. Emilio Cotarelo y Mori, 332–35. Madrid: Casa Editorial Bailly-Baillière.

Mendoza Camaño y Sotomayor, José de, Marquis de Villagarcía. 1859. *Relacion del estado de los reynos del Perú que hace el Excmo. Sr. Marqués de Villagarcía al Excmo. Sr. Don José Manso de Velasco, Conde de Superunda, su sucesor en aquel Virreynato, fecha en 24 de Julio de 1745.* Vol. 3, *Memorias de los vi[r]reyes que han gobernado el Perú durante el tiempo del coloniaje espanol,* ed. Manuel Atanasio Fuentes. 6 vols. Lima, Peru: F. Bailly.

Merchant, N. H. [Attr. to Daniel Defoe]. 1684a. *The Compleat Tradesman, or The Exact Dealers Daily Companion. Instructing Him Thoroughly in all things absolutely Necessary to be known by all those who would thrive in the World; and in the whole ART and MYSTERY OF TRADE and TRAFFIC; and will be of constant use for all MERCHANTS, WHOLE-SALE-MEN, SHOP-KEEPERS, RETAILERS, YOUNG TRADESMEN, COUNTREY-CHAPMEN, INDUSTRIOUS YEOMEN, TRADERS in Petty Villages, and all FARMERS, AND Others that go to Countrey FAIRS and MAR-*

KETS; and for all Men whatsoever, that be of any TRADE, or have any considerable Dealings in the WORLD. 3rd exp. ed. London: John Dunton.

———. [Attr. to Daniel Defoe]. 1684b. *The Pleasant Art of Money-Catching, Newly and Fully Discovered. Being the second and last part of that very useful book intitled The Compleat Tradesman*. London: John Dunton.

Migliorino, Francesco. 1985. *Fama e infamia: Problemi della società medievale nel pensiero giuridico nei secoli XII e XIII*. Catania, Italy: Editrice Giannotta.

Mignolo, Walter. 2002. "Rethinking the Colonial Model." In *Rethinking Literary History*, ed. Linda Hutcheon and Mario J. Valdés, chap. 5. Oxford, England: Oxford University Press.

Millau y Marabal, Francisco. 1772. *Descripción de la Provincia del Río de la Plata y de sus Poblaciones*. Madrid: Biblioteca de Palacio, Colección Miscelánea de Ayala, XV, ms. 2829.

Minsheu, John. 1599. *A Dictionarie in Spanish and English, first published into the English tongue by Ric. Percivale Gent. Now enlarged and amplified with many thousand words, as by this marke * to each of them prefixed may appeere*. London: Edm. Bollifant.

———. 1617. *A Most Copious Spanish Dictionarie, with Latine and English*. London: John Minsheu.

Mondragón, Diego. 1756. *Informe histórico y exacta noticia de las Misiones y Conquistas espirituales hechas en las Indias Occidentales por los Religiosos del Real y Militar Orden de Na. Sa. de la Merced. Hechos heroicos, Vida y muerte de los que más se distinguieron. Trata del profetizao Descubrimiento de la América, de la naturaleza y costumbres de los Indios en general; modo de hacer las Reducciones de los Gentiles*. Madrid: Biblioteca de Palacio, Colección Miscelánea de Ayala, XXVIII, ms. 2842.

Montaigne, Michel Eyquem de. 1988. "Des Coches." In vol. 3. *Essais*, 393v.–402v. Pref. Robert Aulotte. Facs. ed. Geneva, Switzerland: Slatkine-Champion.

Monteiro da Vide, Archbishop Sebastião. 1719. *Constituiçoens primeyras do Arcebispado da Bahia*. Lisbon, Portugal: Oficina de Pascoal da Silva.

Montesquieu, Charles Louis de Secondat, Baron de. 1986. *Lettres Persanes*. Ed. Laurent Versini. Paris: Imprimerie Nationale.

Morcillo Rubio Auñón, Diego, Archbishop and Viceroy. 1720. *Vando que Su Excelencia el Arzobispo mandó publicar para embarazar el Comercio con los dichos Franceses*. Lima, Peru, March 11.

Moreno Cebrián, Alfredo. 1977. *El corregidor de indios y la economía peruana del siglo XVIII*. Madrid: CSIC–Instituto G. Fernández de Oviedo.

Moreno Toscano, Alejandra. 1998. "Economía regional y urbanización: Ciudades y regiones en Nueva España." In *Mercado interno en México: Siglos XVIII–XIX*, ed. Jorge Silva Riquer and Jesús López Martínez, 64–94. Mexico City: Instituto de Investigaciones Históricas–UNAM.

Morgan, Ronald J. 2002. *Spanish American Saints and the Rhetoric of Identity 1600–1810*. Tucson: University of Arizona Press.

Mörner, Magnus. 1967. *Race Mixture in the History of Latin America*. Boston: Little, Brown.

Moureau, François. 1982. *Le Mercure galant de Dufresny (1710–1714) ou le journalisme a la mode: Studies on Voltaire and the Eighteenth Century*, no. 206. Oxford, England: Voltaire Foundation.

Muldoon, James. 2000a. *Empire and Order: The Concept of Empire, 800–1800*. New York: St. Martin's Press, 1999. Reprint, London: Macmillan Press.

_____. 2000b. "Medieval Canon Law and the Conquest of the Americas." *Jahrbuch für Geschichte Lateinamerikas* 37:10–22.

Nebrija, Elio Antonio de. 1951. *Vocabulario Español-Latino (Salamanca ¿1495?)*. Facs. ed. Madrid: Talleres Tipográficos de la Editorial Castalia.

_____. 1979. *Diccionario Latino-Español (Salamanca 1492)*. Introd. Germán Colón and Amadeu-J. Soberanas. Barcelona, Spain: Puvill-Editor.

Neuman and Baretti's Dictionary of the Spanish and English Languages. 1827. Boston: Hilliard, Gray, Little and Wilkins.

Novicow, J. A. 1897. *L'avenir de la race blanche: Critique du pessimisme contemporain*. Paris: Félix Alcan.

Núñez de la Vega, Francisco. 1702. *Constituciones diocesanas del Obispado de Chiappa*. Rome: Caietano Zenobi.

Núñez y Domínguez, José de J. 1927. *Un Virrey limeño en México (Don Juan de Acuña, Marqués de Casa Fuerte)*. Mexico City: Talleres Gráficos del Museo Nacional de Arqueología, Historia y Etnografía.

O'Connor, Patrick J. 1996. "Deleitando, dilatando, delatando: Una multiplicidad de lectores en *El lazarillo de ciegos caminantes*." *Revista Iberoamericana* 175 (April–June): 333–50.

Olabarrieta Medrano, Miguel. 1717. *Recuerdo de las obligaciones del Ministerio Apostolico en la cura de las almas. Manual Moral ordenando primariamente a los señores parochos, o Curas, de este nuevo Mundo, en este Reino del Perú, y los demas de las Indias*. Lima, Peru: Diego de Lira.

Ortega Montañés, Juan de. 1965. *Instrucción reservada al Conde de Moctezuma*. Prol. and ed. Norman F. Martin. Mexico City: Editorial Jus.

Oudin, Cesar. 1607. *Tesoro de las dos lenguas francesa y española. Thresor des deux langues françoise et espagnolle: Auquel est contenu l'explication de toutes les deux respectivement l'une par l'autre: Divisé en deux parties*. Paris: Marc Orry.

_____. 1675. *Trésor des deux langues, Françoise et Espagnole. Reveu, corrigé et augmenté d'une Infinité d'Omissions, Additions, Locutions, Phrases, Proverbes, Sentences, et Recherches tirées du Trésor de Covarruvias*. 2 vols. Lyons, France: Michel Mayer.

Outram, Dorinda. 1995. *The Enlightenment*. Cambridge, England: Cambridge University Press.

Pagden, Anthony. 1987. "Identity Formation in Spanish America." In *Colonial Identity in the Atlantic World, 1500–1800*, ed. Anthony Pagden and Nicholas Canny, 51–93. Princeton, N.J.: Princeton University Press.

_____. 1992. "Fabricating Identity in Spanish America." *History Today* 42 (May): 44–49.

Pallavicino, Ferrante. 1644. *Le Courrier desvalisé publié par Ginifaccio Spironcini et dedié a Monsr. Lelio Talentoni. Tiré de l'Italien*. Villefranche, France: Jean Guibaud.

_____. 1660a. *Continuazione del Corriero svaligiato publicato da Ginifaccio Spironcini. Opere scelte di Ferrante Pallavicino. Di nuovo ristampato, corretto e aggiuntovi la Vita dell'Autore e la Continuazione del Corriero*. Villafranca, Italy: Giovanni Gibaldo.

_____. 1660b. *Il corriero svaliggiato. Opere scelte di Ferrante Pallavicino. Di nuovo ristampato, corretto e aggiuntovi la Vita dell'Autore e la Continuazione del Corriero*. Villafranca, Italy: Giovanni Gibaldo.

_____. 1667. *Il Mercurio postiglione di questo e l'altro mondo.* Villafranca, Italy: Claudio del Monte.

Palma Murga, Gustavo. 1986. "Núcleos de poder local y relaciones familiares en la ciudad de Guatemala a finales del siglo XVIII." *Mesoamérica* 2:241–308.

Palmer, Bryan D. 1990. *Descent into Discourse: The Reification of Language and the Writing of Social History.* Philadelphia: Temple University Press.

Parry, Benita. 1987. "Problems in Current Theories of Colonial Discourse." *Oxford Literary Review* 9.1–2:27–58.

Paz y Salgado, Antonio de. 1747. *Las luces del Cielo de la Iglesia difundidas en el hemisferio de Guathemala.* Santiago de Guatemala: Sebastián de Arévalo.

Peralta Barnuevo Rocha y Benavides, Pedro de. 1708. *Lima triumphante, glorias de América, juegos pythios y jubilos de la Minerva peruana en la entrada que hizo S. Exc. en esta muy noble y leal Ciudad, Emporio y Cabeza del Peru, y en el recibimiento con que fue celebrado por la Real Universidad de S. Marcos.* Lima, Peru: Joseph de Contreras y Alvarado.

_____. 1730. *Historia de España vindicada.* Lima: Francisco Sobrino. 2 vols.

_____. 1732. *Lima fundada, o Conquista del Perú. Poema heroico en que se decanta toda la historia del Descubrimiento y sugeción de sus Provincias por Don Francisco Pizarro, Marqués de los Atabillos, Inclito y Primer Gobernador de este vasto Imperio, y se contiene la serie de los reyes, la Historia de los Virreyes y Arzobispos que ha tenido, y la memoria de los Santos y Varones illustres que la Ciudad y Reino han producido.* Lima, Peru: Francisco Sobrino.

_____. 1733. *Relación del auto de fe.* Lima, Peru: Francisco Sobrino.

_____. 1736. *El cielo en el Parnasso: Certamen poético.* Lima, Peru: Imprenta Real de la Calle de Valladolid.

_____. 1964. *Obras dramáticas cortas.* Ed. Elvira Ampuero. Lima, Peru: Ediciones de la Biblioteca Universitaria.

_____. 1994. *Diálogo de los muertos: La causa académica. Censorship and Art in Pre-Enlightenment Lima: Pedro de Peralta's* Diálogo de los muertos: La causa académica. Ed. and study Jerry M. Williams. Potomac, Maryland: Scripta Humanistica.

_____. 1996a. *Imagen política del gobierno del Excelentísimo Señor Don Diego Ladrón de Guevara.* In *Peralta Barnuevo and the Discourse of Loyalty: A Critical Edition of Four Selected Texts,* ed. Jerry M. Williams, 39–74. Tempe: Arizona State University.

_____. 1996b. *El templo de la Fama vindicado. Peralta Barnuevo and the Discourse of Loyalty: A Critical Edition of Four Selected Texts,* ed. Jerry M. Williams, 117–67. Tempe: Arizona State University.

_____. 2001. *Cartel del Certamen, El Júpiter Olímpico, para la festiva celebración poética que consagra reverentemente la Real Universidad de San Marcos de Lima, Emporio del Perú, al Excmo. Señor D. Fray Diego Morcillo Rubio de Auñon.* In *Peralta Barnuevo and the Art of Propaganda: Politics, Poetry and Religion in Eighteenth-Century Lima,* ed. Jerry M. Williams, 45–69. Newark, Del.: Juan de la Cuesta.

Pérez de Barradas, José. 1976. *Los mestizos de América.* Madrid: Espasa-Calpe.

Pérez de Herrera, Cristóbal. 1733. *Enigmas.* Madrid: Los Herederos de F. del Hierro.

_____. 1943. *Enigmas.* Madrid: Atlas.

Pérez de Lara, Ildefonso. 1767–1768. *De anniversariis et capellaniis Libri Duo. Opus quidem ut pium, e practicabile, ita e utile in utroque foro versantibus, Judicibus, Advocatis, Clericis, e Monachis, e quibuscumque aliis piorum executoribus.* Vol. 1, *Opera Omnia in tres tomos distributa.* 3 vols. Madrid: Antonio Mayoral and Imprenta de Antonio Pérez de Soto.

Peters, Edward. 1990. "Wounded Names: The Medieval Doctrine of Infamy." *Sewanee Mediaeval Studies* 5:43–89.

Petit, Pablo. 1730. *Breve tratado de la enfermedad venerea, o morbo galico, en que se explican sus veraderas causas y su perfecta curacion, segun los verdaderos principios de la Medicina y Cirugia moderna, calificados con la demonstracion de los experimentos.* Lima, Peru: Imprenta de la Calle Real de Palacio.

Phelan, John L. 1972. "El auge y la caída de los criollos en la Audiencia de Nueva Granada, 1700–1781." *Boletín de Historia y Antigüedades* 59:597–618.

Pineda, Pedro. 1740. *A New Dictionary, Spanish and English and English and Spanish.* London: F. Gyles, T. Woodward, T. Cox, J. Clarke, A. Millar, and P. Vaillant.

Pinedo, Luis de. 1964. *Libro de chistes de Luis de Pinedo.* In *Sales Españolas o Agudezas del ingenio nacional,* ed. Antonio Paz y Melia and Ramón Paz, 97–117. 2nd ed. rev. Madrid: Atlas.

Pitt-Rivers, Julian. 1973. "Race in Latin America: The Concept of 'Raza.'" *Archives Européennes de Sociologie* 14:3–31.

Playford, John, Samuel Morland and Israel Falgate. 1766. *Vade mecum, or the Necessary Pocket Companion.* 21st corr. and exp. ed. London: H. Woodfall.

———. 1772. *Vade mecum, or the Necessary Pocket Companion.* 22nd corr. and exp. ed. London: John Rivington.

Pliny. 1940. *Natural History.* Vol. 3. Trans. H. Rackham. Cambridge, Mass.: Harvard University Press; London: William Heinemann.

Postigo Castellanos, Elena. 1988. *Honor y privilegio en la Corona de Castilla: El Consejo de Órdenes y los Caballeros de Hábito en el s. XVII.* Almazán, Spain: Junta de Castilla y León.

Pratt, Mary Louise. 1992. *Imperial Eyes: Travel Writing and Transculturation.* London: Routledge.

Pritanio, Lamindo [Lodovico Antonio Muratori]. 1766. *Delle Riflessioni sopra il Buon Gusto nelle Scienze e nell'Arti.* 2 vols. Venice, Italy: Niccolò Pezzana.

Pupo-Walker, Enrique. 1982. "Notas para una caracterización formal de *El lazarillo de ciegos caminantes.*" *Revista Iberoamericana* 121 (December): 647–70.

Quevedo Villegas, Francisco de. 1945. *El mundo de por dentro.* In *Obras completas en prosa,* ed. Luis Astrana Marín, 224–33. 3rd ed. Madrid: Aguilar.

Ramón, Gabriel. 2002. "El umbral de la urbe: Usos de la Plaza Mayor de Lima (siglos XVIII–XIX)." In *Los espacios públicos de la ciudad: Siglos XVIII y XIX,* ed. Carlos Aguirre Anaya, Marcela Dávalos, and María Amparo Ros, 265–88. Mexico City: Casa Juan Pablos–Instituto de Cultura de la Ciudad de México.

Ramos Pérez, Demetrio. 1967. *Trigo chileno, navieros del Callao y hacendados limeños entre la crisis agrícola del siglo XVII y la comercial de la primera mitad del XVIII.* Madrid: CSIC.

Real Academia de la Historia, ed. 1807. *Las siete partidas del Rey Don Alfonso el Sabio.* 3 vols. Madrid: Imprenta Real.

Real Academia Española. 1979. *Diccionario de autoridades* [*Diccionario de la lengua castellana*]. Facs. ed. 3 vols. Madrid: Gredos.

Real Audiencia de Lima. 1705. *En la Ciudad de los Reyes en veintiocho de septiembre de mil setecientos y cinco años, se juntaron a Acuerdo de Govierno . . . Presidente y Oidores de esta Real Audiencia.* Auto de gobierno, September 28.

Real Díaz, José J. 1956. "Don Alonso Carrió de la Vandera, autor del *Lazarillo de ciegos caminantes.*" *Anuario de Estudios Americanos* 13:1–30.

Recopilación de leyes de los Reynos de las Indias. 1756. 2nd ed. 4 vols. Madrid: Antonio Balbas.

Reyes, Alfonso. 1944. *El Deslinde: Prolegómenos a la teoría literaria.* Mexico City: Colegio de México.

Ripa, Cesare. 1669. *Iconologia divisa in tre libri.* Rev. Gio. Zaratino Castellini. Venice, Italy: Nicolò Pezzana.

Rípodas Ardanaz, Daisy. 1977. *El matrimonio en Indias: Realidad social y regulación jurídica.* Buenos Aires, Argentina: Fundación para la Educación, la Ciencia y la Cultura.

Rivington, John. 1765. *A Complete Guide to All Persons Who Have Any Trade or Concern with the City of London and Parts Adjacent . . . Designed for the Use of Persons of All Degrees, as Well Natives as Foreigners.* 10th rev. and exp. ed. London: J. Rivington.

Robert, Ulysse. 1891. *Les signes d'infamie au Moyen Age: Juifs, sarrasins, hérétiques, lépreux, cagots et filles publiques.* Paris: Honoré Champion, Libraire.

Rodó, José Enrique. 2000. *Ariel.* Ed. Belén Castro. Madrid: Cátedra.

Rodrigo, Enrique. 2000. "Carrió de la Vandera y Dufresny: El uso de interlocutores ficcionales en dos libros de viaje." *Hispanic Journal* 21.1 (Spring): 141–49.

Román Gutiérrez, José Francisco, ed. 1998. *Las reformas borbónicas y el nuevo orden colonial.* Mexico City: Instituto Nacional de Antropología e Historia.

Rubio Mañé, J. Ignacio. 1955. *Introducción al estudio de los virreyes de Nueva España 1535–1746.* Vol. 1, *Orígenes y jurisdicciones, y dinámica social de los virreyes.* Mexico City: Ediciones Selectas.

Rufo, Juan. 1972. *Las seiscientas apotegmas y otras obras en verso.* Ed. and prol. Alberto Blecua. Madrid: Espasa-Calpe.

Saavedra Fajardo, Diego. 1999. *Empresas políticas.* Ed. Sagrario López Poza. Madrid: Cátedra.

Sahlins, Marshall. 1977. "Colors and Cultures." In *Symbolic Anthropology: A Reader in the Study of Symbols and Meanings,* ed. Janet L. Dolgin, David S. Kemnitzer, and David M. Schneider, 165–79. New York: Columbia University Press.

Sáiz, María Dolores. 1996. *Los orígenes: El siglo XVIII.* Vol. 1, *Historia del periodismo en España.* 3 vols. Madrid: Alianza.

Salamiellas, Johan Alvares de. 1998. *Texto y concordancias de El tratado de menescalcia.* Ed. Maria Isabel Montoya Ramírez. Madison, Wis.: HSMS.

Salas Barbadillo, Alonso Jerónimo de. 1911. *Los mirones en la Corte.* Vol. 1, *Colección,* ed. Emilio Cotarelo y Mori, 255–57. Madrid: Casa Editorial Bailly-Bailliére.

Salucio, Agustín. 1975. *Discurso sobre los estatutos de limpieza de sangre.* Facs. ed. Cieza, Spain: A. Pérez y Gómez.

Sampson Vera Tudela, Elisa. 2000. *Colonial Angels: Narratives of Gender and Spirituality in Mexico 1580–1750.* Austin: University of Texas Press.

Sánchez, Luis Alberto. 1967. *El Doctor Océano: Estudios sobre Don Pedro de Peralta Barnuevo.* Lima, Peru: Universidad Nacional Mayor de San Marcos.

_____. 1971. *La Perricholi.* 6th corr. ed. Buenos Aires, Argentina: Editorial Francisco de Aguirre.

Santa Cruz, Melchor de. 1997. *Floresta española.* Ed. and prol. María Pilar Cuartero and Maxime Chevalier. Pref. Maxime Chevalier. Barcelona, Critica.

Santiago Concha, José de, Marquis de Casa Concha. 1726. *Relación instructiva que dio el Marqués de Casa Concha en 26 de Junio de 1726 a su sucesor en la Superintendencia y gobierno de la mina de azogue de Guancavelica.* Madrid: Biblioteca de Palacio, Colección Miscelánea de Ayala, VII, ms. 2822.

Sarmiento, Martín. 1789. *Reflexiones literarias para una Biblioteca Real y para otras bibliotecas publicas, hechas por el R.P. Mtro. F. Martín Sarmiento, Benedictino, en el mes de diciembre de 1743.* Vol. 20, *Semanario Erudito que comprehende varias obras ineditas, criticas, morales, instructivas, politicas, historicas, satiricas, y jocosas de nuestros mejores autores antiguos y modernos,* ed. Antonio Valladares de Sotomayor, 229–99. Madrid: Don Blas Roman.

Schell Hoberman, Louisa, and Susan Migden Socolow, eds. 1986. *Cities and Society in Colonial Latin America.* Albuquerque: University of New Mexico Press.

Schwartz, Stuart B. 1995. "Colonial Identities and the *Sociedad de Castas*." *Colonial Latin American Review* 4.1:185–201.

Secretaría del Supremo Consejo y Cámara de Indias. 1784. "Relación de la literatura, grados, méritos y servicios del doctor D. Estanislao de Recabarren Pardo de Figueroa." Madrid, June 19.

Seed, Patricia. 1982. "Social Dimensions of Race: Mexico City, 1753." *Hispanic American Historical Review* 62:569–606.

———. 1988. *To Love, Honor and Obey in Colonial Mexico: Conflicts over Marriage Choice, 1574–1821.* Stanford, Calif.: Stanford University Press.

Selis, Nicholas Josef. 1761. *L'inoculation du Bon Sens.* London: n.p.

Serra, Màrius. 1991. *Manual d'enigmística.* Barcelona, Spain: Columna.

Seznec, Jean. 1995. *The Survival of the Pagan Gods: The Mythological Tradition and Its Place in Renaissance Humanism and Art.* Trans. Barbara F. Sessions. Princeton, N.J.: Princeton University Press.

Sicroff, Albert A. 1985. *Los estatutos de limpieza de sangre: Controversias entre los siglos XV y XVII.* Trans. Mauro Armiño. Madrid: Taurus.

Silva Riquer, Jorge, and Jesús López Martínez, eds. 1998. *Mercado interno en México: Siglos XVIII–XIX.* Mexico City: Instituto de Investigaciones Históricas–UNAM.

Smart, Jack. n.d. *Jack Smart's Merry Jester, or, The Wit's Compleat* Treasury. London: J. Fuller.

Smedley, Audrey. 1998. "'Race' and the Construction of Human Identity." *American Anthropologist* 100.3 (September): 690–702.

Smith, Paul Julian. 1992. *Representing the Other: "Race," Text, and Gender in Spanish and Spanish American Narrative.* Oxford, England: Clarendon Press.

Sobrino, Francisco. 1721. *Dicionario nuevo de las lenguas española y francesa.* Rev. and enlarged ed. 2 vols. Brussels, Belgium: Casa de Francisco Foppens.

Socolow, Susan Migden. 1987. *The Bureaucrats of Buenos Aires, 1769–1810: Amor al Real Servicio.* Durham, N.C.: Duke University Press.

Solórzano y Pereira, Juan de. 1736–1739. *Política indiana.* Ed. Francisco Ramiro de Valenzuela. 2 vols. Madrid: Matheo Sacristán and Gabriel Ramírez.

———. 1972. *Política indiana.* Facs. ed. Introd. Miguel Angel Ochoa Brun. 5 vols. Madrid: Ediciones Atlas.

Soria Murillo, Victor Manuel. 1994. *La Casa de Moneda de México bajo la administración borbónica 1733–1821.* Mexico City: Universidad Autónoma Metropolitana.

Sousa de Macedo, Antonio de. 1882. *Eva y Ave o María triunfante: Teatro de la erudición y filosofía cristiana en que se representan los dos estados del mundo, caido en Eva y levantado en Ave.* Ed. and trans. Diego Suárez de Figueroa. Murcia, Spain: Librería de Miguel Tornel y Olmos.

Souza Penha, Evaristo de. 1978. "La función ideológica de la ironía en *El lazarillo de ciegos caminantes.*" Ph.D. diss., University of Washington.

Stein, Stanley J., and Barbara H. Stein. 2000. *Silver, Trade and War: Spain and America in the Making of Early Modern Europe.* Baltimore: Johns Hopkins University Press.

Stevens, Captain John. 1706. *A New Spanish and English Dictionary.* London: George Sawbridge.

Stolley, Karen. 1993. El lazarillo de ciegos caminantes*: Un itinerario crítico.* Hanover, N.H.: Ediciones del Norte.

———. 1994. "Concolorcorvo: Guide for Travelers in Eighteenth-Century Spanish America." In *Coded Encounters: Writing, Gender, and Ethnicity in Colonial Latin America,* ed. Francisco Javier Cevallos-Candau, Jeffrey A. Cole, Nina M. Scott, and Nicomedes Suárez-Araúz, 247–54. Amherst: University of Massachusetts Press.

Stuart, Kathy. 1999. *Defiled Trades and Social Outcasts: Honor and Ritual Pollution in Early Modern Germany.* Cambridge, England: Cambridge University Press.

Suárez, Margarita. 1995. *Comercio y fraude en el Perú colonial: Las estrategias de un banquero.* Lima, Peru: IEP Ediciones.

Suárez Argüello, Clara Elena. 1997. *Camino real y carrera larga: La arriería en la Nueva España durante el siglo XVIII.* CIESA–Ediciones de la Casa Chata.

Suárez de Figueroa, Cristóbal. 1615. *Teatro universal de todas ciencias y artes.* Madrid: Luis Sánchez.

———. 1733. *Teatro universal de todas ciencias y artes.* Rev. and exp. anonymous. Madrid, n.p.

Sweet, James H. 1997. "The Iberian Roots of American Racist Thought." *William and Mary Quarterly* 3d. series, 54.1 (January): 143–66.

Tarde, Gabriel. 1903. *The Laws of Imitation.* Trans. Elsie Clews Parsons. Introd. Franklin H. Giddings. New York: Henry Holt.

Taylor, Paul C. 2004. *Race: A Philosophical Introduction.* Cambridge, England: Polity Press.

Tesauro, Emanuele. 1968. *Il Cannocchiale Aristotelico.* Introd. August Buck. Berlin: Bad Homburg.

Timoneda, Joan. 1990. *Buen aviso y Portacuentos: El Sobremesa y alivio de caminantes.* Ed. María Pilar Cuartero and Maxime Chevalier. Madrid: Espasa-Calpe.

Tinagero de la Escalera, Bernardo. n.d. *Proyecto del Príncipe de Santo Bono, Virrey del Perú, sobre establecer un comercio más frecuente de cartas entre la Corte y aquellas provincias, para la más breve respuesta de las que se escribían y que no se experimentase el retardo de dos y tres anos. . . . Discurre sobre todo Don Bernardo Tinagero de la Escalera, y manifiesta no ser útil este Proyecto por las razones en que se funda, y por no experimentarse los retardos referidos, con cuyo dictamen se conforma S.M.* Madrid, Biblioteca de Palacio, Colección Miscelánea de Ayala, LXII, ms. 2875.

Torquemada, Juan de. 1615. *Segunda parte de los veinte y un libros rituales y Monarchia Indiana. Con el Origen y guerras de los Yndias Occidentales. De sus Poblaçones, Descubri-*

Index

www.ingramcontent.com/pod-product-compliance
Lightning Source LLC
Chambersburg PA
CBHW030856270326
41929CB00008B/444